Windows™ Graphics Programming with Borland® C++

Second Edition

Coriolis Group Book

Windows™ Graphics Programming with Borland® C++
Second Edition

Loren Heiny

John Wiley & Sons, Inc.

New York • Chichester • Brisbane • Toronto • Singapore

Library of Congress Cataloging-in-Publication Data

Heiny, Loren.
    Windows graphics programming with Borland C++ / by Loren Heiny. --
2nd ed.
        p. cm.
    Includes index.
    ISBN 0-471-30930-3
    1. Microsoft Windows (Computer file) 2. C++ (Computer program language) 3. Borland C++. 4. ObjectWindows. 5. Computer graphics.
I. Title.
QA76.76.W56H44 1994   94-13118
006.6'785--dc20   CIP

Printed in the United States of America

10 9 8 7 6 5 4 3 2 1

Contents

Preface

When I started writing the first edition of this book back in late 1990, Windows was still a novelty. And most PC graphics programmers berated Windows for its sluggishness and lack of programming ease. Things have changed. Although as a graphics programmer I never have enough speed, tools such as Borland C++ make it a pleasure to program Windows. I can create better looking, more elaborate, and easier to use programs in Windows than ever before.

Part of becoming an effective Windows programmer is building up a collection of programming tools and techniques. In this book I share some of what I find most useful when creating Windows graphics applications. Inside, you'll find lots of code and practical tips spanning a wide variety of graphics topics. Each step along the way I've tried to present the material so that you can begin using it in your own graphics applications right away.

In fact, since the first edition of this book I've received many encouraging letters from readers outlining the projects that they've built using the material presented here. A few that come to mind are a model railroad track layout program, a computer-aided software engineering (CASE) tool, an electronic slot machine, a visual math analysis package, and a sailing navigation app.

But nothing in the computer industry stays current very long. Therefore, my intention in this second edition is to bring the book up to date. I've extended the book in four main areas. First, all the code has been updated to work with Borland C++ version 4 and the latest generation of ObjectWindows library, OWL 2.0. Second, this edition includes a new chapter on Win32 graphics functions—which are sure to become more important as 32-bit Windows technology matures. Third, I've expanded coverage of several topics, most notably I've enhanced the chapter on bitmaps. And fourth, I've refined and extended a few of the applications. For instance, the drawing program covered in Chapters 14 now spans over 70 pages and supports object resizing, reshaping, a drawing surface and much more. I've added these capabilities at the risk of making the code too challenging for the uninitiated, however, I hope you'll find these added capabilities worthwhile.

Here's an overview of what else is inside:

- In-depth coverage of Windows' Graphics Device Interface (GDI)

- Hands-on approach to developing graphics programs and techniques in Windows

- Support for 16- and 32-bit graphics programming
- The fundamentals of two- and three-dimensional graphics programming
- Animation techniques
- Fractal programming
- Interactive drawing tool
- Three-dimensional, solid modeling

WHO THIS BOOK IS FOR

This book is for anyone who wants to learn how to write useful graphics programs for Windows or Windows NT. Although you'll need to know the basics of C++ programming, you don't need to be a Windows programming expert to follow along. In fact, if you are new to Windows and have an adventurous spirit, you'll find plenty of step-by-step examples to help you get through the material.

If you don't know either C or C++, this book may be a significant challenge. A thorough knowledge of C++ is assumed. Of course, the best way to learn is by doing. And this book gives you ample opportunity to learn by programming.

Finally, if you're interested in graphics programming, but have been avoiding Windows, you ought to take a second look. Windows markedly improves the process of writing graphics applications that work on many different graphics devices. Rather than spending your time writing display drivers you can improve what your applications do. This alone makes Windows programming an ideal choice for developing graphics applications.

HOW THIS BOOK IS DIFFERENT

This book is about graphics programming. In particular, it presents Windows programming from a C++ perspective. To get you up and running as quickly as possible, all the programs in this book use the C++ ObjectWindows library (OWL 2.0) included with Borland C++ version 4. Object Windows makes it possible to focus more on the details of graphics programming and less on low-level Windows issues. Of course, C++ brings a whole new flavor to Windows programming. If you're already a C Windows programmer, I think you'll be pleased by C++'s ability to package under one roof many of the details of an application.

I've also tried to do more than just explain Windows' functions. I've included several complete applications of which the drawing program in Chapter 14 is the most extensive. As I see it, too many issues never seem to crop up on small programs. Only by attempting full blown applications do you really begin to understand the important tradeoffs in Windows graphics programming. Of course, when you're done, you'll have a substantial amount of code to use your own graphics applications.

What You'll Need

To compile and run the programs in this book you'll need Borland C++ 4.xx. You'll also need to install the ObjectWindows library that comes with Borland C++. Realize, that the code in the book will not work with earlier versions of the Borland compiler.

You don't need any special hardware beyond that which Borland C++ and Windows require. That is, you must have at least an IBM-compatible 386 computer equipped with DOS 4.01 or higher, at least 4MB of memory (although I find 8MB to be a practical minimum), a mouse, and a Windows-compatible display. However, to get the most out of this book you'll probably want a Super VGA graphics card and color monitor.

A Look Inside

This book progresses from the basics of graphics programming to more advanced topics in a way that lets you put previously learned skills to use quickly. It begins by exploring the fundamentals of Windows programming and the essentials of the Graphics Device Interface (GDI). Then the book explores several graphics topics, such as presentation graphics, animation, and fractals. The last third of the book develops two extensive graphics applications: an object-oriented drawing program and a three-dimensional viewing package. Along the way you'll find numerous code examples, special notes about issues to watch out for, and step-by-step instructions on how to compile the programs and suggestions for modifying them.

About the Code

If you've thumbed through this book, you've already noticed that it includes a number of tools and applications. To save you from having to enter all of this code, I've made the software available in electronic form. A disk order form is located at the back of the book. If you're in a hurry, you can phone in your order. The phone number is included on the order form.

Contacting the Author

If you have comments about the material in this book, problems with some of its programs, or would like to share what you are doing, you can contact me by mail at P.O. Box 122, Tempe, Az 85280, on CompuServe at 73527,2365, or on the BBS mentioned on the disk order page at the back of the book.

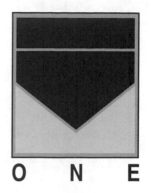

O N E

Introduction to Windows Programming

If you're thinking about writing a new graphics program or updating an existing one, you're probably considering Microsoft Windows as the primary platform. And there's good reason to do so—Windows is rapidly becoming the standard environment for PC users.

However, Windows represents a substantial change for most PC graphics programmers. On the plus side, Windows provides a consistent, mouse-oriented, graphical user interface, complete with pop-up menus, windows, and dialog boxes. Windows also makes it possible to run multiple programs simultaneously and to take advantage of all the memory available on today's PCs. On the downside, Windows demands a style of programming that at first may be a bit overwhelming, but taken in steps is really quite manageable.

This chapter introduces some of the basics of Windows programming. We'll develop three small Windows applications using Borland's ObjectWindows Library (OWL) Version 2.0—an object-oriented, C++ hierarchy for Windows programming. Although these three applications will be short programs, you'll discover that they provide a lot of flexibility. For instance, they all support resizable, graphical windows, numerous display adapters, and multitasking.

THE PROGRAMMING PERSPECTIVE

Windows offers over one thousand functions and support services through its *Application Programmers Interface (API)*. This extensive library hints at the complexity built into Windows. But what really makes Windows programming a challenge is the style of programming required. It's a style quite different from what you are probably accustomed to using.

1

Graphics Windows programming is different for three basic reasons:

1. Programs are organized around events.
2. The computer's resources are shared among applications.
3. Programs don't directly manipulate devices (such as the screen) directly.

The following three sections discuss these differences in more detail.

Programming with Events

In DOS, programs are usually written as a sequence of steps grouped into functions. Windows programs, however, are organized around *events* or *messages*. An event occurs when something within Windows changes. Messages are used to signal that an event has taken place or is about to occur. Table 1.1 lists a handful of the many messages that Windows provides. For example, Windows posts a message called **WM_LBUTTONDOWN** each time you press the left mouse button. A program, then, can be written to watch for messages like **WM_LBUTTONDOWN** and respond to them appropriately.

How does this difference reveal itself in a program? Consider a DOS-based application that determines how long the left mouse button is pressed. You might use a loop that waits until the left mouse button is pressed, get the time, wait until the button is released, get the time again, and then display the difference. This approach is outlined in Figure 1.1. Unfortunately, your program will be tied up in the two loops until the appropriate mouse action is taken. In a Windows program, the story is different.

A Windows application divides the code so that it responds to several internal messages managed by Windows, as shown in Figure 1.1. For instance,

Table 1.1 Common Windows Messages

Message	Description
WM_CHAR	The user has pressed a non-system key
WM_CREATE	The window is about to be created; any initialization steps can be taken at this time
WM_DESTROY	The window is about to be removed; any cleanup can be performed at this time
WM_LBUTTONDOWN	The left mouse button was pressed
WM_LBUTTONUP	The left mouse button was released
WM_MOUSEMOVE	The mouse has been moved
WM_PAINT	A window should paint itself
WM_SIZE	The size of the window has changed

Figure 1.1 Windows and DOS applications are designed differently.

```
                        Dos Application
                              •
                              •
                              •
     // Wait until the button is pressed
     while (MouseStatus() != LEFTBUTTONDOWN);
     Time1 = GetTime();
     // Wait until the button is released
     while (MouseStatus() != LEFTBUTTONUP);
     Time2 = GetTime();
     DurationOfPress = Time2 - Time1;
                              •
                              •
                              •

                     Windows Application
                              •
                              •
                              •
     while (GetMessage(&Message)) {
       switch(Message) {
         case WM_LBUTTONDOWN:
               Time1 = GetTime();
               break;
         case WM_LBUTTONUP;
               Time2 = GetTime();
               DurationOfPress = Time2 - Time1;
               break;
       }
     }
                              •
                              •
                              •
```

the **WM_LBUTTONDOWN** message is sent when the left mouse button is pressed, and **WM_LBUTTONUP** is sent when the button is released. Internally, the messages are simply integer values (constants) that correspond with the events. The constants for Windows' messages are defined in the WINDOWS.H header file.

The benefit of the event-driven approach is that it becomes fairly simple for the operating system to intertwine multiple applications. A program is allowed to run when it has a message to respond to, but is placed on the sidelines when it doesn't have anything to do, thereby freeing the processor to run other applications.

Sharing Resources

Because multiple programs can be executing virtually at the same time, Windows programs must share the computer's resources, such as memory, disk drives, screen, and printers. The sharing of resources comes with a price: you must get permission to access a device before you can use it, and, as soon as you are done with the device, you must release it so that other programs can access it. These "permission slips" come in the form of *handles*. We'll explore handles later in this chapter.

Device-Independent Graphics

If you're like most graphics programmers, you've probably spent a great deal of time rewriting your code to support the endless series of display adapters and printers available. With Windows, much of this can be avoided because Windows takes care of the low-level details of communicating with these devices.

Windows programs are not designed for a specific display device or printer. Instead, you access each device through high-level functions. Windows' device drivers handle the low-level details of manipulating the devices. The drawback to this approach is the overhead involved. Since you won't be accessing the screen directly, graphics operations will be slower than you might be accustomed to.

WINDOWS, OBJECTS, AND C++

By design, Windows is object oriented. All of its interface elements, such as its windows, scroll bars, dialog boxes, and so on, are organized as objects. As is true with objects in C++, a Windows object often has both data and functionality. For instance, an OK button in a dialog box may invoke a function that both verifies the data a user enters and copies it into a set of variables.

As a C++ programmer, you'll probably be comfortable with the fact that both Windows organizes its user-interface elements into objects. However, Windows is not written in an object-oriented language. Consequently, Windows has all the classical signs of objects, without the palatable syntax of a language such as C++.

Windows Programming with ObjectWindows

To exploit the object-oriented features of C++ while programming for Windows, you'll need an object hierarchy built around Windows' functions. We could develop our own, but instead we'll use OWL 2.0, which is included with Borland C++ 4.0.

OWL handles many of the behind-the-scenes issues of Windows programming and enables us to take advantage of C++'s object-oriented programming (OOP) features. As a result, we'll be able to focus on the issues of graphics programming. OWL will take care of much of the application overhead.

Note OWL 2.0 is not code compatible with earlier versions of OWL. There are differences in the class hierarchies as well as the way that OWL hooks into Windows' messaging system. If you have a version of Borland C++ prior to Version 4.0, you must upgrade your compiler (and OWL) to run the programs in this book.

Multiple Platforms and 32-Bit Programming

One of the advantages of using Borland C++ and OWL 2.0 is that with them you can write your programs to run under standard 16-bit Windows or the more powerful 32-bit, Windows NT, or the hybrid Win32s. Most of the platform-specific details are hidden from you, although there are differences that you must be aware of.

For instance, in 32-bit programs Windows uses 32-bit numbers rather than 16-bit numbers, resulting in larger coordinate ranges. Probably more useful, are additional functions, such as Bezier curve drawing routines. Unfortunately, these extended functions are available only on 32-bit versions of Windows, such as Windows NT, and not standard Windows or Win32s. The routines won't cause a run-time error if executed in Windows or Win32s, however, they don't generate any output either.

A BARE-BONES WINDOWS PROGRAM

It's time for some code. In this section, we'll develop one of the smaller Windows applications you'll probably ever want to create. The program, SIMPLE.CPP, displays a resizable window, as shown in Figure 1.2. Because SIMPLE.CPP is a Windows program, it supports all the screen display devices that Windows supports, allows for resizing the window, can run alongside other programs, and supports both the keyboard and mouse. Not bad for a 31-line program!

The code that creates the window is listed next. When you type in the code, remember that C++ is case sensitive. You must adhere to the capitalization shown.

```
// SIMPLE.CPP: Displays a resizable window.

#include <owl\applicat.h>  // Header file for the application class
#include <owl\framewin.h>  // Header file for the window class
```

```
// Derive an application class from OWL's generic application class
class TSimpleApp : public TApplication {
public:
  TSimpleApp() : TApplication() { } // Call the base-class constructor
  void InitMainWindow();
};

// Define the behavior for the window in the program. Here it
// doesn't do anything except call its ancestor's constructor.
class TDoNothingWindow : public TWindow {
public:
  TDoNothingWindow(TWindow *parent, const char* title)
    : TWindow(parent, title) { }
};

// Link the customized window to the application object
void TSimpleApp::InitMainWindow()
{
  MainWindow = new TFrameWindow(0, "SIMPLE PROGRAM",
    new TDoNothingWindow(0, ""));
}

// This is the main entry point for the program
int OwlMain(int /*argc*/, char* /*argv*/[])
{
  return TSimpleApp().Run(); // Create an application object and
}                            // execute its Run member function
```

Figure 1.2 Output of SIMPLE.CPP.

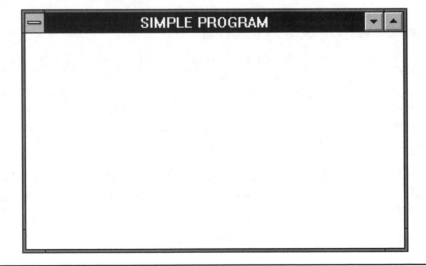

Compiling SIMPLE.CPP

Compiling SIMPLE.CPP is rather simple if you use the Borland C++'s Integrated Development Environment (IDE). Here are the steps to follow:

1. Create a project file for the program by selecting the Project | New project menu option. In the dialog box that appears, set the project name to SIMPLE.IDE and place it in the same directory as the SIMPLE.CPP source code. At this time, make sure that the Target option is set to Windows 3.x (16) (16-bit Windows), the memory model is set to Large, and that the OWL and Dynamic options are selected. These last two options ensure that OWL's *dynamic link libraries (DLLs)* will be used by your application. DLLs are libraries that are linked at run-time in Windows, preventing the library code from having to be embedded into your .EXE files. The DLLs that OWL uses are located in Borland's BIN directory. Realize that you must copy these DLLs (such as BC40RTL.DLL and OWL200.DLL) along with your program's .EXE file if you want to run your program on another machine. Once all the options are correct, select the OK button in the dialog box.

2. The Project window will appear in the lower portion of the screen. It lists the files used to build your program. In this case, it will automatically list the three files SIMPLE.CPP, SIMPLE.DEF, and SIMPLE.RC. SIMPLE.CPP is the program listed earlier. But where did the two additional files come from? The first, SIMPLE.DEF, is expected to be a *module definition file* that specifies various attributes of the executable file, such as the program's stack size. Fortunately, Borland can use default settings, so you can delete this file from the project. The other file, SIMPLE.RC, is supposed to be a *resource file* that contains the program's menus, dialog boxes, and so on. Since our application doesn't require any special attention here, you can delete this file from the project file too.

3. Verify that the pathname to your compiler's include and library directories are correct. These settings are accessible through the Options | Project | Directories menu option. If they aren't correct, your compiler won't be able to find the header files or link the compiled code.

4. Verify that the preprocessor define values are correct. They are accessible through the Options | Project | Compiler | Defines menu option. Normally, the compiler sets the preprocessor defines to:

```
_RTLDLL;_BIDSDLL;_OWLDLL;_OWLPCH;
```

The first two preprocessor define values ensure that the code will be compiled so that your code is compatible with Borland's run-time libraries. The next define value, **_OWLDLL**, selects OWL's code and, finally, **_OWLPCH** specifies that precompiled headers for OWL are used.

5. Select the Debug | Run menu option to compile, link, and run the program.

6. When compiling and linking SIMPLE.CPP, you will get a compiler warning informing you that you did not specify a module definition file. Don't worry; your compiler uses default settings that are sufficient. If you want to get rid of the module definition warning, you can add the following definition file, OWL.DEF (or SIMPLE.DEF, if you prefer), to your project file. To do so, place the following statements in a file named OWL.DEF.

```
EXETYPE WINDOWS
CODE PRELOAD MOVEABLE DISCARDABLE
DATA PRELOAD MOVEABLE MULTIPLE
HEAPSIZE 4096
STACKSIZE 8192
```

Next, add the filename OWL.DEF to SIMPLE.CPP's project list. You can use this definition file with all of the programs in this book. (For more information on definition files refer to Borland's Windows documentation.)

7. Once your program is running, try resizing the window, invoking another instance of the program, or whatever else you feel will prove that everything is in order.

How to Read an OWL Program

It's time to take a detailed look at SIMPLE.CPP. The first several statements include three OWL header files. Two of the header files, APPLICAT.H and FRAMEWIN.H, define or include other files that define the functions, classes, types, and constants used in a typical, OWL-based Windows program. In more complicated applications, you will have to add additional header files to gain access to OWL's other classes and functions. (You can add the optional header file, OWLPCH.H, to tell the compiler to use precompiled headers, which can help in compilation time if you have extra disk space.) In you're familiar with traditional Windows programming, you may be wondering whether we've forgotten to include the standard header file WINDOWS.H, which declares Windows' messages, functions, and so on. We don't need to. APPLICAT.H contains an indirect reference to WINDOWS.H for us.

Next, notice that SIMPLE.CPP defines two classes: **TSimpleApp** and **TDoNothingWindow**. Both are derived from classes provided by OWL: **TApplication** and **TWindow**. Almost all of your Windows applications will be derived from at least these two classes. Briefly, **TApplication** provides the application-level details that Windows requires and **TWindow** specifies what the program will display and its user interaction. If you look closely at the code you'll also see that we're using one other OWL class, **TFrameWindow**. You can think of it as a framing object that contains the program's specific **TWindow** implementation—much like a picture frame contains a specific picture. Figure 1.3 illustrates the relationships among these three classes.

The **TApplication** class hides much of the lengthy, but necessary, support logic that is required in even a simple Windows program. By deriving an application object, **TSimpleApp**, from OWL's default application class, we are able to inherit all of the behind-the-scenes code required by our simple Windows program.

The **TSimpleApp** class redefines **TApplication** in two ways. First, it provides its own constructor **TSimpleApp**, which gets called when an object of type **TSimpleApp** is declared:

```
TSimpleApp() : TApplication() { }
```

In this case, the **TSimpleApp** constructor simply calls **TApplication**'s constructor and doesn't do anything else. Notice that there aren't any arguments passed between these two constructors. Actually, there is a hidden parameter—the name that we want to give to the application. OWL defines this parameter as a *default argument* so that when a name isn't specified, the constructor assigns the application name to a NULL string.

As with most of the classes in the OWL 2.0 class library, there is more than one constructor for the **TApplication** class and more than one way to call them. You'll probably want to spend a little time looking over OWL's documentation to understand the best way to use each of the constructors. Realize that C++ will call the proper constructor for us and handle any default arguments, if they exist.

Note Because all of OWL's classes contain constructors that have parameters, you must always define constructors in classes derived from OWL's classes. In addition, each new constructor must call its parent's constructor, as shown in **TSimpleApp** and **TDoNothingWindow**. You must do this even if the new constructor doesn't do anything else.

Figure 1.3 The class hierarchy used in SIMPLE.CPP.

The second part of **TSimpleApp** overrides the function **InitMainWindow**. It's used by OWL to specify which window the application should display.

The other class in SIMPLE.CPP, **TDoNothingWindow**, is derived from OWL's **TWindow** class:

```
class TDoNothingWindow : public TWindow {
```

The **TDoNothingWindow** class specifies exactly what the displayed window will do, such as what happens when the left mouse button is pressed or what is supposed to be painted in the window. In this program, no special actions are taken, therefore **TDoNothingWindow** doesn't provide any new or over-ridden functions. In fact, **TDoNothingWindow** inherits all its behavior from **TWindow**. Since **TWindow** displays a blank window, so too does **TDoNothingWindow**. The only member function in the derived class is its constructor, which passes along its parameters to its parent class, **TWindow**:

```
TDoNothingWindow(TWindow *parent, const char* title)
  : TWindow(parent, title) { }
```

The first parameter, **parent**, is a pointer to the parent interface object of the **TDoNothingWindow** object. As you'll see later, we'll set this parameter to 0 (a NULL pointer) in both cases to indicate that the displayed Window is not bound to any other object. The other parameter, **title**, is a far pointer to a string that is to appear in the window's title bar.

To show how the **TDoNothingWindow** class is used, we need to turn to the only overridden member function in the **TSimpleApp** class. This function, **InitMainWindow**, is defined as:

```
void TSimpleApp::InitMainWindow()
{
  MainWindow = new TFrameWindow(0, "SIMPLE PROGRAM",
    new TDoNothingWindow(0, ""));
}
```

InitMainWindow sets the variable **MainWindow**, which is contained in the **TApplication** class, to a dynamically allocated **TFrameWindow** object. **TFrameWindow** is a class defined in OWL that integrates a window with the application object. Like its name suggests, **TFrameWindow** is a frame designed to hold something else—in this case a **DoNothingWindow** object. In English, a **TSimpleApp** program pops up a window that has all the properties of a **TDoNothingWindow** object. In particular, this application displays a blank window with the title string "SIMPLE PROGRAM." (Notice that the title of the window is set through the **TFrameWindow** object and not through **TDoNothingWindow**.) Since every program we'll write has a window, you'll see the **InitMainWindow** function overridden in every application in this book.

Where an OWL Program Begins

There's not much that we haven't already covered in SIMPLE.CPP, except the **OwlMain** function. It's the launching pad for an OWL application. **OwlMain** is defined in SIMPLE.CPP as:

```
int OwlMain(int /*argc*/, char* /*argv*/[])
{
  return TSimpleApp().Run(); // Create an application object and
}                            // execute its Run member function
```

If you're new to C++ or event-driven programming, you might be scratching your head over this code. It probably looks too simple and too complex at the same time. Here, **OwlMain** instructs Windows to create a **TSimpleApp** object, perform its **Run** member function, and return the object's status to the operating system.

The OWL **Run** function hides the secret of the event-driven nature of Windows. It contains a **while** loop that continually asks Windows for the next message to process and sends it off to be handled. The loop terminates when the **WM_QUIT** message occurs.

In many ways, **OwlMain** is similar to C++'s **main** function. Like **main**, **OwlMain** accepts a variable number of command-line arguments—although we won't be using them in this book. Realize that in a standard Windows program we'd actually use the Windows function **WinMain** as the entry point for our programs. Therefore, not suprisingly, **OwlMain** hides a call to **WinMain**.

Adding Screen Output

A window isn't of much value if it doesn't display anything. So let's modify the SIMPLE.CPP program to draw a rectangle like the one shown in Figure 1.4. The new code for the program, which we'll call RECTANGL.CPP, is shown next.

 To compile RECTANGL.CPP, follow the same procedure outlined for SIMPLE.CPP. When you run the program, try resizing the window. Notice that the size of the rectangle does not change and that it is clipped to the boundaries of the window.

```
// RECTANGL.CPP: Displays a rectangle in a resizable window.

#include <owl\applicat.h> // Header file for the TApplication class
#include <owl\framewin.h> // Header file for the TFrameWindow class
#include <owl\dc.h>       // Defines OWL's device context class

class TRectangleApp : public TApplication {  // Application class
public:
  TRectangleApp() : TApplication() { }
  void InitMainWindow();
};
```

```
// This time we'll override TWindow's Paint member function
// to alter what the window displays
class TRectangleWindow : public TWindow {
public:
  TRectangleWindow(TWindow *parent, const char* title)
    : TWindow(parent, title) { }
  void Paint(TDC& dc, BOOL, TRect&);
};

// When the window is painted, draw a rectangle in it
void TRectangleWindow::Paint(TDC& dc, BOOL, TRect&)
{
  Rectangle(dc, 20, 10, 300, 100);   // Draw a rectangle
}

void TRectangleApp::InitMainWindow()
{
  MainWindow = new TFrameWindow(0, "RECTANGLE",
    new TRectangleWindow(0, ""));
}

int OwlMain(int /*argc*/, char* /*argv*/[])
{
  return TRectangleApp().Run();
}
```

The RECTANGL.CPP program is similar to SIMPLE.CPP. It is built around two classes: **TRectangleApp** and **TRectangleWindow**. Notice that **TRectangleWindow** contains one new member function, **Paint**. This is a very special virtual function defined in OWL's **TWindow** class. It automatically

Figure 1.4 Output of RECTANGL.CPP.

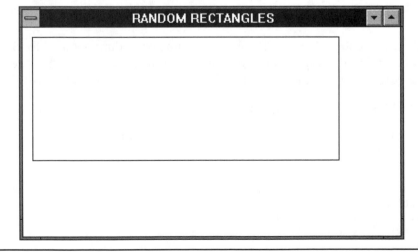

responds to Windows' **WM_PAINT** message requesting that the window repaint itself. The **Paint** function is almost always overridden in order to draw something in the window's interior. By default, as you saw in SIMPLE.CPP, **Paint** doesn't do anything. Here, we are calling the Windows function **Rectangle** and telling it to draw a rectangle that extends from column 20 and row 10 to column 300 and row 100:

```
void TRectangleWindow::Paint(TDC& dc, BOOL, TRect&)
{
  Rectangle(dc, 20, 10, 300, 100);    // Draw a rectangle
}
```

The coordinates in the **Rectangle** function are probably obvious, but what is its first parameter **dc**? This variable actually performs two roles here; however, as far as the **Rectangle** function is concerned, it's used as what Windows calls a *handle* to a *device context*. Before we can describe what a handle to a device context is though, we need to cover what a device context is.

In many respects, a device context is much like a C++ object. Specifically, a device context specifies the drawing parameters to be used in a graphics operation, such as the current color, line style, and fill settings, and also provides access to the drawing routines themselves. In addition, the device context acts as a permission slip that regulates which program can access the screen, avoiding program conflicts.

The handle to a device context is really nothing mysterious. It is simply a unique integer value, assigned by Windows, that is used to locate the device's data and functions stored in the device context. In C++ terms, a device context is like an object, and a handle is a bit like a **this** pointer.

In fact, a device context is so much like an object, that OWL encapsulates all the functions and variables connected with a device context into a class called **TDC**. If you look back at the parameter list, in fact, you'll notice that **dc** is actually of type **TDC**. However, how can **dc** be a **TDC** variable and passed to **Rectangle** as an **HDC**? The answer is in a *type conversion function* that the class **TDC** includes. It performs the conversion for us. If you look at OWL's source code you'll see that all the function does is return an encapsulated **dc** variable.

As part of its job as an object, the **TDC** class supplies its own **Rectangle** function, however, we'll use Windows' standard graphics functions in order to make the code a bit more portable. There really isn't much difference, so if you prefer you could rewrite the call to **Rectangle** as:

```
dc.Rectangle(20, 10, 300, 100);
```

Where does the device context come from? The OWL code hides a call to a Windows function that gains access to the device context handle so that painting functions draw to the screen. Also hidden is that, immediately after **Paint** finishes, the handle to the device context is released by the program so that the display can be used by other programs. Remember, Windows programs must share the screen with other programs. We'll discuss additional details of the device context in Chapter 2.

The last two parameters in **Paint** are not used here. They signal whether the background needs erasing and what area of the window should be updated. Variable names are not specified here so that the compiler won't generate warnings stating that the variables aren't used. By listing only the types in the argument list, the warnings are avoided. If you're wondering, **BOOL** is defined in WINDOWS.H as an unsigned character and **TRect** is an OWL version of Window's **RECT** structure that specifies two opposing corners of a rectangle. We'll explore these structures further in the next chapter.

USING EVENTS AND MESSAGES

An important part of learning how to write Windows programs involves getting used to the event-driven concept. To emphasize this point, we'll add another twist to our first application, SIMPLE.CPP. This time, we'll modify the program so that it draws randomly sized rectangles in response to one of two events: a left mouse click or a keypress. These two Windows events have the names **WM_LBUTTONDOWN** and **WM_CHAR**, respectively. We'll also need to respond to the **WM_SIZE** event, as we'll discuss shortly.

The source code for the new program, RANDRECT.CPP, is listed at the end of this chapter. Although the output varies, Figure 1.5 presents what a typical window looks like.

The RANDRECT program introduces several new aspects of Windows programming. We'll begin by working with what we've already explained—the

Figure 1.5 Typical output of RANDRECT.CPP.

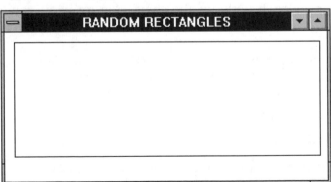

Paint function. Here we've added a call to **random** to return a random number between 0 and 199, inclusive. This value is added as an offset to the width and height of the rectangle drawn:

```
int r = random(200);    // Get a random number between 0 and 199
Rectangle(dc, 10, 10, 300+r, 100+r);
```

The **random** function is initialized in the constructor for our window class by calling the C++ function **randomize**. (Since **Paint** responds to the internal **WM_PAINT** message, each time a **WM_PAINT** message is generated, **Paint** draws a new, randomly sized rectangle.)

Responding to the two user-initiated messages, **WM_LBUTTONDOWN** and **WM_CHAR**, is fairly simple with OWL. All we need to do is override the member functions, **EvLButtonDown** and **EvChar** (accessible through the **TWindow** class), which correspond with these two events. Notice the similarity between the names of these functions and the names of the events. Similar functions can be overridden for any of Windows' other messages.

How do **EvLButtonDown** and **EvChar** in RANDRECT get called by Windows? Internally, OWL manages a *message response table* that lists these functions and the Windows' messages that they correspond to. The table is constructed through a combination of OWL-supplied macros. If you look at the end of the **TRandomRectWindow** class you'll see one such macro:

```
DECLARE_RESPONSE_TABLE(TRandomRectWindow);
```

This macro signals that we'll be needing a message response table for some of the functions in **TRandomRectWindow**. The specific routines are listed in a macro block that appears after **TRandomRectWindow**:

```
DEFINE_RESPONSE_TABLE1(TRandomRectWindow, TWindow)
  EV_WM_LBUTTONDOWN,
  EV_WM_CHAR,
  EV_WM_SIZE,
END_RESPONSE_TABLE;
```

In English, this macro block states that the **TRandomRectWindow** class includes functions to respond to three messages: **WM_LBUTTONDOWN**, **WM_CHAR**, and **WM_SIZE**. The functions that OWL calls are predefined. For example, OWL executes **EvLButtonDown** when the **WM_LBUTTONDOWN** event occurs. In fact, each Windows message has a specific function prototype that it expects, as outlined in the Borland C++'s *OWL Reference Guide*. Table 1.2 lists a few of the common Windows messages and the functions you'll need to supply. Notice that the names of the Windows messages, their macro names, and the response functions are slight variations of one another. For instance, to respond to the Windows event **WM_CHAR**, we must specify the OWL macro

Table 1.2 Common Windows Events and Their OWL Response Functions

Message	Macro	Response Function
WM_LBUTTONDOWN	EV_WM_LBUTTONDOWN	void EvLButtonDown(UINT modkeys, TPoint& point)
WM_SIZE	EV_WM_SIZE	void EvSize(UINT sizeType,TSize& size)
WM_CHAR	EV_WM_CHAR	void EvChar(UINT key,UINT repeatCount, UINT flags)
WM_CLOSE	EV_WM_CLOSE	void EvClose()
WM_MOVE	EV_WM_MOVE	void EvMove(TPoint& client)

EV_WM_CHAR, and provide code for the function **EvChar**. The specific parameters of the response functions depend on the variables provided by Windows through the event. For instance, the **point** parameter in **EvLButtonDown** specifies the location of the mouse when the left mouse button was pressed.

 Note If you leave out the response table entry for a particular function that is expected to respond to a Windows message, the function will never be called. For instance, if you supply a function **EvChar**, but don't list **EV_WM_CHAR** in the window's response table, **EvChar** will never be executed. Put another way, if it appears like your message response functions aren't being called, before you do anything else, check for the correct response table macro.

Now let's take a look at the response functions. The **EvChar** routine, for instance, is defined later in the file as:

```
void TRandomRectWindow::EvChar(UINT, UINT, UINT)
{
  ::InvalidateRect(HWindow, 0, TRUE);
}
```

What does the statement in **EvChar** do? The **InvalidateRect** function is a Windows routine that instructs Windows to post a **WM_PAINT** message to erase and then repaint the display window. Its first parameter, **HWindow** (a variable of the **TWindow** class), tells Windows which window to update; in this instance, **TRandomRectWindow** is updating its own window. The 0 parameter says to repaint the whole window. The third parameter instructs Windows to erase the window before repainting it. (We'll visit **InvalidateRect** again in Chapter 2.) The two colons before the **InvalidateRect** function act as a C++ scoping operator. They are required because OWL supplies a function with the same name. Without the colons the compiler will think you're trying to call OWL's C++ version of the routine and not Window's C-based function.

It's important to understand how **InvalidateRect** is being used. The **Paint** member function, which draws the rectangle, is not called directly within **EvChar**. Instead, **InvalidateRect** generates a **WM_PAINT** message that invokes the **Paint** function. Using messages this way is at the heart of message-driven programming.

The **EvLButtonDown** message response function is similar to **EvChar**, except, of course, that it responds to the **WM_LBUTTONDOWN** message.

The **EvSize** function also performs a paint message. However, **EvSize** responds to the **WM_SIZE** message, which is generated each time the size of the window changes. **EvSize** is important, because whenever the user enlarges the window, a new **WM_PAINT** message is generated to paint the newly exposed areas. Since the code will paint a new, randomly sized rectangle with each **WM_PAINT** message, we may get garbage on the screen, because the old rectangle isn't erased before the new rectangle is drawn. We could add a fill operation to the window to solve the problem, or as we've done here, respond to the **WM_SIZE** message to force the window to completely erase itself and paint a new rectangle.

To compile RANDRECT.CPP, follow the same procedure outlined for SIMPLE.CPP. After you have the program running, try placing other applications over RANDRECT's window and then removing them. Similarly, try resizing the window, clicking the left mouse button, or pressing a key to force the window to repaint. As you do these things, pay attention when RANDRECT draws a new rectangle, so that you can better understand when **WM_PAINT** messages are generated.

```
// RANDRECT.CPP: Randomly displays rectangles in response
// to a left click or a keypress.

#include <owl\applicat.h>
#include <owl\framewin.h>
#include <owl\dc.h>        // For OWL's device context class
#include <stdlib.h>        // For random() function

class TRandomRectApp : public TApplication {
public:
  TRandomRectApp() : TApplication() { }
  void InitMainWindow();
};

class TRandomRectWindow : public TWindow {
public:
  TRandomRectWindow(TWindow *parent, const char* title)
    : TWindow(parent, title)
    { randomize(); }
  void Paint(TDC& dc, BOOL, TRect&);
  void EvLButtonDown(UINT, TPoint&);
```

```
  void EvChar(UINT, UINT, UINT);
  void EvSize(UINT, TSize&);

  DECLARE_RESPONSE_TABLE(TRandomRectWindow);
};

DEFINE_RESPONSE_TABLE1(TRandomRectWindow, TWindow)
  EV_WM_LBUTTONDOWN,
  EV_WM_CHAR,
  EV_WM_SIZE,
END_RESPONSE_TABLE;

// Display a random rectangle
void TRandomRectWindow::Paint(TDC& dc, BOOL, TRect&)
{
  int r = random(200);    // Get a random number between 0 and 199
  // The width and height of the rectangle depends on the
  // random number just retrieved
  Rectangle(dc, 10, 10, 300+r, 100+r);
}

// Force the window to repaint in response to a left click
void TRandomRectWindow::EvLButtonDown(UINT, TPoint&)
{
  ::InvalidateRect(HWindow, 0, TRUE);
}

// Force the window to repaint in response to a keypress
void TRandomRectWindow::EvChar(UINT, UINT, UINT)
{
  ::InvalidateRect(HWindow, 0, TRUE);
}

// Force the window to repaint if the window is resized
void TRandomRectWindow::EvSize(UINT, TSize&)
{
  ::InvalidateRect(HWindow, 0, TRUE);
}

void TRandomRectApp::InitMainWindow()
{
  MainWindow = new TFrameWindow(0, "RANDOM RECTANGLES",
    new TRandomRectWindow(0, ""));
}

int OwlMain(int /*argc*/, char* /*argv*/[])
{
  return TRandomRectApp().Run();
}
```

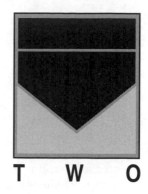

T W O

Working with Display Devices

I n Chapter 1, we explained three simple OWL-based Windows programs to provide you with a basic framework for developing Windows applications. Now we'll turn our attention to Windows' graphics capabilities and detail how you can use them to flesh out a Windows program.

The *Graphics Device Interface (GDI)* is the gateway to graphics programming in Windows. It's a collection of graphics functions that perform such actions as drawing lines, painting bitmaps, setting colors, and so on.

You've already seen the GDI at work in Chapter 1, when we painted rectangles on the screen. In the next several chapters, we'll explain the nuts and bolts of the GDI, giving you a foundation for assembling your own graphics programs.

In this chapter, we'll begin by discussing how Windows treats its display devices. We'll also explore ways of determining the default graphics capabilities of a particular device. This will also give us a chance to explain some of the ways in which Windows manages its output.

Display Devices and Windows

One of the main objectives of the GDI is device-independent graphics programming. The goal is to make it possible for code that works on a monochrome display, for instance, to work equally well on an Super VGA display, or even a printer. Windows partially achieves this independence by designing the graphics functions to work with generic *devices* rather than specific hardware. Windows supports four types of devices: screen displays, hard-copy printers and plotters, bitmaps, and special files known as metafiles.

Under this approach, you won't be burdened with the details of working on different displays. As you might imagine, however, this does not preclude you from having to consider the capabilities of the devices you are using.

Of course, not all output devices can do the same things. For instance, a plotter does not support raster graphics operations for plotting pixels or displaying bitmaps. And some printers don't support graphics at all. For this reason, writing a program that must work on a wide variety of devices leads to many challenging problems.

The Device Context

As you learned in Chapter 1, Windows maintains information about a particular device in what it calls a *device context*, which is your link to sending output to a device. Actually, a device context serves several purposes:

• It houses dozens of drawing parameters used by the GDI functions, such as the pen, fill, and font styles.

• It provides access to the drawing routines and capabilities for a specific device.

• It mediates between multiple applications that want to access the same device. On a display screen, the device context uses clipping to ensure that an application won't draw beyond what it should. On a printer, the device context keeps print operations separate in the Print Manager.

Attributes of the Device Context

A device context contains the current drawing settings that Windows' graphics functions use, such as the line style, fill pattern, and font. Table 2.1 lists the drawing attributes included in the device context and provides their default values.

Handling a Device Context

When you want to use a particular output device, you must have access to its device context. You manipulate a device context indirectly by using a *handle*. Since devices can be shared among programs, the handle to a device context also acts as your permission slip to use the display, printer, or whatever.

After Windows gives you a handle to a device context, you are guaranteed that no other application will interfere with your graphics operations on that device. When you are finished drawing or using a device context, you should return your handle. In Windows parlance, this latter step is called *releasing the device context*. The importance of releasing a device context as soon as you can is underscored by the fact that standard Windows only has room for *five*

Table 2.1 The Display Device-Context Attributes and Their Default Values

Attribute	Default Value	Comments
Background color	White	
Background mode	OPAQUE	Fills gaps in lines, hatch patterns, and text
Brush handle	WHITE_BRUSH	Fill style
Brush origin	(0,0)	
Clipping region	Entire client area	
Color palette	DEFAULT_PALETTE	
Current position	(0,0)	
Drawing mode	R2_COPYPEN	
Font handle	SYSTEM_FONT	
Intercharacter spacing	0	
Mapping mode	MM_TEXT	One unit equals one pixel
Pen handle	BLACK_PEN	
Polygon-filling mode	ALTERNATE	For polygon routines
Stretching mode	BLACKONWHITE	Used by StretchBlt
Text alignment	TA_LEFT, TA_TOP, and TA_NOUPDATECP	
Text color	Black	
Viewport extent	(1,1)	
Viewport origin	(0,0)	
Window extent	(1,1)	
Window origin	(0,0)	

device contexts at a time. 32-bit Windows, such as Windows NT, is not burdened by this restriction; however, it's still not a good idea to consume resources for longer than you need.

Accessing a Device Context

A handle to a device context is defined in WINDOWS.H as the type **HDC**. Therefore, the following statement declares a device-context handle called **hDC**:

```
HDC hDC;
```

How do you gain access to a particular device? There are two common techniques. One is used in response to a **WM_PAINT** message, which as you recall, is generated when a window is to be updated. In this case, the function pair **BeginPaint** and **EndPaint** is used to retrieve and then release a handle to the video display's device context. For instance, the following code excerpt illustrates how to use these two functions to draw a rectangle on the screen:

```
PAINTSTRUCT ps;
HDC hDC = BeginPaint(HWindow, &ps);
Rectangle(ps.hdc, 10, 10, 100, 300);
EndPaint(HWindow, &ps);
```

The **HWindow** parameter to **BeginPaint** is a handle to the window to be updated. (OWL provides the handle to a window for us in the **TWindow** class.) Since the window is displayed on the screen, the device context returned will be associated with the screen.

The other parameter to **BeginPaint**, **ps**, is a structure of type **PAINTSTRUCT**. As you can see, **PAINTSTRUCT** contains a handle to the device context (**ps.hdc**). It also contains the bounding coordinates of the rectangular region in the window to be painted. Here's the complete definition of **PAINTSTRUCT**:

```
typedef struct tagPAINTSTRUCT {
  HDC hdc;                 // Handle to the device context on which to draw
  BOOL fErase;            // 0 if the display was just cleared
  RECT rcPaint;           // Coordinates of region to paint
  BOOL fRestore;          // Used by Windows
  BOOL fIncUpdate;        // Used by Windows
  BYTE rgbReserved[16];   // Used by Windows
} PAINTSTRUCT;
```

One purpose of **BeginPaint** is to set up a clipping region in the device context so that graphics operations will not change the screen outside of the clipping region. (This also implies that only the area within the clipping region is updated.) Because manipulating the screen is often the slow part of graphics operations, this clipping will speed up any window repainting. You can speed up your screen painting further by generating drawing commands in this region only. Of course, doing so will require more code.

The **rcPaint** field in **PAINTSTRUCT** specifies which rectangular region of the window is to be painted. Windows says this region is *invalid*. The bounds of the rectangle are contained in a structure of type **RECT** that is defined in WINDOWS.H as:

```
typedef struct tagRECT {
  int left;
  int top;
  int right;
```

```
    int bottom;
} RECT;
```

Note OWL defines the class **TRect** that contains the same fields as **RECT**, as well as support for manipulating the rectangular region. The **Paint** function in **TWindow**, for instance, uses the **TRect** type.

The **EndPaint** function releases the device context and *validates* the window region that was painted. If the validation isn't done (by not calling **EndPaint**), Windows will continually generate **WM_PAINT** messages, requesting that the window be updated. (Note that after **EndPaint** is called, the device context being used is no longer valid.)

In a non-OWL Windows application, you must use **BeginPaint** and **EndPaint** in response to a **WM_PAINT** message. However, OWL calls these functions for you as long as you use **TWindow**'s **Paint** function. On the other hand, it you chose to override and don't use **TWindow**'s **WM_PAINT** response function, **EvPaint**, you must perform these operations yourself.

Recall from Chapter 1 that a **RECT** structure is passed to the OWL function **Paint**. This rectangle refers to the same area as the **rcPaint** field in **PAINTSTRUCT**. However, be careful when using **PAINTSTRUCT**. Its **rcPaint** field refers to the *clipping region*, not the whole window. Therefore, don't scale your figures based on **rcPaint** or **Paint**'s **RECT** parameter.

Another common way of gaining access to a device context is to use the function **GetDC**:

```
HDC GetDC(HWND hWindow);
```

Once you have the handle, you are free to draw any graphics to it. As you'll see, every drawing routine in the GDI requires that a handle to a device context be passed as its first argument. This is Windows' way of making sure you have permission to use the device and that it knows which device you want to use.

As soon as you are finished drawing, you should immediately return your permission slip to Windows. This is done by releasing your device-context handle using the **ReleaseDC** function:

```
ReleaseDC(HWindow, hDC);
```

The following code, for example, uses **GetDC** and **ReleaseDC** to draw a rectangle in response to a left mouse click:

```
void TExampleWindow::EvLButtonDown(UINT, TPoint&)
{
  HDC hDC = ::GetDC(HWindow);
  Rectangle(hDC, 10, 10, 300, 100);
```

```
    ::ReleaseDC(HWindow, hDC);
}
```

To recap, the difference between **BeginPaint\EndPaint** and **GetDC\ReleaseDC** is that the **BeginPaint** pair sets up a clipping region to improve the speed of painting the window. In addition, OWL sandwiches **TWindow**'s **Paint** member function with calls to **BeginPaint** and **EndPaint**, so we don't have to call them ourselves. The **GetDC** and **ReleaseDC** function pair, on the other hand, is useful when drawing to the screen in response to messages other than **WM_PAINT**.

Note Each time you call **GetDC** or use OWL's **Paint** function, the device-context values are set to their defaults. To save and later restore the settings of a device context, Windows provides the **SaveDC** and **RestoreDC** functions. OWL includes similarly named functions in its **TDC** class.

Displaying a Device's Capabilities

You can retrieve information about a device and the features that it supports by calling the GDI function **GetDeviceCaps** (function parameters are breifly described following the function format):

```
int GetDeviceCaps(HDC hDC, int deviceCode);
```

- **hDC** is a handle to the device context.
- The function returns the device context's value for the field specified by **deviceCode**.

The majority of the valid **deviceCode** values are illustrated in the DEVICE.CPP program. The DEVICE.CPP program (shown later in this section) illustrates how to use **GetDeviceCaps**. The program calls **GetDeviceCaps** several times, passing it various constants, to retrieve and then display most of the settings of the video display. Figures 2.1 and 2.2 present the output of DEVICE.CPP for VGA and Super VGA displays, respectively.

The DEVICE.CPP program is rather large, but is really quite simple. Most of the code lies within the **Paint** function, so we'll begin there. This function contains several calls to **GetDeviceCaps**—each with a different constant passed to it. Each value that **GetDeviceCaps** returns is stored in the string, **buffer**, and passed to **ShowLn** to be displayed. For instance, the following statements retrieve and then display the width of the screen:

```
sprintf(buffer, "%-d", GetDeviceCaps(dc, HORZRES));
ShowLn(hDC, ht*3,  "HORZRES",     buffer,  "Width in pixels");
```

Figure 2.1 Default settings in a VGA device context.

Constant	Value	Description
HORZRES	640	Width in pixels
VERTRES	480	Height in pixels
HORZSIZE	208	Width in mm
VERTSIZE	156	Height in mm
ASPECTX	36	Horizontal aspect
ASPECTXY	51	Diagonal aspect
ASPECTY	36	Vertical aspect
BITSPIXEL	1	Color bits/pixel
LOGPIXELSX	96	Logical pixels/inch
LOGPIXELSY	96	Logical pixels/inch
NUMPENS	80	Number of device-specific pens
NUMBRUSHES	-1	Number of device-specific brushes
NUMFONTS	0	Number of device-specific fonts
NUMCOLORS	16	Number of colors (default)
PLANES	4	Number of color planes

Device Capabilities

Palette not supported

The **ShowLn** function, included in DEVICE.CPP, calls the Windows' function **TextOut** three times to display each of the three strings passed to it in a different column. The row at which the text is displayed depends on the

Figure 2.2 Default settings in a Super VGA device context.

Constant	Value	Description
HORZRES	640	Width in pixels
VERTRES	480	Height in pixels
HORZSIZE	240	Width in mm
VERTSIZE	180	Height in mm
ASPECTX	36	Horizontal aspect
ASPECTXY	51	Diagonal aspect
ASPECTY	36	Vertical aspect
BITSPIXEL	8	Color bits/pixel
LOGPIXELSX	96	Logical pixels/inch
LOGPIXELSY	96	Logical pixels/inch
NUMPENS	100	Number of device-specific pens
NUMBRUSHES	-1	Number of device-specific brushes
NUMFONTS	0	Number of device-specific fonts
NUMCOLORS	20	Number of colors (default)
PLANES	1	Number of color planes
SIZEPALETTE	256	Number of palette entries
NUMRESERVED	20	Palette entries reserved
COLORRES	18	Device's color resolution in bits/pixel

Device Capabilities

calculation made with the variable **ht**. The **ht** variable stores the height of each line of text and is calculated from values returned by the GDI function **GetTextMetrics**. We'll cover **GetTextMetrics** and **TextOut** in detail in Chapter 7 (when we discuss GDI's text features).

You can also use **GetDeviceCaps** to determine whether a device supports a particular operation, such as bitmap operations or curve drawing. When writing generic code that works on a wide range of devices (particularly printers), you'll probably have to do this. For instance, you can test whether a device supports a logical color palette, as shown in DEVICE.CPP. This operation involves two checks. First, the code passes **RASTERCAPS** to **GetDeviceCaps** to see if its return value has the **RC_PALETTE** bit set. Second, it tests whether the device driver is written for Windows 3.0 (or higher):

```
if ((GetDeviceCaps(dc, RASTERCAPS) & RC_PALETTE) &&
    (GetDeviceCaps(dc, DRIVERVERSION) >= 0x300)) {
```

To compile DEVICE.CPP use the procedure outlined in Chapter 1. If your graphics adapter is capable of displaying several different Windows-compatible modes, try running the program each one and compare the results. To change to another display mode, use the SETUP program included with Windows.

```
// DEVICE.CPP: Displays information about the video display.

#include <owl\applicat.h>
#include <owl\framewin.h>
#include <owl\dc.h>
#include <stdio.h>
#include <string.h>

class TDeviceWindow : public TWindow {
public:
  TDeviceWindow(TWindow *parent, const char* title)
    : TWindow(parent, title) { }
  void Paint(TDC& dc, BOOL, TRect&);
  void DisplayLn(TDC& dc, int y,
    char col1[], char col2[], char col3[]);
};

class TDeviceApp : public TApplication {
public:
  TDeviceApp() : TApplication() { }
  virtual void InitMainWindow() {
    MainWindow = new TFrameWindow(0, "Device Capabilities",
      new TDeviceWindow(0, ""));
  }
};

// Shows information about the video display
void TDeviceWindow::Paint(TDC& dc, BOOL, TRect&)
```

```
{
  char buffer[80];
  int ht;
  TEXTMETRIC tm;
  GetTextMetrics(dc, &tm);
  ht = tm.tmHeight + tm.tmExternalLeading;

  DisplayLn(dc, ht,    "Constant",    "Value", "Description");
  DisplayLn(dc, ht*2,  "--------------",
    "----------", "--------------------");
  sprintf(buffer, "%-d", GetDeviceCaps(dc, HORZRES));
  DisplayLn(dc, ht*3, "HORZRES",     buffer, "Width in pixels");
  sprintf(buffer, "%-d", GetDeviceCaps(dc, VERTRES));
  DisplayLn(dc, ht*4, "VERTRES",     buffer, "Height in pixels");
  sprintf(buffer, "%-d", GetDeviceCaps(dc,HORZSIZE));
  DisplayLn(dc, ht*5, "HORZSIZE",    buffer,  "Width in mm");
  sprintf(buffer, "%-d", GetDeviceCaps(dc,VERTSIZE));
  DisplayLn(dc, ht*6, "VERTSIZE",    buffer,  "Height in mm");
  sprintf(buffer, "%-d", GetDeviceCaps(dc,ASPECTX));
  DisplayLn(dc, ht*7, "ASPECTX",     buffer, "Horizontal aspect");
  sprintf(buffer, "%-d", GetDeviceCaps(dc,ASPECTXY));
  DisplayLn(dc, ht*8, "ASPECTXY",    buffer, "Diagonal aspect");
  sprintf(buffer, "%-d", GetDeviceCaps(dc,ASPECTY));
  DisplayLn(dc, ht*9, "ASPECTY",     buffer, "Vertical aspect");
  sprintf(buffer, "%-d", GetDeviceCaps(dc,BITSPIXEL));
  DisplayLn(dc, ht*10, "BITSPIXEL",  buffer, "Color bits/pixel");
  sprintf(buffer, "%-d", GetDeviceCaps(dc,LOGPIXELSX));
  DisplayLn(dc, ht*11, "LOGPIXELSX", buffer, "Logical pixels/inch");
  sprintf(buffer, "%-d", GetDeviceCaps(dc,LOGPIXELSY));
  DisplayLn(dc, ht*12, "LOGPIXELSY", buffer, "Logical pixels/inch");
  sprintf(buffer, "%-d", GetDeviceCaps(dc,NUMPENS));
  DisplayLn(dc, ht*13, "NUMPENS",    buffer, "Number of device-specific pens");
  sprintf(buffer, "%-d", GetDeviceCaps(dc,NUMBRUSHES));
  DisplayLn(dc, ht*14, "NUMBRUSHES", buffer, "Number of device-specific brushes");
  sprintf(buffer, "%-d", GetDeviceCaps(dc,NUMFONTS));
  DisplayLn(dc, ht*15, "NUMFONTS",   buffer, "Number of device-specific fonts");
  sprintf(buffer, "%-d", GetDeviceCaps(dc,NUMCOLORS));
  DisplayLn(dc, ht*16, "NUMCOLORS",  buffer, "Number of colors (default)");
  sprintf(buffer, "%-d", GetDeviceCaps(dc,PLANES));
  DisplayLn(dc, ht*17, "PLANES",     buffer, "Number of color planes");

  if ((GetDeviceCaps(dc,RASTERCAPS) & RC_PALETTE) &&
    (GetDeviceCaps(dc,DRIVERVERSION) >= 0x300)) {
    sprintf(buffer, "%-d", GetDeviceCaps(dc,SIZEPALETTE));
    DisplayLn(dc, ht*18, "SIZEPALETTE", buffer,
      "Number of palette entries");
    sprintf(buffer, "%-d", GetDeviceCaps(dc,NUMRESERVED));
    DisplayLn(dc, ht*19, "NUMRESERVED", buffer,
      "Palette entries reserved");
    sprintf(buffer, "%-d", GetDeviceCaps(dc,COLORRES));
    DisplayLn(dc, ht*20, "COLORRES",    buffer,
      "Device's color resolution in bits/pixel");
  }
}
```

```
    else
      TextOut(dc, 10, ht*18, "Palette not supported", 21);
}

// Display each column of infomation separately so that
// if a variable-pitch font is used, the columns will line up
void TDeviceWindow::DisplayLn(TDC& dc, int y,
  char col1[], char col2[], char col3[])
{
  int x1 = 10;   int x2 = 140;   int x3 = 210;
  TextOut(dc, x1, y, col1, strlen(col1));
  TextOut(dc, x2, y, col2, strlen(col2));
  TextOut(dc, x3, y, col3, strlen(col3));
}

int OwlMain(int /*argc*/, char* /*argv*/[])
{
  return TDeviceApp().Run();
}
```

Another function that returns information about the size of various components of a window and display is **GetSystemMetrics**. For instance, **GetSystemMetrics** can retrieve the pixel width and height of icons on the screen:

```
int iconWidth = GetSystemMetrics(SM_CXICON);
int iconHeight = GetSystemMetrics(SM_CYICON);
```

Similarly, this function can return the pixel height and width of the screen using the following two statements:

```
int screenWidth = GetSystemMetrics(SM_CXSCREEN);
int screenHeight = GetSystemMetrics(SM_CYSCREEN);
```

OWL Encapsulates the Device Context

OWL encapsulates the device context variables and the GDI functions associated with them into the **TDC** class defined in the header file DC.H. Although OWL uses **TDC** rather than **HDC** throughout its code, we'll favor the standard device context Windows type, **HDC**, instead. As a result, we won't be using **TDC**'s encapsulated GDI functions. We'll use the standard Windows functions. If you want to make the code in this book more object-oriented you may want to use the encapsulated routines. For instance, the statements in the DEVICE.CPP program that call the GDI function **TextOut** could be rewritten using the form:

```
dc.TextOut(x3, y, col3, strlen(col3));
```

How Windows Overlaps Windows

To determine how best to write a graphics program, it's necessary to understand how Windows overlaps windows. Whenever one window obscures another, Windows does not attempt to remember what is covered up. Instead, Windows waits until the bottom window becomes visible again and then commands it to repaint itself by posting a **WM_PAINT** message. This prevents Windows from having to remember everything that gets overwritten.

Working with the Screen

Windows applications usually draw on the screen by writing to pop-up windows. A typical window has several components, as shown in Figure 2.3. Usually, you'll be painting to the interior of the window, called the *client area*.

The screen and, of course, its windows are made up of tiny dots called pixels. The pixels are referenced using the default coordinate system shown in Figure 2.4. The top-left coordinate is the point (0,0), with X and Y values increasing to the right and down the screen. Windows also provides other coordinate systems, which we'll cover in a later section of this chapter.

Figure 2.3 Components of a window.

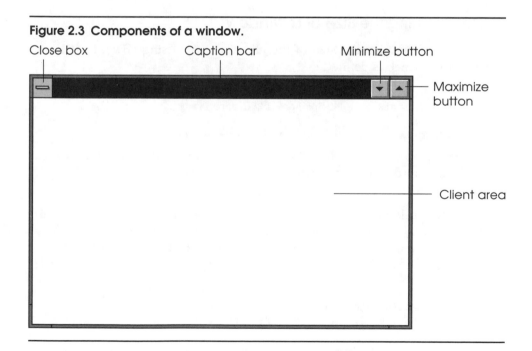

Figure 2.4 Default coordinates of a window.

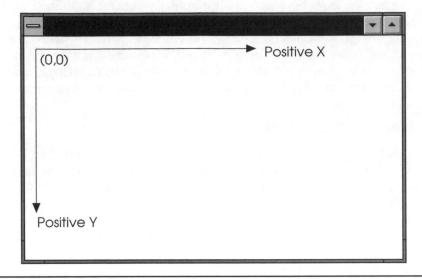

Determining the Size of a Window

You can determine the size of the client area by using GDI's **GetClientRect** function, which is defined as:

```
void GetClientRect(HWND hWindow, RECT* rect);
```

* **hWindow** is a handle to the window (**HWND**).
* **rect** is a pointer to a **RECT** structure that contains the top-left and bottom-right coordinates of the window's client area.

The top-left corner of the client area is always returned as (0,0). Therefore, the right and bottom fields of the **RECT** structure yield the width and height of the client area. The following code uses **GetClientRect** to draw a rectangle the full size of a window's client area:

```
RECT rect;
GetClientRect(HWindow, &rect);
Rectangle(hDC, 0, 0, rect.right, rect.bottom);
```

Note The OWL class, **TWindow**, encapsulates calls to **GetClientRect** and similar functions that pass a handle to a window as their first parameter. These OWL functions pass the handle to the window implicitly. However, as with the device context class, we will be using the standard Windows version of the these functions. Unfortunately, C++ can't be sure which function we're trying to call. Consequently, when we use the standard Windows functions we must place the :: scoping operator before each Windows function call that has a similar routine in **TWindow**:

```
::GetClientRect(HWindow, &rect);
```

Forcing Windows to Repaint

As mentioned earlier, the **Paint** member function in the **TWindow** class responds to Windows' **WM_PAINT** message. In addition, only the client area that is considered invalid is painted. You can manually force regions of the client area to be updated by calling Windows' **InvalidateRect** function. This routine specifies a rectangular region in the client area to be updated and then posts a **WM_PAINT** message in Windows' message queue. Here's its format:

```
void InvalidateRect(HWND hWindow, RECT* rect, BOOL erase);
```

- **hWindow** is a handle to the window (**HWND**).

- **rect** is a far pointer to a rectangular region to be updated; if this argument is NULL then the whole client area is invalidated.

- **erase** is a Boolean flag set to TRUE if the invalid client area should be cleared before repainting; if FALSE, the region is not erased prior to painting it.

Quite often, **InvalidateRect** is used in message response functions that want to change the screen. Rather than change the screen directly, the **InvalidateRect** function is called, which triggers a **WM_PAINT** message and tells OWL's **Paint** function to handle the drawing. We took this approach in the RANDRECT.CPP program in Chapter 1 when we called **InvalidateRect** in response to keypresses and left mouse clicks.

A Window's Coordinates

The coordinate system in a window is based on its current *mapping mode*. Windows provides eight mapping modes, as listed in Table 2.2. Each mapping mode serves two purposes: it specifies the orientation and scale of the client area's coordinate system and it determines how to interpret the units passed to GDI commands.

At this stage, we need to point out that all GDI commands use *logical* coordinates. For example, the statement

```
Rectangle(hDC, 10, 10, 40, 100);
```

draws a rectangle from *logical* coordinate (10,10) to *logical* coordinate (40,100). The mapping mode determines how these logical coordinates are translated into the device's actual units or *physical units.* On a video display, the physical units are its pixels.

The eight mapping modes fall into three categories, based on the logical units that they use. The first mapping mode listed in Table 2.2, **MM_TEXT**, references pixels on the screen. The next five mapping modes express logical units in terms of some real-world measure, such as inches or millimeters. The last two modes enable you to express logical units according to scale factors that you specify.

The origin of the device context is not affected by the selection of the mapping mode. Whenever you gain access to a device context, the origin is set to the top left of the client area. You can, however, change the position of the origin, as we'll see later in this chapter.

Notice that the direction of the positive Y axis is not the same for all modes. The **MM_TEXT** mode has increasing Y values as you move *down* a window; the other mapping modes have increasing Y values as you move *up* the window. Since the origin is at the top left of the client area, all values of positive Y in these modes are above and, therefore, outside of the window. For example, if you select the **MM_LOENGLISH** mode and immediately plot the pixel (10,10), it won't appear. Positive Y values won't show up unless you take additional steps.

Table 2.2 Mapping Modes Supported by Windows

MappingMode	Increasing Logical Unit	X	Y
MM_TEXT	1 pixel	Right	Down
MM_LOENGLISH	0.01 inch	Right	Up
MM_HIENGLISH	0.001 inch	Right	Up
MM_LOMETRIC	0.1 millimeter	Right	Up
MM_HIMETRIC	0.01 millimeter	Right	Up
MM_TWIPS	1/20 point or 1/1440 inch	Right	Up
MM_ISOTROPIC	Variable; scale in X equals scale in Y	Programmable	Programmable
MM_ANISOTROPIC	Variable; scale in X doesn't have to equal Y	Programmable	Programmable

Controlling the Mapping Mode

Windows provides two functions to set and determine the mapping mode:

```
int GetMapMode(HDC hDC);
int SetMapMode(HDC hDC, int newMapMode);
```

- **hDC** is a handle to the device context.
- **newMapMode** is one of the mapping modes shown in Table 2.2.
- **GetMapMode** returns the current mapping mode.
- **SetMapMode** returns the previous mapping mode.

The Default Mapping Mode

By default, a window employs the **MM_TEXT** mapping mode. As previously illustrated in Figure 2.4, **MM_TEXT** arranges the coordinate system so that the point (0,0) is at the top left of the client area, with X values increasing left to right and Y values top to bottom. In addition, coordinates in this mode have a one-to-one correspondence with pixels on the screen. One logical unit equals one pixel. The point (3,2), therefore, is the fourth pixel from the left in the third row of the window.

The **MM_TEXT** mapping mode is commonly used when you want to control which pixels to use in your drawings. This mapping mode has an additional advantage: the coordinate structure of **MM_TEXT** matches those used by the mouse. For these and other reasons, we'll usually use **MM_TEXT** in this book.

Unfortunately, different devices have different pixel sizes and dimensions. Therefore, figures drawn in different display modes or on different devices may be different sizes or proportions. For instance, the following rectangle drawn on a VGA display would appear a mere .1 inch in size on a 300 dots per inch laser printer

```
Rectangle(hDC, 10, 10, 40, 40);
```

You can compensate for these device dependencies by using some of the values accessible through the **GetDeviceCaps** function. For instance, you can adjust each of your drawings by the aspect ratio of the screen. A less tedious approach is to use one of Windows' other mapping modes.

Device-Independent Mapping Modes

Windows provides five mapping modes that express logical units in terms of some real-world dimension, such as inches or millimeters. For example,

MM_LOENGLISH sets each unit equal to 0.01 inch in width and height. Therefore, you can display a one-inch square using 100 of these units:

```
SetMapMode(hDC, MM_LOENGLISH);
Rectangle(hDC, 0, 0, 100, 100);  // Display a one-inch square
```

The **MM_LOENGLISH** mapping mode uses as many pixels as it needs to draw the rectangle one inch in size—regardless of the display's resolution. This is the advantage of using one of these mapping modes.

The **MM_HIENGLISH**, **MM_LOMETRIC**, **MM_HIMETRIC**, and **MM_TWIPS** mapping modes are similar, except that they use different units. The **MM_TWIPS** measure might seem a little odd. This mode bases its measurement on *points*, the standard unit of measure in the publishing world.

If you need to convert from logical coordinates to physical coordinates, you can use the following function:

```
BOOL LPtoDP(HDC hDC, POINT* pointsArray, int numPoints);
```

Similarly, to convert from device coordinates to logical coordinates, you can use:

```
BOOL DPtoLP(HDC hDC, POINT* pointsArray, int numPoints);
```

In both cases, **pointsArray** is an array of **POINT** structures, which contains the coordinates that are converted. The variable **numPoints** is the number of points in the **pointsArray**.

Windows defines **POINT** as a structure that contains the two integer variables, **x** and **y**. OWL provides a similar class, **TPoint**, that contains two integers, **x** and **y**, and a variety of operators and functions to manipulate them.

Setting the Origin

Sometimes you'll want to relocate the origin of the current mapping mode. To accomplish this, you should use the two Windows functions **SetViewportOrgEx** and **SetWindowOrgEx**. The difference between the two routines is based on the units of the coordinates passed to them. The **SetWindowOrgEx** function always refers to coordinates in logical units, and the units passed to **SetViewportOrgEx** are always in device units (pixels). Since the **MM_TEXT** mode has a one-to-one correspondence between its logical coordinates and physical coordinates—they're both pixels—it does not matter which function you use in this mode.

Recall that in non-**MM_TEXT** mapping modes, the origin is at the top left of the window, yet Y values increase as you move up the window. One way to fix this is to call **SetViewportOrgEx** in order to move the origin to the bottom left of the window, as shown in Figure 2.5:

Figure 2.5 Setting the origin to the bottom of the window.

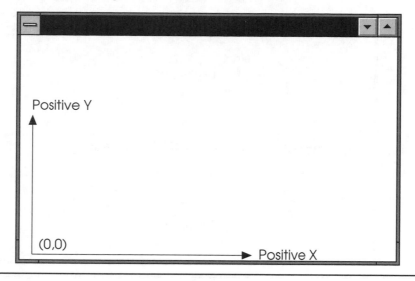

```
GetClientRect(hDC, &rect);
SetViewportOrgEx(hDC, 0, rect.bottom, &prevOrigin);
```

Note   Earlier versions of Windows used viewport and window routines with similar names. For instance, the routine **SetViewportOrgEx** was preceeded by **SetViewportOrg**. Both functions perform the same operation, although the Ex, or *extended*, function has an additional parameter that returns the previous setting. As you work through the following sections you'll notice other routines with the Ex suffix; they also are extended versions of previous Windows functions. Realize that the older routines are not supported in 32-bit targets; therefore, to write the most portable code, you should use the newer, extended functions.

Similarly, to move the origin to the center of the window, as shown in Figure 2.6, you could use:

```
GetClientRect(hDC, &rect);
SetViewportOrgEx(hDC, rect.right/2, rect.bottom/2, &prevOrigin);
```

The last parameter in these two function calls is a pointer to a **POINT** structure that gets loaded with the location of the previous origin.

To determine the current viewport and window origins, Windows provides these routines:

Figure 2.6 Setting the origin to the center of the window.

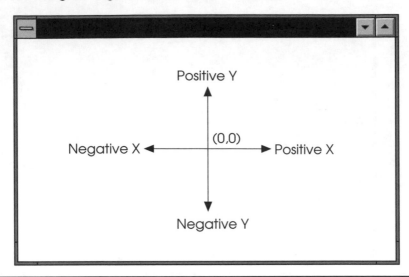

```
BOOL GetViewportOrgEx(HDC hDC, POINT* origin);
BOOL GetWindowOrgEx(HDC hDC, POINT* origin);
```

- **hDC** is a handle to the device context.
- **origin** points to a **POINT** structure that contains the location of the origin.
- Both functions return TRUE if they succeed, 0 otherwise.

Note that **GetViewportOrgEx** always returns the origin in device units and **GetWindowOrgEx** always returns its values in logical units.

User-Defined Scaling of Coordinates

There are two mapping modes we haven't covered yet: **MM_ISOTROPIC** and **MM_ANISOTROPIC**. These two modes allow you to specify the scale factors used in the X and Y directions. Both mapping modes are useful when you need to scale drawings so that they are guaranteed to fit within a window.

In the case of **MM_ISOTROPIC**, the scale of the X and Y dimensions is set equivalently. As a result, a circle will appear as a true circle, not as an ellipse, *regardless of the aspect ratio of the display device*. The **MM_ANISOTROPIC** mode is similar to **MM_ISOTROPIC** except that the X and Y axes do not have to have the same scale factor.

The scale factors are set indirectly by specifying the X and Y extents of the logical coordinates and the client area to be used:

```
BOOL SetViewportExtEx(HDC hDC, int x, int y, SIZE* prevExtents);
BOOL SetWindowExtEx(HDC hDC, int x, int y, SIZE* prevExtents);
```

- **hDC** is a handle to the device context.
- The integer values **x** and **y** are the extents to use.
- **prevExtents** points to a **SIZE** structure that is set to the previous extents.
- Both functions return non-zero if they succeed.

The scale factors depend on the ratio between the extents specified in the two functions.

As was the case with the two functions that set the origin, these two functions differ in the units that they use. The **SetViewportExtEx** function refers to the device's units (pixels), while **SetWindowExtEx** uses logical coordinates. In addition, when the **MM_ISOTROPIC** mode is set, you must call **SetWindowExtEx** before calling **SetViewportExtEx**.

Let's look at an example. The following program uses the **MM_ISOTROPIC** mapping mode to draw a square using the **Rectangle** function, regardless of the window's dimensions or the screen's aspect ratio.

```
// MM_ISO.CPP: Displays a rectangle using the MM_ISOTROPIC mapping mode.

#include <owl\applicat.h>
#include <owl\framewin.h>
#include <owl\dc.h>

class TExampleApp : public TApplication {
public:
  TExampleApp() : TApplication() { }
  void InitMainWindow();
};

class TExampleWindow : public TWindow {
public:
  TExampleWindow(TWindow *parent, const char* title)
    : TWindow(parent, title) { }
  void Paint(TDC& dc, BOOL, TRect&);
  void EvSize(UINT, TSize&);

  DECLARE_RESPONSE_TABLE(TExampleWindow);
};

DEFINE_RESPONSE_TABLE1(TExampleWindow, TWindow)
  EV_WM_SIZE,
END_RESPONSE_TABLE;
```

```
// Display a square in the center of the window
void TExampleWindow::Paint(TDC& dc, BOOL, TRect&)
{
  RECT rect;
  ::GetClientRect(HWindow, &rect);
  SetMapMode(dc, MM_ISOTROPIC);   // Set mapping mode
  SetWindowExtEx(dc, 10000, 10000, &SIZE()); // Set logical unit extent
  SetViewportExtEx(dc, rect.right, rect.bottom, &SIZE()); // Device extent
  // Place the origin in the center of the window
  SetViewportOrgEx(dc, rect.right/2, rect.bottom/2, &POINT());
  // Draw the square using logical coordinates
  Rectangle(dc, -2500, -2500, 2500, 2500);
}

// Force the window to repaint if the window is resized
void TExampleWindow::EvSize(UINT, TSize&)
{
  ::InvalidateRect(HWindow, 0, TRUE);
}

void TExampleApp::InitMainWindow()
{
  MainWindow = new TFrameWindow(0, "MM_ISOTROPIC",
    new TExampleWindow(0, ""));
}

int OwlMain(int /*argc*/, char* /*argv*/[])
{
  return TExampleApp().Run();
}
```

▼ **Note**   If you're new to C++, you may be wondering about the last parameters used in these two statements of the previous program:

```
SetWindowExtEx(dc, 10000, 10000, &SIZE()); // Set logical unit extent
SetViewportExtEx(dc, rect.right, rect.bottom, &SIZE()); // Device extent
```

The somewhat terse syntax, **&SIZE()**, creates a temporary, unnamed **SIZE** structure and passes a pointer to it along to the function. After the function call, the temporary **SIZE** variable is lost and the returned values are unaccessible. This isn't a problem, however, since we don't need the return values, anyway. This technique is useful if you aren't interested in what a parameter returns, yet you still must provide a placeholder for it. Alternatively, you can set the parameters to 0, which informs the functions not to return a value. Either style is acceptable.

Figure 2.7 shows the square as it appears in windows of varying sizes. Note that the size of the figure depends on the dimensions of the window, but that the figure always remains square. The **MM_ISOTROPIC** mode always maintains the shape of figures.

Figure 2.7 Using the MM_ISOTROPIC mapping mode.

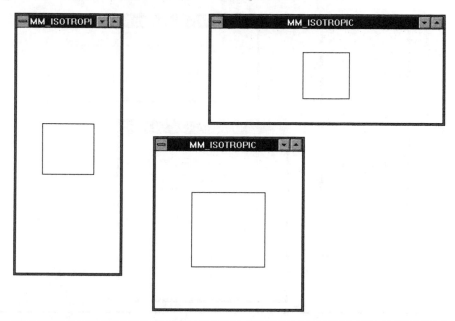

The **MM_ANISOTROPIC** mode allows you to set the extents of the logical and device units also. However, unlike **MM_ISOTROPIC**, you can use different scale factors for the X and Y axes. This will enable you to scale figures so that they fill up an entire window, for instance.

The following code draws a square, using *logical* coordinates, that fills the entire client area:

```
void TExampleWindow::Paint(TDC& dc, BOOL, TRect&)
{
  RECT rect;
  ::GetClientRect(HWindow, &rect);
  dc.SetMapMode(MM_ANISOTROPIC); // Set mapping mode
  SetWindowExtEx(dc, 10000, 10000, 0); // Set logical unit extent
  SetViewportExtEx(dc, rect.right, rect.bottom, &SIZE()); // Device extent
  // Place the origin in the center of the client area
  SetViewportOrgEx(dc, rect.right/2, rect.bottom/2, &POINT());
  // Draw the square using logical coordinates
  Rectangle(dc, -2500, -2500, 2500, 2500);
}
```

Try replacing the **Paint** function in the previous program with this routine. It will generate output such as that shown in Figure 2.8. As you can see, Windows stretches the rectangle so that it fills the interior of the client area. Of

Figure 2.8 Using the MM_ANISOTROPIC mapping mode.

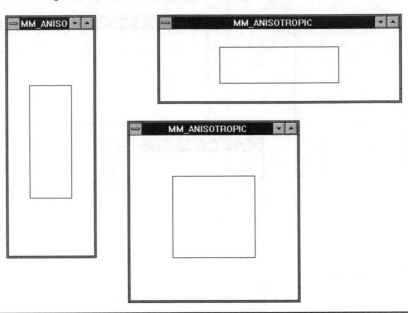

course, it would be a lot easier to draw the rectangle in **MM_TEXT** mode using the client area's dimensions. But when you want to draw figures in logical units and fill an area, **MM_ANISOTROPIC** is quite useful.

Modifying the Origin and Extents

After you have set the origin or extent of a viewport or window, you can easily modify the value using the appropriate function listed here:

```
BOOL OffsetViewportOrgEx(HDC hDC, int x, int y, POINT prevOrigin);
BOOL OffsetWindowOrgEx(HDC hDC, int x, int y, POINT prevOrigin);
```

- **hDC** is a handle to the device context.
- **x** and **y** are integers that represent the new origin.
- **prevOrigin** points to a **POINT** structure that contains the location of the previous origin.
- Both functions return non-zero if they succeed.

Similarly, you can modify a viewport's or window's extent by using one of these two functions:

```
BOOL ScaleViewportExtEx(HDC hDC, int xNum, int xDenom,
  int yNum, int yDenom, SIZE* prevExtents);
BOOL ScaleWindowExtEx(HDC hDC, int xNum, int xDenom,
  int yNum, int yDenom, SIZE* prevExtents);
```

- **hDC** is a handle to a device context.
- **xNum** is an integer that is multiplied by the current X extent.
- **xDenom** is an integer that is divided into the current X extent.
- **yNum** is an integer that is multiplied by the current Y extent.
- **yDenom** is an integer that is divided into the current Y extent.
- **prevExtents** points to a **SIZE** structure that is set to the previous extents.
- Both functions return non-zero if they succeed.

T H R E E

Drawing Lines and Curves

So far we've covered only basic Windows programming concepts. Now it's time to take an up-close look at the GDI routines that draw graphics figures. The next several chapters will serve as your reference to many of GDI's drawing functions.

We'll begin by explaining and demonstrating the functions that draw simple shapes, such as pixels, lines, and arcs. Along the way you'll see how Windows uses the concept of a pen object to prescribe the line styles it uses. We'll also discuss various effects you can achieve by manipulating the pen settings and Windows' other drawing modes.

A DRAWING PROGRAM SHELL

There's no better way to learn something than to try it yourself. Therefore, in this chapter and through Chapter 8, you'll find numerous blocks of code that illustrate various GDI functions. To prevent a lot of redundant code, the code excerpts will be contained in **Paint** member functions that you can pop into the program shell that follows.

The program shell, EXAMPLE.CPP, is very similar to the simple programs you've seen so far. Right now, though, EXAMPLE.CPP doesn't do anything. Later, when you come across a **Paint** function, simply replace the **Paint** function shown in EXAMPLE.CPP with the new one. All the **Paint** functions are written so that they belong to the class **TExampleWindow**, which is defined in EXAMPLE.CPP. These routines should give you a good starting point from which to test aspects of the drawing functions that you're curious about.

```
// EXAMPLE.CPP: A simple program shell that you can use
// with the Paint member functions included in this book.

#include <owl\applicat.h>
#include <owl\framewin.h>
#include <owl\dc.h>

class TExampleApp : public TApplication {
public:
  TExampleApp() : TApplication() { }
  void InitMainWindow();
};

class TExampleWindow : public TWindow {
public:
  TExampleWindow(TWindow* parent, const char* title)
    : TWindow(parent, title) { }
  void Paint(TDC&, BOOL, TRect&);
};

void TExampleApp::InitMainWindow()
{
  MainWindow = new TFrameWindow(0, "", new TExampleWindow(0, ""));
}

int OwlMain(int /*argc*/, char* /*argv*/[])
{
  return TExampleApp().Run();
}

// Replace this function with the Paint code excerpts
// listed in the book
void TExampleWindow::Paint(TDC&, BOOL, TRect&)
{
}
```

Note   Chapters 3 through 7 present the 16-bit versions of many of the standard graphics functions in the GDI. These routines can be called from within 16- and 32-bit applications, although 32-bit applications may implement slight variations of these routines. Chapter 8 highlights the key differences and presents several GDI functions that are exclusive to 32-bit applications running under a true 32-bit version of Windows, such as Windows NT.

MANIPULATING SCREEN PIXELS

One of the most basic graphics operations is the ability to manipulate individual pixels on the screen. To facilitate this, Windows provides the **GetPixel** and **SetPixel** functions:

```
COLORREF GetPixel(HDC hDC, int x, int y);
COLORREF SetPixel(HDC hDC, int x, int y, COLORREF color);
```

- **hDC** is a handle to the device context.
- **x** and **y** are two integers that specify the logical coordinates of the pixel to manipulate.
- **GetPixel** returns the color of the pixel at (**x**,**y**).
- **SetPixel** returns the actual color used or -1 if the pixel is outside of the clipping region.

As with all the GDI functions, the **x**,**y** coordinates are specified in logical units. However, these two functions always operate on a single pixel. The **x**,**y** coordinates simply tell the functions where the pixel are.

Note   The **TDC** class in OWL encapsulates the variables and functions common to a generic device context. In fact, all of the Windows functions that have a device context handle as the first parameter, have matching routines in OWL's **TDC** class. For instance, **TDC** includes the functions **GetPixel** and **SetPixel** that manipulate pixels. There are advantages to using the GDI functions encapsulated in OWL's **TDC** class; however, we'll usually restrict ourselves to the regular GDI versions of the routines. This should make it easier for you to port your code to another compiler or toolkit if you decide to. OWL provides a similar set of classes that encapsulate Windows' colors, pen styles, and so on. Again, we typically won't use these alternative classes.

We won't cover the color system until Chapter 5, but as you can see, both functions use color variables. Windows supports three ways of specifying colors. For now, you only need to know that Windows allows you to specify colors using a combination of red, green, and blue intensity values that can range from 0 to 255. A pixel is set to white, for instance, if its red, green, and blue components are all 255. A pixel appears black if all three color components are 0. A bright red pixel, on the other hand, might have red set to 255 and the other two components set to 0. By combining these three color components, you can specify over 16 million colors. Of course, what you actually get depends on how many colors your hardware can display.

The three color components are normally packed into a double word that WINDOWS.H defines as the type **COLORREF**. Windows provides the **RGB** macro that can merge three intensity values into a double word. For instance, the following code sets the pixel (10,100) to white, and its neighbor to red:

```
SetPixel(hDC, 10, 100, RGB(255,255,255));
SetPixel(hDC, 11, 100, RGB(255,0,0));
```

Similarly, the following **Paint** function draws a diagonal line of pixels that progress from black to white. To test this code, simply place it in the EXAMPLE.CPP program shell given at the beginning of this chapter.

```
// Draw a figure
void TExampleWindow::Paint(TDC& dc, BOOL, TRect&)
{
  // Sequence through 256 possible gray colors; your hardware may
  // not be able to display all 256 levels, however.
  for (int i=0; i<256; i++)
    SetPixel(dc, i, i, RGB(i,i,i));
}
```

Note It's important to realize that the **GetPixel** and **SetPixel** functions work with raster-style devices, such as video displays, but won't work with non-raster devices, such as plotters. If your code must work with a variety of output devices, you may want to call **GetDeviceCaps** to verify that the device you're using supports pixel operations.

DRAWING LINES

To draw lines, you typically use the pair of functions **MoveToEx** and **LineTo**. As Figure 3.1 shows, **MoveToEx** tells Windows where to set the beginning of the line, and **LineTo** specifies where the line ends. Actually, **MoveToEx** updates the *current position* attribute of the device context and **LineTo** draws a line from the current position to the point passed to it. The two functions use the following form:

```
BOOL MoveToEx(HDC hDC, int x, int y, POINT* prevPt);
BOOL LineTo(HDC hDC, int x, int y);
```

- **hDC** is a handle to the device context—the display surface on which the line is drawn.
- The **x** and **y** integers specify the endpoints of the line; assuming that the default mapping mode is used, the **x** and **y** coordinates specify pixel positions.
- **prevPt** points to a **POINT** structure that is set to the previous current position. You can set this parameter to 0 if you do not need the previous setting returned.

Both functions return non-zero if they succeed or zero otherwise. **LineTo** also sets the current position to (**x**,**y**) so that you can easily draw a connecting line using another call to **LineTo**.

Figure 3.1 Lines can be drawn with MoveToEx and LineTo.

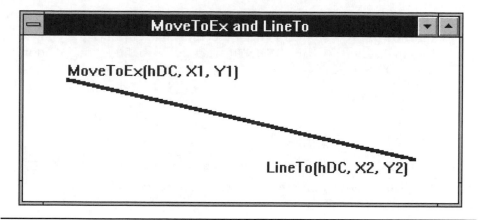

One probably unexpected action, or rather non-action, of **LineTo** is that the *last pixel* of the line does not get painted. This is the case, regardless of the current mapping mode. At first this may seem a bit odd. However, Windows takes this approach so that it's easier for you to connect lines. In this way, Windows won't paint the connecting endpoints twice. This saves a little time, but more importantly avoids any odd painting effects if special screen operators are employed, such as exclusive ORing. We'll explore this further when we discuss the numerous ways that pixels can be combined with the display.

Let's look at an example. The following code draws a triangle with the three vertices (120,40), (200,100), and (40,100):

```
void TExampleWindow::Paint(TDC& dc, BOOL, TRect&)
{
  MoveToEx(dc, 120, 40, 0);
  LineTo(dc, 200, 100);
  LineTo(dc, 40, 100);
  LineTo(dc, 120, 40);
}
```

Note If you want to ensure that the endpoint of the line is drawn, you can call **SetPixel** to display the point passed to **LineTo**.

Drawing Connected Lines and Polygons

When you need to draw a series of connected lines, you'll probably want to turn to the **Polyline** function. Here's the format for this routine:

```
BOOL Polyline(HDC hDC, POINT* endPoints, int count);
```

- **hDC** is a handle to the device context.
- **endPoints** is an array of **POINT** structures that specifies the endpoints of the line segments; the **POINT** structure is defined by Windows (in WINDOWS.H) as:

```
typedef struct tagPOINT {
  int x;
  int y;
} POINT;
```

- **count** is the number of coordinate pairs in **endPoints**.
- **Polyline** returns non-zero if it succeeds and zero otherwise.

The current position is not affected by **Polyline.**

Here's how you can code **Polyline** to draw the triangle discussed in the last section:

```
void TExampleWindow::Paint(TDC& dc, BOOL, TRect&)
{
  POINT triangle[4] = {{120,40}, {200,100}, {40,100}, {120,40}};
  Polyline(dc, triangle, 4);
}
```

Notice that the triangle must be explicitly closed off by setting the first and last points of the **triangle** array to the same coordinate. The **Polyline** function does not automatically close off polygons. Figure 3.2 shows the output of the previous **Paint** function.

Figure 3.2 A triangle drawn with Polyline.

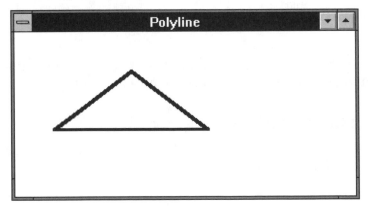

So when should **Polyline** be used rather than a series of **MoveToEx**s and **LineTo**s? Generally, **Polyline** will be faster because it avoids the additional overhead of calling the **MoveToEx** and **LineTo** functions several times. On the downside, **Polyline** requires that you store and then pass it the endpoints of the lines.

Note that, just as is the case with **LineTo**, **Polyline** does not draw the last pixel of the last line specified in the **POINT** array.

DRAWING ARCS

The GDI provides the **Arc** function for drawing elliptical or circular arcs. The **Arc** function is defined in WINDOWS.H as:

```
BOOL Arc(HDC hDC, int x1, int y1, int x2, int y2, int x3, int y3,
    int x4, int y4);
```

- **hDC** is a handle to the device context.
- **x1,y1** and **x2,y2** are integers that specify two opposing corners of a bounding box in which the arc is centered; these corners can either be the upper-left and lower-right or the lower-left and upper-right coordinates.
- **x3,y3** and **x4,y4** specify the starting and ending points of the arc; the arc is drawn counterclockwise from the starting point to the ending point.

Figure 3.3 should give you a better understanding of how the nine parameters of **Arc** relate to the dimensions of the arc drawn. Here's the best way of thinking about them: The bounding box, indicated by **x1,y2** and **x2,y2**, specifies how big and how elliptical the arc will be; the starting and ending points, indicated by **x3,y3** and **x4,y4**, specify where the arc starts and how long it will be.

How do you specify the endpoints of the arc? Fortunately, the endpoints given in the parameter list don't have to fall on the arc itself. Instead, the endpoints actually specify points along two lines that emanate from the arc's center. The endpoints of the arc are set to where the arc intersects these invisible lines. For instance, both statements in Figure 3.4 generate the same arc, but notice that they have different endpoints specified. The same arcs are drawn because the endpoints fall on the same lines. There's a restriction, however. If one of the endpoints is equal to the center of the arc, then the arc is not drawn at all and the function returns zero.

If the starting and ending points are the same, the **Arc** function draws a closed ellipse or circle, instead of a portion of the figure that creates an arc.

As is true with the line-drawing routines, the endpoint (last pixel) of the arc is not drawn along with the rest of the figure.

Figure 3.3 The Arc function.

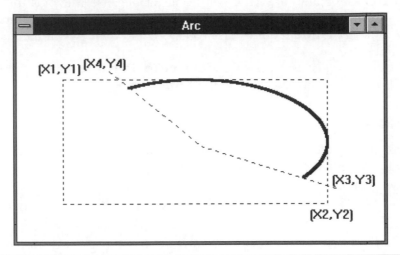

Figure 3.4 Different endpoints can specify the same arc.

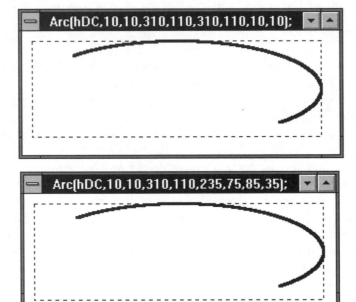

LINE STYLES

Windows allows you to control the color, width, and style of lines and arcs. These three drawing attributes are grouped into what Windows calls a *pen object*. Like the other objects in Windows, pens are manipulated by using handles.

The device context stores a handle to a single pen object. This pen prescribes what line style the GDI's drawing routines will use. By default, the device context contains a handle to a black pen that draws solid lines, one-pixel wide.

To save memory, Windows shares pens between applications. In addition, it predefines three pen styles for drawing black, white, and null (invisible) lines. These pens are known as *stock objects* and have special macro constants defined for them in WINDOWS.H: **BLACK_PEN**, **WHITE_PEN**, and **NULL_PEN**, respectively.

A handle to a pen is defined as follows:

```
HPEN hPen;          // A handle to a pen
```

Switching to another stock pen is a two-step process. First, you must call **GetStockObject** to retrieve a handle to the desired pen. For instance, the following statement declares a handle to a pen and retrieves a handle to the stock white pen object:

```
HPEN hPen = HPEN(GetStockObject(WHITE_PEN));
```

Then, to use the pen, you must place or *select* the pen into the device context using the function **SelectObject**:

```
HPEN hOldPen = HPEN(SelectObject(hDC, hPen));
```

As you can see, **SelectObject** returns a handle to the previously selected pen so that you can later switch back to it, if desired. Once these two steps are taken, subsequent calls to the line-drawing routines will use solid white lines.

Note Notice that the return values in the two previous calls to **GetStockObject** and **SelectObject** are cast to the **HPEN** type. Type conversions are required with these two routines since they don't return object handles of a specific type. This requirement helps to avoid accidentally selecting the wrong type of object and assigning its handle to a variable—a bug that used to be extremely difficult to detect.

The following code draws a line using the default black pen object and then switches to the white pen and draws a white line over half of the existing black line. Since the background of an OWL window is normally white, this latter step has the effect of erasing half the line.

```
void TExampleWindow::Paint(TDC& dc, BOOL, TRect&)
{
  // Use default black pen first to draw a line
  MoveToEx(dc, 0, 0, 0);          // Draw a diagonal line
  LineTo(dc, 300, 300);
  SelectObject(dc, GetStockObject(WHITE_PEN));  // Use white pen
  MoveToEx(dc, 150, 150, 0);   // Erase half the line
  LineTo(dc, 300, 300);
}
```

Note It's important to realize that a device context can only have one pen selected at a time. Therefore, if you want to use several line styles, you must switch back and forth between them using calls to **SelectObject**.

Custom Pens

If you want to draw anything other than black, white, or invisible solid lines, you'll have to create your own pen style. Windows provides two functions for defining custom pen settings:

```
HPEN CreatePen(int penStyle, int width, COLORREF color);
HPEN CreatePenIndirect(LOGPEN* logPen);
```

- **penStyle** is one of the constants shown in Figure 3.5.
- **width** is the line width in logical units.
- **color** is the color of the pen.
- **logPen** points to a **LOGPEN** structure (defined later) that defines the attributes of the pen to create.
- Both functions return a handle to the pen created.

Figure 3.5 shows the seven pen styles. The program that generated this figure, SHOWPENS.CPP, follows this section. You may want to look at it to get a better idea of how pens are used in a program. The program encapsulates the details of creating and using the various pen styles in the function **ShowPenStyle**. Note that each pen object is deleted after it has been used, but not until it has been removed from the device context.

Compile the program using the procedure outlined in Chapter 1. Try changing some of the parameters passed to **ShowPenStyle** to see what affect they have on the lines drawn.

```
// SHOWPENS.CPP: Displays Windows' standard pen styles.
#include <owl\applicat.h>
#include <owl\framewin.h>
#include <owl\dc.h>
```

Figure 3.5 The predefined pen styles.

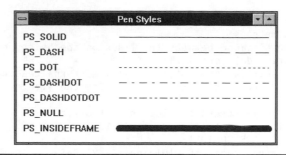

```
class TPenStyleWindow : public TWindow {
public:
  TPenStyleWindow(TWindow *parent, const char* title)
    : TWindow(parent, title) { }
  void TPenStyleWindow::ShowPenStyle(HDC hDC, RECT& r, int x, int y,
    int width, int style, COLORREF color, const char *name);
  virtual void Paint(TDC& dc, BOOL, TRect&);
};

class TPenStyleApp : public TApplication {
public:
  TPenStyleApp() : TApplication() { }
  void InitMainWindow() {
    MainWindow = new TFrameWindow(0, "Pen Styles",
      new TPenStyleWindow(0, ""));
  }
};

// Display a single pen style
void TPenStyleWindow::ShowPenStyle(HDC hDC, RECT& r, int x, int y,
  int width, int style, COLORREF color, const char* name)
{
  // Create the specified pen style
  HPEN hPen = CreatePen(style, width, color);
  // Display the name of the string
  TextOut(hDC, x, y, name, lstrlen(name));
  // You must select a pen into a device context before using it
  HPEN hOldPen = HPEN(SelectObject(hDC, hPen));
  // Draw with the pen
  MoveToEx(hDC, x+150, y+8, 0);
  LineTo(hDC, r.right-10, y+8);
  // Select the original pen style into the device context
  // so that hPen can be deleted. Never delete an object while
  // it is currently selected into a device context!
  SelectObject(hDC, hOldPen);
  DeleteObject(hPen);       // Delete the pen from Windows' memory
}
```

```
// Paint the window with several different pen styles
void TPenStyleWindow::Paint(TDC& dc, BOOL, TRect&)
{
  RECT rect;
  TEXTMETRIC metrics;
  // Base the distance between the lines on the height of the text
  GetTextMetrics(dc, &metrics);
  int yinc = metrics.tmHeight + metrics.tmExternalLeading + 8;
  ::GetClientRect(HWindow, &rect);   // Get the size of the window

  // Draw the seven types of lines one at a time
  ShowPenStyle(dc, rect, 10, 10, 1, PS_SOLID,
    RGB(0,0,0), "PS_SOLID");
  ShowPenStyle(dc, rect, 10, 10+yinc, 1, PS_DASH,
    RGB(0,0,0), "PS_DASH");
  ShowPenStyle(dc, rect, 10, 10+2*yinc, 1, PS_DOT,
    RGB(0,0,0), "PS_DOT");
  ShowPenStyle(dc, rect, 10, 10+3*yinc, 1, PS_DASHDOT,
    RGB(0,0,0), "PS_DASHDOT");
  ShowPenStyle(dc, rect, 10, 10+4*yinc, 1, PS_DASHDOTDOT,
    RGB(0,0,0), "PS_DASHDOTDOT");
  ShowPenStyle(dc, rect, 10, 10+5*yinc, 1, PS_NULL,
    RGB(0,0,0), "PS_NULL");
  ShowPenStyle(dc, rect, 10, 10+6*yinc, 10, PS_INSIDEFRAME,
    RGB(0,0,0), "PS_INSIDEFRAME");
}

int OwlMain(int /*argc*/, char* /*argv*/[])
{
  return TPenStyleApp().Run();
}
```

A pen's width is specified in logical units. Therefore, in the **MM_TEXT** mapping mode, a width of 5 produces a line five pixels wide. Note, however, that specifying a line width of 0 will always generate a one-pixel wide line, regardless of the mapping mode.

During figure drawing, a thick line is always centered about the figure. In other words, if a line is five pixels wide, one pixel will lie along the line's center and two pixels will be on either side. An exception is the **PS_INSIDEFRAME** style, which guarantees that the entire line will lie on the inside of the boundary of an arc, ellipse, or rectangle.

Here's how you can create a solid, black line that is five pixels wide:

```
hPen = CreatePen(PS_SOLID, 5, RGB(0, 0, 0));
```

Figure 3.6 shows several lines with various line widths. Notice that thick lines have rounded tips. In addition, Windows drivers don't support thick dotted or dashed lines. If you request a styled line thicker than one pixel wide, Windows draws a solid line.

Figure 3.6 Lines can vary in width.

When setting the color for a line, it's important to know that Windows always uses "pure" colors. If you specify a color that the display hardware cannot directly generate, Windows finds and uses the closest color it can display. You'll see in the next chapter that filled figures can generate a wider variety of colors by *dithering*—a technique that mixes pixels of different colors to give the impression of different shades.

There is one exception to the way Windows selects colors for lines: if the **PS_INSIDEFRAME** pen style is used, Windows may use a dithered color.

The **CreatePenIndirect** function can also define a pen style. However, it accepts a **LOGPEN** structure, which defines the various aspects of the pen. The **LOGPEN** structure is defined in WINDOWS.H as:

```
typedef struct tagLOGPEN {
  UINT lopnStyle;        // One of the constants in Figure 3.5
  POINT lopnWidth;       // The logical width of the line
  COLORREF lopnColor;    // The color of the line
} LOGPEN;
```

The **x** field of the **POINT** structure specifies the width of the line. Therefore, to create the same pen as the one shown in the **CreatePen** example earlier, you could use:

```
LOGPEN logPen;
logPen.lopnStyle = PS_SOLID;
logPen.lopnWidth.x = 5;
logPen.lopnColor = RGB(0, 0, 0);
HPEN hPen = CreatePenIndirect(&logPen);
```

After you have defined a custom pen style, you must select it into the device context in order to use it. Once again, to accomplish this, use the **SelectObject** function. Selecting a pen into a device context serves two purposes: it tells Windows which pen style to use and it translates the specifications you give to **CreatePen** (or **CreatePenIndirect**) into what the hardware can actually achieve.

Deleting Custom Pens

If you create your own pen style, you must also delete it from Windows' list of objects before your application terminates. If you fail to do this, the memory associated with the pen will be lost. To delete a pen object, call **DeleteObject**:

```
DeleteObject(hCustomPen);
```

However, do not delete a pen object (or any other object) while it is currently selected into a device context. If the pen you want to delete is currently selected, you should first deselect it by selecting another pen object. Alternatively, you can delete a pen after the device context has been released. Deleting custom pens is very important; however, you should *never delete any of the stock pens.*

We're now ready to look at an example. The following **Paint** function illustrates how to correctly use a pen object. In this example, **Paint** creates a dotted, red pen, selects it into the device context, and draws a line. After the line is drawn, the pen object is deleted from the device context after first reselecting the default pen:

```
void TExampleWindow::Paint(TDC& dc, BOOL, TRect&)
{
  // Create a red, dotted pen
  HPEN hRedPen = CreatePen(PS_DOT, 1, RGB(255,0,0));
  // Select the red pen into the device context
  HPEN hOldPen = HPEN(SelectObject(dc, hRedPen));
  MoveToEx(dc, 40, 10, 0);     // Draw a red, dotted line
  LineTo(dc, 200, 300);
  // Select the original pen back into the device context
  // so that you can delete the red pen
  SelectObject(dc, hOldPen);
  DeleteObject(hRedPen);    // Delete the red, dotted pen
}
```

SETTING THE DRAWING MODE

Normally, Windows draws a line, arc, pixel, or filled pixel directly on the screen using the current pen color. However, you can select alternative drawing modes that combine the pen's color in a bitwise manner with what is being overwritten. These are called *raster operations*, or ROPs for short. Windows defines sixteen ROP codes, as listed in Table 3.1. Figure 3.7 illustrates how each of these modes affects white lines drawn over rectangles of various shades. The program that generated this figure, ROP.CPP, follows this section. You may want to modify it to work with lines of other colors so that you can see how the ROP codes impact the display.

Table 3.1 Raster Operations

Constant	Resulting Color
R2_BLACK	Black
R2_COPYPEN	Pen color
R2_MASKNOTPEN	Screen and pen colors are ORed together and the result is negated
R2_MASKPEN	The screen and pen colors are ANDed
R2_MASKPENNOT	The pen is ANDed with the negated screen color
R2_MERGENOTPEN	The negated pen color is ORed with the screen
R2_MERGEPEN	The pen and screen colors are ORed together
R2_MERGEPENNOT	The pen color is ORed with the negated screen color
R2_NOP	The screen color is not changed
R2_NOT	The screen color is inverted
R2_NOTCOPYPEN	The inverted pen color
R2_NOTMASKPEN	The pen and screen are ANDed together and the result is inverted
R2_NOTMERGEPEN	The pen and screen colors are ORed together and the result is inverted
R2_NOTXORPEN	The pen and screen colors are exclusive ORed and then inverted
R2_WHITE	White
R2_XORPEN	The pen and screen colors are exclusive ORed

Figure 3.7 Using the raster operation codes.

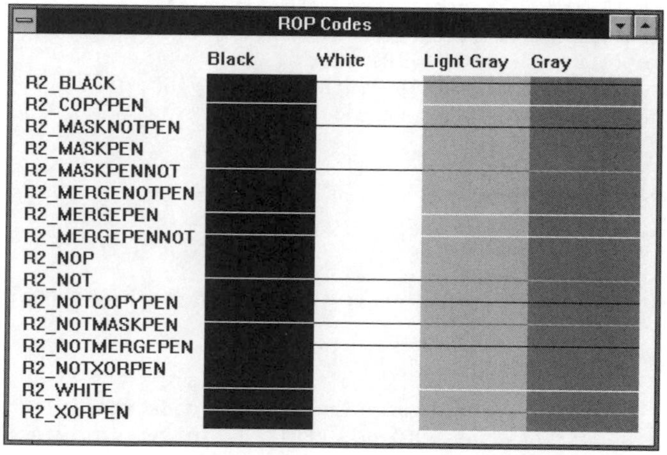

Windows provides two functions for manipulating the ROP mode:

```
int GetROP2(HDC hDC);
int SetROP2(HDC hDC, int mode);
```

- **mode** should be set to one of the constants in Table 3.1.
- **GetROP2** returns the current drawing mode.
- **SetROP2** returns the previous drawing mode.

The default mode is **R2_COPYPEN**, which overwrites screen values with the pen's color. Using some of the other ROP codes can be a bit confusing, especially when you are manipulating a variety of colors. Always remember that you are manipulating the bit patterns. Also, some of the modes have specific purposes. For instance, **R2_XORPEN** and **R2_NOTPEN** are often used to move figures cleanly across the screen. By drawing a white line once with **R2_XORPEN**, the line is guaranteed to show up, no matter what was below it. Then, to remove the line and restore the screen, you simply draw the line again.

 Here's the ROP.CPP program that generates Figure 3.7. Try changing the program so that **ShowLine** draws its lines using pen colors other than white.

```
// ROP.CPP: Illustrates how ROP codes affect white lines drawn
// over various colors.

#include <owl\applicat.h>
#include <owl\framewin.h>
#include <owl\dc.h>

class TROPWindow : public TWindow {
public:
  TROPWindow(TWindow *parent, const char* title)
    : TWindow(parent, title) { }
  void Paint(TDC& hDC, BOOL, TRect&);
  void ShowLine(TDC& dc, RECT& r, int y, int yinc,
    int ROPCode, const char* name);
};

class TROPApp : public TApplication {
public:
  TROPApp() : TApplication() { }
  void InitMainWindow() {
    MainWindow = new TFrameWindow(0, "ROP Codes", new TROPWindow(0, ""));
  }
};

// Display a single white line using the ROP code specified
void TROPWindow::ShowLine(TDC& dc, RECT& r, int y, int yinc,
  int ROPCode, const char* name)
```

```
{
  // You may want to set the pen color to something other
  // than white in order to see what the results are
  SelectObject(dc, GetStockObject(WHITE_PEN));
  TextOut(dc, 10, y, name, lstrlen(name)); // Display ROP name
  int prevMode = SetROP2(dc, ROPCode);     // Set the ROP mode
  MoveToEx(dc, 150, y+yinc/3, 0);          // Draw the line
  LineTo(dc, r.right-12, y+yinc/3);
  SetROP2(dc, prevMode);                   // Restore the ROP mode
}

// Paint lines using several different ROP codes
void TROPWindow::Paint(TDC& dc, BOOL, TRect&)
{
  TRect rect, bar;
  ::GetClientRect(HWindow, &rect);  // Get the size of the window
  int yinc = (rect.bottom - 30 - 10) / 16;  // Line separation

  // Paint four filled rectangles of various shades as a
  // backdrop. The lines will be drawn over these rectangles.
  int barWd = (rect.right - 150 - 10) / 4;
  SetRect(&bar, 150, 30, 150+barWd, rect.bottom-10);
  TextOut(dc, bar.left, 10, "Black", 5);

  FillRect(dc, &bar, HBRUSH(GetStockObject(BLACK_BRUSH)));
  bar.left += barWd;    bar.right += barWd;
  TextOut(dc, bar.left, 10, "White", 5);
  FillRect(dc, &bar, HBRUSH(GetStockObject(WHITE_BRUSH)));
  bar.left += barWd;    bar.right += barWd;
  TextOut(dc, bar.left, 10, "Light Gray", 10);
  FillRect(dc, &bar, HBRUSH(GetStockObject(LTGRAY_BRUSH)));
  bar.left += barWd;    bar.right += barWd;
  TextOut(dc, bar.left, 10, "Gray", 4);
  FillRect(dc, &bar, HBRUSH(GetStockObject(GRAY_BRUSH)));

  // Draw white horizontal lines over the backdrops. Each
  // line is drawn with a different ROP code.
  ShowLine(dc, rect, 30, yinc, R2_BLACK, "R2_BLACK");
  ShowLine(dc, rect, 30+yinc, yinc, R2_COPYPEN, "R2_COPYPEN");
  ShowLine(dc, rect, 30+2*yinc, yinc,
    R2_MASKNOTPEN, "R2_MASKNOTPEN");
  ShowLine(dc, rect, 30+3*yinc, yinc,
    R2_MASKPEN, "R2_MASKPEN");
  ShowLine(dc, rect, 30+4*yinc, yinc,
    R2_MASKPENNOT, "R2_MASKPENNOT");
  ShowLine(dc, rect, 30+5*yinc, yinc,
    R2_MERGENOTPEN, "R2_MERGENOTPEN");
  ShowLine(dc, rect, 30+6*yinc, yinc,
    R2_MERGEPEN, "R2_MERGEPEN");
  ShowLine(dc, rect, 30+7*yinc, yinc,
    R2_MERGEPENNOT, "R2_MERGEPENNOT");
  ShowLine(dc, rect, 30+8*yinc, yinc, R2_NOP, "R2_NOP");
  ShowLine(dc, rect, 30+9*yinc, yinc, R2_NOT, "R2_NOT");
  ShowLine(dc, rect, 30+10*yinc, yinc,
```

```
      R2_NOTCOPYPEN, "R2_NOTCOPYPEN");
  ShowLine(dc, rect, 30+11*yinc, yinc,
      R2_NOTMASKPEN, "R2_NOTMASKPEN");
  ShowLine(dc, rect, 30+12*yinc, yinc,
      R2_NOTMERGEPEN, "R2_NOTMERGEPEN");
  ShowLine(dc, rect, 30+13*yinc, yinc,
      R2_NOTXORPEN, "R2_NOTXORPEN");
  ShowLine(dc, rect, 30+14*yinc, yinc, R2_WHITE, "R2_WHITE");
  ShowLine(dc, rect, 30+15*yinc, yinc, R2_XORPEN, "R2_XORPEN");
}

int OwlMain(int /*argc*/, char* /*argv*/[])
{
  return TROPApp().Run();
}
```

Modes for Dotted and Dashed Lines

If you are using dotted or dashed lines, two additional device-context attributes come into play: background mode and background color. The background mode—the two mode possibilities are shown in Table 3.2—specifies whether the gaps between the dashes or dots should be updated on the screen.

The **OPAQUE** mode fills the gaps within dashed and dotted lines with the background color. The **TRANSPARENT** mode does not. By default, the **OPAQUE** mode is used and the gaps are filled with the default background color, white. You can, however, use **SetBkMode** to switch to the **TRANSPARENT** mode, which tells Windows not to affect the screen where there are gaps in a line. You can change the background color using **SetBkColor**. Here is how the two functions are defined:

```
COLORREF SetBkColor(HDC hDC, COLORREF color);
int SetBkMode(HDC hDC, int bkMode);
```

- **hDC** is a handle to the device context.
- **color** is the color to be used as the background color.
- **bkMode** is either the constant **TRANSPARENT** or **OPAQUE**.
- **SetBkColor** returns the previous color used for the background.
- **SetBkMode** returns the previous background mode.

Table 3.2 Background Modes

Constant	Description
OPAQUE	The background is set to the background color
TRANSPARENT	The background color is not changed

Figure 3.8 Using the two background modes with styled lines.

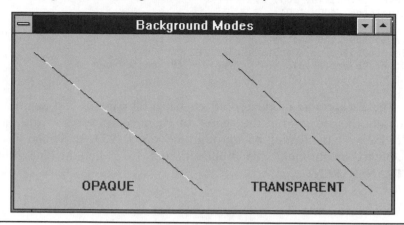

Figure 3.8 illustrates how the background mode affects dashed lines that are drawn over a light gray backdrop. The left line uses the **OPAQUE** mode and the right line uses the **TRANSPARENT** mode. The background color is set to white—the default color. Notice that the **OPAQUE** mode sets the spaces between the line's dashes to white. In most cases, this is probably not what you want. Generally, you should use the **TRANSPARENT** mode when drawing over a backdrop that has a color other than the background color in the device context.

Here's another example. The following **Paint** function displays two solid black lines and then overwrites them with a dashed line. One dashed line is displayed using the **OPAQUE** mode and the other is displayed using the **TRANSPARENT** mode. As you might expect, the dashed line drawn with the **TRANSPARENT** mode does not show up.

```
void TExampleWindow::Paint(TDC& dc, BOOL, TRect&)
{
  MoveToEx(dc, 40, 40, 0); // Draw two black lines next to each other
  LineTo(dc, 400, 40);
  MoveToEx(dc, 40, 100, 0);
  LineTo(dc, 400, 100);
  // Create a black, dashed pen
  HPEN hPen = CreatePen(PS_DASH, 1, RGB(0,0,0));
  SelectObject(dc, hPen);    // Select the pen into the device context
  // The background color is white by default and the background mode
  // is OPAQUE. Overwrite the top line with a black, dashed line.
  MoveToEx(dc, 40, 40, 0);
  LineTo(dc, 400, 40);
  // Now use the TRANSPARENT mode and overwrite the bottom
  // line with the black, dashed line. The line won't show up.
```

```
    SetBkMode(dc, TRANSPARENT);
    MoveToEx(dc, 40, 100, 0);
    LineTo(dc, 400, 100);
    // Select the default pen back into the device context
    // so that the custom pen can be deleted
    SelectObject(dc, GetStockObject(BLACK_PEN));
    DeleteObject(hPen);        // Delete the custom pen
}
```

The background mode also affects hatch fill patterns and text. For instance, normally the area within the "gaps" of characters are set to the background color because the default background mode is **OPAQUE**. Similarly, you'll only be able to "see through" a hatch fill pattern if you switch the background mode to **TRANSPARENT**.

F O U R

Filled Figures

In Chapter 3 we focused on simple figures, such as drawing lines and arcs. Now we'll turn our attention to the GDI routines that draw filled figures. We'll also cover the fill styles and settings that Windows provides.

As with Chapter 3, this chapter will serve as a reference for the functions that are covered. As you read through the chapter, you'll encounter several blocks of code contained in **Paint** functions. You can insert these into the EXAMPLE.CPP program shell listed at the beginning of Chapter 3. Try modifying these code blocks to expand your understanding of the GDI.

DRAWING FILLED FIGURES

Figure 4.1 displays a variety of filled shapes drawn with the functions described in this chapter. As you can see, filled figures can come in a variety of shapes and styles. The outlines of the figures are drawn using the current pen style—the default, black, solid pen. The interiors of the regions are filled with the current fill settings.

Windows organizes fill settings into an object that it calls a *brush*. By default, the device context contains a handle to a solid, white brush, which paints solid white regions. We'll use the default brush until we have a chance to cover brushes in detail later in this chapter.

Drawing Rectangles

The **Rectangle** function is GDI's principal routine for displaying filled rectangles. It draws a rectangle with the current pen style and then fills its interior with the current brush pattern. The **Rectangle** function uses this form:

Figure 4.1 Examples of filled figures.

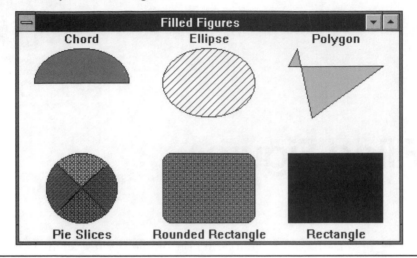

```
BOOL Rectangle(HDC hDC, int x1, int y1, int x2, int y2);
```

- **hDC** is a handle to a device context.
- **x1,y1** and **x2,y2** are the coordinates of opposing corners (in logical units) of the rectangle, as shown in Figure 4.2.
- The function returns TRUE if it succeeds and FALSE otherwise.

Figure 4.2 A sample rectangle.

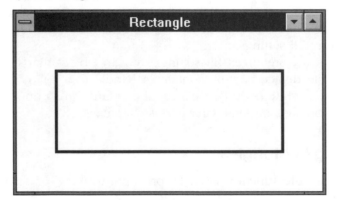

For example, the statement

```
Rectangle(hDC, 10, 10, 300, 100);
```

draws a rectangle that extends from the point (10,10) to (300,100). Well, not quite. Actually, the **Rectangle** routine always draws the right and bottom edges of the rectangle one pixel less than specified. In fact, all rectangular regions fall one pixel short in height and width. For instance, the bounding box of the **Arc** function, which we discussed in Chapter 3, is one pixel smaller than you might expect. This off-by-one oddity has to do with the way Windows determines where filled regions should be drawn.

As you might guess, correctly aligning various figures using the GDI can be a bit tricky. Here's a rule to remember: When you are specifying rectangular areas, Windows will always trim the figure by one pixel in height and width. You might run into a problem when you mix area-oriented function calls— such as **Rectangle**—with pixel, line, or polygon routines. If you give **Polyline** the same coordinates that you pass to **Rectangle**, for instance, the **Polyline** figure will be one pixel wider and taller.

The following **Paint** function does just this. It draws two overlapping rectangles—one with **Rectangle**, the other with **Polyline**. The coordinates are the same for both, but as you'll see when you plug this routine into EXAMPLE.CPP and then run the program, the rectangles won't quite align:

```
void TExampleWindow::Paint(TDC& dc, BOOL, TRect&)
{
  Rectangle(dc, 10, 10, 200, 200);    // Display a rectangle
  // Display a polygon with the same points
  POINT p[5] = {{10,10}, {200,10}, {200,200}, {10,200}, {10,10}};
  Polyline(dc, p, 5);
}
```

Here's another example. Suppose you want to draw a rectangle that fills the entire client area of a window. To do this correctly, just pass **Rectangle** the coordinates that **GetClientRect** retrieves. These coordinates don't cause a problem because both functions are area-oriented.

```
void TExampleWindow::Paint(TDC& dc, BOOL, TRect&)
{
  RECT rect;        // Display a rectangle that covers the entire window
  ::GetClientRect(HWindow, &rect);   // Get the dimensions of the window
  // Display the rectangle
  Rectangle(dc, 0, 0, rect.right, rect.bottom);
}
```

Note   Notice that in the previous example **rect.left** and **rect.top** are not used. The **GetClientRect** function will always return them as zero. In addition, note that

GetClientRect *always* expresses the area of the window in device units (pixels)—regardless of the mapping mode.

Ellipse, Pie, and Chord

Windows provides three routines that draw filled curved figures: **Ellipse**, **Pie**, and **Chord**. Each routine draws the outline of its figure using the currently selected pen style, and fills its interior with the currently selected brush pattern. As with all of the functions that fill figures, none uses or modifies the current position value.

The **Ellipse** function is defined as:

```
BOOL Ellipse(HDC hDC, int x1, int y1, int x2, int y2);
```

- **hDC** is a handle to the device context.
- The ellipse is centered within a bounding box specified by the coordinates **x1,y1** and **x2,y2**. Figure 4.3 shows a sample ellipse.
- The function returns TRUE if it succeeds and FALSE otherwise.

The **Ellipse** function returns a Boolean flag indicating whether the ellipse is drawn. The other fill routines do the same. For instance, **Ellipse** won't draw anything and returns 0 (FALSE) if its bounding box either has a width or height that is fewer than two pixels.

The **Pie** function, which has the format shown next, draws a portion of an ellipse:

```
BOOL Pie(HDC hDC, int x1, int y1, int x2, int y2,
  int startX, int startY, int endX, int endY);
```

- **hDC** is a handle to the device context.
- **x1,y1** and **x2,y2** define the bounding box of the pie slice.
- The pie slice is drawn counterclockwise from the radial line that contains the point **startX,startY** to the radial line that contains the point **endX,endY**.

Figure 4.4 illustrates how these parameters are used to draw a pie slice. If you want to draw a circular pie slice, make the bounding box a square. In addition, you should use a mapping mode, such as **MM_ISOTROPIC**, to guarantee that the X and Y values are scaled the same. Actually, on a VGA display, you don't have to worry about this because the pixels are about the same size in width and height. However, it's not good practice to write code that assumes only one type of display.

Figure 4.3 A sample ellipse.

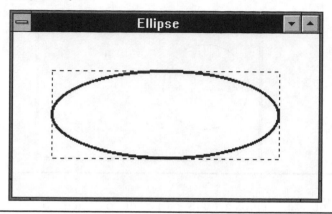

Note   The **Pie** function can draw a complete ellipse (or circle) by making the starting and ending points the same. However, if you use this approach, a line is drawn from the center of the ellipse to this point. For example, the pie slice in Figure 4.5 was created by using the following **Paint** function:

```
void TExampleWindow::Paint(TDC& dc, BOOL, TRect&)
{
  // Draw a pie slice that has a bounding box that stretches from
  // (10,10) to (100,100). The starting and ending points are both (0,0).
  Pie(dc, 10, 10, 100, 100, 0, 0, 0, 0);
}
```

Figure 4.4 Drawing a pie slice.

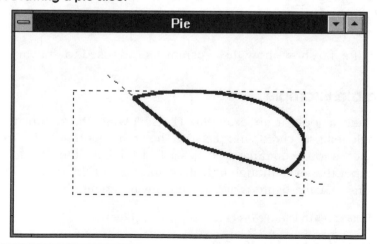

Figure 4.5 The Pie function draws a line inside a complete ellipse.

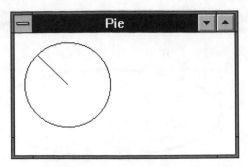

The intruding line is actually part of the pie slice's perimeter. Nonetheless, this is probably not what you want. If you need to draw a complete ellipse, you should use the **Ellipse** function.

The **Chord** routine is the last of the three curve drawing functions. It's similar to the **Arc** function, except that **Chord** joins the endpoints of the arc with a line and fills its interior by using the currently selected brush. Here's how the **Chord** routine is defined:

```
BOOL Chord(HDC hDC, int x1, int y1, int x2, int y2,
  int startX, int startY, int endX, int endY);
```

- The chord is contained in the bounding box specified by the logical coordinates **x1,y1** and **x2,y2**.
- The arc is drawn counterclockwise from **startX,startY** to **endX,endY**; these points specify the starting and ending points of the chord, but they don't have to lie on the chord's arc.

Figure 4.6 shows how these parameters are used to draw a chord.

A Simple Example

Now take a look at an example. The following **Paint** function draws the rectangle, ellipse, chord, and pie slice shown in Figure 4.7. Try experimenting with the various coordinates to get a feel for how these functions operate. Remember that even though only the perimeters of the figures appear to have been drawn, each figure is actually filled with a white brush.

```
void TExampleWindow::Paint(TDC& dc, BOOL, TRect&)
{
  Rectangle(dc, 10,10, 300,300);
```

Figure 4.6 Drawing a chord.

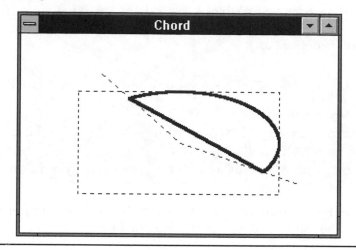

```
    Ellipse(dc, 10,10, 300,300);
    Pie(dc, 30,30, 280,280, 0,0, 280,280);
    Chord(dc, 30,30, 280,280, 260,280, 0,20);
}
```

Figure 4.7 Displaying various shapes.

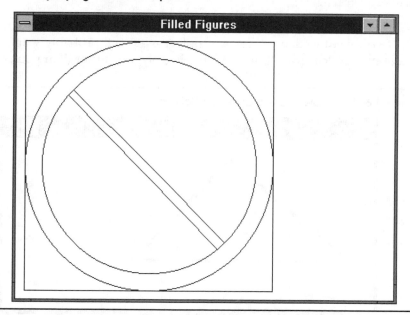

Filling a Polygon

The **Polygon** routine enables you to draw a wide range of filled figures. A similar function, **PolyPolygon**, draws an array of polygons. The **Polygon** function is defined as:

```
BOOL Polygon(HDC hDC, POINT* points, int numPoints);
```

- **hDC** is a handle to the device context.
- **points** is an array of **POINT** structures and contains the endpoints of the lines that make up the polygon.
- **numPoints** is the number of coordinates in the **points** array.

The **Polygon** function draws the outline of the polygon first, using the current pen style. It then fills the interior of the polygon with the currently selected brush.

Unlike **Polyline**, if you don't make the initial and final points in the **points** array the same, **Polygon** will automatically close off the polygon for you. For example, to draw the filled triangle shown in Figure 4.8, which has the three vertices (150,20), (250,125), and (25,125), you could use:

```
void TExampleWindow::Paint(TDC& dc, BOOL, TRect&)
{
  POINT p[3] = {{150,20}, {250,125}, {25,125}};
  Polygon(dc, p, 3);
}
```

If you want to draw a series of polygons, you'll probably want to call the function **PolyPolygon**. It draws multiple polygons faster than you could draw

Figure 4.8 A sample figure drawn with Polygon.

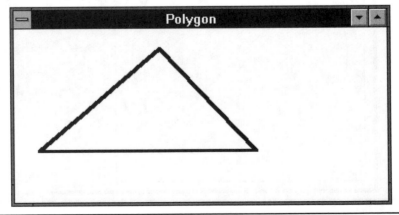

the same polygons with separate calls to **Polygon**. Here's how **PolyPolygon** is defined:

```
BOOL PolyPolygon(HDC hDC, POINT* points, int* polyCounts,
  int count);
```

- **hDC** is a handle to the device context.
- The second parameter, **points**, is a pointer to an array of **POINT** structures that contain the vertices of the polygons to be drawn. Unlike the **Polygon** function, these polygons are not automatically closed.
- **polyCounts** is a pointer to an array of integers that list the number of vertices of each polygon in the **points** array.
- **count** is the number of polygons.
- The function returns TRUE if it succeeds, FALSE otherwise.

Somewhat surprising is the fact that **PolyPolygon** does not automatically close off the polygons that are passed to it. If a polygon is not closed, then its outline is simply drawn and, of course, it is not filled. This partly explains why the GDI doesn't include a function called **PolyPolyline—PolyPolygon** can mimic this behavior.

Consider an example. Figure 4.9 shows three polygons drawn using **PolyPolygon**. The **Paint** function that generated this output is shown here. Notice that only the outline of the rightmost polygon is drawn because we did not close it off by setting its first coordinate equal to its last.

```
void TExampleWindow::Paint(TDC& dc, BOOL, TRect&)
{
  POINT p[11] = {{20,20},  {100,75}, {20,120}, {20,20}, // Left polygon
    {110,20},    {200,120}, {110,120}, {110,20},         // Middle polygon
```

Figure 4.9 Using PolyPolygon.

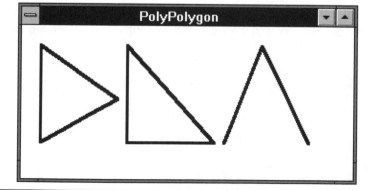

```
      {210,120},  {250,20},  {300,120}};                    // Right polygon
   int counts[3] = {4, 4, 3};  // Number of points in each polygon
   PolyPolygon(dc, p, counts, 3);
}
```

Polygon Fill Mode

Clearly, you can create complex overlapping polygons using the **Polygon** and **PolyPolygon** functions. However, it may surprise you to learn how Windows normally fills the interiors of complex polygons. By default, Windows employs a fill scheme that paints every other closed region of a polygon. Windows calls this the **ALTERNATE** polygon fill mode. To understand how this mode works, look at an example. Figure 4.10 displays a star shape using the **ALTERNATE** polygon filling mode. As you scan from left to right on a line, notice that every other region of the star is filled. The other regions are left unchanged.

Windows also supports the **WINDING** polygon fill mode, which guarantees that every closed region within a polygon is filled. On the right side of Figure 4.10, the same star figure drawn earlier is displayed using the **WINDING** mode. Notice that every region within the star is filled.

Windows provides two functions for manipulating the polygon fill mode (which is stored in the device context):

```
int GetPolyFillMode(HDC hDC);
int SetPolyFillMode(HDC hDC, int polyFillMode);
```

- **hDC** is a handle to the device context.
- **polyFillMode** is either the constant **ALTERNATE** or **WINDING**.
- **GetPolyFillMode** returns the current polygon fill mode.
- **SetPolyFillMode** returns the previous polygon fill mode.

Floodfills

So far we've explored filled figures of specific shapes. Windows also includes the **FloodFill** routine that fills the interior of a bounded region, using the currently selected brush:

```
BOOL FloodFill(HDC hDC, int x, int y, COLORREF color);
```

- **hDC** is a handle to the device context.
- The logical coordinate **x,y** is the starting location of the fill operation.
- The border pixels of the fill operation have the color indicated by the **color** parameter.

Figure 4.10 The ALTERNATE and WINDING polygon fill modes.

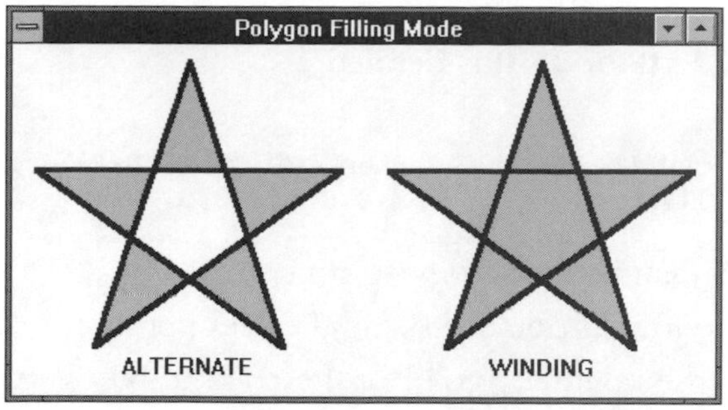

The **FloodFill** routine works much like the paint bucket fill operations typically found in paint programs. You instruct Windows where to start filling and what color to consider its border, and the routine paints the region in all directions—up to the border color specified.

Use **FloodFill** with caution when you are drawing to the screen. The problem is that overlapping windows act as borders to the fill routines. Figure 4.11 illustrates this predicament. Suppose you want to floodfill the region that is partially covered by a window. If you send **FloodFill** the point (10,10), which is in the left part of the region, only the left side of the area gets filled. The pop-up window blocks the progress of the floodfill operation. The right half is unchanged. Clearly this is not what you want.

Figure 4.11 Floodfill operations may not always succeed when drawn to the screen.

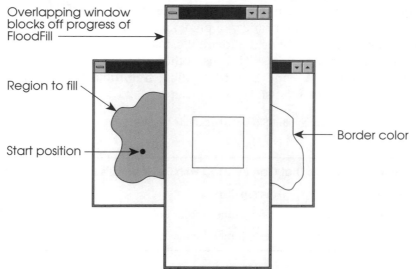

Overlapping window blocks off progress of FloodFill

Region to fill

Start position

Border color

The GDI also includes a similar function, **ExtFloodFill**, which works in one of two ways: It can fill regions up to a particular border, such as **FloodFill** does, or it can *overwrite* neighboring groups of pixels that are a specific color. Here's how **ExtFloodFill** is defined:

```
BOOL ExtFloodFill(HDC hDC, int x, int y, COLORREF color,
  UINT fillType);
```

- **hDC** is a handle to the device context.
- **x,y** is the logical point to begin the fill operation.
- **color** is the boundary color or the color to be overwritten.
- **fillType** specifies the type of fill operation that will take place.

The variable **fillType** can be one of the two constants shown in Table 4.1.

The type of fill operation that **ExtFloodFill** performs depends on the value of its last parameter, **fillType**. If you set **fillType** to **FLOODFILLBORDER**, **ExtFloodFill** operates exactly like **FloodFill**. If, however, you use the **FLOODFILLSURFACE** constant, the routine overwrites all connected pixels of the color specified.

WORKING WITH BRUSHES

Windows paints the interior of filled figures using a *brush*. Much like pens, brushes are objects maintained by Windows. They control the style, color, and pattern used in fill operations. The device context stores a handle to the brush that the fill functions use. The default brush paints regions solid white. A handle to a brush is defined as the type **HBRUSH**.

Windows provides a variety of predefined brush styles called *stock* brushes, which are listed in Table 4.2 and are illustrated in Figure 4.12.

If you want to use a stock brush other than the default white brush, you must first retrieve a handle to it by calling **GetStockObject**. For instance, to gain access to a gray brush, you can use:

```
HBRUSH hGrayBrush = HBRUSH(GetStockObject(GRAY_BRUSH));
```

Table 4.1 Constants That Can Be Used with ExtFloodFill's fillType Argument

Constant	Description
FLOODFILLBORDER	Fill up to the border color; equivalent to FloodFill
FLOODFILLSURFACE	Overwrite all connected pixels that have the color specified

Table 4.2 Stock Brushes

Constant	Description
BLACK_BRUSH	Black brush
DKGRAY_BRUSH	Dark gray brush
GRAY_BRUSH	Gray brush
HOLLOW_BRUSH	Hollow (or null) brush
LTGRAY_BRUSH	Light gray brush
NULL_BRUSH	Null brush, same as HOLLOW_BRUSH
WHITE_BRUSH	White brush

Before a brush can have any effect you must usually select it into the device context by using **SelectObject**. Here's how you can draw a rectangle with a gray interior, for instance:

```
void TExampleWindow::Paint(TDC& dc, BOOL, TRect&)
{
  HBRUSH hGrayBrush = HBRUSH(GetStockObject(GRAY_BRUSH));
  SelectObject(dc, hGrayBrush);
  Rectangle(dc, 10, 10, 50, 100);
}
```

Custom Brushes

If you need a brush pattern other than those that Windows provides, you can create your own using one of the functions in Table 4.3.

Figure 4.12 The stock brush objects.

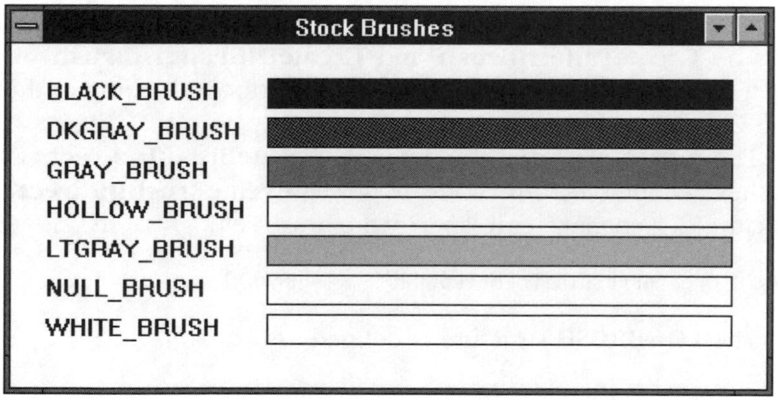

Table 4.3 Functions That Create Brush Objects

Function	Description
CreateBrushIndirect	Uses a logical brush to specify the brush style
CreateDIBPatternBrush	Uses the top-left 8 by 8 pixels in a device-independent bitmap as the brush style
CreateHatchBrush	Builds a brush with a hatch pattern
CreatePatternBrush	Creates a brush from the top-left 8 by 8 pixels of a bitmap
CreateSolidBrush	Creates a solid brush; the colors of the brush may be dithered (explained in Chapter 5)

Of these functions, **CreateSolidBrush** is probably one of the most common. It returns a handle to a solid brush pattern that has a specified color.

```
HBRUSH CreateSolidBrush(color);
```

For example, to create a solid, red brush you could use:

```
HBRUSH hRedBrush = CreateSolidBrush(RGB(255, 0, 0));
```

Remember, the brush may use dithering if the color specified is not supported by the hardware.

The **CreateHatchBrush** function creates a brush with a hatch-style pattern. It uses the form:

```
HBRUSH CreateHatchBrush(int hatchType, COLORREF color);
```

- **hatchType** is one of the constants illustrated in Figure 4.13.
- **color**, which is of type **COLORREF**, is the color of the brush.

The **CreatePatternBrush** and **CreateDIBPatternBrush** functions construct brush patterns from bitmaps. We'll postpone looking at these functions until Chapter 6, when we discuss bitmaps.

The last of the brush functions is **CreateBrushIndirect**, which creates brushes like the other functions; however, **CreateBrushIndirect** uses a single structure as its parameter to specify the brush settings. Here's how it is defined:

```
HBRUSH CreateBrushIndirect(LOGBRUSH* logBrush);
```

The **LOGBRUSH** structure is defined as:

```
typedef struct tagLOGBRUSH {
  UINT lbStyle;      // Style of the brush
```

Figure 4.13 Hatch types available with CreateHatchBrush function.

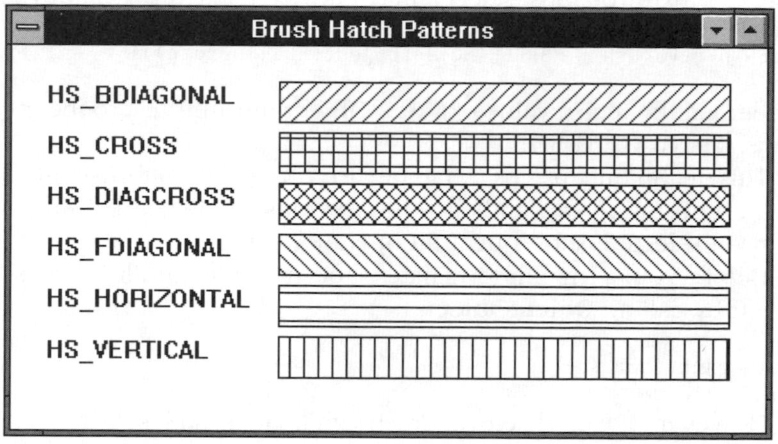

```
   COLORREF lbColor; // The color of the brush
   int lbHatch;        // The hatch style if lbStyle equals BS_HATCHED
} LOGBRUSH;
```

The **lbStyle** field of the **LOGBRUSH** structure specifies the type of brush to create. You can use one of the constants listed in Table 4.4 for this field. If you set **lbStyle** to **BS_HATCHED**, then you should also set the **lbHatch** field to the particular hatch pattern desired. You can use one of the constants in Figure 4.13 for **lbHatch**.

Here's how you can create a solid, red brush using **CreateBrushIndirect**:

```
LOGBRUSH logBrush;
logBrush.lbStyle = BS_SOLID;
logBrush.lbColor = RGB(200, 0, 0);
// The logBrush.lbHatch field is ignored in this example
HBRUSH hBrush = CreateBrushIndirect(&logBrush);
```

Table 4.4 Brush Styles That Can Be Used with LOGBRUSH

Constant	Description
BS_DIPATTERN	A device-independent bitmap is used as the brush pattern
BS_HATCHED	A hatched brush pattern
BS_HOLLOW	An empty brush
BS_NULL	Same as BS_HOLLOW
BS_PATTERN	A memory bitmap is used as the brush pattern
BS_SOLID	A solid brush

Using Custom Brushes

To use a brush, you must select it into a device context by calling **SelectObject**:

```
HBRUSH hPrevBrush = HBRUSH(SelectObject(hDC, hBrush));
```

Remember, the return value of **SelectObject** must be cast to the correct type— in this case to **HBRUSH**.

This technique places a handle to your custom brush into the device context and returns a handle to the previously selected brush. Once a brush has been selected, subsequent fill operations will use it.

Before your program terminates, you must delete all brushes that you've created by calling **DeleteObject**:

```
DeleteObject(hBrush);
```

However, never delete a brush while it is still selected into a device context. If the brush you wish to delete is currently selected, simply select another brush before calling **DeleteObject**. Similarly, you can wait until after you have released the device context before you delete your custom brushes.

When you use one of the functions in Table 4.3 to create a brush, you are merely setting the specifications of the brush. You are creating what Windows calls a *logical* brush. Windows doesn't really turn the logical definition into anything useful until you select it into a device context. When you call **SelectObject**, Windows translates the logical brush settings that you've specified into the actual capabilities that the display device supports. This is when Windows decides, for instance, whether it can draw a solid brush with a single color or whether it must use dithering.

Now let's put all this together. The following **Paint** function creates a red, solid brush and paints a rectangle with it. Try changing the brush color or using one of the other brush creation functions to expand your knowledge of brushes:

```
void TExampleWindow::Paint(TDC& dc, BOOL, TRect&)
{
  HBRUSH hBrush = CreateSolidBrush(RGB(255,0,0));  // Create a red brush
  // Select the brush into the device context
  HBRUSH hOldBrush = HBRUSH(SelectObject(dc, hBrush));
  // Use the red brush to draw a filled rectangle
  Rectangle(dc, 10, 10, 300, 300);
  // Remove the red brush from the device context
  SelectObject(dc, hOldBrush);
  DeleteObject(hBrush);        // Delete the red brush object
}
```

Null Pens and Filled Figures

A null pen is one of the stock objects provided by Windows. Unlike any of the other pen styles, null pens do not actually draw anything on the display device. Sometimes it is useful to select the **NULL_PEN** when drawing filled figures so that the border is not drawn.

How else does a null pen affect filled figures? It may surprise you to learn that the interior of the filled figure will overwrite the top and left sides of the figure. In other words, the **NULL_PEN** object will not draw an outline for the figure, but it also doesn't claim the space around the figure's perimeter. You already saw how filled figures create shapes that appear to be one pixel narrower and shorter than first expected. If you use a **NULL_PEN**, the figure will be yet another pixel shorter and narrower than expected. In practical terms, this means that if you don't want a perimeter to be drawn around your figure, it may be easier to make the pen style the same as the brush or use a routine that doesn't draw a perimeter, such as **FillRect**. The following code illustrates how you can compensate for using a **NULL_PEN** with the **Rectangle** function:

```
SelectObject(hDC, GetStockObject(DKGRAY_BRUSH));
SelectObject(hDC, GetStockObject(NULL_PEN));
Rectangle(hDC, 100, 100, 201, 201);
```

The previouse statement will produce the same figure as the following statements:

```
rect.left = 100;  rect.top = 100;
rect.right = 200; rect.bottom = 200;
FillRect(hDC, &rect, HBRUSH(GetStockObject(DKGRAY_BRUSH)));
```

▼ Note When you are trying to match the pen color used to draw a filled figure with its interior color, remember that the brush may use dithering, but the pen style will not. Therefore, the two colors may be different, even if you specify the same RGB colors. To avoid this problem, you must select a color that the brush will not dither. Chapter 5 provides a method to remedy this situation.

Other Rectangle Functions

We've covered all the standard graphics functions that you might expect the GDI to support. However, Windows includes additional functions for drawing, manipulating, and filling rectangular figures. Let's take a look at some of these.

The **RoundRect** function implements an interesting twist on the **Rectangle** routine. It draws filled rectangles with curved corners, such as the one shown in Figure 4.14. The function has two more parameters than **Rectangle**. These

Figure 4.14 The RoundRect function.

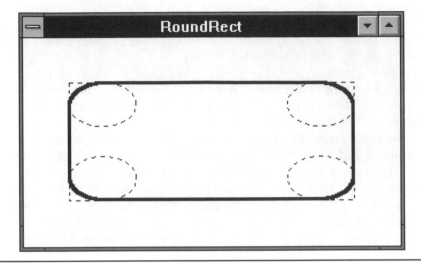

specify the width and height of the ellipse used to draw the rounded corners. Here's the complete function:

```
BOOL RoundRect(HDC hDC, int x1, int y1, int x2, int y2,
  int ellipseWidth, int ellipseHeight);
```

- **hDC** is a handle to the device context.
- **x1,y1** and **x2,y2** specify a box containing the rectangle.
- **ellipseWidth** and **ellipseHeight** specify how curved the corners of the rectangle should be.

The **FillRect** function fills a rectangle region with the brush style passed to it:

```
int FillRect(HDC hDC, RECT* rect, HBRUSH hBrush);
```

- **hDC** is a handle to the device context.
- **rect** is the rectangular region to fill.
- The **hBrush** brush is used to fill the rectangular region.

The return value for this function is not used.

This routine is convenient when you want to fill a rectangular region, but don't want to bother with selecting the brush into a device context first. As with many of the fill routines, **FillRect** does not paint the rightmost column and bottommost row of the rectangle.

The **FrameRect** function draws a rectangle with a border that is one logical unit wide. The interior of the rectangle is not changed. Here is its definition:

```
BOOL FrameRect(HDC hDC, RECT* rect, HBRUSH hBrush);
```

- **hDC** is a handle to the device context.
- **rect**, which is a pointer to a **RECT** structure, specifies the region to draw a frame around.
- The frame is drawn using the brush **hBrush**.

▼ **Note**   The **FrameRect** function doesn't use the selected pen style to draw its rectangle. Instead it uses the *brush style* passed to it. The width of the border is always one logical unit, however.

Windows provides a variety of other functions for manipulating rectangles, such as moving them, testing whether a point lies within a rectangle, setting the clipping region to a rectangle, and so on. A summary of Windows' rectangle functions is listed in Table 4.5. A particularly useful function is **SetRect**, which fills the four fields of a **RECT** structure with four values:

```
void SetRect(RECT* rect, int left, int top, int right, int bottom);
```

- The rightmost four parameters are assigned to the fields in the **RECT** structure **rect**.

For example, the following statement sets the fields in **rect** to the bounding box that extends from (10,100) to (300,200)

```
RECT rect;
SetRect(&rect, 10, 100, 300, 200);
```

Table 4.5 GDI's Rectangle Functions

Function	Description
CopyRect	Copies the coordinates in a RECT structure
EqualRect	Tests whether two rectangles are equal
FillRect	Fills a rectangular region
FrameRect	Draws a frame around the region specified

continued

Table 4.5 GDI's Rectangle Functions (Continued)

Function	Description
InflateRect	Changes the size of a rectangle
InvertRect	Inverts the colors in a rectangular region
OffsetRect	Moves a rectangle
PtInRect	Returns TRUE if a specified point is within a particular rectangle
Rectangle	Displays a rectangle
RoundRect	Displays a rectangle with rounded corners
SetRect	Sets a RECT structure to the values specified
SetRectEmpty	Sets the dimensions of a RECT structure to zero
UnionRect	Determines the union of two rectangles

DRAWING AND CLIPPING WITH REGIONS

Thus far, you've seen how Windows uses a variety of objects, such as pens, brushes, and windows. Windows also includes objects that represent regions. You can combine region objects to create extremely complex shapes. After you have defined a region, you can paint it, invert it, or use it to set the clipping area of your drawings.

We won't be using regions in this book, but for the sake of completeness, the region-related functions are listed in Table 4.6. Most of them should be self-explanatory. Remember, regions are objects; they must be handled like other objects. To use one, you must define the region, retrieve a handle to it, and finally select it into the device context. Similarly, before your program terminates, you must delete the region by calling **DeleteObject** (although not while it is currently selected).

Table 4.6 Region-Related Functions

Function	Description
CreateRectRgn	Makes a rectangular region
CreateRectRgnIndirect	Defines a rectangular region
CreateRoundRectRgn	Creates a rectangular region with rounded corners
CreateEllipticRgn	Defines an elliptical region
CreateEllipticRgnIndirect	Defines an elliptical region
CreatePolygonRgn	Uses a polygon to define a region

continued

Table 4.6 Region-Related Functions (Continued)

Function	Description
CreatePolyPolygonRgn	Uses one or more polygons to define a region
CombineRegion	Creates a new region based on two other regions
EqualRgn	Determines whether two regions are equal
FillRgn	Fills a region with the specified brush
FrameRgn	Draws a frame around the region using the current brush
GetRgnBox	Retrieves the bounding box of the specified region
InvertRgn	Inverts the pixels in the region
OffsetRgn	Moves a region by the amount specified
PaintRgn	Fills the region with the currently selected brush

Regions can also be used to specify areas for clipping. Table 4.7 lists these region-related functions.

Table 4.7 Clipping Functions That Use Regions

Function	Description
ExcludeClipRect	Removes the specified rectangular region from the current clipping region
ExcludeUpdateRgn	Removes the updated region in a window from the current clipping region
InvalidateRgn	Marks the region for repainting
SelectClipRgn	Clips graphics functions to the specified region
ValidateRgn	Validates the region

F I V E

Working with Colors

uch of GDI's flexible nature stems from its use of such features as logical units, generic devices, and high-level function calls. As you might guess, Windows also uses device-independent techniques to support the numerous color capabilities of video displays and printers. In this chapter, you'll learn how to apply these device-independent techniques. In particular, you'll learn how to specify colors in a Windows program and how you can control which colors are available to an application. Although much of what we will cover here applies to all output devices, we'll focus on video displays.

COLORS AND DEVICE DEPENDENCE

Windows is designed to run on a variety of output devices. Therefore, it encounters some challenging problems involved in supporting colors. Graphics adapters can't, unfortunately, display all the same colors and usually don't organize their video memory in the same manner. Table 5.1 illustrates some of the differences for a few of the standard video displays. (We could develop a similar table for other output devices, such as printers and plotters.) At this time, you may want to review the DEVICE.CPP program we developed in Chapter 2, which can display the capabilities of your monitor.

The number of colors that your computer can display depends on the graphics adapter installed. Of equal importance is the device driver you are using with your graphics board. For instance, many SVGA displays enable you to display anywhere from 16 to 16 million simultaneous colors. Specific capabilities depend on which display driver and mode you have selected through Windows' SETUP program.

Table 5.1 Color Capabilities of Several Graphics Adapters

Display Device	VGA	SVGA	8514/A	15-Bit SVGA	24-Bit SVGA
Number of Color Planes	4	1	1	1	1
Bits Per Pixel	4	8	8	15	24
Max Simultaneous Colors	16	256	256	32,768	16 million

You may be surprised to learn—if you haven't already discovered—that just because your display adapter and Windows driver can display 256 simultaneous colors, many commercial applications don't automatically use the extra colors. As a programmer, you must explicitly program your applications to use the colors provided on today's SVGA displays. In this chapter, you'll learn how to accomplish this.

THE SYSTEM PALETTE

Graphics adapters, such as the VGA, can display a wide variety of colors. However, not all colors can be displayed at one time. Therefore, as a compromise, these graphics boards provide a palette that contains a subset of the total number of colors possible. You can draw on the screen with any of the colors in the palette.

By default, Windows also defines a palette for itself, called the *system palette*. This palette is automatically loaded with Windows' standard colors, and is referred to as the *default palette*. On a VGA graphics adapter, the system palette contains 16 colors. On an SVGA display in 256-color (or greater) mode, the system palette has 20 colors. The default colors in these palettes are listed in Table 5.2.

Note Normally, you don't need to know where these colors are located in the palette. Windows does not normally specify colors in terms of palette indexes, but rather as color intensities. The next section discusses this concept further.

Specifying Colors

To support device-independent graphics, Windows does not specify colors in terms of bit planes or implement a specific palette organization. Instead, colors are specified in terms of red, green, and blue (RGB) components. Internally, Windows translates these color components into the actual colors that the hardware can display and sets the appropriate bits.

Table 5.2 Colors in the System Palette

VGA Colors	256-Color SVGA also has:
Black	Pale green
Dark red	Pale blue
Dark green	Off white
Light green	Medium gray
Dark blue	
Lavender	
Slate	
Light gray	
Dark gray	
Bright red	
Bright green	
Yellow	
Bright blue	
Magenta	
Cyan	
White	

Each color component can range from 0 (off) to 255 (fully on). The color white, for instance, has the red, green, and blue components equal to 255. Black has them all set to 0.

The red, green, and blue color components are often grouped into a single double word to represent a color. Windows defines the **COLORREF** type for double words of this form. You've already seen (in Chapters 3 and 4) how Windows uses **COLORREF** to specify colors for pixel operations, pens, and brushes.

Actually, a **COLORREF** variable can have three meanings, depending on the value in its high-order byte, as shown in Table 5.3.

Table 5.3 COLORREF Variable Meanings

Description	High-Order Byte
An explicit RGB value	0
An index to a logical palette entry	1
A palette-relative RGB value	2

If the high-order byte of a **COLORREF** variable is zero, the three other bytes in the **COLORREF** value specify an *explicit* RGB color. The low-order byte specifies the red component, the next byte the green component, and the third byte the blue component. Figure 5.1 shows how these color components fit together. For example, the **COLORREF** value 0x000000FF (binary) represents a purely red color. To create a purely blue color, you would use 0x00FF0000 (binary).

To simplify the process of specifying **COLORREF** colors, Windows provides the **RGB** macro, which accepts three color components and returns an explicit **COLORREF** value. For example, to declare a variable indicating pure red, you could use:

```
COLORREF pureRed = RGB(255,0,0);
```

Similarly, the macro statement

```
RGB(255,128,1)
```

creates the value 0x000180FF.

DITHERING

Windows' system palette is normally restricted to 20 or fewer colors. Fortunately, Windows can paint regions with many more gradations of colors. Windows does this by placing different colors next to each other—in a process called *dithering*. In this way, Windows creates the illusion that it can display more colors. When you request a color that Windows does not have, Windows can create its own.

Figure 5.2 shows an exploded view of two dithered shades of blue. The region on the left was generated using **RGB(128,128,223)**. The color on the right was created using **RGB(64,0,255)**. Notice that Windows uses different groupings of pixels to produce the different shades.

Figure 5.1 Specifying COLORREF's color components.

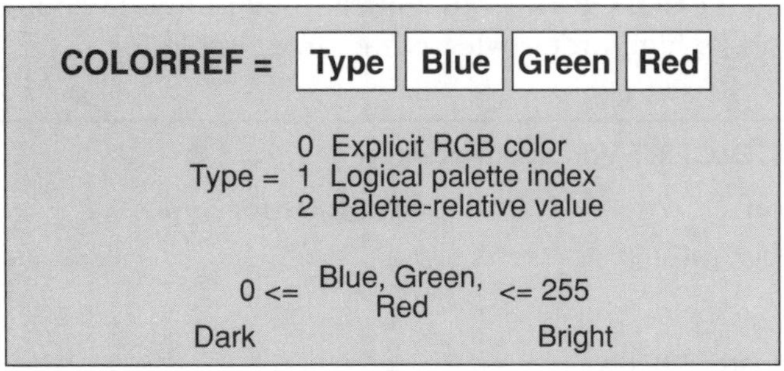

COLORREF = | Type | Blue | Green | Red |

```
            0  Explicit RGB color
Type =      1  Logical palette index
            2  Palette-relative value

              Blue, Green,
     0 <=         Red        <= 255

   Dark                      Bright
```

Figure 5.2 Dithering combines pixels of different colors to produce shades not available in Windows.

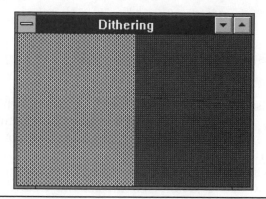

Dithered colors require combinations of neighboring pixels. Therefore, the technique cannot be used when setting individual pixels, drawing lines, and writing text; only *pure* colors (colors in the system palette) are used in these instances. On the other hand, the fill operations support dithered colors. In addition, the **PS_INSIDEFRAME** line style may use dithering if its line width is greater than one pixel.

Two conditions must exist for Windows to go out on its own and use dithering:

• The figure being drawn must support dithering.

• The color requested must not exist in the palette.

If you draw a line or pixel using a color that does not exist in the palette, Windows uses the closest match in the palette. Remember, Windows never dithers lines or individual pixels. You can call the function **GetNearestColor** to determine which color Windows will use for a specific color setting. This function is defined as:

```
COLORREF GetNearestColor(HDC hDC, COLORREF color);
```

• **hDC** is a handle to the device context.

• **color**, which is of type **COLORREF**, is the color to be matched.

• **GetNearesetColor** returns the closest RGB, pure color it could locate.

One way to use **GetNearestColor** is to test whether a particular color is in the palette. If the return value is the same as the color passed in, then the color is a pure color and must be in the palette. The following **if** statement returns TRUE if the color passed to **GetNearestColor** is in the system palette:

```
if ((actualColor=GetNearestColor(hDC, color)) == color) {
  // The color is in the system palette
}
else {
  // The color is not in the system palette
}
```

You can also call **GetNearestColor** to determine which fill color you can use to prevent dithering because **GetNearestColor** returns the closest pure color that matches the color specified. Of course, the color that you get might not be close to what you requested.

The following **Paint** function illustrates how you can use this technique. It fills the window using a pure red brush. The RGB color specified would normally have caused the brush to be dithered, if we had not called **GetNearestColor**. Remember, you can use the following **Paint** function with the EXAMPLE.CPP program shell listed in Chapter 3.

```
void TExampleWindow::Paint(TDC& dc, BOOL, TRect&)
{
  RECT rect;
  ::GetClientRect(HWindow, &rect);
  // Create a brush using a pure color
  HBRUSH hBrush = CreateSolidBrush(GetNearestColor(dc, RGB(200,18,64)));
  FillRect(dc, &rect, hBrush);  // Fill the window with the brush
  DeleteObject(hBrush);
}
```

A Dithered Backdrop

The following program, BACKDROP.CPP, illustrates how powerful Windows' dithering capabilities are. The program displays a graduated, blue backdrop, as shown in Figure 5.3, by sequencing through a series of blue intensities. The top of the client area is set black, and the bottom is bright blue.

The core of the program is the **for** loop in the **Paint** member function:

```
for (i=0; i<numSteps; i++) {
  hBrush = CreateSolidBrush(RGB(0, 0, i*colorInc));
  rect2.top = rect.top + i * stepSize;
  rect2.bottom = rect.top + (i + 1) * stepSize;
  FillRect(hDC, &rect2, hBrush);
  DeleteObject(hBrush);
}
```

This loop creates several filled regions, each with a slightly brighter blue color. Each shade of blue is created with a call to **CreateSolidBrush**. The **FillRect**

Figure 5.3 BACKDROP.CPP displays a dithered blue backdrop.

function displays each color as a horizontal strip. Notice that since **FillRect** takes a brush as a parameter, we don't need to select it into the device context.

Here's the complete BACKDROP program. To compile the program, use the procedure outlined in Chapter 1. Try changing the backdrop color to something other than blue.

```
// BACKDROP.CPP: Displays a graduated blue backdrop.

#include <owl\applicat.h>
#include <owl\framewin.h>
#include <owl\dc.h>

class TBackdropWindow : public TWindow {
public:
  TBackdropWindow(TWindow *parent, const char *title)
    : TWindow(parent, title) { }
  void Paint(TDC& dc, BOOL, TRect&);
};

class TBackdropApp : public TApplication {
public:
  TBackdropApp() : TApplication() { }
  void InitMainWindow();
};

// Paint a blue, graduated backdrop
void TBackdropWindow::Paint(TDC& dc, BOOL, TRect&)
{
  RECT rect, rect2;
  HBRUSH hBrush;
  int i, numSteps, stepSize=8, colorInc;

  ::GetClientRect(HWindow, &rect);
  rect2.left = 0;    rect2.right = rect.right;
```

```
    // Determine how thick to make each strip of color
    numSteps = (rect.bottom - rect.top) / 8 + 1;
    if (numSteps == 1) colorInc = 0;
      else colorInc = 255 / (numSteps-1);
    // Create and display the strips of blue
    for (i=0; i<numSteps; i++) {
      hBrush = CreateSolidBrush(RGB(0, 0, i*colorInc));
      rect2.top = rect.top + i * stepSize;
      rect2.bottom = rect.top + (i + 1) * stepSize;
      FillRect(dc, &rect2, hBrush);
      DeleteObject(hBrush);
    }
}

void TBackdropApp::InitMainWindow()
{
  MainWindow = new TFrameWindow(0, "BACKDROP",
    new TBackdropWindow(0, ""));
}

int OwlMain(int /*argc*/, char* /*argv*/[])
{
  return TBackdropApp().Run();
}
```

Working with a Logical Palette

Specifying colors as RGB triplets gives you a way to logically specify colors. By using triplets, you don't have to worry about the specific colors that a particular graphics adapter supports. However, the pure colors are limited to those colors in the system palette in most modes.

Because numerous graphics adapters support modes that can display many more colors than the ones in the system palette, Windows 3.0 and later versions include another mechanism for specifying colors. In these "additional-color" modes, Windows enables you to use as many colors as can be simultaneously displayed by the hardware (256 on an SVGA display in 256-color mode, for instance). Windows automatically sets aside 20 colors in the extended palette for the colors in the default palette. These are the same 20 colors listed earlier in Table 5.2. You can add colors to this bigger system palette by using what Windows calls a *logical palette*. In this section, we'll discuss how to use the logical palette to get the most colors out of the 256-color mode and break out of the 20-color ceiling.

A logical palette is an array of colors that you want your application to be able to use. The colors that you place in a logical palette are added to the extended system palette as room permits. Realize, however, that an application doesn't have to have a logical palette. You only need to define one if you want to take advantage of the additional colors on an SVGA display. If you don't define a logical palette, your application will simply use the 20 default colors in the system palette.

Different applications can have their own logical palettes. Windows intervenes to give preference to the topmost window. Here's how it works: If a window becomes active and has a logical palette, its palette colors are mapped into the system palette. If a color in the logical palette already exists in the system palette, the color is mapped to the matching color index in the system palette. However, if the color doesn't have a match in the system palette, the color is added to it. Next, the colors from other applications that have logical palettes are mapped into the system palette. When the system palette becomes filled, the closest matching color is selected instead.

Windows implements the palette system this way so that multiple applications can have their own palettes. Yet when a window becomes active, it receives priority regarding the colors that are available in the system palette. When a window is not active, on the other hand, it may not get its first choice of colors. Figure 5.4 illustrates this palette matching process for two windows that utilize logical palettes.

Figure 5.4 Mapping two logical palettes to the system palette.

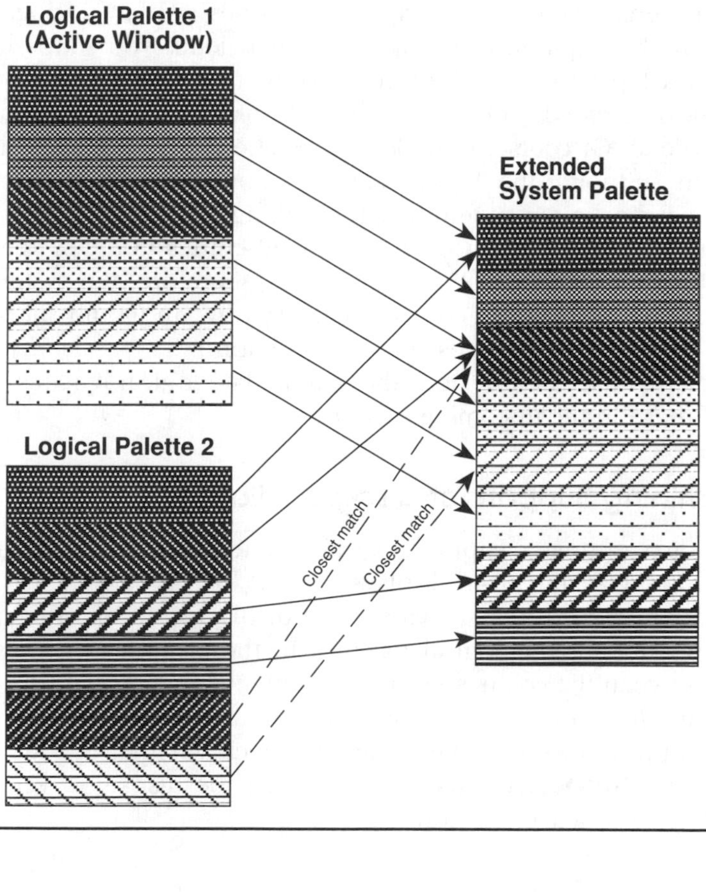

Table 5.4 Logical Palette Manipulation Functions

Function	Description
AnimatePalette	Instantly changes colors on the display
CreatePalette	Defines the palette structure
GetNearestPaletteIndex	Returns the index of a logical palette entry that most closely matches a specified RGB color
GetPaletteEntries	Retrieves logical palette entries
RealizePalette	Maps the entries in the currently selected logical palette to the system palette
SelectPalette	Selects a logical palette into a device context
SetPaletteEntries	Changes entries in a logical palette but does not change the display until it is repainted
UpdateColors	Updates each pixel in a window to the colors in the system palette

---

As I mentioned earlier, an application does not have a logical palette by default. If the application wants a logical palette, you must define one. In addition, a logical palette does not have to resemble the hardware's palette. The logical palette can be as small as one entry or many times larger than the actual palette. Of course, if the logical palette is bigger than what the display hardware supports, the logical palette colors are simply mapped to their closest matches in the system palette. Nothing is gained.

Note also that Windows will occupy 20 entries in the systemwide palette for the default colors. In 256 color modes, therefore, the system palette has room for only 236 custom colors. (Actually, you can modify all but two of the system colors, as we'll discuss in a later section.)

Table 5.4 lists the functions that manipulate logical palettes. We'll explore each of these in the upcoming sections.

Determining Support for a Logical Palette

Not all display drivers support logical palettes. Typically, only the 256-color modes on SVGA and 8514A displays support logical palettes. It's interesting to note that video cards that are capable of displaying 15-bit or even 24-bit color values do *not* support logical palettes. In these modes there's a one-to-one match between the colors specified and the colors displayed.

Here's how to determine whether the installed hardware and display drivers support a logical palette: simply check whether the **RC_PALETTE** bit returned by **GetDeviceCaps** is set and that the display driver is written for Windows 3.0 or a later version:

```
if ((GetDeviceCaps(hDC, RASTERCAPS) & RC_PALETTE) &&
    (GetDeviceCaps(hDC, DRIVERVERSION) >= 0x300))
  // Logical palettes supported
else
  // Logical palettes not supported
```

Creating a Logical Palette

Creating a logical palette requires the following steps:

1. Allocate and initialize a **LOGPALETTE** structure and its colors.
2. Call **CreatePalette** to return a handle to the logical palette.
3. Select the logical palette into the device context by calling **SelectPalette**. Notice that **SelectObject** is not used here.
4. Call **RealizePalette** to transfer the logical palette's colors into the system palette.

Once you've taken these steps, the colors in the logical palette are available to your application. Look at an example. Suppose you want to create a logical palette that has two entries—one for red and the other for blue. You first need to define the palette entries. For this you need a **LOGPALETTE** structure, which is defined in Windows as:

```
typedef struct tagLOGPALETTE {
  WORD palVersion;              // Windows version number
  WORD palNumEntries;           // Number of entries in the palette
  PALETTEENTRY palPalEntry[1];  // Array of PALETTEENTRY
} LOGPALETTE;                   // structures
```

The topmost field must be set to the Windows version number. For instance, the value 0x300 corresponds with Windows 3.0. The second field is the number of entries in the palette. For this example, it would be set to 2. The last field is the array of colors in the palette. Each color is defined by a **PALETTEENTRY** structure, which is defined as:

```
typedef struct tagPALETTEENTRY {
  BYTE peRed;
  BYTE peGreen;
  BYTE peBlue;
  BYTE peFlags;
} PALETTEENTRY;
```

Three of the fields in **PALETTEENTRY** store the red, green, and blue components of the color. The remaining field is one of the flags shown in Table 5.5. These flags tell Windows how you are going to use the color. Windows checks the **peFlags** field to determine how to best match your logical palette to the extended system palette. Usually, you'll want to use a value of zero (NULL), unless you are doing palette animation. (We'll discuss this later.)

Table 5.5 Constants for peFlags Field of a PALETTEENTRY Structure

Constant	Description
NULL (0)	Normal use of palette entry
PC_EXPLICIT	The red and green fields of each PALETTEENTRY specify an entry in the *hardware* palette
PC_NOCOLLAPSE	Do not map this logical palette entry to an existing palette entry, even if it matches an existing entry
PC_RESERVED	This palette entry will change frequently using palette animation; do not map colors from other applications to this color since the color will change

---

Here's how you can allocate and define the color entries in a two-color palette:

```
LOGPALETTE* logPal;
int numColors = 2;
logPal = (LOGPALETTE *)(new char[sizeof(LOGPALETTE) +
  sizeof(PALETTEENTRY) * numColors]);
logPal->palVersion = 0x300;
logPal->palNumEntries = numColors;
logPal->palPalEntry[0].peRed = 175;
logPal->palPalEntry[0].peGreen = 0;
logPal->palPalEntry[0].peBlue = 0;
logPal->palPalEntry[0].peFlags = 0;
logPal->palPalEntry[1].peRed = 0;
logPal->palPalEntry[1].peGreen = 0;
logPal->palPalEntry[1].peBlue = 180;
logPal->palPalEntry[1].peFlags = 0;
```

Now you can call **CreatePalette** to retrieve a handle to a logical palette that meets the criteria you've specified.

```
HPALETTE hLogPal = CreatePalette(logPal);
```

You're not done yet, however. Next you must select the palette into the device context and then call **RealizePalette** to force Windows to map the colors in the logical palette to the system palette. The **SelectPalette** function is defined as:

```
HPALETTE SelectPalette(HDC hDC, HPALETTE hLogPal, BOOL background);
```

- **hDC** is a handle to the device context.
- **hLogPal** is a handle to a logical palette.

- If the function returns non-zero, then the palette is used as a background palette; if the function returns zero, then the palette is a foreground palette.
- The **SelectPalette** function returns a handle to the previously selected palette.

In our example, we could select and realize the palette using these statements:

```
HPALETTE prevPalette = SelectPalette(hDC, hLogPal, 0);
RealizePalette(hDC);
```

Now the two colors you've placed in the logical palette will be available as pure colors. We'll discuss in a moment how to actually request Windows to use these colors.

Note that Windows manages logical palettes as objects. Therefore, like all GDI objects, you must delete your logical palette before your program terminates. This requires that you free the memory associated with the **LOGPALETTE** structure and that you call **DeleteObject** to tell Windows to discard the palette internally:

```
delete(logPal);
DeleteObject(hLogPal);
```

A good place to do this is in your window's destructor or in the **EvDestroy** message-response function. Remember, Windows generates the **WM_DESTROY** message when a window is being closed.

Specifying Colors with a Logical Palette

Now we'll return to techniques for specifying colors. Windows provides two macros that create special **COLORREF** values that are compatible with logical palettes: **PALETTEINDEX** and **PALETTERGB**.

We'll consider **PALETTEINDEX** first. It returns a **COLORREF** value for a specified index of a logical palette entry that contains the color desired. For example, suppose you have realized a logical palette that is initialized with the following settings for index 6:

```
logPal->palPalEntry[6].peRed = 255;
logPal->palPalEntry[6].peGreen = 0;
logPal->palPalEntry[6].peBlue = 0;
logPal->palPalEntry[6].peFlags = 0;
```

Then, if you create a pen with the color **PALETTEINDEX(6)**, the color red will be used.

The third and last way to specify colors is to use the macro **PALETTERGB**, which generates what are known as *palette-relative* colors. The **PALETTERGB** macro accepts three logical color components, as is the case with the macro **RGB**, and returns a **COLORREF** value representing them. If a logical palette exists and the specified color is in the logical palette, its pure color is used. If the color doesn't exist, however, the closest match in the logical palette is selected. In other words, dithering is not used with **PALETTERGB** if a logical palette exists.

A third possibility is also supported by **PALETTERGB**. If a logical palette does not exist, then the value returned by **PALETTERGB** is equivalent to what the **RGB** macro would return.

You may be wondering what happens if you request a color using the **RGB** macro that the currently selected logical palette contains. Will the pure color in the logical palette be used? No. Colors defined using the **RGB** macro never use the logical or extended palettes. They can only "find" colors in the default palette. Therefore, the closest color in the default palette is used or a dithered color is created. To use the colors in the logical palette, you must use **PALETTEINDEX** or **PALETTERGB**.

 Note A logical palette enables you to specify which logical colors you *want* available. However, the colors you actually receive depends on your hardware. For example, VGA and SVGA systems can only display up to 64 shades of any color.

Modifying a Logical Palette

One of the advantages of using a logical palette is that you can easily change or add colors during program execution. In addition, you can update the colors on the screen instantly, by changing the palette entries.

There are two ways you can change the colors currently displayed in a client area in a window. You can first change the colors in the logical palette and then call **AnimatePalette** to instantly transfer these changes to the physical palette. Doing so will force the new colors to replace the old ones on the screen instantly. This technique can be used to animate objects, as we'll explore further in Chapter 9.

Another way to change the palette entries is to call **SetPaletteEntries** first, followed by **RealizePalette**, and then redraw the client area yourself. *The color changes don't take place until the client area is repainted.* The **SetPaletteEntries** function is defined as:

```
UINT SetPaletteEntries(HPALETTE hPalette, UINT startIndex,
   UINT numEntries, PALETTEENTRY* paletteEntries);
```

- **hPalette** is a handle to the palette to update.
- **startIndex** specifies the first location in the logical palette to be changed.

- **numEntries** specifies the number of entries in **paletteEntries**.
- **paletteEntries** is a pointer to an array of **PALETTEENTRY** structures that contains the RGB colors to copy into the logical palette, **hPalette**

If you plan to modify the colors in a palette during program execution, you should set the **peFlags** field of the **PALETTEENTRY** structure to **PC_RESERVED**. This instructs Windows not to let other applications use the color, since you are planning to change it.

Remember, if you modify palette entries using **SetPaletteEntries**, the system palette is not updated until the palette is realized *and* the client area is redrawn.

We'll now look at **AnimatePalette**, which is defined as:

```
void AnimatePalette(HPALETTE hPalette, UINT startIndex, UINT numEntries,
  PALETTEENTRY* newPaletteColors);
```

- **hPalette** is a handle to the palette to update.
- **startIndex** is the first index in the logical palette to be updated.
- **numEntries** is the number of entries in the **newPaletteColors** to be copied to the logical palette.
- **newPaletteColors** is a pointer to an array of **PALETTEENTRY** structures, which contains the colors to be copied into the logical palette, **hPalette**.

Let's say you want to change all pixels on the screen that use the sixth palette entry (which we defined earlier as red). You would first change your copy of the logical palette and then pass it along to **AnimatePalette** to have the display's color updated. Here are the steps to take:

```
logPal->palPalEntry[6].peRed = 255;
logPal->palPalEntry[6].peGreen = 0;
logPal->palPalEntry[6].peBlue = 0;
AnimatePalette(hLogPal, 6, 1, &logPal->palPalEntry[6]);
```

Actually, if you were to do this, you probably would have originally set the **peFlags** field of **PALETTEENTRY** to **PC_RESERVED**.

Palette Messages

An application can rely on two messages to keep track of the palette changes going on in Windows. These messages are listed in Table 5.6. Generally, you don't need to use these messages unless it is critical that your display maintain its true colors while it is not in focus.

Table 5.6. Logical Palette Messages

Message	Description
WM_QUERYNEWPALETTE	Before a window becomes active, this message is generated so that a window can realize its palette
WM_PALETTECHANGED	Another window has changed the palette

When an application receives the **WM_PALETTECHANGED** message, it signals that another program has changed the system palette. The application can respond with one of three actions:

- Do nothing, in which case the colors that should appear in the application may be remapped by other applications with logical palettes.
- Realize its own palette and redraw its client area; some colors may not be restored if the palette is already full.
- Realize its logical palette and use **UpdateColors** to rapidly update the colors; the colors may not all be correct, however, due to the updating process.

A Shaded Backdrop Using a Palette

Now that we've covered many of the basic issues involved in using logical palettes, we can provide an example. The next program, LOGDROP.CPP, revisits the BACKDROP.CPP program developed earlier in this chapter. This time, however, we'll use a logical palette to display pure shades of blue that progress from black to bright blue. Figure 5.5 shows the new, smoother version of the backdrop.

Figure 5.5 Using a logical palette to display a shaded background.

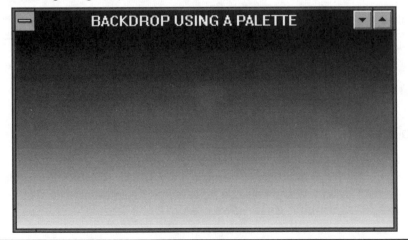

The program uses a logical palette that contains 64 entries. Each entry is a different intensity of blue. The red and green color components are unused. Why only 64 shades of blue? Even though you can specify up to 256 variations of blue, a VGA or an SVGA display only uses 6 bits to determine a color. Therefore, the display can only show up to 64 shades of any given color.

The logical palette is allocated and initialized in the window's **SetupWindow** function. (Alternatively, you could place this code in the **EvCreate** message-response function that is called when Windows posts the **WM_CREATE** message, signaling that a new window is being created.) Here's how the logical palette is allocated to hold 64 entries:

```
int numColors = 64;
logPal = (LOGPALETTE *)(new char[sizeof(LOGPALETTE) +
  sizeof(PALETTEENTRY) * numColors]);
logPal->palVersion = 0x300;
logPal->palNumEntries = numColors;
```

The colors themselves are placed in the logical palette in the **for** loop in **SetupWindow**. Notice that only the blue field of each palette entry is changed. The loop index is multiplied by 4 to stretch the logical intensity values so that they range from 0 (dark) to 255 (bright blue).

```
for (i=0; i<64; i++) {
  // An SVGA supports 64 simultaneous shades of a color
  logPal->palPalEntry[i].peRed = 0;
  logPal->palPalEntry[i].peGreen = 0;
  logPal->palPalEntry[i].peBlue = i*4;
  logPal->palPalEntry[i].peFlags = 0;
}
```

After the colors have been placed in the palette entries, a handle to the logical palette is retrieved by the call:

```
hLogPal = CreatePalette(logPal);
```

The logical palette is not used until the beginning of **Paint**. First, the palette is selected into the device context and then it is realized:

```
SelectPalette(hDC, hLogPal, 0);
RealizePalette(hDC);
```

Now the colors are available to the program.

The **for** loop in **Paint** displays one strip for each of the 64 shades of blue in the logical palette. The height of each strip is calculated just before the loop and is stored in **stepSize**:

```
stepSize = (rect.bottom - rect.top) / numColors + 1;
```

The loop itself creates a brush for each of the 64 colors in the logical palette and calls **FillRect** to display each one.

```
for (i=0; i<numColors; i++) {
  hBrush = CreateSolidBrush(PALETTERGB(0, 0, i*4));
  rect2.top = rect.top + i * stepSize;
  rect2.bottom = rect.top + (i + 1) * stepSize;
  FillRect(hDC, &rect2, hBrush);
  DeleteObject(hBrush);
}
```

Notice that **PALETTERGB** is used to specify the brush color. You could use **PALETTEINDEX**, but the routine will not work if a logical palette does not exist; **PALETTERGB** will.

Finally, **TWindow**'s **EvDestroy()** function is overridden to free the memory associated with the logical palette and delete it from Windows' list of objects. Alternatively, we could have overridden the destructor to perform the same operation. Always remember to clean up after your objects.

```
delete(logPal);
DeleteObject(hLogPal);
TWindow::EvDestroy();
```

 The complete LOGDROP.CPP program is shown next. To run the program you must have an SVGA or 8514/A display. In addition, you should use a 256-color Windows driver. If your current graphics mode does not support a palette, LOGDROP.CPP will produce the same window as BACKDROP.CPP.

```
// LOGDROP.CPP: Displays a graduated backdrop using a logical palette.

#include <owl\applicat.h>
#include <owl\framewin.h>
#include <owl\dc.h>

class TBackdropWindow : public TWindow {
  LOGPALETTE* logPal;     // The logical palette
  HPALETTE hLogPal;       // A handle to the logical palette
public:
  TBackdropWindow(TWindow *parent, const char *title)
    : TWindow(parent, title) { }
  void SetupWindow();
  void Paint(TDC& dc, BOOL, TRect&);
  void EvDestroy();

  DECLARE_RESPONSE_TABLE(TBackdropWindow);
};

DEFINE_RESPONSE_TABLE1(TBackdropWindow, TWindow)
  EV_WM_DESTROY,
END_RESPONSE_TABLE;
```

```
class TBackdropApp : public TApplication {
public:
  TBackdropApp() : TApplication() { }
  void InitMainWindow();
};

// Free up the memory used by the palette. Make sure to call the
// inherited EvDestroy function!
void TBackdropWindow::EvDestroy()
{
  delete(logPal);
  DeleteObject(hLogPal);
  // You must call TWindow's EvDestroy function also
  TWindow::EvDestroy();
}

// Create a logical palette for the program that contains 64 shades of
// blue. Since the VGA and SVGA only have 6 bits of resolution per
// red, green, or blue, this is the maximum number of shades we can get.
void TBackdropWindow::SetupWindow()
{
  TWindow::SetupWindow();    // Call the inherited function!
  int numColors = 64;
  logPal = (LOGPALETTE *)(new char[sizeof(LOGPALETTE) +
    sizeof(PALETTEENTRY) * (numColors-1)]);
  logPal->palVersion = 0x300;
  logPal->palNumEntries = numColors;
  for (int i=0; i<64; i++) {
    // A SVGA supports 64 simultaneous shades of a color
    logPal->palPalEntry[i].peRed = 0;
    logPal->palPalEntry[i].peGreen = 0;
    logPal->palPalEntry[i].peBlue = BYTE(i*4);
    logPal->palPalEntry[i].peFlags = 0;
  }
  hLogPal = ::CreatePalette(logPal);
}

// Paint a blue, graduated backdrop
void TBackdropWindow::Paint(TDC& dc, BOOL, TRect&)
{
  RECT rect, rect2;
  HBRUSH hBrush;
  int i, stepSize;

  SelectPalette(dc, hLogPal, 0);
  RealizePalette(dc);
  ::GetClientRect(HWindow, &rect);
  rect2.left = 0;   rect2.right = rect.right;
  int numColors = 64;
  stepSize = (rect.bottom - rect.top) / numColors + 1;
  for (i=0; i<numColors; i++) {
    hBrush = ::CreateSolidBrush(PALETTERGB(0, 0, i*4));
    rect2.top = rect.top + i * stepSize;
    rect2.bottom = rect.top + (i + 1) * stepSize;
```

```
    FillRect(dc, &rect2, hBrush);
    DeleteObject(hBrush);
  }
}

void TBackdropApp::InitMainWindow()
{
  MainWindow = new TFrameWindow(0, "Backdrop Using a Palette",
    new TBackdropWindow(0, ""));
}

int OwlMain(int /*argc*/, char* /*argv*/[])
{
  return TBackdropApp().Run();
}
```

Determining Color Components

When you need to access one of the color components in a **COLORREF**
variable, you can use one of the following macros:

```
BYTE red = GetRValue(COLORREF color);
BYTE green = GetGValue(COLORREF color);
BYTE blue = GetBValue(COLORREF color);
```

These macros are especially useful when you need to manipulate RGB
colors returned from one of GDI's functions, such as **GetPixel**. The following
Paint function, for instance, determines what RGB colors are displayed when
a pure-color brush is used in conjunction with **GetNearestColor**. (Refer to the
section *Dithering* for a discussion of this function and how it can be used to
select non-dithered brushes.)

```
void TExampleWindow::Paint(TDC& dc, BOOL, TRect&)
{
  RECT rect;
  ::GetClientRect(HWindow, &rect);
  // Create a brush using a pure color
  HBRUSH hBrush = CreateSolidBrush(GetNearestColor(dc, RGB(200,18,64)));
  FillRect(dc, &rect, hBrush);  // Fill the window with the brush
  DeleteObject(hBrush);
  // Determine what color was used and display its RGB values
  char buffer[80];
  COLORREF color = GetPixel(dc, 0, 0);
  wsprintf(buffer, "Red=%d  Green=%d  Blue=%d", GetRValue(color),
    GetGValue(color), GetBValue(color));
  TextOut(dc, 0, 0, Buffer, lstrlen(buffer));
}
```

MANIPULATING THE SYSTEM PALETTE

Although the trend in Windows is to make all the system colors accessible to a program, normally you won't want to change them since these colors are directly tied to the colors of the system menus, and so on. Changing these colors will change the way Windows looks and might confuse your users.

Sometimes, though, you might need the additional colors. In these situations, Windows provides the functions listed in Table 5.7 for manipulating the system colors. You can change all the colors in the system palette except the black and white entries. Looking at it another way: You're always guaranteed that the system palette will contain **RGB(0,0,0)**, which is black, and **RGB(255,255,255)**, which is white.

If you change the system palette, but want to restore it to its original state, you can call **GetStockObject** to retrieve a handle to a palette with the default settings:

```
hPalette = HPALETTE(GetStockObject(DEFAULT_PALETTE));
```

SETTING THE BACKGROUND BRUSH

Normally ObjectWindows erases a window using a white brush. You can, however, change how Windows paints the backdrop. There are two basic approaches:

- Redefine the **hbrBackground** field of the window's class definition—a structure normally hidden by OWL.

- Provide a function that responds to the **WM_ERASEBCKGND** message and paint the window's backdrop yourself.

Setting Windows' **hbrBackground** attribute is probably the most obvious approach. In OWL you can modify a window's class definition by calling the

---

Table 5.7 Functions for Manipulating System Colors

Function	Description
GetNearestColor	Returns the closest match to a color in the system palette
GetSysColor	Retrieves color of a system element
GetSystemPaletteEntries	Copies the portion of the system palette specified
GetSystemPaletteUse	Determines whether an application can fully manipulate the system palette
SetSysColors	Sets one or more system colors
SetSystemPaletteUse	Enables active application to fully manipulate the system palette

TWindow member function **GetWindowClass**. Here's how you could override it to set the background brush to black in a class derived from OWL's **TWindow**:

```
void TExampleWindow::GetWindowClass(WNDCLASS& wndClass)
{
  // Call parent's function first
  TWindow::GetWindowClass(wndClass);
  // Now supply your own window attributes
  wndClass.hbrBackground = HBRUSH(GetStockObject(BLACK_BRUSH));
}
```

This function modifies the window's definition so that it displays a black background. However, the function actually forces *all* windows of the same class name to use the background brush. This may be what you want. On the other hand, you may only want this one instance of the program to have a black background. If this is the case, you must also supply Windows with a new class name. In this way, Windows will keep this new type of window separate from other windows. In OWL you can change a window's class name by overriding **TWindow**'s **GetClassName** function and supplying it with a new name:

```
char* TExampleWindow::GetClassName()
{
  return "NEWCLASSNAME";
}
```

In terms of the second technique, here's how you might override the **EvEraseBkgnd** message-response function to paint the window black:

```
void TExampleWindow::EvEraseBkgnd(HDC hDC)
{
  RECT rect;
  ::GetClientRect(HWindow, &rect);
  FillRect(hDC, &rect, HBRUSH(GetStockObject(BLACK_BRUSH)));
}
```

If you do decide to use the **EvEraseBkgnd** approach, make sure to also include the **EV_WM_ERASEBKGND** macro in your window's message response table. Otherwise, your customized **EvEraseBkgnd** will never be called.

Realize that, in both cases, we haven't modified the background color stored in the device context. Therefore, when Windows erases the gaps within any text or hatch patterns that you display, it will use the device context's background color— normally white. You can set the background color, using **SetBkColor**, to the same color as the brush. If your backdrop is a complex drawing or bitmap, this won't fully solve the problem, however. In these cases, you may want to set the background mode to **TRANSPARENT** so that any text you display won't corrupt the backdrop. A slightly better approach is to select background colors that will use pure colors rather than dithering. This avoids unexpected side effects with some of GDI's graphics functions. The earlier discussion of **GetNearestColor** describes how you can do this.

Working with Bitmaps

Y ou can write most graphics applications exclusively with calls to the GDI's pixel-, line-, and curve-drawing routines. However, there are times when it is more convenient to work with *bitmaps*— rectangular blocks of a picture. Windows uses bitmaps to store and display components of its user interface, such as the Close button in the system menu and the arrows on scroll bars. Similarly, Borland's Resource Workshop pops up a bitmap image when it starts. In each case, the applications display previously drawn bitmap images on the screen.

In this chapter, we'll look at the bitmap support that Windows provides. We'll also explore several ways of using bitmaps in graphics applications. For instance, we'll investigate how to rapidly update the screen using bitmaps, display bitmap files, and add bitmaps in menus. In Chapter 9, we'll explore techniques for animating objects using bitmaps.

OVERVIEW OF BITMAPS

A bitmap is a rectangular array of data that represents a screen image. Each element in the array typically corresponds with a pixel on the screen. Bitmaps can be created in several ways. You can:

- Interactively paint a bitmap with the Resource Workshop, then save the image to a file and later read it into an application

- Hard-code a bitmap's array values in your program

- Allocate memory for a bitmap and then draw on it much like you would other display devices; after the bitmap has been painted, you can copy it to a window

- Allocate memory for a bitmap and then copy portions of the screen into it

Table 6.1 lists the primary bitmap functions Windows provides for constructing bitmaps in a program.

Bitmaps have changed quite a bit since the early days of Windows. Originally, bitmaps were tied quite closely to specific displays. Since display modes use different numbers of bit planes and colors, the bitmaps would not appear the same on different types of graphics adapters. These older style of bitmaps are called *device-specific bitmaps* since they are closely tied to the display on which they were created or displayed.

Device-independent bitmaps (*DIB*) were added with Windows 3.0. This newer class of bitmaps eases the task of using bitmaps in a program. Now you don't have to know what the characteristics of a display are in order to work with a bitmap image. You still can use the device-specific functions, however. In fact, there are times when it's easier to use them.

Table 6.1 Bitmap Construction Functions

Function	Description
CreateBitmap	Creates a device-dependent bitmap
CreateBitmapIndirect	Creates a device-dependent bitmap
CreateCompatibleBitmap	Creates an uninitialized bitmap compatible with a device context
CreateDIBitmap	Creates a device-dependent bitmap from a device-independent bitmap
CreateDiscardableBitmap	Creates a bitmap that can be discarded
CreateDIBPatternBrush	Creates a logical brush that uses the specified device-independent bitmap
CreatePatternBrush	Creates a logical brush that uses a specified bitmap
GetDIBits	Copies a bitmap's values into device-independent structures
GetBitmapBits	Returns an array of bits
GetBitmapDimensions	Retrieves the bitmap's dimensions in 0.1 mm units
GetObject	Retrieves information about a bitmap
LoadBitmap	Loads a bitmap image referenced in a resource file
SetDIBits	Sets the bits in a bitmap to the specified device-independent values
SetDIBitsToDevice	Copies values stored in device-independent format to the display
SetBitmapBits	Copies an array of values to a bitmap
SetBitmapDimensions	Sets the bitmap's dimensions in 0.1 mm units

Bitmaps and Handles

Not surprisingly, Windows manages bitmaps as objects. As with all objects, you don't manipulate the bitmaps directly. Instead, bitmaps are manipulated using handles, which have the type **HBITMAP**. The following declaration defines a handle to a bitmap variable called **hBitmap**:

```
HBITMAP hBitmap;
```

Similarly, in order to draw with a bitmap you must select it into a device context, using **SelectObject**. When you are finished with the bitmap, you must delete it from memory by calling **DeleteObject**. These are the same steps we've been taking with all Windows' objects.

Using a Memory Device Context

Requiring you to select a bitmap into a device context before you can use it is to be expected for an object. However, what device context can you use? So far we've been using a device context associated with the screen. Every time you draw to a screen's device context, you draw to the screen. However, we want to manipulate bitmaps. We want to be able to associate a bitmap with a device context so that every time we manipulate the device context, it operates on the bitmap. In order to accomplish this, Windows provides a special type of device context called a *memory device context.*

A memory device context is much like a screen's device context. It is accessed using a handle of type **HDC** and has a complete set of drawing tools and objects associated with it. However, we want to make a memory device context that is *compatible* with the display. Windows enables you to do this by calling **CreateCompatibleDC**, which makes a copy of the device context that you pass to it. For example, the following statements retrieve a handle to the device context associated with a window, create a compatible memory device context (**hMemDC**), and then release the screen's device context:

```
HDC hDC = GetDC(HWindow);
HDC hMemDC = CreateCompatibleDC(hDC);
ReleaseDC(HWindow, hDC);
```

The **GetDC** and **ReleaseDC** functions are described in Chapter 2, however, the **CreateCompatibleDC** routine is new. Here, it instructs Windows to make a copy of the window's device context. However, **CreateCompatibleDC** does not give the memory device context a useful display surface. We must select a bitmap into the memory device context:

```
SelectObject(hMemDC, hBitmap);
```

Only after calling **SelectObject** does the memory device context actually have something you can draw on.

Now, whenever you use the **hMemDC** device context, you'll actually be working with the bitmap! Further, you can use the memory device context anywhere you would normally use a device context. You can call any of the GDI's functions, pass the function **hMemDC**, and write to the bitmap rather than the screen. We'll look at this further in a moment.

Cleaning Up after Bitmaps

After you are finished with a memory device context, you should release its device context using **DeleteDC**:

```
DeleteDC(hMemDC);
```

Similarly, when you no longer need a bitmap, you should delete it from Windows' memory:

```
DeleteObject(hBitmap);
```

As with all objects, however, never delete a bitmap while it is currently selected into a device context. If you need a bitmap throughout an application, it's often easiest to construct your bitmaps in OWL's **TWindow::SetupWindow** function and delete any bitmap objects in the window object's destructor.

So far we've covered in general terms how to gain access to bitmaps. Now we'll explore the various ways we can generate and use bitmap images.

LOADING AND DISPLAYING BITMAP FILES

One way to create bitmap images is with Borland's Resource Workshop. By using its painting tools, you can interactively draw a bitmap image and store it to a Window's device-independent bitmap file. (These files end with a .BMP extension.) In this section we'll present one technique for displaying bitmap files that is useful when an application displays a non-changing bitmap image, such as in an opening screen. In this case, the bitmap image is attached to the program's executable file. At the end of this chapter, we'll discuss an alternative technique that is ideal for situations when the bitmap image varies, which is typical of a bitmap editing program.

To display a non-changing bitmap image, your application should follow these three steps:

1. Load the bitmap image into memory.
2. Create a memory device context for the bitmap.
3. Copy the bitmap to the device context.

We'll take some time now to discuss each of these steps in detail.

Step 1: Loading a Bitmap

You can use the **LoadBitmap** function to tell Windows which bitmap file to read:

```
HBITMAP hBitmap = LoadBitmap(HINSTANCE hInstance, LPCSTR bitmapFile);
```

Starting from the left, the **LoadBitmap** function returns a handle to the bitmap that it reads. The first parameter is a handle to the program's *instance*. So far, OWL has hidden this Windows term from us; however, now we need it so that Windows will retrieve the correct bitmap image for our application. Windows uses instance handles to help keep track of the various versions of the programs running. (In case you're curious, the **OwlMain** function hides the program instance handle from us, which is passed along to Windows' initialization code.)

You can retrieve the handle to a program's instance, by using the statement:

```
HINSTANCE hInstance = GetApplicationObject()->GetInstance();
```

Now, let's get back to the **LoadBitmap** function. The rightmost parameter in **LoadBitmap** is the name associated with the bitmap file. This is *not* the bitmap's filename, though. So what does this name refer to? To explain, we need to introduce one more Windows programming concept—*resource files*.

So far we've been programming Windows applications like we would any DOS application. Statements are written in a program file, compiled, and then run. However, in Windows you can specify parts of the program in a resource file. A resource file is a text file containing statements that specify which menus, dialog boxes, bitmaps, and so on that your program uses. That is, it includes the program's *resources*. A resource file is compiled (by the Resource Compiler or the Resource Workshop) and combined with your application's executable file when your source files are linked together. In Borland C++ 4.0 you typically include the name of the resource file in your application's project file, just as if it were another source file.

Each resource in a program's resource file uses one or more statements of a special syntax. For instance, you can list which bitmaps a program uses with the **BITMAP** statement:

```
BitmapFile  BITMAP FILENAME.BMP
```

The leftmost string is the internal name of the bitmap file. This is the same name that you use in the **LoadBitmap** statement. The rightmost string is the actual name of the bitmap file.

For example, if the bitmap file is called MYBITMAP.BMP, then the following statement in a resource file will associate the internal name **BitmapFile** with the actual bitmap file MYBITMAP.BMP:

```
BitmapFile  BITMAP  MYBITMAP.BMP
```

Let's put all this to work. Assuming that a resource file uses the statement just shown, you can read the MYBITMAP.BMP file into your application using the statement:

```
HBITMAP hBitmap = LoadBitmap(GetApplicationObject()->GetInstance(),
  BitmapFile);
```

Step 2: Creating a Memory Device Context

The previous statement gives you a handle to the bitmap, but you can't display the bitmap yet. You must first create a memory device context for it and then select the bitmap into this device context:

```
HDC hDC = GetDC(HWindow);
HDC hMemDC = CreateCompatibleDC(hDC);
ReleaseDC(HWindow, hDC);
SelectObject(hMemDC, hBitmap);
```

We're almost there. The next section discusses how to actually display the bitmap on the screen.

Step 3: Displaying a Bitmap

After you have a bitmap associated with a memory device context, you can display it. This is done by copying the bitmap in the memory device context to the screen through the screen's device context. The **BitBlt** function performs this operation:

```
BitBlt(HDC hDestDC, int xDest, int yDest, int width, int height,
  HDC hSrcDC, int xSrc, int ySrc, DWORD rop);
```

- **hDestDC** is a handle to the destination device context.
- **xDest,yDest** specifies the top-left logical coordinate of the destination rectangle.
- **width** and **height** specify the logical width and height of the destination and source.
- **hSrcDC** is the source device context.
- **xSrc,ySrc** is the top-left logical coordinate of the rectangular region to copy from the source device context.
- **rop** is a special code that specifies how the source and destination are to be combined. To copy the source to the destination, use **SRCCOPY**.
- The **BitBlt** fuction returns TRUE if it succeeds and FALSE otherwise.

Figure 6.1 Using the parameters of the BitBlt function.

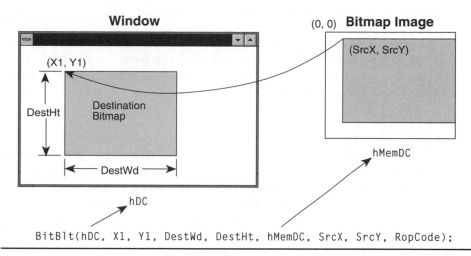

```
BitBlt(hDC, X1, Y1, DestWd, DestHt, hMemDC, SrcX, SrcY, RopCode);
```

Figure 6.1 shows how these parameters relate to the two bitmaps. For example, to display the **hBitmap** image in a 100 by 100 pixel rectangular region at the top of a window, you would use:

```
BitBlt(hDC, 0, 0, 100, 100, hMemDC, 0, 0, SRCCOPY);
```

If the bitmap is larger than the width and height specified, the extra pixels in the bitmap are ignored. If the bitmap is too small, the destination context is left unchanged wherever the bitmap is not defined. Finally, if the colors are different, the source colors are converted to those used by the destination device context.

Notice that you can use **BitBlt** to copy from the screen to a bitmap. All you need to do is swap the device-context parameters:

```
BitBlt(hMemDC, 0, 0, 100, 100, hDC, 0, 0, SRCCOPY);
```

A Simple Example

We've covered quite a few steps here. To clear up any confusion, we'll provide an example. The following **Paint** function reads the bitmap file MYBITMAP.BMP and displays it at the top-left of a window. Here are the steps you'll need to use the **Paint** function:

1. Use the Resource Workshop or a similar program to generate a bitmap and save it into a file with the name MYBITMAP.BMP. This is the bitmap file we'll display.

2. Create a resource file called EXAMPLE.RC. It only needs one line:

```
BitmapFile  BITMAP  MYBITMAP.BMP
```

3. Add the filename, EXAMPLE.RC to your application's project file. As long as you do this, Borland C++ will automatically invoke Resource Workshop to compile the resource file and link the resulting .RES file that it creates to your application's .EXE file.

4. Place the **Paint** function shown next into the EXAMPLE.CPP program stub listed at the beginning of Chapter 3.

Now let's take a look at the code. The **Paint** function uses many of the statements you've already seen. Note that the **BitBlt** function displays the top 100 by 100 portion of the bitmap. If the bitmap is a different size, this won't cause a problem. Also, notice that **Paint** deletes the memory device context and the bitmap after they are no longer needed. These are two very important steps.

```
void TExampleWindow::Paint(TDC& dc, BOOL, TRect&)
{
  HBITMAP hBitmap = LoadBitmap(GetApplicationObject()->GetInstance(),
    "BitmapFile");   // See note that follows
  HDC hMemDC = CreateCompatibleDC(dc);
  SelectObject(hMemDC, hBitmap);
  BitBlt(dc, 0, 0, 100, 100, hMemDC, 0, 0, SRCCOPY);
  DeleteDC(hMemDC);
  DeleteObject(hBitmap);
}
```

▼ Note You really don't want to load the bitmap in the **Paint** function; however, for simplicity's sake, we're calling **LoadBitmap** in the **Paint** routine. To test this **Paint** function, you'll need to create a bitmap in the file MYBITMAP.BMP and define a resource file with the statement:

```
BitmapFile BITMAP MYBITMAP.BMP
```

WORKING WITH ROP CODES

Let's return to the **BitBlt** function. The last parameter of **BitBlt**, **rop**, specifies how a source bitmap is combined with the destination device. The **rop** parameter can actually be one of 256 different values, but Windows only provides constants for 15 of the most common, which are listed in Table 6.2.

The ROP (raster operation) code specifies how the brush selected in the device context, the pixels in the source, and the pixels in the destination are combined. Probably the most commonly used ROP code is **SRCCOPY**, which copies the source bitmap to the destination bitmap.

Table 6.2 Raster Operation Codes Used by BitBlt

Constant	Description
BLACKNESS	Sets all destination pixels black
DSTINVERT	Inverts the destination
MERGECOPY	ANDs the brush pattern and source bitmap
MERGEPAINT	ORs the inverted source bitmap with the destination bitmap
NOTSRCCOPY	Copies the inverted source bitmap to the destination
NOTSRCERASE	Inverts the result of ORing the source and destination bitmaps together
PATCOPY	Copies the brush pattern to the destination bitmap
PATINVERT	Exclusive ORs the brush pattern bitmap with the destination bitmap
PATPAINT	ORs the inverted source bitmap with the brush pattern and then ORs this result with the destination
SRCAND	ANDs the source and destination bitmaps together
SRCCOPY	Copies the source bitmap to the destination
SRCERASE	ANDs the inverted destination bitmap with the source bitmap
SRCINVERT	Exclusive ORs the source and destination bitmaps
SRCPAINT	ORs the source and destination bitmaps together
WHITENESS	Sets all destination pixels white

The following **Paint** function illustrates how the **NOTSRCCOPY** code, which inverts the source bitmap's colors, works. In this example, the display device context is used as the source and destination bitmap; therefore, **NOTSRCCOPY** inverts the screen between (0,0) and (145,130). Its output is shown in Figure 6.2.

```
void TExampleWindow::Paint(TDC& dc, BOOL, TRect&)
{
  POINT p[3] = {{0,125}, {70,0}, {140,125}};
  Polygon(dc, p, 3);        // Draw a triangle
  // Invert the colors where the triangle is
  BitBlt(dc, 0, 0, 145, 130, dc, 0, 0, NOTSRCCOPY);
}
```

CREATING BITMAPS

You can use two basic techniques to create a bitmap from within your application. The first technique hard-codes the bitmap pattern into an array and calls

Figure 6.2 Inverting bitmap colors with NOTSRCCOPY.

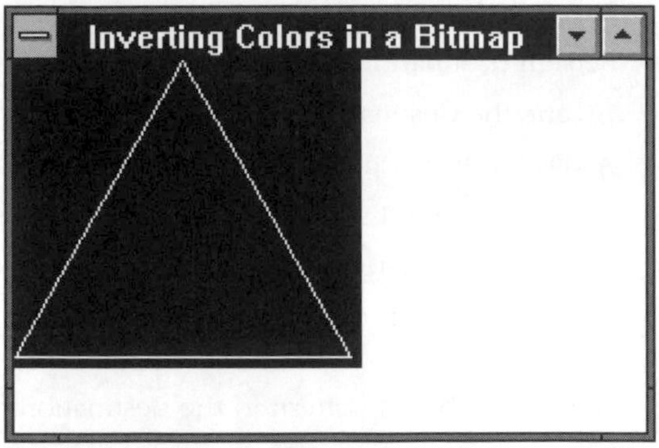

CreateBitmap (or a similar function) to return a handle to a bitmap of the specified type. The other technique is to define a bitmap that is compatible with your display device context and then draw the desired figure on it.

The **CreateBitmap**, **CreateBitmapIndirect**, and **CreateDIBitmap** functions fall into the first category. They all require that you supply the bitmap data in a special format. Further, the **CreateBitmap** and **CreateBitmapIndirect** functions require that you arrange the pattern in the same way that the colors are maintained on the display device. Generally, this isn't practical except in all but the simplest of cases, such as for creating small monochrome bitmaps. The **CreateDIBitmap** function is slightly better because the information can adhere to Windows' device-independent bitmap standard. It's particularly useful when reading device-independent bitmaps from a file, as we'll cover at the end of this chapter.

The second approach is to create a bitmap that you can draw onto. Since this is a common graphics technique, we'll provide an example. The first thing you must do is define a bitmap and select it into a memory device context that is compatible with the display:

```
RECT rect;
GetClientRect(HWindow, &rect);
HDC hMemDC = CreateCompatibleDC(hDC);
SelectObject(hMemDC, hSavedBitmap);
```

Then, you can call **CreateCompatibleBitmap** to actually create a bitmap of a particular size.

```
hSavedBitmap = CreateCompatibleBitmap(hDC, rect.right, rect.bottom);
```

This statement, for instance, specifies that the bitmap will be as large as the window's client area. After the bitmap has been defined, it is selected into the memory device context. However, the bitmap is not ready to use yet. It initially contains undefined values. You'll want to clear these values before using the bitmap. For instance, you might want to call **FillRect** to initialize the bitmap to a solid color, such as white:

```
FillRect(hMemDC, &rect, HBRUSH(GetStockObject(WHITE_BRUSH)));
```

Notice that **hMemDC** specifies the device context. This is the way you tell Windows to draw on the bitmap. Similarly, you can drawn on the bitmap with any of GDI's graphics functions. The following statement, for instance, draws a rectangle on the bitmap:

```
Rectangle(hMemDC, 10, 10, 100, 100);
```

The following **Paint** function further illustrates how you can draw on a bitmap. It creates a bitmap 100 by 100 pixels in size, initializes it to gray, and then draws an ellipse on it. The bitmap is then copied to the top-left of the display window.

```
void TExampleWindow::Paint(TDC& dc, BOOL, TRect&)
{
  RECT rect;
  HBITMAP hSavedBitmap = LoadBitmap(GetApplicationObject()->
    GetInstance(), "BitmapFile");
  HDC hMemDC = CreateCompatibleDC(dc); // Create a memory device context
  SelectObject(hMemDC, hSavedBitmap);
  // Create a bitmap compatible with the display
  HBITMAP hBitmap = CreateCompatibleBitmap(dc, 100, 100);
  rect.left = 0;    rect.top = 0;
  rect.right = 100; rect.bottom = 100;
  // Initialize the bitmap
  FillRect(hMemDC, &rect, HBRUSH(GetStockObject(GRAY_BRUSH)));
  Ellipse(hMemDC, 10, 10, 50, 50);    // Draw an ellipse on the bitmap
  BitBlt(dc, 0, 0, 100, 100, hMemDC, 0, 0, SRCCOPY);
  // Delete the memory device context and the bitmap
  DeleteDC(hMemDC);
  DeleteObject(hBitmap);
  DeleteObject(hSavedBitmap);
}
```

STRETCHING BITMAPS

You've already seen how **BitBlt** copies from one device context to another. However, what if you only want to copy a portion of a bitmap or what if the bitmap is of a different size than its destination? For these instances, Windows provides the **StretchBlt** function. Here's how **StretchBlt** is defined:

```
BOOL StretchBlt(hDestDC, xDest, yDest, widthDest, heightDest,
  hSrcDC, xSrc, ySrc, widthSrc, heightSrc, rop);
```

Figure 6.3 Using the parameters of StretchBlt.

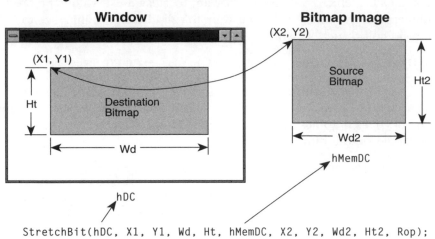

```
StretchBit(hDC, X1, Y1, Wd, Ht, hMemDC, X2, Y2, Wd2, Ht2, Rop);
```

The parameters are the same as **BitBlt**'s except for the **widthSrc** and **heightSrc** arguments that specify the logical width and height of the source bitmap. Figure 6.3 shows how the parameters in **StretchBlt** relate to one another.

When you're working with a bitmap, how can you tell how big it is? If you haven't saved this information, you can call **GetObject**. It returns the specifications of a bitmap in a **BITMAP** structure, which is defined as:

```
typedef struct tagBITMAP {
  int bmType;         // 0
  int bmWidth;        // Pixel width of bitmap
  int bmHeight;       // Pixel height of bitmap
  int bmWidthBytes;   // Number of bytes in each row of bitmap
  BYTE bmPlanes;      // Number of color planes in the bitmap
  BYTE bmBitsPixel;   // Number of bits per pixel
  void* bmBits;       // Points to the raster data
} BITMAP;
```

If a variable **bm** is declared as a **BITMAP** structure, the following call to **GetObject** retrieves information about the bitmap **hBitmap**:

```
GetObject(hBitmap, sizeof(BITMAP), &bm);
```

The **bmWidth** and **bmHeight** fields in **bm** contain the values you must pass to **StretchBlt** to specify the dimensions of a bitmap.

Putting all this together, the following statements stretch a bitmap, called **hSource**, so that it covers the whole client area of a window:

```
RECT rect;
BITMAP bm;
GetClientRect(HWindow, &rect);
HDC hMemDC = CreateCompatibleDC(hDC);
SelectObject(hMemDC, hSource);
GetObject(hBitmap, sizeof(BITMAP), &bm);
StretchBlt(hDC, 0, 0, rect.right, rect.bottom,
  hMemDC, 0, 0, bm.bmWidth, bm.bmHeight, SRCCOPY);
DeleteDC(hMemDC);
```

 Note Because of all the things that **StretchBlt** must do, it is rather slow. Don't expect fast screen updates with this function.

When a bitmap must be reduced in size, **StretchBlt** combines or removes pixels. The way that it reduces the size of a bitmap depends on the stretch mode. Table 6.3 lists the three modes that **StretchBlt** supports. By default, pixels are ANDed together, thereby favoring black pixels over white. This is called the **BLACKONWHITE** mode. However, if your bitmap image consists of a thin white line on a black background, the line will quickly disappear as the bitmap is reduced. The way around this is to select the **WHITEONBLACK** mode, which ORs pixels together as the bitmap is reduced in size. This mode isn't good for color bitmaps, either. In this case, it may be best to select the **COLORONCOLOR** mode. You can select the mode **StretchBlt** uses by calling **SetStretchBltMode** and passing it the mode desired:

```
SetStretchBltMode(hDC, StretchMode);
```

If a bitmap must be expanded, on the other hand, **StretchBlt** duplicates rows or columns of the bitmap. Quite obviously, this can create staircasing in your bitmap or distortion if some rows are duplicated and others are not.

Table 6.3 Stretching Modes Used by StretchBlt

Constant	Description
BLACKONWHITE	Pixels that must be combined are ANDed together, which preserves black pixels over white ones; use when your figure is black and the background is white (the default)
COLORONCOLOR	Lines are deleted without further action; use when your figure is made up of several colors
WHITEONBLACK	Pixels that must be combined are ORed together, which preserves white pixels over black ones; use when your figure is white and the background is black

Mirroring Bitmaps

One interesting way to use **StretchBlt** is to mirror a bitmap image. You simply need to give the height and width parameters of the source and destination bitmaps' opposite signs. The following **Paint** function, for example, draws a triangle on the left side of the screen and then copies it to the right, mirroring the image so it appears upside-down, as shown in Figure 6.4. Notice that the height parameter of the source bitmap is −150 and the destination height is 150. This forces the bitmap to be flipped vertically. Try flipping the image horizontally by giving the width parameters opposite signs.

```
void TExampleWindow::Paint(TDC& dc, BOOL, TRect&)
{
  // Display a triangle on the left side of the screen
  POINT p[3] = {{20,125}, {80,25}, {140,125}};
  Polygon(hDC, p, 3);
  // Copy an inverted image of the triangle to the right
  // side of the display window
  StretchBlt(hDC, 200, 150, 150, -150, hDC, 0, 0, 150, 150, SRCCOPY);
}
```

Creating Bitmap Brushes

You can use the **CreatePatternBrush** or **CreateDIBPatternBrush** functions to define a logical brush pattern from a bitmap. Recall that a brush pattern is an 8 by 8 rectangular array of colors. The pattern is repeated in order to paint large regions. A bitmap brush is created by copying the top-left 8 by 8 pixels of a bitmap image into a brush style. This also means the bitmap must be at least 8 by 8 pixels in size.

The following **Paint** function fills a rectangle with a brush constructed from Windows' combo bitmap. Figure 6.5 shows a version of the **Paint**

Figure 6.4 Mirroring a bitmap image with StretchBlt.

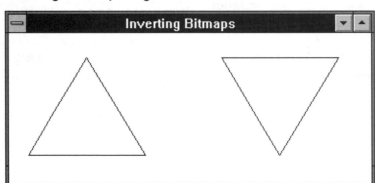

Figure 6.5 Using a bitmap image in a brush.

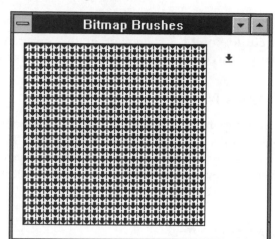

function. It has been modified to also display the combo bitmap on the right side of the filled rectangle.

```
void TExampleWindow::Paint(TDC& dc, BOOL, TRect&)
{
  HBITMAP hBitmap = LoadBitmap(0, (LPSTR)OBM_COMBO);
  HBRUSH hBrush = CreatePatternBrush(hBitmap);
  HBRUSH hOldBrush = HBRUSH(SelectObject(dc, hBrush));
  Rectangle(dc, 10, 10, 200, 200);
  SelectObject(dc, hOldBrush);
  DeleteObject(hBrush);
  DeleteObject(hBitmap);
  // Display the complete bitmap next to it
  hBitmap = LoadBitmap(0, (LPSTR)OBM_COMBO);
  HDC hMemDC = CreateCompatibleDC(dc);
  SelectObject(hMemDC, hBitmap);
  BitBlt(dc, 220, 20, 300, 300, hMemDC, 0, 0, SRCCOPY);
  DeleteDC(hMemDC);
  DeleteObject(hBitmap);
}
```

The **OBM_COMBO** constant passed to **LoadBitmap** is one of several such constants that Windows provides for the bitmaps it uses in its user interface. The **(LPSTR)** casting is required because **OBM_COMBO** is an integer constant, not a string (as **LoadBitmap** expects). Notice that **LoadBitmap**'s first parameter is set to 0. This tells the function to locate the system's bitmaps and not the application's bitmaps.

To get the previous **Paint** function to run, you also must add the statement

```
#define OEMRESOURCE 1
```

before the **#include <owl.h>** statement in the program. This forces your compiler to give you access to the **OBM_XXXX** constants in WINDOWS.H.

BITMAPS AND MAPPING MODES

So far, we've been copying from one device context to another without much care for the logical units that each device context uses. If the logical units are the same, the copying is simple. Each pixel in one bitmap corresponds with a pixel in the other. However, if the mapping modes are different, then you must use **StretchBlt** to resolve the differences.

TESTING FOR BITMAP SUPPORT

Bitmaps are only supported on raster display devices. Plotters, for example, don't support bitmaps. Therefore, when you want to generate printed output of a bitmap, you may want to test whether the output device supports bitmaps. Simply pass the **GetDeviceCaps** function (introduced in Chapter 2) the **RASTERCAPS** constant and test whether the return value has the **RC_BITBLT** bit set:

```
if (GetDeviceCaps(hDC, RASTERCAPS) & RC_BITBLT) {
  // Device supports bitmaps
}
else {
  // Device does not support bitmaps
}
```

Note, however, that all display screens support bitmaps; Windows relies on this fact since it uses bitmaps to display windows. Therefore, you don't need to worry about testing whether your display supports bitmaps.

SAVING THE SCREEN

When you write a program that displays complex graphics, sometimes it's painfully slow to update the screen in response to **WM_PAINT** messages. One way to fix this problem is to use a bitmap to save a copy of the original screen and then copy the bitmap to the window when the window needs to be updated.

The application we show next illustrates how you can use this technique. The **Paint** function either draws a randomly sized rectangle and saves its image into **hBitmap** or repaints the window with the **hBitmap** image. Which path the **Paint** function takes depends on the Boolean flag **SavedScreen**.

The first time through **Paint**, **SavedScreen** is FALSE, so **Rectangle** is used to draw a randomly size rectangle:

```
Rectangle(hDC, 10, 10, random(rect.right), random(rect.bottom));
```

The program then saves the client area of the window in **hBitmap** and the **SavedScreen** flag is set TRUE. The next time **Paint** is called, **SavedScreen** will be TRUE, so it will update the window using the bitmap and not the **Rectangle** function.

To use this technique, we first create a memory device context that is compatible with the window

```
HDC hMemDC = CreateCompatibleDC(hDC);
```

and then create a bitmap that is as large as the window:

```
hBitmap = CreateCompatibleBitmap(hDC, rect.right, rect.bottom);
```

Next, the bitmap is selected into the memory device context and the window is copied into the bitmap:

```
SelectObject(hMemDC, hBitmap);
BitBlt(hMemDC, 0, 0, rect.right, rect.bottom, hDC, 0, 0, SRCCOPY);
```

Finally, the **SavedScreen** flag is set TRUE so that the next time through the code will repaint the window with the bitmap.

If **SavedScreen** is TRUE, the bitmap is painted by selecting it into the memory device context and transferring it to the screen:

```
// Display the saved bitmap
SelectObject(hMemDC, hBitmap);
BitBlt(hDC, 0, 0, rect.right, rect.bottom, hMemDC, 0, 0, SRCCOPY);
```

Note that, since we are using **BitBlt**, the bitmap will not be resized if the window size is changed. This is exactly what we want. The image of the rectangle should not change every time the window is resized.

To reset the state of the **SavedScreen** flag so that the program will draw a new randomly sized rectangle, you must press a key or the left mouse button. These events set the **SavedScreen** flag to FALSE and call **InvalidateRect** to force the window to repaint itself.

Before exiting the program, the **hBitmap** is deleted in the **EvDestroy** message-response function:

```
void TRandomRectWindow::EvDestroy()
{
  DeleteObject(hBitmap);
```

```
    // You must inherit TWindow's EvDestroy function!
    TWindow::EvDestroy();
}
```

Notice that **EvDestroy** calls its **TWindow**'s **EvDestroy** function. This is a very important step. We don't want to replace **EvDestroy** completely. We just want to perform an additional step—deleting the bitmap.

The main drawback to saving the screen, as we have done here, is that high-resolution screens can consume large amounts of memory. However, if your graphics program updates the screen too slowly, the extra memory requirement is a reasonable price to pay.

 The SAVERAND.CPP program that follows implements the details we described in this section. The program doesn't require any special steps to compile beyond those mentioned in Chapter 1.

• SAVERAND.CPP

```
// SAVERAND.CPP: Randomly displays rectangles in response
// to a left click or a keypress. Saves the screen so that
// the randomly generated rectangle can be redisplayed.

#include <owl\applicat.h>
#include <owl\framewin.h>
#include <owl\dc.h>
#include <stdlib.h>  // For random() function

class TRandomRectWindow : public TWindow {
  BOOL SavedScreen;
  HBITMAP HBitmap;
public:
  TRandomRectWindow(TWindow *parent, const char* title)
    : TWindow(parent, title) {
    randomize();
    SavedScreen = FALSE;
    HBitmap = 0;
  }
  void Paint(TDC& dc, BOOL, TRect&);
  void EvLButtonDown(UINT, TPoint&);
  void EvChar(UINT, UINT, UINT);
  void EvDestroy();

  DECLARE_RESPONSE_TABLE(TRandomRectWindow);
};

DEFINE_RESPONSE_TABLE1(TRandomRectWindow, TWindow)
  EV_WM_LBUTTONDOWN,
  EV_WM_CHAR,
  EV_WM_DESTROY,
END_RESPONSE_TABLE;
```

```
class TRandomRectApp : public TApplication {
public:
  TRandomRectApp() : TApplication() { }
  void InitMainWindow();
};

void TRandomRectWindow::Paint(TDC& dc, BOOL, TRect&)
{
  RECT rect;
  ::GetClientRect(HWindow, &rect);
  HDC hMemDC = CreateCompatibleDC(dc);
  if (!SavedScreen) {
    // Display a new randomly sized rectangle. The width and height of
    // the rectangle depends on the random number just retrieved
    Rectangle(dc, 10, 10, random(rect.right), random(rect.bottom));
    // Save the client area. If the bitmap already
    // is in use, delete it first.
    if (HBitmap) DeleteObject(HBitmap);
    HBitmap = CreateCompatibleBitmap(dc, rect.right, rect.bottom);
    SelectObject(hMemDC, HBitmap);
    BitBlt(hMemDC, 0, 0, rect.right, rect.bottom, dc, 0, 0, SRCCOPY);
    SavedScreen = TRUE;
  }
  else {
    SelectObject(hMemDC, HBitmap);  // Display the saved bitmap
    BitBlt(dc, 0, 0, rect.right, rect.bottom, hMemDC, 0, 0, SRCCOPY);
  }
  DeleteDC(hMemDC);
}

// Force the window to repaint in response to a left click
void TRandomRectWindow::EvLButtonDown(UINT, TPoint&)
{
  SavedScreen = FALSE;
  ::InvalidateRect(HWindow, 0, TRUE);
}

// Force the window to repaint in response to a keypress
void TRandomRectWindow::EvChar(UINT, UINT, UINT)
{
  SavedScreen = FALSE;
  ::InvalidateRect(HWindow, 0, TRUE);
}

// Delete the bitmap from Windows' system memory
void TRandomRectWindow::EvDestroy()
{
  DeleteObject(HBitmap);
  TWindow::EvDestroy();  // Call TWindow's WMDestroy function
}

void TRandomRectApp::InitMainWindow()
{
```

```
  MainWindow = new TFrameWindow(0, "Random Rectangles",
    new TRandomRectWindow(0, ""));
}

int OwlMain(int /*argc*/, char* /*argv*/[])
{
  return TRandomRectApp().Run();
}
```

ADDING BITMAPS TO A MENU

One intriguing way to use bitmaps is in menu entries. Although we have not
written any programs that exploit Windows' menuing system, you're probably
already familiar with how they look and operate. You may have even seen
some paint programs that supply examples of line styles in menus rather than
words. In this section you'll learn how to give your programs this feature. The
program that we'll provide, BMPMENU.CPP, displays a single menu with four
line styles in it, as shown in Figure 6.6.

Before we get any further along, we need to lay some groundwork. Earlier
you learned how Windows uses resource files to list the bitmaps that it uses.
Windows does the same for menus. In our case, the resource file BMPMENU.CPP
lists the program's menu entries. Actually, it specifies a single pop-up menu
and lists four *placeholders* for menu entries. We'll replace these placeholders
with bitmap menu images. Here's the complete resource file, BMPMENU.RC:

```
/* BMPMENU.RC: Resource file for BMPMENU.RC. */

100 MENU
{
  POPUP "&Lines"
  {
    MENUITEM "PlaceHolder1", 200
    MENUITEM "PlaceHolder2", 201
    MENUITEM "PlaceHolder3", 202
    MENUITEM "PlaceHolder4", 203
  }
}
```

Figure 6.6 The menu in BMPMENU.CPP contains bitmap images.

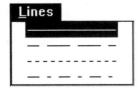

The numbers are used within the program to identify the components of the menu. For instance, the menu itself is referenced in the program using the number 100. The menu entries begin at 200.

Now let's look at the program. The **SetupWindow** function in **TWindow** is overridden to create the bitmap menu. This is a message-response member function that gets triggered before the window is about to be displayed. Notice that the first thing we do is call **TWindow**'s version of **SetupWindow**:

```
TWindow::SetupWindow();
```

This is an important step. We're only adding functionality to **SetupWindow**, not replacing it entirely. We'll do the same for **EvDestroy**, which is called when the window is terminated.

The **SetupWindow** function defines an array of four pens that are used to create the bitmaps in the pop-up menu. The first pen is the stock **BLACK_PEN** object and the other three are custom pens:

```
HPEN hPen[4];       // Use four different pens
hPen[0] = GetStockObject(BLACK_PEN);
hPen[1] = CreatePen(PS_DASH, 1, RGB(0,0,0));
hPen[2] = CreatePen(PS_DOT, 1, RGB(0,0,0));
hPen[3] = CreatePen(PS_DASHDOT, 1, RGB(0,0,0));
```

Next, the width of the bitmap is set to three times an icon's width and one-half an icon's height:

```
int width = GetSystemMetrics(SM_CXICON) * 3;
int height = GetSystemMetrics(SM_CYICON) / 2;
```

The following **for** loop creates a bitmap for each menu entry and places the bitmaps in the menu:

```
for (int i=0; i<4; i++) {
  Bmp[i] = CreateCompatibleBitmap(hDC, width, height);
  SelectObject(hMemDC, Bmp[i]);
  SelectObject(hMemDC, hPen[i]);
  FillRect(hMemDC, &rect, hbrBkgnd);  // Initialize the bitmap
  MoveToEx(hMemDC, 2, height/2, 0);
  LineTo(hMemDC, width-2, height/2);
  // Update the menu entry. Note: This window's parent,
  // which is the frame window, maintains the menu, so get
  // the menu's handle from the parent window.
  ModifyMenu(GetSubMenu(::GetMenu(Parent->HWindow),0), CM_LINE+i,
    MF_BITMAP | MF_BYCOMMAND, CM_LINE+i, (LPSTR)Bmp[i]);
}
```

A handle to each bitmap is stored in the array **Bmp**. The memory device context, **hMemDC**, is shared between the bitmaps and is used to select and paint the bitmaps. Note that **FillRect** is called to initialize the bitmap to the background color since bitmaps are normally undefined. The calls to **MoveToEx** and **LineTo** paint a line centered within the bitmap using the selected pen style specified by **hPen[i]**.

To add the bitmap to the menu, the program calls Windows' **ModifyMenu** routine. This function is passed—from left to right—a handle to the menu, the current menu identifier, the style of the new menu entry, the new menu identifier, and the bitmap to display. The **ModifyMenu** function replaces the menu entry specified by the first menu identifier with the bitmap. Because we're replacing menu entries, we supplied menu placeholders in the resource file. You can't define an empty pop-up menu in a resource file. In case you're wondering, the size of the menu is adjusted to that used by the bitmaps.

Of course, we have to clean up the objects that we've created before terminating the program. A good place to do this is in the **EvDestroy** message-response member function. Here we're deleting each of the four bitmaps and then chaining to **TWindow**'s **EvDestroy** function:

```
for (int i=0; i<4; i++)
  DeleteObject(Bmp[i]);
// You must chain to TWindow's EvDestroy function
TWindow::EvDestroy();
```

The pen styles are deleted after they are used in **SetupWindow**. Notice, however, that the first pen is not deleted since it uses the stock object, **BLACK_PEN**.

The menu entries don't do anything when you select them. However, this example shows you how to place bitmaps into a menu. In Chapter 8, you'll learn how to hook your code into the menu entries.

Compiling BMPMENU.CPP

To compile the BMPMENU.CPP program, you must use a project file and include the files BMPMENU.CPP and BMPMENU.RC. The compiler needs both of these files. The BMPMENU.RC file was listed earlier. Here's the complete BMPMENU.CPP program.

• BMPMENU.CPP

```
// BMPMENU.CPP: Displays a pull-down menu containing bitmaps.

#include <owl\applicat.h>
#include <owl\framewin.h>
#include <owl\dc.h>

#define CM_LINE 200   // First menu entries command value
```

```
class TBmpMenuWindow : public TWindow {
  HBITMAP Bmp[4];      // Four bitmap menu entries
public:
  TBmpMenuWindow(TWindow *parent, const char* title)
    : TWindow(parent, title) { }
  void SetupWindow();
  void EvDestroy();

  DECLARE_RESPONSE_TABLE(TBmpMenuWindow);
};

DEFINE_RESPONSE_TABLE1(TBmpMenuWindow, TWindow)
  EV_WM_DESTROY,
END_RESPONSE_TABLE;

class TBmpMenuApp : public TApplication {
public:
  TBmpMenuApp() : TApplication() { }
  void InitMainWindow();
};

void TBmpMenuWindow::SetupWindow()
{
  TWindow::SetupWindow();
  HPEN hPen[4];       // Use four different pens
  hPen[0] = HPEN(GetStockObject(BLACK_PEN));
  hPen[1] = CreatePen(PS_DASH, 1, RGB(0,0,0));
  hPen[2] = CreatePen(PS_DOT, 1, RGB(0,0,0));
  hPen[3] = CreatePen(PS_DASHDOT, 1, RGB(0,0,0));
  // Each menu entry will be three times the width of a
  // system icon and one third its height
  int width = GetSystemMetrics(SM_CXICON) * 3;
  int height = GetSystemMetrics(SM_CYICON) / 2;
  HDC hDC = GetDC(HWindow);
  HDC hMemDC = CreateCompatibleDC(hDC);
  RECT rect;
  rect.left = 0;    rect.right = width;
  rect.top = 0;     rect.bottom = height;
  HBRUSH hbrBkgnd = CreateSolidBrush(GetBkColor(hDC));
  SelectObject(hMemDC, hbrBkgnd);
  for (int i=0; i<4; i++) {
    Bmp[i] = CreateCompatibleBitmap(hDC, width, height);
    SelectObject(hMemDC, Bmp[i]);
    SelectObject(hMemDC, hPen[i]);
    FillRect(hMemDC, &rect, hbrBkgnd);  // Initialize the bitmap
    MoveToEx(hMemDC, 2, height/2, 0);
    LineTo(hMemDC, width-2, height/2);
    // Update the menu entry. Note: This window's parent,
    // which is the frame window, maintains the menu, so get
    // the menu's handle from the parent window.
    ModifyMenu(GetSubMenu(::GetMenu(Parent->HWindow),0), CM_LINE+i,
      MF_BITMAP | MF_BYCOMMAND, CM_LINE+i, (LPSTR)Bmp[i]);
  }
```

```
    ReleaseDC(HWindow, hDC);
    DeleteDC(hMemDC);
    DeleteObject(hbrBkgnd);
    // Delete the custom pens
    for (i=1; i<4; i++) DeleteObject(hPen[i]);
}

// Delete the menu bitmap at the end of the program
void TBmpMenuWindow::EvDestroy()
{
  for (int i=0; i<4; i++)
    DeleteObject(Bmp[i]);
  // You must chain to TWindow's EvDestroy function
  TWindow::EvDestroy();
}

void TBmpMenuApp::InitMainWindow()
{
  MainWindow = new TFrameWindow(0, "Menu with Bitmaps",
    new TBmpMenuWindow(0, ""));
  // The TFrameWindow takes care of the menu
  MainWindow->AssignMenu(100);

}

int OwlMain(int /*argc*/, char* /*argv*/[])
{
  return TBmpMenuApp().Run();
}
```

FILLING REGIONS WITH PATBLT

Before we continue, we have one loose end to tie up: the **PatBlt** function. This routine fills a region according to the same raster operation codes that **BitBlt** and **StretchBlt** use. Although **PatBlt** is not a bitmap function, we'll mention it here since it uses the same **rop** parameter. Here's **PatBlt**'s format:

```
PatBlt(HDC hDC, int x, int y, int width, int height, DWORD rop);
```

- **hDC** is a handle to the device context.
- **x,y** is the top-left logical coordinate of the region to fill.
- **width** and **height** are the logical width and height of the region to fill.
- **rop** is one of the raster operation codes (listed earlier in Table 6.2) that use the currently selected brush pattern.

The following statements, for instance, are an easy way to clear a window's client area with white:

```
void TExampleWindow::Paint(TDC&, BOOL, TRect&)
{
  RECT rect;
  ::GetClientRect(HWindow, &rect);
  PatBlt(hDC, 0, 0, rect.right, rect.bottom, WHITENESS);
}
```

SIZING A WINDOW TO A BITMAP

Since Windows applications are often large and slow to load, many programs briefly display a bitmap centered on the screen. Besides setting the tone of the application, the *splash* screen gives the user something to look at, adds a little color, and gives the application a chance to display its copyright information. In this section, you'll learn the basics of displaying a bitmap in a window centered on the screen.

We're going to develop a program, called SPLASH.CPP, that displays a bitmap, as shown in Figure 6.7. You can create your own bitmaps, of just about any size, using Borland's Resource Workshop. The code wraps the bitmap in a thin-bordered window that is automatically sized to the dimensions of the bitmap.

The SPLASH program overrides the two OWL classes, **TWindow** and **TFrameWindow**. The **TBitmapWindow**, which is derived from **TWindow**, is responsible for loading the bitmap and displaying it on the screen. The **TSizedFrameWindow** class, which is derived from **TFrameWindow**, holds a **TBitmapWindow** object as its client window and is overridden in order to force the frame to a thin border.

The **SetupWindow** function in **TBitmapWindow** loads the bitmap through the application's resource file, SPLASH.RC:

```
HBitmap = LoadBitmap(GetApplicationObject()->GetInstance(), BMPNAME);
```

Figure 6.7 SPLASH displays a bitmap centered on the screen.

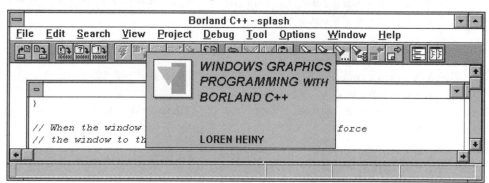

The name of the bitmap is defined in the macro constant **BMPNAME** as **SplashBitmap**. If the **LoadBitmap** function successfully reads the bitmap it sets the **HBitmap** variable to the handle of the bitmap. If, on the other hand, **SetupWindow** can't load the bitmap file, the program displays an error message and quits.

Next, **SetupWindow** retrieves the dimensions of the bitmap using the Windows function **GetObject**:

```
GetObject(HBitmap, sizeof(BmpSize), &BmpSize);
```

The **TBitmapWindow** class defines **BmpSize** as a variable of type **BITMAP**. It receives information about the colors and dimensions of the bitmap, **HBitmap**.

After this, the code retrieves the pixel dimensions of the screen by calling the Windows function **GetSystemMetrics**:

```
int scrnWd = GetSystemMetrics(SM_CXSCREEN);
int scrnHt = GetSystemMetrics(SM_CYSCREEN);
```

Using this information, **SetupWindow** calls the Windows routine **SetWindowPos** to force the bitmap's frame window (its parent window) to the size of the bitmap, centered on the screen:

```
::SetWindowPos(Parent->HWindow, 0,
  (scrnWd-(BmpSize.bmWidth+GetSystemMetrics(SM_CXBORDER)*2)) / 2,
  (scrnHt-(BmpSize.bmHeight+GetSystemMetrics(SM_CYBORDER)*2)) / 2,
  BmpSize.bmWidth, BmpSize.bmHeight, SWP_NOZORDER);
```

The fifth and sixth parameters set the parent window to the width and height of the bitmap. The two preceding parameters tell the parent window where it should place its upper-left corner. In order to center the window properly, we must account for the frame's thickness. The **GetSystemMetrics** function is used to retrieve the pixel thicknesses of the frame. Actually, the frame is only one pixel wide. In fact, we've overridden the **TFrameWindow** class so that the window doesn't have a system menu and a resizable frame. This is accomplished by redefining the attributes field of **TFrameWindow** in the derived class' constructor:

```
Attr.Style = WS_POPUP | WS_BORDER;
```

The **WS_** constants are defined in WINDOWS.H and tell Windows to make a pop-up window with a thin border.

The bitmap is actually displayed in **TBitmapWindow**'s **DrawBitmap** function.

```
HDC hMemDC = CreateCompatibleDC(dc);
HBITMAP hOldBmp = HBITMAP(SelectObject(hMemDC, HBitmap));
```

```
BitBlt(dc, left, top, right, bottom, hMemDC, 0, 0, SRCCOPY);
SelectObject(hMemDC, hOldBmp);
DeleteDC(hMemDC);
```

The **DrawBitmap** routine is called in **TBitmapWindow**'s **Paint** function.

And finally, when SPLASH exits, it deletes the bitmap in **TBitmapWindow**'s destructor:

```
TBitmapWindow::~TBitmapWindow()
{
  DeleteObject(HBitmap);
}
```

To compile and run SPLASH, you'll want to place the files SPLASH.CPP and SPLASH.RC in a project file. The source code for the file SPLASH.CPP and its resource file SPLASH.RC are shown at the end of this section. You'll also need to create a bitmap in a file named SPLASH.BMP. You can use the Resource Workshop to draw your bitmap. The size of the bitmap doesn't matter since the window will automatically size itself to the dimensions of the bitmap.

When you run SPLASH you'll see your bitmap displayed in the center of the screen. The window doesn't have a system menu so you'll need to use the key combination Alt+F4 to close the window and exit the application.

In an actual application, you'd only want the bitmap window to display for a few seconds. The trick is to initiate a timer event that will tell your application when the delay time is over and, therefore, when your application should remove the splash window. Chapter 9 shows how you can define your own timer events in Windows.

• SPLASH.CPP

```
// SPLASH.CPP: Displays a bitmap in a window, centered on the screen.
// The bitmap, named FlashBitmap", is accessed through the resource
// file. You'll need to press Alt+F4 to close the window.

#include <owl\applicat.h>
#include <owl\framewin.h>
#include <owl\dc.h>

#define BMPNAME "SplashBitmap"  // The name of the bitmap file to display

class TSizedFrameWindow : public TFrameWindow {
public:
  TSizedFrameWindow(TWindow *parent, const char* title,
    TWindow* clientWnd);
};

TSizedFrameWindow::TSizedFrameWindow(TWindow *parent, const char* title,
  TWindow* clientWnd) : TFrameWindow(parent, title, clientWnd),
  TWindow(parent, title)
```

```
{
  // Make the frame window that contains the bitmap window
  // a pop-up window with a thin border
  Attr.Style = WS_POPUP | WS_BORDER;
}

class TBitmapWindow : public TWindow {
  HBITMAP HBitmap;
  BITMAP BmpSize;
public:
  TBitmapWindow(TWindow *parent, const char* title)
    : TWindow(parent, title) { HBitmap = 0; }
  ~TBitmapWindow();
  void SetupWindow();
  void Paint(TDC& dc, BOOL, TRect&);
  void DrawBitmap(HDC dc, int left, int top,
    int right, int bottom);
};

class TBitmapApp : public TApplication {
public:
  TBitmapApp() : TApplication() { }
  void InitMainWindow();
};

TBitmapWindow::~TBitmapWindow()
{
  DeleteObject(HBitmap);
}

void TBitmapWindow::SetupWindow()
{
  TWindow::SetupWindow();

  // Load the bitmap from the file
  HBitmap = LoadBitmap(GetApplicationObject()->GetInstance(), BMPNAME);
  if (!HBitmap) {        // The handle will be non-zero if the
    char buff[256];      // bitmap was successfully read
    wsprintf(buff, "Failed to load the bitmap \"%s\"", BMPNAME);
    ::MessageBox(HWindow, buff, "DISPIM", MB_OK);
    PostQuitMessage(0);
  }

  // Get the size of the bitmap
  GetObject(HBitmap, sizeof(BmpSize), &BmpSize);
  // Get the pixel dimensions of the screen
  int scrnWd = GetSystemMetrics(SM_CXSCREEN);
  int scrnHt = GetSystemMetrics(SM_CYSCREEN);
  // The parent window (a TFrameWindow) contains this
  // window. Set the parent window to the dimensions of
  // the bitmap and center it on the screen.
  ::SetWindowPos(Parent->HWindow, 0,
    (scrnWd-(BmpSize.bmWidth+GetSystemMetrics(SM_CXBORDER)*2)) / 2,
    (scrnHt-(BmpSize.bmHeight+GetSystemMetrics(SM_CYBORDER)*2)) / 2,
```

```
                BmpSize.bmWidth, BmpSize.bmHeight, SWP_NOZORDER);
}

// Display the bitmap in the window
void TBitmapWindow::Paint(TDC& dc, BOOL, TRect&)
{
  RECT rect;
  ::GetClientRect(HWindow, &rect);
  DrawBitmap(dc, 0, 0, rect.right, rect.bottom);
}

// Display the bitmap, HBitmap, inside the window
void TBitmapWindow::DrawBitmap(HDC dc, int left, int top,
  int right, int bottom)
{
  HDC hMemDC = CreateCompatibleDC(dc);
  HBITMAP hOldBmp = HBITMAP(SelectObject(hMemDC, HBitmap));
  BitBlt(dc, left, top, right, bottom, hMemDC, 0, 0, SRCCOPY);
  SelectObject(hMemDC, hOldBmp);
  DeleteDC(hMemDC);
}

void TBitmapApp::InitMainWindow()
{
  MainWindow = new TSizedFrameWindow(0, "DISPIM",
    new TBitmapWindow(0, ""));
}

int OwlMain(int /*argc*/, char* /*argv*/[])
{
  return TBitmapApp().Run();
}
```

• SPLASH.RC

```
/* SPLASH.RC: Resource file for SPLASH.CPP. */

SplashBitmap BITMAP "SPLASH.BMP"
```

READING DEVICE-INDEPENDENT BITMAPS

In this section, we'll discuss the basics of reading and displaying a device-independent bitmap file independent of your application. This section is intended only to get you started working with bitmap files. We'll accomplish this by developing the program DISPBMP, which displays device-independent bitmaps in a window.

A device-independent bitmap (DIB) stores each bitmap pixel in sequential order from the bottom row of the bitmap to the top. This contrasts with a device-specific bitmap where the pixels may be divided across multiple bit planes. Earlier we showed the **BITMAP** structure, which holds the format of a

Figure 6.8 The format of a device-independent bitmap in memory.

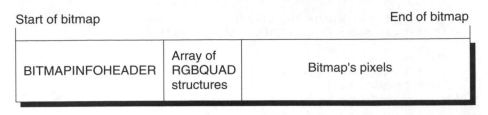

device-specific bitmap. A DIB, in contrast, has the organization in memory shown in Figure 6.8.

On disk, a device-independent bitmap is only slightly different. A .BMP file begins with a header, which conforms to the Windows structure **BITMAPFILEHEADER**, followed by the DIB data itself. Therefore, you can read a .BMP file in two steps. First, read the **BITMAPFILEHEADER** (checking that the **bfType** field contains the BM characters indicating that the file holds a .BMP image). Second, read the rest of the file into a DIB memory block.

Although these steps aren't that complicated, OWL provides the **TDib** class that performs these operations for us. Therefore, to keep our sample program simple we'll use the **TDib** class to read a .BMP file and later display it to the screen. A pointer to a **TDib** object is located at the top of the main window's class declaration in DISPBMP:

```
class TBmpWindow : public TWindow {
public:
  TDib* Dib;
```

The bitmap object isn't allocated until a bitmap is read from memory. This takes place in DISPBMP's **ReadBitmap** function:

```
BOOL TBmpWindow::ReadBitmap(char* filename)
{
  delete Dib;                    // Delete the existing bitmap
  try {
    Dib = new TDib(filename);    // Read the bitmap file
  }
  catch(TGdiBase::TXGdi) {       // Catch any exceptions
    ::MessageBox(HWindow, "Failed to read bitmap", "DISPBMP", MB_OK);
    return FALSE;                // Return failure flag
  }
  return TRUE;                   // Return success flag
}
```

ReadBitmap is called to allocate a new **TDib** object and read the .BMP file specified by **filename**. The function also frees any previously allocated object by calling **delete**.

ReadBitmap also illustrates how to use C++'s new exception handling facilities. *Exceptions* provide a way to jump out of a block and code and perform any necessary actions. They are particularly useful for error handling, which is what our code does here. Exceptions have three components, two of which are shown here. The **try** block encompasses the code in which to anticipate an exception. Similarly, the **catch** block captures exceptions that occur. The parameter in the **catch** statement is used to differentiate between various exceptions. In this case, the **catch** block is executed only if the exception is passed the parameter **TGdiBase::TXGdi**, which is a type defined in OWL. The exception itself is generated in the **try** block's code by executing a **throw** statement and passing a parameter that the **catch** block tests for.

Displaying a Device-Independent Bitmap

The **Paint** function displays the bitmap using a device-independent version of **BitBlt**. The Windows function, **SetDIBitsToDevice**, writes a bitmap to a display device. The function is declared as:

```
BOOL SetDIBitsToDevice(HDC hDC, int xDest, int yDest, int wd, int ht,
  int xSrc, int ySrc, int startScanLine, int numScanLines, void* dibBits,
  BITMAPINFO* bmpInfo, UINT colorUse);
```

- **hDC** is a handle to the device context to display the bitmap on.
- **xDest**,**yDest** and **wd**,**ht** is the region to display the bitmap in.
- **xSrc**,**ySrc** is the top-left coordinate of the bitmap to use.
- **startScanLine** specifies the first scan line in the bitmap to use and **numScanLines** is the number of scan lines to display.
- **dibBits** is the bitmap's pixel data.
- **bmpInfo** points to a **BITMAPINFO** structure that contains information on the bitmap.
- **colorUse** specifies whether the bitmap uses true RGB values or palette indexes to specify each pixel's color.

This awkward collection of parameters suggests that **SetDIBitsToDevice** has a lot to do. It does. **SetDIBitsToDevice** converts the device-independent bitmap into a bitmap that the display device can actually display.

Here's how **SetDIBitsToDevice** is used in DISPBMP's **Paint** function:

```
if (Dib) {              // This will be 0 if a bitmap doesn't exist
  // Display the bitmap
  SetDIBitsToDevice(dc, 0, 0, Dib->Width(), Dib->Height(), 0, 0, 0,
    Dib->NumScans(), Dib->GetBits(), Dib->GetInfo(), Dib->Usage());
}
```

Because **SetDIBitsToDevice** has a lot to do, there is a better way of displaying a device-independent bitmap. It's a good idea to convert the bitmap to a device-specific bitmap once and then display this converted bitmap using **BitBlt**. This approach requires an additional bitmap, but it speeds up the bitmap painting.

Working with Scrollers

The DISPBMP program displays the bitmap at the top-left of the window; however, if the window is too small, the right and bottom edges of the bitmap may extend beyond the bounds of the window. When this occurs, DISPBMP adds two scroll bars to the window frame.

Adding scroll bars to an OWL application requires two simple steps:

1. Add the Windows style constants **WS_HSCROLL** and **WS_VSCROLL** to the **Attr.Style** field in your **TWindow**'s class. You'll want to bitwise-OR these constants to **Attr.Style** in your window's constructor:

```
Attr.Style |= WS_HSCROLL | WS_VSCROLL;
```

2. Also in the window's constructor, create a **TScroller** object and assign its pointer to the OWL-supplied **Scroller** field in **TWindow**:

```
Scroller = new TScroller(this, 1, 1, 200, 200);
```

The first two numbers in **TScroller**'s argument list specify the number of pixels in the X and Y dimensions that the window should be scrolled each time the scroll bar is advanced. The last two numbers specify the extents or *range* of the scroll bars.

These two steps will add horizontal and vertical scroll bars to any application. OWL will automatically scroll the window's client area whenever the scroll bars are moved. However, there are a few more steps we must take to make the scroll bars function properly. For instance, the DISPBMP program also:

• Hides the scroll bars when the bitmap completely fits within the window
• Sets the scroll bar range to reflect the size of the bitmap in the window
• Readjusts the scroll bars each time the size of the window is changed
• Resets the location of the scroll bars when a new bitmap is displayed

The **SetScrollers** function is called when a new bitmap file is read and the size of the window changes. It sets the range of the scroll bars to the length of the bitmap that extends beyond the window. If the bitmap fits completely within the window, the code sets the range to 0, which removes the scroll bars.

In either case, **SetScrollers** calls **InvalidateRect** to force the window to repaint itself with the new scroll bar settings. Here's the complete function:

```
void TBmpWindow::SetScrollers()
{
  if (Dib) {
    RECT rect;
    ::GetClientRect(HWindow, &rect);
    int xRange = (Dib->Width() > rect.right) ?
      (Dib->Width()-rect.right) / SCROLLINC + 2 : 0;
    int yRange = (Dib->Height() > rect.bottom) ?
      (Dib->Height()-rect.bottom) / SCROLLINC + 2 : 0;
    Scroller->SetRange(xRange, yRange);  // Set the scroll ranges
  }
  else    // No bitmap present
    Scroller->SetRange(0, 0);  // Remove the scroll bars
  ::InvalidateRect(HWindow, 0, TRUE); // Display the bitmap and scrollers
}
```

When a new bitmap file is read, **SetScrollers** is called to recompute the ranges of the scroll bars. The code also resets locations of the scroll bars so that the top-left of the image is displayed:

```
Scroller->ScrollTo(0, 0);   // Set the window to the top left
```

Specifying a Filename

The DISPBMP program includes two menu options. Both menu options are listed in the program's resource file DISPBMP.RC. The name of the bitmap file is retrieved from the user using the common dialog box shown in Figure 6.9, which is provided with Windows.

Figure 6.9 The File Open dialog box is provided with Windows to standardize file selection.

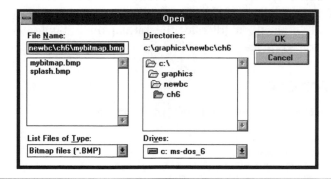

To use the File Open dialog box, DISPBMP:

- Includes OWL's header file OPENSAVE.H in your application.
- Declares a **TOpenSaveDialog::TData** object that passes information to and from the dialog box:

```
static TOpenSaveDialog::TData data (
  OFN_HIDEREADONLY | OFN_FILEMUSTEXIST | OFN_NOREADONLYRETURN,
  "Bitmap files (*.BMP)|*.bmp|", 0, "", "BMP");
```

The bitwise-ORed values specify the types of files to display in the dialog box. The constants are defined in Windows and fairly straightforward. The next set of parameters specify the types of file extensions to look for.

- Calls a **TFileOpenDialog** object to create the dialog box. Its **Execute** function returns **IDOK** if the user selects the OK button:

```
if (TFileOpenDialog(this, data).Execute() == IDOK) {
```

- Retrieves the name of the file entered by calling **TOpenSaveDialog**'s **GetFileTitle** function:

```
TOpenSaveDialog::GetFileTitle(data.FileName, filename, MAXPATH);
```

You can find these statements in the **CmFileOpen** function, which is called whenever the user selects the Open image menu option.

To compile and run DISPBMP you'll want to place the files DISPBMP.CPP and DISPBMP.RC in a project file. The source code for the file DISPBMP.CPP and its resource file DISPBMP.RC follow this section. You'll also need a bitmap to display. You might want to try one of the standard bitmaps that comes with Windows such as ARCHES.BMP, which is located in the \WINDOWS directory.

Realize that DISPBMP can display an device-independent bitmap, however, its appearance depends on the actual display capabilities of the video adapter. For instance, if you try to display a 24-bit image on a 16-color display, **SetDIBitsToDevice** will convert the bitmap to a 16-color version and display it. In addition, if the bitmap uses a palette, the code currently doesn't customize DISPBMP's palette to display the bitmap in full-color. You may want to modify the program to handle this case.

• DISPBMP.CPP

```
// DISPBMP.CPP: Displays an image in a bitmap file.

#include <owl\applicat.h>
#include <owl\framewin.h>
#include <owl\dc.h>
#include <owl\opensave.h>    // For FILE Open dialog box
```

```
#include <owl\scroller.h>    // For OWL's scroller support
#include <owl\editfile.rh>   // For OWL's standard menu commands
#include <dir.h>             // For MAXPATH constant

const SCROLLINC = 8;    // Move 8 pixels at a time while scrolling

class TBmpWindow : public TWindow {
public:
  TDib* Dib;
  TBmpWindow(TWindow *parent, const char* title);
  ~TBmpWindow();
  BOOL ReadBitmap(char* filename);
  void SetScrollers();
  void Paint(TDC& dc, BOOL, TRect&);
  void EvSize(UINT sizeType, TSize& size);
  void CmFileOpen();

  DECLARE_RESPONSE_TABLE(TBmpWindow);
};

DEFINE_RESPONSE_TABLE1(TBmpWindow, TWindow)
  EV_WM_SIZE,
  EV_COMMAND(CM_FILEOPEN, CmFileOpen),
END_RESPONSE_TABLE;

class TBmpApp : public TApplication {
public:
  TBmpApp() : TApplication() { }
  void InitMainWindow();
};

// Add the scroll bars to the window in the window's constructor
TBmpWindow::TBmpWindow(TWindow *parent, const char* title)
  : TWindow(parent, title)
{
  // Tell Windows to add scroll bars to the window
  Attr.Style |= WS_HSCROLL | WS_VSCROLL;
  // Tell OWL about the scrollers and set up their default ranges.
  // Increment the scrollers in SCROLLINC-pixel steps and set their
  // ranges to 0, so that the scroll bars aren't display yet.
  Scroller = new TScroller(this, SCROLLINC, SCROLLINC, 0, 0);
  Dib = 0;  // Make sure to initialize the bitmap pointer
}

// Free the bitmap object when the program quits
TBmpWindow::~TBmpWindow()
{
  delete Dib;
}


// Retrieve the name of the bitmap file, read the file, display it,
// and set the scroll bars
void TBmpWindow::CmFileOpen()
```

```
{
  static TOpenSaveDialog::TData data (
    OFN_HIDEREADONLY | OFN_FILEMUSTEXIST | OFN_NOREADONLYRETURN,
    "Bitmap files (*.BMP)|*.bmp|", 0, "", "BMP");
  if (TFileOpenDialog(this, data).Execute() == IDOK) {
    char filename[MAXPATH];
    TOpenSaveDialog::GetFileTitle(data.FileName, filename, MAXPATH);
    if (ReadBitmap(filename)) {    // Read the bitmap file
      SetScrollers();              // Modify the scroll bar ranges
      Scroller->ScrollTo(0, 0);    // Set the window to the top left
    }
  }
}

// Set the scroll bar ranges for this image and the current window
// dimensions. Add 2 extra scroll units so that the image scrolls a
// little beyond the edge. This way the user can see that they really
// are at the edge of the image.
void TBmpWindow::SetScrollers()
{
  if (Dib) {
    RECT rect;
    ::GetClientRect(HWindow, &rect);
    int xRange = (Dib->Width() > rect.right) ?
      (Dib->Width()-rect.right) / SCROLLINC + 2 : 0;
    int yRange = (Dib->Height() > rect.bottom) ?
      (Dib->Height()-rect.bottom) / SCROLLINC + 2 : 0;
    Scroller->SetRange(xRange, yRange);  // Set the scroll ranges
  }
  else    // No bitmap present
    Scroller->SetRange(0, 0);  // Remove the scroll bars
  ::InvalidateRect(HWindow, 0, TRUE); // Display the bitmap and scrollers
}

// Whenever the window is resized (and the window is not iconic),
// the scroll bars need to be changed
void TBmpWindow::EvSize(UINT sizeType, TSize& size)
{
  TWindow::EvSize(sizeType, size);
  if (sizeType != SIZEICONIC) {    // Is the window iconic?
    SetScrollers();                // If not, reset the scrollers
    ::InvalidateRect(HWindow, 0, FALSE);  // Repaint everything
  }
}

// Free the old bitmap and then read the specified bitmap file into a
// new bitmap object. The try and catch statements process any
// errors generated when the bitmap is read.
BOOL TBmpWindow::ReadBitmap(char* filename)
{
  delete Dib;                      // Delete the existing bitmap
  try {
    Dib = new TDib(filename);  // Read the bitmap file
  }
```

```
    catch(TGdiBase::TXGdi) {       // Catch any exceptions
      ::MessageBox(HWindow, "Failed to read bitmap", "DISPBMP", MB_OK);
      return FALSE;                 // Return failure flag
    }
    return TRUE;                    // Return success flag
}

// Paint the bitmap
void TBmpWindow::Paint(TDC& dc, BOOL, TRect&)
{
   if (Dib) {            // This will be 0 if a bitmap doesn't exist
      // Display the bitmap
      SetDIBitsToDevice(dc, 0, 0, Dib->Width(), Dib->Height(), 0, 0, 0,
       Dib->NumScans(), Dib->GetBits(), Dib->GetInfo(), Dib->Usage());
   }
}

void TBmpApp::InitMainWindow()
{
   MainWindow = new TFrameWindow(0, "DISPBMP", new TBmpWindow(0, ""));
   MainWindow->AssignMenu("MENU_1");  // Add the menu to the application
}

int OwlMain(int /*argc*/, char* /*argv*/[])
{
   return TBmpApp().Run();
}
```

• DISPBMP.RC

```
/* DISPBMP.RC: Resource file for DISPBMP program. */

#include <owl\editfile.rh>

MENU_1 MENU
{
 POPUP "&File"
 {
  MENUITEM "&Open image", CM_FILEOPEN
  MENUITEM SEPARATOR
  MENUITEM "E&xit", CM_EXIT
 }
}
```

S E V E N

Text and Fonts

Text output is probably not the first topic that graphics programmers think about. However, text is often an integral part of graphics applications. Fortunately, Windows provides a variety of text display functions. In this chapter, we'll explore these functions and discuss techniques for using them. We'll begin with the simple text routines—some of which you've already seen. Then we'll progress into Windows' highly programmable text features that support scalable fonts and a variety of font styles.

DISPLAYING TEXT

Windows provides the five functions listed in Table 7.1 for displaying text. The function you select depends on the number of lines of text you want to display and how the text is to be formatted. In the next several sections, we'll describe how each function works. We'll also explore the various support functions that Windows provides.

Table 7.1 Text Display Routines

Function	Description
DrawText	Displays text within a rectangle according to the format specified
ExtTextOut	Displays a string within a specified rectangle
GrayText	Displays a gray text string
TabbedTextOut	Displays a string using specified tab locations
TextOut	Displays a string at a specified location

Displaying a Text String

The most common text output function you'll use is **TextOut**, which displays a single line of text at a specified location. Here is **TextOut**'s format:

```
BOOL TextOut(HDC hDC, int x, int y, LPCSTR str, int strLen);
```

- **hDC** is a handle to the display context.
- **x,y** is the logical coordinate where the text is displayed.
- **str** is the string to be displayed.
- **strLen** is the length of the string.
- The function returns TRUE if it succeeds; otherwise it returns FALSE.

For example, the following statement displays the string "Sample text" at the top left of a window:

```
TextOut(hDC, 0, 0, "Sample text", 11);
```

You'll often use **TextOut** in conjunction with **wsprintf**, which enables you to construct a formatted string. This function is similar to C++'s **sprintf** function and is prototyped in WINDOWS.H. The **wsprintf** function works much like **printf**, except it places the output into a buffer that can be passed along to **TextOut** and displayed. Windows provides similar string functions, such as **lstrlen** and **lstrcmp**. All these functions are designed to work with the long pointers that Windows uses. However, since the programs in this book are assumed to be compiled in large memory model, you can use the standard string functions, if you prefer. The following statements, for instance, create a string and then display it to the screen:

```
int x = 10;
char buffer[80];
wsprintf(buffer, "This number is 10 => %d", x);
TextOut(x, y, buffer, strlen(buffer));
```

The positioning of the text relative to the (X,Y) coordinate depends on the current text alignment settings in the device context. By default, text is displayed so that the (X,Y) point is to the left and at the top of the string. These positions correspond with Windows' constants **TA_LEFT** and **TA_TOP**.

You can control the text alignment by calling the **SetTextAlign** function and passing it a combination of flags ORed together. Tables 7.2 and 7.3 lists the vertical and horizontal text alignment flags you can use. Figure 7.1 shows strings displayed with each of these settings. For example, the following statement right-justifies text:

```
SetTextAlign(hDC, TA_RIGHT | TA_TOP);
```

Table 7.2 Vertical Text Alignment Settings

Constant	Description
TA_TOP	The top of the text is aligned to this point
TA_BASELINE	The baseline of the text is aligned to this point
TA_BOTTOM	The bottom of the text is aligned to this point

Table 7.3 Horizontal Text Alignment Settings

Constant	Description
TA_CENTER	The horizontal center of the text is placed at this point (the current position is not affected if used)
TA_LEFT	The left side of the text is aligned to this point
TA_RIGHT	The right side of the text is aligned to this point

Note If you supply only one text alignment constant to **SetTextAlign**, the other text alignment setting is reset to its default state.

When using **TextOut** with the default (system) font, you should be aware that it may be difficult to display multiple columns of text properly. The problem is that the default font is variable-width; not all characters have the same width. The character "W," for instance, is much wider than a comma. As a result, characters will not line up vertically in the columns.

Figure 7.1 The text alignment settings.

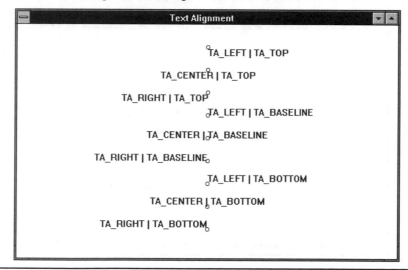

One solution is to display each column with a separate call to **TextOut** (as we did with DEVICE.CPP in Chapter 2). An alternative is to use the function **TabbedTextOut** (shown later), which allows you to specify tab positions. Another possibility is to select a fixed-width font (shown later).

To determine what the current text alignment settings are in the device context, you can call **GetTextAlign**. It returns a word value that you can AND with the various alignment flags to test which ones are set. For example, the following statement retrieves the alignment flags:

```
UINT AlignFlags = GetTextAlign(hDC);
```

The Current Position and Text

How does the **TextOut** function affect the current position? By default, it doesn't. You must OR the **TA_UPDATECP** flag with your other text settings when you call **SetTextAlign** in order to have the current position updated. If you don't include the **TA_UPDATECP** flag in a call to **SetTextAlign**, the **TA_NOUPDATECP** flag is effectively used, which instructs Windows not to update the current position. Figure 7.2 presents a version of Figure 7.1 that shows the current position before and after calls to **TextOut**.

Displaying Text with Tabs

Earlier, the problem of displaying multiple columns of text was described. One solution is to use the **TabbedTextOut** function, which can display a string that

Figure 7.2 The current position can be changed by TextOut.

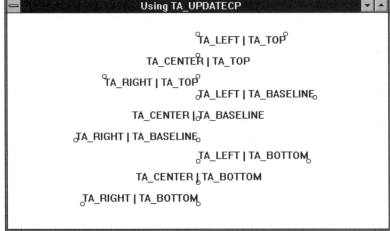

contains tab characters (\t). The tabs can be used to align the columns of text. Here's the format of **TabbedTextOut**:

```
DWORD TabbedTextOut(HDC hDC, int x, int y, LPCSTR str, int count,
  int numTabPositions, int tabStopPositions[], int tabOrigin);
```

- **hDC** is a handle to the device context.
- **x,y** specifies the logical coordinate to start writing the text.
- **str** is a long pointer to the string to be displayed.
- **count** is the number of characters in the string.
- **numTabPositions** specifies the number of tab stops in the **tabStopPositions** array.
- **tabStopPositions** is an integer array of tab positions, in pixels.
- **tabOrigin** specifies the logical X-coordinate where the tabs begin.
- The high-order word of the return value specifies the height of the string and the low-order word its width.

If you need to, you can call the **GetTabbedTextExtent** routine to compute the width and height of a line of text containing tab characters:

```
DWORD GetTabbedTextExtent(HDC hDC, LPCSTR str, int count,
  int numTabPositions, int tabStopPositions[]);
```

The following program demonstrates how **TabbedTextOut** can display columns of text. Its output is shown in Figure 7.3. In this case, a list of names, addresses, and phone numbers is displayed. The tab positions are initialized in the **Tabs** array to pixel columns 140 and 275.

• COLTXT.CPP

```
// COLTXT.CPP: Displays three columns of text using TabbedTextOut.

#include <owl\applicat.h>
#include <owl\framewin.h>
#include <owl\dc.h>
#include <string.h>

class TExampleWindow : public TWindow {
public:
  TExampleWindow(TWindow *parent, const char* title)
    : TWindow(parent, title) { }
  void Paint(TDC& dc, BOOL, TRect&);
};
```

Figure 7.3 TabbedTextOut can display strings using tabs.

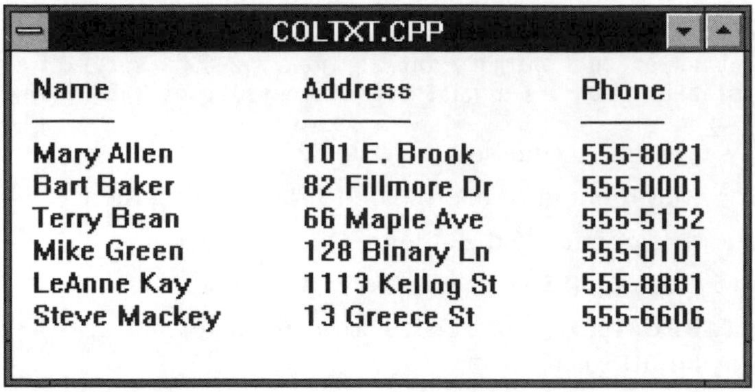

```
                            COLTXT.CPP                   ▼ ▲

   Name                 Address             Phone
   ─────                ───────             ─────
   Mary Allen           101 E. Brook        555-8021
   Bart Baker           82 Fillmore Dr      555-0001
   Terry Bean           66 Maple Ave        555-5152
   Mike Green           128 Binary Ln       555-0101
   LeAnne Kay           1113 Kellog St      555-8881
   Steve Mackey         13 Greece St        555-6606
```

```
class TColTxtApp : public TApplication {
public:
  TColTxtApp() : TApplication() { }
  void InitMainWindow();
};

void TExampleWindow::Paint(TDC& dc, BOOL, TRect&)
{
  static char* table[8] = {"Name\tAddress\tPhone",
    "----------\t------------\t----------",
    "Scott Merritt \t101 E. Brook \t555-8021",
    "Lori Kay \t82 Fillmore Dr \t555-0001",
    "Darin DeForest \t66 Maple Ave \t555-5152",
    "Duke Markee \t128 Binary Ln \t555-0101",
    "Rachel Rosita \t1113 Kellog St \t555-8881",
    "Mike Kollwitz \t13 Green St \t555-6606"};
  static int tabs[2] = {140, 275};  // Tab positions
  SIZE size;
  GetTextExtentPoint(dc, "A", 1, &size);
  for (int i=0; i<8; i++)
    TabbedTextOut(dc, 10, 10+i*size.cy, table[i],
      strlen(table[i]), 2, tabs, 0);
}

void TColTxtApp::InitMainWindow()
{
  MainWindow = new TFrameWindow(0, "COLTXT Program",
    new TExampleWindow(0, ""));
}

int OwlMain(int /*argc*/, char* /*argv*/[])
{
  return TColTxtApp().Run();
}
```

Displaying a Message

Windows makes it easy to display a debugging or warning message by using the **MessageBox** function. It pops up a window containing a single line of text that you pass to it and waits until the user selects one of its buttons or closes the window. The **MessageBox** function is defined as:

```
int MessageBox(HDC hDC, LPCSTR str, LPCSTR caption, UINT flags);
```

The last parameter determines which buttons appear in the pop-up window. Windows provides a variety of choices, but probably the most common one you'll use is **MB_OK**. It displays an OK button that the user can click on to close the window.

The **MessageBox** function is ideal for debugging messages. You can easily place brief debugging statements in your code and then have Windows pop up the message at the appropriate time. Realize that you can place formatted text in the pop-up window's title as well as in its display area. Of course, the pop-up window will suspend the program while the message is displayed.

Dimensions of Characters

As you'll see in upcoming sections, Windows supports a wide range of font styles and sizes. This can make your applications look nice; however, writing the code can be tedious. The difficulty is that your code must be flexible enough to work equally well on different displays. One aspect of writing generic code, therefore, involves adjusting for the actual dimensions of the currently selected font. For this, Windows provides the function **GetTextMetrics**, which returns font characteristics in a **TEXTMETRICS** structure.

The **TEXTMETRICS** structure is the key to retrieving general information about the currently selected font (the font in the device context). Its format is:

```
typedef struct tagTEXTMETRIC {
  int tmHeight;
  int tmAscent;
  int tmDescent;
  int tmInternalLeading;
  int tmExternalLeading;
  int tmAveCharWidth;
  int tmMaxCharWidth;
  int tmWeight;
  int tmItalic;
  BYTE tmUnderlined;
  BYTE tmStruckOut;
  BYTE tmFirstChar;
  BYTE tmLastChar;
  BYTE tmDefaultChar;
  BYTE tmBreakChar;
```

```
    BYTE tmPitchAndFamily;
    BYTE tmCharSet;
    int tmOverhang;
    int tmDigitizedAspectX;
    int tmDigitizedAspectY;
} TEXTMETRIC;
```

Most of the 24 fields in this structure are self-explanatory. Take some time, however, to match the top five fields with the character dimensions shown in Figure 7.4. Realize that **TEXTMETRICS** stores its measurement in logical units. If the mapping mode is **MM_TEXT**, therefore, the units are pixel dimensions.

The next several fields of the structure describe additional information about the dimensions of the current font. The **tmExternalLeading** is the size of the line space between rows of text. Quite often you can ignore this dimension since the internal leading (space above letters) is enough to keep lines of text separated. Two other fields, **tmAveCharWidth** and **tmMaxCharWidth**, specify the average width of lowercase characters and the width of the widest character, respectively.

The remaining **TEXTMETRICS** fields describe various aspects of the current font. We'll encounter these fields later in this chapter.

Figure 7.4 The dimensions of a character.

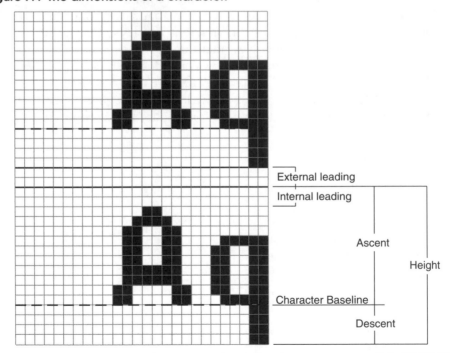

Take a look at an example. The following **Paint** function declares a variable of type **TEXTMETRICS**, calls **GetTextMetrics** to retrieve information about the current font, and uses the **tmHeight** field to display two separate consecutive lines of text:

```
void TExampleWindow::Paint(TDC& dc, BOOL, TRect&)
{
  TEXTMETRIC tm;
  GetTextMetrics(dc, &tm);
  TextOut(dc, 0, 0, "First line", 10);
  TextOut(dc, 0, tm.tmHeight, "This line is below the first", 28);
}
```

The **GetTextMetrics** function is useful for determining general information about the current font. However, if you want to determine the precise length of a string, an alternative choice is **GetTextExtentPoint**. This routine, shown next, returns the logical height and width of a text string in a **SIZE** structure. Here's how the **GetTextExtentPoint** function is defined in WINDOWS.H:

```
BOOL GetTextExtentPoint(HDC hDC, LPCSTR str, int strLen, SIZE* size);
```

- **hDC** is a handle to the device context.
- **str** is the string to measure.
- **strLen** is the number of characters in **str**.
- **size** points to a **SIZE** structure that is to contain the string's dimensions in logical units. The structure's **cx** field is set to the string's width and the **cy** field is set to the string's height.
- The function returns TRUE if it succeeds, FALSE otherwise.

Note **GetTextExtentPoint** was introduced in Windows 3.1. Earlier versions of Windows provided the **GetTextExtent** function, which returned the string's dimensions in a packed, double word. However, **GetTextExtent** is not supported in Win32 platforms. Therefore, to ensure that your code is ready for 32-bit environments, you should use the newer, **GetTextExtentPoint** routine.

WINDOWS FONTS

Windows 3.1 provides three types of fonts: raster (bitmapped), stroke, and TrueType fonts. Raster fonts are represented as small blocks of pixels, as shown in Figure 7.5. Windows provides several sizes of raster fonts and styles and can scale them to create additional sizes if it must. However, as raster-based characters get larger, they display an unattractive staircase effect.

Figure 7.5 A sample raster character.

Stroke characters, on the other hand, are made up of line segments and can readily be scaled to a wide variety of sizes. Figure 7.6 shows a sample stroke character. The drawback to stroke fonts is that as their sizes increase, the gaps between the strokes become larger and more visible.

Lastly, TrueType fonts generally display text the fastest and with the best result. The fonts store the outlines of the characters as a series of lines and curves, called *glyphs*. In addition, the characters include "hints" that help produce text with the best appearance when scaled to various sizes.

Windows includes the six stock font styles listed in Table 7.4. The default font, which Windows uses in its menus and captions, is a raster font. This accounts for its good quality. Like other elements of Windows, fonts are

Figure 7.6 A sample stroke font character.

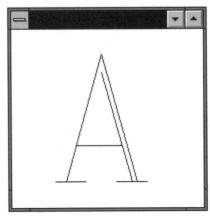

Table 7.4 Stock Logical Fonts

Font	Description
ANSI_FIXED_FONT	ANSI fixed-pitch font (Courier)
ANSI_VAR_FONT	ANSI variable-pitch system font (Helv)
DEVICE_DEFAULT_FONT	Equivalent to SYSTEM_FONT on most video displays; printers may use a font that doesn't require graphics mode
OEM_FIXED_FONT	IBM-PC compatible character set for DOS windows
SYSTEM_FONT	Proportional font used by default; used in menus, window captions, and so on
SYSTEM_FIXED_FONT	Fixed ANSI font used before Windows 3.0

treated as objects; the device context contains a handle to the currently se-lected font. A handle to a font has the type name **HFONT**.

To use one of the other stock fonts, you must first call **GetStockObject** to retrieve a handle to the font and then the **SelectObject** to associate the font with the display context. Here's how to switch to the **ANSI_FIXED_FONT**, for instance:

```
HFONT hNewFont = HFONT(GetStockObject(ANSI_FIXED_FONT)));
HFONT hOldFont = HFONT(SelectObject(hDC, hNewFont));
```

Remember, these are stock objects, therefore they should never be deleted.

Creating Custom Fonts

You don't have much control over the appearance of text when you use Windows' stock fonts. However, Windows allows you to specify a font with the size, style, and typeface you desire. A font specified in this manner is called a *logical font*. The specifications you provide for the logical font are later mapped to the actual capabilities of the hardware being used. Therefore, the font that you request and the one you actually get might be quite different. Table 7.5 lists several of the common fonts available in Windows. Figure 7.7 shows a sampling of these fonts at various sizes.

Before we go any further, there are a few issues related to Windows' fonts that we need to resolve. You've already seen how Windows has three types of font styles: raster, stroke, and TrueType. The fonts are also divided between two types of character sets: ANSI and OEM. The latter is the character set that DOS normally contains. The ANSI character set is a machine-independent character set. In addition, the fonts are divided into families based on their font style. For instance, the Times New Roman typeface is part of the FF_ROMAN family and the Arial typeface is part of the FF_SWISS family. All these details will become important when creating a logical font.

Figure 7.7 Windows supports a variety of fonts.

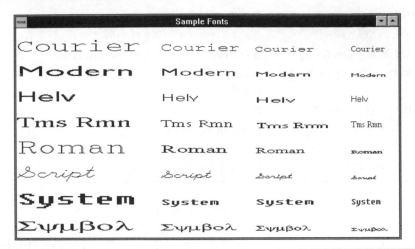

Defining a Logical Font

When you specify a logical font, you can control its typeface, height, width, and style. The following steps outline how to create and use a custom font:

1. Define the specifications of the font using **CreateFont** or **CreateFontIndirect** (these functions are described shortly). Both return a handle to the logical font, which is of type **HFONT**.

Table 7.5 Sample Windows Fonts

Face Name	Family	Type	Character Set
Arial	FF_SWISS	TrueType	ANSI
Courier	FF_MODERN	Raster	ANSI
Courier New	FF_MODERN	TrueType	ANSI
MS Sans Serif	FF_SWISS	TrueType	ANSI
Roman	FF_ROMAN	Stroke	OEM
Script	FF_SCRIPT	Stroke	OEM
Symbol	FF_DECORATIVE	Raster	——
System	FF_SWISS	Raster	ANSI
Terminal	FF_MODERN	Raster	OEM
Times New Roman	FF_ROMAN	TrueType	ANSI

2. Select the logical font into a device context by using **SelectObject**. Windows chooses the available "real" font that best matches the logical font definition. You can call **GetTextFace** and **GetTextMetrics** to determine which font is selected and its characteristics.

3. Use the font.

4. Before your program terminates or when you are finished using the font, you must delete it from Windows by calling **DeleteObject**. However, don't delete the custom font while it is selected into a device context and never delete one of the stock objects.

We'll provide some code in a moment, but first we should review these steps in greater detail. Windows includes the following two functions for defining a logical font:

```
HFONT hFont = CreateFont(int height, int width, int escapement,
   int orientation, int weight, BYTE italic, BYTE underline,
   BYTE strikeOut, BYTE charSet, BYTE outputPrecision,
   BYTE clipPrecision, BYTE quality, BYTE pitchAndFamily,
   LPCSTR fontName);
HFONT hFont = CreateFontIndirect(&logFont);
```

Both return handles to the logical font that meets the specifications you give. The difference between the two functions is obviously in their parameters. The **CreateFont** routine requires that you pass 14 arguments and **CreateFontIndirect** encompasses these parameters into a single **LOGFONT** structure. The **LOGFONT** structure is defined in WINDOWS.H as:

```
typedef struct tagLOGFONT {
  int lfHeight;
  int lfWidth;
  int lfEscapement;
  int lfOrientation;
  int lfWeight;
  BYTE lfItalic;
  BYTE lfUnderline;
  BYTE lfStrikeOut;
  BYTE lfCharSet;
  BYTE lfOutPrecision;
  BYTE lfClipPrecision;
  BYTE lfQuality;
  BYTE lfPitchAndFamily;
  BYTE lfFaceName[LF_FACESIZE];
} LOGFONT;
```

Next we'll describe each of the parameters passed to **CreateFont** and the fields included in the **LOGFONT** structure:

• The **lfHeight** and **lfWidth** fields specify the height and average width of the font.

- The **lfEscapement** and **lfOrientation** fields specify the escapement and orientation of the characters, respectively. Both are specified in tenths of degrees, measured counterclockwise from the three o'clock position. (We'll visit these fields again in the section *Rotating Text* at the end of this chapter.)

- The **lfWeight** field specifies the boldness or weight of the characters as a range from 1 (light) to 1000 (heavy). A zero value selects the default weight. Windows defines several constants to use; however, in actuality, only two settings are typically supported: **FW_NORMAL** (400) and **FW_BOLD** (700).

- The **lfItalic**, **lfUnderline**, and **lfStrikeOut** fields, if non-zero, specify that the text should be italic, underlined, or have strike out markings, respectively.

- The **lfCharSet** field indicates the desired character set. You can set it to one of the following constants: **ANSI_CHARSET**, **SYMBOL_CHARSET**, or **OEM_CHARSET**.

- The **lfOutPrecision** field instructs Windows how closely the requested font should match the output. Although it can be one of the following constants— **OUT_DEFAULT_PRECIS**, **OUT_STRING_PRECIS**, **OUT_CHARACTER_PRECIS**, or **OUT_STROKE_PRECIS**—you'll usually want to use **OUT_DEFAULT_PRECIS**.

- The **lfClipPrecision** field determines how Windows clips characters. The three possibilities are: **CLIP_DEFAULT_PRECIS**, **CLIP_CHARACTER_PRECIS**, and **CLIP_STROKE_PRECIS**.

- The **lfQuality** field tells Windows how closely to match the logical font to the real font. It can be one of the following constants: **DEFAULT_QUALITY**, **DRAFT_QUALITY**, and **PROOF_QUALITY**.

- The **lfPitchAndFamily** field is one of the font family constants (listed in Table 7.4) ORed with the desired pitch. The pitch can either be **DEFAULT_PITCH**, **FIXED_PITCH**, or **VARIABLE_PITCH**.

- The **lfFaceName** field specifies the name of the typeface, such as Courier, Arial, and so on. These names are listed in Table 7.5. Setting **lfFaceName** to **NULL** forces Windows to use a default font.

Now that we've defined the various parameters that you can use to define a logical font, we can continue to explain how logical fonts are used. As mentioned earlier, the device context specifies the current font that text routines, such as **TextOut**, use. To change this font, you must select another font into the device context. We can, therefore, use **SelectObject** to select a custom font into the device context. This step serves two purposes. It requests that Windows select from its available font files the closest matching font and adjust it as necessary. Second, **SelectObject** changes the font in the device context so that subsequent text functions will use the custom font.

Since Windows doesn't really create a new font, but rather finds the closest match, the font selected can be quite different from the one actually specified.

The font might be a different type style, face, weight, or size. You should call **GetTextMetrics** and **GetTextFace** to determine the characteristics of the actual font selected.

A Logical Font Example

It's time to look at an example. The following sample **Paint** member function defines a 40 point, bold, Arial font and displays a string in the middle of the client area of a window.

```
void TExampleWindow::Paint(TDC& dc, BOOL, TRect&)
{
  RECT rect;
  rect.left = 0; rect.top = 0;
  rect.right = 400; rect.bottom = 300;
  Rectangle(dc, rect.left, rect.top, rect.right, rect.bottom);
  // Define the logical font
  HFONT hFont = CreateFont(40, 36, 0, 0, FW_BOLD, 0, 0, 0,
    ANSI_CHARSET, OUT_DEFAULT_PRECIS, CLIP_DEFAULT_PRECIS,
    PROOF_QUALITY, FF_SWISS | VARIABLE_PITCH, "Arial");
  // Select the logical font into the device context
  HFONT hOldFont = HFONT(SelectObject(dc, hFont));
  SetTextAlign(dc, TA_CENTER | TA_BASELINE); // Center the text
  // Display the text
  TextOut(dc, rect.right/2, rect.bottom/2, "A sample string", 15);
  SelectObject(dc, hOldFont);   // Deselect the logical font
  DeleteObject(hFont);          // Delete the logical font from memory
}
```

Although, we used **CreateFont** here, the **CreateFontIndirect** function is often easier to use. The reason is that **CreateFontIndirect** is designed so that fields set to 0 in the structure select the default settings. Therefore, if you allocate a **LOGFONT** structure and initialize it to 0 or declare it as static so that its fields are set to 0, you'll only have to set the fields that are required for your custom font.

 Note   If you want to use one of the stroke fonts, you *must* set the character-set field (**lfCharSet**) to **OEM_CHARSET**. Otherwise, Windows will select a compatible raster font.

CONTROLLING TEXT COLOR

The device context contains three parameters that control the text color, background color, and background mode used to display text. The text color is black by default. However, it can be any one of the pure colors available to you; text is *never dithered*. To set the color, you can use **SetTextColor**:

```
COLORREF SetTextColor(HDC hDC, COLORREF color);
```

- **hDC** is a handle to the device context.
- The **color** parameter, which is a **COLORREF** variable, specifies the color to use for the text.
- Returns the previous color.

For instance, to force Windows to write red text, you could use:

```
SetTextColor(hDC, RGB(255, 0, 0));
```

The background mode indicates whether the gaps within and around each character are painted to a background color. By default, the gaps are filled with white. This effectively erases anything below the text so that it will appear correctly. Recall from Chapters 3 and 4 that the background mode and color affect hatch patterns and styled lines. To set the background mode, use **SetBkMode** and pass it the desired setting: **OPAQUE** (default) or **TRANSPARENT**. The background color can be set using **SetBkColor**.

Setting Text Justification

The device context also includes a parameter that allows you to control the spacing between characters. The **SetTextCharacterExtra** function specifies the number of additional pixels (or logical units) to place between characters. The following statement, for instance, adds three pixels between characters:

```
SetTextCharacterExtra(hDC, 3);
```

Similarly, the following **Paint** function stretches a text string across a rectangle that is 200 pixels wide. Its output is shown in Figure 7.8:

Figure 7.8 Using SetTextCharacterExtra to justify text.

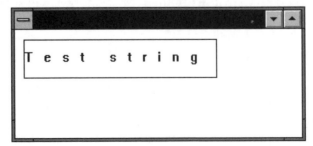

```
void TExampleWindow::Paint(TDC& dc, BOOL, TRect&)
{
  char buffer[12] = "Test string";
  SIZE size;
  GetTextExtentPoint(dc, buffer, 11, &size);
  int wd = (200 - size.cx) / 11;
  SetTextCharacterExtra(dc, wd);
  Rectangle(dc, 9, 0, 209, 50);
  TextOut(dc, 10, 20, buffer, 11);
}
```

Scaling Text within a Box

Scaling text so that it fits within a rectangular region is fairly easy with Windows. The following program, SCALETXT.CPP, illustrates one way to do this. Its output is shown in Figure 7.9.

In Windows, the problem of scaling text so that it fits within a box becomes one of determining which logical font to create so that its text will fit within the rectangular region. Therefore, the SCALETXT.CPP program simply calls **CreateFont** with the desired dimensions. The height parameter is straightforward; it is set to the height of the rectangle. The character width of the desired font, however, must be calculated; it is set to the width of the rectangle divided by the number of characters in the string and adjusted by a small scale factor:

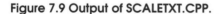

```
(rect.right-rect.left) / lstrlen(Str) * 2 / 3;
```

Figure 7.9 Output of SCALETXT.CPP.

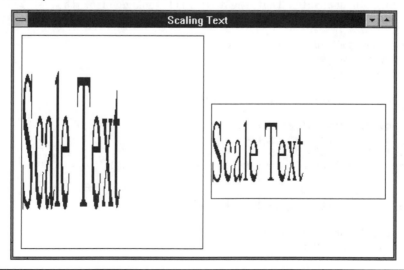

The scale factor of 2/3 is required because the width value used by **CreateFont** corresponds with the *average* width of the characters. Since many characters are wider than the average width, the string displayed would usually be too long without the scale factor. Actually, even in this program, a string of letter *M*s might even extend beyond the bounds of the rectangle since the letter *M* is one of the wider characters.

Try adjusting the size of the display window to various sizes. You'll discover that, although this technique scales the text so that it fits within the box, it doesn't guarantee that the text will be readable or that it will fill the entire box. You may want to experiment with other techniques that adjust both the height and width of the requested font so that the text both fits within the box and is readable.

Also notice that a vector font, in this case the Roman font, is used. A raster font could also have been used; however, Windows cannot scale raster fonts to the degree that it can scale vector fonts. As a result, raster fonts might not fit in the region specified.

The complete SCALETXT.CPP program is shown next. In order to get a better understanding of how Windows scales fonts, try changing the **CreateFont** statement in **ScaleText** so that the program uses a font other than Roman.

• SCALETXT.CPP

```cpp
// SCALETXT.CPP: Given a box of a particular size, this program
// scales the text so that it fits within the box. This routine
// guarantees that the text string will fit in the box, but it
// doesn't guarantee that the text will look good or that it will be
// readable. This can happen if the box is too small for the text.

#include <owl\applicat.h>
#include <owl\framewin.h>
#include <owl\dc.h>

class TScaleTxtWindow : public TWindow {
public:
  TScaleTxtWindow(TWindow *parent, const char* title)
    : TWindow(parent, title) {  }
  void Paint(TDC& dc, BOOL, TRect&);
  void ScaleText(HDC hDC, RECT& rect, char *str);
};

class TScaleTxtApp : public TApplication {
public:
  TScaleTxtApp() : TApplication() { }
  void InitMainWindow();
};
```

```
void TScaleTxtWindow::Paint(TDC& dc, BOOL, TRect&)
{
  RECT rect;
  ::GetClientRect(HWindow, &rect);
  RECT txtBox;
  txtBox.left = 10;                  txtBox.top = 10;
  txtBox.right = rect.right/2;   txtBox.bottom = rect.bottom-10;
  ScaleText(dc, txtBox, "Scale Text");
  txtBox.left = rect.right/2+10; txtBox.top = rect.bottom/3;
  txtBox.right = rect.right-10;  txtBox.bottom = rect.bottom*3/4;
  ScaleText(dc, txtBox, "Scale Text");
}

// Displays the string str within the rectangular region specified by
// rect. It first creates a font the size needed to display the string.
// A stroke font is used since it can be scaled to many different sizes.
// The font is deleted after the string is displayed.
void TScaleTxtWindow::ScaleText(HDC hDC, RECT& rect, char *str)
{
  HFONT hFont = CreateFont(rect.bottom-rect.top,
    (rect.right-rect.left)/lstrlen(str)*2/3, 0, 0, FW_NORMAL, 0, 0, 0,
    ANSI_CHARSET, OUT_DEFAULT_PRECIS, CLIP_DEFAULT_PRECIS,
    DEFAULT_QUALITY, FF_ROMAN, "Roman");
  SelectObject(hDC, hFont);
  TextOut(hDC, rect.left, rect.top, str, lstrlen(str));
  FrameRect(hDC, &rect, HBRUSH(GetStockObject(BLACK_BRUSH)));
  DeleteObject(hFont);
}

void TScaleTxtApp::InitMainWindow()
{
  MainWindow = new TFrameWindow(0, "Scaling Text",
    new TScaleTxtWindow(0, ""));
}

int OwlMain(int /*argc*/, char* /*argv*/[])
{
  return TScaleTxtApp().Run();
}
```

Rotating Text

We briefly mentioned that the **lfEscapement** and **lfOrientation** fields of the **LOGFONT** structure control the orientation of text. The **lfEscapement** field specifies the angle of the string measured in .1 degree increments, counter-clockwise from the three o'clock position. For example, setting the escapement field to 450 will display a text string at 45 degrees. The **lfOrientation** field, also specified in .1 degree increments, tells Windows how much to rotate the individual characters within the text string. Although these two fields may seem a bit confusing, they're actually quite easy to use in practice. If you simply want to rotate a text string about a point, you only need to set both fields to the angle desired.

The following program, for instance, rotates the string "Howdy!" about the center of the client area. A sample output of the screen is shown in Figure 7.10. Each time you press a key or click the left mouse button, the string is rotated counterclockwise by 10 degrees.

```
// ROTATE.CPP: Rotates a text string each time you click the
// left mouse button or press a key.

#include <owl\applicat.h>
#include <owl\framewin.h>
#include <owl\dc.h>

class TRotateWindow : public TWindow {
  int TextAngle;
public:
  TRotateWindow(TWindow *parent, const char* title)
    : TWindow(parent, title) { TextAngle = 0; }
  void Paint(TDC& dc, BOOL, TRect&);
  void EvLButtonDown(UINT modKeys, TPoint& point);
  void EvChar(UINT key, UINT repCount, UINT flags);
  void EvSize(UINT, TSize&);

  DECLARE_RESPONSE_TABLE(TRotateWindow);
};

DEFINE_RESPONSE_TABLE1(TRotateWindow, TWindow)
  EV_WM_LBUTTONDOWN,
```

Figure 7.10 Sample output of ROTATE.CPP.

```
    EV_WM_CHAR,
    EV_WM_SIZE,
END_RESPONSE_TABLE;

class TRotateApp : public TApplication {
public:
  TRotateApp() : TApplication() { }
  void InitMainWindow();
};

void TRotateWindow::Paint(TDC& dc, BOOL, TRect&)
{
  RECT rect;
  static LOGFONT lf;                    // Use a static variable so values are
  char *szTextString = "Howdy!";        // initialized to zero
  ::GetClientRect(HWindow, &rect);
  lf.lfWeight = FW_HEAVY;               // Make text bold
  lf.lfCharSet = OEM_CHARSET;           // Use ANSI character set
  lf.lfPitchAndFamily = FF_SCRIPT;      // Use the script family
  lf.lfHeight = 100;                    // Make text 100 pixels tall
  lf.lfEscapement = TextAngle;          // This is the text angle
  lf.lfOrientation = TextAngle;         // and orientation
  HFONT hFont = CreateFontIndirect(&lf);
  SelectObject(dc, hFont);
  TextOut(dc, rect.right/2, rect.bottom/2,
    szTextString, lstrlen(szTextString));
  DeleteObject(hFont);
}

void TRotateWindow::EvChar(UINT, UINT, UINT)
{
  // Increment the angle of the font
  if (TextAngle == 3500) TextAngle = 0;
    else TextAngle += 100;
  ::InvalidateRect(HWindow, 0, TRUE);  // Repaint the text
}

void TRotateWindow::EvLButtonDown(UINT, TPoint&)
{
  // Increment the angle of the font
  if (TextAngle == 3500) TextAngle = 0;
    else TextAngle += 100;
  ::InvalidateRect(HWindow, 0, TRUE);  // Repaint the text
}

// Force the window to repaint if the window is resized
void TRotateWindow::EvSize(UINT, TSize&)
{
  ::InvalidateRect(HWindow, 0, TRUE);
}

void TRotateApp::InitMainWindow()
{
```

```
    MainWindow = new TFrameWindow(0, "Rotate Text",
      new TRotateWindow(0, ""));
}

int OwlMain(int /*argc*/, char* /*argv*/[])
{
  return TRotateApp().Run();
}
```

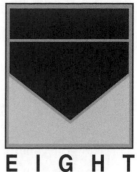

EIGHT

Win32 Drawing Functions

In the previous chapters, we explored numerous GDI drawing functions that work in both 16-bit and 32-bit Windows applications. However, if you're programming soley for 32-bit Windows, such as Windows NT, you'll have additional graphics functions available. For instance, Windows NT supports irregularly shaped curves, extended pen styles, and collections of drawing commands, called *paths*. In this chapter, we'll survey these additional functions and explain how you can use them in your applications. (Chapter 12 describes several 32-bit GDI functions that define useful transformations.)

Realize that these Win32 functions are not available in standard 16-bit Windows or Win32s. Therefore if you are planning to develop an application equally capable in standard Windows and Windows NT, you probably won't want to use the routines presented here. However, if you do execute any of these 32-bit oriented routines in Win32s, the worst thing that will happen is that they return FALSE and won't draw anything.

DRAWING ARCS

The standard Windows API includes the **Arc** function that draws a simple arc. Win32 applications, however, have access to the four additional arc functions listed in Table 8.1.

The **ArcTo** function is similar to the standard **Arc** function; however, it performs two extra steps. First, it draws a line from the current position to the starting point of the arc. Second, after the arc is drawn, **ArcTo** moves the current position to the end of the arc. As with many of the pixel-oriented GDI drawing routines, **ArcTo** does not draw the last pixel of the arc.

167

Table 8.1 32-Bit Extended Arc Functions

Function	Description
AngleArc	Draws an arc and a connecting line segment
ArcTo	Draws an arc and updates the current position
GetArcDirection	Retrieves the direction arcs are drawn
SetArcDirection	Sets the direction an arc is drawn

The **ArcTo** function is declared as:

```
BOOL ArcTo(HDC hDC, int left, int top, int right, int bottom,
    int x1Radius, int y1Radius, int x2Radius, int y2Radius);
```

- **hDC** is a handle to the device context.
- **left**, **top**, **right**, and **bottom** are the logical coordinates of a rectangle that bounds the arc.
- The starting point of the curve is located at the interesection of the arc and an imaginary line that extends from the center of the arc's bounding box to the point **x1Radius,y1Radius**. Similarly, the ending point is located at the intersection of the arc and an imaginary line that extends from the center of the arc's bounding box to **x2Radius,y2Radius**.
- **ArcTo** returns TRUE if the function succeeds, FALSE otherwise.

The following **Paint** function illustrates how the **ArcTo** function works. It generates the drawing shown in Figure 8.1. You can use this **Paint** function,

Figure 8.1 The ArcTo function draws an arc and updates the location of the current position.

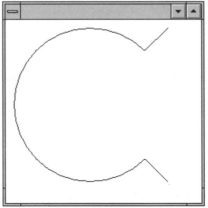

and the other ones in this chapter, with the EXAMPLE.CPP source file listed in Chapter 3. You will need to set the compiler's target to Win32, however, to generate code that can run in Windows NT.

```
void TExampleWindow::Paint(TDC& dc, BOOL, TRect&)
{
  MoveToEx(dc, 200, 10, 0);
  ArcTo(dc, 10, 10, 200, 200, 200, 10, 200, 200);
  LineTo(dc, 200, 200);
}
```

Specifying the endpoints of an arc using the **Arc** and **ArcTo** functions is tedious. An easier way is to use the **AngleArc** routine. It enables you to specify the endpoints of the arc in degrees. The function prototype for **AngleArc** is:

```
BOOL AngleArc(HDC hDC, int x, int y, int radius, int startAngle,
  int sweepAngle);
```

- **hDC** is a handle to the device context.
- The point **x,y** is the center of the arc in logical units.
- **radius** is the radius of the arc along the x axis. It is in logical units and must be positive.
- **startAngle** specifies the angle, in degrees, to the starting point of the arc relative to the x axis.
- **sweepAngle** specifies the sweep angle of the arc, in degrees, relative to the start of the arc.
- **AngleArc** returns TRUE if the function succeeds, FALSE otherwise.

AngleArc draws an arc starting at an angle **startAngle** degrees from the X axis. The sweep of the arc extends **sweepAngle** number of degrees. By default, these angles are measured in the counterclockwise direction. The function uses the current pen to draw the arc and does not affect the current position or fill the figure. If the sweep angle is greater than 360 degrees an ellipse is drawn.

The following **Paint** function illustrates how **AngleArc** draws an arc. Figure 8.2 shows the output of this **Paint** function.

```
void TExampleWindow::Paint(TDC& dc, BOOL, TRect&)
{
  MoveToEx(dc, 200, 10, 0);
  AngleArc(dc, 110, 110, 90, 45, 315);
  LineTo(dc, 200, 200);
}
```

Figure 8.2 The AngleArc function draws an arc using angular measurements.

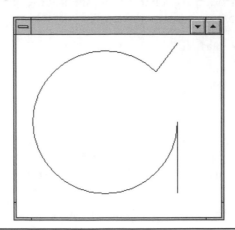

Controlling the Painting Direction

You can alter the direction **AngleArc** draws its arc using the **SetArcDirection** function. For instance, by default **AngleArc** measures its angles in a counterclockwise direction. You can instead, force **AngleArc** to draw its arc in a clockwise direction. To retrieve the current drawing direction, you can call the **GetArcDirection** function. These two routines are declared as:

```
int GetArcDirection(HDC hDC);
int SetArcDirection(HDC hDC, int arcDirection);
```

- **hDC** is a handle to the device context.
- **arcDirection** is a constant that specifies the direction to draw arcs.
- **GetArcDirection** returns the current arc direction. If there is an error, however, it returns zero.
- **SetArcDirection** returns the previous arc direction, or zero if an error occurs.

To make **AngleArc** draw its arc clockwise, you must set the **arcDirection** parameter to the **AD_CLOCKWISE** constant. Similarly, to make the arc routines draw arcs in a counterclockwise manner you must set **arcDirection** to **AD_COUNTERCLOCKWISE**.

The following **Paint** function demonstrates how the arc direction affects the output of the **AngleArc** function. The first call to **AngleArc** draws an arc in a clockwise direction. The second call to **AngleArc**, in contrast, paints the arc in a counterclockwise direction. The output of this function is shown in Figure 8.3.

Figure 8.3 The SetArcDirection function controls the direction that an arc is drawn.

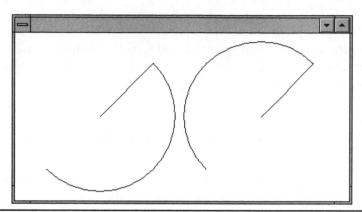

```
void TExampleWindow::Paint(TDC& dc, BOOL, TRect&)
{
  SetArcDirection(dc, AD_CLOCKWISE);
  MoveToEx(dc, 105, 105, 0);
  ArcTo(dc, 10, 10, 200, 200, 200, 10, 10, 200);
  SetArcDirection(dc, AD_COUNTERCLOCKWISE);
  MoveToEx(dc, 305, 105, 0);
  ArcTo(dc, 210, 10, 400, 200, 400, 10, 210, 200);
}
```

Although the name doesn't suggest it, **SetArcDirection** also affects the direction of all the GDI routines bounded by rectangles. These routines are **Arc**, **ArcTo**, **Chord**, **Ellipse**, **Pie**, **Rectangle**, and **RoundRect**. We'll explore what it means to set the drawing direction of these other shapes in the section *Working with Paths*.

EXTENDED POLYGON FUNCTIONS

Win32 supplies two new polygon drawing routines. The first, **PolylineTo**, updates the current position as it draws one or more line segments. The second function, **PolyPolyline**, draws sets of connected line segments or polygons. Both functions draw the line segments using the current pen syle and do not fill the interiors of the polygons. The two functions are defined as:

```
BOOL PolylineTo(HDC hDC, POINT points[], DWORD numPts);
BOOL PolyPolyline(HDC hDC, POINT points[], DWORD numPtsArray[],
  DWORD numPolys);
```

• **hDC** is a handle to a device context.

- **points** is an array of **POINT** structures that specifies the endpoints of the line segments.

- **numPts** is the number of points in the points array.

- **numPtsArray** is an array of **DWORD**s that specifies the number of points in each set of line segments in points; each set of line segments must have at least two points.

- **numPolys** is the number of independent sets of line segments in the points array.

- **PolylineTo** and **PolyPolyline** return TRUE if they succeed, FALSE otherwise.

The following **Paint** function illustrates how **PolylineTo** uses and updates the current position. This routine generates the output shown in Figure 8.4. Only the diagonal line is actually specified in the list of polyline points. The top line is drawn from the current position, which is set by **MoveToEx**, to the first point in the array of points. The bottom line is drawn by the **LineTo** function and illustrates how the current position is set to the last point in the vertices list when **PolylineTo** is finished.

```
void TExampleWindow::Paint(TDC& dc, BOOL, TRect&)
{
  POINT p[2] = {{200,10}, {10,200}};
  MoveToEx(dc, 10, 10, 0); // PolylineTo draws from the current position
  PolylineTo(dc, p, 2);
  LineTo(dc, 200, 200);    // Draw a line from the new current position
}
```

Figure 8.4 The PolylineTo function updates the current position after drawing a polygon.

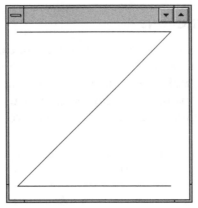

Notice that **PolylineTo** draws a line from the current position to the first coordinate in the **points** array. Similarly, it moves the current position to the last coordinate of the **points** array.

In contrast, the **PolyPolyline** function does not use or change the current position. It's useful if you need to draw a set of unconnected, unfilled polygons. The **Paint** function that follows illustrates how **PolyPolyline** operates. The single call to **PolyPolyline** in this case generates a pair of polygons.

```
void TExampleWindow::Paint(TDC& dc, BOOL, TRect&)
{
  POINT p[7] = {{10,10}, {200,10}, {100,200},
    {210,10}, {400,10}, {300,200}, {210,10}};
  DWORD numPts[2] = {3, 4};
  PolyPolyline(dc, p, numPts, 2);
}
```

DRAWING IRREGULAR CURVES

One of the more powerful extensions that Win32 includes is its ability to draw irregular curves, commonly known as Bézier curves or splines. The two primary spline routines are **PolyBezier** and **PolyBezierTo**. Both functions draw a series of connected curves using the current pen style and do not fill the figures that they draw. Here are the function prototypes for these two routines:

```
BOOL PolyBezier(HDC hDC, POINT points[], DWORD numPts);
BOOL PolyBezierTo(HDC hDC, POINT points[], DWORD numPts);
```

- **hDC** is a handle to the device context.
- **points** is a **POINT** array that contains the endpoints of a series of connected curves and control points that specify the curvature the arc at each endpoint.
- **numPts** is the number of endpoints and control points in the points array.
- Both functions return TRUE if they succeed, FALSE otherwise.

Specifying a Bézier curve is done by supplying a series of arc endpoints and *control* points that specify how much to bend the curve at each endpoint. As Figure 8.4 illustrates, the curve is bent so that it is tangent to an imaginary line drawn to its control point (indicated in the figure by a dashed line). The longer theses lines are, the harder they tug on the curve and the sharper the curve. In addition, the position of the control points relative to the endpoints that they are connected to, controls the direction of the curve.

From a programming standpoint, you specify a Bézier curve by intermixing the coordinates of the arc endpoints and the control points. These points are stored in a array of **POINT** structures. The smallest curve you can specify

Figure 8.4 The PolyBezier function draws irregular curves.

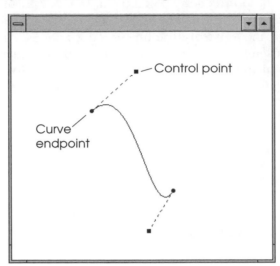

requires four points: the curve's two endpoints and their matching control points. Specifically, the first array location specifies the starting coordinate of the curve. The next array location contains the starting coordinate's control point. The next index location stores the control point for the opposite end of the curve. And finally, the fourth point is the ending coordinate of the arc. You can append additional arc segments to the curve by adding three points for each segment. The last point of the previous arc becomes the new arc's starting coordinate. The first of the new three points becomes the control point for the start of the appended arc. The second array location contains the control point for the third point, which is the new endpoint of the curve. Figure 8.5 displays the output of the following **Paint** function that draws two connecting splines.

```
void TExampleWindow::Paint(TDC& dc, BOOL, TRect&)
{
  POINT p[13] = {{175,50}, {165,55}, {200,70}, {200,75}, {200,80},
    {25,95}, {25,100}, {25,105}, {200,120}, {200,125}, {200,130},
    {165,145}, {175,150}};
  PolyBezier(dc, p, 13);
}
```

PolyBezierTo is different than **PolyBezier** in that it updates the current position. **PolyBezierTo** draws a line from the current position to the first coordinate in the **points** array and moves the current position to the position of the last coordinate in the array.

Figure 8.5 An array of POINT structures specifies how to draw a Bézier curve.

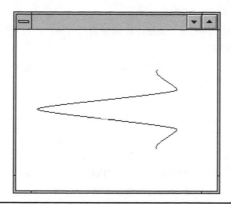

Win32 actually provides a third way to draw Bézier curves, using the **PolyDraw** function. This routine, in fact, enables you to draw a mixture of connected line segments and splines. The **PolyDraw** function is defined as:

```
BOOL PolyDraw(HDC hDC, POINT points[], BYTE types[], int numPts);
```

- **hDC** is a handle to the device context.
- **points** is an array of **POINT** structures that lists the endpoints and control points of the figure.
- **types** is an array that specifies what each value in the **points** array represents.
- **numPts** is the number of points in the **points** array.

The **points** array specifies a series of coordinates. For each coordinate in the **points** array there is a corresponding value in the **types** array that tells **PolyDraw** how to interpret the coordinate. In all, there are three accepted interpretations. These are listed in Table 8.2.

In addition, the **PT_CLOSEFIGURE** constant can be bitwise-ORed to a drawing type to signal that the figure should be closed off. The figure is not filled, however. Also, the lines and curves are drawn using the current pen style.

The following **Paint** function demonstrates how the **PolyDraw** function works. It displays two line segments connected to a spline as shown in Figure 8.6.

```
void TExampleWindow::Paint(TDC& dc, BOOL, TRect&)
{
  const int numPts = 5;
  POINT pts[numPts] = {{40,40}, {65,15},
    {170,130}, {200,100}, {40,100}};
```

Table 8.2 Graphics Operations Supported in PolyDraw

Type Constant	Description
PT_MOVETO	Moves the current position to the corresponding coordinate in the points array
PT_LINETO	Draws a line from the current position to the corresponding coordinate in the points array; the current position is moved to the endpoint of this line segment
PT_BEZIERTO	Specifies a control point or the endpoint of a curve

Figure 8.6 The PolyDraw function can display connected line segments and splines.

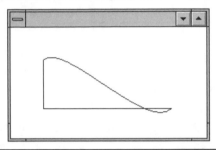

```
BYTE ptTypes[numPts] = {PT_MOVETO, PT_BEZIERTO,
  PT_BEZIERTO, PT_BEZIERTO, PT_LINETO | PT_CLOSEFIGURE};
PolyDraw(dc, pts, ptTypes, numPts);
}
```

EXTENDED PEN STYLES

The pen styles in standard Windows are adequate for many applications, however, Win32 takes the concept much further. Using the **ExtCreatePen** function and its companion structure **EXTLOGPEN** you can define thick pens with patterns, bitmaps, user-defined styles, and more. In addition, you can miter or bevel the endpoints of lines that are joined together.

The **ExtCreatePen** function is declared as:

```
HPEN ExtCreatePen(DWORD penStyle, DWORD width, LOGBRUSH* logBrush,
  DWORD numStyleBits, DWORD* styleBits);
```

• **penStyle** specifies the type of pen to create.

• **width** is the logical width of the pen.

- **logBrush** is a pointer to a **LOGBRUSH** structure that specifies various attributes of the pen.

- **styleBits** and **numStyleBits** specify an optional user-defined pen style.

- **ExtCreatePen** returns a handle to a pen that adheres to the specifications provided or zero if the function fails.

- Normally, **ExtCreatePen** returns a handle to a pen that you can select into a device context. If, however, you execute **ExtCreatePen** in standard Windows, the function will return a handle set to zero. If you later pass this pen handle to **SelectObject**, Windows won't complain, but at the same time, it won't change the current pen style either.

There are two types of extended pens: *cosmetic* and *geometric*. Cosmetic pens are always one pixel wide. They can differ from standard lines, in that it is possible to customize the bit patterns used in the line. Geometric pens, on the other hand, can have a variety of widths and appearances.

Why does Win32 support two different types of pens? One valuable use is in drawing programs that use Windows' function to zoom into a drawing. Cosmetic pens will always be one pixel wide, no matter what the zoom factor is. Geometric pens, on the other hand, become thicker as the drawing is enlarged.

The pen style is a combination of several constants. There are four properties of the pen that you may want to set. First, you must specify whether you are defining a cosmetic or geometric pen style, by setting **penStyle** to either the **PS_COSMETIC** or **PS_GEOMETRIC** constant. In addition, you may want to bitwise-OR the variable **penStyle** with one or more of the values in Tables 8.3, 8.4, and 8.5. Table 8.3 specifies the form of the pen style, whether the line

Table 8.3 ExtCreatePen Supports These Pen Styles

Constant	Description
PS_ALTERNATE	Every other pixel is set; available only with cosmetic pens
PS_SOLID	Draws solid lines
PS_DASH	Draws dashed lines
PS_DOT	Draws dotted lines
PS_DASHDOT	Draws lines with alternating dashes and dots
PS_DASHDOTDOT	Draws lines with alternating dashes and pairs of dots
PS_NULL	Draws invisible lines
PS_USERSTYLE	Draws user-specified line styles
PS_INSIDEFRAME	Draws solid lines that are drawn on the interior edges of bounding shapes; available only with geometric pens

Table 8.4 Geometric Pens Can Have One of These End Cap Styles

Constant	Description
PS_ENDCAP_ROUND	Draws lines and arcs with rounded ends
PS_ENDCAP_SQUARE	Draws lines and arcs with a square appended to each end
PS_ENDCAP_FLAT	Draws lines and arcs with flat ends that do not extend beyond the endpoints of the figures

is dashed, solid, and so on. The constants in Table 8.4 control the appearance of the endpoints of lines drawn with the pen style. And finally, Table 8.5 specifies how lines are connected together; that is, if the functions drawing them support this feature.

Minimally, you only need to set **penStyle** to **PS_COSMETIC** or **PS_GEOMETRIC**. By default, the lines are drawn solid with rounded ends and connections.

The EXTPEN.CPP program that follows shows how to use the **ExtCreatePen** function. Pay special attention to how the function uses brush patterns to define the fill patterns of thick pens. In particular, the routine uses a **LOGBRUSH** structure to specify the characteristics of the pen style. The **lbStyle** field of a **LOGBRUSH** structure specifies its style, whether it's solid, a hatch pattern, or bitmap. The **lbColor** field controls the color of the pen and the **lbHatch** field specifies the type of hatch pattern used, if any. The following statements, for instance, create a red, crosshatched, 16-unit wide pen with flat ends:

```
LOGBRUSH lb;
lb.lbStyle = BS_HATCHED;
lb.lbColor = RGB(0,0,0);
lb.lbHatch = HS_CROSS;
HPEN hPen = ExtCreatePen(PS_GEOMETRIC | PS_SOLID | PS_ENDCAP_SQUARE,
  16, &lb, 0, 0);
```

Figure 8.7 shows a few of the many types of line styles you can generate with **ExtCreatePen**. The EXTPEN.CPP program, shown next, generates the line styles in the figure. To compile and run the program you must specify a Win32 target.

Table 8.5 Geometric Pens Can Join Lines and Curves

Constant	Description
PS_JOIN_BEVEL	Bevels the connection between two figures
PS_JOIN_MITER	Connected figures are mitered if they are within the limit set by SetMiterLimit; if it exceeds the limit, the figures are beveled together
PS_JOIN_ROUND	Joins are rounded together

Figure 8.7 The EXTPEN program displays several line styles using the Win32 function ExtCreatePen.

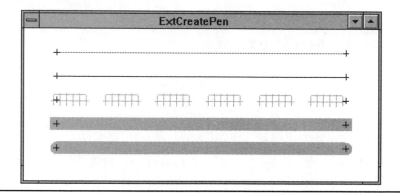

• EXTPEN.CPP

```
// EXTPEN.CPP: Illustrates some of the features of the ExtCreatePen
// function. This extended GDI routine only works correctly with Win32.

#include <owl\applicat.h>
#include <owl\framewin.h>
#include <owl\dc.h>

const CROSSWD = 4;
const LEFT = 40;
const RIGHT = 400;
const INC = 30;

class TExampleWindow : public TWindow {
public:
  TExampleWindow(TWindow *parent, const char* title)
    : TWindow(parent, title) { }
  void Mark(HDC dc, int x, int y);
  void ShowLine(HDC hDC, HPEN hPen, int x1, int x2, int y);
  void Paint(TDC& dc, BOOL, TRect&);
};

class TExampleApp : public TApplication {
public:
  TExampleApp() : TApplication() { }
  void InitMainWindow();
};

void TExampleApp::InitMainWindow()
{
  MainWindow = new TFrameWindow(0, "ExtCreatePen",
    new TExampleWindow(0, ""));
}
```

```cpp
int OwlMain(int /*argc*/, char* /*argv*/[])
{
  return TExampleApp().Run();
}

// Draw a figure
void TExampleWindow::Paint(TDC& dc, BOOL, TRect&)
{
  int y = INC;
  LOGBRUSH lb;                       // Creates a single-pixel wide line
  lb.lbStyle = BS_SOLID;             // with every other pixel set black
  lb.lbColor = RGB(0,0,0);
  HPEN hPen1 = ExtCreatePen(PS_COSMETIC | PS_ALTERNATE, 1, &lb, 0, 0);
  ShowLine(dc, hPen1, LEFT, RIGHT, y);
  y += INC;
  lb.lbStyle = BS_SOLID;             // Creates a solid, single-pixel wide,
  lb.lbColor = RGB(0,0,0);           // black line
  HPEN hPen2 = ExtCreatePen(PS_COSMETIC | PS_SOLID, 1, &lb, 0, 0);
  ShowLine(dc, hPen2, LEFT, RIGHT, y);
  y += INC;
  lb.lbStyle = BS_HATCHED;           // Creates a dashed, gray line, 16
  lb.lbColor = RGB(192,192,192); // pixels wide
  lb.lbHatch = HS_CROSS;
  HPEN hPen3 = ExtCreatePen(PS_GEOMETRIC | PS_DASH, 16, &lb, 0, 0);
  ShowLine(dc, hPen3, LEFT, RIGHT, y);
  y += INC;
  lb.lbStyle = BS_SOLID;             // Creates a 16-pixel wide, gray line
  lb.lbColor = RGB(192,192,192); // with a crosshatch pattern. The
  lb.lbHatch = HS_CROSS;             // line has square endcaps
  HPEN hPen4 = ExtCreatePen(PS_GEOMETRIC | PS_SOLID | PS_ENDCAP_SQUARE,
    16, &lb, 0, 0);
  ShowLine(dc, hPen4, LEFT, RIGHT, y);
  y += INC;
  lb.lbStyle = BS_SOLID;             // Same as above, but with rounded
  lb.lbColor = RGB(192,192,192); // ends
  HPEN hPen5 = ExtCreatePen(PS_GEOMETRIC | PS_SOLID | PS_ENDCAP_ROUND,
    16, &lb, 0, 0);
  ShowLine(dc, hPen5, LEFT, RIGHT, y);
  // Select the default pen back into the device context
  // so that the custom pens can be deleted
  SelectObject(dc, GetStockObject(BLACK_PEN));
  DeleteObject(hPen1);       // Delete the custom pen
  DeleteObject(hPen2);       // Delete the custom pen
  DeleteObject(hPen3);       // Delete the custom pen
  DeleteObject(hPen4);       // Delete the custom pen
  DeleteObject(hPen5);       // Delete the custom pen
}

// Display a crosshair centered at the coordinate (x,y)
void TExampleWindow::Mark(HDC dc, int x, int y)
{
  HPEN hOldPen = HPEN(SelectObject(dc, GetStockObject(BLACK_PEN)));
  MoveToEx(dc, x-CROSSWD, y, 0);
  LineTo(dc, x+CROSSWD, y);
```

```
      MoveToEx(dc, x, y-CROSSWD, 0);
      LineTo(dc, x, y+CROSSWD);
      SelectObject(dc, hOldPen);
}

// Show the specified line and display a crosshair at each end
void TExampleWindow::ShowLine(HDC hDC, HPEN hPen,
    int x1, int x2, int y)
{
  HPEN hOldPen = HPEN(SelectObject(hDC, hPen));
  SelectObject(hDC, hPen);    // Select the pen into the device context
  MoveToEx(hDC, x1, y, &POINT());
  LineTo(hDC, x2, y);
  SelectObject(hDC, hOldPen);
  Mark(hDC, x1, y);
  Mark(hDC, x2, y);
}
```

Joining Line Segments

As mentioned in the last section, you can tell **ExtCreatePen** to define a thick pen style with one of three different connecting styles. Figure 8.8 shows what affect these join styles have on two connecting lines. Although the figure doesn't show it, the join styles also influence the way Windows connects arcs and Bézier splines.

If you specify mitered joins, you have one additional control over them: You can switch to beveled joins if the connecting lines produce too sharp of a mitered cut. This can occur, for instance, if two thick lines are joined together at a very small angle. Fortunately, Windows defines a miter limit that it uses to determine if it should use beveled rather than mitered joins. The miter limit is the ratio of the width of the join and the width of the lines, as shown in Figure 8.9. By default, Windows draws mitered joins up to the point where the join width is ten times greater than the line width. If you want to avoid drawing mitered

Figure 8.8 The ExtCreatePen enables you to specifiy how lines and curves are joined.

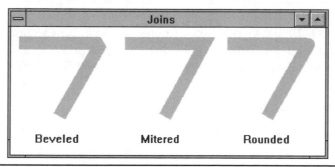

Beveled   Mitered   Rounded

Figure 8.9 The GDI calculates a miter ratio when determining if it should draw mitered joins.

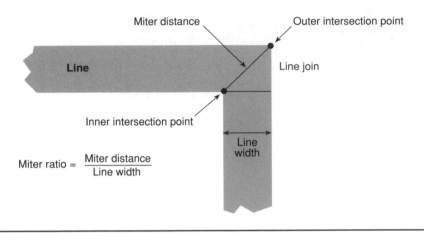

---

joins between two lines at small angles, you can decrease the miter limit using the **SetMiterLimit** function. To retrieve the current miter limit you can call the function **GetMiterLimit**. These two functions are defined as:

```
BOOL SetMiterLimit(HDC hDC, FLOAT newLimit, FLOAT* oldLimit);
BOOL GetMiterLimit(HDC hDC, FLOAT* currLimit);
```

- **hDC** is a handle to the device context.
- **newLimit** is the miter limit to use.
- **oldLimit** is a pointer to a **FLOAT** value that will receive the previous miter limit setting. If you want to ignore this value, you can set it to 0.
- **currLimit** is a pointer to a **FLOAT** value that is set to the current miter limit.
- Both functions return TRUE if they succeed, FALSE otherwise.

Figure 8.10 shows two sets of mitered joins; the top lines use the default miter limit and the bottom ones use a miter limit of 3.0. Notice that the rightmost joins are drawn differently because they have different miter limits.

WORKING WITH PATHS

In the last section, we mentioned that Windows needs to know what lines or curves it's connecting before the GDI can join the figures correctly. One way to

Figure 8.10 The miter limit affects whether the GDI should draw mitered joins or beveled connections.

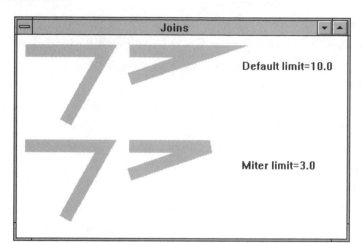

get around this problem is with *paths*. A path is a sequence of curves and lines that can be rendered or manipulated as a group.

A path is another component of a device context and consists of a series of drawing commands. By default, a device context has an empty path. You can build a path by placing GDI drawing functions between the functions **BeginPath** and **EndPath**:

```
BeginPath();
// GDI functions here
EndPath();
```

The GDI functions inside the **BeginPath\EndPath** pair do not render anything, instead they add to the current path. Other functions are used to draw the path, as you'll learn in the next section. A list of the path-related functions is shown in Table 8.6.

The path is not available in the device context until you call the **EndPath** function. However, once you've constructed a path, you can:

- Redraw the outline or interior of the path
- Convert the path to a region
- Use the path to define a clipping region
- Change the pen width used in the path
- Retrieve the coordinates of the path
- Replace all curves in the path with line segments

Table 8.6 Path-Related Functions in 32-Bit Windows

Function	Description
AbortPath	Closes and discards the current path
BeginPath	Begins creating a new path for a device context
CloseFigure	Closes the currently defined path
EndPath	Ends the path
FillPath	Fills the interior of the current path
FlattenPath	Replaces all curves in the path with line segments
GetMiterLimit	Retrieves the join limits for mitered connections
GetPath	Retrieves the current path
PathToRegion	Converts a path to a region
SelectClipPath	Defines a clip region based on the current path
StrokeAndFillPath	Draws the perimeter of the current path and fills its interior
StrokePath	Draws the perimeter of the current path
WidenPath	Redefines the current path to use the currently selected pen

---

Almost all of the path functions listed in Table 8.6 take a single parameter: a handle to the device context that contains the path. In addition, all the functions return TRUE if they succeed and FALSE otherwise.

Drawing a Path

To draw a path, you can use the functions **StrokePath**, **FillPath**, and **StrokeAndFillPath**:

```
BOOL StrokePath(hDC);
BOOL FillPath(hDC);
BOOL StrokeAndFillPath(hDC);
```

• **hDC** is a handle to the device context.

The **StrokePath** function draws the lines and curves in a path using the currently selected pen. Put another way, any pen styles selected in the **BeginPath\EndPath** pair are not used to draw the path. It also means that the whole path is drawn with the same pen. The **FillPath** function, similarly, fills the interior of a path using the currently selected brush. It also automatically closes all paths and subpaths with straight lines. And finally, the

StrokeAndFillPath function draws the interior of the path and then pens its lines and curves. The following **Paint** function, for instance, illustrates how to define a path and later display it using these three functions. It generates the drawing in Figure 8.11.

```
void TExampleWindow::Paint(TDC& dc, BOOL, TRect&)
{
  LOGBRUSH lb;                    // Create a pen to use in the paths
  lb.lbStyle = BS_SOLID;
  lb.lbColor = RGB(0,0,0);
  HPEN hPen = ExtCreatePen(
    PS_GEOMETRIC | PS_SOLID | PS_ENDCAP_FLAT | PS_JOIN_BEVEL,
    16, &lb, 0, 0);
  SelectObject(dc, hPen);    // Select the pen into the device context
  SelectObject(dc, GetStockObject(DKGRAY_BRUSH)); // Select a brush

  BeginPath(dc);    // Begin defining a path
  POINT triangle[4] = {{120,40}, {200,100}, {40,100}, {120,40}};
  Polygon(dc, triangle, 4);
  EndPath(dc);       // End the path definition
  StrokePath(dc);
  TextOut(dc, 90, 140, "StrokePath", 10);

  BeginPath(dc);    // Begin defining a path
  POINT triangle2[4] = {{120+200,40}, {200+200,100},
    {40+200,100}, {120+200,40}};
  Polygon(dc, triangle2, 4);
  EndPath(dc);       // End the path definition
  FillPath(dc);
  TextOut(dc, 290, 140, "FillPath", 8);

  BeginPath(dc);    // Begin defining a path
  POINT triangle3[4] = {{120+400,40}, {200+400,100},
    {40+400,100}, {120+400,40}};
  Polygon(dc, triangle3, 4);
  EndPath(dc);       // End the path definition
  StrokeAndFillPath(dc);
  TextOut(dc, 460, 140, "StrokeAndFillPath", 17);
}
```

Figure 8.11 Windows provides three functions for displaying a path.

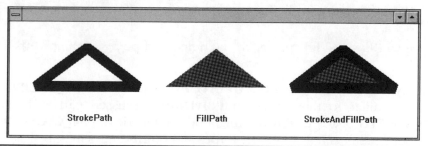

Note The **FillPath** function destroys the path after it displays the path. To restore the path use Windows' **SaveDC** and **RestoreDC** functions:

```
SaveDC(hDC);
FillPath(hDC); // FillPath fills the interior of the path, but destroys the path
RestoreDC(hDC, -1); // Restore the device context and path
// Other path operations
```

Functions that change the current position inside a path begin a new *subpath*. Each subpath is independent and is not mitered or beveled with the other subpaths.

Since a path can contain portions of a figure that overlap itself, it's possible to set the window mode to fill every other region. Recall from Chapter 4 that you can pass the constant **ALTERNATE** to the **SetPolyFillMode** function to produce this affect. Because paths can contain subpaths, it's possible to produce complex overlapping shapes. To give you the greatest flexibility over what it means to fill every other region, Windows allows you to control the drawing direction of the rectangle-based GDI drawing routines, such as **Rectangle** and **Ellipse**. Although it may not seem like it's correct, you can call the **SetArcDirection** function to specify whether these GDI function should render their figures in a clockwise or counterclockwise direction.

You can close a path within the **BeginPath\EndPath** pair by calling **ClosePath**. It adds a connecting line from the last point in the current subpath to its first. Realize, **ClosePath** will not work outside of the path block.

Determining the Current Path

You can retrieve an array that contains the points that make up the current path by calling the **GetPath** function. It is defined as:

```
int GetPath(HDC hDC, POINT points[], BYTE types[], int numPts);
```

- **hDC** is a handle to the device context.
- **points** is an array of **POINT** structures that is set to the endpoints and control points in the path's figures.
- **types** is an array of **BYTE** values that is set to the type of each point in the path.
- **numPts** should be passed as the number of points in the **points** array.

The **types** array contains **PT_MOVETO**, **PT_LINETO**, and **PT_BEZIERTO** constants similar to those used in **PolyDraw** discussed earlier. In addition, **PT_LINETO** or **PT_BEZIERTO** might be combined with **PT_CLOSEFIGURE** if the path or subpath is closed. The **types** and **points** arrays must be large enough to hold all the points in the path. To determine how many points to allocate space for, you can call **GetPath** with **numPts** set to 0. In this case, **GetPath** returns the number of points and does not write to the **types** or **points** buffers. When retrieving the path data, **numPts** should be set to the number of points in the path. If this number is too small, **GetPath** will return –1, signaling an error.

▼ **Note**   Raster fonts do not add to a path and do not display anything if they are located within a path block. Vector fonts do add to the path as strokes. Similarly, the outlines of TrueType characters are added as closed paths.

Creating Extended Regions

One way to use a path is to convert the area that it encompasses into a Windows region. Recall that regions are useful for specifying areas that Windows can update or exclude from updating. To convert the current path to a region, you must call the function **PathToRegion**. It is defined as:

```
HRGN PathToRegion(hDC);
```

- **hDC** is a handle to the device context.
- **HRGN** is a handle to the region that corresponds to the current path.

Two additional region functions that Win32 applications have access to are **ExtCreateRegion** and **GetRegionData**. The **ExtCreateRegion** function creates a region based on a series of transformations and **GetRegionData** retrieves the information about a particular region.

Using Paths to Control Clipping

One way to use paths is to define them as clipping regions—areas of the screen that are not allowed to be updated. Any portion of the window outside of the clipping region can change. Because you can use various GDI functions to create paths of complex shapes, it's possible to create complex clipping regions from paths.

To convert the current path to a clipping region you can call the **SelectClipPath** function, which is defined as:

```
BOOL SelectClipPath(HDC hDC, int iMode);
```

- **hDC** is a handle to the device context.
- **iMode** is one of the constants listed in Table 8.7 that specifies how the path should be combined with the current clip region.

Table 8.7 Clip Path Operations

Constant	Description
RGN_AND	The region becomes the intersection of the current clipping region and the current path
RGN_COPY	The clipping region is set to the current path
RGN_DIFF	The areas in the current path are removed from the current clipping region
RGN_OR	The current path is added to the current clipping region
RGN_XOR	The clipping region becomes the union of the current clipping region and the current path minus the common areas

The following **Paint** function illustrates how you can use a path to define a clipping region. It uses the outlines of a TrueType string to define a path, sets the clipping region to the path, and then draws a series of horizontal lines across the text. Figure 8.12 shows the final output of the **Paint** function.

```
void TExampleWindow::Paint(TDC& dc, BOOL, TRect&)
{
  // Select a TrueType font
  HFONT hFont = CreateFont(120, 0, 0, 0, FW_BOLD, 0, 0, 0,
    ANSI_CHARSET, OUT_DEFAULT_PRECIS, CLIP_DEFAULT_PRECIS,
    PROOF_QUALITY, FF_SWISS | VARIABLE_PITCH, "Helv");
  // Select the logical font into the device context
  HFONT hOldFont = HFONT(SelectObject(dc, hFont));
  SIZE size;    // Get the size of the text
  GetTextExtentPoint(dc, "Graphics", 8, &size);
  BeginPath(dc);    // Make a path out of the outline of the text
  TextOut(dc, 20, 20, "Graphics", 8);
  EndPath(dc);
  SelectClipPath(dc, RGN_DIFF); // Remove the path as the clip region
  SelectObject(dc, hOldFont);
  DeleteObject(hFont);
  // Draw to the window a series of horizontal lines. These lines
  for (int y=20; y<20+size.cy; y+=5) { // will be clipped to the outline
    MoveToEx(dc, 20, y, 0);              // of the text in the path
    LineTo(dc, 20+size.cx, y);
  }
```

Figure 8.12 You can use a path to define complex clipping regions, as shown here.

N I N E

Presentation Graphics

You've probably heard the term *presentation graphics* about as often as you've heard about user interfaces. In fact, many of the popular Windows applications, such as Excel, provide presentation graphics features for displaying data as pictures and graphs. Many people find that pictures, rather than columns of numbers, are an easier way to view and study information.

Fortunately, presentation graphics are relatively easy to program with Windows. In this chapter, we'll explore techniques for drawing bar graphs, coin graphs, and pie charts. We'll also develop a set of tools, built around C++ classes, for displaying various graph types. By using classes, we'll be able to take advantage of C++'s object-oriented nature and more easily keep the graph-generation code separate from our application code. As a result, it will be easier for you to integrate these graph-drawing objects into your own applications.

A BAR GRAPH CLASS

Every presentation toolkit needs code for displaying bar graphs. We'll start by developing a C++ class, **TBarGraph**, that encompasses all the details of painting a bar graph in a window. The class definition for **TBarGraph** and its code are contained in the two source files BARGRAPH.H and BARGRAPH.CPP (which we'll show in a moment). We'll also develop a program called BARTEST.CPP to test the **TBarGraph** class.

The bar graphs we'll create have four primary components: a rectangular backdrop, a title, labels on the X and Y axes, and the bars themselves. The bar graph class, **TBarGraph**, implements everything we need to initialize the

189

values of a bar graph and to draw the graph in a window. Here's the definition of the bar graph class included in BARGRAPH.H:

```
class TBarGraph {          // The bar graph class
  int BarValues[MAXBARS]; // The bar values
  char BarLabels[MAXBARS][LABELLEN]; // Labels for each bar
  char Title[TITLELEN];    // Title of chart
  int NumRules;            // Number of horizontal rules
  int MaxBarValue;         // Largest bar value on the graph
  int NumBars;             // Number of bars
public:
  TBarGraph(char *title, int numRules=4) {
    NumBars = 0;  strcpy(Title, title);  NumRules = numRules;
  }
  virtual void Display(HDC hDC, int left, int top, int right, int bottom);
  void DrawChart(HDC hDC, int left, int top, int right, int bottom);
  int GetMax();
  virtual void DrawBar(HDC hDC, int left, int top, int right, int bottom);
  void SetTitle(char *title) { strcpy(Title, title); }
  BOOL AddBar(int barValue, char *barLabel);
  void NewGraph() { NumBars = 0;  NumRules = 4; }
};
```

The **TBarGraph** class includes six private variables that store information about the bar graph, such as the values to place along the axes, the bar graph's title, and so on. Some of these variables have default values that are set in the class's constructor, although all of the defaults can be modified. The key variable is **BarValues**, which is an integer array that contains a value for each bar. Figure 9.1 shows the various components of a typical bar graph and how they relate to the **TBarGraph** class.

Table 9.1 lists and briefly describes each member function in **TBarGraph**.

Table 9.1 Member Functions in the TBarGraph Class

Function	Description
TBarGraph	Constructor for the class; sets the chart's title and number of horizontal rules used in the chart; by default, a bar chart doesn't have any bars in it
Display	High-level function to draw a bar chart
DrawChart	Internal routine to draw the bar chart
GetMax	Internal routine to determine the maximum bar value
DrawBar	Draws a bar in the chart
SetTitle	Optional function that can be called to set the bar chart's title
AddBar	User-level routine to add a bar to the chart
NewGraph	Removes all bars from the current chart

Figure 9.1 The components of a bar chart.

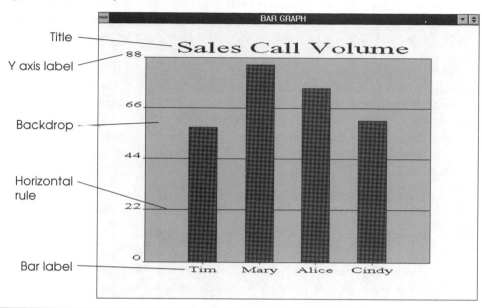

CREATING A BAR CHART

Using **TBarGraph** to draw a bar chart involves three steps:

1. Create and initialize a **TBarGraph** object. You can pass the title of the bar graph to the **TBarGraph** constructor.
2. Place bars in the graph by calling **TBarGraph::AddBar**.
3. Call **TBarGraph::Display** to paint the bar chart.

Now we'll walk through these steps to create the bar graph shown in Figure 9.1. (We'll look at a complete program later.) First, you must create a **TBarGraph** object:

```
TBarGraph* barGraph = new TBarGraph("Sales Call Volume");
```

This statement dynamically allocates and initializes a **TBarGraph** object pointed to by **barGraph**. The constructor gives the bar chart the title "Sales Call Volume."

The bars are added from left to right, using these four statements:

```
barGraph->AddBar(57, "Tim");
barGraph->AddBar(83, "Mary");
barGraph->AddBar(71, "Alice");
barGraph->AddBar(58, "Cindy");
```

The first parameter to **AddBar** is the bar's value and the second is its label. The bar values are stored in the array **BarValues** and the labels are placed in the character array **BarLabels**. In addition, each call to **AddBar** increments **NumBars**, which keeps track of the number of bars in the chart.

Note   The **TBarGraph** constructor actually accepts *two* parameters. The first is the title, which is always required (although it can be a NULL string). The second parameter is optional. It specifies how many horizontal rules are drawn on the backdrop. This value is saved in **NumRules**. It also indirectly specifies how many labels are placed on the Y axis since each horizontal rule has a label next to it. A default value of 4 is given to **NumRules** if a parameter is not specified. (See BARGRAPH.H.):

```
TBarGraph(char *title, int numRules=4) {
  NumBars = 0;  strcpy(Title, title);  NumRules = numRules;
}
```

Therefore, by default, a bar chart has four horizontal rules and four labels on the Y axis. Similarly, if you want a bar chart that does not have a title or any labels on the Y axis, you should use the constructor:

```
TBarGraph* barGraph = new TBarGraph(""); // No title or Y axis labels
```

Displaying a Bar Chart

To display a bar chart, you call TBarGraph's **Display** function. You pass it the handle to the device context and the pixel boundaries of the backdrop. (The title and Y axis labels are painted outside of this region.) For example, you might call **Display** so that it draws a chart leaving a 50 pixel boundary around the chart:

```
RECT rect;
GetClientRect(HWindow, &rect):
Display(hDC, 50, 50, rect.right-50, rect.bottom-50);
```

Normally, you place the call to **Display** in your **Paint** function.

The **Display** function actually takes only three actions:

- Displays the bar chart's title
- Determines the maximum bar value
- Calls **DrawChart** to display the rest of the chart

The real workhorse is **DrawChart**, which draws the chart's backdrop, the bars, and labels. We'll explain this function in a moment, but first we need to show how **Display** writes the title.

Writing the Title

A chart can be many different sizes. To compensate for this, the chart's title is scaled so that it fits within the region above the bar chart.

The font is selected by calling the GDI function **CreateFont**. A request is made for a Roman font that is as tall as it is wide. In particular, the font size is set to one-half the distance between the top of the bar chart and the top of the window:

```
HFONT hFont = CreateFont(top/2, top/2, 0, 0, 0, 0,
  0, 0, 0, 0, 0, 0, 0, "Arial");
HFONT hOldFont = HFONT(SelectObject(hDC, hFont));
```

A problem may occur if the title is too long, however, since we are basing the size of the text on the vertical space above the chart and not on the actual width of the chart. GDI's **GetTextExtentPoint** function is used, therefore, to see how long the text will actually be. The statement for this test is located in the **if** statement:

```
SIZE size;
GetTextExtentPoint(hDC, Title, strlen(Title), &size);
if (size.cx > (right-left)*2/3) {
```

If the text is longer than two-thirds the width of the chart, a new font is selected by calling **CreateFont** again. In this case, the width of the text is selected so that it squeezes the text evenly across the top of the chart:

```
// Select another sized font that will size the
// text so that it fits within the width of the chart
hFont = CreateFont(top/2, (right-left)/strlen(Title),
  0, 0, 0, 0, 0, 0, 0, 0, 0, 0, 0, "Arial");
SelectObject(hDC, hFont);
```

After the title's font has been created, the text alignment is modified in order to center the string, and then the title is displayed:

```
SetTextAlign(hDC, TA_CENTER | TA_BOTTOM);
TextOut(hDC, (left+right)/2, top-2, Title, strlen(Title));
```

The next statements in **Display** determine the maximum value to be displayed in the bar chart and save this value in **MaxBarValue**. All bars are scaled to this maximum value. Then, the execution proceeds to the member function **DrawChart**, which finishes drawing the bar chart.

Painting a Backdrop

The foundation of the bar chart is its backdrop. Therefore, one of the first tasks of **DrawChart** is to draw a backdrop. For our purposes, the backdrop simply draws a gray rectangle. The dimensions of the bar chart passed to the **Display** function are actually the dimensions of the backdrop and are sent along to **Rectangle** after the currently selected brush is set to light gray:

```
SelectObject(hDC, GetStockObject(LTGRAY_BRUSH));
Rectangle(hDC, left, top, right, bottom);  // The backdrop
```

You may want to extract the code that draws the backdrop and place it into a virtual function. In this way, you can readily override the function in derived classes in order to provide other styles of backdrops.

Displaying Labels

The labels along the Y axis and the horizontal rules are painted in **DrawChart** after the backdrop is displayed. Remember, the number of labels and horizontal rules depends on the **NumRules** parameter passed to **TBarGraph**'s constructor.

As with the chart's title, the labels for the Y axis are scaled based on the size of the chart. In this case, the width and height of the selected font is set to one-sixth of the vertical pixel separation between the horizontal rules. This separation is calculated in **DrawChart** and stored in the variable **offset**. Notice that the labels are displayed right justified.

```
// Calculate how many pixels apart the horizontal rules should be
int offset = (bottom - top) / NumRules;
incr = MaxBarValue / NumRules;

// Create a font for labeling of the horizontal hash marks. Its
// height is based the distance between the hash marks.
HFONT hFont = CreateFont(offset/5, 0, 0, 0, FW_BOLD,
  0, 0, 0, 0, 0, 0, 0, 0, "Times New Roman");
HFONT hOldFont = HFONT(SelectObject(hDC, hFont));
SetTextAlign(hDC, TA_RIGHT | TA_BASELINE);
```

The strings that appear below the bars on the X axis are written with the same font. Labels for the bars, which are specified in calls to **AddBar**, are stored in the **BarLabels** array. If a label is not desired for a particular bar, its corresponding value in **BarLabels** can be set to NULL. Since it's possible that a bar's label may extend over the label of the neighboring bar, only the first five characters of each string are displayed. As a finishing touch, a small vertical hash mark is also placed above each string.

The **for** loop located at the end of **DrawChart** displays a bar for each value in **BarValues**, a label, and a hash mark:

```
for (i=0; i<NumBars; i++) {
  if (strcmp(BarLabels[i], "") != 0) {
    // Show hash mark only if a string is to be written
    MoveToEx(hDC, left+(i+1)*offset, bottom, &POINT());
```

```
        LineTo(hDC, left+(i+1)*offset, bottom+hashMarkSize);
        TextOut(hDC, left+(i+1)*offset, bottom+hashMarkSize+2,
        BarLabels[i], strlen(BarLabels[i]));
    }
    // Draw the bars for the values. Make the total width of one of the
    // bars equal to half the distance between two of the hash marks on
    // the horizontal bar.
    height = BarValues[i] * scale;
    DrawBar(hDC, left+(i+1)*offset-offset/4, bottom-height,
        left+(i+1)*offset+offset/4, bottom);
}
```

Drawing a Bar

Within the **for** loop is a call to the member function **DrawBar** that displays each bar. However, when you look at **DrawBar**, you'll see that it simply calls **Rectangle**. If this is the only use for **DrawBar**, why is the extra function used? Simple. We want to be able to use **TBarGraph** in other applications that may paint different types of graphs. By placing the code that actually draws each bar in the virtual function **DrawBar**, we'll be able to override it in classes derived from **TBarGraph** to draw other types of bars. In fact, we'll do exactly this when we create a coin graph later in this chapter.

The height of each bar depends on the scale factor shown next. Its value is based on the overall height of the bar chart and the maximum value in the chart, **MaxBarValue**:

```
scale = double(bottom - top) / MaxBarValue;
```

The pixel height of a bar in the graph, therefore, is calculated by multiplying the numeric value of the bar with the scale factor:

```
height = BarValues[i] * scale;
```

Determining the width and spacing of the bars is a bit more complex. The basic idea is to divide the horizontal axis evenly among the bars, as outlined in Figure 9.2. The following calculation determines the amount of this separation and stores the result in **offset**:

```
offset = (right - left) / (NumBars + 1);
```

The centers of the bars are then placed **offset** number of pixels apart. In addition, the width of each bar is set to one-half the width of **offset**. In other words, half of each bar, which is one-fourth of **offset**, extends to the left of the center point and one-fourth to the right. This accounts for the divide-by-four calculation in the call to **DrawBar**:

```
DrawBar(hDC, left+(i+1)*offset-offset/4, bottom-height,
    left+(i+1)*offset+offset/4, bottom);
```

Figure 9.2 Dimensions of the bars in TBarGraph.

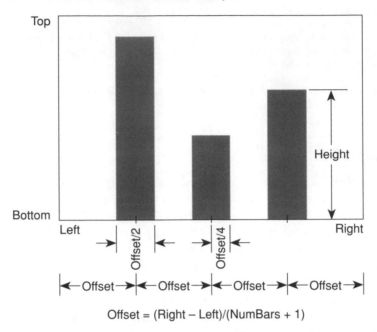

$$Offset = (Right - Left)/(NumBars + 1)$$

Testing the Bar Chart Object

Now we'll put the bar chart object to work. The program BARTEST.CPP uses the BARGRAPH.CPP utility to display the bar chart shown in Figure 9.3. Since all the intricacies of displaying the bar chart are hidden in the **TBarGraph** class, the main program is quite short.

The **TBarGraphWindow** class, derived from **TWindow**, contains the code that uses **TBarGraph**. This class includes the variable **BarGraph**, which is a pointer to a **TBarGraph** object. The **TBarGraphWindow** constructor dynamically allocates and initializes the **BarGraph** object so that it uses the title "Sales (in thousands)" and has four bars:

```
TBarGraphWindow(TWindow *parent, const char* title)
  : TWindow(parent, title) {
  BarGraph = new TBarGraph(" Sales (in thousands) ");
  BarGraph->AddBar(5, "Jan");
  BarGraph->AddBar(4, "Feb");
  BarGraph->AddBar(7, "Mar");
  BarGraph->AddBar(6, "Apr");
}
```

Figure 9.3 BARTEST.CPP creates this bar graph.

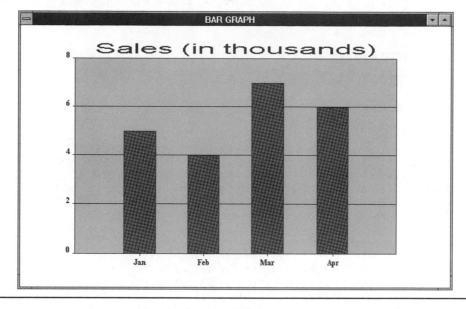

The **TBarGraphWindow**'s **Paint** function calls **TBarGraph::Display** to draw the chart in the program's window:

```
void TBarGraphWindow::Paint(TDC& dc, BOOL, TRect&)
{
  RECT rect;
  ::GetClientRect(HWindow, &rect);
  int sizeX = rect.right / 8;       int sizeY = rect.bottom / 8;
  BarGraph->Display(dc, sizeX, sizeY,
    rect.right-sizeX, rect.bottom-sizeY);
}
```

Remember, the chart boundaries passed to **Display** do not include the room used to display the title or the axes' labels to the left and below the bar graph.

Compiling and Using BARTEST.CPP

To compile BARTEST.CPP, you must include the files BARTEST.CPP and BARGRAPH.CPP in a project file.

After you have the program running, try resizing the window to make sure that the bar chart is resized correctly. The fonts in the bar chart should automatically adjust to the size of the bar chart. In addition, the separation between the bars should change too. You might also try temporarily placing another window over the BARTEST.CPP window and then removing it to verify that repainting is handled correctly. This is a common test you'll want to perform when verifying your own graphics code.

• BARGRAPH.H

```
// BARGRAPH.H: Header file for BARGRAPH.CPP.

#ifndef BARGRAPHH
#define BARGRAPHH
#include <string.h>

#define TITLELEN 30      // The graph's title can be this long + 1
#define INTLEN 10        // An integer string's length + 1
#define STRLEN 15        // A string length used in a dialog box + 1
#define LABELLEN 6       // Maximum length of a bar's string + 1
#define MAXBARS 4        // Maximum number of bars in chart

// The bar graph class
class TBarGraph {          // The bar graph class
  int BarValues[MAXBARS]; // The bar values
  char BarLabels[MAXBARS][LABELLEN]; // Labels for each bar
  char Title[TITLELEN];    // Title of chart
  int NumRules;            // Number of horizontal rules
  int MaxBarValue;         // Largest bar value on chart
  int NumBars;             // Number of bars
public:
  TBarGraph(char *title, int numRules=4) {
    NumBars = 0;  strcpy(Title, title);  NumRules = numRules;
  }
  virtual void Display(HDC hDC, int left, int top, int right, int bottom);
  void DrawChart(HDC hDC, int left, int top, int right, int bottom);
  int GetMax();
  virtual void DrawBar(HDC hDC, int left, int top, int right, int bottom);
  void SetTitle(char *title) { strcpy(Title, title); }
  BOOL AddBar(int barValue, char *barLabel);
  void NewGraph() { NumBars = 0;  NumRules = 4; }
};
#endif
```

• BARGRAPH.CPP

```
// BARGRAPH.CPP: Implements a simple bar graph class.

#include <windows.h>
#include <stdio.h>
#include <stdlib.h>
#include "bargraph.h"

// After declaring a TBarGraph object call this member function
// to add each bar to the graph. Returns TRUE if successful.
```

```
BOOL TBarGraph::AddBar(int barValue, char *barLabel)
{
  if (NumBars < MAXBARS) {
    BarValues[NumBars] = barValue;
    if (strlen(barLabel) < LABELLEN)
      strcpy(BarLabels[NumBars], barLabel);
    else {
      strncpy(BarLabels[NumBars], barLabel, LABELLEN-1);
      BarLabels[NumBars][LABELLEN-1] = '\0';
    }
    NumBars++;
    return TRUE;
  }
  return FALSE;
}

// High-level routine that displays a bar graph
void TBarGraph::Display(HDC hDC, int left, int top, int right, int bottom)
{
  if (NumRules < 0) NumRules = 1;  // Make sure NumRules is > zero

  // Display the title at the top. Create a font for the title that
  // fits just above the bar graph unless this will lead to the
  // title being too long. If so, squeeze the size.
  HFONT hFont = CreateFont(top/2, top/2, 0, 0, 0, 0,
    0, 0, 0, 0, 0, 0, 0, "Arial");
  HFONT hOldFont = HFONT(SelectObject(hDC, hFont));

  SIZE size;
  GetTextExtentPoint(hDC, Title, strlen(Title), &size);
  if (size.cx > (right-left)*2/3) {
    // Is the title string wider than the chart?
    // Select another sized font that will size the
    // text so that it fits within the width of the chart
    hFont = CreateFont(top/2, (right-left)/strlen(Title),
      0, 0, 0, 0, 0, 0, 0, 0, 0, 0, 0, "Arial");
    SelectObject(hDC, hFont);
    DeleteObject(hOldFont);
  }
  SetTextAlign(hDC, TA_CENTER | TA_BOTTOM);
  TextOut(hDC, (left+right)/2, top-2, Title, strlen(Title));

  // Determine a maximum value for the chart scale. It should be at least
  // as large as the largest bar value and a multiple of the number
  // of horizontal rules that the user desires. NumRules should not
  // be greater than MaxBarValue.
  MaxBarValue = GetMax();      // Get the largest bar value
  while ((MaxBarValue % NumRules) != 0)
    MaxBarValue++;
  DrawChart(hDC, left, top, right, bottom);
  SelectObject(hDC, hOldFont);
  DeleteObject(hFont);
}
```

```cpp
// Draws the backdrop and the chart itself
void TBarGraph::DrawChart(HDC hDC, int left, int top,
  int right, int bottom)
{
  double scale;
  int i, height, incr, hashMarkSize;
  char buffer[10];

  // Make a border around the backdrop
  SelectObject(hDC, GetStockObject(LTGRAY_BRUSH));
  Rectangle(hDC, left, top, right, bottom);  // The backdrop
  if (NumBars <= 0) return;         // There isn't anything to display

  // Calculate how many pixels apart the horizontal rules should be
  int offset = (bottom - top) / NumRules;
  incr = MaxBarValue / NumRules;

  // Create a font for labeling of the horizontal hash marks. Its
  // height is based the distance between the hash marks.
  HFONT hFont = CreateFont(offset/5, 0, 0, 0, FW_BOLD,
    0, 0, 0, 0, 0, 0, 0, 0, "Times New Roman");
  HFONT hOldFont = HFONT(SelectObject(hDC, hFont));
  SetTextAlign(hDC, TA_RIGHT | TA_BASELINE);

  // Base the hash mark's width on the width of the characters
  SIZE size;
  GetTextExtentPoint(hDC, "A", 1, &size);
  hashMarkSize = size.cx/3+1;
  for (i=0; i<NumRules; i++) {
    // Draw horizontal rule
    MoveToEx(hDC, left-hashMarkSize, top+i*offset, &POINT());
    LineTo(hDC, right, top+i*offset);
    // Show hash mark
    sprintf(buffer, "%d", incr*(NumRules-i));
    TextOut(hDC, left-2*hashMarkSize-1,
      top+i*offset, buffer, strlen(buffer));
  }
  // Display the 0 label. It may not line up exactly if the
  // number of rules does not divide evenly into the pixel
  // height of the backdrop.
  MoveToEx(hDC, left-hashMarkSize, bottom-1, &POINT());
  LineTo(hDC, right, bottom-1);
  TextOut(hDC, left-2*hashMarkSize-1, top+i*offset, "0", 1);

  // Calculate the amount to scale all bars. Note: The cast to
  // "double" is required.
  scale = double(bottom - top) / MaxBarValue;

  // Fill the bars with dark gray
  SelectObject(hDC, GetStockObject(DKGRAY_BRUSH));
  offset = (right - left) / (NumBars + 1);
  SetTextAlign(hDC, TA_CENTER | TA_TOP);
  for (i=0; i<NumBars; i++) {
```

```
      if (strcmp(BarLabels[i], "") != 0) {
        // Show hash mark only if a string is to be written
        MoveToEx(hDC, left+(i+1)*offset, bottom, &POINT());
        LineTo(hDC, left+(i+1)*offset, bottom+hashMarkSize);
        TextOut(hDC, left+(i+1)*offset, bottom+hashMarkSize+2,
        BarLabels[i], strlen(BarLabels[i]));
      }
      // Draw the bars for the values. Make the total width of one of the
      // bars equal to half the distance between two of the hash marks on
      // the horizontal bar.
      height = BarValues[i] * scale;
      DrawBar(hDC, left+(i+1)*offset-offset/4, bottom-height,
        left+(i+1)*offset+offset/4, bottom);
    }
    SelectObject(hDC, hOldFont);
    DeleteObject(hFont);
}

// Draws a single bar in the chart
void TBarGraph::DrawBar(HDC hDC, int left, int top,
  int right, int bottom)
{
  Rectangle(hDC, left, top, right, bottom);
}

// Finds and returns the largest value in the array of bar values
int TBarGraph::GetMax()
{
  int largest=1;
  for (int i=0; i<NumBars; i++)
    if (BarValues[i] > largest)
      largest = BarValues[i];
  return largest;
}
```

● BARTEST.CPP

```
// BARTEST.CPP: Displays a simple bar graph.

#include <owl\applicat.h>
#include <owl\framewin.h>
#include <owl\dc.h>
#include <stdlib.h>
#include "bargraph.h"

class TBarGraphWindow : public TWindow {
  TBarGraph *BarGraph;
public:
  TBarGraphWindow(TWindow *parent, const char* title)
    : TWindow(parent, title) {
    BarGraph = new TBarGraph(" Sales (in thousands) ");
    BarGraph->AddBar(5, "Jan");
    BarGraph->AddBar(4, "Feb");
```

```
      BarGraph->AddBar(7, "Mar");
      BarGraph->AddBar(6, "Apr");
   }
   virtual ~TBarGraphWindow() { delete BarGraph; }
   void Paint(TDC& dc, BOOL, TRect&);
   void EvSize(UINT, TSize&);

   DECLARE_RESPONSE_TABLE(TBarGraphWindow);
};

DEFINE_RESPONSE_TABLE1(TBarGraphWindow, TWindow)
   EV_WM_SIZE,
END_RESPONSE_TABLE;

class TBarGraphApp : public TApplication {
public:
   TBarGraphApp() : TApplication() { }
   void InitMainWindow();
};

void TBarGraphWindow::Paint(TDC& dc, BOOL, TRect&)
{
   RECT rect;
   ::GetClientRect(HWindow, &rect);
   int sizeX = rect.right / 8;      int sizeY = rect.bottom / 8;
   BarGraph->Display(dc, sizeX, sizeY,
      rect.right-sizeX, rect.bottom-sizeY);
}

// Repaint the whole bar graph if the size of the window changes
void TBarGraphWindow::EvSize(UINT, TSize&)
{
   ::InvalidateRect(HWindow, 0, TRUE);
}

void TBarGraphApp::InitMainWindow()
{
   MainWindow = new TFrameWindow(0, "BAR GRAPH",
      new TBarGraphWindow(0, ""));
}

int OwlMain(int /*argc*/, char* /*argv*/[])
{
   return TBarGraphApp().Run();
}
```

INTERACTIVELY CREATING A BAR GRAPH

In the previous section, we displayed a bar chart by hard-coding its title, number of bars, labels, and so on in a test program. But this doesn't take advantage of Windows' user-interface features. In this section, we'll develop a program that opens a dialog box allowing the user to interactively set the title,

Figure 9.4 Use the dialog box in BARTEST2.CPP to create a custom bar chart.

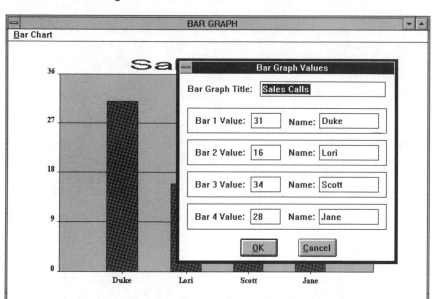

values, and labels for the bar chart. The new program, called BARTEST2.CPP, will be presented in a moment. A sample screen of the new program and its dialog box is shown in Figure 9.4.

Working with Dialog Boxes

Adding a dialog box to an OWL program requires the following four steps:

1. Design the dialog box using Borland's Resource Workshop or enter commands to create the dialog box in a resource (RC) file.
2. Dynamically create objects for the dialog box and each of its controls. These objects associate the dialog box's elements with OWL.
3. Provide a mechanism for copying the data to and from the dialog box.
4. Add the resource file to your project file.

This is the first time we'll integrate a dialog box into an application. However, we won't go into the details involved in designing and creating a dialog box. Information on doing this is thoroughly described in Borland's documentation. Instead, we'll focus on what is required to integrate the dialog box into our application.

Dialog Boxes and Resource Files

The format of dialog boxes (like menus) is not placed in a Windows program. Instead, it's put into a *resource file* that is compiled and linked with your application. To use a resource file you must add the name of the resource file to your project file, as if it were another program module. BARTEST2.RC (shown later) provides the resource file for the bar chart application, BARTEST2.

The resource file describes the dialog box and its elements. The following three statements form the top of the dialog box definition in BARTEST2.RC. The number 200 is an I.D that the application and Windows use to identify the dialog box. The four other numbers in the first statement provide the dialog box's position and the next line its caption. The third statement specifies the form of the dialog box. The Resource Workshop typically generates these statements for you when you interactively create a dialog box.

```
200 DIALOG 24, 24, 168, 146
STYLE DS_MODALFRAME | WS_POPUP | WS_CAPTION | WS_SYSMENU
CAPTION "Bar Graph Values"
```

Listed after these statements are the various components of the dialog box, called *controls*. The dialog box uses four types of controls:

- Static fields that display text, such as user prompts
- Edit fields that enable the user to enter text
- Button controls for the OK and Cancel buttons
- Rectangle controls that display black boxes

The text fields begin with the command **LTEXT**, signaling that text is to be displayed left justified. For instance, the first statement after the dialog box's header declares a static text control. It displays the string "Bar Graph Title:" at the position indicated by the last four numbers in the following statement:

```
LTEXT "Bar Graph Title:", -1, 6, 8, 52, 8
```

The -1 is a placeholder for the control's I.D. By setting it to -1, we're saying that we don't care about the text field's I.D; we're not going to refer to the text string in the program, so we don't need an I.D for it.

The **EDITTEXT** fields are used for user input. The input field that corresponds with the bar graph's title, for instance, has the form:

```
EDITTEXT 201, 63, 6, 98, 12
```

Again, the last four numbers indicate the position of the edit field. The first number, 201 in this case, is the edit field's I.D. There are nine edit fields: one for the chart title, four for the bar values, and four for the bar labels.

The BARTEST2.RC file also includes statements for two buttons: an OK button and a Cancel button. The OK button is defined as the default button:

```
DEFPUSHBUTTON "&OK", 1, 48, 129, 30, 14
PUSHBUTTON "&Cancel", 2, 94, 129, 30, 14
```

Finally, the dialog box contains four rectangles that are drawn around the four groups of bar values:

```
CONTROL "", -1, "STATIC", SS_BLACKFRAME | WS_CHILD | WS_VISIBLE,
    6, 27, 156, 20
CONTROL "", -1, "STATIC", SS_BLACKFRAME | WS_CHILD | WS_VISIBLE,
    6, 52, 156, 20
CONTROL "", -1, "STATIC", SS_BLACKFRAME | WS_CHILD | WS_VISIBLE,
    6, 77, 156, 20
CONTROL "", -1, "STATIC", SS_BLACKFRAME | WS_CHILD | WS_VISIBLE,
    6, 102, 156, 20
```

Connecting Dialogs Boxes with OWL

Commands that are placed in the resource file tell Windows how to create the dialog box, but we also need to give it functionality. This is where OWL steps in. A dialog box object derived from OWL's **TDialog** class is used to associate the dialog box with OWL and connect it with your code. The **TDialog** class provides all of the *default* behavior for a dialog box. We have, however, derived the class **TValuesDlg** from **TDialog** so that we can tell OWL about our particular editing controls.

The edit controls are used to enter the values for the bars, their labels, and the title of the chart. Each editing field and the text in the dialog box is added as a control to the dialog box in the resource file. In addition, the editing fields are added as objects to the **TValuesDlg** object, within its constructor, using statements such as:

```
new TEdit(this, 201, sizeof(TransferStruct.Title));
```

The **TEdit** class is also included in OWL and handles all the details for an editing field. The **this** pointer tells the **TEdit** object which object **TEdit** is being added to—in this case, a **TValuesDlg**. The second parameter is the I.D corresponding with the edit control statement in the resource file. In this case, the number 201 corresponds with the edit control statement listed in the last section.

The third parameter in **TEdit**'s constructor says how big to make the editing field. It reveals the mechanism we'll use for accessing the data in the edit fields. Here we're using a special feature built into OWL, called a *Transfer Buffer*, that automatically copies data to and from the dialog box. All we need to do is provide OWL with a structure that can hold the data from the dialog box. This is the purpose of the following structure:

```
struct TTransferStruct {
  char Title[TITLELEN];
  char Val1[INTLEN];
  char String1[STRLEN];
  char Val2[INTLEN];
  char String2[STRLEN];
  char Val3[INTLEN];
  char String3[STRLEN];
  char Val4[INTLEN];
  char String4[STRLEN];
};
```

As you can see, each field in **TTransferStruct** corresponds with one editing field in the dialog box. The **TransferStruct** field in the **TValuesDlg** dialog box is set to a **TTransferStruct** structure that is initialized in **TBarGraphWindow**'s constructor.

Adding a Menu

The previous code shows how the various components of a dialog box are hooked into an OWL program, but we're still not done. We need a way for the user to activate the dialog box from within our application. For this purpose, we'll add a single menu item, which contains the string "Bar Chart," to the program. Integrating the menu into our program requires two steps. First, we must add the appropriate commands to the resource file:

```
100 MENU
{
 MENUITEM "&Bar Chart", 101
}
```

The 101 is the menu item's identifier, which is used internally when the menu option is selected. Windows uses the identifier to differentiate between each menu selection. This assumes, however, that each menu option within the application has a unique identifier.

The second step in hooking a menu into an application is to load the menu into the application. For this, OWL provides the **AssignMenu** function in the **TFrameWindow** class to perform this task. You can find the call to **AssignMenu** in **TBarGraphApp**'s **InitMainWindow** function:

```
MainWindow->AssignMenu(100);      // Set up the menu
```

The 100 in **AssignMenu** corresponds to the 100 used in the menu's declaration in the resource file. Notice that the menu is assigned to the **MainWindow** variable, which **InitMainWindow** defines as a **TFrameWindow**.

We'll use the function **CmBars**, defined in the **TBarGraphWindow** class, to respond to the menu's single item. It's defined in the **TBarGraphWindow** class as:

```
void CmBars();
```

Notice that the function is declared without any parameters. This is OWL's format for functions that are to respond to menu options. The **CmBars** function is also included in the message response macro located after **TBarGraphWindow**:

```
DEFINE_RESPONSE_TABLE1(TBarGraphWindow, TWindow)
  EV_COMMAND(101, CmBars),
```

The EV_COMMAND macro ties the function **CmBars** with the identifier 101—the identifier for the Bar Chart menu option. As a result, when the Bar Chart menu item is selected, **CmBars** is called.

The **CmBars** function, in turn, pops up the dialog box by calling Windows' **Execute** function. If the **Execute** function returns **IDOK**—meaning that the user has pressed the OK button—then its data is used to define a new bar graph. The following code excerpt, for instance, illustrates how **CmBars** copies the dialog box's data, using the fields of **TransferStruct**, to the application:

```
TValuesDlg* ValuesDlg = new TValuesDlg(this, "ValuesDlg");
if ((ValuesDlg->Execute()) == IDOK) {
  BarGraph->SetTitle(TransferStruct.Title);
  BarGraph->NewGraph();   // Initialize the bar chart's values
  if (strcmp(TransferStruct.Val1, "") != 0) {
    BarGraph->AddBar(atoi(TransferStruct.Val1),
      TransferStruct.String1);
```

The top statement in the **if** statement, for example, sets the title of the bar chart to the **Title** field of the dialog box. The other **if** statements test whether the numeric fields in the dialog box are empty. If so, these fields are ignored. If, on the other hand, the fields contain values, bars are added to the bar graph for each field.

Compiling and Using the Program

 Compiling BARTEST2.CPP requires that you include the files BARTEST2.CPP, BARGRAPH.CPP, and BARTEST2.RC in your project file. Then, to create a bar chart, select the Bar Chart menu option, which brings up the dialog box that allows you to enter your own chart values. You must fill in the dialog box fields from top to bottom, although you don't need to supply a title or labels for the bars.

Extending the Program

Currently the **TBarChart** class only accommodates four bars in a single chart. This limitation is forced by the constant **MAXBARS**, which is set to 4, and the number of fields provided in the dialog box. You may want to modify the program so that a chart can have more bars.

Other ways to extend BARTEST2.CPP include adding a dialog box to specify the colors of the bars, backdrop, strings, or window background. You might also want to modify the program so that you can read or write the chart information directly from a database or spreadsheet file.

• BARTEST2.RC

```
/* BARTEST2.RC: Resource file for BARTEST2.CPP. */

100 MENU
{
 MENUITEM "&Bar Chart", 101
}

200 DIALOG 24, 24, 168, 146
STYLE DS_MODALFRAME | WS_POPUP | WS_CAPTION | WS_SYSMENU
CAPTION "Bar Graph Values"
{
 LTEXT "Bar Graph Title:", -1, 6, 8, 52, 8
 EDITTEXT 201, 63, 6, 98, 12
 LTEXT "Bar 1 Value:", -1, 12, 33, 42, 8
 EDITTEXT 202, 56, 31, 24, 12
 LTEXT "Name:", -1, 86, 34, 22, 8
 EDITTEXT 203, 110, 31, 46, 12
 LTEXT "Bar 2 Value:", -1, 12, 58, 42, 8
 EDITTEXT 204, 56, 56, 24, 12
 LTEXT "Name:", -1, 86, 58, 22, 8
 EDITTEXT 205, 110, 56, 46, 12
 LTEXT "Bar 3 Value:", -1, 12, 83, 42, 8
 EDITTEXT 206, 56, 81, 24, 12
 LTEXT "Name:", -1, 86, 83, 22, 8
 EDITTEXT 207, 110, 81, 46, 12
 LTEXT "Bar 4 Value:", -1, 12, 108, 42, 8
 EDITTEXT 208, 56, 106, 24, 12
 LTEXT "Name:", -1, 86, 108, 22, 8
 EDITTEXT 209, 110, 106, 46, 12
 DEFPUSHBUTTON "&OK", 1, 48, 129, 30, 14
 PUSHBUTTON "&Cancel", 2, 94, 129, 30, 14
 CONTROL "", -1, "STATIC", SS_BLACKFRAME | WS_CHILD | WS_VISIBLE,
    6, 27, 156, 20
 CONTROL "", -1, "STATIC", SS_BLACKFRAME | WS_CHILD | WS_VISIBLE,
    6, 52, 156, 20
 CONTROL "", -1, "STATIC", SS_BLACKFRAME | WS_CHILD | WS_VISIBLE,
    6, 77, 156, 20
```

```
CONTROL "", -1, "STATIC", SS_BLACKFRAME | WS_CHILD | WS_VISIBLE,
    6, 102, 156, 20
}
```

• BARTEST2.CPP

```cpp
// BARTEST2.CPP: Interactively allows you to create a bar graph.

#include <owl\applicat.h>
#include <owl\framewin.h>
#include <owl\dc.h>
#include <owl\dialog.h>
#include <owl\edit.h>
#include <stdio.h>
#include <stdlib.h>
#include <string.h>
#include "bargraph.h"

// Structure used to transfer data to and from the dialog box
struct TTransferStruct {
  char Title[TITLELEN];
  char Val1[INTLEN];
  char String1[STRLEN];
  char Val2[INTLEN];
  char String2[STRLEN];
  char Val3[INTLEN];
  char String3[STRLEN];
  char Val4[INTLEN];
  char String4[STRLEN];
};

// OWL class used with the dialog box
class TValuesDlg : public TDialog {
public:
  TValuesDlg(TWindow* parent, const char* far name);
};

TTransferStruct TransferStruct;

class TBarGraphWindow : public TWindow {
  TBarGraph *BarGraph;       // Pointer to a bar graph object
public:
  TValuesDlg *ValuesDlg;    // The dialog box object
  TBarGraphWindow(TWindow *parent, const char far* title)
    : TWindow(parent, title) {
    BarGraph = new TBarGraph("");  // Create a bar graph
  }
  virtual ~TBarGraphWindow() { delete BarGraph; }
  void SetupWindow();
  void Paint(TDC& dc, BOOL, TRect&);
  void CmBars();
  void EvSize(UINT, TSize&);
```

```
    DECLARE_RESPONSE_TABLE(TBarGraphWindow);
};

DEFINE_RESPONSE_TABLE1(TBarGraphWindow, TWindow)
  EV_COMMAND(101, CmBars),
  EV_WM_SIZE,
END_RESPONSE_TABLE;

void TBarGraphWindow::SetupWindow()
{
  TWindow::SetupWindow();
  memset(&TransferStruct, 0x00, sizeof(TransferStruct));
}

// Paint the bar graph
void TBarGraphWindow::Paint(TDC& dc, BOOL, TRect&)
{
  RECT rect;
  ::GetClientRect(HWindow, &rect);
  int sizeX = rect.right / 8;       int sizeY = rect.bottom / 8;
  ::FillRect(dc, &rect, HBRUSH(GetStockObject(WHITE_BRUSH)));
  BarGraph->Display(dc, sizeX, sizeY,
    rect.right-sizeX, rect.bottom-sizeY);
}

// Respond to the "Bar Chart" menu option. Retrieve the user
// input from the dialog box. Force the window to repaint itself
// with the new settings.
void TBarGraphWindow::CmBars()
{
  TValuesDlg* ValuesDlg = new TValuesDlg(this, "ValuesDlg");
  if ((ValuesDlg->Execute()) == IDOK) {
    BarGraph->SetTitle(TransferStruct.Title);
    BarGraph->NewGraph();    // Initialize the bar chart's values
    if (strcmp(TransferStruct.Val1, "") != 0) {
      BarGraph->AddBar(atoi(TransferStruct.Val1),
        TransferStruct.String1);
      if (strcmp(TransferStruct.Val2, "") != 0) {
        BarGraph->AddBar(atoi(TransferStruct.Val2),
          TransferStruct.String2);
        if (strcmp(TransferStruct.Val3, "") != 0) {
          BarGraph->AddBar(atoi(TransferStruct.Val3),
            TransferStruct.String3);
          if (strcmp(TransferStruct.Val4, "") != 0) {
            BarGraph->AddBar(atoi(TransferStruct.Val4),
              TransferStruct.String4);
          }
        }
      }
    }
    ::InvalidateRect(HWindow, 0, FALSE);
  }
}
```

```
// When the window is resized, repaint the bar graph
void TBarGraphWindow::EvSize(UINT, TSize&)
{
  ::InvalidateRect(HWindow, 0, FALSE);
}

// Associate each of the editing fields in the dialog box with OWL
TValuesDlg::TValuesDlg(TWindow* parent, const char* far name)
  : TDialog(parent, name), TWindow(parent)
{
  new TEdit(this, 201, sizeof(TransferStruct.Title));
  new TEdit(this, 202, sizeof(TransferStruct.Val1));
  new TEdit(this, 203, sizeof(TransferStruct.String1));
  new TEdit(this, 204, sizeof(TransferStruct.Val2));
  new TEdit(this, 205, sizeof(TransferStruct.String2));
  new TEdit(this, 206, sizeof(TransferStruct.Val3));
  new TEdit(this, 207, sizeof(TransferStruct.String3));
  new TEdit(this, 208, sizeof(TransferStruct.Val4));
  new TEdit(this, 209, sizeof(TransferStruct.String4));
  SetTransferBuffer(&TransferStruct);
}

class TBarGraphApp : public TApplication {
public:
  TBarGraphApp() : TApplication() { }
  void InitMainWindow();
};

void TBarGraphApp::InitMainWindow()
{
  MainWindow = new TFrameWindow(0, "BAR GRAPH",
    new TBarGraphWindow(0, ""));
  MainWindow->AssignMenu(100);        // Set up the menu
}

int OwlMain(int /*argc*/, char* /*argv*/[])
{
  return TBarGraphApp().Run();
}
```

COIN GRAPHS

One variation on the idea of a bar graph is a coin graph, which uses small images stacked like coins, rather than bars. In fact, coin graphs are so similar to bar graphs that we'll derive a coin graph class from **TBarGraph**. This will enable us to inherit many of the details of creating a coin chart from those we developed for bar charts. This new class, called **TCoinGraph**, is included in the files COINGRPH.H and COINGRPH.CPP (which appear later in this chapter).

A test program, COINTEST.CPP generates the coin graph shown in Figure 9.5. The chart represents the sales of computer monitors for four computer salespeople. To make the chart interesting, a small picture of a monitor is used to

Figure 9.5 COINTEST.CPP displays a bar graph using coins instead of bars.

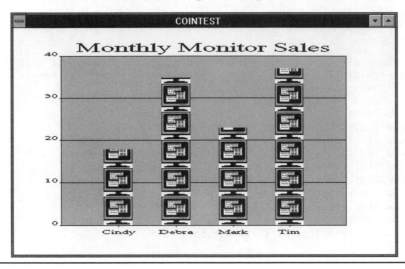

create a stack representing a sales total. The picture is actually a small bitmap created with Borland's Resource Workshop.

Here's the class definition for **TCoinGraph**:

```
class TCoinGraph : public TBarGraph {
public:
  HBITMAP HCoinFig;
  HBRUSH HCoinBrush;
  TCoinGraph(char *title) : TBarGraph(title) { }
  virtual void DrawBar(HDC hDC, int left, int top, int right, int bottom);
  void DisplayCoin(HDC hDC, int x, int y, int wd, int ht);
};
```

The principal change we need to make to **TBarGraph** is to override **DrawBar** so that we can display a stack of bitmaps rather than simple rectangles. We've also added the member function **DisplayCoin** and the variables **hCoinFig** and **hCoinBrush** to draw the bitmaps.

The bitmap image was created with the Resource Workshop and stored in the file COINFIG.BMP. It's loaded into the application in the COINTEST.CPP **Paint** function:

```
CoinGraph->HCoinFig = LoadBitmap(GetModule()->GetInstance(), "coinfig");
```

The name of the bitmap is actually specified in the resource file COINTEST.RC, which associates the internal name "coinfig" with the real filename COINFIG.BMP. In fact, the resource file only has one statement:

```
COINFIG BITMAP coinfig.bmp
```

You can add your own bitmap, but if you do, you must ensure that the name of the icon file in COINTEST.RC corresponds with the bitmap's actual filename.

The **DrawBar** function, as mentioned earlier, is overridden to display each stack of coin images. The function displays as many square bitmap images as it can within the allotted height of the bar. Since the height of the bitmap images might not divide evenly into the height of the bar, a clipping region is first set up so that the topmost bitmap is trimmed to size, if necessary:

```
// Save the current clipping region
RECT clipRect;
GetClipBox(hDC, &clipRect);
HRGN hRgn = CreateRectRgn(left, top, right, bottom);
SelectClipRgn(hDC, hRgn);
```

The following **for** loop calls **DisplayCoin** to display the bitmap images. After the bitmaps are painted, the clipping region is restored.

```
for (j=pictHeight; j<=(bottom-top)+pictHeight; j+=pictHeight)
  DisplayCoin(hDC, left, bottom-1-j, right-left, right-left);
// Restore the clipping region to the clip area
hRgn = CreateRectRgn(clipRect.left, clipRect.top,
  clipRect.right, clipRect.bottom);
SelectClipRgn(hDC, hRgn);
```

The size of the bitmap image depends on the width of the bar. For convenience, the height of each bitmap image is set equal to its width. The GDI's **StretchBlt** function is then used to stretch or compress the image to the desired size:

```
void TCoinGraph::DisplayCoin(HDC hDC, int x, int y,
  int wd, int ht)
{
  // Draw the bitmap once as a test
  HDC hMemDC = CreateCompatibleDC(hDC);
  HBITMAP OldBitmap = HBITMAP(SelectObject(hMemDC, HCoinFig));
  BITMAP bm;
  GetObject(HCoinFig, sizeof(BITMAP), (LPSTR)&bm);
  StretchBlt(hDC, x, y, wd, ht,
    hMemDC, 0, 0, bm.bmWidth, bm.bmHeight, SRCCOPY);
  SelectObject(hMemDC, OldBitmap);
  DeleteDC(hMemDC);
}
```

Compiling COINTEST.CPP

To compile COINTEST.CPP you must have a project file that includes BARGRAPH.CPP, COINGRPH.CPP, COINTEST.CPP, and COINTEST.RC.

• COINGRPH.H

```
// COINGRPH.H: Header file for COINGRPH.CPP.

#include "bargraph.h"

// The coin chart class is derived from the bar graph class
class TCoinGraph : public TBarGraph {
public:
  HBITMAP HCoinFig;
  HBRUSH HCoinBrush;
  TCoinGraph(char *title) : TBarGraph(title) { }
  virtual void DrawBar(HDC hDC, int left, int top, int right, int bottom);
  void DisplayCoin(HDC hDC, int x, int y, int wd, int ht);
};
```

• COINGRPH.CPP

```
// COINGRPH.CPP: Implements a coin graph object.

#include <windows.h>
#include "bargraph.h"
#include "coingrph.h"

// High-level member function that you should call to display
// a coin graph
void TCoinGraph::DisplayCoin(HDC hDC, int x, int y,
  int wd, int ht)
{
  // Draw the bitmap once as a test
  HDC hMemDC = CreateCompatibleDC(hDC);
  HBITMAP OldBitmap = HBITMAP(SelectObject(hMemDC, HCoinFig));
  BITMAP bm;
  GetObject(HCoinFig, sizeof(BITMAP), (LPSTR)&bm);
  StretchBlt(hDC, x, y, wd, ht,
    hMemDC, 0, 0, bm.bmWidth, bm.bmHeight, SRCCOPY);
  SelectObject(hMemDC, OldBitmap);
  DeleteDC(hMemDC);
}

// Draws a single pie slice
void TCoinGraph::DrawBar(HDC hDC, int left, int top,
  int right, int bottom)
{
  int j, pictHeight = (right - left);

  // Save the current clipping region
  RECT clipRect;
  GetClipBox(hDC, &clipRect);
  HRGN hRgn = CreateRectRgn(left, top, right, bottom);
  SelectClipRgn(hDC, hRgn);

  for (j=pictHeight; j<=(bottom-top)+pictHeight; j+=pictHeight)
    DisplayCoin(hDC, left, bottom-1-j, right-left, right-left);
```

```
    // Restore the clipping region to the clip area
    hRgn = CreateRectRgn(clipRect.left, clipRect.top,
      clipRect.right, clipRect.bottom);
    SelectClipRgn(hDC, hRgn);
}
```

• COINTEST.RC

```
/* COINTEST.RC: Resource file for COINTEST.CPP */

COINFIG BITMAP coinfig.bmp
```

• COINTEST.CPP

```
// COINTEST.CPP: Displays a coin graph.

#include <owl\applicat.h>
#include <owl\framewin.h>
#include <owl\dc.h>
#include "coingrph.h"

class TCoinGraphWindow : public TWindow {
  TCoinGraph *CoinGraph;
public:
  TCoinGraphWindow(TWindow *parent, const char* title)
    : TWindow(parent, title) {
    CoinGraph = new TCoinGraph("Monthly Monitor Sales");
    CoinGraph->AddBar(18, "Cindy");
    CoinGraph->AddBar(35, "Debra");
    CoinGraph->AddBar(23, "Mark");
    CoinGraph->AddBar(37, "Tim");
  };
  void SetupWindow();
  void Paint(TDC& dc, BOOL, TRect&);
  void EvSize(UINT, TSize&);

  DECLARE_RESPONSE_TABLE(TCoinGraphWindow);
};

DEFINE_RESPONSE_TABLE1(TCoinGraphWindow, TWindow)
  EV_WM_SIZE,
END_RESPONSE_TABLE;

class TCoinGraphApp : public TApplication {
public:
  TCoinGraphApp() : TApplication() { }
  void InitMainWindow();
};

void TCoinGraphWindow::SetupWindow()
{
  TWindow::SetupWindow();
```

```
    // Load the bitmap to be used for the coin chart.
    // The bitmap should be in the file COINFIG.BMP.
    CoinGraph->HCoinFig = LoadBitmap(GetModule()->GetInstance(), "coinfig");
    if (CoinGraph->HCoinFig == NULL) {
      ::MessageBox(HWindow, "Could not load bitmap file: COINFIG.BMP",
        0, MB_OK);
      PostQuitMessage(0);
    }
}

void TCoinGraphWindow::Paint(TDC& dc, BOOL, TRect&)
{
  RECT rect;
  ::GetClientRect(HWindow, &rect);
  int sizeX = rect.right / 8;      int sizeY = rect.bottom / 8;
  // Erase the window before painting the chart
  ::FillRect(dc, &rect, HBRUSH(GetStockObject(WHITE_BRUSH)));
  CoinGraph->Display(dc, sizeX, sizeY, rect.right-sizeX,
    rect.bottom-sizeY);
}

// When the window is resized, invalidate the whole window so that the
// window is completely repainted. However, pass FALSE to InvalidateRect
// so that the background won't be erased. The Paint routine will white
// out the background to reduce any screen flicker.
void TCoinGraphWindow::EvSize(UINT, TSize&)
{
  ::InvalidateRect(HWindow, 0, FALSE);
}

void TCoinGraphApp::InitMainWindow()
{
  MainWindow = new TFrameWindow(0, "COINTEST",
    new TCoinGraphWindow(0, ""));
  MainWindow->AssignMenu(100);    // Set up the menu
}

int OwlMain(int /*argc*/, char* /*argv*/[])
{
  return TCoinGraphApp().Run();
}
```

THREE-DIMENSIONAL BAR CHARTS

The bar chart applications developed earlier are attractive, but can we do better? Yes. With a little creative programming, we can handcraft a professional-looking, *three-dimensional* bar chart, as shown in Figure 9.6.

Unfortunately, Windows does not have an all-in-one function that paints three-dimensional bar charts, we have to build our own. One solution is provided in the **TThreeDBar** class included in the source files 3DBAR.H and

Figure 9.6 3DTEST.CPP displays this three-dimensional bar graph.

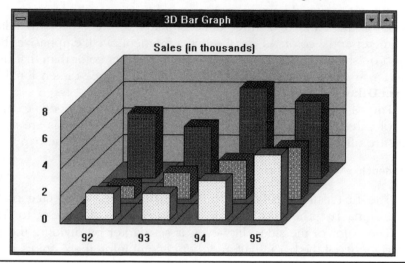

3DBAR.CPP. Like the **TBarChart** class, this new class contains all the functionality we need for painting a three-dimensional bar chart.

As you might guess, **TThreeDBar** is a bit more complex than its two-dimensional counterpart. It supplies the logic for drawing each three-dimensional bar, creating a three-dimensional backdrop, and writing all the necessary labels on the chart. We'll also write **TThreeDBar** so that we can have more than one row of bars. Here's the class definition for **TThreeDBar**:

```
class TThreeDBar {
public:
  static int BarValues[3][4];    // 3 rows of 4 values maximum
  static char *BarLabels[4];
  static char Title[23];
  static int NumRules;
  static int NumValues;
  static int NUM_GRAPHS;
  int NumGraphs;
  int MaxBarValue;
  static COLORREF Colors[3];
  TThreeDBar() { }
  void ThreeDBar(HDC hDC, int left, int top,
    int right, int bottom, COLORREF color);
  void Display(HDC hDC, int left, int top, int right, int bottom);
  void DrawChart(HDC hDC, int left, int top, int right, int bottom);
  int GetMax();
};
```

Adding the Third Dimension

For two-dimensional bars, we only needed to specify the location, height, and width of the bar. For a three-dimensional bar, we'll need to add a depth parameter and a color. As you'll see in a moment, we'll emphasize the sense of depth by shading the sides of the bar with a darker color than that used on the front. You can locate the code for drawing each three-dimensional bar in the **ThreeDBar** member function.

Part of the illusion of depth is created by adding polygons to the side and top of a rectangle, as shown in Figure 9.7. These polygons are sized so that they are offset by 25 percent of the width of the front of the bar.

```
int depth = (right - left) / 4;
```

The first call to **Polygon** in **ThreeDBar** draws the face of the three-dimensional bar. The fill color of the bar is set to the color passed to **ThreeDBar**.

The color of the sides, however, is set darker by dividing the RGB color components of the bar in half and then recombining these colors into a brush:

```
BYTE red = GetRValue(color) / 2;
BYTE green = GetGValue(color) / 2;
BYTE blue = GetBValue(color) / 2;
hBrush = CreateSolidBrush(RGB(red, green, blue));
hOldBrush = HBRUSH(SelectObject(hDC, hBrush));
```

The top and right sides of the three-dimensional bar are then displayed by calls to **Polygon**.

Figure 9.7 The dimensions of a three-dimensional bar.

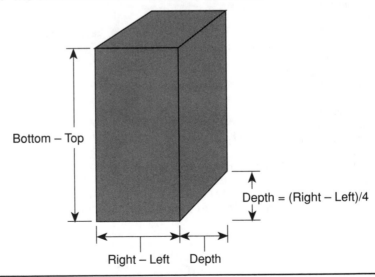

Bottom – Top

Depth = (Right – Left)/4

Right – Left   Depth

A Three-Dimensional Backdrop

Part of **TThreeDBar**'s complexity is due to its three-dimensional backdrop. The geometry of the backdrop is similar to that used to draw a three-dimensional bar. In fact, in many respects the backdrop is one of the three-dimensional bars turned over. Again, two different brushes are used to enhance the sense of depth. The vertical panels are painted with a light gray brush (**LTGRAY_BRUSH**) and the floor of the backdrop with a darker brush (**GRAY_BRUSH**).

A few comments about the code are necessary. Notice that the backside of the backdrop is drawn using **Rectangle** and that the left and bottom panels are drawn with **Polygon**. Because these two functions align pixels differently, we must slightly adjust for the bottom and right edges of the panel drawn with **Rectangle**.

```
Rectangle(hDC, left+dOffset, top-dOffset,
  right+dOffset+1, bottom-dOffset+1);
```

We could have used **Polygon** throughout and avoided this. However, doing so would have required a few more statements to load the rectangle's coordinates into an array and pass them along to **Polygon**.

The Finishing Touches

We still need to add a title and a set of labels to our chart. To keep our task simple, we'll use the default font rather than dynamically scaling a font. In addition, we've written the code so that several rows of bars can be displayed. As a result, the **BarValues** array is now a two-dimensional array. Also, the function **GetMax** is provided to search the whole **BarValues** array for the greatest Y value.

The 3DTEST.CPP program, tests the three-dimensional bar charting class. It displays the chart shown earlier in Figure 9.5. The code is fairly straightforward, so we won't go into it here.

Compiling 3DBAR.CPP

To compile 3DBAR.CPP, you'll need to include the files 3DBAR.CPP and 3DTEST.CPP in your project file.

• 3DBAR.H

```
// 3DBAR.H: Header file for 3DBAR.CPP.

#ifndef THREEDBAR
#define THREEDBAR

#include <windows.h>
```

```
class TThreeDBar {
public:
  static int BarValues[3][4];    // 3 rows of 4 values maximum
  static char *BarLabels[4];
  static char Title[23];
  static int NumRules;
  static int NumValues;
  static int NUM_GRAPHS;
  int NumGraphs;
  int MaxBarValue;
  static COLORREF Colors[3];
  TThreeDBar() { }
  void ThreeDBar(HDC hDC, int left, int top,
    int right, int bottom, COLORREF color);
  void Display(HDC hDC, int left, int top, int right, int bottom);
  void DrawChart(HDC hDC, int left, int top, int right, int bottom);
  int GetMax();
};
#endif
```

• 3DBAR.CPP

```
// 3DBAR.CPP: Displays a three-dimensional bar graph.

#include <stdio.h>
#include <string.h>
#include "3dbar.h"

// High-level routine to display a three-dimensional bar chart
void TThreeDBar::Display(HDC hDC, int left, int top, int right, int bottom)
{
  if (NumRules < 0) NumRules = 1;  // Make sure NumRules is > zero

  // Determine a maximum value for the chart scale. It should be at least
  // as large as the largest list of values and a multiple of the number
  // of rules that the user desires. NumRules should not be greater than
  // MaxBarValue.
  MaxBarValue = GetMax();      // Get the largest bar value
  while ((MaxBarValue % NumRules) != 0)
    MaxBarValue++;
  DrawChart(hDC, left, top, right, bottom);
}

#define HASH_WIDTH 8      // Amount to offset pixels
#define THREEDDEPTH 0.25  // Percentage amount of depth to use
#define ADDEDDEPTH 0.025  // Spacing around bars

// Draws the chart's backdrop and the bars themselves
void TThreeDBar::DrawChart(HDC hDC, int left, int top,
  int right, int bottom)
{
  double scale;
  int i, j, height, incr;
```

```
            char buffer[10];
            int offset;      // Draw a horizontal rules this many pixels apart

            // Make a border around the backdrop
            SelectObject(hDC, GetStockObject(LTGRAY_BRUSH));

            // Draw backdrop of graph. The depth of the frame depends
            // on how rows of graphs there are and the width of the
            // graph itself.
            int bdOffset = (right - left) / NumValues *
              (THREEDDEPTH + 2 * ADDEDDEPTH);
            int dOffset = bdOffset * NumGraphs;
            // Reset the height of the bar graph based on the number
            // of rows
            top += dOffset;
            right -= dOffset;

            // Note the +1 added to the right and bottom sides of this
            // rectangle. They are required so that the rectangle
            // will line up with the polygons drawn next.
            Rectangle(hDC, left+dOffset, top-dOffset,
              right+dOffset+1, bottom-dOffset+1);

            POINT poly[4];
            poly[0].x = left;           poly[0].y = top;
            poly[1].x = left+dOffset;   poly[1].y = top-dOffset;
            poly[2].x = left+dOffset;   poly[2].y = bottom-dOffset;
            poly[3].x = left;           poly[3].y = bottom;
            Polygon(hDC, poly, 4);

            poly[0].x = left;           poly[0].y = bottom;
            poly[1].x = left+dOffset;   poly[1].y = bottom-dOffset;
            poly[2].x = right+dOffset;  poly[2].y = bottom-dOffset;
            poly[3].x = right;          poly[3].y = bottom;
            // Draw the bottom dark gray
            SelectObject(hDC, GetStockObject(GRAY_BRUSH));
            Polygon(hDC, poly, 4);

            // Write the title above the chart
            SetTextAlign(hDC,TA_CENTER | TA_BOTTOM);
            TextOut(hDC, (left+right+dOffset)/2, top-2-dOffset,
              Title, strlen(Title));

            offset = (bottom - top) / NumRules;
            incr = MaxBarValue / NumRules;

            // Use the default font for labeling the horizontal hash marks
            SetTextAlign(hDC, TA_RIGHT | TA_BASELINE);
            for (i=0; i<NumRules; i++) {
              // Draw horizontal rules on back of frame
              MoveToEx(hDC, left+dOffset, top-dOffset+i*offset, 0);
              LineTo(hDC, right+dOffset, top-dOffset+i*offset);
              // Draw rules on left side of frame
              MoveToEx(hDC, left, top+i*offset, 0);
```

```
      LineTo(hDC, left+dOffset, top-dOffset+i*offset);
      // Display scale text to left of frame
      sprintf(buffer, "%d", incr*(NumRules-i));
      TextOut(hDC, left-2*HASH_WIDTH,
        top+i*offset, buffer, strlen(buffer));
  }
  // Write out the "0" value by itself, without a horizontal line
  TextOut(hDC, left-2*HASH_WIDTH, top+NumRules*offset, "0", 1);

  // Write out the values for the horizontal axis.
  // Figure the amount to scale all bars.
  scale = (bottom - top) / MaxBarValue;
  offset = (right - left) / NumValues;

  // Use the default font for labeling the bars
  SetTextAlign(hDC, TA_CENTER | TA_TOP);
  for (i=0; i<NumValues; i++) {
    TextOut(hDC, left+i*offset+offset/2, bottom+HASH_WIDTH+2,
      BarLabels[i], strlen(BarLabels[i]));
    // Draw lines between the three-dimensional bars.
    // Don't draw one at the end though. It's not needed.
    if (i < NumValues-1) {
      MoveToEx(hDC, left+(i+1)*offset, bottom, 0);
      LineTo(hDC, left+(i+1)*offset+dOffset, bottom-dOffset);
    }
  }
  // Draw the bars
  for (j=0; j<NumGraphs; j++) {
    for (i=0; i<NumValues; i++) {
      height = BarValues[j][i] * scale;
      ThreeDBar(hDC,
        left+i*offset+dOffset-bdOffset*j+bdOffset/4,
        bottom-height-dOffset+(j+1)*bdOffset-bdOffset/4,
        left+i*offset+offset/2+dOffset-bdOffset*j+bdOffset/4,
        bottom-dOffset+(j+1)*bdOffset-bdOffset/4, Colors[j]);
    }
    // Draw a horizontal line between the rows of bars. Don't
    // draw a line for the last set, however. It's not needed.
    if (j < NumGraphs-1) {
      MoveToEx(hDC, left+dOffset-bdOffset*(j+1),
        bottom-dOffset+bdOffset*(j+1), 0);
      LineTo(hDC, right+dOffset-bdOffset*(j+1),
        bottom-dOffset+bdOffset*(j+1));
    }
  }
}

// Display a three-dimensional bar. The left, top, right, and
// bottom variables specify the pixel boundaries of the bar's face.
void TThreeDBar::ThreeDBar(HDC hDC, int left, int top,
  int right, int bottom, COLORREF color)
{
  POINT poly[4];
  int depth = (right - left) / 4;
```

```
    // Draw front of three-dimensional bar
    poly[0].x = left;        poly[0].y = top;
    poly[1].x = right;       poly[1].y = top;
    poly[2].x = right;       poly[2].y = bottom;
    poly[3].x = left;        poly[3].y = bottom;
    HBRUSH hBrush = CreateSolidBrush(color);
    HBRUSH hOldBrush = HBRUSH(SelectObject(hDC, hBrush));
    Polygon(hDC, poly, 4);
    SelectObject(hDC, hOldBrush);
    DeleteObject(hBrush);

    // Make the color a little darker for the top and sides
    // by cutting the brush's RGB color components in half
    BYTE red = GetRValue(color) / 2;
    BYTE green = GetGValue(color) / 2;
    BYTE blue = GetBValue(color) / 2;
    hBrush = CreateSolidBrush(RGB(red, green, blue));
    hOldBrush = HBRUSH(SelectObject(hDC, hBrush));

    // Draw top of three-dimensional bar
    poly[0].x = left;        poly[0].y = top;
    poly[1].x = left+depth;  poly[1].y = top-depth;
    poly[2].x = right+depth; poly[2].y = top-depth;
    poly[3].x = right;       poly[3].y = top;
    Polygon(hDC, poly, 4);
    // Draw side of three-dimensional bar
    poly[0].x = right;       poly[0].y = top;
    poly[1].x = right+depth; poly[1].y = top-depth;
    poly[2].x = right+depth; poly[2].y = bottom-depth;
    poly[3].x = right;       poly[3].y = bottom;
    Polygon(hDC, poly, 4);
    SelectObject(hDC, hOldBrush);
    DeleteObject(hBrush);
}

// Find and return the largest value in the array of bar values
int TThreeDBar::GetMax()
{
    int i, j, largest=1;

    for (j=0; j<NumGraphs; j++)
      for (i=0; i<NumValues; i++)
        if (BarValues[j][i] > largest)
      largest = BarValues[j][i];
    return largest;
}
```

• 3DTEST.CPP

```
// 3DTEST.CPP: Displays a three-dimensional bar graph.

#include <owl\applicat.h>
#include <owl\framewin.h>
```

```
#include <owl\dialog.h>
#include <owl\dc.h>
#include <stdio.h>
#include <string.h>
#include "3dbar.h"

class TThreeDBarWindow : public TWindow {
public:
  TThreeDBar* ThreeDGraph;    // A three-dimensional graph object
  TThreeDBarWindow(TWindow* parent, const char* title)
    : TWindow(parent, title) {
    ThreeDGraph = new TThreeDBar();
  }
  virtual ~TThreeDBarWindow() { delete ThreeDGraph; }
  void Paint(TDC& dc, BOOL, TRect&);
  void EvSize(UINT, TSize&);

  DECLARE_RESPONSE_TABLE(TThreeDBarWindow);
};

DEFINE_RESPONSE_TABLE1(TThreeDBarWindow, TWindow)
  EV_WM_SIZE,
END_RESPONSE_TABLE;

// Here are the hard-coded settings of the bar graph
int TThreeDBar::BarValues[3][4] = {{5,4,7,6},{1,2,3,4},{2,2,3,5}};
char *TThreeDBar::BarLabels[4] = {"92","93","94","95"};
char TThreeDBar::Title[23] = " Sales (in thousands) ";
int TThreeDBar::NumValues = 4;
int TThreeDBar::NumRules = 4;       // Use four rules on the backdrop
int TThreeDBar::NUM_GRAPHS = 3;     // Three sets of bars
// Colors of the bars--back to front
COLORREF TThreeDBar::Colors[] = {
  RGB(128, 0, 32), RGB(250, 200, 100), RGB(0, 200, 225)};

class TThreeDBarApp : public TApplication {
public:
  TThreeDBarApp() : TApplication() { }
  void InitMainWindow();
};

void TThreeDBarWindow::Paint(TDC& dc, BOOL, TRect&)
{
  int sizeX, sizeY;
  RECT rect;

  ThreeDGraph->NumGraphs = ThreeDGraph->NUM_GRAPHS;
  ::GetClientRect(HWindow, &rect);
  sizeX = rect.right / 8;      sizeY = rect.bottom / 8;

  // Note: This chart is shifted down a little compared
  // to the one drawn in BARGRAPH.CPP since its depth
  // takes up space. This helps to center the chart vertically.
```

```
    ThreeDGraph->Display(dc, sizeX, sizeY,
      rect.right-sizeX, rect.bottom-sizeY);
}

// Force the window to completely repaint when the user
// resizes the window
void TThreeDBarWindow::EvSize(UINT, TSize&)
{
  ::InvalidateRect(HWindow, 0, TRUE);
}

void TThreeDBarApp::InitMainWindow()
{
  MainWindow = new TFrameWindow(0, "3D Bar Graph",
    new TThreeDBarWindow(0, ""));
}

int OwlMain(int /*argc*/, char* /*argv*/ [])
{
  return TThreeDBarApp().Run();
}
```

PIE CHARTS

The pie chart provides yet another technique for graphically displaying information. In this section, we'll develop the C++ class **TPieChart**, which encompasses all the details for drawing a simple pie chart and a legend. The source code for **TPieChart** is included in the files PIE.H and PIE.CPP, listed at the end of this chapter. In addition, a program that puts **TPieChart** to work, PIETEST.CPP, is provided. The output from this program is shown in Figure 9.8.

Figure 9.8 PIETEST.CPP creates this pie chart.

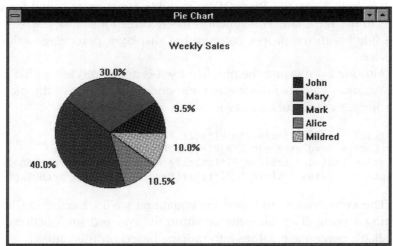

The **TPieChart** class is similar to the other graphing classes created earlier in this chapter, so we'll just focus on its differences. The **Display** member function is the high-level routine you should call to display a pie chart.

Drawing a Slice

In Chapter 4, we introduced the **Pie** function. Here, we'll use it to draw each slice of our pie chart. Our task then is to determine how to relate a set of data to the various slices. Typically, each slice represents the proportion, or percentage, of a particular piece of data in relation to the whole chart.

For our program, we'll assume that we have a series of percentage values. Each percentage value corresponds with one pie slice and all the slices total 100 percent. In some applications, you may need to convert a set of raw data into an appropriate set of percentage values. To keep our program simple, however, we'll assume that these percentages are already available.

Clearly, we want the pie chart that is displayed to be circular. However, if we use the **MM_TEXT** mapping mode, we won't be guaranteed this. Therefore, one of the first steps of the pie chart class is to switch to the **MM_ISOTROPIC** mapping mode:

```
SetMapMode(hDC, MM_ISOTROPIC);
SetWindowExtEx(hDC, rect.right, rect.bottom, 0);
SetViewportExtEx(hDC, rect.right, rect.bottom, 0);
```

In addition, the origin is temporarily set to the position that will become the center of the pie chart:

```
SetViewportOrgEx(hDC, rect.right/4+10, rect.bottom/2, 0);
```

The radius of the pie chart is also calculated to be one-fourth the width of the window. Next, the **PieceOfPie** member function is called for each of the slices in the pie chart. This function has two responsibilities: to display the pie slice filled with the proper color and to display a percentage value alongside the slice.

Although displaying the pie slice itself is accomplished with a single call to **Pie**, we must calculate the starting and ending positions of the pie slice. These coordinates are calculated as follows:

```
startLocX = radius * cos(2*M_PI*startPercentage/100.0);
startLocY = -radius * sin(2*M_PI*startPercentage/100.0);
endLocX = radius * cos(2*M_PI*(startPercentage+slicePercentage)/100.0);
endLocY = -radius * sin(2*M_PI*(startPercentage+slicePercentage)/100.0);
```

The coordinates are based on equations we'll describe in Chapter 11 for rotating a point. The calculations within the cos and sin functions convert the pie slice's percentage values into radians based on this ratio:

$$\frac{\text{Angle (in radians)}}{2 * \text{PI}} = \frac{\text{Percentage}}{100 \text{ percent}}$$

The **StartPercentage** variable specifies the sum of the pie slice percentages, up to the pie slice being displayed. The **SlicePercentage** value is the percentage of the slice itself. The results of these calculations are passed along to **Pie** to draw the slice:

```
Pie(hDC, -radius, -radius, radius, radius,
  startLocX, startLocY, endLocX, endLocY);
```

Remember, the center of the window's coordinate system is set to the center of the pie chart. Also, the fill color of each pie slice is stored in the **TPieChart**'s **Colors** array.

Determining where to display the percentage values requires similar calculations. However, here the radius is extended by a scale factor of 1.2. In addition, to compensate for the various positions of the text around the pie chart, the text justification attributes are adjusted based on the angle at which the text is located.

Displaying a Legend

At the end of **TPieChart**'s **Display** function, the **ShowKey** routine is called for each pie slice to display an entry for the slice in the legend. The legend shows one rectangle and a label for each pie slice, on the right side of the screen. The **Rectangle** function is used to draw filled boxes, which are 16 by 16 pixels in size. Note that the mapping mode in **Display** is set back to **MM_TEXT** in order to make the calculations simpler.

Compiling PIETEST.CPP

To compile PIETEST.CPP, you must create a project file that includes the files PIETEST.CPP and PIE.CPP.

• PIE.H

```
// PIE.H: Header file for PIE.CPP.

#ifndef PIEH
#define PIEH

class TPieChart {
public:
  static double PercentValues[5];
  static char* Labels[5];
  static char Title[13];
```

```
  static int NumValues;
  static COLORREF Colors[5];
  TPieChart() { }
  void PieceOfPie(HDC hDC, int radius,
    double startPercentage, double showPercentage, COLORREF color);
  void Display(HDC hDC, RECT& rect);
  void ShowKey(HDC hDC, int x, int y, COLORREF color, char *label);
};
#endif
```

• PIE.CPP

```
// PIE.CPP: A Windows-compatible pie chart object.

#include <windows.h>
#include <stdio.h>
#include <string.h>
#include <math.h>
#include "pie.h"

#define min(a,b)              (((a) < (b)) ? (a) : (b))

// High-level routine to display a pie chart
void TPieChart::Display(HDC hDC, RECT& rect)
{
  double runningSum=0;
  int i, radius = min(rect.bottom/4, rect.right/4);

  SetTextAlign(hDC, TA_CENTER);    // Display the title
  TextOut(hDC, rect.right/2, rect.bottom/12, Title, strlen(Title));
  // Use a mapping mode which has 1:1 aspect ratio
  // so that the pie chart will be circular
  SetMapMode(hDC, MM_ISOTROPIC);
  SetWindowExtEx(hDC, rect.right, rect.bottom, 0);
  SetViewportExtEx(hDC, rect.right, rect.bottom, 0);
  // Place the origin in the center
  SetViewportOrgEx(hDC, rect.right/4+10, rect.bottom/2, 0);
  // Display the pie slices
  for (i=0; i<NumValues; i++) {
    PieceOfPie(hDC, radius, runningSum, PercentValues[i],
      Colors[i]);
    runningSum += PercentValues[i];
  }
  // Display a legend
  SetMapMode(hDC, MM_TEXT);
  SetViewportOrgEx(hDC, 0, 0, 0);  // Restore the origin
  for (i=0; i<NumValues; i++)
    ShowKey(hDC, rect.right*3/4, rect.bottom/4+i*20,
      Colors[i], Labels[i]);
}

// Display a pie slice. This routine is called while the
// MM_ISOTROPIC mode is being used.
```

```
void TPieChart::PieceOfPie(HDC hDC, int radius,
  double startPercentage, double slicePercentage,
  COLORREF color)
{
  int startLocX, startLocY, endLocX, endLocY, labelAngle, x, y;
  double labelLoc, lRadius, startAngle, endAngle;
  char buffer[10];

  // Offset label radius by a factor of 1.2. This value
  // is dependent on the size of characters you are using.
  lRadius = (double)radius * 1.2;

  startLocX = radius * cos(2*M_PI*startPercentage/100.0);
  startLocY = -radius * sin(2*M_PI*startPercentage/100.0);
  endLocX = radius * cos(2*M_PI*(startPercentage+slicePercentage)/100.0);
  endLocY = -radius * sin(2*M_PI*(startPercentage+slicePercentage)/100.0);

  startAngle = startPercentage / 100.0 * 360.0;
  endAngle = (startPercentage + slicePercentage) / 100.0 * 360.0;
  labelAngle = (startAngle + endAngle) / 2;
  labelLoc = labelAngle * 0.017453;  // Convert to radians

  // Create a brush to fill the pie slice with
  HBRUSH hBrush = CreateSolidBrush(color);
  HANDLE oldBrush = SelectObject(hDC, hBrush);
  // Draw the pie slice
  Pie(hDC, -radius, -radius, radius, radius,
    startLocX, startLocY, endLocX, endLocY);
  // Set up to write its label
  x = cos(labelLoc) * lRadius;
  y = -sin(labelLoc) * lRadius;
  // Set text alignment depending upon location of the pie slice
  if (labelAngle >= 300 || labelAngle < 60)
    SetTextAlign(hDC, TA_LEFT | TA_BOTTOM | TA_NOUPDATECP);
  else if (labelAngle >= 60 && labelAngle < 120)
    SetTextAlign(hDC, TA_CENTER | TA_TOP | TA_NOUPDATECP);
  else if (labelAngle >= 120 && labelAngle < 240)
    SetTextAlign(hDC, TA_RIGHT | TA_BOTTOM | TA_NOUPDATECP);
  else
    SetTextAlign(hDC, TA_CENTER | TA_TOP | TA_NOUPDATECP);

  sprintf(buffer, "%3.1lf%%", slicePercentage);
  TextOut(hDC, x, y, buffer, strlen(buffer));
  startPercentage += slicePercentage;
  SelectObject(hDC, oldBrush);
  DeleteObject(hBrush);
}

// Display an entry in the legend for a pie slice
void TPieChart::ShowKey(HDC hDC, int x, int y,
  COLORREF color, char *label)
{
  HBRUSH hBrush = CreateSolidBrush(color);
  HBRUSH hOldBrush = HBRUSH(SelectObject(hDC, hBrush));
```

```
      Rectangle(hDC, x, y, x+16, y+16);
      SetTextAlign(hDC, TA_LEFT | TA_TOP);
      TextOut(hDC, x+20, y, label, strlen(label));
      SelectObject(hDC, hOldBrush);
      DeleteObject(hBrush);
}
```

• PIETEST.CPP

```
// PIETEST.CPP: Displays a pie chart.

#include <owl\applicat.h>
#include <owl\framewin.h>
#include <owl\dc.h>
#include <stdio.h>
#include <string.h>
#include <math.h>
#include "pie.h"

double TPieChart::PercentValues[] = {9.5, 30, 40, 10.5, 10};
char* TPieChart::Labels[] = {"John", "Mary", "Mark",
  "Alice", "Mildred"};
char TPieChart::Title[] = "Weekly Sales";
int TPieChart::NumValues = 5;
COLORREF TPieChart::Colors[] = {RGB(128, 0, 0), RGB(0, 128, 0),
  RGB(0, 0, 128), RGB(128, 0, 128), RGB(64, 64, 0)};

class TPieChartWindow : public TWindow {
public:
  TPieChart *PieChart;
  TPieChartWindow(TWindow *parent, const char* title)
    : TWindow(parent, title)
    { PieChart = new TPieChart(); }
  virtual ~TPieChartWindow() { delete PieChart; }
  void Paint(TDC& dc, BOOL, TRect&);
  void EvSize(UINT, TSize&);

  DECLARE_RESPONSE_TABLE(TPieChartWindow);
};

DEFINE_RESPONSE_TABLE1(TPieChartWindow, TWindow)
  EV_WM_SIZE,
END_RESPONSE_TABLE;

class TPieChartApp : public TApplication {
public:
  TPieChartApp() : TApplication() { }
  void InitMainWindow();
};

// Erase the window and then repaint the pie chart
void TPieChartWindow::Paint(TDC& dc, BOOL, TRect&)
{
```

```
  RECT rect;
  ::GetClientRect(HWindow, &rect);
  FillRect(dc, &rect, HBRUSH(GetStockObject(WHITE_BRUSH)));
  PieChart->Display(dc, rect);
}

// Repaint the whole pie chart if the size of the window changes
void TPieChartWindow::EvSize(UINT, TSize&)
{
  ::InvalidateRect(HWindow, 0, TRUE);
}

void TPieChartApp::InitMainWindow()
{
  MainWindow = new TFrameWindow(0, "Pie Chart",
    new TPieChartWindow(0, ""));
}

int OwlMain(int /*argc*/, char* /*argv*/[])
{
  return TPieChartApp().Run();
}
```

T E N

Animation

nimation has many uses. It can help draw attention to a portion of a display, demonstrate how something works, or simply make a program more visually interesting. And, of course, animation is at the heart of most computer games.

You may have heard that Windows does not offer much for the animation programmer. Actually, it might surprise you to learn what you *can* do. In this chapter, we'll explore some of the animation techniques possible with Windows. In particular, we'll focus on techniques for inbetweening, moving images across the screen, and animating objects by changing palette colors.

INBETWEENING

Inbetweening is at the heart of many forms of animation; it is this technique that creates the illusion of fluid movement. The prodecure to create inbetweening is simple. The basic idea is to specify the start and stop coordinates of an object and then calculate and display the object as it progresses from its initial state to its final one. Let's take a simple case. Suppose you want to animate a single pixel by moving it from the point (0,0) to the coordinate (150,150) in 15 incremental steps. A routine that can do this merely performs a linear interpolation between the start and stop positions of the point and plots the pixel at these calculated locations. Here's one solution:

```
numberOfSteps = 15;
stepSize = (stopX - startX) / numberOfSteps;
for (j=0; j<numberOfSteps; j++) {
  incAmount = stepSize * j;
```

```
  SetPixel(hDC, startX + incAmount,
    startY + incAmount, RGB(0,0,0));   // Paint pixel black
  SetPixel(hDC, startX + incAmount,
    startY + incAmount, RGB(255,255,255));   // Erase pixel
}
// Draw the final location of the pixel
SetPixel(hDC, x+incAmount, y+incAmount, RGB(0,0,0));
```

The **StepSize** variable determines the amount the pixel is moved between each step. The distance depends on the number of intermediate states that are desired (in this case, 15) and the total distance to travel. The **for** loop steps through each of the intermediate positions, plotting the pixel black by a call to **SetPixel** and then erasing it by another call to **SetPixel**—setting it white. In this example, the X and Y directions are incremented equally, but you can easily modify the code so that the X and Y directions change by different amounts.

This example shows you how to move a point across the screen, but what about animating an *object*? The transition is simple. If you have an object that is drawn as a series of line segments, for instance, all you need to do is run the inbetweening algorithm on each of the endpoints of the line segments and draw the lines between the points at each step in the process. We'll look at this procedure later; first we need to address some Windows programming issues.

Event-Driven Animation

In the last section you saw how to move a point across the screen using a simple **for** loop. However, forcing Windows to stay in a loop like this is not really consistent with Windows' event-driven nature. A better approach is to write the code so that the location of the point is updated in response to an event. What event can you use? Fortunately, Windows permits you to generate events based on the computer's clock. Specifically, you can call **SetTimer** to have Windows trigger events at regular intervals. Here's the format of the **SetTimer** function:

```
UINT SetTimer(HWND hWindow, UINT timerId, UINT time,
  FARPROC lpFunction);
```

- **hWindow** is a handle to the window; remember, OWL provides this for us through the **TWindow** class.

- **timerId** is an integer code that you can use to distinguish between different timer events.

- **time** specifies how often the event should be generated; its units are in milliseconds.

- **lpFunction** can be set to an optional function that is invoked whenever the timer events occur; we'll trap for **WM_TIMER** messages instead and, therefore, set this parameter to 0.
- **SetTimer** returns the timer's identifier or zero if the function fails.

Take a look at an example. The following statement sets up a one second timer with an ID of 1:

```
SetTimer(HWindow, 1, 1000, 0);
```

To turn off the timer, you call **KillTimer** with a handle to the window and the timer ID:

```
KillTimer(HWindow, 1);
```

Responding to timer events involves trapping for the **WM_TIMER** message. First, you must include a **EvTimer** message-response function in your class that is derived from **TWindow**. The function must have the form:

```
void EvTimer(UINT timerId);
```

The **timerId** parameter is the ID of the timer event, which was specified in **SetTimer**. Assuming the **EvTimer** function is part of the class **TExampleWindow**, we also must supply the **EV_WM_TIMER** macro in the window's response table:

```
DEFINE_RESPONSE_TABLE1(TExampleWindow, TWindow)
  EV_WM_TIMER,
END_RESPONSE_TABLE;
```

The **EvTimer** function that actually traps for one or more of its timers uses the form:

```
void TExampleWindow::EvTimer(UINT timerId)
{
  if (timerId == 1)
    // Timer 1 triggered this event
}
```

The idea is to determine whether the timer that caused the current timer event, identified by the **timerId** parameter, is the ID we're waiting for. The previous code, for instance, catches all of timer 1's events.

This covers the basics of using timers in a Windows program. In the next section you'll see how a timer can be integrated into a Windows program that implements inbetweening.

ANIMATING A LINE

To animate an object, we must be able to draw the object, remove it from the screen, draw it in a new position, erase it, draw it at the next location, and so on. However, if we remove the figure by overwriting it with the background color, as we suggested with the pixel example, the window will quickly become a mess if the animated figure crosses over any other objects in the window. Clearly, this is not what we want.

The solution is to exclusive-OR each pixel in the object with the colors on the screen that they overwrite. Because of the nature of exclusive-ORing, this will guarantee that the pixel will be visible. It also means that we can remove the figure simply by drawing it again. To enable exclusive-ORing, we must set the raster operation mode passed to the function **SetROP2** (discussed in Chapter 3) to **R2_XORPEN**. Then, if we draw objects as a series of line segments, we can move the lines across the screen by relying on the **R2_XORPEN** mode.

Well, not quite.

The problem is that the default pen color is black, and we won't change anything by exclusive-ORing the value of black, which is zero, with the screen. Therefore, to effectively use the **R2_XORPEN** mode, we must also switch the pen object to **WHITE_PEN**.

Note   You can also use the **R2_NOT** mode, which negates the screen color. Therefore, applying the operator twice will restore the screen.

WORKING WITH INBETWEENING

Now we'll integrate **SetROP2** and **WM_TIMER** messages into an inbetweening program so that we can animate a set of line segments. The INBTWEEN.CPP application, shown at the end of this section, does just this. It moves a rectangle across the screen, as shown in Figure 10.1.

Most of the variables that control the inbetweening are located in the **TInbetweenWindow** class definition. The starting vertices of the rectangle are stored in the static array **StartPoints**, which is built from **POINT** structures. The final location of the rectangle is stored in the static array **StopPoints**.

As you'll see later, the **Polyline** function is used in the program to draw the lines; therefore, the arrays are declared so that their first and last coordinates are the same—in order to close off the rectangle. An additional array, **Points**, is provided to hold and display each intermediate state of the animated rectangle. (**Points** is initialized with the coordinates in **StartPoints**, in the **TInbetweenWindow** constructor.) The constant **NUM_STEPS** defines the number of intermediate steps used in the animation. In this example, **NUM_STEPS** is set to an integer value of 100. The **StepNdx** variable is used to specify where in the inbetweening process the program currently is, and begins as zero.

Figure 10.1 Time-lapsed output of INBTWEEN.CPP.

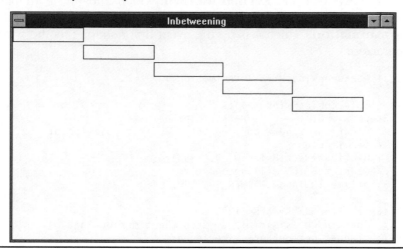

This takes care of the setup code. Now we can discuss how the program moves the rectangle. The application includes two functions that draw to the window. The **Paint** member function is one of these. It merely calls **Polyline** to draw the current position of the rectangle. The **Paint** function is particularly important for drawing the initial position of the rectangle and refreshing the screen when the window is resized, obscured by another window, and so on.

The other painting function is **Inbetween**, which is called in response to **WM_TIMER** messages and is used to move the rectangle one step at a time across the window. The **Inbetween** function first sets the ROP mode to **R2_XORPEN** and switches to a **WHITE_PEN**. Then it tests whether the rectangle has reached the ending position. If so, the code skips to the **KillTimer** statement to terminate the animation.

Otherwise, the top part of the **if-else** statement is executed. It erases the current location of the rectangle by calling **Polyline**, calculates the rectangle's new positions, and then calls **Polyline** to display it. Here you can clearly see the exclusive-ORing action at work:

```
if (StepNdx < NUM_STEPS) {
  Polyline(hDC, Points, LENGTH);   // Erase the lines
  // Calculate new position of figure
  float incAmount = StepNdx * StepSize;
  for (int j=0; j<LENGTH; j++) {
    Points[j].x = StartPoints[j].x + incAmount *
      (StopPoints[j].x - StartPoints[j].x);
    Points[j].y = StartPoints[j].y + incAmount *
      (StopPoints[j].y - StartPoints[j].y);
  }
  Polyline(hDC, Points, LENGTH);   // Draw lines
```

The INBTWEEN.CPP program also includes the two message-response functions **EvChar** and **EvLButtonDown**, which initiate the animation whenever a keypress or left-button mouse click is detected. Both call the function **StartAnimation**, which sets up the event timer as long as the window is not minimized:

```
void TInbetweenWindow::StartAnimation()
{
  if (!::IsIconic(HWindow)) {
    StepNdx = 0;          // Restart the animation
    // Clear the window and repaint the first position of
    // the figure
    ::InvalidateRect(HWindow, 0, TRUE);
    // Start the 100 millisecond timer
    ::SetTimer(HWindow, TIMER_ID, 100, 0);
  }
  else if (StepNdx <= NUM_STEPS)
    // The window is minimized. Stop the timer so that
    // it does not get any timer events.
    ::KillTimer(HWindow, TIMER_ID);
}
```

 Note You don't want the timer triggering painting messages while the program is minimized. If the program doesn't stop the timer, painting commands would cause the icon to flicker.

 The source code for the INBTWEEN.CPP program follows. Try changing the coordinates in the **StartPoints** and **EndPoints** arrays so that the program displays different figures.

• INBTWEEN.CPP

```
// INBTWEEN.CPP: A simple program that demonstrates inbetweening.
// It moves a rectangle across the screen or turns a rectangle
// into a triangle. The animation starts or restarts whenever
// the left mouse button is pressed or a non-system key is pressed.

#include <owl\applicat.h>
#include <owl\framewin.h>
#include <owl\dc.h>

#define TIMER_ID 1     // Identifies this application's timer

const int NUM_STEPS = 100;   // Number of inbetweening steps
const int LENGTH = 5;        // Length of Points array
class TInbetweenWindow : public TWindow {
  static POINT StartPoints[LENGTH];
  static POINT StopPoints[LENGTH];
  POINT Points[LENGTH];        // Contains points to be drawn
```

```
    int StepNdx;
    float StepSize;              // Amount to move each step
  public:
    TInbetweenWindow(TWindow *parent, const char* title);
    void Inbetween();
    void StartAnimation();
    void EvTimer(UINT timerId);
    void EvLButtonDown(UINT, TPoint&);
    void EvChar(UINT, UINT, UINT);
    void Paint(TDC& dc, BOOL, TRect&);

    DECLARE_RESPONSE_TABLE(TInbetweenWindow);
  };

  DEFINE_RESPONSE_TABLE1(TInbetweenWindow, TWindow)
    EV_WM_TIMER,
    EV_WM_LBUTTONDOWN,
    EV_WM_CHAR,
  END_RESPONSE_TABLE;

  POINT TInbetweenWindow::StartPoints[LENGTH] =
    {{0,0}, {100,0}, {100,20}, {0,20}, {0,0}};
  POINT TInbetweenWindow::StopPoints[LENGTH] =
    {{400,100}, {500,100}, {500,120}, {400,120}, {400,100}};

  // The constructor for the TInbetweenWindow class
  TInbetweenWindow::TInbetweenWindow(TWindow *parent, const char* title)
    : TWindow(parent, title) {
    StepNdx = 0;
    StepSize = 1.0 / (NUM_STEPS - 1);
    for (int i=0; i<LENGTH; i++) {
      Points[i].x = StartPoints[i].x;
      Points[i].y = StartPoints[i].y;
    }
  }

  class TInbetweenApp : public TApplication {
  public:
    TInbetweenApp() : TApplication() { }
    void InitMainWindow();
  };

  void TInbetweenApp::InitMainWindow()
  {
    MainWindow = new TFrameWindow(0, "Inbetweening",
      new TInbetweenWindow(0, ""));
  }

  // Paint the figure wherever it currently is
  void TInbetweenWindow::Paint(TDC& dc, BOOL, TRect&)
  {
    Polyline(dc, Points, LENGTH);
  }
```

```cpp
// Call this routine to animate the polygon
void TInbetweenWindow::Inbetween()
{
  HDC hDC = GetDC(HWindow);
  SelectObject(hDC, GetStockObject(WHITE_PEN));
  SetROP2(hDC, R2_XORPEN);  // Exclusive-OR lines
  StepNdx++;
  if (StepNdx < NUM_STEPS) {
    Polyline(hDC, Points, LENGTH);   // Erase the lines
    // Calculate new position of figure
    float incAmount = StepNdx * StepSize;
    for (int j=0; j<LENGTH; j++) {
      Points[j].x = StartPoints[j].x + incAmount *
        (StopPoints[j].x - StartPoints[j].x);
      Points[j].y = StartPoints[j].y + incAmount *
        (StopPoints[j].y - StartPoints[j].y);
    }
    Polyline(hDC, Points, LENGTH);   // Draw lines
  }
  else {
    // Reached the end of the animation sequence. Stop the timer.
    StepNdx--;
    ::KillTimer(HWindow, TIMER_ID);
  }
  ReleaseDC(HWindow, hDC);
}

// Call Inbetween() to animate the figure each time
// this application's timer event occurs.
void TInbetweenWindow::EvTimer(UINT timerId)
{
  if (timerId == TIMER_ID)
    Inbetween();
}

// A key was pressed. Start the animation over.
void TInbetweenWindow::EvChar(UINT, UINT, UINT)
{
  StartAnimation();
}

// The left mouse button was pressed. Start the animation over.
void TInbetweenWindow::EvLButtonDown(UINT, TPoint&)
{
  StartAnimation();
}

void TInbetweenWindow::StartAnimation()
{
  if (!::IsIconic(HWindow)) {
    StepNdx = 0;        // Restart the animation
    // Clear the window and repaint the first position of
    // the figure
    ::InvalidateRect(HWindow, 0, TRUE);
```

```
    // Start the 100 millisecond timer
    ::SetTimer(HWindow, TIMER_ID, 100, 0);
  }
  else if (StepNdx <= NUM_STEPS)
    // The window is minimized. Stop the timer so that
    // it does not get any timer events.
    ::KillTimer(HWindow, TIMER_ID);
}

int OwlMain(int /*argc*/, char* /*argv*/[])
{
  return TInbetweenApp().Run();
}
```

One intriguing feature of inbetweening: the first and last images of the object being animated do not have to be the same. Figure 10.2 shows the time-lapsed output of the INBTWEEN.CPP program modified so that it transforms a rectangle into a triangle. You need to keep in mind one restriction, though: *the number of line segments in the beginning and ending figures must be the same.*

Since the number of line segments must be the same in the start and stop states, but clearly the rectangle and triangle have different numbers of vertices, **StopPoints** is declared so that its last coordinate is specified twice. In other words, one of the line segments in the rectangle shrinks to a line of zero length. Therefore, although the same number of line segments is declared in the arrays, it appears that the triangle has fewer lines than the rectangle. Here are the array declarations for generating Figure 10.2:

```
POINT TInbetweenWindow::StartPoints[LENGTH] =
  {{0,0}, {539,0}, {539,199}, {0,199}, {0,0}};
```

Figure 10.2 Using inbetweening to convert a rectangle into a triangle.

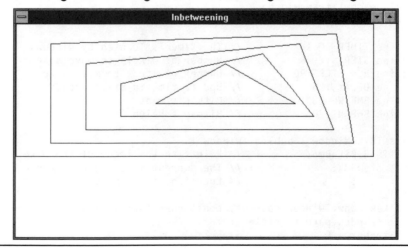

```
POINT TInbetweenWindow::StopPoints[LENGTH] =
  {{210,120}, {315,60}, {420,120}, {210,120}, {210,120}};
```

Realize that you can make the beginning and ending figures quite different from one another. In fact, one trick you can use is to add extra lines or figures to the final drawing. This technique emphasizes the differences even more. For instance, you could supply a set of line segments that transform a square into a face. You can also rotate and scale objects. Of course, supplying all the coordinates to draw these figures is a little tedious.

ANIMATING WITH BITBLT

One of the drawbacks to inbetweening is that the animated objects must be redrawn at each step along the way. For complex figures, this process can be slow. An alternative method is to draw each object on a bitmap and then move the bitmap images across the screen using the **BitBlt** function. (Refer to Chapter 6 for more details on bitmaps and **BitBlt**.)

For example, the BIKE.CPP program (listed next) uses **BitBlt** to move a bicycle image across the screen. A time-lapsed view of the program is shown in Figure 10.3. Here's the complete code for BIKE.CPP.

• BIKE.CPP

```cpp
// BIKE.CPP: Demonstrates how to perform animation using the GDI's
// BitBlt function. The program creates a bitmap image of a
// bicycle and copies the image of the bike across the screen
// using the exclusive-OR option of BitBlt.

#include <owl\applicat.h>
#include <owl\framewin.h>
#include <owl\dc.h>

#define TIMER_ID 1          // The timer's ID used by Windows
#define STEP_SIZE 5         // Number of pixels to move bike
#define NUM_STEPS 80        // Number of steps to move bike
#define DELAY 125           // Update time in milliseconds
#define BMP_WD 130          // Bitmap's width
#define BMP_HT 70           // Bitmap's height

class TBikeWindow : public TWindow {
  HBITMAP BikeBmp;          // Points to the image of the bike
  int StepNdx;              // The current intermediate step
  int X, Y;                 // Location of the bitmap
public:
  TBikeWindow(TWindow *parent, const char far* title)
    : TWindow(parent, title) {
    StepNdx = 0;
```

Figure 10.3 Time-lapsed output of BIKE.CPP.

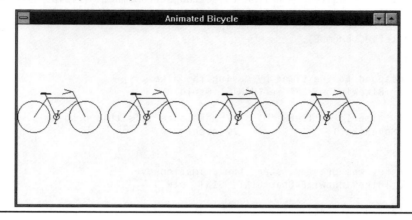

```
    DrawBike();                  // Create the bike's bitmap
  }
  void DrawBike();
  void MoveBike();
  void StartAnimation();
  void EvTimer(UINT timerId);
  void EvLButtonDown(UINT, TPoint&);
  void EvChar(UINT, UINT, UINT);
  void Paint(TDC& dc, BOOL, TRect&);

  DECLARE_RESPONSE_TABLE(TBikeWindow);
};

DEFINE_RESPONSE_TABLE1(TBikeWindow, TWindow)
  EV_WM_TIMER,
  EV_WM_LBUTTONDOWN,
  EV_WM_CHAR,
END_RESPONSE_TABLE;

class TBikeApp : public TApplication {
public:
  TBikeApp() : TApplication() { }
  void InitMainWindow();
};

void TBikeApp::InitMainWindow()
{
  MainWindow = new TFrameWindow(0, "Animated Bicycle",
    new TBikeWindow(0, ""));
}

// Paint the figure of the bike wherever it currently is
void TBikeWindow::Paint(TDC& dc, BOOL, TRect&)
{
```

```
    HDC hMemDC = CreateCompatibleDC(HDC(dc));
    HBITMAP oldBitmap = HBITMAP(SelectObject(hMemDC, BikeBmp));
    BitBlt(dc, X, Y, BMP_WD, BMP_HT, hMemDC, 0, 0, NOTSRCCOPY);
    SelectObject(hMemDC, oldBitmap);
    DeleteDC(hMemDC);
}

// Respond to the timer by moving the bike
void TBikeWindow::EvTimer(UINT timerId)
{
  if (timerId == TIMER_ID)    // Make sure it's this program's
    MoveBike();               // event
}

// A key was pressed; start the animation over.
void TBikeWindow::EvChar(UINT, UINT, UINT)
{
  StartAnimation();
}

// The left mouse button was pressed. Start the animation over.
void TBikeWindow::EvLButtonDown(UINT, TPoint&)
{
  StartAnimation();
}

void TBikeWindow::StartAnimation()
{
  if (!::IsIconic(HWindow)) {
    StepNdx = 0;          // Restart the animation
    X = 0;  Y = 100;
    ::InvalidateRect(HWindow, 0, TRUE);
    ::SetTimer(HWindow, TIMER_ID, DELAY, 0);    // Start the timer
  }
  else if (StepNdx <= NUM_STEPS) {
    // The window is minimized. Stop the timer to
    // avoid any unnecessary timer events.
    ::KillTimer(HWindow, TIMER_ID);
  }
}

// Draw a bicycle in the BikeBmp bitmap using calls to
// Ellipse and MoveToEx/LineTo.
void TBikeWindow::DrawBike()
{
  X = 0;  Y = 100;
  HDC hDC = GetDC(HWindow);
  SetMapMode(hDC, MM_ISOTROPIC);
  RECT rect;
  ::GetClientRect(HWindow, &rect);
  SetViewportExtEx(hDC, rect.right, -rect.bottom, 0);
  SetViewportOrgEx(hDC, 0, rect.bottom, 0);
  HDC hBikeDC = CreateCompatibleDC(hDC);
  BikeBmp = CreateCompatibleBitmap(hDC, BMP_WD, BMP_HT);
```

```
     HBITMAP hOldBmp = HBITMAP(SelectObject(hBikeDC, BikeBmp));
     ReleaseDC(HWindow, hDC);

     SetRect(&rect, 0, 0, BMP_WD, BMP_HT);
     FillRect(hBikeDC, &rect, HBRUSH(GetStockObject(BLACK_BRUSH)));
     SelectObject(hBikeDC, GetStockObject(BLACK_BRUSH));
     SelectObject(hBikeDC, GetStockObject(WHITE_PEN));
     Ellipse(hBikeDC, 0, 20, 50, 70);      // Rear wheel
     Ellipse(hBikeDC, 80, 20, 130, 70);    // Front wheel
     Ellipse(hBikeDC, 55, 40, 65, 50);     // Pedal wheel
     MoveToEx(hBikeDC, 25, 45, 0);
     LineTo(hBikeDC, 45, 15);          // Rear wheel fork
     LineTo(hBikeDC, 89, 15);          // Horizontal bar of frame
     MoveToEx(hBikeDC, 42, 9, 0);
     LineTo(hBikeDC, 59, 45);          // Rear diagonal frame bar
     MoveToEx(hBikeDC, 85, 5, 0);
     LineTo(hBikeDC, 105, 45);         // Front fork
     MoveToEx(hBikeDC, 59, 45, 0);
     LineTo(hBikeDC, 91, 19);          // Front diagonal bar of frame
     MoveToEx(hBikeDC, 84, 5, 0);
     LineTo(hBikeDC, 68, 9);           // Handlebars
     MoveToEx(hBikeDC, 84, 5, 0);
     LineTo(hBikeDC, 71, 1);
     MoveToEx(hBikeDC, 36, 7, 0);
     LineTo(hBikeDC, 44, 7);           // Seat
     MoveToEx(hBikeDC, 35, 8, 0);
     LineTo(hBikeDC, 51, 8);
     MoveToEx(hBikeDC, 35, 9, 0);
     LineTo(hBikeDC, 52, 9);
     MoveToEx(hBikeDC, 57, 55, 0);
     LineTo(hBikeDC, 63, 35);          // Pedals
     MoveToEx(hBikeDC, 61, 35, 0);
     LineTo(hBikeDC, 65, 35);
     MoveToEx(hBikeDC, 59, 55, 0);
     LineTo(hBikeDC, 55, 55);

     SelectObject(hBikeDC, hOldBmp);
     DeleteDC(hBikeDC);
}

// Move bike across the screen in increments of STEP_SIZE
void TBikeWindow::MoveBike()
{
  if (StepNdx < NUM_STEPS) {
    HDC hDC = GetDC(HWindow);
    HDC hMemDC = CreateCompatibleDC(hDC);
    HBITMAP oldBitmap = HBITMAP(SelectObject(hMemDC, BikeBmp));
    BitBlt(hDC, X, Y, BMP_WD, BMP_HT, hMemDC, 0, 0, SRCINVERT);
    X = StepNdx * STEP_SIZE;
    // Draw the bike
    BitBlt(hDC, X, Y, BMP_WD, BMP_HT, hMemDC, 0, 0, SRCINVERT);
    SelectObject(hMemDC, oldBitmap);
    DeleteDC(hMemDC);
    ReleaseDC(HWindow, hDC);
```

```
      StepNdx++;
    }
  else if (StepNdx == NUM_STEPS) {
    StepNdx--;                    // The bike has reached the end
    ::KillTimer(HWindow, TIMER_ID);   // Stop the timer events
    }
  }
}

int OwlMain(int /*argc*/, char* /*argv*/[])
{
  return TBikeApp().Run();
}
```

The bitmap image of the bike is painted in the **CreateBike** function. The bitmap itself is formed by making a memory device context that is compatible with the screen, creating the bitmap, and then selecting the bitmap into the memory device context:

```
HDC hBikeDC = CreateCompatibleDC(hDC);
BikeBmp = CreateCompatibleBitmap(hDC, BMP_WD, BMP_HT);
HBITMAP hOldBmp = SelectObject(hBikeDC, BikeBmp);
```

Once the bitmap is selected into the memory device context, **hBikeDC**, you can draw into the bitmap. Notice that the first step taken with the bitmap is to initialize it with black. The bike's figure will be drawn in white. Notice also that the **hBikeDC** variable is passed to each of the GDI calls. Remember, we're drawing to the bitmap, not the window.

The function **MoveBike** is called to move the bicycle image in **BikeBmp** across the screen. In particular, **MoveBike** is called once every 125 milliseconds in response to a **WM_TIMER** message. The timer is set up when the user presses a key or clicks the left mouse button in the **EvChar** and **EvLButtonDown** functions.

In this example, the image of the bike is moved from the coordinate (0,100) to (500,100) in steps of 5 pixels. The movement is accomplished by erasing the bike at its current position and then displaying it at the next location in the **MoveBike** function:

```
if (StepNdx < NUM_STEPS) {
  HDC hDC = GetDC(HWindow);
  HDC hMemDC = CreateCompatibleDC(hDC);
  HBITMAP oldBitmap = HBITMAP(SelectObject(hMemDC, BikeBmp));
  BitBlt(hDC, X, Y, BMP_WD, BMP_HT, hMemDC, 0, 0, SRCINVERT);
  X = StepNdx * STEP_SIZE;
  // Draw the bike
  BitBlt(hDC, X, Y, BMP_WD, BMP_HT, hMemDC, 0, 0, SRCINVERT);
  SelectObject(hMemDC, oldBitmap);
  DeleteDC(hMemDC);
  ReleaseDC(HWindow, hDC);
  StepNdx++;
}
```

The first call to **BitBlt** erases the current image of the bicycle image by exclusive-ORing **BikeBmp** to the window. The second call displays the bicycle image at its next location, using the **SCRINVERT** option. If the bike has reached its destination, the timer is turned off by calling **KillTimer**.

A Pedaling Bicycle

We can improve on BIKE.CPP by rotating the bicycle's pedals as the bike moves. The basic idea is to create several images of the bike, each with the pedals at different orientations, and then sequence through them to make it look like the pedals are turning. We can accomplish this in two ways: We could make several images of the entire bicycle with the pedals at different orientations, and then sequence through them; or, we could have one complete image of the bicycle and a series of smaller images that just show the pedals at various positions. With the second technique, we must overlay the pedal images with the bike image to create the motion.

You may be wondering why we would want to have two sets of images, one for the bicycle and one for animating the pedals. One important reason, which isn't critical here, is that for large pictures we can speed up the animation process and save memory by swapping images only of the regions that must be changed. In addition, several images of the entire bicycle can consume a lot more memory than a single bitmap of the bicycle and a companion set of smaller bitmaps. In high-resolution graphics modes, it is very easy to consume an excessive amount of memory.

Now we'll return to the task of animating the bicycle pedals. The following program, BIKE2.CPP, animates the bicycle by moving it across the screen as well as rotating its pedals. The program accomplishes this by creating four different images of the bike, each with different pedal orientations, and sequencing through these bitmaps. The program is complicated by the extra bitmaps, but is otherwise quite similar to BIKE.CPP.

• BIKE2.CPP

```
// BIKE2.CPP: Moves a bicycle across the screen using the GDI's
// BitBlt function. The program creates four images of a
// bicycle--each with its pedals in a different orientation--so
// that when the images are played back it looks like the pedals
// are rotating.

#include <owl\applicat.h>
#include <owl\framewin.h>
#include <owl\dc.h>

#define TIMER_ID 1     // The timer's ID used by Windows
```

```
#define STEP_SIZE 5     // Number of pixels to move bike each time
#define NUM_STEPS 80    // Number of steps to "inbetween"
#define DELAY 125       // Update time in milliseconds
#define BMP_WD 130      // Width of the bitmaps
#define BMP_HT 70       // Height of the bitmaps

class TBikeWindow : public TWindow {
  HBITMAP BikeBmp1;             // The images of the bike
  HBITMAP BikeBmp2;
  HBITMAP BikeBmp3;
  HBITMAP BikeBmp4;
  int StepNdx;                  // The current intermediate step
  int X, Y;                     // Location of bike
public:
  TBikeWindow(TWindow *parent, const char far* title)
    : TWindow(parent, title) {
    StepNdx = 0;
    CreateBike();               // Draw the bike bitmaps
  }
  void CreateBike();
  void MoveBike();
  void StartAnimation();
  void EvTimer(UINT timerId);
  void EvLButtonDown(UINT, TPoint&);
  void EvChar(UINT, UINT, UINT);
  void Paint(TDC& dc, BOOL, TRect&);

  DECLARE_RESPONSE_TABLE(TBikeWindow);
};

DEFINE_RESPONSE_TABLE1(TBikeWindow, TWindow)
  EV_WM_TIMER,
  EV_WM_LBUTTONDOWN,
  EV_WM_CHAR,
END_RESPONSE_TABLE;

class TBikeApp : public TApplication {
public:
  TBikeApp() : TApplication() { }
  void InitMainWindow();
};

void TBikeApp::InitMainWindow()
{
  MainWindow = new TFrameWindow(0, "Pedaling Bicycle",
    new TBikeWindow(0, ""));
}

// Paint the bike wherever it currently is
void TBikeWindow::Paint(TDC& dc, BOOL, TRect&)
{
  HBITMAP oldBitmap;
  HDC memDC = CreateCompatibleDC(dc);
```

```
    switch(StepNdx % 4) {      // Select the bitmap to draw
      case 0: oldBitmap = HBITMAP(SelectObject(memDC, BikeBmp1)); break;
      case 1: oldBitmap = HBITMAP(SelectObject(memDC, BikeBmp2)); break;
      case 2: oldBitmap = HBITMAP(SelectObject(memDC, BikeBmp3)); break;
      case 3: oldBitmap = HBITMAP(SelectObject(memDC, BikeBmp4)); break;
    }
    BitBlt(dc, X, Y, BMP_WD, BMP_HT, memDC, 0, 0, NOTSRCCOPY);
    SelectObject(memDC, oldBitmap);
    DeleteDC(memDC);
}

// Respond to the timer by moving the bike
void TBikeWindow::EvTimer(UINT timerId)
{
  if (timerId == TIMER_ID)
    MoveBike();
}

// A key was pressed. Start the animation over.
void TBikeWindow::EvChar(UINT, UINT, UINT)
{
  StartAnimation();
}

// The left mouse button was pressed. Start the animation over.
void TBikeWindow::EvLButtonDown(UINT, TPoint&)
{
  StartAnimation();
}

void TBikeWindow::StartAnimation()
{
  if (!::IsIconic(HWindow)) {
    X = 0;   Y = 100;          // Restart the animation
    StepNdx = 0;
    ::InvalidateRect(HWindow, 0, TRUE);
    ::SetTimer(HWindow, TIMER_ID, DELAY, 0);
  }
  else if (StepNdx < NUM_STEPS)
    // The window is minimized. Stop the animation if it hasn't
    // finished in order to avoid unnecessary timer events.
    ::KillTimer(HWindow, TIMER_ID);
}

// Paint four bitmap images of a bicycle--each with
// different pedal positions
void TBikeWindow::CreateBike()
{
  X = 0;   Y = 100;
  HDC hDC = GetDC(HWindow);
  RECT rect;
  ::GetClientRect(HWindow, &rect);
  SetMapMode(hDC, MM_ISOTROPIC);
```

```
SetViewportExtEx(hDC, rect.right, -rect.bottom, 0);
SetViewportOrgEx(hDC, 0, rect.bottom, 0);
HDC hBikeDC = CreateCompatibleDC(hDC);
BikeBmp1 = CreateCompatibleBitmap(hDC, BMP_WD, BMP_HT);
HBITMAP hOldBmp = HBITMAP(SelectObject(hBikeDC, BikeBmp1));
ReleaseDC(HWindow, hDC);

SetRect(&rect, 0, 0, BMP_WD, BMP_HT);
FillRect(hBikeDC, &rect, HBRUSH(GetStockObject(BLACK_BRUSH)));
SelectObject(hBikeDC, GetStockObject(BLACK_BRUSH));
SelectObject(hBikeDC, GetStockObject(WHITE_PEN));
Ellipse(hBikeDC, 0, 20, 50, 70);    // Rear wheel
Ellipse(hBikeDC, 80, 20, 130, 70);  // Front wheel
Ellipse(hBikeDC, 55, 40, 65, 50);   // Pedal wheel
MoveToEx(hBikeDC, 25, 45, 0);
LineTo(hBikeDC, 45, 15);                 // Rear wheel fork
LineTo(hBikeDC, 90, 15);                 // Horizontal bar of frame
MoveToEx(hBikeDC, 42, 9, 0);
LineTo(hBikeDC, 60, 45);                 // Rear diagonal frame bar
MoveToEx(hBikeDC, 85, 5, 0);
LineTo(hBikeDC, 105, 45);                // Front fork
MoveToEx(hBikeDC, 60, 45, 0);
LineTo(hBikeDC, 92, 19);                 // Front diagonal bar of frame
MoveToEx(hBikeDC, 84, 5, 0);
LineTo(hBikeDC, 68, 9);                  // Handlebars
MoveToEx(hBikeDC, 84, 5, 0);
LineTo(hBikeDC, 71, 1);
MoveToEx(hBikeDC, 36, 7, 0);
LineTo(hBikeDC, 44, 7);                  // Draw seat
MoveToEx(hBikeDC, 35, 8, 0);
LineTo(hBikeDC, 51, 8);
MoveToEx(hBikeDC, 35, 9, 0);
LineTo(hBikeDC, 52, 9);

HDC hBike2DC = CreateCompatibleDC(hBikeDC);
SelectObject(hBike2DC, GetStockObject(WHITE_PEN));
BikeBmp2 = CreateCompatibleBitmap(hBikeDC, BMP_WD, BMP_HT);
HBITMAP hOldBmp2 = HBITMAP(SelectObject(hBike2DC, BikeBmp2));
BitBlt(hBike2DC, 0, 0, BMP_WD, BMP_HT, hBikeDC, 0, 0, SRCCOPY);
MoveToEx(hBike2DC, 66, 39, 0); // Draw pedals
LineTo(hBike2DC, 54, 51);
MoveToEx(hBike2DC, 64, 39, 0);
LineTo(hBike2DC, 68, 39);
MoveToEx(hBike2DC, 52, 51, 0);
LineTo(hBike2DC, 56, 51);

BikeBmp3 = CreateCompatibleBitmap(hBikeDC, BMP_WD, BMP_HT);
SelectObject(hBike2DC, BikeBmp3);
SelectObject(hBike2DC, GetStockObject(WHITE_PEN));
BitBlt(hBike2DC, 0, 0, BMP_WD, BMP_HT, hBikeDC, 0, 0, SRCCOPY);
MoveToEx(hBike2DC, 50, 45, 0); // Draw pedals
LineTo(hBike2DC, 70, 45);
MoveToEx(hBike2DC, 50, 44, 0);
```

```
   LineTo(hBike2DC, 50, 45);
   MoveToEx(hBike2DC, 70, 44, 0);
   LineTo(hBike2DC, 70, 47);

   // Note that each time a compatible device context is
   // created we must reselect the pen style
   BikeBmp4 = CreateCompatibleBitmap(hBikeDC, BMP_WD, BMP_HT);
   SelectObject(hBike2DC, BikeBmp4);
   SelectObject(hBike2DC, GetStockObject(WHITE_PEN));
   BitBlt(hBike2DC, 0, 0, BMP_WD, BMP_HT, hBikeDC, 0, 0, SRCCOPY);
   MoveToEx(hBike2DC, 54, 39, 0); // Draw pedals
   LineTo(hBike2DC, 66, 51);
   MoveToEx(hBike2DC, 52, 39, 0);
   LineTo(hBike2DC, 56, 39);
   MoveToEx(hBike2DC, 64, 51, 0);
   LineTo(hBike2DC, 68, 51);
   SelectObject(hBike2DC, hOldBmp2);
   DeleteDC(hBike2DC);

   MoveToEx(hBikeDC, 60, 37, 0);  // Draw pedals
   LineTo(hBikeDC, 60, 53);
   MoveToEx(hBikeDC, 58, 37, 0);
   LineTo(hBikeDC, 62, 37);
   MoveToEx(hBikeDC, 58, 53, 0);
   LineTo(hBikeDC, 62, 53);
   SelectObject(hBikeDC, hOldBmp);
   DeleteDC(hBikeDC);
}

// Move the bike across the screen in increments of STEP_SIZE
void TBikeWindow::MoveBike()
{
  HBITMAP oldBitmap;
  StepNdx++;
  if (StepNdx < NUM_STEPS) {
    HDC hDC = GetDC(HWindow);
    HDC memDC = CreateCompatibleDC(hDC);
    switch(StepNdx % 4) {
      case 0:      // Erase the current image of the bike first
        oldBitmap = HBITMAP(SelectObject(memDC, BikeBmp4));
        BitBlt(hDC, X, Y, BMP_WD, BMP_HT, memDC, 0, 0, SRCINVERT);
        SelectObject(memDC, BikeBmp1);  // Select next bitmap
        break;
      case 1:
        oldBitmap = HBITMAP(SelectObject(memDC, BikeBmp1));
        BitBlt(hDC, X, Y, BMP_WD, BMP_HT, memDC, 0, 0, SRCINVERT);
        SelectObject(memDC, BikeBmp2);
        break;
      case 2:
        oldBitmap = HBITMAP(SelectObject(memDC, BikeBmp2));
        BitBlt(hDC, X, Y, BMP_WD, BMP_HT, memDC, 0, 0, SRCINVERT);
        SelectObject(memDC, BikeBmp3);
        break;
```

```
      case 3:
        oldBitmap = HBITMAP(SelectObject(memDC, BikeBmp3));
        BitBlt(hDC, X, Y, BMP_WD, BMP_HT, memDC, 0, 0, SRCINVERT);
        SelectObject(memDC, BikeBmp4);
        break;
    }
    X = StepNdx * STEP_SIZE;       // Draw bike
    BitBlt(hDC, X, Y, BMP_WD, BMP_HT, memDC, 0, 0, SRCINVERT);
    SelectObject(memDC, oldBitmap);
    DeleteDC(memDC);
    ReleaseDC(HWindow, hDC);
  }
  else if (StepNdx == NUM_STEPS) {
    StepNdx--;
    ::KillTimer(HWindow, TIMER_ID);
  }
}

int OwlMain(int /*argc*/, char* /*argv*/[])
{
  return TBikeApp().Run();
}
```

Sparkling Text

The following program, SPARKTXT.CPP, uses a sequence of bitmaps in a slightly different way. It briefly displays small, sparkling, specular highlights on a text string. This simple animation effect is an excellent way to add a touch of class to your opening screens, demos, or About boxes.

The highlights are drawn directly to the screen using a variety of star-like patterns, as shown in Figure 10.4. In all, the program displays three sets of highlights. The centers of the three highlights are specified in the **Sparks** array:

```
POINT Sparks[NUMSPARKS] = {{50,50}, {125,52}, {140,60}};
```

Figure 10.4 SPARKTXT animates a series of star-like bursts to add specular highlights to a text string.

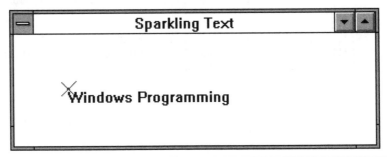

Each of the three highlights follows the same animation pattern, which is specified by the **Offsets** array:

```
POINT Offsets[NUMSTEPS*2] = {{0,4}, {4,0}, {0,9}, {9,0},
  {0,0}, {0,0}, {0,4}, {4,0}, {7,7}, {7,-7}, {0,4}, {4,0}};
```

The **Offsets** array is a sequence of **POINT** structures in which each point specifies the pixel offsets (from the center) of a branch of a single phase of a highlight. Since the highlights are symmetric, offsets for only two of the four branches are specified in consecutive pairs of the **POINT** structures in **Offsets**. For instance, the first two **POINT** structures create a crosshair pattern that is eight pixels in height and width. Since two **POINT** structures define each phase of a highlight, and the highlights go through **NUMSTEPS** of phases, the **Offsets** array is declared to hold **NUMSTEPS*2** elements.

The highlights are drawn in the **UpdateSparkle** function using a red pen. If the branches of the highlight are relatively long (greater than four pixels), a few extra pixels are placed at the center of the highlight to give it a heavier appearance. To remove a highlight SPARKTXT.CPP saves a bitmap of the original screen so that it can later copy the bitmap back to the screen to remove the highlight.

The **Iterations** variable keeps track of which of the three highlights is displayed. Similarly, **StepNdx** selects the current highlight drawn. These variables are incremented every 60 milliseconds in response to a **WM_TIMER** event that is initiated whenever the user presses a key or clicks the left mouse button.

 There are no special instructions required for compiling SPARKTXT.CPP, however, once you have it up and running you might want to try adding more variability to the placements of the specular highlights.

• SPARKTXT.CPP

```
// SPARKTXT.CPP: Displays text with sparkling specular highlights.

#include <owl\applicat.h>
#include <owl\framewin.h>
#include <owl\dc.h>

#define TIMER_ID 1          // The timer's ID used by Windows
#define DELAY 60            // Update time in milliseconds
#define SPARKWD 10          // Specular highlight's pixel width
#define SPARKHT 10          // Specular highlight's pixel height
#define NUMSPARKS 3         // Number of highlights to show
#define NUMSTEPS 6          // Number of components in highlight
#define BIGLEN 5            // If a highlight offset is longer
                            // than this add a circle to its center
```

```
#define STRING "Windows Programming"
// Offsets used to build specular highlights at each step
// Each pair of points specifies how to build a highlight
// The first point gives the "vertical" offset of the highlight
// and the second point gives the "horizontal" offset
// The offsets are added to the highlight's center point
// in the positive and negative directions
POINT Offsets[NUMSTEPS*2] = {{0,4}, {4,0}, {0,9}, {9,0},
  {0,0}, {0,0}, {0,4}, {4,0}, {7,7}, {7,-7}, {0,4}, {4,0}};
POINT Sparks[NUMSPARKS] = {{50,50}, {125,52}, {140,60}};

class TSparklingTextWindow : public TWindow {
  int StepNdx;
  int X, Y;          // Center of sparkle
  int Iterations;
  HPEN SparkPen;
  HBITMAP ScreenBmp;
  HDC MemDC;
public:
  TSparklingTextWindow(TWindow *parent, const char far* title)
    : TWindow(parent, title) {
    StepNdx = 0;
    Iterations = 0;
    X = Sparks[Iterations].x;  Y = Sparks[Iterations].y;
  }
  ~TSparklingTextWindow() {
    ::KillTimer(HWindow, TIMER_ID);
    DeleteObject(SparkPen);
    DeleteObject(ScreenBmp);
  }
  void SetupWindow();
  void UpdateSparkle();
  void StartAnimation();
  void EvTimer(UINT timerId);
  void EvLButtonDown(UINT, TPoint&);
  void EvChar(UINT, UINT, UINT);
  void Paint(TDC& dc, BOOL, TRect&);

  DECLARE_RESPONSE_TABLE(TSparklingTextWindow);
};

DEFINE_RESPONSE_TABLE1(TSparklingTextWindow, TWindow)
  EV_WM_TIMER,
  EV_WM_LBUTTONDOWN,
  EV_WM_CHAR,
END_RESPONSE_TABLE;

class TSparklingTextApp : public TApplication {
public:
  TSparklingTextApp() : TApplication() { }
  void InitMainWindow();
};
```

```
void TSparklingTextApp::InitMainWindow()
{
  MainWindow = new TFrameWindow(0, "Sparkling Text",
    new TSparklingTextWindow(0, ""));
}

void TSparklingTextWindow::SetupWindow()
{
  TWindow::SetupWindow();
  // Use a red pen for the highlights
  SparkPen = CreatePen(PS_SOLID, 1, RGB(255,0,0));
}

void TSparklingTextWindow::Paint(TDC& dc, BOOL, TRect&)
{
  TextOut(dc, X, Y, STRING, strlen(STRING));
}

// Respond to the timer by updating the specular highlights
void TSparklingTextWindow::EvTimer(UINT timerId)
{
  if (timerId == TIMER_ID)    // Make sure it's this program's
    UpdateSparkle();          // event
}

// A key was pressed. Start the animation over again.
void TSparklingTextWindow::EvChar(UINT, UINT, UINT)
{
  StartAnimation();
}

// The left mouse button was pressed. Start the animation over.
void TSparklingTextWindow::EvLButtonDown(UINT, TPoint&)
{
  StartAnimation();
}

void TSparklingTextWindow::StartAnimation()
{
  if (!::IsIconic(HWindow)) {
    StepNdx = 0;        // Restart the animation
    Iterations = 0;
    X = Sparks[0].x;  Y = Sparks[0].y;
    ::InvalidateRect(HWindow, 0, TRUE);
    ::SetTimer(HWindow, TIMER_ID, DELAY, 0);    // Start the timer
  }
  else if (StepNdx <= NUMSTEPS*2) {
    // The window is minimized. Stop the timer to
    // avoid any unnecessary timer events.
    ::KillTimer(HWindow, TIMER_ID);
  }
}
```

```
// Update the specular highlight on the text
void TSparklingTextWindow::UpdateSparkle()
{
  if (StepNdx < NUMSTEPS*2) {
    HDC hDC = GetDC(HWindow);
    SelectObject(hDC, SparkPen);
    MemDC = CreateCompatibleDC(hDC);
    if (!StepNdx) {
      // The first time through save the area where the highlight
      // will appear
      ScreenBmp = CreateCompatibleBitmap(hDC, 20, 20);
      SelectObject(MemDC, ScreenBmp);
      BitBlt(MemDC, 0, 0, 20, 20, hDC, X-10, Y-10, SRCCOPY);
    }
    else {
      // Restore the screen where the previous highlight was
      SelectObject(MemDC, ScreenBmp);
      BitBlt(hDC, X-10, Y-10, 20, 20, MemDC, 0, 0, SRCCOPY);
    }
    DeleteDC(MemDC);

    // Draw the new highlight
    MoveToEx(hDC, X+Offsets[StepNdx].x, Y+Offsets[StepNdx].y, 0);
    LineTo(hDC, X-Offsets[StepNdx].x, Y-Offsets[StepNdx].y);
    StepNdx++;
    MoveToEx(hDC, X+Offsets[StepNdx].x, Y+Offsets[StepNdx].y, 0);
    LineTo(hDC, X-Offsets[StepNdx].x, Y-Offsets[StepNdx].y);
    if (Offsets[StepNdx].x > 4 || Offsets[StepNdx].y > 4) {
      SetPixel(hDC, X-1, Y-1, RGB(255,0,0));
      SetPixel(hDC, X, Y-1, RGB(255,0,0));
      SetPixel(hDC, X+1, Y-1, RGB(255,0,0));
      SetPixel(hDC, X+1, Y, RGB(255,0,0));
      SetPixel(hDC, X+1, Y+1, RGB(255,0,0));
      SetPixel(hDC, X+1, Y, RGB(255,0,0));
      SetPixel(hDC, X-1, Y+1, RGB(255,0,0));
      SetPixel(hDC, X-1, Y, RGB(255,0,0));
    }
    StepNdx++;
    ReleaseDC(HWindow, hDC);
  }
  else {
    if (Iterations >= NUMSPARKS-1)
      ::KillTimer(HWindow, TIMER_ID);    // Stop the timer events
    // Erase the highlight
    HDC hDC = GetDC(HWindow);
    MemDC = CreateCompatibleDC(hDC);
    SelectObject(MemDC, ScreenBmp);
    BitBlt(hDC, X-10, Y-10, 20, 20, MemDC, 0, 0, SRCCOPY);
    DeleteDC(MemDC);
    ReleaseDC(HWindow, hDC);
    StepNdx = 0;                   // This is the end

    if (Iterations <= NUMSPARKS) {
      // Move the specular highlight
```

```
      Iterations++;
      X = Sparks[Iterations].x;  Y = Sparks[Iterations].y;
    }
  }
}

int OwlMain(int /*argc*/, char* /*argv*/[])
{
  return TSparklingTextApp().Run();
}
```

ANIMATING OBJECTS ON A BACKDROP

So far we've been using **BitBlt** to move objects across a plain background. Unfortunately, this does not represent a realistic animation situation. In most animation applications, you'll probably have several objects in the background. We could, for example, add a country-scene backdrop to the bicycle animation programs. However, if we put objects on the screen that the bicycle must cross over, the bicycle might change its color as it overlaps with other objects. The reason is that the animated object and the screen are exclusive-ORed together. Wherever the bitmap image contains a non-zero value, copying the image to the screen will change its corresponding pixel color if the screen also has a non-zero value at that location. Fortunately, there is a way around this problem.

The solution is to use the object image in conjunction with a second, special bitmap. The second bitmap contains a black-and-white representation of the image to be animated. We'll call this the AND mask, because it is ANDed with the screen before the object image is combined with the screen. Essentially, the AND mask is used to select which pixels in the screen are to be changed and which ones are to stay the same. After the AND mask is applied, the object bitmap image is ORed with the screen. As a result, wherever the AND mask is black, the OR mask color will be visible; in turn, wherever the AND mask is white, the screen will show through. This process is summarized in Figure 10.5. (Of course, all this assumes that the AND mask only has black pixels where the figure is to be drawn.)

Figure 10.5 Using two masks to display objects without disturbing the backdrop.

And Mask Value	Image Mask Value	Resulting Screen Value
0	0	0
0	1	1
1	0	Screen unchanged
1	1	This state is not used

To remove the object, we'll save the screen region where the masks are to be displayed. Then, to erase the masks, we'll simply overwrite them with the saved portion of the screen.

Unfortunately, this animation technique can be slow because we must deal with several screen images. First, we must save the screen, then AND a bitmap, followed by ORing an image, and later restoring the screen to its original state by copying back the saved screen image. This can take a great deal of time—especially when the size of the object being animated is large. Therefore, BALL.CPP, located at the end of this section, only moves a small ball across a backdrop, as shown in Figure 10.6. The ball is drawn to the screen using two masks, as outlined earlier.

The two masks that make up the ball are shown in Figure 10.7. They are accessed through the bitmaps **AndBmp** and **BallBmp**. A third bitmap, **CoveredBmp**, is used to save the portion of the screen that is covered by the masks at each step of the animation.

The ball's image is constructed from two concentric ellipses in the function **DrawBall**. The outer one is white, while the inner one is black. This effectively cuts out a hole in the ball.

```
SelectObject(hBallDC, GetStockObject(WHITE_PEN));
Ellipse(hBallDC, 0, 0, BMP_WD, BMP_HT);
// Paint a black hole in the ball
SelectObject(hBallDC, GetStockObject(BLACK_BRUSH));
Ellipse(hBallDC, BMP_WD/4, BMP_HT/4,
  BMP_WD-BMP_WD/4, BMP_HT-BMP_HT/4);
```

Figure 10.6 The moving ball does not disturb the backdrop in BALL.CPP.

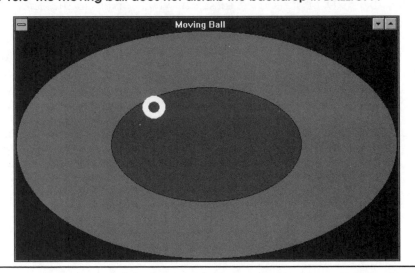

Figure 10.7 The two masks used in BALL.CPP.

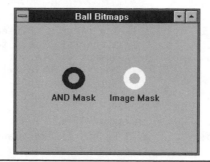

The AND mask in this case is merely the inverted image of the ball's bitmap. Therefore, **BitBlt** is used to create it:

```
BitBlt(hANDDC, 0, 0, BMP_WD, BMP_HT, hBallDC, 0, 0, NOTSRCCOPY);
```

The process of moving the circle across the screen is encapsulated by the four calls to **BitBlt** in the function **MoveBall**:

```
SelectObject(hMemDC, CoveredBmp);
BitBlt(hDC, X, Y, BMP_WD, BMP_HT, hMemDC, 0, 0, SRCCOPY);
X = StepNdx * STEP_SIZE;
// Save the area where the ball will appear
BitBlt(hMemDC, 0, 0, BMP_WD, BMP_HT, hDC, X, Y, SRCCOPY);
// Draw the ball at its new location using the two bitmaps
SelectObject(hMemDC, ANDBmp);
BitBlt(hDC, X, Y, BMP_WD, BMP_HT, hMemDC, 0, 0, SRCAND);
SelectObject(hMemDC, BallBmp);
BitBlt(hDC, X, Y, BMP_WD, BMP_HT, hMemDC, 0, 0, SRCPAINT);
```

The first call to **BitBlt** overwrites the current position of the ball by using the **CoveredBmp** bitmap. The next call saves the screen where the ball will next appear. The last two **BitBlt**s write the two masks to the screen and draw the ball.

 The BALL.CPP program is shown next. Once you have the program running, try creating your own moving object. You'll need to modify the **DrawBall** function so that it draws your custom figure in **hBallDC** and paints a mask for it in **hANDDC**.

• BALL.CPP

```
// BALL.CPP: Moves a ball across a colored backdrop using two
// bitmaps.
```

```
#include <owl\applicat.h>
#include <owl\framewin.h>
#include <owl\dc.h>

#define TIMER_ID 1          // The timer's ID used by Windows
#define STEP_SIZE 5         // Number of pixels to move bike
#define NUM_STEPS 80        // Number of steps to move bike
#define DELAY 125           // Update time in milliseconds
#define BMP_WD 35           // Bitmap's width
#define BMP_HT 35           // Bitmap's height

class TBallWindow : public TWindow {
  HBITMAP BallBmp;          // Points to the image of the ball
  HBITMAP ANDBmp;           // The AND mask
  HBITMAP CoveredBmp;       // Saves window below ball
  HBRUSH RedBrush;          // A red brush
  HBRUSH BlueBrush;         // A blue brush
  int StepNdx;              // The current intermediate step
  int X, Y;                 // Location of the bitmap
public:
  TBallWindow(TWindow *parent, const char* title)
    : TWindow(parent, title) {
    StepNdx = 0;
    DrawBall();              // Create the ball's bitmap
  }
  void DrawBall();
  void MoveBall();
  void StartAnimation();
  void EvTimer(UINT timerId);
  void EvLButtonDown(UINT, TPoint&);
  void EvChar(UINT, UINT, UINT);
  void EvDestroy();
  BOOL EvEraseBkgnd(HDC);
  void Paint(TDC& dc, BOOL, TRect&);

  DECLARE_RESPONSE_TABLE(TBallWindow);
};

DEFINE_RESPONSE_TABLE1(TBallWindow, TWindow)
  EV_WM_TIMER,
  EV_WM_LBUTTONDOWN,
  EV_WM_CHAR,
  EV_WM_DESTROY,
  EV_WM_ERASEBKGND,
END_RESPONSE_TABLE;

class TBallApp : public TApplication {
public:
  TBallApp() : TApplication() { }
  void InitMainWindow();
};

void TBallApp::InitMainWindow()
{
```

```
      MainWindow = new TFrameWindow(0, "Moving Ball",
        new TBallWindow(0, ""));
    }

    // Paint the figure of the ball wherever it currently is
    void TBallWindow::Paint(TDC& dc, BOOL, TRect&)
    {
      HDC hMemDC = CreateCompatibleDC(dc);
      // Save the screen where the ball will appear
      SelectObject(hMemDC, CoveredBmp);
      BitBlt(hMemDC, 0, 0, BMP_WD, BMP_HT, dc, X, Y, SRCCOPY);
      // Draw the ball using the two bitmaps
      SelectObject(hMemDC, ANDBmp);
      BitBlt(dc, X, Y, BMP_WD, BMP_HT, hMemDC, 0, 0, SRCAND);
      SelectObject(hMemDC, BallBmp);
      BitBlt(dc, X, Y, BMP_WD, BMP_HT, hMemDC, 0, 0, SRCPAINT);
      DeleteDC(hMemDC);
    }

    // Paint the window's background black
    BOOL TBallWindow::EvEraseBkgnd(HDC)
    {
      RECT rect;
      ::GetClientRect(HWindow, &rect);
      HDC hDC = GetDC(HWindow);
      FillRect(hDC, &rect, HBRUSH(GetStockObject(BLACK_BRUSH)));
      SelectObject(hDC, RedBrush);
      Ellipse(hDC, 0, 0, rect.right, rect.bottom);
      SelectObject(hDC, BlueBrush);
      Ellipse(hDC, rect.right/4, rect.bottom/4,
        rect.right-rect.right/4, rect.bottom-rect.bottom/4);
      ReleaseDC(HWindow, hDC);
      return TRUE;
    }

    // Respond to the timer by moving the ball
    void TBallWindow::EvTimer(UINT timerId)
    {
      if (timerId == TIMER_ID)    // Make sure it's this
        MoveBall();               // program's event
    }

    // A key was pressed. Start the animation over.
    void TBallWindow::EvChar(UINT, UINT, UINT)
    {
      StartAnimation();
    }

    // The left mouse button was pressed. Start the animation over.
    void TBallWindow::EvLButtonDown(UINT, TPoint&)
    {
      StartAnimation();
    }
```

```cpp
// Delete the bitmap objects created in DrawBall
void TBallWindow::EvDestroy()
{
  DeleteObject(ANDBmp);
  DeleteObject(BallBmp);
  DeleteObject(CoveredBmp);
  DeleteObject(RedBrush);
  DeleteObject(BlueBrush);
  TWindow::EvDestroy();
}

void TBallWindow::StartAnimation()
{
  if (!::IsIconic(HWindow)) {
    StepNdx = 0;          // Restart the animation
    X = 0;   Y = 100;
    ::InvalidateRect(HWindow, 0, TRUE);
    ::SetTimer(HWindow, TIMER_ID, DELAY, 0);    // Start timer
  }
  else if (StepNdx <= NUM_STEPS) {
    // The window is minimized. Stop the timer to
    // avoid any unnecessary timer events.
    ::KillTimer(HWindow, TIMER_ID);
  }
}

// Draw a ball in the BallBmp bitmap and a black and
// white version of it in ANDBmp
void TBallWindow::DrawBall()
{
  X = 0;   Y = 100;
  HDC hDC = GetDC(HWindow);
  RECT rect;
  ::GetClientRect(HWindow, &rect);
  HDC hBallDC = CreateCompatibleDC(hDC);
  CoveredBmp = CreateCompatibleBitmap(hDC, BMP_WD, BMP_HT);
  BallBmp = CreateCompatibleBitmap(hDC, BMP_WD, BMP_HT);
  SelectObject(hBallDC, BallBmp);
  HDC hANDDC = CreateCompatibleDC(hDC);
  ANDBmp = CreateCompatibleBitmap(hDC, BMP_WD, BMP_HT);
  SelectObject(hANDDC, ANDBmp);
  ReleaseDC(HWindow, hDC);

  // Draw a white ball on a black backdrop
  SetRect(&rect, 0, 0, BMP_WD, BMP_HT);
  FillRect(hBallDC, &rect, HBRUSH(GetStockObject(BLACK_BRUSH)));
  SelectObject(hBallDC, GetStockObject(WHITE_PEN));
  Ellipse(hBallDC, 0, 0, BMP_WD, BMP_HT);
  // Paint a black hole in the ball
  SelectObject(hBallDC, GetStockObject(BLACK_BRUSH));
  Ellipse(hBallDC, BMP_WD/4, BMP_HT/4,
    BMP_WD-BMP_WD/4, BMP_HT-BMP_HT/4);
```

```
    // Create the AND mask. Set each of its pixels to black
    // where the BallBmp has a non-black pixel. Set all other
    // pixels to white. In this case the AND mask is an simply
    // an inverted copy of the ball's bitmap.
    BitBlt(hANDDC, 0, 0, BMP_WD, BMP_HT, hBallDC, 0, 0, NOTSRCCOPY);

    DeleteDC(hANDDC);
    DeleteDC(hBallDC);

    // Create a red and blue brush for the background
    RedBrush = CreateSolidBrush(RGB(255,0,0));
    BlueBrush = CreateSolidBrush(RGB(0,0,255));
}

// Move ball across the screen in increments of STEP_SIZE
void TBallWindow::MoveBall()
{
  if (StepNdx < NUM_STEPS) {
    HDC hDC = GetDC(HWindow);
    HDC hMemDC = CreateCompatibleDC(hDC);
    // Restore the window where the ball is
    SelectObject(hMemDC, CoveredBmp);
    BitBlt(hDC, X, Y, BMP_WD, BMP_HT, hMemDC, 0, 0, SRCCOPY);
    X = StepNdx * STEP_SIZE;
    // Save the area where the ball will appear
    BitBlt(hMemDC, 0, 0, BMP_WD, BMP_HT, hDC, X, Y, SRCCOPY);
    // Draw the ball at its new location using the two bitmaps
    SelectObject(hMemDC, ANDBmp);
    BitBlt(hDC, X, Y, BMP_WD, BMP_HT, hMemDC, 0, 0, SRCAND);
    SelectObject(hMemDC, BallBmp);
    BitBlt(hDC, X, Y, BMP_WD, BMP_HT, hMemDC, 0, 0, SRCPAINT);
    DeleteDC(hMemDC);
    ReleaseDC(HWindow, hDC);
    StepNdx++;
  }
  else if (StepNdx == NUM_STEPS) {
    StepNdx--;                  // The ball has reached the end
    ::KillTimer(HWindow, TIMER_ID);   // Stop the timer events
  }
}

int OwlMain(int /*argc*/, char* /*argv*/[])
{
  return TBallApp().Run();
}
```

ANIMATION USING THE PALETTE

Typically, animation is performed by drawing an object as it moves across the screen or by moving an image of an object across the screen. However, an alternative method of animation, which is sometimes quite dramatic and simple, uses the hardware palette to produce animation.

The basic idea is to draw objects on the screen using different palette colors. Then, the colors in the palette are changed. When this is done, objects drawn with the altered colors immediately change on the screen. With judicious selection of colors, you can easily make objects rotate, move, appear, or disappear.

A common example of palette animation displays a mountain scene with flowing water. The motion of the water is induced by a series of changes to the palette. Since it would take a great deal of time and programming to create a good-looking mountain scene, we'll construct a simpler example.

The program, SUNSET.CPP, displays an island view of a sunset. As the sun slowly lowers from the sky and evening progresses, the palette colors are darkened by decreasing their RGB values equally, as shown in Figure 10.8.

The **WM_ERASEBKGND** message is overwritten to display the base of the scene, which contains the sky, the ocean, and the top of the island. The sun is displayed in the **Paint** function. Unquestionably, this island scene is simple. You can spruce up your version of the program as your tastes desire by adding palm trees, a hammock, or whatever.

The key to the animation is to use the colors in a logical palette to paint the elements of the backdrop. In **SetupWindow**, a three-color palette is created that contains one color for the sky, another for the island, and a third for the ocean. Solid brushes for each of these colors are also created in **SetupWindow**:

```
SkyBr = CreateSolidBrush(PALETTEINDEX(0));     // Light blue
IslandBr = CreateSolidBrush(PALETTEINDEX(1));  // Brown
OceanBr = CreateSolidBrush(PALETTEINDEX(2));   // Dark blue
```

The first position of the sun is displayed in the **Paint** function using the **Ellipse** routine. Once the user presses a key or the left mouse button, a timer begins. The function **EvTimer** is called to update the position of the sun by moving it down one line in the window every half second. Notice, however,

Figure 10.8 Palette animation is used to darken the window as the sun lowers in SUNSET.CPP.

that the sun is not painted directly onto the screen. Instead, it is drawn onto an intermediate, blue-sky bitmap that is copied to the screen using **BitBlt**.

Note Drawing into a temporary bitmap, as SUNSET.CPP does, illustrates a useful animation technique. By drawing the sun into a blue-sky bitmap and transferring the sky bitmap to the screen, the sun is shown in its new position and the old location of the sun is overwritten in one step. This helps to reduce screen flicker as the window is updated. Compare this to the screen flicker you observed in the BIKE programs.

When the sun reaches the horizon, each of the palette colors used in the scene is decreased. Then **AnimatePalette** is called to instantaneously update the screen.

```
for (int i=0; i<NUM_COLORS; i++) {
  if (LogPal->palPalEntry[i].peRed > ColorDec)
    LogPal->palPalEntry[i].peRed -= BYTE(ColorDec);
  else if (LogPal->palPalEntry[i].peRed)
    LogPal->palPalEntry[i].peRed--;
  if (LogPal->palPalEntry[i].peGreen > ColorDec)
    LogPal->palPalEntry[i].peGreen -= BYTE(ColorDec);
  else if (LogPal->palPalEntry[i].peGreen)
    LogPal->palPalEntry[i].peGreen--;
  if (LogPal->palPalEntry[i].peBlue > ColorDec)
    LogPal->palPalEntry[i].peBlue -= BYTE(ColorDec);
  else if (LogPal->palPalEntry[i].peBlue)
    LogPal->palPalEntry[i].peBlue--;
}
AnimatePalette(HLogPal, 0, NUM_COLORS, LogPal->palPalEntry);
```

The SUNSET.CPP program is shown next. Remember, to use palette animation you'll need a video driver that supports palettes, such as a 256-color driver. The program won't run without palette support. In fact, with the increasing popularity of 24-bit graphics modes, which don't support color palettes, there's probably good reason to use alternative animation techniques. However, for some applications, palette animation is hard to beat.

• SUNSET.CPP

```
// SUNSET.CPP: A simple oceanside sunset that illustrates palette
// animation. Each figure in the drawing is drawn using a color in a
// logical palette. As the sun in the sky falls all the logical
// palette colors are made darker until the sun has set. Click the
// mouse in the window or press a key to start the animation.

#include <owl\applicat.h>
#include <owl\framewin.h>
#include <owl\dc.h>
```

```
#define TIMER_ID 1        // The timer's ID used by Windows
#define DELAY 500         // Update time in milliseconds
#define NUM_COLORS 3      // Number of colors in the logical palette

class TSunsetWindow : public TWindow {
  int SunX, SunY;         // Location of the sun
  int SunWd;              // Diameter of sun
  int ColorDec;          // Amount to darken each color
  BOOL Done;              // TRUE when sun has set
  HBRUSH SkyBr;           // The sky's color
  HBRUSH OceanBr;         // The ocean's color
  HBRUSH SunBr;           // The sun's color
  HBRUSH IslandBr;        // The island's color
  LOGPALETTE* LogPal;     // Pointer to a logical palette
  HPALETTE HLogPal;       // Handle to the logical palette
  BOOL PalSupport;        // TRUE if hardware supports a palette
public:
  TSunsetWindow(TWindow *parent, const char* title)
    : TWindow(parent, title) {
    Done = FALSE;
    PalSupport = FALSE;
  }
  void StartAnimation();
  void SetLogPaletteColors();
  void EvTimer(UINT timerId);
  void EvLButtonDown(UINT, TPoint&);
  void EvChar(UINT, UINT, UINT);
  void SetupWindow();
  void EvDestroy();
  void EvSize(UINT, TSize&);
  void Paint(TDC& hDC, BOOL, TRect&);

  DECLARE_RESPONSE_TABLE(TSunsetWindow);
};

DEFINE_RESPONSE_TABLE1(TSunsetWindow, TWindow)
  EV_WM_TIMER,
  EV_WM_LBUTTONDOWN,
  EV_WM_CHAR,
  EV_WM_DESTROY,
  EV_WM_SIZE,
END_RESPONSE_TABLE;

// Create a logical palette and initialize it with the colors
// for the sky, ocean, and island. If a logical palette is
// not supported by the hardware, set PalSupport to FALSE.
void TSunsetWindow::SetupWindow()
{
  TWindow::SetupWindow();    // Call the inherited SetupWindow function
  HDC hDC = GetDC(HWindow);
  if (RC_PALETTE & GetDeviceCaps(hDC, RASTERCAPS)) {
    LogPal = (LOGPALETTE *)new char[sizeof(LOGPALETTE) +
      sizeof(PALETTEENTRY) * NUM_COLORS];
    if (LogPal != NULL) {
```

```
        LogPal->palVersion = 0x300;
        LogPal->palNumEntries = NUM_COLORS;
        SetLogPaletteColors();
        HLogPal = CreatePalette(LogPal);
        PalSupport = TRUE;
        // Create brushes for the scene
        SkyBr = CreateSolidBrush(PALETTEINDEX(0));      // Light blue
        IslandBr = CreateSolidBrush(PALETTEINDEX(1));   // Brown
        OceanBr = CreateSolidBrush(PALETTEINDEX(2));    // Dark blue
        SunBr = CreateSolidBrush(RGB(255, 255, 64));    // Yellow
    }
  }
  ReleaseDC(HWindow, hDC);
}

// Clean up after the program. Delete any memory used and
// stop the timer.
void TSunsetWindow::EvDestroy()
{
  if (PalSupport) {
    // These objects weren't created if the hardware
    // does not support logical palettes
    DeleteObject(SkyBr);
    DeleteObject(IslandBr);
    DeleteObject(OceanBr);
    DeleteObject(SunBr);
    DeleteObject(HLogPal);
    delete LogPal;
  }
  ::KillTimer(HWindow, TIMER_ID);
  TWindow::EvDestroy();
}

// Paint the initial ocean scene
void TSunsetWindow::Paint(TDC& dc, BOOL, TRect&)
{
  RECT rect, rect2;
  if (!PalSupport) {
    // The video driver doesn't support a logical palette.
    // A 256-color video driver is required.
    ::MessageBox(HWindow, "256-Color Video Mode Driver Required",
      "Program Termination", MB_OK);
    // Tell the program to quit
    ::SendMessage(HWindow, WM_CLOSE, 0, 0L);
    return;
  }
  SelectPalette(dc, HLogPal, 0);  // Use the logical palette
  RealizePalette(dc);
  // Make sure the program is using the initial palette colors
  SetLogPaletteColors();
  AnimatePalette(HLogPal, 0, NUM_COLORS, LogPal->palPalEntry);
  // Determine how big the window and sky are
  ::GetClientRect(HWindow, &rect);
  CopyRect(&rect2, &rect);
```

```
        rect2.bottom = rect.bottom / 2;
        FillRect(dc, &rect2, SkyBr);
        rect2.top = rect2.bottom;   rect2.bottom = rect.bottom;
        // Display the sky
        FillRect(dc, &rect2, OceanBr);
        // Draw the crest of the island
        SelectObject(dc, IslandBr);
        SelectObject(dc, GetStockObject(NULL_PEN));
        Ellipse(dc, 0, rect.bottom-rect.bottom/8,
          rect.right, rect.bottom+rect.bottom/8);
        // Display the sun
        SunWd = rect.bottom / 8;
        SunX = rect.right / 2;    SunY = rect.bottom/4;
        SelectObject(dc, SunBr);
        Ellipse(dc, SunX-SunWd, SunY-SunWd, SunX+SunWd, SunY+SunWd);
        // Determine how much to darken each color as the sun drops.
        // You want the brightest color to turn black, so divide it
        // by the width of the sun.
        ColorDec = 255 / SunWd / 2;
}

// Respond to the timer by lowering the sun
void TSunsetWindow::EvTimer(UINT timerId)
{
  // Make sure it's this program's event
  if (timerId == TIMER_ID && !Done) {
    RECT rect;
    HDC hDC = GetDC(HWindow);
    SelectPalette(hDC, HLogPal, 0);  // Use the logical palette
    RealizePalette(hDC);
    ::GetClientRect(HWindow, &rect);
    if (SunY-SunWd < rect.bottom/2) {
      // Move the sun by painting its new position into
      // a bitmap and then copying the bitmap onto the
      // screen. This reduces screen flicker since the
      // sun does not have to be erased.
      RECT skyRect;
      CopyRect(&skyRect, &rect);
      skyRect.bottom /= 2;   // Bottom of sky extends to mid window
      HDC hMemDC = CreateCompatibleDC(hDC);
      HBITMAP hSkyBmp = CreateCompatibleBitmap(hDC,
        skyRect.right, skyRect.bottom);
      SelectObject(hMemDC, hSkyBmp);
      // The logical palette must be selected into
      // the memory context too!
      SelectPalette(hMemDC, HLogPal, 0);  // Use the logical palette
      RealizePalette(hMemDC);
      FillRect(hMemDC, &skyRect, SkyBr);
      SelectObject(hMemDC, GetStockObject(NULL_PEN));
      SunY++;                          // Draw sun at this line
      SelectObject(hMemDC, SunBr);
      Ellipse(hMemDC, SunX-SunWd, SunY-SunWd, SunX+SunWd, SunY+SunWd);
      // Copy the sky bitmap to the window
      BitBlt(hDC, 0, 0, skyRect.right, skyRect.bottom,
```

```
          hMemDC, 0, 0, SRCCOPY);
        // NOTE: ReleaseDC is NOT used here. ReleaseDC is used
        // with GetDC only.
        DeleteDC(hMemDC);
        DeleteObject(hSkyBmp);
        // When the sun reaches the horizon, darken all the
        // colors in the palette and then call AnimatePalette
        // to update the screen
        if (SunY > rect.bottom/2-SunWd) {
          for (int i=0; i<NUM_COLORS; i++) {
            if (LogPal->palPalEntry[i].peRed > ColorDec)
              LogPal->palPalEntry[i].peRed -= BYTE(ColorDec);
            else if (LogPal->palPalEntry[i].peRed)
              LogPal->palPalEntry[i].peRed--;
            if (LogPal->palPalEntry[i].peGreen > ColorDec)
              LogPal->palPalEntry[i].peGreen -= BYTE(ColorDec);
            else if (LogPal->palPalEntry[i].peGreen)
              LogPal->palPalEntry[i].peGreen--;
            if (LogPal->palPalEntry[i].peBlue > ColorDec)
              LogPal->palPalEntry[i].peBlue -= BYTE(ColorDec);
            else if (LogPal->palPalEntry[i].peBlue)
              LogPal->palPalEntry[i].peBlue--;
          }
          AnimatePalette(HLogPal, 0, NUM_COLORS, LogPal->palPalEntry);
        }
      }
      else {
        Done = TRUE;
        ::KillTimer(HWindow, TIMER_ID);   // Stop the timer events
      }
      ReleaseDC(HWindow, hDC);
  }
}

void TSunsetWindow::EvSize(UINT, TSize&)
{
  StartAnimation();
}

// A key was pressed. Start the animation over.
void TSunsetWindow::EvChar(UINT, UINT, UINT)
{
  StartAnimation();
}

// The left mouse button was pressed. Start the animation over.
void TSunsetWindow::EvLButtonDown(UINT, TPoint&)
{
  StartAnimation();
}

// Begin the animation sequence by resetting the colors in the
// logical palette and forcing the window to repaint. It doesn't
// restart the animation if the window is currently minimized.
```

```
void TSunsetWindow::StartAnimation()
{
  if (!::IsIconic(HWindow)) {  // Is the window an icon?
    // Reset the colors used in the display
    SetLogPaletteColors();
    // Redisplay the scene from the beginning
    ::InvalidateRect(HWindow, 0, TRUE);
    Done = FALSE;
    ::SetTimer(HWindow, TIMER_ID, DELAY, 0);   // Start timer
  }
  else if (!Done) {
    // The window is minimized. Stop the timer to
    // avoid any unnecessary timer events.
    Done = TRUE;
    ::KillTimer(HWindow, TIMER_ID);
  }
}

// This routine sets the colors in the logical palette to those
// required to display the blue sky, brown island, and blue ocean
void TSunsetWindow::SetLogPaletteColors()
{
  LogPal->palPalEntry[0].peRed = 128;    // Light blue sky
  LogPal->palPalEntry[0].peGreen = 255;
  LogPal->palPalEntry[0].peBlue = 255;
  LogPal->palPalEntry[0].peFlags = PC_RESERVED;
  LogPal->palPalEntry[1].peRed = 128;    // Brown
  LogPal->palPalEntry[1].peGreen = 64;
  LogPal->palPalEntry[1].peBlue = 58;
  LogPal->palPalEntry[1].peFlags = PC_RESERVED;
  LogPal->palPalEntry[2].peRed = 0;      // Dark blue ocean
  LogPal->palPalEntry[2].peGreen = 0;
  LogPal->palPalEntry[2].peBlue = 255;
  LogPal->palPalEntry[2].peFlags = PC_RESERVED;
}

class TSunsetApp : public TApplication {
public:
  TSunsetApp() : TApplication() { }
  void InitMainWindow();
};

void TSunsetApp::InitMainWindow()
{
  MainWindow = new TFrameWindow(0, "Island Sunset",
    new TSunsetWindow(0, ""));
}

int OwlMain(int /*argc*/, char* /*argv*/[])
{
  return TSunsetApp().Run();
}
```

E L E V E N

Fractal Landscapes

F
ractals are intriguing. With only a small amount of code and data you can generate highly detailed, complex scenes. In this chapter, we'll use fractals to paint natural-looking landscape scenes. We'll develop three applications that use fractals in slightly different ways to add realism to a scene. The first application displays a two-dimensional view of a mountain and a shoreline. The second program moves to the desert and portrays an animated lightning storm. The last fractal example displays a three-dimensional, snow-capped mountain scene.

INTRODUCTION TO FRACTALS

If you want to write a program that generates a scene, you would probably start by supplying the program with a list of shapes and coordinates to display. The more detail you'd want in the figure, the more shapes and figures you would supply. Clearly, for highly detailed or complex scenes, this approach would require that you supply a large amount of data.

Fractals provide a way around this problem. With fractals, you only need to provide a crude representation of a scene. The algorithm breaks this representation up into smaller and smaller pieces, offsetting each piece in order to create the desired effect. In fact, fractals are an excellent way of modeling nature's complexity. With fractals, it's possible to create highly detailed, realistic scenes of mountains, leaves, lakes, bolts of lightning, and so on.

The success of fractal geometry is based on its randomness. As a region that makes up a scene is successively divided, its smaller components are *perturbed* based on some scale factor and random number. The random number gives the figure its natural appearance and the scale factor guides its

271

overall appearance. A decay factor is also employed to lessen the scale factor with each successively smaller region. By selecting the appropriate scale and decay factors, you can make jagged mountains or rolling hills.

We'll begin by fractalizing line segments and restricting ourselves to two dimensions: X and Y. This restriction will make it easier for you to see how fractalization works. Later, we'll add the third dimension and work with planes and polygons.

A MOUNTAIN SKYLINE

The first fractal program, FRACTAL.CPP, displays a randomly generated mountain skyline with a lake at its base and a glowing sun above it. A sample scene created by FRACTAL.CPP is shown in Figure 11.1. The contours of the mountains and the shoreline are created with fractals.

Fractalizing a Line

The contour lines of the mountains and the ocean actually begin as straight lines that extend across the screen. The procedure **Fractal** is invoked to contort these lines so that they take on the jaggedness of a mountain skyline or the meanderings of a shoreline.

The **Fractal** procedure calls the routine **Subdivide**, which actually performs the fractalization. This function takes a line segment, calculates the midpoint between its endpoints, and then perturbs the midpoint up or down

Figure 11.1 FRACTAL.CPP creates this moutain skyline.

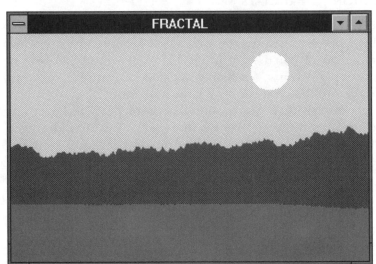

by a random amount. This adjusted midpoint is saved in the array **frctl** and later used to determine the Y value of the figure at that point.

The fractalization continues by taking the line segments to the left and right of the midpoint and bending these segments at their midpoints, too. Their segments are subdivided and perturbed in a similar fashion and the process is repeated until the segments become too small to subdivide. At the end, **frctl** contains a series of small, connected segments that vary in the Y direction. Figure 11.2 shows the stages of the fractalization of a sample line segment. Note that the amount the line segment is perturbed decreases as the line segment is subdivided into smaller pieces.

Using the Fractal Routine

The degree to which a midpoint is perturbed is randomly calculated. This gives the final figure a reasonably natural look. However, there are several variables passed to the **Fractal** function that help control the way the lines are generated. Here is the complete **Fractal** routine:

```
void TFractalWindow::Fractal(int y1, int y2, int last,
  double h, double scale, int frctl[])
{
  int first = 0;
  frctl[first] = y1;                        // Use y1 and y2 as end
  frctl[last] = y2;                         // points of line
  double ratio = 1.0 / pow(2.0, h);         // Defines fractalization
  double std = scale * ratio;               // decays at each level
  Subdivide(first, last, std, ratio, frctl); // Start fractalization
}
```

The **y1** and **y2** variables are the Y values of the endpoints of the line to fractalize. The **Fractal** routine calls **Subdivide** to perturb the Y values between

---

Figure 11.2 The process of fractalizing a line.

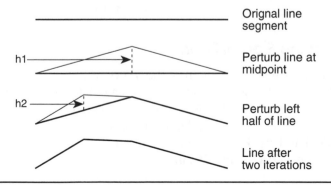

Orignal line segment

Perturb line at midpoint

Perturb left half of line

Line after two iterations

---

these two parameters and places the results in the **frctl** array. The **last** parameter specifies the last index location to use in **frctl**; the **y2** value is placed here.

The **scale** parameter partially defines the amount of the perturbation at each step in the fractalization. In addition, **scale**'s preceding parameter, **h**, specifies a decay factor that is multiplied (indirectly) against the current perturbation value in **scale**, at each subdivision of the line. This reduces the size of **scale** with each successively smaller line segment. As a result, line segments initially vary greatly, but as they get smaller they are perturbed less and less. This creates a realistic roughness in many scenes.

It is the combination of these two values, **scale** and **h**, that controls the outcome of the fractal line. For example, in this program the mountain skyline is much rougher than the shoreline so its **h** decay factor is set to only 0.5 (1 is the smoothest and close to 0 is the roughest). In addition, the mountains should be large, so **scale** is initially set to a rather large value of 50. The shoreline, however, is supposed to be much smoother, so its **h** factor is 0.9, and **scale** is assigned a value of 30.

You may also want to experiment with the **h** and **scale** values passed to the fractal routine for the mountains and shoreline—to see what effect these parameters have on the fractalized surface.

Randomness Is Natural

The key to fractal geometry is the randomness that is applied to the line, surface, or shape that is being fractalized. Here, the Borland C++ routines **random** and **randomize** are combined to return a random value based on the clock in the PC. The statement **random(16)**, for instance, returns a random number between 0 and 15, inclusive. These random values are used to determine how much to perturb each line segment.

Since the **Fractal** routine is based on random numbers, the program generates a different landscape scene each time the program is started. In addition, FRACTAL.CPP is designed to calculate a new scene each time the user presses a key or clicks the left mouse button.

Displaying the Fractal Scene

The fractalized values placed into the **frctl** array (passed to **Fractal**) are actually Y *offsets*. The points displayed are calculated from the values in **frctl** and stored in an array of **POINT** structures, which is passed to **Polygon** to display the figure. For example, the **SkyFractal** array contains the fractalized Y offsets, calculated by **Fractal**, for the mountain's skyline. These points are copied into the **POINT** array **Skyline**:

```
for (i=0, x=-1; i<l; i++, x+=xInc) {    // Draw one line at a time
  Skyline[i].x = x;
  Skyline[i].y = y + SkyFractal[i];     // using y values in frctl
}
Skyline[i].x = rect.right + 1;
Skyline[i++].y = rect.bottom + 1;
Skyline[i].x = rect.left - 1;
Skyline[i++].y = rect.bottom + 1;
SkyLen = i;
```

The **y** variable specifies the overall height of the mountains. The variable is set to the middle row of the window. Notice that the **POINT** array is closed off by extending its vertices to the bottom of the window. The **xInc** variable is used in the **for** loop to spread out the mountain's fractal values across the width of the window.

After the fractal values have been loaded into a **POINT** array, the proper brush style (**MtnBr**) is selected and **Polygon** is called to display the mountains. (Earlier, the program selected the **NULL_PEN** object so that a border is not drawn):

```
SelectObject(dc, MtnBr);
Polygon(dc, Skyline, SkyLen);  // Draw the mountain
```

The additional **POINT** array, **Skyline**, allows us to stretch or compress the fractal values in **SkyFractal** so that they fit within the window. The fractalized values, therefore, are independent of the size of the window. If the window size is changed, we simply recalculate **Skyline**'s values, not the fractal values in **SkyFractal**.

Note

If we recalculated the fractal values each time the **Paint** routine is called, the scene would quickly become a mess. Remember, the fractal values are based on random numbers. Therefore, each time the values are calculated, they are different.

Since the **Paint** function can be called to restore a portion of the window, we need to save the currently displayed fractal values in order to repaint them. However, we can't recalculate the fractal values—unless we also store the random numbers that went along with them.

The program uses the Boolean flag **Calculated** to determine when it needs to recalculate the scene. If **Calculated** is TRUE, the precalculated values in the fractal arrays are used. If **Calculated** is FALSE, however, a new scene is created by calling **Fractal**. The flag is required so that the program won't recalculate the whole scene whenever a portion of the scene must be repainted.

Displaying the shoreline is similar to the approach used to paint the mountains. The sky, however, is painted by the **EvEraseBkgnd** message response function. Since OWL programs normally paint the backdrop white, we have to change the background color to avoid Windows painting the window white and then repainting it with the sky's color. Another way to change the background color is to set the **hbrBackground** field in the class definition to the sky's color.

The **WM_CHAR** and **WM_LBUTTONDOWN** messages are captured in order to force the program to generate a new scene each time the user presses a key or clicks the left mouse button. The new scene is generated by setting the **Calculated** flag to FALSE and calling **InvalidateRect** to erase the entire window and then repaint it:

```
void TFractalWindow::EvChar(UINT, UINT, UINT)
{
  Calculated = FALSE;      // Force recalculation of fractals
  ::InvalidateRect(HWindow, 0, TRUE);
}
```

The arrays used in FRACTAL.CPP are dynamically allocated in **SetupWindow**, which is called when the window is being created. Similarly, the arrays are deallocated by **EvDestroy**, which is called when the window is being closed. In addition, the brushes used to paint the sky, mountains, water, and sun are created and destroyed by these two functions.

Compiling FRACTAL.CPP

To compile the FRACTAL program you only need one source file, FRACTAL.CPP.

• FRACTAL.CPP

```
// FRACTAL.CPP: Creates a fractalized mountain scene. The scene
// changes each time you press a key or click the left mouse button.

#include <owl\applicat.h>
#include <owl\framewin.h>
#include <owl\dc.h>
#include <math.h>

const int MAXSIZE = 1000;    // The fractalized array has this room

class TFractalWindow : public TWindow {
  int SkyLen;             // Length of Skyline array
  int ShoreLen;           // Length of Shoreline array
  BOOL Calculated;        // TRUE if fractal offsets are calculated
  POINT* Skyline;         // Points to display for skyline
  POINT* Shoreline;       // Points to display for shoreline
  int* ShoreFractal;      // Fractal offsets for shoreline
  int* SkyFractal;        // Fractal offsets for skyline
  HBRUSH SkyBr;           // Brush for sky
```

```
    HBRUSH MtnBr;         // Brush for mountain
    HBRUSH LakeBr;        // Brush for lake
    HBRUSH SunBr;         // Brush for sun
public:
  TFractalWindow(TWindow *parent, const char* title)
    : TWindow(parent, title) {
    randomize();          // Initialize random function
    Calculated = FALSE;
    // Allocate memory for the polygons
    Shoreline = new POINT[MAXSIZE];
    Skyline = new POINT[MAXSIZE];
    ShoreFractal = new int[MAXSIZE];
    SkyFractal = new int[MAXSIZE];
  }
  void Fractal(int y1, int y2, int last,
    double h, double scale, int frctl[]);
  void Subdivide(int p1, int p2, double std,
    double ratio, int frctl[]);
  void SetupWindow();
  void EvDestroy();
  void EvChar(UINT, UINT, UINT);
  void EvLButtonDown(UINT, TPoint&);
  BOOL EvEraseBkgnd(HDC hDC);
  void Paint(TDC& dc, BOOL, TRect&);
  void EvSize(UINT, TSize&);

  DECLARE_RESPONSE_TABLE(TFractalWindow);
};

DEFINE_RESPONSE_TABLE1(TFractalWindow, TWindow)
  EV_WM_DESTROY,
  EV_WM_CHAR,
  EV_WM_LBUTTONDOWN,
  EV_WM_ERASEBKGND,
  EV_WM_SIZE,
END_RESPONSE_TABLE;

// Create the brushes used in the program
void TFractalWindow::SetupWindow()
{
  TWindow::SetupWindow();
  SkyBr = CreateSolidBrush(RGB(128, 255, 255)); // Light blue
  MtnBr = CreateSolidBrush(RGB(128, 64, 58));   // Brown
  LakeBr = CreateSolidBrush(RGB(0, 0, 255));    // Dark blue
  SunBr = CreateSolidBrush(RGB(255, 255, 64));  // Yellow
}

// This routine cleans up after the program
void TFractalWindow::EvDestroy()
{
  // Delete the brushes created in SetupWindow
  DeleteObject(SkyBr);
  DeleteObject(MtnBr);
  DeleteObject(LakeBr);
```

```
    DeleteObject(SunBr);
    // Free the memory allocated in the constructor
    delete Shoreline;
    delete Skyline;
    delete ShoreFractal;
    delete SkyFractal;
    TWindow::EvDestroy();
}

// Draw the mountain scene. Don't recompute the scene if
// the Calculated flag is TRUE.
void TFractalWindow::Paint(TDC& dc, BOOL, TRect&)
{
  RECT rect;
  int i, x, xInc, l, y;

  ::GetClientRect(HWindow, &rect);
  // Don't outline the filled figures. Use an invisible pen.
  SelectObject(dc, GetStockObject(NULL_PEN));
  // Draw a sun using a filled ellipse
  int radius = rect.bottom / 14;  // The radius of the sun
  SelectObject(dc, SunBr);
  Ellipse(dc, rect.right*3/4-radius, rect.bottom/4-radius,
    rect.right*3/4+radius, rect.bottom/4+radius);
  // Calculate approximate height of mountain
  y = (rect.bottom - rect.top) / 2;
  l = MAXSIZE - 3;
  xInc = (rect.right-rect.left+2) / (l-1) + 1;
  if (!Calculated) {    // Fractalize the mountain's skyline
    Fractal(0, 0, l, 0.5, 50.0, SkyFractal);
  }
  // Fill the polygon with the points just calculated
  for (i=0, x=-1; i<l; i++, x+=xInc) {    // Draw one line at a time
    Skyline[i].x = x;
    Skyline[i].y = y + SkyFractal[i];    // using y values in frctl
  }
  Skyline[i].x = rect.right + 1;
  Skyline[i++].y = rect.bottom + 1;
  Skyline[i].x = rect.left - 1;
  Skyline[i++].y = rect.bottom + 1;
  SkyLen = i;
  SelectObject(dc, MtnBr);
  Polygon(dc, Skyline, SkyLen);  // Draw the mountain
  // Calculate approximate "height" of the water in the scene
  y = (rect.bottom - rect.top) * 3 / 4;
  if (!Calculated) {
    // Fractalize the shoreline. Make it smooth.
    Fractal(0, 0, l, 0.9, 30.0, ShoreFractal);
    Calculated = TRUE;    // The fractal lines have been calculated
  }
  // Copy the fractalized values to an array. This array is
  // passed to Polygon in order to draw the lake.
  for (i=0, x=-1; i<l; i++, x+=xInc) {
```

```
      Shoreline[i].x = x;
      Shoreline[i].y = y + ShoreFractal[i];
    }
    Shoreline[i].x = rect.right + 1;
    Shoreline[i++].y = rect.bottom + 1;
    Shoreline[i].x = rect.left - 1;
    Shoreline[i++].y = rect.bottom + 1;
    ShoreLen = i;
    SelectObject(dc, LakeBr);
    Polygon(dc, Shoreline, ShoreLen);    // Paint the lake
}

// The user has pressed a key. Recalculate and repaint the
// landscape scene.
void TFractalWindow::EvChar(UINT, UINT, UINT)
{
  Calculated = FALSE;      // Force recalculation of fractals
  ::InvalidateRect(HWindow, 0, TRUE);
}

// The user has clicked the left mouse button. Recalculate
// and repaint the landscape scene.
void TFractalWindow::EvLButtonDown(UINT, TPoint&)
{
  Calculated = FALSE;     // Recalculate fractals
  ::InvalidateRect(HWindow, 0, TRUE);
}

// Repaint the scene if the window is resized
void TFractalWindow::EvSize(UINT, TSize&)
{
  Calculated = FALSE;     // Recalculate fractals
  ::InvalidateRect(HWindow, 0, TRUE);
}

// This is the main fractal routine. It fractalizes a line in one
// dimension only. The fractalized line is put into the array frctl.
// The parameter h is a number between 0 and 1 that specifies the
// roughness of the line (1 is smoothest), and scale is a scale
// factor that tells how much to perturb each line segment.
void TFractalWindow::Fractal(int y1, int y2, int last,
  double h, double scale, int frctl[])
{
  int first = 0;
  frctl[first] = y1;                    // Use y1 and y2 as end
  frctl[last] = y2;                     // points of line
  double ratio = 1.0 / pow(2.0, h);     // Defines fractalization
  double std = scale * ratio;           // decays at each level
  Subdivide(first, last, std, ratio, frctl); // Start fractalization
}

// This is the work-horse routine for the fractalization function. It
// computes the midpoint between the two points: p1 and p2, and then
```

```
// perturbs it by a random factor that is scaled by std. Then it
// calls itself to fractalize the line segments to the left and
// right of the midpoint. This process continues until no further
// divisions can be made.
void TFractalWindow::Subdivide(int p1, int p2, double std,
  double ratio, int frctl[])
{
  double stdmid;
  // Break the line at the midpoint of point 1 and point 2
  int midpnt = (p1 + p2) / 2;
  // If the midpoint is unique from point 1 and point 2,
  // then perturb it randomly according to the equation shown
  if (midpnt != p1 && midpnt != p2) {
    frctl[midpnt] = ((double)(frctl[p1] + frctl[p2])) / 2 +
      (double)((random(16) - 8)) / 8.0 * std;
    // Then fractalize the line segments to the left and right of the
    // midpoint by calling subdivide again. Note that the scale factor
    // used to perturb each fractalized point is decreased with each call
    // by the amount in ratio.
    stdmid = std * ratio;
    // Fractalize left segment
    Subdivide(p1, midpnt, stdmid, ratio, frctl);
    // Fractalize right segment
    Subdivide(midpnt, p2, stdmid, ratio, frctl);
  }
}


// Paint the background of the window the sky color
BOOL TFractalWindow::EvEraseBkgnd(HDC hDC)
{
  RECT rect;
  ::GetClientRect(HWindow, &rect);
  FillRect(hDC, &rect, SkyBr);
  return TRUE;
}

class TFractalSceneApp : public TApplication {
public:
  TFractalSceneApp() : TApplication() { }
  void InitMainWindow();
};

void TFractalSceneApp::InitMainWindow()
{
  MainWindow = new TFrameWindow(0, "FRACTAL",
    new TFractalWindow(0, ""));
}

int OwlMain(int /*argc*/, char* /*argv*/[])
{
  return TFractalSceneApp().Run();
}
```

A DESERT STORM

After I wrote the original FRACTAL program, a colleague of mine, Bryan Flamig, modified it to display a desert mountain scene during a lightning storm—complete with flashing bolts of lightning. His program, written as a DOS application, included fast line-drawing routines and register-level palette animation, so I expected it would be a challenge to port to Windows. However, it didn't turn out to be difficult. I think you'll find the result intriguing and I hope it serves as a launching pad for your own ideas and modifications.

The program, entitled STORM.CPP, is similar to FRACTAL.CPP in that it displays a two-dimensional fractalized mountain scene. However, STORM also includes two layers of fractalized clouds behind the mountains, bolts of lightning, and randomly generated saguaro cacti. In addition, the scene is set at night during a full moon. As you'll discover, the random function is liberally called in order to provide variety in the scenes generated.

The lightning bolts are generated by briefly exclusive-ORing fractalized lines with the screen. They are triggered in response to a one-second timer. The position, duration, and, in fact, whether the lightning bolt is displayed at all, are randomly determined. Similarly, two banks of distant clouds light up from time to time. Palette animation is used here to achieve this effect. The two fractalized cloud banks, normally black, use different palette entries that are randomly set to various shades of gray to create the illusion of distant lightning.

Additionally the program displays small saguaro cactus plants scattered near the bottom of the scene. Palette animation is employed here, too. Normally, the cacti are a muted green that blend with the mountain backdrop. However, when a lighting bolt flashes, the cactus color is momentarily switched to a lighter green. Figure 11.3 displays a frame that STORM created.

 Note   Since STORM.CPP uses palette animation, your display hardware must support logical palettes.

Figure 11.3 STORM.CPP creates this desert storm scene.

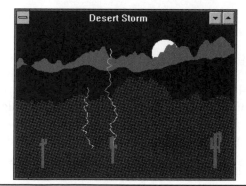

Now we'll walk through the various components of the program. The **Paint** member function divides the process of drawing the scene into painting the moon, the two banks of clouds, the mountains, and then the cacti. The backdrop is initially filled black by the **EvEraseBkgnd** message-response function.

Displaying Clouds and Mountains

The **Paint** function calls **CloudBank** to display each of the two cloud banks. The outline of clouds is created using a series of fractalized line segments similar to those used to create the outline of the mountains. However, the fractal lines are bent into two pieces so that a peak exists:

```
int last = MAXCLOUD - 1;
CloudFractal[0] = 0;
CloudFractal[last/2] = rect.bottom / 8;
CloudFractal[last] = 0;
double ratio = 1.0 / pow(2.0,0.5);   // Defines fractalization
double std = 50.0 * ratio;           // decays at each level
Subdivide(0, last/2, std, ratio, CloudFractal);
Subdivide(last/2, last, std, ratio, CloudFractal);
```

Adding this initial offset helps to make the clouds appear more like thunderheads. The fractal values are stored in the array **CloudFractal**. This array is used to draw both sets of clouds. The two cloud banks are made slightly different, however, by placing them at different heights in the window and stretching them by different amounts. For instance, the clouds farthest away are incremented by four pixels in the X direction and the closer ones by ten pixels. Both cloud banks are initially set to black. However, they use different palette entries so that later we can modify their colors individually. The **CloudBank** function also draws a series of ellipses along the perimeter of the cloud line. This helps to add a little puffiness to the tops of the clouds.

The **MountainSkyline** routine draws the mountains. It follows the same procedure as the one used in FRACTAL.CPP.

Displaying Saguaro Cacti

The **Saguaro** function displays up to 11 saguaro cacti of random height and position. The details of the function may be a little obscure due to the randomness it employs. Basically, the code attempts to paint cactus plants that are not too tall and that diminish in size as they get farther away (higher in the scene).

Similarly, the pen width used to draw a cactus is based on its height. Taller cacti are drawn with thicker pens. Two branches of random height are placed near the top of each saguaro—one branch on each side. A muted green color, stored in the third index location of the logical palette, is used to draw the cacti. You'll see later how this palette color is temporarily changed to a brighter green whenever a lightning bolt is displayed.

Timing the Animation

A one-second timer is set up in the **SetupWindow** function. The **EvTimer** function performs the storm's animation by doing one or more of the following: flashing the cloud banks, displaying a bolt of lightning, and/or temporarily making the cacti brighter. The **random** function is used again to reduce how frequently the animation is performed. For instance, **EvTimer** calls **random** with a parameter of 3 to reduce the probability of displaying a bolt of lightning to 30 percent.

A lightning bolt is simply a fractalized line. Actually, it's the same fractal surface used to display the mountains, which is stored in **SkyFractal**. The difference is that the **SkyFractal** values are copied into the **x** field of the **Lightning** array, rather than the **y** field. The lightning is displayed by calling **Polyline** after setting the drawing mode to **R2_XORPEN**. Remember, the **R2_XORPEN** mode exclusive-ORs the pen color with the screen. Later, the lighting flash is removed by redrawing it. A random delay is introduced so that the lightning remains on the screen long enough to be visible.

▼ **Note** The colors displayed where the lightning bolts are exclusive-ORed with the screen depend on two things: the original screen color and the color in the hardware palette that corresponds with the result of the exclusive-OR operation.

During the lightning flash, the cactus plants are highlighted by changing their palette color to a brighter green. Palette index 2 stores the color of the saguaros. The **AnimatePalette** function makes the palette change instantly visible on the screen:

```
SetPaletteEntry(2, 100, 128, 100);
AnimatePalette(HLogPal, 2, 1, &LogPal->palPalEntry[2]);
```

In addition to the lightning bolts, **EvTimer** may also brighten the two layers of clouds. The brightness of the clouds is randomly selected between black and gray—between 0 and 127:

```
// Use palette animation to flash the banks of clouds
BYTE flashColor = random(128);  // Randomly pick a cloud color
if (random(2))
  SetPaletteEntry(0, flashColor, flashColor, flashColor);
// Randomly flash the other bank of clouds
flashColor = random(128);
if (random(2))
  SetPaletteEntry(1, flashColor, flashColor, flashColor);
```

```
// Perform the palette animation
AnimatePalette(HLogPal, 0, 2, LogPal->palPalEntry);
```

Again, the program delays a random amount before restoring the clouds' palette colors to black.

The logical palette holds the key to the palette animation. The **SetupWindow** function creates a logical palette with three entries—two for the clouds and one for the saguaros. For convenience, the function **SetPaletteEntry** is also included to set the entries in the logical palette to a particular RGB value.

Compiling STORM.CPP

To run the STORM program you only need to compile the source file STORM.CPP. Remember, STORM uses a logical palette; therefore it can only run if a 256-mode Windows video driver is installed.

• STORM.CPP

```
// STORM.CPP: A variation on the fractal landscape program that
// uses palette animation to produce a fairly realistic
// representation of a night-time desert lightning storm.
// The program requires logical palette support. Therefore,
// you must run it with a 256-color video driver.

#include <owl\applicat.h>
#include <owl\framewin.h>
#include <owl\dc.h>
#include <math.h>

#define MAXSKY 100    // The sky's fractalized array has this room
#define MAXCLOUD 175 // Cloud array
#define MAXBOLT 75    // Lightning bolt array size
#define TIMER_ID 1    // The timer's ID used by Windows
#define NCOLORS 3     // Number of colors in the logical palette

int Delay(int k);    // A simple delay routine

class TStormWindow : public TWindow {
  int SkyLen;
  int CloudLen;
  int LightningLen;
  BOOL PalSupport;         // TRUE if hardware supports a palette
  BOOL Calculated;
  LPLOGPALETTE LogPal;
  HPALETTE HLogPal;
  LPPOINT SkyLine;
  LPINT SkyFractal;
  LPPOINT CloudLine;
```

```
    LPINT CloudFractal;
    LPPOINT Lightning;
public:
  TStormWindow(TWindow *parent, const char* title)
    : TWindow(parent, title) {
    randomize();              // Initialize random function
    PalSupport = FALSE;
    Calculated = FALSE;
  }
  void Fractal(int y1, int y2, int last, double h,
    double scale, int frctl[]);
  void Subdivide(int p1, int p2, double std,
    double ratio, int frctl[]);
  void CloudBank(HDC hDC, RECT& rect, COLORREF color,
    int xInc, int yOffset);
  void MountainSkyline(HDC hDC, RECT& rect);
  void Cactus(HDC hDC, RECT& rect);
  void SetPaletteEntry(int indx, BYTE red, BYTE green, BYTE blue);
  void SetupWindow();
  void EvDestroy();
  void EvTimer(UINT timerId);
  void EvLButtonDown(UINT, TPoint&);
  void EvChar(UINT, UINT, UINT);
  BOOL EvEraseBkgnd(HDC hDC);
  void EvSize(UINT, TSize&);
  void Paint(TDC& dc, BOOL, TRect&);

  DECLARE_RESPONSE_TABLE(TStormWindow);
};

DEFINE_RESPONSE_TABLE1(TStormWindow, TWindow)
  EV_WM_DESTROY,
  EV_WM_TIMER,
  EV_WM_LBUTTONDOWN,
  EV_WM_CHAR,
  EV_WM_ERASEBKGND,
  EV_WM_SIZE,
END_RESPONSE_TABLE;

// Fill the background with black
BOOL TStormWindow::EvEraseBkgnd(HDC hDC)
{
  RECT rect;
  ::GetClientRect(HWindow, &rect);
  FillRect(hDC, &rect, HBRUSH(GetStockObject(BLACK_BRUSH)));
  return TRUE;
}

// Paint the mountain backdrop
void TStormWindow::Paint(TDC& dc, BOOL, TRect&)
{
  if (!PalSupport) {
    // The video driver doesn't support a logical palette.
```

```
    // A 256-color video driver is required.
    ::MessageBox(HWindow, "256-Color Video Mode Driver Required",
      "Program Termination", MB_OK);
    // Tell the program to quit
    PostQuitMessage(0);
    return;
  }
  SelectPalette(dc, HLogPal, 0);  // Use the logical palette
  RealizePalette(dc);
  RECT rect;
  ::GetClientRect(HWindow, &rect);
  // Draw a white moon
  Ellipse(dc, rect.right-120, 20, rect.right-80, 60);
  // Display the farthest-away layer of fractalized clouds
  CloudBank(dc, rect, PALETTEINDEX(0), 4, 0);
  // Draw another layer of clouds a bit "closer." Use a
  // different palette index so that flashes in the clouds
  // can be shown using palette animation.
  CloudBank(dc, rect, PALETTEINDEX(1), 10, 10);
  MountainSkyline(dc, rect);
  Cactus(dc, rect);
  Calculated = TRUE;    // The values have been calculated
}


// When the user clicks the left mouse button recalculate the scene
void TStormWindow::EvLButtonDown(UINT, TPoint&)
{
  Calculated = FALSE;    // Force recalculation of fractals
  ::InvalidateRect(HWindow, 0, TRUE);  // Redraw scene
}


// When the user presses a key recalculate the scene
void TStormWindow::EvChar(UINT, UINT, UINT)
{
  Calculated = FALSE;    // Force recalculation of fractals
  ::InvalidateRect(HWindow, 0, TRUE);  // Redraw scene
}


// Repaint the whole window if the user resizes the window
void TStormWindow::EvSize(UINT, TSize&)
{
  ::InvalidateRect(HWindow, 0, TRUE);  // Redraw scene
}


// Called at each timer event. Perform one step of the animation.
void TStormWindow::EvTimer(UINT timerId)
{
  int i, oldMode;
  HPEN hOldPen;

  if (timerId != TIMER_ID) return;
  // Respond to the timer message randomly
  if (Calculated && !random(3)) {
    HDC hDC = GetDC(HWindow);
```

```
// Display a lighting only 30% of the time
BOOL displayBolt = (random(3) == 0) ? 1 : 0;
if (displayBolt) {
  RECT rect;
  ::GetClientRect(HWindow, &rect);
  // Randomly place the lightning bolt in the X direction, but
  // don't place it too close to the border.
  int x = random(rect.right-20) + 10;
  // Randomly place the top of the lightning bolt
  int y = random(100);
  int boltTop = (SkyLine[y].y + CloudLine[y].y) / 2;
  // Place the bottom somewhere between the bottom of the
  // window and the top of the lightning bolt. Use
  // the skyline fractal as the lightning bolt pattern.
  int boltBttm = rect.bottom - random(boltTop);
  for (i=0; y<boltBttm && i<MAXBOLT; i++, y+=4) {
    Lightning[i].x = x - SkyFractal[i];
    Lightning[i].y = y;
  }
  LightningLen = i-1;
  hOldPen = HPEN(SelectObject(hDC, GetStockObject(WHITE_PEN)));
  oldMode = SetROP2(hDC, R2_XORPEN);
  Polyline(hDC, Lightning, LightningLen);  // Draw lightning
  // Show the cacti. Notice which palette entry is used.
  SetPaletteEntry(2, 100, 128, 100);
  AnimatePalette(HLogPal, 2, 1, &LogPal->palPalEntry[2]);
  Delay(5+random(20));
  Polyline(hDC, Lightning, LightningLen);  // Erase lightning
  SetPaletteEntry(2, 50, 67, 41);
  AnimatePalette(HLogPal, 2, 1, &LogPal->palPalEntry[2]);
}
// Use palette animation to flash the banks of clouds
BYTE flashColor = random(128);  // Randomly pick a cloud color
if (random(2))
  SetPaletteEntry(0, flashColor, flashColor, flashColor);
// Randomly flash the other bank of clouds
flashColor = random(128);
if (random(2))
  SetPaletteEntry(1, flashColor, flashColor, flashColor);
// Perform the palette animation
AnimatePalette(HLogPal, 0, 2, LogPal->palPalEntry);
if (displayBolt) {
  Polyline(hDC, Lightning, LightningLen);  // Draw
  // Show the cacti as green
  SetPaletteEntry(2, 100, 128, 100);
  AnimatePalette(HLogPal, 2, 1, &LogPal->palPalEntry[2]);
  Delay(20+random(10));
  Polyline(hDC, Lightning, LightningLen);  // Erase
  // Hide the cacti again
  SetPaletteEntry(2, 50, 67, 41);
  AnimatePalette(HLogPal, 2, 1, &LogPal->palPalEntry[2]);
  SetROP2(hDC, oldMode);
  SelectObject(hDC, hOldPen);
}
```

```
      ReleaseDC(HWindow, hDC);
      Delay(15+random(10));
      // Restore the palette
      SetPaletteEntry(0, 0, 0, 0);
      SetPaletteEntry(1, 0, 0, 0);
      AnimatePalette(HLogPal, 0, 2, LogPal->palPalEntry);
  }
}

// Set up the memory and drawing parameters for the application
void TStormWindow::SetupWindow()
{
  TWindow::SetupWindow();

  // Create a timer event that triggers every second
  ::SetTimer(HWindow, TIMER_ID, 1000, 0);
  // Allocate memory for the polygons
  SkyLine = new POINT[MAXSKY];
  SkyFractal = new int[MAXSKY];
  CloudLine = new POINT[MAXCLOUD];
  CloudFractal = new int[MAXCLOUD];
  Lightning = new POINT[MAXBOLT];
  // Create a logical palette, if supported by the hardware
  HDC hDC = GetDC(HWindow);
  if (RC_PALETTE & GetDeviceCaps(hDC, RASTERCAPS)) {
    LogPal = (LOGPALETTE *)(new char[sizeof(LOGPALETTE) +
      sizeof(PALETTEENTRY) * NCOLORS]);
    LogPal->palVersion = 0x300;
    LogPal->palNumEntries = NCOLORS;
    SetPaletteEntry(0, 0, 0, 0);
    LogPal->palPalEntry[0].peFlags = PC_RESERVED;
    SetPaletteEntry(1, 0, 0, 0);
    LogPal->palPalEntry[1].peFlags = PC_RESERVED;
    SetPaletteEntry(2, 50, 67, 41);
    LogPal->palPalEntry[2].peFlags = PC_RESERVED;
    HLogPal = CreatePalette(LogPal);
    PalSupport = TRUE;
  }
  ReleaseDC(HWindow, hDC);
}

// Cleanup routine
void TStormWindow::EvDestroy()
{
  ::KillTimer(HWindow, TIMER_ID);
  if (PalSupport) {
    DeleteObject(HLogPal);
    delete LogPal;
  }
  delete SkyLine;
  delete SkyFractal;
  delete CloudFractal;
  delete CloudLine;
  delete Lightning;
```

```
    TWindow::EvDestroy();
}


// This is the main fractal routine. It fractalizes a line in one
// dimension only. The fractalized line is put into the array frctl.
// The parameter h is a number between 0 and 1 that specifies the
// roughness of the line (1 is smoothest), and "scale" is a scale
// factor that tells how much to perturb each line segment.
void TStormWindow::Fractal(int y1, int y2, int last,
  double h, double scale, int frctl[])
{
  int first=0;
  double ratio, std;

  frctl[first] = y1;               // Use y1 and y2 as end
  frctl[last] = y2;                // points of line
  ratio = 1.0 / pow(2.0, h);       // Defines fractalization
  std = scale * ratio;             // decays at each level
  Subdivide(first, last, std, ratio, frctl);  // Start fractalization
}


// This is the work-horse routine for the fractalization function. It
// computes the midpoint between the two points: p1 and p2, and then
// perturbs it by a random factor that is scaled by std. Then it
// calls itself to fractalize the line segments to the left and
// right of the midpoint. This process continues until no further
// divisions can be made.
void TStormWindow::Subdivide(int p1, int p2, double std,
  double ratio, int frctl[])
{
  // Break the line at the midpoint of point 1 and point 2
  int midpnt = (p1 + p2) / 2;
  // If the midpoint is unique from point 1 and point 2, then
  // perturb it randomly according to the equation shown
  if (midpnt != p1 && midpnt != p2) {
    frctl[midpnt] = ((double)(frctl[p1] + frctl[p2])) / 2 +
      (double)((random(17) - 8)) / 8.0 * std;
    // Then fractalize the line segments to the left and right of the
    // midpoint by calling subdivide again. Note that the scale factor
    // used to perturb each fractalized point is decreased with each call
    // by the amount in ratio.
    double stdmid = std * ratio;
    // Fractalize left segment
    Subdivide(p1, midpnt, stdmid, ratio, frctl);
    // Fractalize right segment
    Subdivide(midpnt, p2, stdmid, ratio, frctl);
  }
}


// Display a cloud bank using the palette color specified.
// xInc parameter specifies how spread out to draw the
// fractalized polygons. yOffset shifts the cloud bank down
// in the scene, creating the illusion that the clouds are
// closer than those behind and taller than it.
```

```
void TStormWindow::CloudBank(HDC hDC, RECT& rect, COLORREF color,
  int xInc, int yOffset)
{
  int i, x;

  if (!Calculated) {
    int last = MAXCLOUD - 1;
    CloudFractal[0] = 0;
    CloudFractal[last/2] = rect.bottom / 8;
    CloudFractal[last] = 0;
    double ratio = 1.0 / pow(2.0,0.5);  // Defines fractalization
    double std = 50.0 * ratio;           // decays at each level
    Subdivide(0, last/2, std, ratio, CloudFractal);
    Subdivide(last/2, last, std, ratio, CloudFractal);
  }
  // Fill the polygon with the calculated points
  int cloudLeft = 0;
  // Center cloud bank at top 1/4 of scene
  int cloudBottom = rect.bottom / 4;
  for (i=0, x=cloudLeft; i<MAXCLOUD; i++, x+=xInc) {
    CloudLine[i].x = x;
    CloudLine[i].y = cloudBottom - CloudFractal[i] + yOffset;
  }
  CloudLine[MAXCLOUD-2].x = rect.right;  // Right extent of cloud
  CloudLine[MAXCLOUD-2].y = rect.bottom;
  CloudLine[MAXCLOUD-1].x = -1;
  CloudLine[MAXCLOUD-1].y = rect.bottom;
  CloudLen = MAXCLOUD;
  HPEN hOldPen = HPEN(SelectObject(hDC, GetStockObject(NULL_PEN)));
  HBRUSH hCloudBrush = CreateSolidBrush(color);
  HBRUSH hOldBrush = HBRUSH(SelectObject(hDC, hCloudBrush));
  Polygon(hDC, CloudLine, CloudLen);
  // Add some puffiness to the clouds by placing ellipses
  // along the perimeter of the cloud. Center the ellipses
  // around every third point on the cloud's curve.
  int eWd = rect.right / CloudLen / 12;
  for (i=0; i<CloudLen; i+=3) {
    Ellipse(hDC, CloudLine[i].x-eWd, CloudLine[i].y-4,
      CloudLine[i].x+eWd, CloudLine[i].y+20);
  }
  SelectObject(hDC, hOldPen);
  SelectObject(hDC, hOldBrush);
  DeleteObject(hCloudBrush);
}

// Create and draw a fractalized mountain skyline
void TStormWindow::MountainSkyline(HDC hDC, RECT& rect)
{
  int xInc = (rect.right-rect.left+2) / (MAXSKY-2) + 1;
  int y = (rect.bottom - rect.top) / 2;
  SelectObject(hDC, GetStockObject(GRAY_BRUSH));
  SelectObject(hDC, GetStockObject(NULL_PEN));
  if (!Calculated)   // Fractalize the mountain's skyline
    Fractal(0, 0, MAXSKY-3, 0.5, 50.0, SkyFractal);
```

```
    // Fill the polygon with the points just calculated
    for (int i=0, x=-1; i<MAXSKY-2; i++, x+=xInc) {
      SkyLine[i].x = x;
      SkyLine[i].y = y + SkyFractal[i];
    }
    SkyLine[MAXSKY-2].x = rect.right + 1;
    SkyLine[MAXSKY-2].y = rect.bottom + 1;
    SkyLine[MAXSKY-1].x = rect.left - 1;
    SkyLine[MAXSKY-1].y = rect.bottom + 1;
    SkyLen = MAXSKY;
    HBRUSH hbrMtn = CreateSolidBrush(RGB(64, 32, 29));  // Brown
    HBRUSH hOldBrush = HBRUSH(SelectObject(hDC, hbrMtn));
    Polygon(hDC, SkyLine, SkyLen);   // Paint the mountain
    SelectObject(hDC, hOldBrush);
    DeleteObject(hbrMtn);
}


// Display a random number of saguaro cacti
void TStormWindow::Cactus(HDC hDC, RECT& rect)
{
    // Place cactus plants in the foreground. They blend with
    // the mountain, but are visible during lightning strikes.
    HPEN hCactusPen, hBranchPen;
    int maxCactusHt = (rect.bottom - SkyLine[0].y) / 2;
    int cactusBttm, x, branchHt, cactusTop, cactusHt, dist;
    int cnt = random(8) + 3;
    for (int i=0; i<cnt; i++) {
      dist = random(maxCactusHt) + maxCactusHt / 4;
      cactusBttm = rect.bottom - dist;
      // The height of each saguaro depends on how low it is
      // in the scene. The "lower" it is, the closer the plant
      // and the taller it can be.
      cactusHt = random(maxCactusHt-dist) + maxCactusHt/4;
      cactusTop = cactusBttm - cactusHt;
      x = random(rect.right);
      // Create a pen for drawing the main part of the cactus
      // plant. Base its thickness on the height of the plant.
      hCactusPen = CreatePen(PS_SOLID, cactusHt/8, PALETTEINDEX(2));
      SelectObject(hDC, hCactusPen);
      MoveToEx(hDC, x, cactusBttm, 0);
      LineTo(hDC, x, cactusTop);

      // Create a pen for drawing the branches that has a
      // thickness that is based on the height of the plant
      hBranchPen = CreatePen(PS_SOLID, cactusHt/10, PALETTEINDEX(2));
      SelectObject(hDC, hBranchPen);
      branchHt = cactusTop + random(cactusHt/2)+3;
      MoveToEx(hDC, x, branchHt, 0);
      LineTo(hDC, x-cactusHt/8, branchHt);
      LineTo(hDC, x-cactusHt/8, branchHt-random(branchHt-cactusTop+3));
      branchHt = cactusTop + random(cactusHt/2)+2;
      MoveToEx(hDC, x, branchHt, 0);
      LineTo(hDC, x+cactusHt/8, branchHt);
      LineTo(hDC, x+cactusHt/8, branchHt-random(branchHt-cactusTop+2));
```

```
      SelectObject(hDC, GetStockObject(BLACK_PEN));
      DeleteObject(hCactusPen);
      DeleteObject(hBranchPen);
   }
}

// Handy routine that sets a palette entry to the colors specified
void TStormWindow::SetPaletteEntry(int indx, BYTE red,
   BYTE green, BYTE blue)
{
  LogPal->palPalEntry[indx].peRed = red;
  LogPal->palPalEntry[indx].peGreen = green;
  LogPal->palPalEntry[indx].peBlue = blue;
}

class TStormApp : public TApplication {
public:
   TStormApp() : TApplication() { }
   void InitMainWindow();
};

void TStormApp::InitMainWindow()
{
   MainWindow = new TFrameWindow(0, "Desert Storm",
     new TStormWindow(0, ""));
}

// Delay routine
int Delay(int k)
{
   int i, j, l;

   for (j=0; j<k; j++)
     for (i=0; i<8000; i++)
       l = i * 7;
   return l;
}

int OwlMain(int /*argc*/, char* /*argv*/[])
{
   return TStormApp().Run();
}
```

THREE-DIMENSIONAL MOUNTAINS

There are many ways to add the sensation of depth to two-dimensional scenes. The STORM.CPP program, for instance, layers clouds to enhance the impression of depth. Similarly, in Chapter 8, we shaded the sides of polygons to create a three-dimensional bar chart. The next program, 3DFRACT.CPP, uses contour lines to create the illusion of three-dimensional mountains. Figure 11.4 presents a typical scene generated by 3DFRACT.CPP.

Figure 11.4 3DFRACT.CPP generates a random three-dimensional mountain scene.

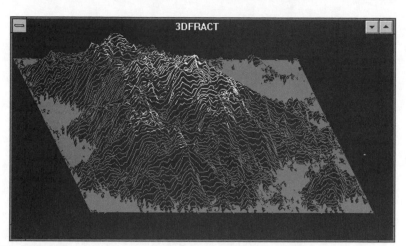

Working with Planes

Because we'll be working in three dimensions, the 3DFRACT.CPP program fractalizes polygons, not lines. It begins with a single plane positioned so that its four corners lie flat. Each corner has a height of zero; that is, the Z values equal zero. This plane is divided into four pieces as shown in Figure 11.5 and the height (Z value) of the center of the original plane is perturbed randomly.

The fractalization process continues by subdividing and perturbing the four smaller polygons in a similar fashion and then subdividing their polygons, and so on. After several iterations, a line is drawn across the middle of each small polygon. Remember, the X and Y positions are not perturbed—only the Z values are. Viewed from the top, therefore, you would only see a series of horizontal lines. By viewing the figure from an angle, however, the Z values come into play and you get the sense of depth.

Now we'll walk through a few iterations of the fractalization process. The top-left coordinate of the polygon to fractalize is the point (**x1,y1**) and the bottom-right point (**x2,y2**). The corners of the polygon are labeled **z1**, **z2**, **z3**, and **z4** as you view clockwise around the polygon. At first, these corners are all zero. The first step in the fractalization process is to divide the polygon into four pieces. This is accomplished by breaking the polygon at its midpoint (**xMid,yMid**).

The Z coordinate of the midpoint is then perturbed. It is calculated as the average height of the four corners and offset by a random amount. This part should sound familiar:

Figure 11.5 The process of fractalizing a polygon.

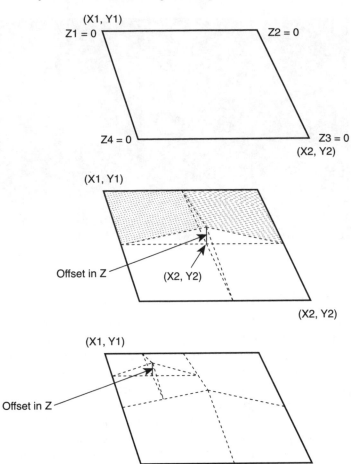

```
int newZ = (z1 + z2 + z3 + z4) / 4 +
  (double)(random(17) - 8) / 8.0 * std;
```

The process is repeated for each of the four smaller polygons. When we have performed the iteration enough times, we'll draw a contour line for the mountain across the middle of each polygon. Of course, what we have now is a three-dimensional line that must be drawn on a two-dimensional screen. The following equations are used to convert our three-dimensional line to the flat screen:

```
ScreenX = Y1 / 2 + X1;
ScreenY = Y1 + Z;
```

Painting the Scene

To make the generated scene more interesting, three colors are used to draw the mountain contour lines. At lower elevations, a green pen is used; higher up, a brown pen is selected, and at very high elevations a snow-white pen is selected.

Before the appropriate line is displayed, the area where the polygon exists is first erased by painting the screen black:

```
// Clear the area where the mountain lines are to appear
POINT p[4];
p[0].x = y1 / 2 + x1;      p[0].y = y1 + z1;
p[1].x = y1 / 2 + x2;      p[1].y = y1 + z2;
p[2].x = y2 / 2 + x2;      p[2].y = y2 + z3;
p[3].x = y2 / 2 + x1;      p[3].y = y2 + z4;
SelectObject(hDC, GetStockObject(NULL_PEN));
SelectObject(hDC, GetStockObject(BLACK_BRUSH));
Polygon(hDC, p, 4);
```

Why is this done? It removes surfaces on the scene that should be hidden. If you look carefully at the code or watch the output as the program executes, you'll see that the program always displays the scene starting from the top-right corner (the farthest point away) and works its way to the left and down the screen. The closest contour line is drawn last. By painting polygons that are farther away first, the program always covers up regions that are supposed to be hidden.

The polygon patches are painted black to clear the way for the contour lines, which are drawn by the following statements:

```
// Display the contour line. Select either the mountain
// or snow color based on the height of Z.
if (z1 >= -(60+random(25)))
  SelectObject(hDC, GreenPen);
else if (z1 >= -(100+random(25)))    // Z values are inverted!
  SelectObject(hDC, MtnPen);
else
  SelectObject(hDC, SnowPen);
MoveToEx(hDC, yMid / 2 + x2, yMid + z23, 0);
LineTo(hDC, yMid / 2 + x1, yMid + z41);
```

The pen selected depends on the value of **z1** as described earlier.

An ocean (or lake) is included in the scene by designating that all Z values below the variable **Sealevel**, which is randomly determined, are drawn as water. Rather than draw each patch of water separately, the program paints the ocean as a single blue polygon before the fractalization process begins.

```
POINT water[4];
water[0].x = 0;            water[0].y = 0;
water[1].x = right;        water[1].y = 0;
```

```
water[2].x = right+bottom/2;   water[2].y = bottom;
water[3].x = bottom/2;         water[3].y = bottom;
SelectObject(dc, WaterBrush);  // Select the water's brush
Polygon(dc, water, 4);         // Paint the water
```

Interrupting the Painting Process

The 3DFRACT program is noticeably slow at generating the fractal scene and painting it, even on a speeding 66MHz 486. This can pose a problem. Normally, whenever Windows is processing a function, such as the fractalizing routine in 3DFRACT.CPP, the application can't do anything else. As a result, the user is locked out from selecting any other applications, modifying Windows settings, and so on. Switching to an hour glass mouse cursor or displaying a status message, helps to tell the user that the application is busy. There is a better technique, however. The idea is have the greedy application manually process any Windows' events that pile up in the message queue. This is precisely what 3DFRACT does. Let's see how.

The **DoPendingMsgs** function holds the answer. It's a routine in 3DFRACT.CPP that is periodically called to check Windows' message queue and process any messages that it finds. It's called at the end of each iteration of the **Fractal** function. Here's the complete routine:

```
void TFractalWindow::DoPendingMsgs()
{
  MSG msg;
  while (PeekMessage(&msg, 0, 0, 0, PM_REMOVE))
    if (!GetApplication()->ProcessAppMsg(msg)) {
      TranslateMessage(&msg);
      if (msg.hwnd == HWindow && msg.message == WM_PAINT)
        // Another painting message is pending. Go do it right now.
        throw(1);
      DispatchMessage(&msg);
    }
}
```

The **while** loop calls the Windows function **PeekMessage** to retrieve a pending message, if one exists. If there isn't a message, the function returns FALSE and the loop doesn't do anything. However, if there is a pending message, it's passed back in the **msg** structure and the body of the **while** loop is executed.

The **ProcessAppMsg** at the top of the loop processes messages for an application's modeless dialog boxes, accelerators, and MDI accelerator messages. Since 3DFRACT doesn't have any of these elements; **ProcessAppMsg** doesn't do anything here except return FALSE. Similarly, **TranslateMessage** is a Windows routine that converts virtual key commands; since 3DFRACT doesn't use them, this function doesn't contribute anything either. Many applications, however, do contain these features, so it's a good idea to plan ahead for them. The remaining Windows function **DispatchMessage** actually processes the queued Windows message.

The **if** statement in the middle of the **while** loop is a little different. It watches for any pending paint messages for 3DFRACT. If one is encountered, the code throws an exception, using the **throw** keyword. Exceptions are the secret 3DFRACT uses to interrupt its drawing process and start over again.

Back in the **Paint** function you may have noticed this odd-looking code segment:

```
try {
  Fractal(0, 0, right, bottom, 0, 0, 0, 0,
    MAXLEVEL, std, ratio);
}
catch(int) {        // Break out and start painting the window again
  ::InvalidateRect(HWindow, 0, TRUE);
}
```

These statements set up the exception handling. The **try** block simply calls the **Fractal** function to generate the scene and display it. However, if a **throw** is encountered while executing **Fractal** (which can occur inside **DoPendingMsgs**), the code unwinds back to the **catch** shown here and calls **InvalidateRect** to repaint the window.

One other thing 3DFRACT now has to contend with is the case when the program is terminated in the middle of a paint operation. The solution is to block the program from terminating while generating a scene. A Boolean flag, **Painting**, is set TRUE while executing a **Paint** function. In addition, we've overridden **TWindow**'s **CanClose** function, which gets called to verify that the window can be closed, to check to make sure this flag is FALSE. If **Painting** is not FALSE, **CanClose** beeps and returns FALSE, ensuring that the window won't close. Only after the **Paint** function is finished will **Painting** be set FALSE and the program will indeed terminate if a close request is made.

Compiling 3DFRACT.CPP

To compile 3DFRACT you only need the source file 3DFRACT.CPP. When you use 3DFRACT, notice that the program must repaint the entire window any time any portion of the window must be updated. This is because the program does not save the fractal values of the scene, as was done in FRACTAL.CPP and STORM.CPP.

• 3DFRACT.CPP

```
// 3DFRACT.CPP: Creates a three-dimensional, contour map of
// fractalized mountains. The scene changes each time you click
// the left mouse button, or press a key.
```

```
#include <owl\applicat.h>
#include <owl\framewin.h>
#include <owl\dc.h>
#include <math.h>

#define MAXLEVEL 8     // Number of recursive iterations

class TFractalWindow : public TWindow {
  HPEN MtnPen;         // Pen to paint the mountains
  HPEN SnowPen;        // Pen to paint the snow
  HPEN GreenPen;       // Low portions of the mountains
  HBRUSH WaterBrush;   // Brush for painting water
  HDC hDC;             // The display's device context handle
  int Sealevel;        // The level of the water
  BOOL Painting;       // TRUE if the program is currently painting
  unsigned Seed;       // Current random number generator seed
public:
  TFractalWindow(TWindow *parent, const char* title)
    : TWindow(parent, title) {
    Seed = unsigned(time(0));   // Seed the random number generator
    Painting = FALSE;           // We're not painting yet
  }
  void Fractal(int x1, int y1, int x2, int y2, int z1, int z2,
    int z3, int z4, int iteration, double std, double ratio);
  void DoPendingMsgs();
  void SetupWindow();
  void EvDestroy();
  void EvChar(UINT, UINT, UINT);
  void EvLButtonDown(UINT, TPoint&);
  BOOL EvEraseBkgnd(HDC hDC);
  void Paint(TDC& dc, BOOL, TRect& r);
  void EvSize(UINT, TSize&);
  BOOL CanClose();

  DECLARE_RESPONSE_TABLE(TFractalWindow);
};

DEFINE_RESPONSE_TABLE1(TFractalWindow, TWindow)
  EV_WM_DESTROY,
  EV_WM_CHAR,
  EV_WM_LBUTTONDOWN,
  EV_WM_ERASEBKGND,
  EV_WM_SIZE,
END_RESPONSE_TABLE;

// Draw the whole mountain scene
void TFractalWindow::Paint(TDC& dc, BOOL, TRect&)
{
  Painting = TRUE;     // Painting is about to begin
  srand(Seed);         // Seed the random number generator
  RECT rect;
  ::GetClientRect(HWindow, &rect);  // Get the size of the window
  // Move the origin down the window
  SetViewportOrgEx(dc, 0, rect.bottom/8, 0);
```

```
  // Calculate the dimensions of the scene
  int right = rect.right * 3 / 4;
  int bottom = rect.bottom * 3 / 4;
  // Paint a water backdrop using one call to Polygon
  POINT water[4];
  water[0].x = 0;                    water[0].y = 0;
  water[1].x = right;                water[1].y = 0;
  water[2].x = right+bottom/2;       water[2].y = bottom;
  water[3].x = bottom/2;             water[3].y = bottom;
  SelectObject(dc, WaterBrush); // Select the water's brush
  Polygon(dc, water, 4);        // Paint the water
  double h = 0.75;              // Set up the fractal constants
  double scale = bottom;
  double ratio = 1.0 / pow(2.0,h);
  double std = scale * ratio;
  Sealevel = random(18) - 8;  // Randomly determine the sealevel
  hDC = HDC(dc);              // Save a handle to the device context
  // Perform the fractal routine; however, also prepare to have the
  // code do a "throw," signaling that the painting should be restarted
  try {
    Fractal(0, 0, right, bottom, 0, 0, 0, 0,
      MAXLEVEL, std, ratio);
  }
  catch(int) {          // Break out and start painting the window again
    ::InvalidateRect(HWindow, 0, TRUE);
  }
  Painting = FALSE;  // Painting is done now
}


// The user has pressed a key. Recalculate and repaint the
// landscape scene.
void TFractalWindow::EvChar(UINT, UINT, UINT)
{
  Seed = unsigned(time(0));   // Reseed the random number generator
  ::InvalidateRect(HWindow, 0, TRUE);  // Paint the window
}


// The user has clicked the left mouse button. Recalculate
// and repaint the landscape scene.
void TFractalWindow::EvLButtonDown(UINT, TPoint&)
{
  Seed = unsigned(time(0));   // Reseed the random number generator
  ::InvalidateRect(HWindow, 0, TRUE);  // Paint the window
}


// This OWL function is set TRUE if the window can close. It won't
// let the application close, for instance, if the window is painting.
BOOL TFractalWindow::CanClose()
{
  if (Painting) {      // Is the window painting right now?
    MessageBeep(0);    // Yes it is. Warn the user with a beep.
    return FALSE;      // Don't close the widow yet
  }
  return TRUE;         // OK to close the window
}
```

```
// Create the brushes used in the program
void TFractalWindow::SetupWindow()
{
  TWindow::SetupWindow();      // Call the inherited function
  MtnPen = CreatePen(PS_SOLID, 1, RGB(118, 0, 0));
  SnowPen = CreatePen(PS_SOLID, 2, RGB(255, 255, 255));
  GreenPen = CreatePen(PS_SOLID, 1, RGB(0, 128, 0));
  WaterBrush = CreateSolidBrush(RGB(0, 0, 128));
}

// This routine cleans up after the program
void TFractalWindow::EvDestroy()
{
  DeleteObject(MtnPen);         // Delete the pens and brushes
  DeleteObject(SnowPen);
  DeleteObject(GreenPen);
  DeleteObject(WaterBrush);
  TWindow::EvDestroy();         // Call the inherited function
}

// Paint the background black
BOOL TFractalWindow::EvEraseBkgnd(HDC hDC)
{
  RECT rect;
  ::GetClientRect(HWindow, &rect);  // Get the size of the window
  PatBlt(hDC, 0, 0, rect.right, rect.bottom, BLACKNESS);
  return TRUE;
}

// Repaint the scene if the window is resized. There's no reason to
// reseed the random number generator here because the window will be
// a different size and this will change the number of times the
// random function is called and hence the random numbers generated.
void TFractalWindow::EvSize(UINT, TSize&)
{
  ::InvalidateRect(HWindow, 0, TRUE);
}

void TFractalWindow::Fractal(int x1, int y1, int x2, int y2, int z1,
  int z2, int z3, int z4, int iteration, double std, double ratio)
{
  int xMid = (x1 + x2) / 2;
  int yMid = (y1 + y2) / 2;
  int z23 = (z2 + z3) / 2;
  int z41 = (z4 + z1) / 2;
  int newZ = (z1 + z2 + z3 + z4) / 4 +
    (double)(random(17) - 8) / 8.0 * std;
  iteration--;
  if (iteration) {
    int z12 = (z1 + z2) / 2;
    int z34 = (z3 + z4) / 2;
    double stdmid = std * ratio;
    // Iterate from right to left, top to bottom
```

```
      Fractal(xMid, y1, x2, yMid, z12, z2, z23, newZ,
        iteration, stdmid, ratio);
      Fractal(x1, y1, xMid, yMid, z1, z12, newZ, z41,
        iteration, stdmid, ratio);
      Fractal(xMid, yMid, x2, y2, newZ, z23, z3, z34,
        iteration, stdmid, ratio);
      Fractal(x1, yMid, xMid, y2, z41, newZ, z34, z4,
        iteration, stdmid, ratio);
    }
    else {  // Draw the surface
      if (newZ <= Sealevel) {       // Mountains
        // Clear the area where the mountain lines are to appear
        POINT p[4];
        p[0].x = y1 / 2 + x1;        p[0].y = y1 + z1;
        p[1].x = y1 / 2 + x2;        p[1].y = y1 + z2;
        p[2].x = y2 / 2 + x2;        p[2].y = y2 + z3;
        p[3].x = y2 / 2 + x1;        p[3].y = y2 + z4;
        SelectObject(hDC, GetStockObject(NULL_PEN));
        SelectObject(hDC, GetStockObject(BLACK_BRUSH));
        Polygon(hDC, p, 4);
        // Display the contour line. Select either the mountain
        // or snow color based on the height of Z.
        if (z1 >= -(60+random(25)))
          SelectObject(hDC, GreenPen);
        else if (z1 >= -(100+random(25)))   // Z values are inverted!
          SelectObject(hDC, MtnPen);
        else
          SelectObject(hDC, SnowPen);
        MoveToEx(hDC, yMid / 2 + x2, yMid + z23, 0);
        LineTo(hDC, yMid / 2 + x1, yMid + z41);
      }
    }
  DoPendingMsgs();   // Do any pending Windows messages
}

// Process other messages when doing lengthy drawing to the screen
void TFractalWindow::DoPendingMsgs()
{
  MSG msg;
  while (PeekMessage(&msg, 0, 0, 0, PM_REMOVE))
    if (!GetApplication()->ProcessAppMsg(msg)) {
      TranslateMessage(&msg);
      if (msg.hwnd == HWindow && msg.message == WM_PAINT)
        // Another painting message is pending. Go do it right now.
        throw(1);
      DispatchMessage(&msg);
    }
}

class TFractalSceneApp : public TApplication {
public:
  TFractalSceneApp() : TApplication() { }
  void InitMainWindow();
};
```

```
void TFractalSceneApp::InitMainWindow()
{
  MainWindow = new TFrameWindow(0, "3DFRACT",
    new TFractalWindow(0, ""));
}

int OwlMain(int /*argc*/, char* /*argv*/[])
{
  return TFractalSceneApp().Run();
}
```

Two-Dimensional Graphics Techniques

n this chapter, we'll discuss various techniques for manipulating two-dimensional scenes. We'll begin by exploring the relationship between screen and world coordinates. Then, we'll introduce the concept of transformations, and we'll describe how objects in world coordinates can be manipulated in two dimensions. As part of our exploration, we'll develop a package called MATRIX.CPP that implements many of the concepts presented. Then, we'll discuss how some of these transformations can be performed at the pixel level. Finally, we'll build a collection of transformation functions that are available in true 32-bit Windows applications.

SCREEN AND WORLD COORDINATES

So far, we've usually been working with pixels in the **MM_TEXT** mapping mode, in which corrdinates are expressed in relation to the screen. However, many graphics operations are more naturally expressed if you use *world coordinates*—inches, feet, meters, and so on—which are coordinates that are related to the figures being drawn. This is why Windows also supports mapping modes such as, **MM_LOENGLISH** and **MM_LOMETRIC**.

For instance, in a CAD program, it's usually easier to work with objects in world coordinates. The mapping modes help, but you'll also need a way to manipulate the objects internally. For example, if you want to scale your internal representation of a room or rotate it to another perspective, you'll need your own set of support functions. In the following sections, we'll develop the MATRIX.CPP package that provides these types of functions.

TRANSFORMATIONS

Transformations are a basic mathematical operation used in graphics programming. Quite literally, a transform is a function (or equation) that defines how one set of data is to be changed or transformed into another. For example, let's say we have a picture of a wheel on the screen that we want to rotate. We can use a rotation transformation to determine how the wheel is supposed to be appear as it is moved.

The basic transformations are *translation*, *rotation*, and *scaling*. In this section, we'll explore each of these transformations in detail and add routines to MATRIX.H and MATRIX.CPP to perform these operations. A list of the routines in MATRIX.CPP is shown in Table 12.1.

The object-oriented drawing program we'll develop in Chapter 13 uses the MATRIX.CPP unit to translate and rotate objects. When we explore three-dimensional graphics in Chapter 14, we'll rely on transforms to generate perspective views of three-dimensional objects. For now, however, we'll concern ourselves with objects in two dimensions.

Translation

One of the simplest transforms produces a translation. Essentially, a translation defines how a point is supposed to be moved from one location in space to another. For example, if we have a box drawn on the left side of the screen and we want to move it to the right, we can use a translation transformation to specify how each point must be moved.

For instance, translating a pixel on the screen can be done by adding an appropriate value to each of the X and Y coordinates to which the point is to be moved. This can be written in C++ as:

```
NewX = X + TranslateX;
NewY = Y + TranslateY;
```

Table 12.1 Two-Dimensional Transformations Supported in MATRIX.CPP

Function	Description
ToRadians	Converts an angle in degrees to radians
WorldTranslatePoly	Translates a polygon
WorldScalePoly	Scales a polygon
WorldRotatePoly	Rotates a polygon
WorldShearPoly	Shears a polygon
CopyPoly	Copies one polygon to another

Figure 12.1 You can use a transformation to translate an object.

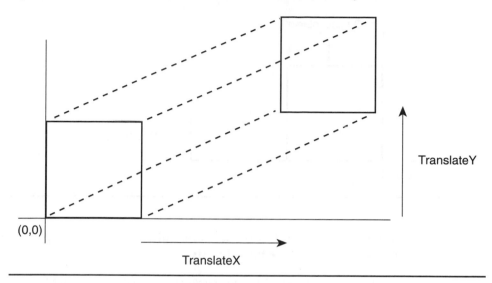

The values **TranslateX** and **TranslateY** can be either positive or negative and define how far the point (X,Y) should be translated in the X and Y directions, respectively.

Translating an object, like a polygon, is only a matter of translating each point that makes up the polygon, as illustrated in Figure 12.1. A routine in MATRIX.CPP that does this is called **WorldTranslatePoly**.

```
void WorldTranslatePoly(POINT poly[], int numPoints, double tx, double ty)
{
  for (int i=0; i<numPoints; i++) {
    poly[i].x = poly[i].x + tx;
    poly[i].y = poly[i].y + ty;
  }
}
```

Scaling a Two-Dimensional Polygon

Scaling a two-dimensional polygon can be accomplished by multiplying each of the coordinates of the original polygon by a scale factor. For example, assume we want to scale the box shown in Figure 12.2 by 2 in the X direction and by 1/2 in the Y direction. This can be done by applying the following equations to each of the coordinates of the box:

```
ScaleDx = X * ScaleX;
ScaleDy = Y * ScaleY;
```

Figure 12.2 Scaling an object by 2 in X and 1/2 in Y.

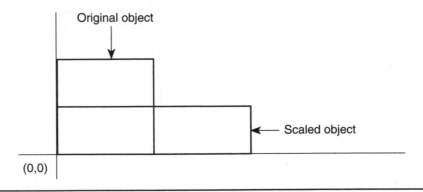

The routine in MATRIX.CPP that performs this operation for a polygon in world coordinates is called **WorldScalePoly**.

```
void WorldScalePoly(POINT poly[], int numPoints, double sx, double sy)
{
  for (int i=0; i<numPoints; i++) {
    poly[i].x = poly[i].x * sx;
    poly[i].y = poly[i].y * sy;
  }
}
```

Merely calling **WorldScalePoly** to scale an object does not always produce the desired results. Since each coordinate in the object is multiplied by a scale factor, the object may be moved as well as scaled, as shown in Figure 12.3—that is, unless one of the coordinates is (0,0). This coordinate would stay the same.

Therefore, if you want to scale an object, yet keep one of its points stationary, two additional steps must be taken. First, the object must be translated so that the point you want to scale about (keep fixed) moves to the origin. Second, after applying the scaling transformation, the object must be translated back by the amount that it was translated earlier.

The net effect is that the object is scaled, but the point that is translated to the origin and back again remains stationary. This scaling sequence, as illustrated in Figure 12.4, is actually more useful than the first.

For example, the following code doubles the size of the polygon in the array **Poly** by translating it so that its first point is at the origin, scaling it, and then translating the polygon back.

```
Px = Poly[0].x;
Py = Poly[0].y;
```

Figure 12.3 Scaling an object not at the origin changes its size *and* location.

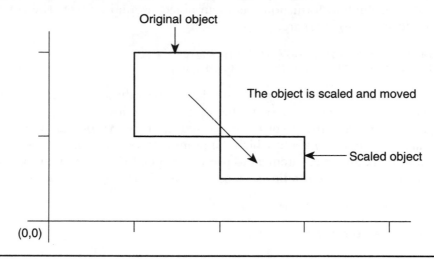

```
WorldTranslatePoly(Poly, NumPoints, -Px, -Py);
WorldScalePoly(Poly, NumPoints, 2.0, 2.0);
WorldTranslatePoly(Poly, NumPoints, Px, Py);
```

Figure 12.4 Use this process to properly scale an object not at the origin.

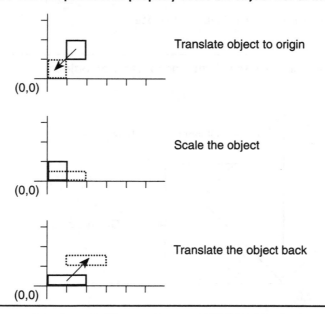

Rotating a Two-Dimensional Polygon

Another useful transformation rotates an object around a point. The equations to perform the rotation are:

```
RotatedX = X * cos(Angle) - Y * sin(Angle);
RotatedY = X * sin(Angle) + Y * cos(Angle);
```

Rather than explain the geometry that derives these equations, we'll look at them from a user's standpoint. The **X** and **Y** variables on the right side of the equation represent the point being rotated, and the **Angle** variable specifies the angle (in radians) about which the point is to be rotated. Because degrees are a more natural measurement to use when specifing angles, you can use the following function, **ToRadians**, to convert angles in degrees to radians:

```
double ToRadians(double degrees)
{
  return degrees * 0.017453292;
}
```

Actually, to rotate an object successfully, we need to pick a point around which the object is to be rotated, translate it to the origin, rotate the polygon, and then translate the object back. The routine in MATRIX.CPP that performs the rotation operation is called **WorldRotatePoly** and can be used to rotate a polygon, as shown in Figure 12.5.

```
void WorldRotatePoly(POINT poly[], int numPoints, double angle)
{
  double x, y, radians, cosTheta, sinTheta;
```

Figure 12.5 You can use a transformation to rotate an object.

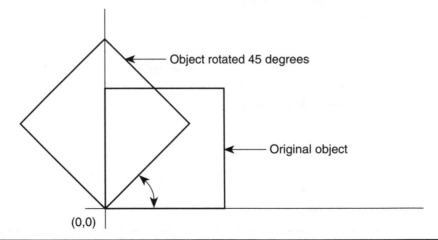

```
radians = ToRadians(angle);
cosTheta = cos(radians);    sinTheta = sin(radians);
for (int i=0; i<numPoints; i++) {
  x = poly[i].x;    y = poly[i].y;
  poly[i].x = x * cosTheta - y * sinTheta;
  poly[i].y = x * sinTheta + y * cosTheta;
  }
}
```

The Shear Transform

Some transformations produce some rather interesting effects. One of the more common transformations shears the objects to which it is applied, as shown in Figure 12.6. This transformation involves multiplying each of the coordinates of the object by a scale factor and adding an offset. The equations that produce the shear effect are:

```
ShearedX = X + C * Y;
ShearedY = D * X + Y;
```

As with rotations, we want to shear the polygon about a point, so we must translate the polygon to the origin, apply the shear transform, and then translate the object back. **WorldShearPoly** is the routine that you use to shear a polygon situated at the origin:

```
void WorldShearPoly(POINT poly[], int numPoints, double c, double d)
{
  double x, y;

  for (int i=0; i<numPoints; i++) {
    x = poly[i].x;    y = poly[i].y;
```

Figure 12.6 You can use a transformation to shear an object.

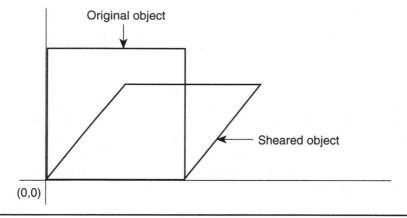

Original object

Sheared object

(0,0)

```
    poly[i].x = x + c * y;
    poly[i].y = d * x + y;
  }
}
```

A Matrix Demo

The program, MTXTEST.CPP, listed after this section tests the matrix operations included in MATRIX.CPP. It applies several of the transformations developed in MATRIX.CPP to the polygon in the array **Points**. After displaying the result of each transforms, you must press a key or click the left mouse button to proceed to the next one.

The heart of the output is in the **Paint** member function. However, this function is a little different than any of the **Paint** functions you've seen before. The **Paint** routine is *state driven*. The variable **State**, located in the class derived from **TWindow**, determines which part of a **switch** statement will display graphics in the window. For instance, **State** is initially zero; therefore, it selects the code that tests the translation function:

```
switch(State) {
  case 0:
    // Test translate polygon
    WorldTranslatePoly(Points, NUMPOINTS, -px, -py);
    Polygon(dc, Points, NUMPOINTS);
    break;
```

To sequence through the steps, you can press any key. Similarly, to start the sequence from the beginning, momentarily depress the left mouse button. To support these two actions, the message-response functions **EvChar** and **EvLButtonDown** are overridden. Each function modifies the **State** variable and calls **InvalidateRect** to display the proper window. Here's the **EvChar** function that supports a keypress:

```
void TMatrixWindow::EvChar(UINT, UINT, UINT)
{
  ::InvalidateRect(HWindow, 0, TRUE);  // Display this state
  State++;
  if (State > 3) State = 0;
}
```

For the function to operate as you would expect, it must use a mapping mode that adjusts the screen's pixels so that measurements are equal in the X and Y directions. For instance, the program uses the **MM_LOENGLISH** mapping mode so that all units are 0.01 inches in size. Further, the program sets the origin near the bottom left of the window so that it becomes easier to tell what the program is doing:

```
SetMapMode(dc, MM_LOENGLISH);
// Set the origin to the center of the window
SetViewportOrgEx(dc, rect.right/4, rect.bottom*3/4, 0);
```

 To compile MTXTEST.CPP you must add the files MTXTEST.CPP and MAXTRIX.CPP to a project file.

● **MTXTEST.CPP**

```
// MTXTEST.CPP: Tests the transforms defined in MATRIX.CPP by
// manipulating a polygon. You will be required to press a key
// or click the left mouse button after each operation is
// performed in order to go on to the next operation.

#include <owl\applicat.h>
#include <owl\framewin.h>
#include <owl\dc.h>
#include "matrix.h"

#define NUMPOINTS 5      // Number of points in the polygon

class TMatrixWindow : public TWindow {
  POINT Points[NUMPOINTS];
  POINT PolyCopy[NUMPOINTS];
  int State;
public:
  TMatrixWindow(TWindow *parent, const char* title)
    : TWindow(parent, title)
    { State = 0; }
  void Paint(TDC& dc, BOOL, TRect&);
  void EvChar(UINT, UINT, UINT);
  void EvLButtonDown(UINT, TPoint&);
  void EvSize(UINT, TSize&);

  DECLARE_RESPONSE_TABLE(TMatrixWindow);
};

DEFINE_RESPONSE_TABLE1(TMatrixWindow, TWindow)
  EV_WM_CHAR,
  EV_WM_LBUTTONDOWN,
  EV_WM_SIZE,
END_RESPONSE_TABLE;

// Display a figure on the screen, depending on the value
// in the State variable
void TMatrixWindow::Paint(TDC& dc, BOOL, TRect&)
{
  RECT rect;
  ::GetClientRect(HWindow, &rect);
  // Draw axes
  MoveToEx(dc, rect.right/4, 0, 0);
  LineTo(dc, rect.right/4, rect.bottom);
```

```
      MoveToEx(dc, 0, rect.bottom*3/4, 0);
      LineTo(dc, rect.right, rect.bottom*3/4);
      TextOut(dc, rect.right/4+10, rect.bottom*3/4+10, "(0,0)", 5);

      // Use a real-world logical mapping mode
      SetMapMode(dc, MM_LOENGLISH);
      // Set the origin to the center of the window
      SetViewportOrgEx(dc, rect.right/4, rect.bottom*3/4, 0);
      // Initialize the array of points
      Points[0].x = 150;  Points[0].y = 80;
      Points[1].x = 400;  Points[1].y = 80;
      Points[2].x = 400;  Points[2].y = 150;
      Points[3].x = 150;  Points[3].y = 150;
      Points[4].x = 150;  Points[4].y = 80;
      int px = Points[0].x;
      int py = Points[0].y;
      Polygon(dc, Points, NUMPOINTS);
      switch(State) {
        case 0:
          // Test translate polygon
          WorldTranslatePoly(Points, NUMPOINTS, -px, -py);
          Polygon(dc, Points, NUMPOINTS);
          break;
        case 1:
          // Scale the polygon about the point (px,py)
          WorldTranslatePoly(Points, NUMPOINTS, -px, -py);
          WorldScalePoly(Points, NUMPOINTS, 1.5, 1.5);
          WorldTranslatePoly(Points, NUMPOINTS, px, py);
          Polyline(dc, Points, NUMPOINTS);
          break;
        case 2:
          // Rotate the figure around the point (px,py) by 45 degrees
          WorldTranslatePoly(Points, NUMPOINTS, -px, -py);
          WorldRotatePoly(Points, NUMPOINTS, 45.0);
          WorldTranslatePoly(Points, NUMPOINTS, px, py);
          Polygon(dc, Points, NUMPOINTS);
          break;
        case 3:
          // Shear the object about the point (px,py)
          WorldTranslatePoly(Points, NUMPOINTS, -px, -py);
          WorldShearPoly(Points, NUMPOINTS, 0.5, 0.5);
          WorldTranslatePoly(Points, NUMPOINTS, px, py);
          Polygon(dc, Points, NUMPOINTS);
          break;
      }
    }

// Go to the next display state if there is a keypress
void TMatrixWindow::EvChar(UINT, UINT, UINT)
{
  ::InvalidateRect(HWindow, 0, TRUE);  // Display this state
  State++;
  if (State > 3) State = 0;
}
```

```
// Start the display process over again when the left mouse
// button is clicked
void TMatrixWindow::EvLButtonDown(UINT, TPoint&)
{
  State = 0;                              // Start over
  ::InvalidateRect(HWindow, 0, TRUE);  // Repaint window
}


// Force the window to repaint the current state if the
// window is resized
void TMatrixWindow::EvSize(UINT, TSize&)
{
  ::InvalidateRect(HWindow, 0, TRUE);
}

class TMatrixApp : public TApplication {
public:
  TMatrixApp() : TApplication() { }
  void InitMainWindow();
};

void TMatrixApp::InitMainWindow()
{
  MainWindow = new TFrameWindow(0, "MATRIX TEST",
    new TMatrixWindow(0, ""));
}

int OwlMain(int /*argc*/, char* /*argv*/[])
{
  return TMatrixApp().Run();
}
```

32-Bit Transform Functions

If you're developing for 32-bit platforms, such as Windows NT, the GDI makes available a series of two-dimensional transformation capabilities similar to those outlined in this chapter, as shown in Figure 12.7. In true 32-bit targets, the device context includes a transform that it applies to the graphics output. By setting the transform you'll be able to rotate, shear, translate or scale GDI output. In particular, each world coordinate (x,y) is converted into (x',y') using these equations:

```
x' = x * eM11 + y * eM21 + eDx
y' = x * eM12 + y * eM22 + eDy
```

Notice that these equations are a generalized form of what we presented in the earlier sections. With appropriate values you can perform a variety of transformations.

The variables **eM11**, **eM21**, and so on are part of the world transform structure mentioned earlier, which is defined as:

```
typedef struct tagXFORM {
  FLOAT eM11;
  FLOAT eM12;
  FLOAT eM21;
  FLOAT eM22;
  FLOAT eDx;
  FLOAT eDy;
} XFORM;
```

To define a specific transform, you must pass an **XFORM** structure with the appropriate settings to the **SetWorldTransform** function.

Table 12.2 shows what settings you'll need to produce specific types of transformations

Actually, there's an important step you must perform before you use Windows' world transformation functions. You must enable the world transformation capabilities by passing the **GM_ADVANCED** setting to the **SetGraphicsMode** function:

```
SetGraphicsMode(dc, GM_ADVANCED);
```

Once this routine is executed, the GDI routines will use the current transform configuration.

The following **Paint** function illustrates how you can use the world transform structure to rotate a rectangle. Actually, the routine displays two rectangles. The first is drawn without using Windows' transform capabilities. The second rectangle, however, uses a modified transform that rotates, translates, and slightly scales first rectangle. It's drawn with a red pen.

```
void TExampleWindow::Paint(TDC& dc, BOOL, TRect&)
{
  Rectangle(dc, 20, 20, 100, 100);    // Draw a rectangle
  SetGraphicsMode(dc, GM_ADVANCED);    // Enable the advanced capabilities
  XFORM xform;                         // Define a transformation
```

Table 12.2 Transformation Settings for Individual Operations

Operation	eM11	eM12	eM21	eM22	eDx	eDy
Rotation	Cosine	Sine	Negative sine	Cosine	—	—
Scaling	Horizontal scale factor	—	—	Vertical scale factor	—	—
Shear	—	Horizontal shear factor	Vertical shear factor	—	—	—
Reflection	Horizontal scale	—	—	Vertical scale	—	—
Translation	—	—	—	—	Horizontal	Vertical

Figure 12.7 Win32 provides the ability to rotate, scale, shear, and translate GDI drawings.

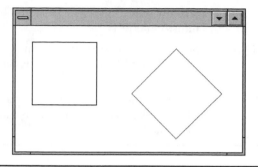

```
    xform.eM11 = cos(M_PI_4);
    xform.eM12 = sin(M_PI_4);
    xform.eDx = 200;
    xform.eM21 = -sin(M_PI_4);
    xform.eM22 = cos(M_PI_4);
    SetWorldTransform(dc, &xform);        // Use the new transform
    // Draw the transformed rectangle with a red pen
    HPEN hPen = CreatePen(PS_SOLID, 1, RGB(255,0,0));
    HPEN hOldPen = HPEN(SelectObject(dc, hPen));
    Rectangle(dc, 20, 20, 100, 100);    // Draw a rotated rectangle
    SelectObject(dc, hOldPen);
    DeleteObject(hPen);
}
```

Note You must compile the previous **Paint** function as a 32-bit Windows (Win32) target. If you don't, you'll get compiler errors. In addition, the routine will run properly only on a true 32-bit platform, such as Windows NT. If you try running the example on a Win32 platform, on the other hand, the transformation functions won't have any affect.

You can reset the current transform or combine multiple transforms using the **ModifyWorldTransform** function:

```
BOOL ModifyWorldTransform(HDC hDC, XFORM* xform, DWORD mode)
```

- **hDC** is a handle to the device context.
- **xform** is a pointer to an **XFORM** structure that contains transform settings.
- **mode**, which can be one of the constants listed in Table 12.3, specifies how the **XFORM** structure is to be used.

Table 12.3 ModifyWorldTransform Supports Three Types of Operations

Constant	Description
MWT_IDENTITY	Sets the transform to the default, identity matrix—no transform effects
MWT_LEFTMULTIPLY	Multiplies the current transform data by the values in XFORM; the XFORM structure is handled as the left multiplicand
MWT_RIGHTMULTIPLY	Multiplies the current transform data by the values in XFORM; the XFORM structure is handled as the right multiplicand

Having the ability to combine multiple transforms is very important. For instance, to properly rotate an object, you really should first translate the figure to the origin, perform the rotation, and then translate the object back. You can set this up by calling **ModifyWorldTransform** three times with the three components of the matrix operation: one for the translation, one for the rotation, and a final **XFORM** structure for the translation back.

• MATRIX.H

```
// MATRIX.H: Header file for MATRIX.CPP.
#ifndef MATRIXH
#define MATRIXH

#include <windows.h>

// Functions provided by MATRIX.CPP:
double ToRadians(double degrees);
void WorldTranslatePoly(POINT poly[], int numPoints, double tx, double ty);
void WorldScalePoly(POINT poly[], int numPoints, double sx, double sy);
void WorldRotatePoly(POINT poly[], int numPoints, double angle);
void WorldShearPoly(POINT poly[], int numPoints, double c, double d);
void CopyPoly(POINT polyFrom[], int numPoints, POINT polyTo[]);
#endif
```

• MATRIX.CPP

```
// MATRIX.CPP: The following set of matrix operations perform
// various transformations in world and screen coordinates.
#include <windows.h>
#include <math.h>
#include "matrix.h"

// Convert degrees to radians
double ToRadians(double degrees)
```

```
{
  return degrees * 0.017453292;
}

// Translates a two-dimensional polygon by tx and ty.
// The polygon should be in world coordinates.
void WorldTranslatePoly(POINT poly[], int numPoints, double tx, double ty)
{
  for (int i=0; i<numPoints; i++) {
    poly[i].x = poly[i].x + tx;
    poly[i].y = poly[i].y + ty;
  }
}

// Scales a polygon by sx in the x dimension and sy in
// the y dimension. The polygon must be in world coordinates.
void WorldScalePoly(POINT poly[], int numPoints, double sx, double sy)
{
  for (int i=0; i<numPoints; i++) {
    poly[i].x = poly[i].x * sx;
    poly[i].y = poly[i].y * sy;
  }
}

// Rotates a polygon by the number of degrees specified
// in angle. The polygon must be in world coordinates.
void WorldRotatePoly(POINT poly[], int numPoints, double angle)
{
  double x, y, radians, cosTheta, sinTheta;

  radians = ToRadians(angle);
  cosTheta = cos(radians);   sinTheta = sin(radians);
  for (int i=0; i<numPoints; i++) {
    x = poly[i].x;     y = poly[i].y;
    poly[i].x = x * cosTheta - y * sinTheta;
    poly[i].y = x * sinTheta + y * cosTheta;
  }
}

// Shears a polygon by applying c to the x dimension and d to
// the y dimension. The polygon must be in world coordinates.
void WorldShearPoly(POINT poly[], int numPoints, double c, double d)
{
  double x, y;

  for (int i=0; i<numPoints; i++) {
    x = poly[i].x;   y = poly[i].y;
    poly[i].x = x + c * y;
    poly[i].y = d * x + y;
  }
}

// Copies from one world polygon to another
void CopyPoly(POINT polyFrom[], int numPoints, POINT polyTo[])
```

```
{
  for (int i=0; i<numPoints; i++) {
    polyTo[i].x = polyFrom[i].x;
    polyTo[i].y = polyFrom[i].y;
  }
}
```

THIRTEEN

Interactive Drawing Tools

U ser interaction is one of the most important elements of a success-
ful program. This is particularly true for graphics applications.
Although Windows provides many user-interface elements and
graphics functions, you're on our own when it comes to *interactively* drawing figures on the screen with a mouse.

In this chapter, we'll develop a set of tools for interactively drawing rubber
banding lines, rectangles, ellipses, and polygons. In addition, we'll create a
tool palette that holds icons for each of these drawing tools. Both of these
packages are good starting points for your own drawing or CAD program. In
fact, in the next chapter we'll use them to build a sophisticated object-oriented
drawing program.

AN INTERACTIVE GRAPHICS PACKAGE

The interactive drawing package (DRAW.CPP) in this chapter includes eight
drawing tools. Each tool is implemented as a separate class (see Table 13.1)
and shares a common ancestor—the **TDrawingTool** class. The object hierarchy is shown in Figure 13.1.

As the details of the various classes unfold, you'll see how you can use
object-oriented programming (OOP) as a powerful means of sharing code and
as a great way to leave the door open for extending a toolkit—which is exactly
what we'll be doing in the object-oriented drawing program in Chapter 14. In
Chapter 14, we'll add the ability to store the figures drawn with the tools we
create in this chapter in an object list so that your drawings can readily be
edited and saved to files.

The **TDrawingTool** class outlines the basic flow of the user interaction
and provides a common programming interface for the drawing routines. Since

Table 13.1 Interactive Drawing Objects Included in DRAW.CPP

Class	Description
TDrawingTool	Base class for all interactive drawing classes
TLineTool	Draws lines
TRectangleTool	Draws filled rectangles
TEmptyRectangleTool	Draws empty rectangles
TPolylineTool	Draws open polygons
TPolygonTool	Draws filled polygons
TEllipseTool	Draws filled ellipses
TEmptyEllipseTool	Draws empty ellipses
TTextTool	Supports text entry

all of the tools are built from the same *base class*, **TDrawingTool**, we'll be able to take full advantage of code sharing and *polymorphism*—the ability of a single function call to have many behaviors.

The source code for the drawing classes are included in the source files DRAW.H and DRAW.CPP, which are listed at the end of this chapter.

DRAWING CONVENTIONS

All of the interactive drawing classes (tools) adhere to several conventions. First, they only support mouse interaction. Second, the tools assume that they are called by the *drawing window* that they are to draw in. Third, the drawing

Figure 13.1 The figure shows the interactive tool hierarchy in DRAW.CPP.

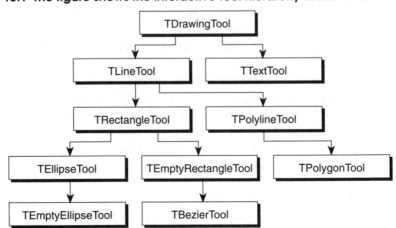

settings that the tools should use to draw a figure are specified in a class called **TPaintContext**.

The **TPaintContext** class is defined at the top of DRAW.H as:

```
class TPaintContext {
public:
  TDrawingTool* Tool;          // Pointer to currently selected tool
  int PenWd;                   // Width of pen
  COLORREF PenColor;           // Color of pen
  COLORREF BrushColor;         // Color of brush
  HWND DrawingWnd;             // The window to draw on
  TWindow* OWLWindow;          // The drawing window's OWL object
  double Zoom;                 // Zoom factor
  int Offsx, Offsy;            // Offset of drawing window's coordinates
  int SnapWd, SnapHt;          // "Snap to grid" width and height
  BOOL SnapOn;                 // Enables the snap to grid feature
  TPaintContext();
  void SetSnapToGrid(int snapWd, int snapHt);
  POINT SnapToGrid(POINT& pt);
  BOOL SetSnapToGridOn(BOOL snapOn);
};
```

The **TPaintContext** class places, in one package, all the common drawing settings required to display a figure. In many respects, **TPaintContext** acts much like a Windows device context. For instance, **TPaintContext** contains a handle to the pen style and brush color to use to draw a figure. The painting context also has a zoom factor, scroller offset, and grid dimensions. In addition, **TPaintContext** holds a pointer to the currently selected drawing tool and a handle and pointer to the drawing window itself. The **TPaintContext** constructor sets these variables to various default settings. The remaining three member functions control the grid settings. You'll see these in action in Chapter 14.

The **TPaintContext** class is widely used by the drawing tools and a necessary element of any program that uses the tools. An application is responsible for allocating and managing a global **TPaintContext** object. It is this object that holds the current drawing settings to use in a new drawing. However, each tool owns its own copy of a **TPaintContext** object, which specifies the object's color, brush style, and so on. Initially, these internal drawing parameters are set to the values in the global **TPaintContext** object.

A Close Look at the DRAW.CPP Tools

We'll now walk through the hierarchy of interactive drawing classes in DRAW.CPP. The base class, **TDrawingTool**, defines the basic shell of the drawing tools. Here is its definition:

```
class TDrawingTool {
public:
  POINT Pt1, Pt2;                     // Current and last mouse position
```

```
        TPaintContext* PC;                  // Drawing parameters
        HDC hDC;                            // Display surface's device context
        HPEN hPen;                          // The drawing pen style
        HBRUSH hBrush;                      // The brush style
        HCURSOR hCursor;                    // The tool's cursor
        virtual void Select(TPaintContext* pc); // Tool selected
        virtual void Deselect() { }         // Deselect the tool
        // Starts the interactive drawing process
        virtual BOOL LButtonDown(POINT& pt);
        // Interactively draws figure
        virtual void MouseMove(POINT& pt);
        virtual BOOL LButtonUp(POINT& pt); // Finalizes drawing
        virtual BOOL RButtonDown(POINT& pt) { return LButtonUp(pt); }
        virtual void Start() { Show(hDC, PC->Zoom, PC->Offsx, PC->Offsy); }
        virtual void Finish();              // Display the permanent settings
        virtual void Show(HDC, double zoom, int offsx=0, int offsy=0) { }
        virtual HICON GetIcon() { return 0; } // Get the icon for the tool
        virtual void UpdateCursor(POINT& pt) { } // Set the mouse cursor
        virtual void SortPoints();
        virtual void SelectCursor(int id);
    };
```

The **TDrawingTool** class begins with the two instance variables **Pt1** and **Pt2**, which keep track of the original and current locations of the mouse. These coordinates specify where a figure is to be displayed as it is being interactively drawn.

The **hPen** and **hBrush** members are the pen and brush styles used while drawing the figure. (Don't get these confused with the pen and brush settings in **TPaintContext**, which are used to draw the *final* figure.)

The **TDrawingTool** class also contains a handle to a device context, **hDC**. This is the device context of the drawing window. Finally, a handle to the cursor used while drawing the figure is stored in the data member **hCursor**.

Table 13.2 provides a brief description of each of **TDrawingTool**'s member functions. These functions fall into two categories: support functions and actual drawing routines. The functions **Select**, **Deselect**, **SetCursor**, and **GetIcon** make sure the application uses the tool's own icon and cursor. The remaining functions actually do the drawing.

Each drawing tool is allocated and managed by the main application. You'll see how this is done later in this chapter when we develop a simple drawing program. For now, we'll walk through the code that implements each of the drawing tools.

Selecting a Tool

The first step in using a tool is to select it by calling the **Select** member function. This function is invoked when the user has chosen the tool from a tool palette or menu. By default, it takes two actions. First, it associates the tool with the **TPaintContext** object passed to it. (Remember, the **TPaintContext**

Table 13.2 TDrawingTool's Member Functions

Function	Description
Deselect	Invoked when a tool is no longer being used
Finish	Draws the figure in its final form
GetIcon	Returns a handle to the tool's icon
LButtonDown	Called when the left mouse button is pressed while in the drawing window; starts the interactive drawing process
LButtonUp	Called when the drawing window receives a WM_LBUTTONUP message; this function usually ends the interactive drawing and draws the figure permanently in the window
MouseMove	Used when the drawing window receives WM_MOUSEMOVE messages; updates the figure being drawn
RButtonDown	Called when the drawing window receives WM_RBUTTONDOWN messages; used by the polygon tools to end the drawing process
Select	Called when a tool is initially selected
SelectCursor	Sets the hCursor data member to the mouse cursor to use while drawing
Show	Displays the figure at the location and size
Start	Begins drawing the figure
SortPoints	Sort the Pt1 and Pt2 points so that Pt1 is to the left and above Pt2
UpdateCursor	Used by some tools to modify the cursor

object tells the tool how the figure it draws is to appear.) Second, it loads the tool's cursor by calling the **SelectCursor** member function:

```
void TDrawingTool::Select(TPaintContext* pc)
{
  PC = pc;            // Save a pointer to the painting context
  SelectCursor(-1);   // Select the tool's default cursor
}
```

In the next chapter, we'll develop some additional tools that override **Select** in order to take immediate action when the tool is selected. For instance, a delete tool will delete an object from the screen as soon as the delete tool is selected.

The −1 passed to **SelectCursor** in the previous code segment tells the routine to use the tool's default cursor. For instance, the **TDrawingTool** version of **SelectCursor** executes the following statement to load an arrow mouse cursor:

```
hCursor = LoadCursor(0, IDC_ARROW);
```

The Windows function **LoadCursor** loads the indicated cursor and saves a handle to it in **TDrawingTool** 's **hCursor** variable. The drawing window handles the details of switching to the cursor. We'll get to this later in the chapter.

The **LoadCursor** function is new, but rather simple. Its two parameters specify which cursor to return a handle to. The first parameter is usually a handle to an application's instance. In this case it's 0 (**NULL**); therefore, we're requesting one of Windows' predefined cursors. In particular, we're gaining access to the default arrow cursor **IDC_ARROW**. A tool can override **SelectCursor** to specify a different mouse cursor. Some of the drawing tools, for example, use Windows' crosshair cursor, which is accessed using the constant **IDC_CROSS**.

The argument passed to **SelectCursor** can be used to select among a variety of cursors. For instance, a tool may need to use a different mouse cursor when editing a figure. The meaning of the argument is completely up to the object. In the next chapter, you'll see how we'll put this parameter to use in order to select another cursor when resizing an object.

The **Deselect** member function is **Select**'s alter ego. **Deselect** is called when the tool is no longer active. This typically occurs when another tool is selected. The function doesn't do anything by default, but again, some tools derived in the next chapter will use it.

Drawing with Events

You may be wondering where the drawing takes place. As you'll see, it is spread across several functions. There are two reasons for all these routines. First, tasks are divided into small functions so that they can easily be overridden in derived classes. Second, the code is organized around specific mouse events that Windows generates.

In particular, when we interactively draw figures, three mouse events are important: button presses, mouse movement, and button releases. You're already familiar with the button press message **WM_LBUTTONDOWN**. Now, we'll also check for **WM_MOUSEMOVE**, **WM_LBUTTONUP**, and **WM_RBUTTONDOWN**, which occur when the mouse is moved, the left button is released, and the right mouse button is pressed, respectively.

It's natural to think of the process of drawing a figure in terms of these events. Drawing begins when the left button is pressed. Then, as the user drags the mouse while holding down the button, the figure's size is updated. When the mouse button is released, the figure is frozen and the tool is ready to draw another object. (In case you're wondering, the right button is used by the polygon tool to close off polygons. For all other tools, it chains to the function associated with **WM_LBUTTONUP**.)

What will trap for these mouse messages? The drawing window will. When the drawing window detects a mouse event, it calls one of the functions

LButtonDown, **MouseMove**, **LButtonUp**, or **RButtonDown** for the desired tool. They all accept a single parameter: a **POINT** structure that specifies the X and Y location of the mouse (in device coordinates). In addition, **LButtonUp** and **RButtonDown** return TRUE as long as a figure is being drawn and return FALSE when the drawing is complete.

Beginning to Draw

Now we'll step through the sequence of functions in **TDrawingTool** to see how a figure is drawn. The **LButtonDown** function is the first routine in the process. **LButtonDown** is called when the left mouse button is pressed. Its chores include gaining access to the drawing window's device context, performing some initialization, and drawing the initial form of the figure.

A handle to the drawing window's device context is retrieved and stored in **TDrawingTool**'s variable **hDC**:

```
hDC = GetDC(PC->DrawingWnd);
```

Notice that the handle to the window passed to **GetDC** comes from the **DrawingWnd** variable in the **TPaintContext** structure.

The next statement in **LButtonDown** introduces a new Windows feature:

```
SetCapture(PC->DrawingWnd);
```

What does **SetCapture** do? Normally, the mouse sends its status information to the window that it is above. However, while drawing, we want the mouse to be able to move outside of the window without terminating the drawing process. (We'll rely on Windows to clip the figure to the drawing window.) The **SetCapture** function solves the problem. It tells Windows to temporarily send all mouse messages to the window specified—in this case, the drawing window, **PC->DrawingWnd**. The drawing window will call the drawing tool's functions when it receives the mouse messages. We'll release the mouse when the drawing is complete, as you'll see later.

Next, **LButtonDown** creates and selects a dotted pen. This is the pen used to draw the figure while the user is interactively setting its size. Then the current location of the mouse, passed to **LButtonDown**, is saved in **Pt1**. This coordinate will be the fixed location of the interactive figure.

After all these preliminaries have been completed, **TDrawingTool**'s **Start** function is called. **Start** is typically used to perform any additional initialization and to draw the initial state of the figure. The figure is actually drawn by calling another member function, **Show**. The base class doesn't draw anything, so **Show** is left empty. Derived classes will override **Show** to display their figures.

Finally, the **LButtonDown** function returns TRUE, indicating that the drawing tool is in the process of interactively drawing a figure.

Sizing the Drawing

A figure is resized as the mouse is moved while the left button is pressed. In an application, the drawing window will trap for **WM_MOUSEMOVE** messages and call the drawing tool's **MouseMove** function to update the figure. **MouseMove** is where the real interaction takes place, but it is surprisingly simple:

```
void TDrawingTool::MouseMove(POINT& pt)
{
  Show(hDC, PC->Zoom);    // Actually removes the figure
  Pt2 = pt;               // Save the object's updated location
  Show(hDC, PC->Zoom);    // Draw the figure
}
```

The mouse's coordinate is passed to **MouseMove** as **pt** and is used to specify the new location of the figure. The two calls to **Show** actually update the figure on the screen. For most objects, **Show** draws a figure from the point (**Pt1.x,Pt1.y**) to the current (**Pt2.x,Pt2.y**). Therefore, the first call redraws the figure at its current location. Actually, the call erases the figure at its current location, as you'll see in a bit. After **Pt2** is updated with the mouse's new position, **Show** is called again to display the figure at its new location.

How can **Show** be used to both erase and display a figure? The function could keep track of whether it should hide or display the figure based on how often it has been called. However, we'll override **TDrawingTool**'s **Start** function later so that the tools will exclusive-OR their figures. In this way, the drawing can be displayed by calling **Show** once, and erased by calling **Show** again.

Ending the Interactive Drawing

Typically, in order to fix the location of the figure being drawn, the user releases the left mouse button. This generates the **WM_LBUTTONUP** message, which the drawing window watches for. When this event occurs, the **LButtonUp** function is called for the drawing tool being used.

The **LButtonUp** routine releases the resources it is using, draws the figure with its permanent settings, and returns FALSE to signal the end of the drawing process.

The first steps taken are to return the device context that was borrowed for the drawing window, release the mouse, and delete the dotted pen object used to interactively draw the figure:

```
ReleaseDC(PC->DrawingWnd, hDC);
ReleaseCapture();
DeleteObject(hPen);          // Delete the dotted pen style
```

Next, the **Finish** member function is called to display the figure with its permanent settings. Although the base class doesn't draw anything, **Finish** performs several operations common to all the drawing tools.

First, **Finish** prepares to draw the figure with its permanent color and fill settings. It retrieves a handle to the drawing window's device context and then creates a pen and brush using the colors specified in **TPaintContext**:

```
hDC = GetDC(PC->DrawingWnd);
hPen = CreatePen(PS_SOLID, PC->PenWd, PC->PenColor);
hBrush = CreateSolidBrush(PC->BrushColor);
SelectObject(hDC, hPen);
SelectObject(hDC, hBrush);
```

With these settings, **Finish** calls **Show** to display the figure

```
Show(hDC, PC->Zoom);
```

and then releases the settings just used:

```
ReleaseDC(PC->DrawingWnd, hDC);
DeleteObject(hBrush);
DeleteObject(hPen);
SortPoints();  // Save sorted versions of the object's coordinates
```

That completes the process of interactively drawing a figure.

Deriving Drawing Tools

To implement a specific drawing tool, you must override parts of **TDrawingTool**. Foremost, the **Show** function should be overridden to display the desired figure. Optionally, you may want to override the **GetIcon** function in order to supply a custom icon for the tool. We'll look at this function later when we develop a tool palette. You may need to override other functions to supply specific behavior. For instance, we'll override **LButtonDown** for the polygon and text tools so that we can change the way these tools respond to mouse events.

DRAWING LINES

Now that we've pulled apart the components of **TDrawingTool**, we can show how it is used to derive a specific drawing tool. We'll begin with **TLineTool**, which draws line segments, as shown in Figure 13.2.

TLineTool lets you draw a line by pointing to where the line is to begin, pressing and holding down the left mouse button, and then dragging the mouse to the desired endpoint. When the button is released, the line is frozen. However, while the button is pressed, **TLineTool** continues to draw the line from the initial location of the mouse, where the button was pressed, to the mouse's current position. Therefore, as the mouse is moved around the screen, the line will shrink and stretch as needed. While you are drawing the line, it is shown as a dotted line, as shown in Figure 13.3.

Figure 13.2 You use the TLineTool class to draw lines.

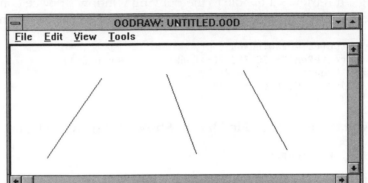

This type of line is called a *rubber-banding* line because the line segment appears to be flexible, like a rubber band. Anyway, to draw more lines, you simply repeat the process.

Deriving a tool, like **TLineTool** from **TDrawingTool**, is a matter of overriding those member functions where we need to replace the inherited object's routines or supplement them. The **TLineTool** class definition, therefore, indicates which functions we have overridden to implement the line-drawing tool. Here's its definition:

```
class TLineTool : public TDrawingTool {  // Draws single lines
public:
  void Start();
  void SelectCursor(int id);
  void Show(HDC hDC, double zoom, int offsx=0, int offsy=0);
  HICON GetIcon();
};
```

Figure 13.3 A dotted line is used while interactively drawing a line.

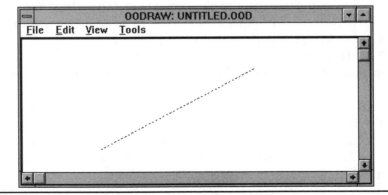

The **Start** function is overridden so that we can change the raster operation mode in order to create the rubber-banding effect. We're using the exclusive-OR mode **R2_XORPEN**:

```
void TLineTool::Start()
{
  SetROP2(hDC, R2_XORPEN);    // Exclusive-OR line while drawing
  TDrawingTool::Start();
}
```

Note Recall that the pen color used to draw the interactive figure is black. Will the pen change anything on the screen since we are using the exclusive-OR mode **R2_XORPEN**? After all, exclusive ORing a black pen with a window won't show up on the screen. However, we can use the exclusive-OR mode here because we are using a *dotted* pen. Remember that, by default, the gaps in the dotted lines are set with the background color, which is normally white. Therefore, when we exclusive-OR the dotted pen to the window, it will appear on the screen due to the white gaps, *not* the black dotted lines.

The **Show** method is overridden to draw the line by calling **MoveToEx** and **LineTo**. The line is drawn from the fixed point (**Pt1.x,Pt1.y**) to the moving point (**Pt2.x,Pt2.y**):

```
void TLineTool::Show(HDC hDC, double zoom, int offsx, int offsy)
{
  MoveToEx(hDC, Pt1.x*zoom-offsx+0.5, Pt1.y*zoom-offsy+0.5, 0);
  LineTo(hDC, Pt2.x*zoom-offsx+0.5, Pt2.y*zoom-offsy+0.5);
}
```

The **hDC** parameter is a handle to the device context for the drawing window. Similarly, the **zoom**, **offsx**, and **offsy** parameters are the drawing window's zoom factor and scroller offsets. By default, **offsx** and **offsy** are set to 0 and normally, **zoom** will be equal to 1. These values are combined with the current object's coordinates to determine the object's pixel location. The 0.5 value is added to the results so that the calculations are *rounded* off. Otherwise C++ will simply truncate the floating point calculations to the integer parameters. Truncating the coordinates can lead to round off errors in certain situations; therefore, *it's a good idea to round off all scaled coordinates.*

The line-drawing tool also modifies the cursor so that it uses a crosshair rather than the default arrow:

```
void TLineTool::SelectCursor(int id)
{
  if (id == -1) hCursor = LoadCursor(0, IDC_CROSS);
    else TDrawingTool::SelectCursor(id);
}
```

Similarly, the line tool provides its own icon by overriding **GetIcon**, but we'll discuss this feature later.

DRAWING RECTANGLES

The drawing tool package can draw either filled or empty rectangles, as shown in Figure 13.4. Filled rectangles are drawn using **TRectangleTool** and hollow rectangles using **TEmptyRectangleTool**.

Both tools work the same way. When you press the left mouse button, the drawing process begins by fixing one corner of the rectangle to the current location of the mouse. The opposing corner of the rectangle floats as you drag the mouse. When you release the left mouse button, the rectangle is drawn with its current settings. The rubber-banding rectangle is drawn using the dotted pen and the permanent rectangle is drawn using the settings in **TPaintContext**. We'll begin by looking at **TRectangleTool**.

As you might imagine, drawing a rectangle is very similar to drawing rubber-banding lines. The only difference is that we want to draw a rectangle rather than a line. Therefore, the **TRectangleTool** class is derived from **TLineTool**. The **TRectagleTool** class definition is:

```
class TRectangleTool : public TLineTool { // Draws a filled rectangle
public:
  void Start();
  void Show(HDC hDC, double zoom, int offsx=0, int offsy=0);
  HICON GetIcon();
};
```

The **Show** function is overridden so that the tool displays a rectangle that extends from the fixed point (**Pt1.x**,**Pt1.y**) to the floating point (**Pt2.x**,**Pt2.y**):

Figure 13.4 You can draw filled and hollow rectangles with the rectangle tools.

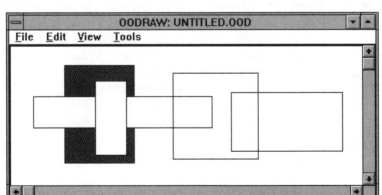

```
void TRectangleTool::Show(HDC hDC, double zoom, int offsx, int offsy)
{
  POINT Pt1b=Pt1, Pt2b=Pt2;    // Sort the two corners of the rectangle
  Sort2Pts(Pt1b, Pt2b);        // so that Pt1 is the top, left value
  Rectangle(hDC, Pt1b.x*zoom-offsx+0.5, Pt1b.y*zoom-offsy+0.5,
    Pt2b.x*zoom-offsx+0.5+1, Pt2b.y*zoom-offsy+0.5+1);
}
```

Why is the **Show** function more complicated than its line drawing tool's counterpart? The extra code adjusts for the fact that Windows draws rectangles one pixel smaller in width and height than specified. As a result, the **Rectangle** statement adds a 1 to the right and bottom edges of the rectangle to draw. But this isn't enough. The situation can worsen if the user drags the mouse to the left and above the original point **Pt1**. We must sort the coordinates **Pt1** and **Pt2** so that **Pt2** is always to the right and below **Pt1**. This is the purpose of **Sort2Pts**. We're using temporary variables to hold the sorted coordinates because the user may drag the mouse to the right and below **Pt1** where the coordinates don't need to be sorted.

If this is all we need to do to draw a rubber-banding rectangle, why is **Start** also overridden? Recall that the GDI **Rectangle** function normally draws a *filled* rectangle. However, we don't want the rubber-banding rectangle to be filled. Only the final figure needs to be. Therefore, the **Start** function is overridden so that we can also select a hollow brush.

```
void TRectangleTool::Start()
{
  TLineTool::Start();          // Do what TLineTool does
  // Use a NULL brush so the interior won't be filled. Since
  // this is a stock object we won't have to delete it later.
  hBrush = HBRUSH(GetStockObject(NULL_BRUSH));
  SelectObject(hDC, hBrush);
}
```

Of course, we still want to do everything else that the line tool does to start the drawing process; therefore, **Start** also calls the inherited function **TLineTool::Start**.

The **TRectangleTool** class also overrides **GetIcon** to supply its own icon, as do all the drawing tools.

Drawing empty rectangles is similar to drawing filled rectangles; therefore the **TEmptyRectangleTool** class is derived from **TRectangleTool**. **TEmptyRectangleTool** overrides **GetIcon** and **Show**. The **Show** function is modified so that the tool always draws hollow rectangles:

```
void TEmptyRectangleTool::Show(HDC hDC, double zoom, int offsx, int offsy)
{
  HBRUSH hOldBrush = HBRUSH(SelectObject(hDC, GetStockObject(NULL_BRUSH)));
  POINT Pt1b=Pt1, Pt2b=Pt2;    // Sort the two corners of the rectangle
  Sort2Pts(Pt1b, Pt2b);        // so that Pt1 is the top, left value
```

```
Rectangle(hDC, Pt1b.x*zoom-offsx+0.5, Pt1b.y*zoom-offsy+0.5,
  Pt2b.x*zoom-offsx+0.5+1, Pt2b.y*zoom-offsy+0.5+1);
SelectObject(hDC, hOldBrush);
}
```

Why is the brush only temporarily changed to a **NULL_BRUSH**? The **Show** function can be called on two different occasions: while interactively drawing the figure and when drawing the figure with its permanent settings. In the latter case, **TDrawingTool::Finish** sets up the brush settings and calls **Show**. By switching to a **NULL_BRUSH** in **Show**, we override this brush style. We must restore the brush style, however, because **Finish** deletes **hBrush** and we don't want to delete the stock brush **NULL_BRUSH**.

DRAWING ELLIPSES

The drawing tool package includes two functions that draw ellipses. The **TEllipseTool** class draws filled ellipses, and **TEmptyEllipseTool** draws hollow ellipses.

The process of interactively drawing ellipses is similar to that used to draw rectangles. You press the left mouse button where you want to locate one corner of the ellipse's bounding box. Then you drag the mouse to change the location of the opposing corner of the bounding box. While you are drawing the ellipse, it is shown with a dotted pen style. When you release the left mouse button, the ellipse is drawn with its permanent settings. Several simple ellipses are shown in Figure 13.5.

Although ellipses aren't drawn with straight lines, the process of interactively drawing them is similar to that used to draw rectangles. Recall that the GDI specifies the coordinates of an ellipse using its bounding box—a rectangle. Therefore, we'll derive our ellipse tools from **TRectangleTool**:

Figure 13.5 You can draw filled and hollow ellipses with the ellipse tools.

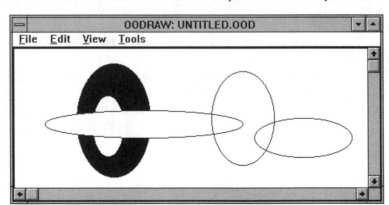

```
class TEllipseTool : public TRectangleTool {  // Draws an ellipse
public:
  void Show(HDC hDC, double zoom, int offsx=0, int offsy=0);
  HICON GetIcon();
};
```

The key modification we need to make here is to override **Show** so that the tool draws ellipses:

```
void TEllipseTool::Show(HDC hDC, double zoom, int offsx, int offsy)
{
  POINT Pt1b=Pt1, Pt2b=Pt2;
  Sort2Pts(Pt1b, Pt2b);
  Ellipse(hDC, Pt1b.x*zoom-offsx+0.5, Pt1b.y*zoom-offsy+0.5,
    Pt2b.x*zoom-offsx+0.5+1, Pt2b.y*zoom-offsy+1+0.5);
}
```

That's all we need to do!

To draw hollow ellipses, the **TEmptyEllipseTool** class is derived from **TEllipseTool** and overrides the **Show** function to force the routine to use a hollow brush:

```
void TEmptyEllipseTool::Show(HDC hDC, double zoom, int offsx, int offsy)
{
  HBRUSH hOldBrush = HBRUSH(SelectObject(hDC, GetStockObject(NULL_BRUSH)));
  POINT Pt1b=Pt1, Pt2b=Pt2;
  Sort2Pts(Pt1b, Pt2b);
  Ellipse(hDC, Pt1b.x*zoom-offsx+0.5, Pt1b.y*zoom-offsy+0.5,
    Pt2b.x*zoom-offsx+1+0.5, Pt2b.y*zoom-offsy+1+0.5);
  SelectObject(hDC, hOldBrush);
}
```

This is the same technique we used to draw empty rectangles in **TEmptyRectangleTool**.

DRAWING POLYGONS

There are two classes in our toolkit that allow you to draw polygons—**TPolylineTool** and **TPolygonTool**. The first class, **TPolylineTool**, allows you to draw a series of lines connected at their endpoints, as shown in Figure 13.6. The second class, **TPolygonTool**, draws closed polygons and fills the interior with the brush style specified in the **TPaintContext** variable. A sample figure drawn with **TPolygonTool** is shown in Figure 13.7.

In effect, **TPolylineTool** is nothing more than a variation of the line-drawing tool; therefore **TPolylineTool** is derived from **TLineTool**. Similarly, **TPolygonTool** operates just like **TPolylineTool**, except for the fact that it draws filled polygons; consequently, it is derived from **TPolylineTool**. Our object hierarchy is really paying off since we are able to share code in the inherited functions.

Figure 13.6 You can draw connected lines with TPolylineTool.

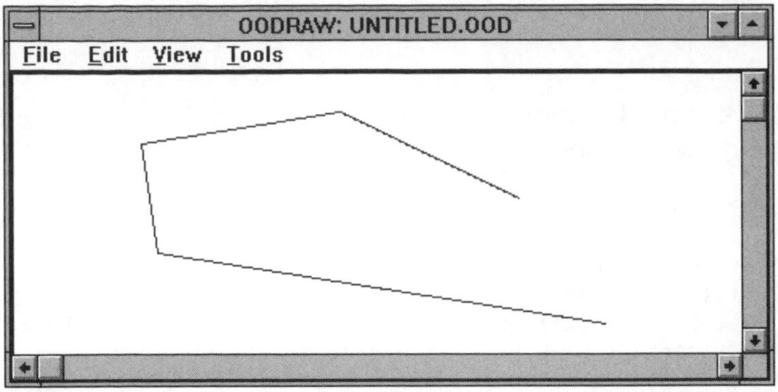

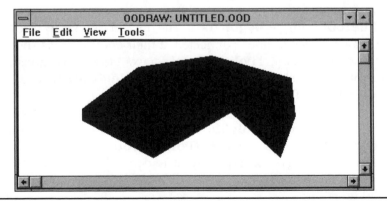

Both polygon classes operate in a similar manner, although they work differently from the drawing tools previously discussed. The polygon classes begin drawing after the first press of the left mouse button. Next, they draw a rubber-banding line as the mouse is moved around the screen until the left button is released. The current line is then frozen and this line becomes the first side of the polygon. When you press the left mouse button again to begin another line, the starting point of the new rubber-banding line is drawn starting from the first line's endpoint.

You can repeat this process to add additional sides to the polygon. When you want to stop drawing, simply press the right mouse button. If **TPolygonTool** is used, the figure is closed off and its interior is filled.

The **TPolylineTool** class is defined as:

```
const int MAXPOLYSIZE = 40;                     // Can have this many edges
class TPolylineTool : public TLineTool {  // Draws connected lines
```

Figure 13.7 You can draw a closed, filled polygon with TPolygonTool.

```
protected:
  BOOL Drawing;              // TRUE if a polygon is being drawn
public:
  POINT Poly[MAXPOLYSIZE];   // List of points in the figure
  int NumPts;                // Number of coordinates in polygon
  TPolylineTool() { Drawing = FALSE; }
  BOOL LButtonDown(POINT& pt);
  BOOL LButtonUp(POINT& pt);
  BOOL RButtonDown(POINT& pt);
  void Start();
  void Show(HDC hDC, double zoom, int offsx=0, int offsy=0);
  HICON GetIcon();
};
```

The connected points of the polygon are stored in the new array variable **Poly**. The number of points in **Poly** is indicated by **NumPts**. The **Poly** array can hold up to **MAXPOLYSIZE** (40) coordinate pairs. The class also contains a third new variable, **Drawing**, which is a Boolean flag that is TRUE while a polygon is being interactively drawn. The functions use **Drawing** to decide how to interpret left button presses. The first time through, **Drawing** is FALSE, indicating that a new polygon is to be started. If **Drawing** is TRUE, however, it means that a polygon is being drawn and the button press can be ignored.

Since the user interaction is different, DRAW.CPP overrides the three mouse-related member functions **LButtonDown**, **LButtonUp**, and **RButtonDown**. The **RButtonDown** function is introduced here so that the tool can check for the closing signal—a right button press.

The **LButtonDown** function only responds to mouse events if the **Drawing** flag is FALSE. If so, a new figure is being started and the function calls **TLineTool**'s **LButtonDown** function to draw the new line:

```
else {                       // Begin a new polygon. Call the
  Drawing = TRUE;            // inherited LButtonDown function
  TLineTool::LButtonDown(pt); // which calls TPolyline::Start.
}
```

This sets up the drawing process. The **Drawing** flag is set TRUE to indicate that a polygon is now being interactively drawn.

The **Start** function is overridden to save the first position of the polygon in the **Poly** array:

```
void TPolylineTool::Start()
{
  Poly[0] = Pt1;             // Save current location of mouse
  NumPts = 1;                // One coordinate pair is saved
  TLineTool::Start();
}
```

The code calls **TLineTool**'s **Start** function to switch the raster operation mode to **R2_XORPEN**. Remember, switching to this mode allows us to draw rubber-banding lines.

The **LButtonUp** function builds up the **Poly** array. Each time the left button is released, the current coordinates of the mouse are placed in **Poly**:

```
if (NumPts < MAXPOLYSIZE) {
  Show(hDC, PC->Zoom);
  Pt2 = pt;
  Poly[NumPts++] = Pt2;
  Show(hDC, PC->Zoom);
  Pt1 = pt;            // A new line starts here
  Show(hDC, PC->Zoom);
  return TRUE;         // Signal that we are still drawing
}
```

Why are there three calls to **Show**? The first two update the location of the edge of the polygon just drawn. The bottom call to **Show** starts drawing the *next* edge of the polygon.

Notice that the code checks whether the **Poly** list is full. If too many edges have been added to the polygon array, then a message is displayed, and the drawing process is terminated.

```
MessageBox(PC->DrawingWnd, "Too many points in polygon",
  GetApplicationObject()->GetName(), MB_OK);
Drawing = FALSE;
TDrawingTool::LButtonUp(pt);
return FALSE;      // Signal the end of the drawing
```

When the right button is pressed, the current location of the mouse is saved:

```
if (Drawing) {
  Drawing = FALSE; // Stop interactively drawing the polygon
  if (NumPts < MAXPOLYSIZE)
    Poly[NumPts++] = Pt2;
```

This is the last line segment of the figure; therefore the function sets **Drawing** to FALSE and returns FALSE.

The line segments are drawn by **Show**, in one of two ways. While the figure is being interactively drawn, rubber-banding lines drawn by **TLineTool** are used. Remember, in this situation the Boolean flag **Drawing** is TRUE. When the final polygon is to be permanently drawn, however, **Drawing** is FALSE and **Polyline** is used to display the points in **Poly** with their proper settings:

```
void TPolylineTool::Show(HDC hDC, double zoom, int offsx, int offsy)
{
  if (Drawing)
    TLineTool::Show(hDC, zoom, offsx, offsy);
  else {
    POINT* pointsZ = new POINT[NumPts];
    if (!pointsZ) {
      MessageBox(PC->DrawingWnd, "Out of Memory",
```

```
        GetApplicationObject()->GetName(), MB_OK | MB_ICONEXCLAMATION);
        return;
    }
    for (int i=0; i<NumPts; i++) {
      pointsZ[i].x = Poly[i].x * zoom - offsx + 0.5;
      pointsZ[i].y = Poly[i].y * zoom - offsy + 0.5;
    }
    Polyline(hDC, pointsZ, NumPts);
    delete pointsZ;
  }
}
```

You'll notice that the code doesn't simply call the **Polyline** routine to display the polygon. The additional code creates a scaled version of the polygon's coordinates that is placed in the temporary **pointsZ** array. These are the actual points displayed.

Drawing filled polygons is similar to drawing connected lines. Therefore, **TPolygonTool** is derived from **TPolylineTool**. The **Show** function mirrors the **Show** routine in **TPolylineTool** except that it calls **Polygon** rather than **Polyline**:

DRAWING TEXT

The **TTextTool** object allows you to enter a single line of text in the drawing window. To use **TTextTool**, you click the left mouse button where you want to begin entering text. The dialog box shown in Figure 13.8 will appear. You use it to enter the text string. If you select the OK button in the dialog box, the string is displayed in the window at the location where the mouse was clicked.

Because the user interaction with **TTextTool** is quite different than with the other drawing tools, **TTextTool** overrides each of the mouse-related member functions in **TDrawingTool**:

Figure 13.8 This dialog box allows you to enter text.

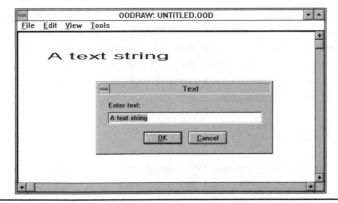

```
const int DEFAULTWD = 20;    // Default width and height of the text
const int DEFAULTHT = 20;
const int MAXSTRING = 80;                  // A string can be this long
class TTextTool : public TDrawingTool {  // Text entry class
public:
  int Wd, Ht;                             // Width and height of the text
  char Str[MAXSTRING];                    // String entered
  TTextTool() {
    Str[0] = '\0';                        // Default string
    Wd = DEFAULTWD; Ht = DEFAULTHT;       // Set default text dimensions
  }
  BOOL LButtonDown(POINT& pt) { return TRUE; }   // Text objects don't
  BOOL RButtonDown(POINT&) { return FALSE; }     // support these
  void MouseMove(POINT& pt) { }                  // four functions
  void Start() { }
  BOOL LButtonUp(POINT&);
  void Show(HDC hDC, double zoom, int offsx=0, int offsy=0);
  HICON GetIcon();
  void GetTextSize(SIZE& size);
  void SelectCursor(int id);
};
```

The text string is saved in the variable **Str**. The tool's constructor initializes the string to a **NULL** string.

Text entry is handled by **LButtonUp**, which pops up a text entry dialog box. Fortunately, OWL provides the **TInputDialog** class, which handles all the details we need for retrieving a text string entered in the dialog box. The specifications for the dialog box are contained in the OWL file INPUTDIA.DLG. This file is located in the \INCLUDE directory of the OWL subdirectory with Borland's compiler.

The **LButtonUp** function begins by popping up a **TInputDialog**:

```
if (TInputDialog(PC->OWLWindow, "Text", "Enter text:",
  Str, MAXSTRING).Execute() == IDOK) {
```

If the user selects the OK button, the input string is placed in **Str**. The code then retrieves a handle to the drawing window's device context and saves the bounds of the string (as it would appear on the screen) in **Pt1** and **Pt2**. We'll use the coordinates of the text's bounding box in the next chapter.

The **Show** function is overridden to display the text string returned by the dialog box. It performs three steps. First, it sets the background mode to transparent—so that the background behind the text is not affected—and switches to the color to draw the text.

```
SetBkMode(hDC, TRANSPARENT);
SetTextColor(hDC, PC->PenColor);
```

Next, a font is temporarily created that fits within the dimensions of a rectangle specified by **Pt1** and **Pt2** and the text is displayed to the screen:

```
HFONT hFont = CreateFont(Ht*zoom, Wd*zoom, 0, 0, 0, 0, 0, 0,
  0, 0, 0, 0, 0, "Arial");
HFONT hOldFont = HFONT(SelectObject(hDC, hFont));
TextOut(hDC, Pt1.x*zoom-offsx+0.5, Pt1.y*zoom-offsy+0.5,
  Str, lstrlen(Str));
```

This code is a little wasteful since it must create the font each time the **Show** function is called. Therefore, you may want to modify the code to create the font once or whenever it must change.

To use **TInputDialog**, you must include the following statements in a resource file that is bound with your application program:

```
#include "windows.h"

/* Required for TInputDialog object, which is used in DRAW.CPP */
rcinclude owl\inputdia.rc
```

Note All applications that use DRAW.CPP must include a resource file that contains these statements. If you don't supply them, the program will still compile and link. However, if you select the **TTextTool** and the resource statements were not used, you will receive a run-time error.

USING ICONS WITH THE TOOLS

Now you have the basic ingredients for using the DRAW.CPP package. However, one component is still missing. Remember that each of the tools provides its own icon in the member function **GetIcon**. Let's look at how this works.

Recall that the **GetIcon** function returns a handle to an icon. For example, the **TLineTool** class defines **GetIcon** as:

```
HICON TLineTool::GetIcon()
{
  return LoadIcon(GetApplicationObject()->GetInstance(), "linetool");
}
```

GetIcon calls the Windows function **LoadIcon** to retrieve a handle to the **linetool** icon. The **LoadIcon** function is defined as:

```
HICON LoadIcon(HANDLE hInstance, LPSTR iconName);
```

- **hInstance** is the instance of the program, and tells Windows which .EXE file contains the specified icon.
- **iconName** is a string that specifies the name of the icon; the icon's name is not a filename, but a string listed in a resource file's **ICON** statement. The string is not case sensitive.

For example, the following **ICON** statement in a resource file associates the internal name **linetool** with an icon's actual filename: LINE.ICO:

```
linetool ICON line.ico
```

If the icon file LINE.ICO exists, the call to **GetIcon** will then retrieve the line's icon. Actually, Windows doesn't go to the icon file to find the icon. Instead, each icon file listed in the resource file is bound with the .EXE file at link time.

Creating an Icon

You can create icons using the Resource Workshop. Figure 13.9 shows several icons that we'll use with the drawing tools presented here and with the tools we'll create in Chapter 14. Each icon is saved in a separate binary file that ends with an .ICO extension.

The icons are all 32 by 32 pixels in size. Although you can use any colors you want, the icons shown here are all set to light gray with black figures. In addition, the left and bottom edges are trimmed in black and the top and right sides of the icon with white. This gives the icon a raised, three-dimensional appearance.

Note   If you don't supply icons for the tools, the DRAW.CPP toolkit can still be used; however the icons will be undefined.

Figure 13.9 The icons in this figure are used in this book.

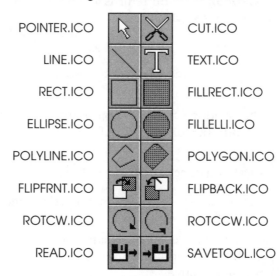

POINTER.ICO	CUT.ICO
LINE.ICO	TEXT.ICO
RECT.ICO	FILLRECT.ICO
ELLIPSE.ICO	FILLELLI.ICO
POLYLINE.ICO	POLYGON.ICO
FLIPFRNT.ICO	FLIPBACK.ICO
ROTCW.ICO	ROTCCW.ICO
READ.ICO	SAVETOOL.ICO

A Simple Drawing Program

We'll now build a simple drawing program that puts these tools to work. The application is named SIMDRAW.CPP. A sample of its output is shown in Figure 13.10.

One of the intriguing aspects of SIMDRAW is its draggable tool palette, which contains an icon for each tool in DRAW.CPP. The tool palette is a pop-up window that you can drag around the screen at will. This is especially convenient when you want instant access to the drawing tools, but don't want to set aside part of the display for a permanent palette. You can select a drawing tool by simply clicking on its icon in the palette.

A Tool Palette

Constructing a palette is rather simple. We'll use a palette here to hold each drawing tool's icon. You can, however, use a similar technique to create a palette of colors, brush patterns, or whatever. In the next chapter, we'll also create a color palette.

The code for the tool palette is contained in the class **TToolsPalette**, which in turn is contained in SIMDRAW.CPP:

```
class TToolsPalette : public TFrameWindow {
public:
  HICON HIcons[NUMICONSWIDE*NUMICONSHIGH];
  TDrawingTool* Tools[NUMICONSWIDE*NUMICONSHIGH];   // Drawing tools
  int IconWd, IconHt; // Width and height of an icon
  int ToolNdx;        // Index of the currently select tool
  int WndWd, WndHt;   // Width and height of palette
  TPaintContext *PC;  // The tools use the paint context
  TToolsPalette(TWindow* parent, const char* title, TPaintContext *pc);
```

Figure 13.10 SIMDRAW.CPP allows you to create this and similar scenes.

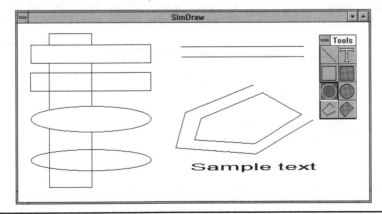

```
void HighlightIcon(HDC hDC, int i);
void Paint(TDC& dc, BOOL, TRect&);
void EvLButtonDown(UINT, TPoint& pt);
void EvClose();

DECLARE_RESPONSE_TABLE(TToolsPalette);
};
```

The tool palette is derived from **TFrameWindow**. However, the **TToolsPalette** constructor reveals the special nature of the window. The tool palette is a pop-up window that has a caption and is initially visible. These settings are assigned to the **Style** field of the **Attr** structure defined in OWL:

```
Attr.Style = WS_POPUPWINDOW | WS_CAPTION | WS_VISIBLE;
```

TToolsPalette then creates one tool object for each tool in the palette. A pointer to each tool is stored in the **Tools** array:

```
Tools[0] = new TLineTool;
Tools[1] = new TTextTool;
Tools[2] = new TEmptyRectangleTool;
Tools[3] = new TRectangleTool;
Tools[4] = new TEmptyEllipseTool;
Tools[5] = new TEllipseTool;
Tools[6] = new TPolylineTool;
Tools[7] = new TPolygonTool;
```

In addition, the constructor saves a handle to each tool's icon by calling each of their **GetIcon** functions:

```
for (int i=0; i<NUMICONSHIGH*NUMICONSWIDE; i++)
  hIcons[i] = Tools[i]->GetIcon();
```

These handles are later used to display the icons themselves. The icons are placed in the palette window from left to right, top to bottom. The width and height of the tool palette is specified by the constants **NUMICONSWIDE** and **NUMICONSHIGH**. In SIMDRAW.CPP, the palette is two icons wide and four icons tall.

The **TToolsPalette** constructor also determines the dimensions of an icon:

```
IconWd = GetSystemMetrics(SM_CXICON);
IconHt = GetSystemMetrics(SM_CYICON);
```

The dimensions are necessary so that the program can set the size of the palette's window based on the number of icons that it contains. The dimensions of the window are stored in the variables **WndWd** and **WndHt**:

```
WndWd = IconWd * NUMICONSWIDE + GetSystemMetrics(SM_CXBORDER) * 2;
WndHt = IconHt * NUMICONSHIGH + GetSystemMetrics(SM_CYBORDER) +
  GetSystemMetrics(SM_CYCAPTION);
```

Finally, the **ToolNdx** is set, which specifies the currently selected tool. In this case, it is set to zero, which selects the line tool. The **TPaintContext** structure is also updated so that it points to this tool:

```
PC = pc;
PC->Tool = Tools[ToolNdx];   // Default tool
```

All these steps are required to set up the palette. But to paint it, all we have to do is supply a **Paint** function for **TToolsPalette**:

```
void TToolsPalette::Paint(TDC& dc, BOOL, TRect&)
{
  for (int j=0; j<NUMICONSHIGH; j++)
    for (int i=0; i<NUMICONSWIDE; i++)
      DrawIcon(dc, i*IconWd, j*IconHt, HIcons[j*NUMICONSWIDE+i]);
  HighlightIcon(dc, ToolNdx);
}
```

Notice that it calls **HighlightIcon**. This is another member function in **TToolsPalette** that highlights the currently selected icon by inverting its colors. **HighlightIcon** is also called when a new tool is deselected.

How can you change which tool is selected? Simply determine which icon the mouse cursor is over when the left mouse button is pressed. This operation is performed in **LButtonDown**. If you check the code, you'll see that the icon images for the currently selected tool and the new tool are inverted to signal the change in tools. In addition, the **Tool** field of the **TPaintContext** structure is updated to point to the new tool.

THE SIMDRAW PROGRAM

The tool palette itself is allocated in the constructor for the program's main window object, **TSimDrawWindow**:

```
PC = new TPaintContext;
ToolPalette = new TToolsPalette(this, "Tools", PC);
```

This constructor also sets the **TPaintContext, PC**, so that it uses its window as the drawing window:

```
PC->DrawingWnd = HWindow;  // This window is the window to draw in
PC->OWLWindow = this;      // Save a pointer to this window
```

Positioning the Palette

The initial location of the palette is set by the window that owns the palette. In SIMDRAW, **TSimDrawWindow** sets the beginning position of the palette. It does this in its **EvSize** function, which responds to **WM_SIZE** messages. These messages occur each time the main window's size is changed, such as when the window is initially created.

The program places the tool palette at the upper-right corner of the main window. The **EvSize** function calls Windows' **MoveWindow** to accomplish this:

```
::MoveWindow(ToolPalette->HWindow, p.x, p.y,
  ToolPalette->WndWd, ToolPalette->WndHt, TRUE);
```

The **MoveWindow** function is written:

```
MoveWindow(HWND hWindow, int x, int y, int width, int height, BOOL redraw);
```

- **hWindow** is a handle to the window to relocate.
- **x** and **y** are the *screen* locations of the window.
- **width** and **height** are the dimensions of the window in device units.
- Set the Boolean flag **redraw** TRUE when you want to have the window repainted when it is moved.

In this case, the width and height of the tool palette are calculated in the tool palette's constructor. The top-left location of the tool palette, however, depends on the width of the window and its border:

```
RECT rect;
::GetClientRect(HWindow, &rect);
int border = GetSystemMetrics(SM_CYCAPTION) + 2;

POINT p;
// Place the tool palette at the top right
p.x = rect.right - ToolPalette->WndWd - border;
p.y = border;
::ClientToScreen(HWindow, &p);
```

Processing Mouse Events

The drawing window is responsible for identifying mouse events, such as button presses. When these events occur, the appropriate drawing tool functions are called. For instance, when a **WM_LBUTTONDOWN** message is received, the current tool's **LButtonDown** function is called.

```
void TSimDrawWindow::EvLButtonDown(UINT, TPoint& pt)
{
  PC->DrawingWnd = HWindow;
  if (!DrawingMode)
    // Tell that tool to start drawing. Note: The drawing mode
    // may change if the figure can't be drawn.
    DrawingMode = PC->Tool->LButtonDown(pt);
}
```

The **DrawingMode** variable is a Boolean flag that is set to TRUE as long as the tool is being used to draw a figure. When the figure has been completed, the flag is set to FALSE. This flag prevents the program from calling a mouse function unnecessarily when the drawing tool is not being used. For instance, mouse movement messages (**WM_MOUSEMOVE**) only call **MouseMove** when **DrawingMode** is TRUE:

```
void TSimDrawWindow::EvMouseMove(UINT, TPoint& pt)
{
  if (DrawingMode)
    PC->Tool->MouseMove(pt);
}
```

The **pt** parameter appearing in the **MouseMove** function holds the position of the mouse at the time of the mouse event. It's passed along to the drawing tool, as shown in the code segment. The mouse coordinate is passed in a similar fashion to the **LButtonDown** and **RButtonDown** routines.

Note Windows always specifies the mouse position in device units (pixels), regardless of the mapping mode.

Changing the Mouse Cursor

Another chore of the drawing window is to control the mouse cursor. When the mouse cursor is over the drawing window, we want the program to switch to the current tool's cursor. Recall that each tool defines the function **SetCursor**, which sets its **hCursor** variable to the cursor to use. This is done in the tool's **Select** function. However, these steps don't change the cursor itself. The drawing window must take this step.

Windows provides the **WM_SETCURSOR** message that signals when the cursor has moved over the client area of the window. All we need to do, therefore, is have the drawing window watch for this message and then switch to the currently selected tool's cursor when the message occurs. The **EvSetCursor** function in **TSimDrawWindow** performs this operation:

```
BOOL TSimDrawWindow::EvSetCursor(HWND hWndCursor, UINT hitTest,
  UINT mouseMsg)
{
  if (hitTest == HTCLIENT) {          // Cursor is in the client area
    ::SetCursor(PC->Tool->hCursor);   // Use the current tool's
    return TRUE;                       // cursor style; otherwise, chain
  }                                    // to the inherited function
  return TWindow::EvSetCursor(hWndCursor, hitTest, mouseMsg);
}
```

The **if** statement tests the **hitTest** parameter to ensure that it equals **HTCLIENT**. This statement is true only when the mouse is within the client area of the window.

Compiling the Program

Compiling SIMDRAW requires several source files. You'll need SIMDRAW.CPP and DRAW.CPP. In addition, you'll need the resource file SIMDRAW.RC (shown later), which lists the icons and the **TInputDialog** definition used in DRAW.CPP. Because several files are involved, you must use a project file that includes SIMDRAW.CPP, DRAW.CPP, and SIMDRAW.RC. Finally, don't forget that you'll need the icons for the drawing tools. Sample icons were shown earlier in Figure 13.9.

When you run SIMDRAW, notice that your drawings are lost if the window is resized or another window temporarily overwrites the drawing window. The program doesn't make any effort to save what's in the window so that it can repaint the window. We could use a bitmap to store the drawing, or we could save each figure on the screen as an object in a list. To repaint the window using this last method, we simply sequence through the list, drawing the objects that are no longer visible. This, in fact, is the approach we'll take in the next chapter.

• DRAW.H

```
// DRAW.H: Header file for the interactive drawing utilities
// used in the drawing program.

#ifndef DRAWH
#define DRAWH

#include <owl\applicat.h>
#include <owl\framewin.h>
#include <owl\dc.h>
#include <stdio.h>
#include <math.h>

#define NOHANDLE -1
#define NWHANDLE 0          // IDs for each of the resize
#define NHANDLE 1           // handles on an object's resize
#define NEHANDLE 2          // frame. These are used to specify
#define EHANDLE 3           // which mouse cursor to currently
#define SEHANDLE 4          // use with the object.
#define SHANDLE 5
#define SWHANDLE 6
#define WHANDLE 7
#define SIZEFRAME 8
#define LASTHANDLE 8        // Next available handle ID

class TDrawingTool;         // Forward declaration

// Maintains the current drawing parameters and the object's specific
// color, fill color, and so on
class TPaintContext {
```

```
public:
  TDrawingTool* Tool;        // Pointer to currently selected tool
  int PenWd;                 // Width of pen
  COLORREF PenColor;         // Color of pen
  COLORREF BrushColor;       // Color of brush
  HWND DrawingWnd;           // The window to draw on
  TWindow* OWLWindow;        // The drawing window's OWL object
  double Zoom;               // Zoom factor
  int Offsx, Offsy;          // Offset of drawing window's coordinates
  int SnapWd, SnapHt;        // "Snap to grid" width and height
  BOOL SnapOn;               // Enables the snap to grid feature
  TPaintContext::TPaintContext();
  void SetSnapToGrid(int snapWd, int snapHt);
  POINT SnapToGrid(POINT& pt);
  BOOL SetSnapToGridOn(BOOL snapOn);
};

// The base class that defines the basic format of the drawing tools
class TDrawingTool {
public:
  POINT Pt1, Pt2;                    // Current and last mouse position
  TPaintContext* PC;                 // Drawing parameters
  HDC hDC;                           // Display surface's device context
  HPEN hPen;                         // The drawing pen style
  HBRUSH hBrush;                     // The brush style
  HCURSOR hCursor;                   // The tool's cursor
  virtual void Select(TPaintContext* pc); // Tool selected
  virtual void Deselect() { }        // Deselect the tool
  // Starts the interactive drawing process
  virtual BOOL LButtonDown(POINT& pt);
  // Interactively draws figure
  virtual void MouseMove(POINT& pt);
  virtual BOOL LButtonUp(POINT& pt); // Finalizes drawing
  virtual BOOL RButtonDown(POINT& pt) { return LButtonUp(pt); }
  virtual void Start() { Show(hDC, PC->Zoom, PC->Offsx, PC->Offsy); }
  virtual void Finish();             // Display the permanent settings
  virtual void Show(HDC, double zoom, int offsx=0, int offsy=0) { }
  virtual HICON GetIcon() { return 0; } // Get the icon for the tool
  virtual void UpdateCursor(POINT& pt) { } // Set the mouse cursor
  virtual void SortPoints();
  virtual void SelectCursor(int id);
};

class TLineTool : public TDrawingTool {  // Draws single lines
public:
  void Start();
  void SelectCursor(int id);
  void Show(HDC hDC, double zoom, int offsx=0, int offsy=0);
  HICON GetIcon();
};

class TRectangleTool : public TLineTool { // Draws a filled rectangle
public:
  void Start();
```

```
  void Show(HDC hDC, double zoom, int offsx=0, int offsy=0);
  HICON GetIcon();
};

// Draws an empty rectangle
class TEmptyRectangleTool : public TRectangleTool {
public:
  void Show(HDC hDC, double zoom,
  int offsx=0, int offsy=0);
  HICON GetIcon();
};

const int MAXPOLYSIZE = 40;             // Can have this many edges
class TPolylineTool : public TLineTool {  // Draws connected lines
protected:
  BOOL Drawing;               // TRUE if a polygon is being drawn
public:
  POINT Poly[MAXPOLYSIZE];  // List of points in the figure
  int NumPts;                 // Number of coordinates in polygon
  TPolylineTool() { Drawing = FALSE; }
  BOOL LButtonDown(POINT& pt);
  BOOL LButtonUp(POINT& pt);
  BOOL RButtonDown(POINT& pt);
  void Start();
  void Show(HDC hDC, double zoom, int offsx=0, int offsy=0);
  HICON GetIcon();
};

// Draws a filled polygon. It's just like TPolylineTool
// except that it draws a filled polygon.
class TPolygonTool : public TPolylineTool {
public:
  void Show(HDC hDC, double zoom, int offsx=0, int offsy=0);
  HICON GetIcon();
};

class TEllipseTool : public TRectangleTool {  // Draws an ellipse
public:
  void Show(HDC hDC, double zoom, int offsx=0, int offsy=0);
  HICON GetIcon();
};

// Draws an empty ellipse
class TEmptyEllipseTool : public TEllipseTool {
public:
  void Show(HDC hDC, double zoom, int offsx=0, int offsy=0);
  HICON GetIcon();
};

const int DEFAULTWD = 20;    // Default width and height of the text
const int DEFAULTHT = 20;
const int MAXSTRING = 80;                 // A string can be this long
class TTextTool : public TDrawingTool { // Text entry class
```

```
public:
  int Wd, Ht;                        // Width and height of the text
  char Str[MAXSTRING];               // String entered
  TTextTool() {
    Str[0] = '\0';                   // Default string
    Wd = DEFAULTWD; Ht = DEFAULTHT;  // Set default text dimensions
  }
  BOOL LButtonDown(POINT& pt) { return TRUE; }  // Text objects don't
  BOOL RButtonDown(POINT&) { return FALSE; }    // support these
  void MouseMove(POINT& pt) { }                 // four functions
  void Start() { }
  BOOL LButtonUp(POINT&);
  void Show(HDC hDC, double zoom, int offsx=0, int offsy=0);
  HICON GetIcon();
  void GetTextSize(SIZE& size);
  void SelectCursor(int id);
};
#endif
```

• DRAW.CPP

```
// DRAW.CPP: Interactive drawing utilities used in the drawing program.

#include <owl\applicat.h>
#include <owl\framewin.h>
#include <owl\dc.h>
#include <owl\inputdia.h>     // Required for OWL's TInputDialog class
#include <math.h>
#include "draw.h"

// Initialize the drawing style and various variables used by the
// drawing tool. Call this function when the mouse button has been pressed
// in the drawing window.
BOOL TDrawingTool::LButtonDown(POINT& pt)
{
  // Get a handle to a device context for the drawing window
  hDC = GetDC(PC->DrawingWnd);
  SetCapture(PC->DrawingWnd); // Capture the mouse in the drawing window
  // As the object is drawn, paint it using a dotted, black pen
  hPen = CreatePen(PS_DOT, 1, RGB(0,0,0));
  SelectObject(hDC, hPen);    // Select the dotted pen
  Pt1 = pt;   Pt2 = Pt1;      // Remember the object's starting point
  Start();                    // Begin drawing the object
  return TRUE;                // Signal that the drawing is in progress
}

// Complete the figure being drawn. Call this function from the
// drawing window whenever the mouse is moved. The pt parameter
// contains the location of the mouse.
void TDrawingTool::MouseMove(POINT& pt)
{
  Show(hDC, PC->Zoom);  // Actually removes the figure
  Pt2 = pt;             // Save the object's updated location
```

```
      Show(hDC, PC->Zoom);  // Draw the figure
    }


    // Perform any final operations that must be made to finish the
    // drawing. Call this function from the drawing window when the
    // left mouse button is released. Finish off the drawing as
    // needed. For instance, figures that are drawn with exclusive-ORed
    // lines must be redrawn with the exclusive-OR feature disabled
    // so that the figure's color will come out correctly.
    BOOL TDrawingTool::LButtonUp(POINT&)
    {
      ReleaseDC(PC->DrawingWnd, hDC); // Release the window's device context
      ReleaseCapture();   // Release the mouse captured in LButtonDown
      DeleteObject(hPen); // Delete the dotted pen style
      Finish();           // Display the object with its permanent settings
      return FALSE;       // Turn off the drawing mode
    }


    // End the interactive drawing. Display the figure with its
    // permanent settings.
    void TDrawingTool::Finish()
    {
      hDC = GetDC(PC->DrawingWnd);
      hPen = CreatePen(PS_SOLID, PC->PenWd, PC->PenColor);
      hBrush = CreateSolidBrush(PC->BrushColor);
      SelectObject(hDC, hPen);
      SelectObject(hDC, hBrush);
      Show(hDC, PC->Zoom);
      ReleaseDC(PC->DrawingWnd, hDC);
      DeleteObject(hBrush);
      DeleteObject(hPen);
      SortPoints();  // Save sorted versions of the object's coordinates
    }


    // The tool is selected
    void TDrawingTool::Select(TPaintContext* pc)
    {
      PC = pc;            // Save a pointer to the painting context
      SelectCursor(-1);   // Select the tool's default cursor
    }


    // Switch to a cursor based on the ID specified. If ID is -1
    // the default arrow cursor is used. Otherwise the ID specifies
    // the cursor to use while over one of the object's handles.
    void TDrawingTool::SelectCursor(int id)
    {
      switch (id) {
        case NEHANDLE:
        case SWHANDLE:
          hCursor = LoadCursor(0, IDC_SIZENESW); break;
        case NWHANDLE:
        case SEHANDLE:
          hCursor = LoadCursor(0, IDC_SIZENWSE); break;
```

```
      case SIZEFRAME:
        hCursor = LoadCursor(0, IDC_SIZE); break;
      default:
        hCursor = LoadCursor(0, IDC_ARROW);
    }
}

// Sort the two points so that Pt1 is to the left and above Pt2
void Sort2Pts(POINT& pt1, POINT& pt2)
{
  POINT pt;
  if (pt1.x > pt2.x) {
    pt.x = pt1.x;      pt1.x = pt2.x;      pt2.x = pt.x;
  }
  if (pt1.y > pt2.y) {
    pt.y = pt1.y;      pt1.y = pt2.y;      pt2.y = pt.y;
  }
}

// Sort the two points so that Pt1 is to the left and above Pt2
void TDrawingTool::SortPoints()
{
  POINT pt;
  if (Pt1.x > Pt2.x || Pt1.y > Pt2.y) {
    pt = Pt1;      Pt1 = Pt2;      Pt2 = pt;
  }
}

// Exclusive-OR the line color while the line is being sized.
// Even though the line is black, this works because the line style
// is dotted and the OPAQUE background color is white. Note: You don't
// have to switch out of exclusive-OR mode because the device context
// is released before painting the final version of the object. It
// retrieves a device context which has the default painting mode.
void TLineTool::Start()
{
  SetROP2(hDC, R2_XORPEN);    // Exclusive-OR line while drawing
  TDrawingTool::Start();
}

// The line tool overrides this function to select the crosshair cursor
// rather than the default arrow cursor. Many of the other drawing
// tools inherit the use of the crosshair cursor through this function.
void TLineTool::SelectCursor(int id)
{
  if (id == -1) hCursor = LoadCursor(0, IDC_CROSS);
    else TDrawingTool::SelectCursor(id);
}

// Draw a line from a fixed point where the mouse button was pressed (which
// was saved in LButtonDown) to its current location. During
// interactive drawing the code uses exclusive-ORing, so this routine
// can also be used to remove the line.
```

```
void TLineTool::Show(HDC hDC, double zoom, int offsx, int offsy)
{
  MoveToEx(hDC, Pt1.x*zoom-offsx+0.5, Pt1.y*zoom-offsy+0.5, 0);
  LineTo(hDC, Pt2.x*zoom-offsx+0.5, Pt2.y*zoom-offsy+0.5);
}

// Return the handle for the line tool's icon
HICON TLineTool::GetIcon()
{
  return LoadIcon(GetApplicationObject()->GetInstance(), "linetool");
}

void TRectangleTool::Start()
{
  TLineTool::Start();          // Do what TLineTool does
  // Use a NULL brush so the interior won't be filled. Since
  // this is a stock object we won't have to delete it later.
  hBrush = HBRUSH(GetStockObject(NULL_BRUSH));
  SelectObject(hDC, hBrush);
}

// Drawing a rectangle is similar to drawing a line, except that
// Rectangle() is called rather than MoveToEx/LineTo
void TRectangleTool::Show(HDC hDC, double zoom, int offsx, int offsy)
{
  POINT Pt1b=Pt1, Pt2b=Pt2;    // Sort the two corners of the rectangle
  Sort2Pts(Pt1b, Pt2b);         // so that Pt1 is the top, left value
  Rectangle(hDC, Pt1b.x*zoom-offsx+0.5, Pt1b.y*zoom-offsy+0.5,
    Pt2b.x*zoom-offsx+0.5+1, Pt2b.y*zoom-offsy+0.5+1);
}

// Return the handle for the rectangle tool's icon
HICON TRectangleTool::GetIcon()
{
  return LoadIcon(GetApplicationObject()->GetInstance(), "rectangletool");
}

// Draw an empty rectangle
void TEmptyRectangleTool::Show(HDC hDC, double zoom, int offsx, int offsy)
{
  HBRUSH hOldBrush = HBRUSH(SelectObject(hDC, GetStockObject(NULL_BRUSH)));
  POINT Pt1b=Pt1, Pt2b=Pt2;    // Sort the two corners of the rectangle
  Sort2Pts(Pt1b, Pt2b);         // so that Pt1 is the top, left value
  Rectangle(hDC, Pt1b.x*zoom-offsx+0.5, Pt1b.y*zoom-offsy+0.5,
    Pt2b.x*zoom-offsx+0.5+1, Pt2b.y*zoom-offsy+0.5+1);
  SelectObject(hDC, hOldBrush);
}

// Return the handle for the empty rectangle tool's icon
HICON TEmptyRectangleTool::GetIcon()
{
  return LoadIcon(GetApplicationObject()->GetInstance(),
    "emptyrectangletool");
}
```

```
// Draw an ellipse
void TEllipseTool::Show(HDC hDC, double zoom, int offsx, int offsy)
{
  POINT Pt1b=Pt1, Pt2b=Pt2;
  Sort2Pts(Pt1b, Pt2b);
  Ellipse(hDC, Pt1b.x*zoom-offsx+0.5, Pt1b.y*zoom-offsy+0.5,
    Pt2b.x*zoom-offsx+0.5+1, Pt2b.y*zoom-offsy+1+0.5);
}

// Return the handle for the ellipse tool's icon
HICON TEllipseTool::GetIcon()
{
  return LoadIcon(GetApplicationObject()->GetInstance(), "ellipsetool");
}

// Draw an empty ellipse
void TEmptyEllipseTool::Show(HDC hDC, double zoom, int offsx, int offsy)
{
  HBRUSH hOldBrush = HBRUSH(SelectObject(hDC, GetStockObject(NULL_BRUSH)));
  POINT Pt1b=Pt1, Pt2b=Pt2;
  Sort2Pts(Pt1b, Pt2b);
  Ellipse(hDC, Pt1b.x*zoom-offsx+0.5, Pt1b.y*zoom-offsy+0.5,
    Pt2b.x*zoom-offsx+1+0.5, Pt2b.y*zoom-offsy+1+0.5);
  SelectObject(hDC, hOldBrush);
}

// Return the handle for the empty ellipse tool's icon
HICON TEmptyEllipseTool::GetIcon()
{
 return LoadIcon(GetApplicationObject()->GetInstance(), "emptyellipsetool");
}

void TPolylineTool::Start()
{
  Poly[0] = Pt1;                  // Save current location of mouse
  NumPts = 1;                     // One coordinate pair is saved
  TLineTool::Start();
}

// The left mouse button was pressed. Either a new figure is
// to be started (Drawing is FALSE) or a polygon is already
// started. If it's a new figure, chain to the line tool's
// LButtonDown() function. Otherwise, ignore the event.
BOOL TPolylineTool::LButtonDown(POINT& pt)
{
  if (Drawing)
    return TRUE;
  else {                         // Begin a new polygon. Call the
    Drawing = TRUE;              // inherited LButtonDown function,
    TLineTool::LButtonDown(pt); // which calls TPolyline::Start.
  }
  return TRUE;
}
```

```
// Each time the left mouse button is released, start
// drawing a new line, which is connected to the previous line.
BOOL TPolylineTool::LButtonUp(POINT& pt)
{
  if (Drawing) {
    if (NumPts < MAXPOLYSIZE) {
      Show(hDC, PC->Zoom);
      Pt2 = pt;
      Poly[NumPts++] = Pt2;
      Show(hDC, PC->Zoom);
      Pt1 = pt;            // A new line starts here
      Show(hDC, PC->Zoom);
      return TRUE;         // Signal that we are still drawing
    }
    else {
      MessageBox(PC->DrawingWnd, "Too many points in polygon",
        GetApplicationObject()->GetName(), MB_OK);
      Drawing = FALSE;
      TDrawingTool::LButtonUp(pt);
      return FALSE;        // Signal the end of the drawing
    }
  }
  return FALSE;
}

// End the polygon figure
BOOL TPolylineTool::RButtonDown(POINT& pt)
{
  if (Drawing) {
    Drawing = FALSE; // Stop interactively drawing the polygon
    if (NumPts < MAXPOLYSIZE)
      Poly[NumPts++] = Pt2;
    else {
      MessageBox(PC->DrawingWnd, "Too many points in polygon",
        GetApplicationObject()->GetName(), MB_OK);
      TDrawingTool::LButtonUp(pt);
      return FALSE;
    }
    return TDrawingTool::LButtonUp(pt);
  }
  return FALSE;
}

// Display the polygon. While interactively drawing use the
// TLineTool's Show() function, since the last line in the
// polygon is the only segment that needs to be updated.
void TPolylineTool::Show(HDC hDC, double zoom, int offsx, int offsy)
{
  if (Drawing)
    TLineTool::Show(hDC, zoom, offsx, offsy);
  else {
    POINT* pointsZ = new POINT[NumPts];
    if (!pointsZ) {
```

```
        MessageBox(PC->DrawingWnd, "Out of Memory",
          GetApplicationObject()->GetName(), MB_OK | MB_ICONEXCLAMATION);
        return;
      }
      for (int i=0; i<NumPts; i++) {
        pointsZ[i].x = Poly[i].x * zoom - offsx + 0.5;
        pointsZ[i].y = Poly[i].y * zoom - offsy + 0.5;
      }
      Polyline(hDC, pointsZ, NumPts);
      delete pointsZ;
    }
}

// Return the handle for the polyline tool's icon
HICON TPolylineTool::GetIcon()
{
  return LoadIcon(GetApplicationObject()->GetInstance(), "polylinetool");
}

// Display the filled polygon. While interactively drawing use
// the TLineTool's Show() function, since the last line in the
// polygon is the only segment that needs to be updated.
void TPolygonTool::Show(HDC hDC, double zoom, int offsx, int offsy)
{
  if (Drawing)
    TLineTool::Show(hDC, zoom, offsx, offsy);
  else {
    POINT* pointsZ = new POINT[NumPts];
    if (!pointsZ) {
      MessageBox(PC->DrawingWnd, "Out of Memory",
        GetApplicationObject()->GetName(), MB_OK | MB_ICONEXCLAMATION);
      return;
    }
    for (int i=0; i<NumPts; i++) {
      pointsZ[i].x = Poly[i].x * zoom - offsx + 0.5;
      pointsZ[i].y = Poly[i].y * zoom - offsy + 0.5;
    }
    Polygon(hDC, pointsZ, NumPts);
    delete pointsZ;
  }
}

// Return the handle for the filled polygon tool's icon
HICON TPolygonTool::GetIcon()
{
  return LoadIcon(GetApplicationObject()->GetInstance(), "polygontool");
}

// Select a crosshair icon for setting the text location
void TTextTool::SelectCursor(int id)
{
  if (id == -1) hCursor = LoadCursor(0, IDC_CROSS);
    else TDrawingTool::SelectCursor(id);
}
```

```
// Place the text string in Str where the user has pressed the left
// mouse button. Pop up a dialog box that requests the string to display.
BOOL TTextTool::LButtonUp(POINT& pt)
{
  // Pop up a dialog box that retrieves the string to display
  if (TInputDialog(PC->OWLWindow, "Text", "Enter text:",
    Str, MAXSTRING).Execute() == IDOK) {
    hDC = GetDC(PC->DrawingWnd);
    HFONT hFont = CreateFont(Ht, Wd, 0, 0, 0, 0,
      0, 0, 0, 0, 0, 0, 0, "Arial");
    SelectObject(hDC, hFont);
    Pt1 = pt;       // Save the position of the text
    SIZE size;      // Calculate the extents of the text
    GetTextExtentPoint(hDC, Str, lstrlen(Str), &size);
    POINT apt;
    apt.x = size.cx;      apt.y = size.cy;
    apt = PC->SnapToGrid(apt);
    Pt2.x = Pt1.x + apt.x;      Pt2.y = Pt1.y + apt.y;
    // Release the window's device context
    ReleaseDC(PC->DrawingWnd, hDC);
    Finish();       // The object is displayed by calling Finish()
  }
  return FALSE;
}


// Get the string's number of rows and columns
void TTextTool::GetTextSize(SIZE& size)
{
  size.cy = (lstrlen(Str)) ? 1 : 0;
  size.cx = lstrlen(Str);
}


void TTextTool::Show(HDC hDC, double zoom, int offsx, int offsy)
{
  // Use transparent text so that the area around the
  // text won't be disturbed
  SetBkMode(hDC, TRANSPARENT);
  SetTextColor(hDC, PC->PenColor);
  // Create the font to use. Scale it to the bounds of the rectangle
  // it should fit in. Also, account for the current zoom factor.
  HFONT hFont = CreateFont(Ht*zoom, Wd*zoom, 0, 0, 0, 0, 0, 0,
    0, 0, 0, 0, 0, "Arial");
  HFONT hOldFont = HFONT(SelectObject(hDC, hFont));
  TextOut(hDC, Pt1.x*zoom-offsx+0.5, Pt1.y*zoom-offsy+0.5,
    Str, lstrlen(Str));
  SelectObject(hDC, hOldFont);
  DeleteObject(hFont);
}


// Return the handle for the text tool's icon
HICON TTextTool::GetIcon()
{
  return LoadIcon(GetApplicationObject()->GetInstance(), "texttool");
}
```

```cpp
//------------------------------------------------------------------

// Constructor for TPaintContext. Set its default values.
TPaintContext::TPaintContext()
{
  // Set the drawing parameters to default values
  Tool = NULL;              // No drawing tool selected
  PenWd = 1;                // One-pixel wide lines
  PenColor = RGB(0,0,0);    // Black pen color
  BrushColor = RGB(255,255,255);   // White brush color
  Offsx = Offsy = 0;
  SnapWd = SnapHt = Zoom = 1;
  SnapOn = TRUE;
  // NOTE: The DrawingWnd and OWLWindow fields are not
  // initialized until after the drawing window is selected
}

// Set the "Snap to grid" pixel dimensions of the drawing window
void TPaintContext::SetSnapToGrid(int snapWd, int snapHt)
{
  SnapWd = (snapWd <= 0) ? 1 : snapWd;
  SnapHt = (snapHt <= 0) ? 1 : snapHt;
}

// Snap the point pt to the current grid
POINT TPaintContext::SnapToGrid(POINT& pt)
{
  if (!SnapOn) return pt;  // Don't snap the point to a grid
  // Round of the point, pt, to the values in SnapWd and SnapHt
  POINT snappedPt;
  snappedPt.x = floor(pt.x / Zoom / (float)SnapWd + 0.5) * SnapWd;
  snappedPt.y = floor(pt.y / Zoom / (float)SnapHt + 0.5) * SnapHt;
  snappedPt.x = snappedPt.x * Zoom + 0.5;
  snappedPt.y = snappedPt.y * Zoom + 0.5;
  return snappedPt;
}

// Enable or disable the "Snap to grid" action for the drawing window
BOOL TPaintContext::SetSnapToGridOn(BOOL snapOn)
{
  BOOL oldSnapOn = SnapOn;
  SnapOn = snapOn;
  return oldSnapOn;
}
```

• SIMDRAW.RC

```
/* SIMDRAW.RC: Resource file for SIMDRAW.CPP */

#include "windows.h"

/* Required for TInputDialog object which is used in DRAW.CPP */
rcinclude owl\inputdia.rc
```

```
/* Icons used in the SIMDRAW program: */
linetool ICON line.ico
emptyrectangletool ICON rect.ico
rectangletool ICON fillrect.ico
emptyellipsetool ICON ellipse.ico
ellipsetool ICON fillelli.ico
polylinetool ICON polyline.ico
polygontool ICON polygon.ico
texttool ICON text.ico
```

• SIMDRAW.CPP

```
// SIMDRAW.CPP: A simple drawing program that illustrates how to
// use the drawing tools in DRAW.CPP. The program displays a palette
// of eight drawing tools. Select the desired tool by clicking on
// its icon; then draw in the main window.

#include <owl\applicat.h>
#include <owl\framewin.h>
#include <owl\dc.h>
#include "draw.h"

#define NUMICONSWIDE 2  // Number of icons wide in the palette
#define NUMICONSHIGH 4  // Number of rows of icons in the palette

// This pop-up window holds the icons for each tool
class TToolsPalette : public TFrameWindow {
public:
  HICON HIcons[NUMICONSWIDE*NUMICONSHIGH];
  TDrawingTool* Tools[NUMICONSWIDE*NUMICONSHIGH];    // Drawing tools
  int IconWd, IconHt; // Width and height of an icon
  int ToolNdx;        // Index of the currently select tool
  int WndWd, WndHt;   // Width and height of palette
  TPaintContext *PC;  // The tools use the paint context
  TToolsPalette(TWindow* parent, const char* title, TPaintContext *pc);
  void HighlightIcon(HDC hDC, int i);
  void Paint(TDC& dc, BOOL, TRect&);
  void EvLButtonDown(UINT, TPoint& pt);
  void EvClose();

  DECLARE_RESPONSE_TABLE(TToolsPalette);
};

DEFINE_RESPONSE_TABLE1(TToolsPalette, TFrameWindow)
  EV_WM_LBUTTONDOWN,
  EV_WM_CLOSE,
END_RESPONSE_TABLE;

// The main window is used as the drawing window
class TSimDrawWindow : public TWindow {
public:
  TToolsPalette *ToolPalette;
  TPaintContext *PC;
```

```
    BOOL DrawingMode;  // TRUE while interactively drawing a figure
    TSimDrawWindow(TWindow *parent, const char* title);
    void EvSize(UINT, TSize&);
    void EvLButtonDown(UINT, TPoint& pt);
    void EvLButtonUp(UINT, TPoint& pt);
    void EvRButtonDown(UINT, TPoint& pt);
    void EvMouseMove(UINT, TPoint& pt);
    BOOL EvSetCursor(HWND hWndCursor, UINT hitTest, UINT mouseMsg);

    DECLARE_RESPONSE_TABLE(TSimDrawWindow);
};

DEFINE_RESPONSE_TABLE1(TSimDrawWindow, TWindow)
  EV_WM_SIZE,
  EV_WM_LBUTTONDOWN,
  EV_WM_LBUTTONUP,
  EV_WM_RBUTTONDOWN,
  EV_WM_MOUSEMOVE,
  EV_WM_SETCURSOR,
END_RESPONSE_TABLE;

// Constructor for the tool palette
TToolsPalette::TToolsPalette(TWindow *parent, const char* title,
  TPaintContext *pc) : TFrameWindow(parent, title)
{
  // The tool palette is a pop-up window that has a caption
  // and is initially visible
  Attr.Style = WS_POPUPWINDOW | WS_CAPTION | WS_VISIBLE;
  // Create the tools that the icons represent. The tools
  // are displayed left to right, top to bottom.
  Tools[0] = new TLineTool;
  Tools[1] = new TTextTool;
  Tools[2] = new TEmptyRectangleTool;
  Tools[3] = new TRectangleTool;
  Tools[4] = new TEmptyEllipseTool;
  Tools[5] = new TEllipseTool;
  Tools[6] = new TPolylineTool;
  Tools[7] = new TPolygonTool;
  // Save a handle to each tool's icon
  for (int i=0; i<NUMICONSHIGH*NUMICONSWIDE; i++)
    HIcons[i] = Tools[i]->GetIcon();
  IconWd = GetSystemMetrics(SM_CXICON);
  IconHt = GetSystemMetrics(SM_CYICON);
  // Size the palette window so that it can hold NUMICONSWIDE
  // columns of NUMICONSHIGH rows of icons
  WndWd = IconWd * NUMICONSWIDE + GetSystemMetrics(SM_CXBORDER) * 2;
  WndHt = IconHt * NUMICONSHIGH + GetSystemMetrics(SM_CYBORDER) +
    GetSystemMetrics(SM_CYCAPTION);
  ToolNdx = 0;                    // Index of currently selected tool
  PC = pc;
  PC->Tool = Tools[ToolNdx];   // Default tool
  // Don't call Select() yet. The drawing window has
  // not been initialized.
}
```

```
// Paint the icons in the window
void TToolsPalette::Paint(TDC& dc, BOOL, TRect&)
{
  for (int j=0; j<NUMICONSHIGH; j++)
    for (int i=0; i<NUMICONSWIDE; i++)
      DrawIcon(dc, i*IconWd, j*IconHt, HIcons[j*NUMICONSWIDE+i]);
  HighlightIcon(dc, ToolNdx);
}


// Invert the icon specified in the tool palette. This
// gives allows the user to see which icon is selected.
void TToolsPalette::HighlightIcon(HDC hDC, int i)
{
  RECT rect;
  rect.top = i / NUMICONSWIDE * IconHt;
  rect.left = i % NUMICONSWIDE * IconWd;
  rect.bottom = rect.top + IconHt;
  rect.right = rect.left + IconWd;
  InvertRect(hDC, &rect);
}


// The mouse was pressed while over the tool palette. Determine
// which icon is selected, deselect the current tool, and select
// the tool that corresponds to the selected icon.
void TToolsPalette::EvLButtonDown(UINT, TPoint& pt)
{
  POINT pti;
  pti.x = pt.x / IconWd;     pti.y = pt.y / IconHt;
  int i = pti.y * NUMICONSWIDE + pti.x;
  HDC hDC = GetDC(HWindow);
  PC->Tool->Deselect();         // Deselect the current tool
  HighlightIcon(hDC, ToolNdx);  // Restore highlighted icon
  ToolNdx = i;                  // This is the tool selected
  PC->Tool = Tools[ToolNdx];    // Save a pointer to the tool selected
  HighlightIcon(hDC, ToolNdx);  // Highlight this new tool's icon
  ReleaseDC(HWindow, hDC);
  PC->Tool->Select(PC);         // Select the new tool
}


// When the user selects the close button on the tool palette don't
// really close the window. Instead, hide the window. This technique
// makes it easier to turn the tool palette off and on.
void TToolsPalette::EvClose()
{
  ::ShowWindow(HWindow, SW_HIDE);
}


// The constructor sets up the tool palette and creates a
// TPaintContext structure. The window acts as the drawing window.
TSimDrawWindow::TSimDrawWindow(TWindow *parent, const char* title)
  : TWindow(parent, title)
{
  PC = new TPaintContext;
```

```
    // Create the tool palette
    ToolPalette = new TToolsPalette(this, "Tools", PC);
    PC->DrawingWnd = HWindow;   // This window is the window to draw in
    PC->OWLWindow = this;       // Save a pointer to this window
    // Select the default tool to use in the drawing window
    PC->Tool->Select(PC);
    DrawingMode = FALSE;   // The selected tool is not drawing right now
}

// The left mouse button was just pressed in the drawing window
void TSimDrawWindow::EvLButtonDown(UINT, TPoint& pt)
{
  PC->DrawingWnd = HWindow;
  if (!DrawingMode)
    // Tell that tool to start drawing. Note: The drawing mode
    // may change if the figure can't be drawn.
    DrawingMode = PC->Tool->LButtonDown(pt);
}

// The left mouse button was just released in the drawing window
void TSimDrawWindow::EvLButtonUp(UINT, TPoint& pt)
{
  if (DrawingMode)
    DrawingMode = PC->Tool->LButtonUp(pt);
}

// Used by the polygon tool to end a drawing. The other drawing
// tools treat it the same as a left button release. In other
// words, it terminates the current drawing.
void TSimDrawWindow::EvRButtonDown(UINT, TPoint& pt)
{
  if (DrawingMode)
    DrawingMode = PC->Tool->RButtonDown(pt);
}

// The mouse is being moved while in the drawing window
void TSimDrawWindow::EvMouseMove(UINT, TPoint& pt)
{
  if (DrawingMode)
    PC->Tool->MouseMove(pt);
}

// Switch to the current drawing tool's cursor when the cursor
// is over the window's client area
BOOL TSimDrawWindow::EvSetCursor(HWND hWndCursor, UINT hitTest,
  UINT mouseMsg)
{
  if (hitTest == HTCLIENT) {          // Cursor is in the client area
    ::SetCursor(PC->Tool->hCursor);   // Use the current tool's
    return TRUE;                      // cursor style; otherwise, chain
  }                                   // to the inherited function
  return TWindow::EvSetCursor(hWndCursor, hitTest, mouseMsg);
}
```

```cpp
// When creating the program's environment, position the tool
// palette at the top right of the window
void TSimDrawWindow::EvSize(UINT, TSize&)
{
  RECT rect;
  ::GetClientRect(HWindow, &rect);
  int border = GetSystemMetrics(SM_CYCAPTION) + 2;
  // Because the palette is a pop-up window, the X and Y locations
  // in MoveWindow are screen coordinates, not client coordinates.
  // We want to place the palette relative to the main program's
  // client coordinates so we must call ClientToScreen to convert them.
  POINT p;
  // Place the tool palette at the top right
  p.x = rect.right - ToolPalette->WndWd - border;
  p.y = border;
  ::ClientToScreen(HWindow, &p);
  ::MoveWindow(ToolPalette->HWindow, p.x, p.y,
    ToolPalette->WndWd, ToolPalette->WndHt, TRUE);
}

class TSimDrawApp : public TApplication {
public:
  TSimDrawApp() : TApplication() { }
  void InitMainWindow();
};

void TSimDrawApp::InitMainWindow()
{
  MainWindow = new TFrameWindow(0, "SimDraw",
    new TSimDrawWindow(0, ""));
}

int OwlMain(int /*argc*/, char* /*argv*/[])
{
  return TSimDrawApp().Run();
}
```

FOURTEEN

An Object-Oriented Drawing Program

I n the previous chapter, we developed a simple drawing program that illustrates how to use the interactive drawing tools presented in that chapter. In this chapter, we'll extend the program in several important ways. Most significantly, our updated application will internally store its drawings as a list of objects so that you can edit your drawings and save your work to files.

But don't think of this program as an untouchable, glass-sealed museum piece. An important goal of this chapter is to give you a solid and flexible framework from which you can build your own custom graphics applications.

OVERVIEW OF THE DRAWING PROGRAM

The environment for the new drawing program, OODRAW, is shown in Figure 14.1. Although at first glance the environment may appear to be similar to its predecessor (SIMDRAW) in Chapter 13, it differs significantly. The major differences are listed here:

- Each figure is saved as an object in an object list.
- Objects can be selected, moved, resized, reordered, and reshaped.
- A color palette is included, which you can use to select the pen and brush colors.
- Drawings can be read from and written to files.
- The environment provides a print function.
- The user draws on a "paper" surface that can be scrolled and scaled.
- The environment displays an optional alignment grid.

Figure 14.1 This figure shows the object-oriented drawing program's environment.

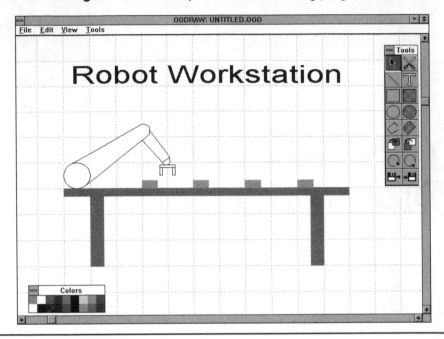

This list hints at the extensive amount of work that lies ahead. We'll build upon some of the tools we've developed in prior chapters to ease some of the work. But most of the coding will be done in this chapter.

The missing ingredients are handled by four primary files:

- GOBJECT.CPP provides a series of objects that are used to represent each figure drawn.

- GOBJLIST.CPP maintains a list of the graphics objects.

- GOBJTOOL.CPP supplies tools derived from DRAW.CPP (listed in Chapter 13) that add drawn figures to the object list.

- OODRAW.CPP provides the code for the four major elements of the environment: the tool palette, the color palette, the drawing window, and the program's main window.

Using Graphics Objects

Our drawing program will use objects to represent each figure. Specifically, each graphics figure is stored as an object derived from the **TGObject** class. The code for **TGObject** is included in GOBJECT.H and GOBJECT.CPP. Table 14.1 lists each of the functions in the class.

Table 14.1 The TGObject Class Functions

Function	Description
TGObject	One of two constructors
~TGObject	The destructor for the class
UpdateBounds	Recalculates the object's bounds
GetBounds	Returns the bounds of the object
Display	Displays the object
Rotate	Rotates the object
Translate	Translates the object
Save	Saves the object to a file
HasSize	Returns TRUE if the object is greater than a minimum size
Scale	Scales the object
Offset	Adjusts the position of the object
DrawHandles	Draws resizing handles around the object
DrawResizingObject	Draws the object as it is being resized
Resize	Resizes the object to fit within a bounded region
ResizeFrame	Resizes a bounding frame according to a handle being moved
Dup	Returns a copy of an object
PtOnResizeHandle	Returns TRUE if a specified point is on a resizing handle
PtOnReshapeHandle	Returns TRUE if a specified point is on a reshaping handle
PtOnFrame	Returns TRUE if a specified point is on the object's bounding frame
PtInObject	Returns TRUE if a specified point is within an object's bounds
ScaleToRect	Resizes the object to fit within a rectangular region
Reshape	Changes the object's shape or moves one of its points

The **TGObject** class forms the basis for a class hierarchy similar to the hierarchy we used in the drawing tools. For instance, GOBJECT.CPP includes the **TLineObj** class, which is derived from **TGObject**, to represent information about a line segment. A specific **TGObject** object is created for each object you draw. The information about the object is copied from the interactive tool that draws it. The complete class hierarchy is presented in Figure 14.2.

The idea is to give each class enough information and flexibility so that it can draw a figure and allow it to be selected, moved, resized, and reshaped. A **TGObject** object does not store the actual coordinates of an object. Instead, it

Figure 14.2 The TGObject class objects extend the interactive drawing tools.

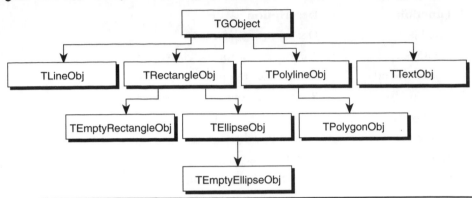

contains a pointer to a **TDrawingTool** that performs these chores. If you're wondering, yes, you can collapse the **TGObject** class into the **TDrawingTool** class. We didn't take this approach here because the material divides nicely and can be explained more readily if taken in pieces. This is the way to think of these two classes: The **TDrawingTool** objects provide a way to interactively draw each object and a place to store its coordinates. The **TGObject** classes extend these tools so that you can move, resize, and reshape the object's drawn.

MANAGING THE GRAPHICS OBJECTS

The **TGObjList** class, located in GOBJLIST.H and GOBJLIST.CPP, contains the list of figures in the drawing window and a collection of functions that manipulate the list. Table 14.2 provides a brief description of each member function in **TGObjList**. The **GObjects** array in the class is an array of pointers to **TGObject**. It holds the list of graphics objects. The size of the array is declared large enough to hold **NUMGOBJECTS** objects, which is defined in GOBJLIST.H as 100. The object list is declared in the program's main window; however, a pointer to the list is shared with the drawing window object. As you'll see later, the drawing window's **Paint** function uses the figure list to display what is in the current drawing.

A graphics object is added to the **GObjects** array by calling the **Add** member function. **Add** simply appends a **TGObject** object passed into the function to the **GObjects** array if there is room. Also, **Add** increments the **NextObj** variable that specifies the next free location in the **GObjects** array. Initially, **NextObj** starts at 0.

The remaining member functions in **TGObjList** are also used to manipulate the graphics figures in the **GObjects** array. These functions determine

Table 14.2 TGObjList Member Functions

Function	Description
TGObjList	The constructor for the class
~TGObjList	The class destructor
Add	Adds an object to the list
Delete	Deletes the selected object from the list
DeleteAll	Deletes all the objects in the list
DisplayAll	Displays all the objects in the list
FlipToBack	Moves the selected object below all the other objects in the list
FlipToFront	Moves the selected object to the top of the list of objects
Rotate	Rotates an object
Read	Reads an object list from a file
Save	Saves the object list to a file
Copy	Copies the selected object to the object buffer
Empty	Returns TRUE if the object list is empty
ObjectSelected	Returns TRUE if there is an object selected
SetSelectedObj	Sets the selected object and returns the previously selected object
Repaint	Repaints the drawing that falls within a rectangular region

which objects are displayed and in what order. For instance, there are functions to delete, copy, and move graphics objects on the screen. Only one object can be manipulated at a time. Specifically, the **SelectedObj** index variable in **TGObjList** points to the object that can manipulated. We'll look at these components as we discuss the various aspects of the OODRAW program.

Drawing Objects

The drawing window, **TDrawingWindow**, is defined in DRAWTOOL.H. This function paints the drawing window and ties together the drawing window's mouse events with the object list. The drawing window supports a variety of features including a paper drawing surface, a scrollable window, a zoom capability, a drawing grid, and a snap-to-grid option.

The drawing window is also the place where the objects drawn are added to the object list. When the user finishes drawing an object, such as when the right mouse button is released, the information in the tool's **TDrawingTool** object is duplicated and copied to a **TGObject**. This object is then added to the object list:

```
if (gObj->HasSize()) {
  // If the object just drawn has size, then add it to the drawing
  // list. Actually, add a copy of the object to the figure list.
  TGObject *nuObj = gObj->Dup();
  // Add in the current scroller offsets of the drawing window
  nuObj->Offset(TPoint((Scroller->XPos*Scroller->XUnit)/PC->Zoom,
    (Scroller->YPos*Scroller->YUnit)/PC->Zoom));
  nuObj->UpdateBounds();              // Update the object's bounds
  Figures->Add(nuObj);
}
```

This code provides a brief view of how objects are added to the drawing list. Later, we'll discuss the mechanics of the **Dup** function and the other components of this code.

Selecting an Object

In order to manipulate an object, it must first be selected. To select an object, click on the arrow icon in the toolbox. Then press the left mouse button while the mouse is over the desired object. A bounding box, shown in Figure 14.3, usually will appear signifying that the object is selected. If several objects are stacked, one on top of one another, you can click the left mouse button again to select the next object in the list. To deselect the object, click the mouse inside the drawing window but outside of all the objects.

Behind the scenes, the **TSelectObjTool** class, which is a **TDrawingTool** object nested in **TSelectObj**, provides the code for selecting an object. Its code is a little complicated because the selection tool also holds the user interaction code for moving, resizing, and reshaping objects. We'll get to these actions in a bit. For now it's only important to know that the index of the selected object is assigned to the **SelectedObj** variable in the **TGObjList** object. If no object is

Figure 14.3 The selected object is normally enlcosed within a bounding box.

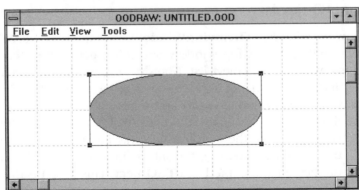

selected, **SelectedObj** is set to -1. The source for **TSelectObjTool** is located in the GOBJTOOL.CPP file.

Deleting Objects

Deleting an object involves two steps: First, you must select the object using the selection (arrow) tool; then, you select the scissors tool to delete the object.

The code for deleting an object is contained in **TGObjList**'s **Delete** function. The routine begins by making sure that the figure list is not empty (there is something to delete). This is a little trickier than you might expect. The problem is that a selected object is actually deselected whenever a new tool is selected—which is exactly what happens when the scissors tool is chosen. To get around this problem, the code saves the previously selected object in the variable **PrevSelectedObj**. If **PrevSelectedObj** *is not* –1, and **SelectedObj** *is* –1, then it holds a valid object that is considered selected. Here's the code in the **Delete** function that performs this check:

```
if (SelectedObj == -1 && PrevSelectedObj == -1) return;
// Restore the selected object, which gets reset after each
// press of the rotate tool
if (SelectedObj == -1) SelectedObj = PrevSelectedObj;
```

Next, the bounds of the currently selected object are saved:

```
RECT bounds;
CopyRect(&bounds, GObjects[SelectedObj]->GetBounds(FALSE));
```

Later in the chapter we'll discuss the code that forces Windows to repaint this area after the object is removed from the figure list.

Then, the object is deleted by removing it from the **GObjects** array and shifting all the objects that follow it down one index location:

```
delete(GObjects[SelectedObj]);
for (int i=SelectedObj; i<NextObj-1; i++)
  GObjects[i] = GObjects[i+1];
```

The **NextObj** variable, which points to the next object location in **GObjects**, is then decremented by one. In addition, **SelectedObj** is set to -1 signaling that no object is selected:

```
NextObj--;
SelectedObj = -1; // There is not a selected object
```

The area where the object was located, saved earlier in **bounds**, is then invalidated so that the drawing window will repaint the area:

```
Repaint(-1, &bounds); // Repaint the window where the object was
```

The area to repaint is set to the object's bounding box. This use of a bounding box provides an efficient way to reduce the amount of repainting required in the window. The **Repaint** function is included in **TGObjList** and encapsulates the code required to properly scale and offset the bounds of the object when the user has zoomed in on the drawing.

How does the delete tool get called? The high-level delete tool is a drawing tool derived from **TGObject**. However, its interaction is really accomplished in its nested **TDrawingTool** object. In addition, unlike the tools we developed in the previous chapter, the delete tool takes action when the **Select** function is called. Remember, **Select** is invoked as soon as the tool's icon is chosen. Therefore, when the tool's icon is selected, the **Select** function is called and the tool deletes the current object immediately. Several of the other new drawing tools also work in this way.

Another new aspect of the delete tool is revealed in its **Select** function:

```
void Select(TPaintContext* pc) {
  TDrawingTool::Select(pc);
  // Send the drawing window a message to delete its
  // currently selected object
  SendMessage(PC->DrawingWnd, WM_UDELETE, 0, 0);
}
```

What's going on here? Earlier we said that the drawing tools don't know about the object list. In the line tool, we used a typecast of the drawing window's pointer to access the object list. Here's another approach. In this function, we're sending the drawing window a *user-defined message* (described in the next section) to delete the object itself.

Using User-Defined Messages

User-defined messages provide a powerful and flexible way to communicate among objects in a big application. To create a user-defined message you must define your own constant, starting at **WM_USER**. For example, the delete user-defined message is specified in GOBJTOOL.H as:

```
#define WM_UDELETE    (WM_USER + 1) // Delete an object
```

The receiving window is responsible for watching for the message. For instance, the drawing window class, **TDrawingWindow**, has a message-response function that checks for **WM_UDELETE** messages:

```
EV_MESSAGE(WM_USER+1, EvUDeleteObject),
```

The **EvUDeleteObject** processes the message by calling **TGObjList**'s **Delete** function:

```
LRESULT TDrawingWindow::EvUDeleteObject(WPARAM, LPARAM)
{
  Figures->Delete();
  return 0;
}
```

Rotating an Object

Two additional functions provided in the OODRAW program allow you to rotate an object around its center. One function rotates lines and polygons clockwise 45 degrees, and the other function rotates them counterclockwise in 45-degree increments.

Rotating objects begins with the **Rotate** member function in the **TGObjList** class. This function, in turn, calls the object's **Rotate** function to rotate itself. To rotate the figure, we begin by calculating the object's center:

```
UpdateBounds();  // Get the current object's bounds
double cx = (DevBounds.left + DevBounds.right) / 2.0;
double cy = (DevBounds.top + DevBounds.bottom) / 2.0;
```

The **DevBounds RECT** structure contains the coordinates of the object's bounding box. The code calls the object's **UpdateBounds** function first to compute the current pixel bounds of the object and place them into **DevBounds**.

Next, the object is translated to the origin, rotated, and then translated back. For instance, the **TPolylineObj**'s **Rotate** function performs these translations using the following statements:

```
CopyToWPoly(((TPolylineTool *)Obj)->Poly, numPts, wPoints);
WTranslatePoly(wPoints, numPts, -cx, -cy);
WRotatePoly(wPoints, numPts, angle);
WTranslatePoly(wPoints, numPts, cx, cy);
CopyFromWPoly(wPoints, numPts, ((TPolylineTool *)Obj)->Poly);
```

The **Rotate** function in **TGObjList** forces the drawing window to repaint itself so that the rotated figure will appear. This is accomplished by forcing the drawing window to repaint itself where the object initially was positioned and where it now exists. **Rotate** saves the bounds of the figure before it is rotated

```
CopyRect(&beforeBounds, GObjects[SelectedObj]->GetBounds(TRUE));
```

then rotates the object and retrieves the rotated object's new bounding box:

```
GObjects[SelectedObj]->Rotate(-angle);
CopyRect(&afterBounds, GObjects[SelectedObj]->GetBounds(TRUE));
```

Finally, the two bounding boxes are repainted by calling the **Repaint** function in **TGObjList**:

```
UnionRect(&clipRect, &beforeBounds, &afterBounds);
Repaint(-1, &clipRect);
```

Changing the Drawing Order

Each time **DisplayAll** is called, it draws each object in the **GObjects** array, starting from the zero index and working toward the last location in the array (which is just before the **NextObj** index). Because this drawing order is always followed, objects at the beginning of the list are always drawn first. Consequently, if two objects overlap, the object closer to the beginning of the **GObjects** array is drawn below the other.

The OODRAW program allows you to modify the order in which objects are displayed by swapping the positions of objects in the **GObjects** array. For instance, moving an object behind all the others is simply a matter of moving the object to the beginning of the list. This is what the **TGObjList** member function **FlipToBack** does. Similarly, the member function **FlipToFront** moves an object from its current location to the tail of the list so that it will be displayed last and, therefore, on top of all the other objects. Since both functions are similar, we'll just focus on **FlipToFront**.

The function begins by determining if an object is selected. If not, the routine returns with no action taken. Next, a temporary pointer, **temp**, is used to save the object indexed by **SelectedObj**. This is the object that will be moved to the end of the **GObjects** array. Then, each object above **SelectedObj** is shifted down one position in the array by the loop:

```
TGObject* temp = GObjects[SelectedObj];
for (int i=SelectedObj; i<NextObj-1; i++)
  GObjects[i] = GObjects[i+1];
```

Finally, the object, which was saved in **temp**, is copied to the end of the object list and the **SelectedObj** index is updated so that it still points to the same object, even though it is not at the end of the list.

```
GObjects[i] = temp;
SelectedObj = i;
Dirty = TRUE;
```

After the object list has been modified, the drawing window is updated by clearing the screen and displaying all objects in the array that are within the bounding box of the current object:

```
Repaint(SelectedObj, 0); // Repaint area where object is located
```

The remaining part of the window does not have to be updated.

Moving Objects

You can move a selected object by using the selection tool, which is located in the top-left corner of the tool palette. To move a selected figure, press and hold down the left mouse button while the mouse cursor is over the dotted bounding rectangle. Then drag the object to the desired location and release the left mouse button.

The code for selecting and moving objects is located in the new **TSelectObj** class. This object includes the **TSelectObjTool** that is derived from the **TDrawingTool** class. Since the user interaction is quite different from the other drawing tools, several of its member functions override the inherited functions. **TSelectObjTool** also includes a new function, **PtOnRect**, that tests whether the mouse is located on the figure's bounding box. Notice, too, that the code takes special care to handle the current mouse's coordinates and the object's absolute coordinate on the paper. This is particularly important when interactively manipulating the **TGObject** objects. Remember, the mouse coordinates are always specified in terms of pixels and the object's data is stored in world (absolute) coordinates.

Resizing an Object

The **TSelectObj** class also includes code to interactively resize a selected object. To resize an object, first click on an object using the selection tool. A frame will appear with a series of small black rectangles. The rectangles are handles that you can click and drag with the mouse. When the mouse is over a valid handle it will change to a resizing cursor. This action takes place in the **UpdateCursor** function in the selection tool's code.

When the mouse is released, the **Finish** function in **TSelectObjTool** is called to set the size of the object to the new frame. Not all of the object's are resized in the same way. For instance, the user resizes the bounding frame of polygons and rectangles. Lines, on the other hand, don't have a bounding frame. Instead, the handles of the lines are moved directly.

To provide this flexibility, objects supply three functions that are used for resizing: **Resize**, **ResizeFrame**, and **DrawResizingObject**. An object may use one or all of these functions to resize itself. Generally, **DrawResizingObject** is the primary routine that draws the object as it is being resized. Most objects draw a frame that is actually resized, for instance. The **Resize** function is used by line objects to drag one of the line's endpoints. And finally, **ResizeFrame** is used by some of the objects to scale the object to the final size of the frame when the mouse is released.

Each object also is responsible for drawing its own handles through the **DrawHandles** function. For instance, line objects only draw two handles—one at each endpoint of the line, as shown in Figure 14.4. Elliptical objects, in

Figure 14.4 Resizing handles appear on the selected object as small, black rectangles.

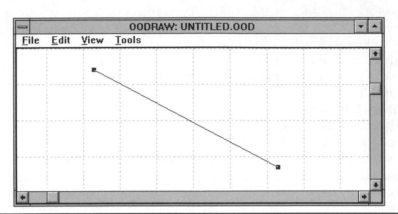

contrast, have four handles—one at each corner of the bounding rectangle. (See Figure 14.3.) A series of constants, defined in GOBJECT.H are used to keep track of which handle is selected and being moved. It's up to each object, however, to interpret what the handle identifier means. The **PtOnResizeHandle** function is used to determine when the mouse is positioned over one of handles of an object. If the mouse is over a handle, the handle's identifier is returned.

Reshaping an Object

Some objects, such as polygons, allow the user to modify the locations of existing points. To change the shape of a figure, first select the object. As mentioned earlier, a frame will appear around the object and a series of rectangles will be drawn around each of the object's coordinates, as shown in Figure 14.5. These are the points that you can move. To relocate a point, press and hold down the Ctrl key and click and drag the desired point. When you release the mouse, the object will be drawn with its new shape. Most of the code for reshaping an object is located in the GOBJECT source file and in the selection tool in GOBJTOOL.CPP.

Although it may seem to be a little strange, editing text is supported through the reshaping functions. To change the string in a text object, select the object, hold down the Ctrl key, and then click the mouse over the text. The edit dialog box appears, allowing you to enter a new text string.

The code for reshaping objects is included in the selection tool and mirrors many of the resizing routines. Most objects, however, do not supply any code for the reshaping routines, since for them the action is equivalent to resizing.

Figure 14.5 The points of a selected polygon are outlined with small rectangles and can be moved to change the object's shape.

Copying and Pasting Objects

The OODRAW program allows you to copy the current object to a buffer and paste it wherever you want. Both operations are accessible through the Edit pull-down menu. To copy the current object, select the Copy menu option. Then, to paste the object on the screen, select the Paste option, and click the left mouse button in the drawing window. The object will be pasted to the center of the drawing window. You can paste additional copies of the same object by clicking the left mouse button again.

The copy operation is provided by the **GObjList** class and the objects themselves. The **GObjList** class provides a buffer, **ObjBuffer**, to hold the copy of the object. This buffer is declared as a **TGObject** pointer; therefore, it can point to any of the derived graphics figure classes—such as **TLineObj**, **TEllipseObj**, and so on.

Here's the **Copy** function in **TGObjList**:

```
void TGObjList::Copy()
{
  if (SelectedObj == -1) return;         // No object selected
  if (!CopyBuffer) delete CopyBuffer;    // Free any existing object
  // Copy the currently selected object to the object buffer
  CopyBuffer = GObjects[SelectedObj]->Dup();
}
```

The function is only called when the Copy option is selected. If the object buffer already has something in it, the previously buffered object is deleted. Then, **ObjBuffer** is set to point to a copy of the current object.

Each **TGObject** has its own **Dup** routine in the GOBJECT.CPP file to duplicate itself. The **Dup** function in the **TLineObj** class, for instance, looks like this:

```
TGObject* Dup() {
  TGObject* gObj = new TLineObj(*this);
  gObj->Obj = new TLineTool(*(TLineTool*)Obj);
  gObj->Obj->PC = new TPaintContext(*(((TLineTool*)Obj)->PC));
  return gObj;
}
```

The call to the **TLineObj**, **TLineTool**, and **TPaintContext** constructors create the nested objects that represent the figure. These constructors, called *copy constructors*, duplicate the information passed to them about the current object.

The paste operation is handled by a **TPasteObj** object. When this tool is selected, it pastes whatever is in **ObjBuffer** to the screen. Inside **TPasteObj** is a **TPasteObjTool** tool that manages the tool's user interaction. This internal tool is derived from **TDrawingTool** and overrides the **LButtonUp** member function. This is where the paste operation takes place. The object in **ObjBuffer** is first duplicated

```
TGObject* obj = Figures->CopyBuffer->Dup();
```

then it is translated so that its center is at the location of the mouse:

```
CopyRect(&bounds, obj->GetBounds(FALSE));
obj->Translate(pt.x-(bounds.left+bounds.right)/2,
  pt.y-(bounds.top+bounds.bottom)/2);
```

Finally, the object is added to the object list and displayed:

```
Figures->Add(obj);
HDC hDC = GetDC(PC->DrawingWnd);
obj->Display(hDC, PC->Zoom);
ReleaseDC(PC->DrawingWnd, hDC);
```

You may be wondering why we are displaying the object directly, using the **Display** function. Shouldn't we call **InvalidateRect** to correctly position the figure on the screen in relation to the other figures? No, that isn't necessary; a pasted object is always placed on top of all other objects.

SETTING UP THE ENVIRONMENT

Although we have the basic form of the drawing program under control, a handful of functions still need to be fleshed out. These functions will all be packaged in OODRAW.CPP. We've already touched on some of them briefly, such as **TToolsPalette** in Chapter 13.

The drawing program consists of five key objects:

- The drawing window
- The main window
- A color palette
- A tool palette
- The object list

The **TOODrawWindow** class, defined in OODRAW.CPP, packages these objects under one roof. It also provides access to the application's main window, which contains the drawing window. The tool and color palettes are displayed by default; however, you can open and close them as you desire. In addition, the drawing window optionally displays an alignment grid. The spacing of the grid is 50 units apart, by default. The size of the grid is set in the **TDrawingWindow** class constructor, which is located in the header file DRAWTOOL.H.

The **DrawGrid** function in DRAWTOOL.CPP paints the drawing "paper" and grid. The paper is drawn the size of an 8-1/2 by 11-inch sheet of paper with a light gray, dashed grid. The remainder of the window is also painted at this time. Manually painting the window's background this way helps to save painting time and reduces screen flicker.

Adding a Menu

Unlike its counterpart in Chapter 13, OODRAW contains a menu. There are four submenus: File, Edit, View, and Tools. The statements for defining the menu are listed in the OODRAW.RC resource file and the command code constants are located in OODRAW.H. The menu options are normally managed by OWL, although the code takes special attention to gray out menu options when there aren't any drawings available. In addition, some of the menu options must be checked when they are selected. The following code, for instance, manages the checkmark next to the 50% view menu option:

```
void TOODrawWindow::CeCheckView50(TCommandEnabler& ce)
{
  ce.SetCheck((DrawingWindow->ZoomMode == VIEW50) ?
    TCommandEnabler::Checked : TCommandEnabler::Unchecked);
}
```

If you're familiar with Windows programming, but are new to OWL 2.0, this code may look a little strange. It sets the checkmark state of the menu option depending on whether the drawing window's zoom mode is **VIEW50**. OWL calls this constant to make sure that the checkmark is shown correctly. The **TCommandEnabler** class, as you might expect, is defined by OWL.

378 ▲ Chapter 14

Saving Object Files

An important capability of a drawing program is the ability to save drawings to disk. Therefore, the **TGObjList** and **TGObject** types contain functions to support reading and writing files.

The information is saved as an ASCII text file so that it is easy to debug and work with. You can even use your text editor to tweak any values. The files begin with a two-line header. The first line contains the string "OODRAW2." The second line specifies the number of objects in the file. For example, if there are 23 graphic objects in a file, the header would be:

```
OODRAW2
23
```

The task of saving the object list is handled by the **Save** member function of **TGObjList**. Actually, all this function does is call each object in the **GObjects** array to save itself:

```
void TGObjList::Save(FILE* fp)
{
  // Write a header to the object file
  fprintf(fp, "OODRAW2\n%d\n", NextObj);
  // Save each object's data to the file
  for (int i=0; i<NextObj; i++)
    GObjects[i]->Save(fp);
  Dirty = FALSE;   // The drawing was saved; reset the dirty flag
}
```

Each derived **TGObject** class overrides the **Save** function in order to save its object data to a file. For instance, **TLineObj** uses the following routine to save the pen width, pen color, and the endpoints of the line:

```
void TLineObj::Save(FILE *fp)
{
  fprintf(fp, "%d %d %ld %d %d %d %d\n", LINEOBJ, Obj->PC->PenWd,
    Obj->PC->PenColor, Obj->Pt1.x, Obj->Pt1.y, Obj->Pt2.x, Obj->Pt2.y);
}
```

Remember, the pen color is a **COLORREF** value (double word); therefore, it requires a **%ld** format statement.

What is the **LINEOBJ** value? This is a unique integer value that is used when the object information is read from the file, and indicates the type of object in the file. A constant for each object type is defined in GOBJECT.H.

Reading the object information from a file is a little different. The **Read** member function in **TGObjList** initiates the process by reading the object header to ensure the file is the right type:

```
fscanf(fp, "%8s", buffer);
if (lstrcmp(buffer, "OODRAW2") != 0) return -1;
```

If this test succeeds, the number of objects in the file is read. Then, a **for** loop reads through the file, one line at a time. It reads the integer code that begins each object statement and then uses the **switch** statement to branch to the correct statement and read the rest of the object's data:

```
switch(objType) {
  case LINEOBJ:
    fscanf(fp, "%d %ld %d %d %d %d", &t1, &pc, &t2, &t3, &t4, &t5);
    obj = new TLineObj(PC->DrawingWnd, t2, t3, t4, t5, t1, pc, PC, TRUE);
    Add(obj);
    break;
```

The call to **TGObjList**'s **Add** function adds the object to the list. Reading the data for objects such as lines and ellipses is simple. We just need a single **fscanf** statement, like the one shown previously.

Polygons and text strings, however, require additional processing because their figures can be of different lengths. Each contains a length count that is used to properly read the data. Here are the statements for reading in a polygon:

```
case POLYGONOBJ:
  fscanf(fp, "%d %ld %ld %d", &t1, &pc, &bc, &t2);
  for (j=0; j<t2; j++)
    fscanf(fp, "%d %d", &p[j].x, &p[j].y);
  obj = new TPolygonObj(PC->DrawingWnd, p, t2, t1, pc, bc, PC, TRUE);
  Add(obj);
  break;
```

After all the objects have been read, the entire drawing window is repainted by calling **InvalidateRect**:

```
InvalidateRect(PC->DrawingWnd, 0, objectsExist);
```

The **objectsExist** parameter is a Boolean flag that is set to TRUE if there were any figures on the screen before the object list was read. This parameter controls whether the program erases the drawing window before repainting itself. If there are no objects in the object list, there isn't any reason to erase the window first.

One important detail that we need to consider is the constructor calls to the **TGObject** objects. Notice that these calls have one more parameter than we used earlier to create the objects. This forces the code to use the version of the **TGObject** constructor that assumes the incoming coordinates are already in world coordinates.

Adding a File Open Dialog Box

The object files are opened in response to one of three file menu options that are captured by **TOODrawWindow**. However, these response functions don't perform any file operations themselves. Instead, they send messages to the drawing window to read a file or save the current object list to a file. For example, the **CmFileOpen** function, which is called when the Open menu option is chosen, sends the user message **WM_UREADOBJLIST** to the drawing window:

```
void TOODrawWindow::CmFileOpen()
{
  if (CanClose() &&  // Call CanClose to save the current drawing
    ::SendMessage(DrawingWindow->HWindow, WM_UREADOBJLIST, 0, 0) == 1) {
    SetTitleTo(DrawingWindow->GetFilename());
  }
}
```

The **EvUReadObjList** function that responds to this message in **TDrawingWindow** reveals how the filename is entered and where the file is opened. First, **EvUReadObjList** brings up a file open dialog box, provided by OWL and Windows. It handles all the details of retrieving a filename from the user.

The dialog box is made displayed with the following two statements:

```
TFileOpenDialog *fileDlg = new TFileOpenDialog(this, FilenameData);
if (fileDlg->Execute() == IDOK) {
```

If the user selects the OK button in the dialog box, the file is opened for reading. The user-supplied filename appears in the **FileName** field of the **FilenameData** variable:

```
if ((fp = fopen(FilenameData.FileName, "r")) == NULL) {
  strcpy(buffer, "Could not open file: ");
  ::MessageBox(HWindow, strcat(buffer,FilenameData.FileName),
  GetApplicationObject()->GetName(), MB_OK | MB_ICONEXCLAMATION);
}
```

If the file is successfully opened, the object list is called to read the file:

```
switch (readStatus=Figures->Read(fp)) {
```

The **switch** statement is used to process any error codes. After this operation has been completed, the file is closed and the function terminates.

Finally, in **CmFileOpen** the name of the file just opened is added to the titlebar using:

```
wsprintf(TitleBarStr, "OODRAW: %s", str);  // Append the string
::SetWindowText(HWindow, TitleBarStr);     // Display the new title
```

Zoom and Scrolling

The drawing window allows you to scale or scroll the drawing. The code for these functions is located in two places. You can find the low-level code in the

TDrawingWindow class in the source file DRAWTOOL.CPP. And the code that integrates the drawing window with the application, such as with its menu, is located in OODRAW.CPP.

Fortunately, OWL takes care of a lot of the scrolling details for us. We do, however, have to compensate for the current offset of the window when determining the current mouse location. For instance, if the window is scrolled horizontally 50 units, we must add 50 to the x location of the mouse. You'll uncover numerous places in the code that perform this type of operation. Usually, the window's current offset is available in the **Offsx** and **Offsy** fields of the global **PC TPaintContext** structure.

Supporting the zoom feature further complicates the problem of determining where the mouse actually is and how to draw any figures. The OODRAW.CPP source file enables the user to change the zoom setting to one of several values. The code doesn't have one single location that adjusts the scale of the drawing, however, the current zoom setting is accessible in the **Zoom** variable in the global **PC** structure. The code manually scales the drawings based on its value. For example, if **Zoom** equals 0.5, the drawing is scaled to 50% of its actual size.

▼**Note** I manually scale the drawing. If you use Windows' mapping mode functions to scale the drawing window, the logical widths of the pens will affect the thickness of displayed lines. A line will get thicker as you zoom in on it. In OODRAW, however, we're only scaling the coordinates of the figures; therefore, when you scale a figure its line thicknesses won't change. This may or may not be what you want in your application.

CREATING A COLOR PALETTE

The OODRAW program includes a color palette that enables you to interactively select the pen and brush colors used by the drawing tools. The color palette is similar to the tool palette we created in the previous chapter and which we'll also use in OODRAW. Of course, the main difference is that our new palette holds blocks of colors and not icons, as shown in Figure 14.6.

The top-left color in the palette displays the current pen color and the bottom-left cell displays the brush color. To change the current pen color, click the left mouse button while the pointer is over the desired color in the palette. Clicking the right mouse button updates the brush color. If you click on the color palette when an object is selected, only the color of the selected object is changed.

The code for the color palette is contained in the OODRAW.CPP source file. In particular, you'll find it located in the **TColorPalette** class. We'll focus on its differences from the tool palette.

Figure 14.6 The color palette is used to select the pen and brush colors.

The colors displayed are listed in the **DefColors** constant, which is defined as an array of **COLORREF** values:

```
const COLORREF DefColors[NUMCOLORSHIGH*NUMCOLORSWIDE] = {
  // Note: The first color position holds the currently
  // selected color. The color below it shows the current
  // fill pattern. The color below is index location 1.
  RGB(0,0,0), RGB(255,255,255),     // Draw color and fill color
  RGB(255,255,255), RGB(0,0,0),     // White and black
  RGB(128,128,128), RGB(64,64,64),  // Gray and dark gray
  RGB(255,0,0), RGB(128,0,0),       // Reds
  RGB(0,255,0), RGB(0,128,0),       // Greens
  RGB(0,0,255), RGB(0,0,128),       // Blues
  RGB(255,255,0), RGB(128,128,0),   // Yellows
  RGB(0,255,255), RGB(0,128,128),   // Cyans
  RGB(255,0,255), RGB(128,0,128)};  // Magentas
```

In the **TColorPalette** constructor, these colors are copied to the array **Colors** so that they can be modified. The colors are displayed in the palette top to bottom and left to right. Since the top-left color in the palette displays the current pen color and the bottom-left cell the brush color, the first two locations in the **Colors** array are reserved for the pen and brush colors. The program copies **Colors[0]** to **TPaintContext**'s **PenColor** field and **Colors[1]** to **BrushColor**. (Remember from Chapter 12 that the drawing tools use **TPaintContext** to determine which color to draw their figures.)

The **EvLButtonDown** message-response function watches for left-button presses, signaling that the user is selecting a new pen color. First, **EvLButtonDown** calculates the index of the color cell that corresponds with the mouse's position. The mouse location is passed to the function in the **pt** parameter:

```
int ix = pt.x / ColorWd;
int iy = pt.y / ColorHt;
int i = ix * NUMCOLORSHIGH + iy;
```

Then, the corresponding pen color in the **Colors** array and **TPaintContext** structure are updated:

```
Colors[0] = GetNearestColor(hDC, Colors[i]);
PC->PenColor = Colors[0];
```

Remember, pen colors are never dithered. Therefore, the **GetNearestColor** function is called to display the closest match for the color selected. This shows the user exactly which color will appear.

If an object is currently selected, however, the color of that object is changed:

```
((TDrawingTool *)obj->Obj)->PC->PenColor = Colors[0];
```

In both cases, the function calls **InvalidateRect** to update the appropriate region of the screen. For instance, if no object is selected, the region where the pen color is displayed is invalidated so that the color palette will show the new color:

```
rect.left = 0;        rect.top = 0;
rect.right = ColorWd;  rect.bottom = ColorHt;
::InvalidateRect(HWindow, &rect, FALSE);
```

The **EvRButtonDown** function is similar to **EvLButtonDown** except that **EvRButtonDown** changes the brush color when the user presses the right mouse button while the pointer is over the color palette.

Displaying the Color Palette

By default, the color palette is displayed at the lower-left corner of the drawing window. You can move the palette freely around the screen or close it if you want. To toggle the display of the color palette, use the Color Palette option in the Tools menu. The message-response function **CmColorPal** responds to this menu entry. Notice that a checkmark appears in the Color Palette option when the program begins. This tells the user that the color palette is selected.

A quick glance at **CmColorPal** will show that several new Windows functions are introduced. Let's take a look. Here's the entire **CmColorPal** routine:

```
void TOODrawWindow::CmColorPal()
{
  if (::IsWindowVisible(ColorPalette->HWindow))
    ::ShowWindow(ColorPalette->HWindow, SW_HIDE);
  else {  // Display the color palette, but don't make it active
    ::ShowWindow(ColorPalette->HWindow, SW_SHOWNOACTIVATE);
    ::InvalidateRect(ColorPalette->HWindow, 0, TRUE);
  }
}
```

Remember, this function gets called when the user wants to toggle the color palette display on or off. Therefore, the routine first determines whether the color palette is visible. For this purpose, Windows provides the **IsWindowVisible** function, which is defined as:

```
BOOL IsWindowVisible(HWND hWindow);
```

- **hWindow** is a handle to the window that is tested for visibility.
- The function returns TRUE if the window exists.

In this case, the code passes **IsWindowVisible** the **HWindow** field of the **ColorPalette** object. If the color palette is already popped up, then **IsWindowVisible** returns non-zero at the top of the **if** statement is executed. Here again, we encounter a few new Windows features. The next statement calls the Windows function **ShowWindow**, which is used to control whether child and pop-up windows are visible. Here's how **ShowWindow** is defined:

```
BOOL ShowWindow(HWND hWindow, int command);
```

- **hWindow** is a handle to the pop-up or child window.
- **command** is one of several possible integer constants defined in Windows; these constants have the **SW_** prefix—for example, **SW_HIDE** hides the specified window and **SW_SHOW** displays it.
- This function returns the previous state of the window.

Our code, therefore, removes the color palette window with the statement:
```
ShowWindow(ColorPalette->HWindow, SW_HIDE);
```

 Note Don't use **CloseWindow** with child and pop-up windows.

The **SW_SHOWNOACTIVATE** option is used if the color palette is to be redisplayed. This option displays the pop-up window at its most recent location and size. In addition, the currently active window remains active.

PRINTING YOUR DRAWINGS

Displaying graphics on the screen is nice, but it's just as important to be able to print a hardcopy of your efforts. Like screen operations, printing can be an involved endeavor in Windows.

On the positive side, Windows handles all the low-level details of communicating with a wide range of printers. In addition, Windows does all this and yet still provides a fairly consistent, device-independent programming interface. In fact, the printer is treated much like other devices, such as the screen and memory device contexts. That is, you manipulate the printer using a handle to a device context. You can use all the same GDI functions that you've been using with the screen; however, rather than using a handle to a device context for the screen, you use one for the printer.

Unfortunately, printers vary widely and there is only so much that Windows can do to make printing a snap. You must make sure the printer is capable of printing what you are sending it. In addition, printer errors are very common. A good program watches for these errors.

Finally, printing graphics can require a lot of memory. You may want to optimize your code to work with some printers that can't readily handle the load of graphics printing.

Fortunately, OWL provides the **TPrintout** class that supplies many of the features we need for printing. The OODRAW application derives the **TWindowPrintout** class from **TPrintout** in order to supply a custom **PrintPage** function that prints the drawing. We'll get to the **PrintPage** function in a bit. The variable **Printer** in **TOODrawWindow** points to a **TWindowPrintout** object. It's created in the **TOODrawWindow** constructor:

```
Printer = new TPrinter;          // Allocate a printer object
```

The **CmPrint** routine launches the printing action and is invoked in response to the Print menu option. **CmPrint** is located in the **TOODrawWindow** class in OODRAW.CPP and is defined as:

```
void TOODrawWindow::CmPrint()
{
  if (Printer) {    // If the printer object exists
    TWindowPrintout printout(DrawingWindow->GetFilename(), DrawingWindow);
    printout.SetBanding(TRUE);
    Printer->Print(DrawingWindow, printout, TRUE);
  }
}
```

This code indirectly calls **TWindowPrintout**'s **PrintPage** that actually prints the drawing. This function is a little involved because we must scale the drawing to the size of the paper. To keep things simple the code sets the printing size so that it fits within the page, regardless of its orientation. In addition, the code turns off the grid and temporarily removes the selection frame from any selected objects.

COMPILING THE OODRAW PROGRAM

The OODRAW program uses several tools that we developed earlier in the book and in this chapter. A listing of these files and the chapters in which they are discussed is shown in Table 14.3. You must have access to all of these files when compiling the program. The best approach is to have the files in the same directory as the OODRAW.CPP file. In addition, you'll need all the icon

Table 14.3 Files Used in the OODRAW Program

Source file	Chapter	Description
DRAW.H	13	Header file for DRAW.CPP
DRAW.CPP	13	Interactive drawing tools
DRAWTOOL.CPP	14	Drawing window routines
DRAWTOOL.H	14	Header file for DRAWTOOL.CPP
GOBJECT.H	14	Header file for GOBJECT.CPP
GOBJECT.CPP	14	Represents each figure as an object
GOBJLIST.H	14	Header file for GOBJLIST.CPP
GOBJLIST.CPP	14	Stores a series of graphics objects
GOBJTOOL.H	14	Header file for GOBJTOOL.CPP
GOBJTOOL.CPP	14	Associates the drawing tools with the object list
MATRIX.H	12	Header file for MATRIX.CPP
MATRIX.CPP	12	Provides matrix operations
OODRAW.H	14	Header file for OODRAW.CPP
OODRAW.CPP	14	The main program file
OODRAW.RC	14	The resource file for the program

files that you created in Chapter 13. Your project file should include the following files: OODRAW.CPP, OODRAW.RC, DRAW.CPP, GOBJECT.CPP, GOBJLIST.CPP, GOBJTOOL.CPP, DRAWTOOL.CPP, and MATRIX.CPP.

Using the Drawing Program

Once you have a compiled and linked version of OODRAW, you can give it a test run. The program's environment should be like that shown earlier in Figure 14.1. If you have any difficulty, make sure you have all of the icon files and DLLs in their appropriate location.

The program is easy to run. You can use the mouse to select tools in the palette and to draw in the window. The drawing functions should all work as described in Chapter 13. Most of the other functions that we have added have been described earlier in this chapter.

Enhancing the Drawing Program

Although the complete drawing program is large, there are many features you might want to add. You should not have too much difficulty in carrying your ideas out; in fact, the program was designed so that additions could easily be made.

Generally, here the steps to follow to add a new drawing-related function:

1. Create an icon using Borland's Resource Workshop, that reflects the functionality of the new feature.

2. Derive a class from **TDrawingTool** and **TGObject** that implements the desired feature.

3. Modify the **NUMICONSWIDE** and **NUMICONSHIGH** constants as desired. In addition, dynamically allocate your tool in the **TToolsPalette** constructor, and save a pointer to the tool in the **Tools** array.

With just a little thought, it's possible to create a long list of features that can be added to OODRAW. Here are a few ideas:

- Add brush styles and variable pen widths.

- Expand some of the existing tools. For instance, you could modify **TTextTool** so that the user can select a font style and size. You could also allow the user to rotate the text.

- Add Clipboard support.

- Associate the drawing's units with actual units. Create a ruler that enables the user to accurately measure, size, and place objects in the scene.

- Expand the selection tool and object list to allow objects to be grouped together.

- Add dimensioning lines and lines with arrowheads.

• DRAWTOOL.H

```
// DRAWTOOL.H: Defines a drawing window for OODRAW.
#ifndef DRAWTOOLH
#define DRAWTOOLH

#include <owl\applicat.h>
#include <owl\framewin.h>
#include <owl\dc.h>
#include <owl\scroller.h>
#include "draw.h"
#include "gobjlist.h"

#define FITINWINDOW 0        // Scale factors
#define VIEW25 1             // 25% scale factor
#define VIEW50 2             // 50% scale factor
#define VIEW100 3            // 100% scale factor
#define VIEW200 4            // 200% scale factor
#define PAPERWD 17           // Paper's width (in number of grid cells)
#define PAPERHT 22           // Paper's width (in number of grid cells)
#define GRIDINCWD 10         // Scroll the window horizontally and
#define GRIDINCHT 10         // vertically in 10 pixel steps
```

```
class TDrawingWindow : public TWindow {
public:
  int GridWd, GridHt;        // Width and height of grid
  BOOL GridOn;               // Display a grid in the window
  BOOL DrawingMode;
  TPaintContext* PC;
  TGObjList* Figures;
  int ZoomMode;              // The zoom mode
  TGObject* CurrObjTool;     // Current drawing tool being used
  char Filename[128];        // The file being edited
  TDrawingWindow(TWindow* parent, const char* title,
    TPaintContext* pc, TGObjList* figures);
  void DrawGrid(HDC hDC);
  char* GetFilename() { return Filename; }
  void SetFilename(char* name) { strcpy(Filename, name); }
  int SaveDrawing(char* filename);
  void Paint(TDC& dc, BOOL, TRect&);
  void EvLButtonDown(UINT, TPoint&);
  void EvLButtonUp(UINT, TPoint&);
  void EvMouseMove(UINT, TPoint&);
  void EvRButtonDown(UINT, TPoint&);
  BOOL EvSetCursor(HWND hWndCursor, UINT hitTest, UINT mouseMsg);
  int SetZoom(int zoomMode, double userScale=0);
  BOOL SetGridOn(BOOL gridOn);
  // The following functions respond to user messages:
  LRESULT EvUDeleteObject(WPARAM, LPARAM);
  LRESULT EvUDeleteAll(WPARAM, LPARAM);
  LRESULT EvUFlipToBack(WPARAM, LPARAM);
  LRESULT EvUFlipToFront(WPARAM, LPARAM);
  LRESULT EvURotateCCW(WPARAM, LPARAM);
  LRESULT EvURotateCW(WPARAM, LPARAM);
  LRESULT EvUReadObjList(WPARAM, LPARAM);
  LRESULT EvUSaveObjList(WPARAM, LPARAM);
  void EvHScroll(UINT code, UINT ps, HWND wnd);
  void EvVScroll(UINT code, UINT ps, HWND wnd);

  DECLARE_RESPONSE_TABLE(TDrawingWindow);
};
#endif
```

• DRAWTOOL.CPP

```
// DRAWTOOL.CPP: Ties together the drawing tools with a drawing window.
#include <owl\opensave.h>  // For the TOpenSaveDialog
#include "drawtool.h"

DEFINE_RESPONSE_TABLE1(TDrawingWindow, TWindow)
  EV_WM_LBUTTONDOWN,
  EV_WM_LBUTTONUP,
  EV_WM_RBUTTONDOWN,
  EV_WM_MOUSEMOVE,
  EV_WM_SETCURSOR,
  EV_WM_HSCROLL,
```

```
    EV_WM_VSCROLL,
    EV_MESSAGE(WM_USER+1, EvUDeleteObject),
    EV_MESSAGE(WM_USER+2, EvUDeleteAll),
    EV_MESSAGE(WM_USER+3, EvUFlipToBack),
    EV_MESSAGE(WM_USER+4, EvUFlipToFront),
    EV_MESSAGE(WM_USER+5, EvURotateCCW),
    EV_MESSAGE(WM_USER+6, EvURotateCW),
    EV_MESSAGE(WM_USER+7, EvUReadObjList),
    EV_MESSAGE(WM_USER+8, EvUSaveObjList),
END_RESPONSE_TABLE;

TDrawingWindow::TDrawingWindow(TWindow* parent, const char* title,
  TPaintContext* pc, TGObjList* figures) : TWindow(parent, title) {
    Attr.Style = WS_CHILD | WS_BORDER | WS_VISIBLE;
    GridWd = 50;  GridHt = 50;    // Each grid is 50 by 50 pixels
    DrawingMode = FALSE;          // You're not doing any drawing yet
    GridOn = TRUE;                // Draw a grid by default
    ZoomMode = VIEW100;           // Start with a 100% scale factor
    PC = pc;                      // The drawing window's paint context
    Figures = figures;            // The figures in the window
    SetFilename("UNTITLED.OOD"); // Default filename
    Attr.Style |= WS_VSCROLL | WS_HSCROLL;  // Use scrollers
    Scroller = new TScroller(this, 10, 10, PAPERWD*GridWd/GRIDINCWD,
      PAPERHT*GridHt/GRIDINCHT);
}

// Set the GridOn flag and return the previous setting of the flag.
// If GridOn is TRUE, a grid is displayed in the drawing window.
BOOL TDrawingWindow::SetGridOn(BOOL gridOn)
{
    BOOL oldGridOn = GridOn;
    GridOn = gridOn;
    return oldGridOn;
}

// Display a "paper" background and a grid
void TDrawingWindow::DrawGrid(HDC hDC)
{
    const int SHADOWDIM = 8;    // Pixel width and height of shadow
    RECT rect;
    ::GetClientRect(HWindow, &rect);
    rect.left = rect.right-1;    rect.top = rect.bottom-1;
    // Create the background color
    HBRUSH hBackgrnd = CreateSolidBrush(RGB(130,255,249));
    HBRUSH hOldBrush = HBRUSH(SelectObject(hDC, hBackgrnd));
    // Make sure the background is not completely clipped. Otherwise,
    // it won't show up when scrolling.
    PatBlt(hDC, PAPERWD*GridWd*PC->Zoom+1, 0, 16000, 16000, PATCOPY);
    PatBlt(hDC, 0, PAPERHT*GridHt*PC->Zoom+1, 16000, 16000, PATCOPY);
    SelectObject(hDC, hOldBrush);
    DeleteObject(hBackgrnd);
    SelectObject(hDC, GetStockObject(WHITE_BRUSH));
    Rectangle(hDC, 0, 0, PAPERWD*GridWd*PC->Zoom+1, // Draw the "paper"
```

```
      PAPERHT*GridHt*PC->Zoom+1);                        // in the window
  // Draw a small, gray shadow to the right and left of the paper
  HBRUSH saveBrush = HBRUSH(SelectObject(hDC, GetStockObject(LTGRAY_BRUSH)));
  PatBlt(hDC, PAPERWD*GridWd*PC->Zoom+1, SHADOWDIM,
    SHADOWDIM, PAPERHT*GridHt*PC->Zoom+1, PATCOPY);
  PatBlt(hDC, SHADOWDIM, PAPERHT*GridHt*PC->Zoom+1,
    PAPERWD*GridWd*PC->Zoom+1, SHADOWDIM, PATCOPY);
  SelectObject(hDC, saveBrush);
  if (GridOn) {   // Draw the grid if GridOn is TRUE
    // The grid is made from dotted lines
    HPEN hThinnerDotPen = CreatePen(PS_DOT, 1, RGB(192,192,192));
    POINT scaledPt, pt, pt2, scaledPt2;
    HPEN hOldPen = HPEN(SelectObject(hDC, hThinnerDotPen));
    for (int i=GridHt, j=0; i<PAPERHT*GridHt; i+=GridHt, j++) {
      pt.x = 0;    pt.y = i;                         // Draw the grid's
      ScalePt(scaledPt, pt, PC->Zoom);               // horizontal lines
      scaledPt = PC->SnapToGrid(scaledPt);
      pt2.x = PAPERWD*GridHt;    pt2.y = i;
      ScalePt(scaledPt2, pt2, PC->Zoom);
      scaledPt2 = PC->SnapToGrid(scaledPt2);
      MoveToEx(hDC, 0, scaledPt.y, 0);
      LineTo(hDC, scaledPt2.x-1, scaledPt2.y);
    }
    for (i=GridWd, j=0; i<PAPERWD*GridWd; i+=GridWd, j++) { // Draw the grid's
      pt.x = i;    pt.y = 0;                          // vertical lines
      pt = PC->SnapToGrid(pt);
      ScalePt(scaledPt, pt, PC->Zoom);
      pt2.x = i;    pt2.y = PAPERHT*GridWd;
      pt2 = PC->SnapToGrid(pt2);
      ScalePt(scaledPt2, pt2, PC->Zoom);
      MoveToEx(hDC, scaledPt.x, 0, 0);
      LineTo(hDC, scaledPt2.x, scaledPt2.y-1);
    }
    SelectObject(hDC, hOldPen);
    DeleteObject(hThinnerDotPen);
  }
}


// Call the figure list's DisplayAll function to display the picture
void TDrawingWindow::Paint(TDC& dc, BOOL, TRect&)
{
  DrawGrid(dc);
  Figures->DisplayAll(dc); // Display the objects in the figure list
}


// The left mouse button was just pressed in the drawing window
void TDrawingWindow::EvLButtonDown(UINT, TPoint& pt)
{
  // In general, the scroller units can reach long values, but because
  // of the size of the drawing window this won't occur here so
  // integer values for the offsets are okay.
  PC->Offsx = (int)Scroller->XPos*Scroller->XUnit;
  PC->Offsy = (int)Scroller->YPos*Scroller->YUnit;
  PC->OWLWindow = this;
```

```
    PC->DrawingWnd = HWindow;
    if (!DrawingMode) {              // Are we already drawing an object?
      POINT scaledPt;                // Start drawing a new object. Note: The
      pt = PC->SnapToGrid(pt);       // drawing mode may change if the figure
      ScalePt(scaledPt, pt, 1/PC->Zoom);              // can't be drawn.
      DrawingMode = PC->Tool->LButtonDown(scaledPt);
    }
}

// The left mouse button was just released in the drawing window
void TDrawingWindow::EvLButtonUp(UINT, TPoint& pt)
{
  pt = PC->SnapToGrid(pt);
  POINT scaledPt;
  ScalePt(scaledPt, pt, 1/PC->Zoom);
  if (DrawingMode) {                // Are we drawing?
    TGObject* gObj = CurrObjTool;
    DrawingMode = PC->Tool->LButtonUp(scaledPt);
    if (!DrawingMode) {             // If the drawing is now done,
      if (gObj->HasSize()) {   // add it to the list
        // If the object just drawn has size, then add it to the drawing
        // list. Actually, add a copy of the object to the figure list.
        TGObject *nuObj = gObj->Dup();
        // Add in the current scroller offsets of the drawing window
        nuObj->Offset(TPoint((Scroller->XPos*Scroller->XUnit)/PC->Zoom,
          (Scroller->YPos*Scroller->YUnit)/PC->Zoom));
        nuObj->UpdateBounds();            // Update the object's bounds
        Figures->Add(nuObj);
      }
    }
  }
}

// Used by polygon function to end drawing
void TDrawingWindow::EvRButtonDown(UINT, TPoint& pt)
{
  pt = PC->SnapToGrid(pt);
  POINT scaledPt;
  ScalePt(scaledPt, pt, 1/PC->Zoom);
  if (DrawingMode) {                    // The right mouse button is
    TGObject* gObj = CurrObjTool;   // used to end the polygon routines
    DrawingMode = gObj->Obj->RButtonDown(scaledPt);
    if (!DrawingMode) {
      // If the drawing is now done, add it to the list
      if (gObj->HasSize()) {
        // If the object has size, add a copy of it to the drawing list
        TGObject *nuObj = gObj->Dup();
        nuObj->Offset(TPoint((Scroller->XPos*Scroller->XUnit)/PC->Zoom,
          (Scroller->YPos*Scroller->YUnit)/PC->Zoom));
        nuObj->UpdateBounds();                // Update the object's bounds
        Figures->Add(nuObj);
      }
    }
  }
}
```

```
// The mouse is being moved while in the drawing window
void TDrawingWindow::EvMouseMove(UINT, TPoint& pt)
{
  if (DrawingMode) {
    pt = PC->SnapToGrid(pt);
    POINT scaledPt;
    ScalePt(scaledPt, pt, 1/PC->Zoom);
    PC->Tool->MouseMove(scaledPt);
  }
  else // Update the cursor as the mouse moves
    PC->Tool->UpdateCursor(pt);
}

// Switch to the current drawing tool's cursor when the cursor
// is over the window's client area
BOOL TDrawingWindow::EvSetCursor(HWND hWndCursor, UINT hitTest,
  UINT mouseMsg)
{
  if (hitTest == HTCLIENT) {        // Cursor is in the client area
    ::SetCursor(PC->Tool->hCursor); // Use the current tool's
    return TRUE;                    // cursor style; otherwise, chain
  }                                 // to the inherited function
  return TWindow::EvSetCursor(hWndCursor, hitTest, mouseMsg);
}

// Delete the current object in the figure list. Repaint the
// window where the object was located.
LRESULT TDrawingWindow::EvUDeleteObject(WPARAM, LPARAM)
{
  Figures->Delete();
  return 0;
}

// Delete all objects in the figure list. Repaint the window.
LRESULT TDrawingWindow::EvUDeleteAll(WPARAM, LPARAM)
{
  Figures->DeleteAll();
  return 0;
}

// Move the current object to the back of the object list.
// Repaint the window where the object is.
LRESULT TDrawingWindow::EvUFlipToBack(WPARAM, LPARAM)
{
  Figures->FlipToBack();
  return 0;
}

// Move the current object to the front of the object list.
// Repaint the portion of the window where the object is.
LRESULT TDrawingWindow::EvUFlipToFront(WPARAM, LPARAM)
{
  Figures->FlipToFront();
  return 0;
}
```

```
// Rotate the current object counterclockwise by 45 degrees
LRESULT TDrawingWindow::EvURotateCCW(WPARAM, LPARAM)
{
  Figures->Rotate(45);
  return 0;
}

// Rotate the current object clockwise by 45 degrees
LRESULT TDrawingWindow::EvURotateCW(WPARAM, LPARAM)
{
  Figures->Rotate(-45);
  return 0;
}

// Save the drawing to the specified file
int TDrawingWindow::SaveDrawing(char* filename)
{
  FILE* fp;
  char buffer[256];
  if ((fp = fopen(filename, "w")) == NULL) {
    strcpy(buffer, "Could not open file: ");
    ::MessageBox(HWindow, strcat(buffer,filename),
    GetApplicationObject()->GetName(), MB_OK | MB_ICONEXCLAMATION);
    return 0;
  }
  else {
    SetFilename(filename);
    Figures->Save(fp);
    fclose(fp);
    return 1;
  }
}

// Save the object list to a file. This function is used by Save
// and Save As. If the filename is UNTITLED.OOD or saveAs is 1,
// then the Save As dialog box appears and asks the user to enter
// a filename. Otherwise, the file is simply saved.
LRESULT TDrawingWindow::EvUSaveObjList(WPARAM saveAs, LPARAM)
{
  if (saveAs || (lstrcmp(Filename, "UNTITLED.OOD") == 0)) {
    TOpenSaveDialog::TData data(
      OFN_HIDEREADONLY | OFN_PATHMUSTEXIST | OFN_OVERWRITEPROMPT,
      "Figures (*.OOD)|*.OOD|", 0, "", "OOD");
    TOpenSaveDialog *saveDlg = new TFileSaveDialog(this, data);
    if (saveDlg->Execute() == IDOK)  // The user pressed the OK button
      return SaveDrawing(data.FileName);  // Save the drawing
  }
  else
    return SaveDrawing(Filename);   // Save the drawing to "Filename"
  return 0;                         // Return a failure flag
}

// Read the object list from a file and display it
LRESULT TDrawingWindow::EvUReadObjList(WPARAM, LPARAM)
```

```
{
  TFileOpenDialog::TData FilenameData(
    OFN_FILEMUSTEXIST | OFN_HIDEREADONLY | OFN_PATHMUSTEXIST,
    "Figures (*.OOD)|*.OOD|", 0, "", "OOD");
  TFileOpenDialog *fileDlg = new TFileOpenDialog(this, FilenameData);
  if (fileDlg->Execute() == IDOK) {
    char buffer[255];
    FILE *fp;
    // Open the file
    if ((fp = fopen(FilenameData.FileName, "r")) == NULL) {
      strcpy(buffer, "Could not open file: ");
      ::MessageBox(HWindow, strcat(buffer,FilenameData.FileName),
        GetApplicationObject()->GetName(), MB_OK | MB_ICONEXCLAMATION);
    }
    else {
      int readStatus;
      switch (readStatus=Figures->Read(fp)) {
        case -1: // File wasn't read. Keep the current file.
          strcpy(buffer, "Incorrect file format: ");
          ::MessageBox(HWindow, strcat(buffer,FilenameData.FileName),
          GetApplicationObject()->GetName(), MB_OK | MB_ICONEXCLAMATION);
          break;
        case -2: // File was partially read. Use new filename.
          strcpy(buffer, "Unexpected end of file: ");
          ::MessageBox(HWindow, strcat(buffer,FilenameData.FileName),
          GetApplicationObject()->GetName(), MB_OK | MB_ICONEXCLAMATION);
          SetFilename(FilenameData.FileName);
          break;
        default: // The read operation succeeded. Use new filename.
          SetFilename(FilenameData.FileName);
      }
      fclose(fp);
      return readStatus;
    }
  }
  return 0;        // Return a failure flag
}

// Set the paper's zoom factor. Return the old setting.
int TDrawingWindow::SetZoom(int zoomMode, double userScale)
{
  double oldZoomMode = ZoomMode;
  ZoomMode = zoomMode;
  switch(zoomMode) {
    case FITINWINDOW: PC->Zoom = userScale; break;
    case VIEW25: PC->Zoom = .25; break;
    case VIEW50: PC->Zoom = .5; break;
    case VIEW100: PC->Zoom = 1; break;
    case VIEW200: PC->Zoom = 2; break;
    default: PC->Zoom = userScale;
  }
  return oldZoomMode;
}
```

```
// Update the scroller position of the drawing window and paper
void TDrawingWindow::EvHScroll(UINT code, UINT pos, HWND wnd)
{
  TWindow::EvHScroll(code, pos, wnd);
  PC->Offsx = (int)Scroller->XPos*Scroller->XUnit;
}

void TDrawingWindow::EvVScroll(UINT code, UINT pos, HWND wnd)
{
  TWindow::EvVScroll(code, pos, wnd);
  PC->Offsy = (int)Scroller->YPos*Scroller->YUnit;
}
```

• GOBJECT.H

```
// GOBJECT.H: Defines resizable graphics objects supported in OODRAW.
#ifndef GOBJECTH
#define GOBJECTH

#include <stdio.h>
#include "matrix.h"
#include "draw.h"

#define LINEOBJ 1           // Flags used to identify the
#define RECTANGLEOBJ 2      // types of objects saved to
#define ELLIPSEOBJ 3        // a file
#define POLYLINEOBJ 4
#define POLYGONOBJ 5
#define TEXTOBJ 6
#define EMPTYRECTANGLEOBJ 7
#define EMPTYELLIPSEOBJ 8
#define HANDLEWD 3       // The pixel width of a resizing handle

// The base class from which all graphics objects are derived
class TGObject {
public:
  RECT DevBounds;            // Boundary in device units
  TDrawingTool* Obj;         // The object that is drawn
  TGObject(HWND drawingWnd, int penWd, COLORREF penColor,
    COLORREF brushColor, TDrawingTool* obj, TPaintContext* pc) { }
  TGObject(HWND drawingWnd, int x1, int y1, int x2, int y2, int penWd,
    COLORREF penColor, COLORREF brushColor, TPaintContext* pc) { }
  virtual ~TGObject() { delete Obj; } // Free the nested object too
  virtual void UpdateBounds();  // Recalculate the object's bounds
  RECT* GetBounds(BOOL frame);  // Get the bounds of the object
  virtual void Display(HDC hDC, double zoom);  // Display the object
  virtual void Rotate(double /*angle*/) { }    // Rotate the object
  virtual void Translate(int transx, int transy);
  virtual void Save(FILE* /*fp*/) { }
  virtual BOOL HasSize();
  virtual void Scale(float scale);  // Scale the object's settings
  virtual void Offset(POINT& pt);   // Offset the object's location
  virtual void DrawHandles(HDC hDC, double zoom, int offsx, int offsy);
```

```cpp
    virtual void DrawResizingObject(HDC hDC, RECT& frame, double zoom,
      int offsx, int offsy, BOOL moving);
    virtual void Resize(HDC hDC, POINT& pt, int handleId,
      double zoom, int offsx, int offsy) { }
    virtual void ResizeFrame(RECT& frame, int handleId, POINT& pt,
      TPaintContext* pc);
    virtual TGObject* Dup() {
      TGObject* gObj = new TGObject(*this);
      gObj->Obj = new TDrawingTool(*Obj);
      return gObj;
    }
    virtual int PtOnResizeHandle(POINT& pt, double zoom, POINT& hPt);
    virtual int PtOnReshapeHandle(POINT& pt, double zoom)
      { return NOHANDLE; }
    virtual BOOL PtOnFrame(RECT* rect, POINT& pt);
    virtual BOOL PtInObject(POINT& pt);
    virtual void ScaleToRect(int handleId, RECT& rect);
    virtual void Reshape(int handleId, POINT& pt, BOOL ignore=0) { }
};

class TLineObj : public TGObject {  // Line object
public:
  TLineObj(BOOL allocObj) : TGObject(0, 0, 0, 0, 0, 0)
    { if (allocObj) Obj = new TLineTool; }  // Contained class
  TLineObj(HWND window, int x1, int y1, int x2, int y2, int penWd,
    COLORREF penColor, TDrawingTool* obj, TPaintContext* pc) :
    TGObject(window, penWd, penColor, 0, obj, pc) {
    Obj = new TLineTool(*(TLineTool*)Obj);
    Obj->Pt1.x = x1;    Obj->Pt1.y = y1;
    Obj->Pt2.x = x2;    Obj->Pt2.y = y2;
  }
  // Alternative constructor used for reading file data. It
  // doesn't convert points to world coordinates.
  TLineObj(HWND window, int x1, int y1, int x2, int y2,
    int penWd, COLORREF penColor, TPaintContext* pc, BOOL allocObj);
  void UpdateBounds();
  void Rotate(double angle);
  void Save(FILE* fp);
  void DrawHandles(HDC hDC, double zoom, int offsx, int offsy);
  void DrawResizingObject(HDC hDC, RECT& frame, double zoom,
    int offsx, int offsy, BOOL moving);
  void Resize(HDC hDC, POINT& pt, int handleId,
    double zoom, int offsx, int offsy);
  void ScaleToRect(int handleId, RECT& rect) { }
  TGObject* Dup() {
    TGObject* gObj = new TLineObj(*this);
    gObj->Obj = new TLineTool(*(TLineTool*)Obj);
    gObj->Obj->PC = new TPaintContext(*(((TLineTool*)Obj)->PC));
    return gObj;
  }
  BOOL PtOnFrame(RECT*, POINT& pt);
  BOOL PtInObject(POINT& pt);
};
```

```
class TRectangleObj : public TGObject {    // Rectangle object
public:
  TRectangleObj(BOOL allocObj) : TGObject(0, 0, 0, 0, 0, 0)
    { if (allocObj) Obj = new TRectangleTool; }
  TRectangleObj(HWND window, int x1, int y1, int x2, int y2, int penWd,
    COLORREF penColor, COLORREF brushColor, TPaintContext* pc) :
    TGObject(window, penWd, penColor, brushColor, 0, pc) {  }
  // Used when creating a rectangle a file
  TRectangleObj(HWND window, int x1, int y1, int x2, int y2, int penWd,
    COLORREF penColor, COLORREF brushColor, TPaintContext* pc, BOOL allocObj);
  void Save(FILE* fp);
  TGObject* Dup() {
    TGObject* gObj = new TRectangleObj(*this);
    gObj->Obj = new TRectangleTool(*(TRectangleTool*)Obj);
    gObj->Obj->PC = new TPaintContext(*(((TDrawingTool *)Obj)->PC));
    return gObj;
  }
  void ResizeFrame(RECT& frame, int handleId, POINT& pt,
    TPaintContext* pc);
  void ScaleToRect(int handleId, RECT& size);   // Scale figure
  int PtOnResizeHandle(POINT& pt, double zoom, POINT& hPt);
  BOOL PtOnFrame(RECT* rect, POINT& pt)
    { return TGObject::PtOnFrame(rect, pt); }
  BOOL PtInObject(POINT& pt) { return TGObject::PtInObject(pt); }
};

// Empty rectangle object
class TEmptyRectangleObj : public TRectangleObj {
public:
  TEmptyRectangleObj(BOOL allocObj) : TRectangleObj(FALSE)
    { if (allocObj) Obj = new TEmptyRectangleTool; }
  TEmptyRectangleObj(HWND window, int x1, int y1, int x2, int y2,
    int penWd, COLORREF penColor, TPaintContext* pc) :
    TRectangleObj(window, x1, y1, x2, y2, penWd, penColor, 0, pc) { }
  TEmptyRectangleObj(HWND window, int x1, int y1, int x2, int y2,
    int penWd, COLORREF penColor, TPaintContext* pc, BOOL allocObj);
  void Save(FILE* fp);
  TGObject* Dup() {
    TGObject* gObj = new TEmptyRectangleObj(*this);
    gObj->Obj = new TEmptyRectangleTool(*(TEmptyRectangleTool*)Obj);
    gObj->Obj->PC = new TPaintContext(*(((TDrawingTool *)Obj)->PC));
    return gObj;
  }
};

class TEllipseObj : public TRectangleObj {  // Ellipse object
public:
  TEllipseObj(BOOL allocObj) : TRectangleObj(FALSE) {
    if (allocObj) Obj = new TEllipseTool;
  }
  TEllipseObj(HWND window, int x1, int y1, int x2, int y2,
    int penWd, COLORREF penColor, COLORREF brushColor,
    TPaintContext* pc) : TRectangleObj(window, x1, y1,
    y2, y2, penWd, penColor, brushColor, pc) { }
```

```
      TEllipseObj(HWND window, int x1, int y1, int x2, int y2,
        int penWd, COLORREF penColor, COLORREF brushColor,
        TPaintContext* pc, BOOL allocObj);
      void Save(FILE* fp);
      TGObject* Dup() {
        TGObject* gObj = new TEllipseObj(*this);
        gObj->Obj = new TEllipseTool(*(TEllipseTool*)Obj);
        gObj->Obj->PC = new TPaintContext(*(((TDrawingTool *)Obj)->PC));
        return gObj;
      }
  };

  class TEmptyEllipseObj : public TEllipseObj {  // Empty ellipse object
  public:
      TEmptyEllipseObj(BOOL allocObj) : TEllipseObj(FALSE)
        { if (allocObj) Obj = new TEmptyEllipseTool; }
      TEmptyEllipseObj(HWND window, int x1, int y1,
        int x2, int y2, int penWd, COLORREF penColor, TPaintContext* pc) :
        TEllipseObj(window, x1, y1, x2, y2, penWd, penColor, 0, pc) { }
      TEmptyEllipseObj(HWND window, int x1, int y1, int x2, int y2,
        int penWd, COLORREF penColor, TPaintContext* pc, BOOL allocObj);
      void Save(FILE* fp);
      TGObject* Dup() {
        TGObject* gObj = new TEmptyEllipseObj(*this);
        gObj->Obj = new TEmptyEllipseTool(*(TEmptyEllipseTool*)Obj);
        gObj->Obj->PC = new TPaintContext(*(((TDrawingTool *)Obj)->PC));
        return gObj;
      }
  };

  class TPolylineObj : public TGObject {  // Draw connected lines
  public:
      TPolylineObj(BOOL allocObj) : TGObject(0, 0, 0, 0, 0, 0)
        { if (allocObj) Obj = new TPolylineTool; }
      TPolylineObj(HWND window, POINT points[], int numPts,
        int penWd, COLORREF penColor, TPaintContext* pc) :
        TGObject(window, penWd, penColor, 0, 0, pc) { }
      TPolylineObj(HWND window, POINT points[], int numPts, int penWd,
        COLORREF penColor, TPaintContext* pc, BOOL allocObj);
      void UpdateBounds();
      void Rotate(double angle);
      void Translate(int transx, int transy);
      void Save(FILE* fp);
      BOOL HasSize() { return ((TPolylineTool *)Obj)->NumPts > 0; }
      void DrawHandles(HDC hDC, double zoom, int offsx, int offsy);
      TGObject* Dup() {
        TGObject* gObj = new TPolylineObj(*this);
        gObj->Obj = new TPolylineTool(*(TPolylineTool*)Obj);
        gObj->Obj->PC = new TPaintContext(*(((TDrawingTool *)Obj)->PC));
        return gObj;
      }
      void Scale(float scale);  // Scale the polygon
      void Offset(POINT& pt);    // Offset the polygon's location
      int PtOnResizeHandle(POINT& pt, double zoom, POINT& hPt);
```

```
    int PtOnReshapeHandle(POINT& pt, double zoom);
    BOOL PtOnFrame(RECT* rect, POINT& pt)
      { return TGObject::PtOnFrame(rect, pt); }
    BOOL PtInObject(POINT& pt);
    void ScaleToRect(int handleId, RECT& size);            // Scale figure
    void Reshape(int handleId, POINT& pt, BOOL ignore=0); // Reshape figure
};

class TPolygonObj : public TPolylineObj {  // A filled polygon
public:
  TPolygonObj(BOOL allocObj) : TPolylineObj(FALSE)
    { if (allocObj) Obj = new TPolygonTool; }
  TPolygonObj(HWND window, POINT points[], int numPts, int penWd,
    COLORREF penColor, COLORREF brushColor, TPaintContext* pc) :
    TPolylineObj(window, points, numPts, penWd, penColor, pc) {
  }
  TPolygonObj(HWND window, POINT points[], int numPts, int penWd,
    COLORREF penColor, COLORREF brushColor, TPaintContext* pc,
    BOOL allocObj);
  void Save(FILE* fp);
  TGObject* Dup() {
    TGObject* gObj = new TPolygonObj(*this);
    gObj->Obj = new TPolygonTool(*(TPolygonTool*)Obj);
    gObj->Obj->PC = new TPaintContext(*(((TDrawingTool *)Obj)->PC));
    return gObj;
  }
};

// Text object. Note that rotation of text is not supported.
class TTextObj : public TRectangleObj {
public:
  TTextObj(BOOL allocObj) : TRectangleObj(FALSE)
    { if (allocObj) Obj = new TTextTool; }
  TTextObj(HWND window, int x1, int y1, int x2, int y2,
    char* string, COLORREF penColor, TPaintContext* pc) :
    TRectangleObj(window, x1, y1, x2, y2, 0, penColor, 0, pc) { }
  TTextObj(HWND window, int x1, int y1, int x2, int y2, int wd, int ht,
    char* string, COLORREF penColor, TPaintContext* pc, BOOL allocObj);
  void Save(FILE* fp);
  BOOL HasSize() { return lstrlen(((TTextTool *)Obj)->Str) > 0; }
  TGObject* Dup() {
    TGObject* gObj = new TTextObj(*this);
    gObj->Obj = new TTextTool(*(TTextTool *)Obj);
    gObj->Obj->PC = new TPaintContext(*(((TDrawingTool *)Obj)->PC));
    return gObj;
  }
  void ScaleToRect(int handleId, RECT& size);
  int PtOnReshapeHandle(POINT& pt, double zoom);
  void Reshape(int, POINT&, BOOL ignore=0);  // Edit text
};
// Support functions
POINT OffsetPt(POINT& pt, int x, int y);
POINT ScalePt(POINT& scaledPt, POINT& pt, float scale);
RECT ScaleRect(RECT& scaledRect, RECT& rect, float scale);
```

```
int PtOnPoint(POINT poly[], int numPts, POINT& pt);
BOOL PtOnLine(POINT& pt1, POINT& pt2, POINT& pt);
BOOL PtOnPolygon(POINT& pt, POINT poly[], int numPts);
BOOL PtInArea(POINT& pt, POINT& center, int range);
// These functions are used to help rotate lines and polygons
void CopyToWPoly(POINT polyFrom[], int numPoints, double polyTo[]);
void CopyFromWPoly(double polyFrom[], int numPoints, POINT polyTo[]);
void WRotatePoly(double poly[], int numPoints, double angle);
void WTranslatePoly(double poly[], int numPoints, double tx, double ty);
#endif
```

• GOBJECT.CPP

```
// GOBJECT.CPP: Defines the functions used to support graphics figures
// as objects in OODRAW. The objects defined here are maintained
// in a list by the class TGObjList which is defined in GOBJLIST.CPP.
#include <owl\applicat.h>
#include <owl\framewin.h>
#include <owl\dc.h>
#include <owl\inputdia.h>      // Required for OWL's TInputDialog class
#include <stdio.h>
#include <math.h>
#include "matrix.h"
#include "gobject.h"
#include "gobjlist.h"

// Scale the object's settings by a scale factor
void TGObject::Scale(float scale)
{
  Obj->Pt1.x = Obj->Pt1.x*scale+0.5;  Obj->Pt1.y = Obj->Pt1.y*scale+0.5;
  Obj->Pt2.x = Obj->Pt2.x*scale+0.5;  Obj->Pt2.y = Obj->Pt2.y*scale+0.5;
}

// Offset the object's location by the value in the pt
void TGObject::Offset(POINT& pt)
{
  Obj->Pt1.x += pt.x;  Obj->Pt1.y += pt.y;
  Obj->Pt2.x += pt.x;  Obj->Pt2.y += pt.y;
}

// Draw a frame around the object using a green pen. Also, draw black
// rectangles at each handle location. By default, the object handles,
// which are used to resize the object, are placed at the four corners
// of the object.
void TGObject::DrawHandles(HDC hDC, double zoom, int offsx, int offsy)
{
  int oldROP = SetROP2(hDC, R2_XORPEN);
  HPEN hPen = CreatePen(PS_SOLID, 1, RGB(0,255,0));
  HPEN hOldPen = HPEN(SelectObject(hDC, hPen));
  HBRUSH hOldBrush = HBRUSH(SelectObject(hDC, GetStockObject(NULL_BRUSH)));
  Rectangle(hDC, Obj->Pt1.x*zoom-offsx+0.5, Obj->Pt1.y*zoom-offsy+0.5,
    Obj->Pt2.x*zoom-offsx+0.5+1, Obj->Pt2.y*zoom-offsy+0.5+1);
```

```
    // Paint four handles at each corner of the object. Use white
    // since the rectangles will be exclusive-ORed.
    SelectObject(hDC, GetStockObject(WHITE_BRUSH));
    SelectObject(hDC, GetStockObject(WHITE_PEN));
    Rectangle(hDC, Obj->Pt1.x*zoom-offsx-HANDLEWD+0.5,
      Obj->Pt1.y*zoom-offsy-HANDLEWD+0.5,
      Obj->Pt1.x*zoom-offsx+0.5+HANDLEWD,
      Obj->Pt1.y*zoom-offsy+0.5+HANDLEWD);
    Rectangle(hDC, Obj->Pt2.x*zoom-offsx+0.5-HANDLEWD,
      Obj->Pt1.y*zoom-offsy+0.5-HANDLEWD,
      Obj->Pt2.x*zoom-offsx+0.5+HANDLEWD,
      Obj->Pt1.y*zoom-offsy+0.5+HANDLEWD);
    Rectangle(hDC, Obj->Pt2.x*zoom-offsx+0.5-HANDLEWD,
      Obj->Pt2.y*zoom-offsy+0.5-HANDLEWD,
      Obj->Pt2.x*zoom-offsx+0.5+HANDLEWD,
      Obj->Pt2.y*zoom-offsy+0.5+HANDLEWD);
    Rectangle(hDC, Obj->Pt1.x*zoom-offsx+0.5-HANDLEWD,
      Obj->Pt2.y*zoom-offsy+0.5-HANDLEWD,
      Obj->Pt1.x*zoom-offsx+0.5+HANDLEWD,
      Obj->Pt2.y*zoom-offsy+0.5+HANDLEWD);
    SelectObject(hDC, hOldBrush);
    SelectObject(hDC, hOldPen);
    DeleteObject(hPen);
    SetROP2(hDC, oldROP);
}

// Draw the frame that is used while resizing the object. By default,
// a green frame is used with a dashed line drawn over it.
void TGObject::DrawResizingObject(HDC hDC, RECT& frame, double zoom,
  int offsx, int offsy, BOOL)
{
  // Draw a green line below a dashed line to help the border stand out
  int hOldROP = SetROP2(hDC, R2_XORPEN);
  HPEN hGreenPen = CreatePen(PS_SOLID, 1, RGB(0,255,0));
  HPEN hOldPen = HPEN(SelectObject(hDC, hGreenPen));
  HBRUSH hOldBrush = HBRUSH(SelectObject(hDC,
    GetStockObject(NULL_BRUSH)));
  Rectangle(hDC, (frame.left-offsx)*zoom+0.5, (frame.top-offsy)*zoom+0.5,
    (frame.right-offsx)*zoom+0.5+1, (frame.bottom-offsy)*zoom+0.5+1);
  SelectObject(hDC, hOldPen);
  Rectangle(hDC, (frame.left-offsx)*zoom+0.5, (frame.top-offsy)*zoom+0.5,
    (frame.right-offsx)*zoom+0.5+1, (frame.bottom-offsy)*zoom+0.5+1);
  DeleteObject(hGreenPen);
  SelectObject(hDC, hOldBrush);
  SetROP2(hDC, hOldROP);
}

// Resize the frame of the object
void TGObject::ResizeFrame(RECT& frame, int handleId, POINT& pt,
  TPaintContext* pc)
{
  switch(handleId) {
    case NWHANDLE:
      frame.left = pt.x+pc->Offsx/pc->Zoom + 0.5;
```

```
          frame.top = pt.y+pc->Offsy/pc->Zoom + 0.5;
          break;
      case NEHANDLE:
          frame.right = pt.x+pc->Offsx/pc->Zoom + 0.5;
          frame.top = pt.y+pc->Offsy/pc->Zoom + 0.5;
          break;
      case SEHANDLE:
          frame.right = pt.x+pc->Offsx/pc->Zoom + 0.5;
          frame.bottom = pt.y+pc->Offsy/pc->Zoom + 0.5;
          break;
      case SWHANDLE:
          frame.left = pt.x+pc->Offsx/pc->Zoom + 0.5;
          frame.bottom = pt.y+pc->Offsy/pc->Zoom + 0.5;
          break;
  }
}

// Return the device unit bounds of the object including room for
// its frame if "frame" is TRUE
RECT* TGObject::GetBounds(BOOL frame)
{
  UpdateBounds();
  if (frame) {
    DevBounds.left -= HANDLEWD;  DevBounds.top -= HANDLEWD;
    DevBounds.right += HANDLEWD; DevBounds.bottom +=HANDLEWD;
  }
  return &DevBounds;
}

// Determine the size of the object's bounding box and place it's
// coordinates into the DevBounds rectangle
void TGObject::UpdateBounds()
{
  int temp;

  if (Obj->Pt1.x > Obj->Pt2.x) {
    temp = Obj->Pt1.x;
    Obj->Pt1.x = Obj->Pt2.x;
    Obj->Pt2.x = temp;
  }
  if (Obj->Pt1.y > Obj->Pt2.y) {
    temp = Obj->Pt1.y;
    Obj->Pt1.y = Obj->Pt2.y;
    Obj->Pt2.y = temp;
  }
  DevBounds.left = Obj->Pt1.x;     DevBounds.right = Obj->Pt2.x;
  DevBounds.top = Obj->Pt1.y;      DevBounds.bottom = Obj->Pt2.y;
}

// Display the object
void TGObject::Display(HDC hDC, double zoom)
{
  HPEN hPen = CreatePen(PS_SOLID, Obj->PC->PenWd, Obj->PC->PenColor);
  HPEN hOldPen = HPEN(SelectObject(hDC, hPen));
```

```
   HBRUSH hBrush = HBRUSH(CreateSolidBrush(Obj->PC->BrushColor));
   HBRUSH hOldBrush = HBRUSH(SelectObject(hDC, hBrush));
   Obj->Show(hDC, zoom);
   SelectObject(hDC, hOldPen);
   SelectObject(hDC, hOldBrush);
   DeleteObject(hPen);
   DeleteObject(hBrush);
}

// Scale the rectangle to fit inside the "rect" rectangle. The
// handleId point should not change.
void TGObject::ScaleToRect(int handleId, RECT& rect)
{
  int nuWd = rect.right - rect.left;
  int nuHt = rect.bottom - rect.top;
  switch(handleId) {
    case SEHANDLE:  // Point 2 was moved
      Obj->Pt2.x = Obj->Pt1.x + nuWd;
      Obj->Pt2.y = Obj->Pt1.y + nuHt;
      break;
    case NWHANDLE:    // Point 1 was moved
      Obj->Pt1.x = Obj->Pt2.x - nuWd;
      Obj->Pt1.y = Obj->Pt2.y - nuHt;
      break;
  }
}

// Translate the object in by transx and transy
void TGObject::Translate(int transx, int transy)
{
  Obj->Pt1.x += transx;  Obj->Pt1.y += transy;
  Obj->Pt2.x += transx;  Obj->Pt2.y += transy;
}

// Return TRUE if the specified point is on the border of the
// object. This routine is used to determine when the mouse is on the
// bounding rectangle that appears when an object is selected. Allow
// a several-pixel fudge factor to make it easier to select the frame.
BOOL TGObject::PtOnFrame(RECT* rect, POINT& pt)
{
  const int extra = 5;
  if ((rect->top-extra <= pt.y && rect->top+extra >= pt.y) ||
      (rect->bottom-extra <= pt.y && rect->bottom+extra >= pt.y)) {
    return (rect->left <= pt.x && rect->right >= pt.x) ? TRUE : FALSE;
  }
  else if ((rect->left-extra <= pt.x && rect->left+extra >= pt.x) ||
    (rect->right-extra <= pt.x && rect->right+extra >= pt.x)) {
    return (rect->top <= pt.y && rect->bottom >= pt.y) ? TRUE : FALSE;
  }
  return FALSE;
}

// Return TRUE if pt is inside the bounding region of the object
BOOL TGObject::PtInObject(POINT& pt)
```

```
{
  RECT rect;
  rect.left = Obj->Pt1.x;    rect.right = Obj->Pt2.x;
  rect.top = Obj->Pt1.y;     rect.bottom = Obj->Pt2.y;
  return PtInRect(&rect, pt);
}

// Return TRUE if the object is more than a point
BOOL TGObject::HasSize()
{
  return (Obj->Pt1.x != Obj->Pt2.x || Obj->Pt1.y != Obj->Pt2.y);
}

// Determine if the point pt is on one of the object's handles.
// If so, return the ID for that handle. (Handles are used to
// resize the object.) In the base class there are only two
// handles, one for Pt1 and one for Pt2.
int TGObject::PtOnResizeHandle(POINT& pt, double /*zoom*/, POINT& hPt)
{
  if (PtInArea(pt, Obj->Pt1, HANDLEWD)) {
    hPt = Obj->Pt1;
    return NWHANDLE;
  }
  else if (PtInArea(pt, Obj->Pt2, HANDLEWD)) {
    hPt = Obj->Pt2;
    return SEHANDLE;
  }
  return NOHANDLE;
}

// Constructor for a line object
TLineObj::TLineObj(HWND window, int x1, int y1, int x2, int y2,
  int penWd, COLORREF penColor, TPaintContext* pc, BOOL allocObj):
  TGObject(window, x1, y1, x2, y2, penWd, penColor, 0, pc)
{
  if (allocObj) {
    Obj = new TLineTool();
    Obj->Pt1.x = x1;    Obj->Pt1.y = y1;
    Obj->Pt2.x = x2;    Obj->Pt2.y = y2;
    Obj->PC = new TPaintContext(*pc);
    Obj->PC->PenWd = penWd;
    Obj->PC->PenColor = penColor;
  }
}

// Get the bounds of the line. The code is a little tricky because you
// need to make sure that the top left of the bounding box is correct.
void TLineObj::UpdateBounds()
{
  if (Obj->Pt1.x <= Obj->Pt2.x) {    // Pt1.x is to the left of Pt2.x
    DevBounds.left = Obj->Pt1.x;
    DevBounds.right = Obj->Pt2.x;
  }
```

```
  else {
    DevBounds.left = Obj->Pt2.x;
    DevBounds.right = Obj->Pt1.x;
  }
  if (Obj->Pt1.y <= Obj->Pt2.y) {      // Pt1.y is above Pt2.y
    DevBounds.top = Obj->Pt1.y;
    DevBounds.bottom = Obj->Pt2.y;
  }
  else {
    DevBounds.top = Obj->Pt2.y;
    DevBounds.bottom = Obj->Pt1.y;
  }
}

// Rotate a line. The function rotates the figure using floating-point
// operations to avoid round-off errors. The .5 values added at the end
// make sure to round off the rotated coordinates rather than
// simply truncating them.
void TLineObj::Rotate(double angle)
{
  double cx, cy, pts[4];
  cx = (Obj->Pt1.x + Obj->Pt2.x) / 2.0;    // Get the center of the line
  cy = (Obj->Pt1.y + Obj->Pt2.y) / 2.0;
  pts[0] = Obj->Pt1.x;  pts[1] = Obj->Pt1.y; // Store the line's end
  pts[2] = Obj->Pt2.x;  pts[3] = Obj->Pt2.y; // points in an array
  WTranslatePoly(pts, 2, -cx, -cy);
  WRotatePoly(pts, 2, angle);
  WTranslatePoly(pts, 2, cx, cy);
  Obj->Pt1.x = pts[0] + 0.5;  Obj->Pt1.y = pts[1] + 0.5;
  Obj->Pt2.x = pts[2] + 0.5;  Obj->Pt2.y = pts[3] + 0.5;
}

// Save the line's information
void TLineObj::Save(FILE *fp)
{
  fprintf(fp, "%d %d %ld %d %d %d %d\n", LINEOBJ, Obj->PC->PenWd,
    Obj->PC->PenColor, Obj->Pt1.x, Obj->Pt1.y, Obj->Pt2.x, Obj->Pt2.y);
}

// A line does not have a bounding rectangle. Instead, handles are
// only placed on the endpoints of the line.
void TLineObj::DrawHandles(HDC hDC, double zoom, int offsx, int offsy)
{
  int oldROP = SetROP2(hDC, R2_XORPEN);
  HBRUSH hOldBrush = HBRUSH(
    SelectObject(hDC, GetStockObject(WHITE_BRUSH)));
  HPEN hOldPen = HPEN(SelectObject(hDC, GetStockObject(WHITE_PEN)));
  Rectangle(hDC, Obj->Pt1.x*zoom-offsx-HANDLEWD+0.5,
    Obj->Pt1.y*zoom-offsy-HANDLEWD+0.5, Obj->Pt1.x*zoom-offsx+HANDLEWD+0.5,
    Obj->Pt1.y*zoom-offsy+HANDLEWD + 0.5);
  Rectangle(hDC, Obj->Pt2.x*zoom-offsx-HANDLEWD+0.5,
    Obj->Pt2.y*zoom-offsy-HANDLEWD+0.5, Obj->Pt2.x*zoom-offsx+HANDLEWD+0.5,
    Obj->Pt2.y*zoom-offsy+HANDLEWD+0.5);
```

```
    SelectObject(hDC, hOldPen);
    SelectObject(hDC, hOldBrush);
    SetROP2(hDC, oldROP);
}


// Don't draw a frame around a line while resizing it. However, when
// moving the line (moving is TRUE), do draw a frame.
void TLineObj::DrawResizingObject(HDC hDC, RECT& frame, double zoom,
  int offsx, int offsy, BOOL moving)
{
  if (moving)
    TGObject::DrawResizingObject(hDC, frame, zoom, offsx, offsy, moving);
  else {
    int hOldROP = SetROP2(hDC, R2_XORPEN);
    // While exclusive-ORing the line, make sure to use a white pen!
    HPEN hOldPen = HPEN(SelectObject(hDC, GetStockObject(WHITE_PEN)));
    MoveToEx(hDC, (Obj->Pt1.x-offsx)*zoom+0.5,
      (Obj->Pt1.y-offsy)*zoom+0.5, 0);
    LineTo(hDC, (Obj->Pt2.x-offsx)*zoom+0.5, (Obj->Pt2.y-offsy)*zoom+0.5);
    SelectObject(hDC, hOldPen);
    SetROP2(hDC, hOldROP);
  }
}


// Draw the object while it is being resized. The point pt is in mouse
// coordinates and specifies where the new point is. handleId indicates
// which point of the object is being moved.
void TLineObj::Resize(HDC, POINT& pt, int handleId,
  double zoom, int offsx, int offsy)
{
  switch (handleId) {  // Which handle of the line is being moved?
    case NWHANDLE:      // Pt1 is being moved
      Obj->Pt1.x = (pt.x + offsx) / zoom + 0.5;
      Obj->Pt1.y = (pt.y + offsy) / zoom + 0.5;
      break;
    case SEHANDLE:      // Pt2 is being moved
      Obj->Pt2.x = (pt.x + offsx) / zoom + 0.5;
      Obj->Pt2.y = (pt.y + offsy) / zoom + 0.5;
      break;
    default: return;    // Error: invalid resizing handle for a line
  }
}


// Returns TRUE if the specified point is on the line. Parametric
// equations are used to determine if p is on the line.
BOOL TLineObj::PtOnFrame(RECT*, POINT& pt)
{
  POINT ptb = pt;
  if (abs(Obj->Pt1.y-Obj->Pt2.y) > abs(Obj->Pt1.x-Obj->Pt2.x)) {
    // The line is steep. Allow for a slight variation in x.
    for (ptb.x=pt.x-HANDLEWD; ptb.x<pt.x+HANDLEWD; ptb.x++)
      if (PtOnLine(Obj->Pt1, Obj->Pt2, ptb)) return TRUE;
  }
```

```
    else {   // The line is shallow. Allow for a slight variation in y.
      for (ptb.y=pt.y-HANDLEWD; ptb.y<pt.y+HANDLEWD; ptb.y++)
        if (PtOnLine(Obj->Pt1, Obj->Pt2, ptb)) return TRUE;
    }
    return FALSE;
}

BOOL TLineObj::PtInObject(POINT& pt)
{
  return PtOnLine(Obj->Pt1, Obj->Pt2, pt);
}

TRectangleObj::TRectangleObj(HWND window, int x1, int y1, int x2, int y2,
  int penWd, COLORREF penColor, COLORREF brushColor, TPaintContext* pc,
  BOOL allocObj) : TGObject(window, x1, y1, x2, y2, penWd, penColor,
  brushColor, pc)
{
  if (allocObj) {
    Obj = new TRectangleTool();
    Obj->Pt1.x = x1;    Obj->Pt1.y = y1;
    Obj->Pt2.x = x2;    Obj->Pt2.y = y2;
    Obj->PC = new TPaintContext(*pc);
    Obj->PC->PenWd = penWd;
    Obj->PC->PenColor = penColor;
    Obj->PC->BrushColor = brushColor;
  }
}

// Update the size of the frame based on the handle being stretched and
// the current point pt. Don't let rectangular objects fold back on
// themselves. They must stay greater than some minimum size. Otherwise,
// you'll run into problems with the figures being off by one in size.
void TRectangleObj::ResizeFrame(RECT& frame, int handleId, POINT& pt,
  TPaintContext* pc)
{
  int minsize = HANDLEWD * 3;
  switch(handleId) {
    case NWHANDLE:
      frame.left = (pt.x+pc->Offsx/pc->Zoom <= frame.right-minsize) ?
        pt.x+pc->Offsx/pc->Zoom + 0.5 : frame.right-minsize;
      frame.top = (pt.y+pc->Offsy/pc->Zoom <= frame.bottom-minsize) ?
        pt.y+pc->Offsy/pc->Zoom + 0.5 : frame.bottom-minsize;
      break;
    case NEHANDLE:
      frame.right = (pt.x+pc->Offsx/pc->Zoom >= frame.left+minsize) ?
        pt.x+pc->Offsx/pc->Zoom + 0.5 : frame.left+minsize;
      frame.top = (pt.y+pc->Offsy/pc->Zoom <= frame.bottom-minsize) ?
        pt.y+pc->Offsy/pc->Zoom + 0.5 : frame.bottom-minsize;
      break;
    case SEHANDLE:
      frame.right = (pt.x+pc->Offsx/pc->Zoom >= frame.left+minsize) ?
        pt.x+pc->Offsx/pc->Zoom + 0.5 : frame.left+minsize;
      frame.bottom = (pt.y+pc->Offsy/pc->Zoom >= frame.top+minsize) ?
        pt.y+pc->Offsy/pc->Zoom + 0.5 : frame.top+minsize;
```

```
          break;
        case SWHANDLE:
          frame.left = (pt.x+pc->Offsx/pc->Zoom <= frame.right-minsize) ?
            pt.x+pc->Offsx/pc->Zoom + 0.5 : frame.right-minsize;
          frame.bottom = (pt.y+pc->Offsy/pc->Zoom >= frame.top+minsize) ?
            pt.y+pc->Offsy/pc->Zoom + 0.5 : frame.top+minsize;
          break;
      }
    }

// Determine if the point pt is on one of the object's handles. If so,
// return the handle's ID. (Handles are used to resize the object.)
int TRectangleObj::PtOnResizeHandle(POINT& pt, double zoom, POINT& hPt)
{
  int handleId = TGObject::PtOnResizeHandle(pt, zoom, hPt);
  if (handleId == NOHANDLE) {
    // A rectangle has two additional resize handles--one
    // at each of the additional two corners of the rectangle
    POINT p;
    p.x = Obj->Pt2.x;  p.y = Obj->Pt1.y;
    if (PtInArea(pt, p, HANDLEWD)) {
      hPt = p;  return NEHANDLE;
    }
    p.x = Obj->Pt1.x;  p.y = Obj->Pt2.y;
    if (PtInArea(pt, p, HANDLEWD)) {
      hPt = p;  return SWHANDLE;
    }
    return NOHANDLE;
  }
  else
    return handleId;
}

// Scale the rectangle to fit inside the "size" rectangle. The
// handleId point should not change.
void TRectangleObj::ScaleToRect(int handleId, RECT& size)
{
  int nuWd = size.right - size.left;
  int nuHt = size.bottom - size.top;
  switch(handleId) {
    case SEHANDLE:  // Point 2 was moved
      Obj->Pt2.x = Obj->Pt1.x + nuWd;  Obj->Pt2.y = Obj->Pt1.y + nuHt;
      break;
    case SWHANDLE:    // Southwestern point was moved
      Obj->Pt1.x = Obj->Pt2.x - nuWd;  Obj->Pt2.y = Obj->Pt1.y + nuHt;
      break;
    case NWHANDLE:    // Point 1 was moved
      Obj->Pt1.x = Obj->Pt2.x - nuWd;  Obj->Pt1.y = Obj->Pt2.y - nuHt;
      break;
    case NEHANDLE:    // Northeastern point was moved
      Obj->Pt2.x = Obj->Pt1.x + nuWd;  Obj->Pt1.y = Obj->Pt2.y - nuHt;
      break;
  }
}
```

```
// Save a rectangle object to a file
void TRectangleObj::Save(FILE *fp)
{
  fprintf(fp, "%d %d %ld %ld %d %d %d %d\n", RECTANGLEOBJ,
    Obj->PC->PenWd, Obj->PC->PenColor, Obj->PC->BrushColor,
    Obj->Pt1.x, Obj->Pt1.y, Obj->Pt2.x, Obj->Pt2.y);
}

// Constructor for an empty rectangle object
TEmptyRectangleObj::TEmptyRectangleObj(HWND window, int x1, int y1,
  int x2, int y2, int penWd, COLORREF penColor, TPaintContext* pc,
  BOOL allocObj) : TRectangleObj(window, x1, y1, x2, y2, penWd,
  penColor, 0, pc, FALSE)
{
  if (allocObj) {
    Obj = new TEmptyRectangleTool();
    Obj->Pt1.x = x1;    Obj->Pt1.y = y1;
    Obj->Pt2.x = x2;    Obj->Pt2.y = y2;
    Obj->PC = new TPaintContext(*pc);
    Obj->PC->PenWd = penWd;
    Obj->PC->PenColor = penColor;
  }
}

// Save an empty rectangle object to a file
void TEmptyRectangleObj::Save(FILE *fp)
{
  fprintf(fp, "%d %d %ld %d %d %d %d\n", EMPTYRECTANGLEOBJ,
    Obj->PC->PenWd, Obj->PC->PenColor, Obj->Pt1.x, Obj->Pt1.y,
    Obj->Pt2.x, Obj->Pt2.y);
}

TEllipseObj::TEllipseObj(HWND window, int x1, int y1, int x2, int y2,
  int penWd, COLORREF penColor, COLORREF brushColor, TPaintContext* pc,
  BOOL allocObj) : TRectangleObj(window, x1, y1, x2, y2, penWd,
  penColor, brushColor, pc, FALSE)
{
  if (allocObj) {
    Obj = new TEllipseTool();
    Obj->Pt1.x = x1;    Obj->Pt1.y = y1;
    Obj->Pt2.x = x2;    Obj->Pt2.y = y2;
    Obj->PC = new TPaintContext(*pc);
    Obj->PC->PenWd = penWd;
    Obj->PC->PenColor = penColor;
    Obj->PC->BrushColor = brushColor;
  }
}

// Save the ellipse object to a file
void TEllipseObj::Save(FILE *fp)
{
  fprintf(fp, "%d %d %ld %ld %d %d %d %d\n", ELLIPSEOBJ,
    Obj->PC->PenWd, Obj->PC->PenColor, Obj->PC->BrushColor,
```

```
        Obj->Pt1.x, Obj->Pt1.y, Obj->Pt2.x, Obj->Pt2.y);
}

TEmptyEllipseObj::TEmptyEllipseObj(HWND window, int x1, int y1,
  int x2, int y2, int penWd, COLORREF penColor, TPaintContext* pc,
  BOOL allocObj) : TEllipseObj(window, x1, y1, x2, y2, penWd,
  penColor, 0, pc, FALSE)
{
  if (allocObj) {
    Obj = new TEmptyEllipseTool();
    Obj->Pt1.x = x1;      Obj->Pt1.y = y1;
    Obj->Pt2.x = x2;      Obj->Pt2.y = y2;
    Obj->PC = new TPaintContext(*pc);
    Obj->PC->PenWd = penWd;
    Obj->PC->PenColor = penColor;
  }
}

// Save an empty ellipse object to a file
void TEmptyEllipseObj::Save(FILE *fp)
{
  fprintf(fp, "%d %d %ld %d %d %d %d\n", EMPTYELLIPSEOBJ, Obj->PC->PenWd,
    Obj->PC->PenColor, Obj->Pt1.x, Obj->Pt1.y, Obj->Pt2.x, Obj->Pt2.y);
}

TPolylineObj::TPolylineObj(HWND window, POINT points[], int numPts,
  int penWd, COLORREF penColor, TPaintContext* pc, BOOL allocObj) :
  TGObject(window, penWd, penColor, 0, 0, pc)
{
  if (allocObj) {
    Obj = new TPolylineTool();
    TPolylineTool* obj = (TPolylineTool *)Obj;
    CopyPoly(points, numPts, obj->Poly);
    obj->NumPts = numPts;
    obj->PC = new TPaintContext(*pc);
    obj->PC->PenWd = penWd;
    obj->PC->PenColor = penColor;
  }
}

// Scale the polygon's settings by the scale factor
void TPolylineObj::Scale(float scale)
{
  for (int i=0; i<((TPolylineTool *)Obj)->NumPts; i++) {
    ((TPolylineTool *)Obj)->Poly[i].x =
      ((TPolylineTool *)Obj)->Poly[i].x * scale + 0.5;
    ((TPolylineTool *)Obj)->Poly[i].y =
      ((TPolylineTool *)Obj)->Poly[i].y * scale + 0.5;
  }
}

// Offset the polygon's location by the value in the pt
void TPolylineObj::Offset(POINT& pt)
```

```
{
  for (int i=0; i<((TPolylineTool *)Obj)->NumPts; i++) {
    ((TPolylineTool *)Obj)->Poly[i].x += pt.x;
    ((TPolylineTool *)Obj)->Poly[i].y += pt.y;
  }
}

// Place the bounds of the polygon into the DevBounds rectangle
void TPolylineObj::UpdateBounds()
{
  RECT rect;
  rect.left = 32767;   rect.right = -32767;
  rect.top = 32767;    rect.bottom = -32767;
  TPolylineTool* obj = (TPolylineTool *)Obj;
  for (int i=0; i<obj->NumPts; i++) {
    if (obj->Poly[i].x < rect.left) rect.left = obj->Poly[i].x;
    if (obj->Poly[i].x > rect.right) rect.right = obj->Poly[i].x;
    if (obj->Poly[i].y < rect.top) rect.top = obj->Poly[i].y;
    if (obj->Poly[i].y > rect.bottom) rect.bottom = obj->Poly[i].y;
  }
  DevBounds = rect;
  Obj->Pt1.x = DevBounds.left;    Obj->Pt1.y = DevBounds.top;
  Obj->Pt2.x = DevBounds.right;   Obj->Pt2.y = DevBounds.bottom;
}

// Rotate a polygon by the amount in "angle"
void TPolylineObj::Rotate(double angle)
{
  int numPts = ((TPolylineTool *)Obj)->NumPts;
  double *wPoints = new double[numPts*2];
  if (!wPoints) {
    MessageBox(GetActiveWindow(), "Out of Memory",
      GetApplicationObject()->GetName(), MB_OK | MB_ICONEXCLAMATION);
    return;
  }
  UpdateBounds();  // Get the current object's bounds
  double cx = (DevBounds.left + DevBounds.right) / 2.0;
  double cy = (DevBounds.top + DevBounds.bottom) / 2.0;
  CopyToWPoly(((TPolylineTool *)Obj)->Poly, numPts, wPoints);
  WTranslatePoly(wPoints, numPts, -cx, -cy);
  WRotatePoly(wPoints, numPts, angle);
  WTranslatePoly(wPoints, numPts, cx, cy);
  CopyFromWPoly(wPoints, numPts, ((TPolylineTool *)Obj)->Poly);
}

void TPolylineObj::Translate(int transx, int transy)
{
  TPolylineTool* obj = (TPolylineTool *)Obj;
  for (int i=0; i<obj->NumPts; i++) {
    obj->Poly[i].x += transx;   obj->Poly[i].y += transy;
  }
  UpdateBounds();   // Update the bounds of the polygon
}
```

```cpp
void TPolylineObj::DrawHandles(HDC hDC, double zoom,
  int offsx, int offsy)
{
  TGObject::DrawHandles(hDC, zoom, offsx, offsy);
  // In addition to drawing the bounding box, draw white,
  // exclusive-ORed rectangles over each segment's endpoint
  int oldROP = SetROP2(hDC, R2_XORPEN);
  HBRUSH hOldBrush = HBRUSH(SelectObject(hDC,
    GetStockObject(BLACK_BRUSH)));
  HPEN hOldPen = HPEN(SelectObject(hDC, GetStockObject(WHITE_PEN)));
  TPolylineTool* gObj = (TPolylineTool *)Obj;
  for (int i=0; i<gObj->NumPts; i++)
    Rectangle(hDC, gObj->Poly[i].x*zoom-offsx-HANDLEWD+0.5,
      gObj->Poly[i].y*zoom-offsy-HANDLEWD+0.5,
      gObj->Poly[i].x*zoom-offsx+HANDLEWD+0.5,
      gObj->Poly[i].y*zoom-offsy+HANDLEWD+0.5);
  SelectObject(hDC, hOldPen);
  SelectObject(hDC, hOldBrush);
  SetROP2(hDC, oldROP);
}

// Determine if the point pt is on one of the object's resize
// handles. If so, return the handle's ID.
int TPolylineObj::PtOnResizeHandle(POINT& pt, double zoom, POINT& hPt)
{
  int handleId = TGObject::PtOnResizeHandle(pt, zoom, hPt);
  if (handleId != NOHANDLE)
    return handleId;
  else if (handleId == NOHANDLE) {
    // A rectangle has to additional resize handles--one
    // at each of the additional two corners of the rectangle
    POINT p;
    p.x = Obj->Pt2.x;  p.y = Obj->Pt1.y;
    if (PtInArea(pt, p, HANDLEWD)) {
      hPt = p;  return NEHANDLE;
    }
    p.x = Obj->Pt1.x;  p.y = Obj->Pt2.y;
    if (PtInArea(pt, p, HANDLEWD)) {
      hPt = p;  return SWHANDLE;
    }
  }
  return NOHANDLE;
}

// Determine if the point pt is near one of the points in the
// polygon. If so, return that point's index.
int TPolylineObj::PtOnReshapeHandle(POINT& pt, double zoom)
{
  POINT pt2;
  pt2.x = pt.x * zoom;  pt2.y = pt.y * zoom;
  TPolylineTool* obj = (TPolylineTool *)Obj;
  int handleId = PtOnPoint(obj->Poly, obj->NumPts, pt2);
  if (handleId >= 0)    // Is pt on one of the object's points?
```

```
      return handleId;     // Return the handle
    return NOHANDLE;       // pt was not near any of the points
}

// Return TRUE if the point pt is on the polygon's boundary. This is
// done by testing whether pt is on one of the polygon's line segments.
BOOL PtOnPolygon(POINT& pt, POINT poly[], int numPts)
{
  for (int i=1; i<numPts; i++)
    if (PtOnLine(poly[i-1], poly[i], pt)) return TRUE;
  return FALSE;
}

// See if pt is inside the object or on its boundary
BOOL TPolylineObj::PtInObject(POINT& pt)
{
  RECT rect;
  TPolylineTool* obj = (TPolylineTool *)Obj;
  CopyRect(&rect, GetBounds(FALSE));
  if (PtInRect(&rect, pt)) return TRUE;
    // You have to test whether pt is on the border, because if the
    // polygon is just a straight line, the code wouldn't select it
    else return PtOnPolygon(pt, obj->Poly, obj->NumPts);
}

// Return the index of the point in the poly array that the
// coordinate pt is near. If pt is not near any point, return -1.
int PtOnPoint(POINT poly[], int numPts, POINT& pt)
{
  for (int i=0; i<numPts; i++)
    if (PtInArea(pt, poly[i], HANDLEWD))
      return i;
  return -1;
}

// Scale the polygon to fit inside the "size" rectangle. The handleId
// point should not change. Note: If the object is currently just a
// vertical or horizontal line (the width or height is 0), this routine
// won't have any affect on the object.
void TPolylineObj::ScaleToRect(int handleId, RECT& size)
{
  TPolylineTool* obj = (TPolylineTool *)Obj;
  RECT rect;
  CopyRect(&rect, GetBounds(FALSE));
  float wd = rect.right - rect.left;
  float ht = rect.bottom - rect.top;
  float nuWd = size.right - size.left;
  float nuHt = size.bottom - size.top;
  int i;
  switch(handleId) {
    case SEHANDLE:  // Point 2 was moved
      for (i=0; i<obj->NumPts; i++) {
        obj->Poly[i].x = (wd == 0) ? rect.left :
```

```
            rect.left + nuWd / wd * (obj->Poly[i].x - rect.left);
          obj->Poly[i].y = (ht == 0) ? rect.top :
            rect.top + nuHt / ht * (obj->Poly[i].y - rect.top);
        }
        break;
    case SWHANDLE:    // Southwestern point was moved
        for (i=0; i<obj->NumPts; i++) {
          obj->Poly[i].x = (wd == 0) ? rect.right :
            rect.right + nuWd / wd * (obj->Poly[i].x - rect.right);
          obj->Poly[i].y = (ht == 0) ? rect.top :
            rect.top + nuHt / ht * (obj->Poly[i].y - rect.top);
        }
        break;
    case NWHANDLE:    // Point 1 was moved
        for (i=0; i<obj->NumPts; i++) {
          obj->Poly[i].x = (wd == 0) ? rect.right :
            rect.right + nuWd / wd * (obj->Poly[i].x - rect.right);
          obj->Poly[i].y = (ht == 0) ? rect.bottom :
            rect.bottom + nuHt / ht * (obj->Poly[i].y - rect.bottom);
        }
        break;
    case NEHANDLE:
        for (i=0; i<obj->NumPts; i++) {
          obj->Poly[i].x = (wd == 0) ? rect.left :
            rect.left + nuWd / wd * (obj->Poly[i].x - rect.left);
          obj->Poly[i].y = (ht == 0) ? rect.bottom :
            rect.bottom + nuHt / ht * (obj->Poly[i].y - rect.bottom);
        }
        break;
  }
  UpdateBounds();
}


// Move the point in the polygon--that corresponds to the
// ID handleId--to the point pt.
void TPolylineObj::Reshape(int handleId, POINT& pt, BOOL ignore)
{
  if (ignore) return;
  TPolylineTool* obj = (TPolylineTool *)Obj;
  // For safety sake, is handleId valid? If not, quit.
  if (handleId < 0 || handleId >= obj->NumPts) return;
  obj->Poly[handleId] = pt;
  UpdateBounds();
}


// Save the series of line segments to a file
void TPolylineObj::Save(FILE *fp)
{
  TPolylineTool* obj = (TPolylineTool *)Obj;
  fprintf(fp, "%d %ld %d %d", POLYLINEOBJ,
    Obj->PC->PenWd, Obj->PC->PenColor, obj->NumPts);
  for (int i=0; i<obj->NumPts; i++)
    fprintf(fp, " %d %d", obj->Poly[i].x, obj->Poly[i].y);
```

```
    fprintf(fp, "\n");
}

TPolygonObj::TPolygonObj(HWND window, POINT points[], int numPts,
  int penWd, COLORREF penColor, COLORREF brushColor, TPaintContext* pc,
  BOOL allocObj) : TPolylineObj(window, points, numPts, penWd,
  penColor, pc, FALSE)
{
  if (allocObj) {
    Obj = new TPolygonTool();
    TPolygonTool* obj = (TPolygonTool *)Obj;
    CopyPoly(points, numPts, obj->Poly);
    obj->NumPts = numPts;
    obj->PC = new TPaintContext(*pc);
    obj->PC->PenWd = penWd;
    obj->PC->PenColor = penColor;
    obj->PC->BrushColor = brushColor;
  }
}

// Save the settings for this closed polygon
void TPolygonObj::Save(FILE *fp)
{
  TPolygonTool* obj = (TPolygonTool *)Obj;
  fprintf(fp, "%d %d %ld %ld %d", POLYGONOBJ, Obj->PC->PenWd,
    Obj->PC->PenColor, Obj->PC->BrushColor, obj->NumPts);
  for (int i=0; i<obj->NumPts; i++)
    fprintf(fp, " %d %d", obj->Poly[i].x, obj->Poly[i].y);
  fprintf(fp, "\n");
}

TTextObj::TTextObj(HWND window, int x1, int y1, int x2, int y2, int wd,
  int ht, char* string, COLORREF penColor, TPaintContext* pc,
  BOOL allocObj) : TRectangleObj(window, x1, y1, x2, y2, 0, penColor,
  0, pc, FALSE)
{
  if (allocObj) {
    Obj = new TTextTool();
    Obj->Pt1.x = x1;    Obj->Pt1.y = y1;
    Obj->Pt2.x = x2;    Obj->Pt2.y = y2;
    TTextTool* obj = (TTextTool *)Obj;
    lstrcpy(obj->Str, string);
    obj->Wd = wd;
    obj->Ht = ht;
    obj->PC = new TPaintContext(*pc);
    obj->PC->PenColor = penColor;
  }
}

// Reshaping text works differently than for the other objects.
// Clicking anywhere inside the boundary of the text brings up the
// edit dialog box so the user can edit the text.
int TTextObj::PtOnReshapeHandle(POINT& pt, double zoom)
```

```
{
  POINT pt2;
  pt2.x = pt.x * zoom;  pt2.y = pt.y * zoom;
  RECT frame;
  int temp;
  if (Obj->Pt1.x > Obj->Pt2.x) {
    temp = Obj->Pt1.x;  Obj->Pt1.x = Obj->Pt2.x;  Obj->Pt2.x = temp;
  }
  if (Obj->Pt1.y > Obj->Pt2.y) {
    temp = Obj->Pt1.y;  Obj->Pt1.y = Obj->Pt2.y;  Obj->Pt2.y = temp;
  }
  frame.left = Obj->Pt1.x;    frame.right = Obj->Pt2.x;
  frame.top = Obj->Pt1.y;     frame.bottom = Obj->Pt2.y;
  return PtInRect(&frame, pt2);
}

// Scale the text to fit inside the "size" rectangle. The
// handleId point should not change. The code assumes that the size
// of the bounding rectangle is not negative.
void TTextObj::ScaleToRect(int handleId, RECT& size)
{
  TRectangleObj::ScaleToRect(handleId, size);
  int nuWd = size.right - size.left;
  int nuHt = size.bottom - size.top;
  TTextTool* obj = (TTextTool *)Obj;
  SIZE chSize;
  obj->GetTextSize(chSize);
  obj->Wd = (chSize.cx > 0) ? (float)nuWd / chSize.cx : 0;
  obj->Ht = (chSize.cy > 0) ? (float)nuHt / chSize.cy : 0;
  // Determine a font width and height that will make the string
  // fit exactly inside the bounds of the resized frame
  HDC hDC = GetDC(0);   // Use the main screen to figure out
  BOOL done = FALSE;    // what font to use since it's handy
  while (!done) {
    // Create the new font
    HFONT hFont = CreateFont(obj->Ht, obj->Wd, 0, 0, 0, 0,
      0, 0, 0, 0, 0, 0, 0, "Arial");
    HFONT hOldFont = HFONT(SelectObject(hDC, hFont));
    SIZE size;     // Calculate the extents of the text
    GetTextExtentPoint(hDC, obj->Str, lstrlen(obj->Str), &size);
    done = TRUE;
    if (size.cx > nuWd) {
      // Cut the text back in width by the scale factor
      // that the text extends beyond the desired boundary
      if (obj->Wd) {
        obj->Wd *= ((float)nuWd / size.cx);
        done = FALSE;
      }
    }
    if (size.cy > nuHt) {
      if (obj->Ht) {
        obj->Ht *= ((float)nuHt / size.cy);
        done = FALSE;
      }
```

```
      }
      SelectObject(hDC, hOldFont);
      DeleteObject(hOldFont);
   }
   ReleaseDC(0, hDC);
}

// Reshaping text actually allows the user to edit the text string
void TTextObj::Reshape(int, POINT&, BOOL ignore)
{
   if (!ignore) return;   // Text uses the inverse of this flag
   TTextTool* obj = (TTextTool *)Obj;
   // Pop up a dialog box that retrieves the string to display
   if (TInputDialog(obj->PC->OWLWindow, "Text", "Edit text:",
      obj->Str, MAXSTRING).Execute() == IDOK) {
      // Using the same font, determine the new text's bounding box
      HFONT hFont = CreateFont(obj->Ht, obj->Wd, 0, 0, FW_NORMAL, 0, 0, 0,
         ANSI_CHARSET, OUT_DEFAULT_PRECIS, CLIP_DEFAULT_PRECIS,
         DEFAULT_QUALITY, FF_SWISS | 0x04, "Arial");
      HDC hDC = GetDC(obj->PC->DrawingWnd);
      HFONT hOldFont = HFONT(SelectObject(hDC, hFont));
      SIZE size;     // Calculate the extents of the text
      GetTextExtentPoint(hDC, obj->Str, lstrlen(obj->Str), &size);
      // The top-left position of the text doesn't change, but
      // recalculate the right-bottom edge of the new text
      POINT apt;
      apt.x = size.cx;    apt.y = size.cy;
      apt = obj->PC->SnapToGrid(apt);
      obj->Pt2.x = obj->Pt1.x + apt.x;   obj->Pt2.y = obj->Pt1.y + apt.y;
      ReleaseDC(obj->PC->DrawingWnd, hDC);
      SelectObject(hDC, hOldFont);
      DeleteObject(hFont);
   }
}

// Save the text object to a file
void TTextObj::Save(FILE *fp)
{
   TTextTool* obj = (TTextTool *)Obj;
   fprintf(fp, "%d %ld %d %d %d %d %d %d %d %s\n", TEXTOBJ,
      Obj->PC->PenColor, Obj->Pt1.x, Obj->Pt1.y, Obj->Pt2.x, Obj->Pt2.y,
      obj->Wd, obj->Ht, lstrlen(obj->Str), obj->Str);
}

// Copies from one world polygon to another
void CopyToWPoly(POINT polyFrom[], int numPoints, double polyTo[])
{
   for (int i=0; i<numPoints; i++) {
      polyTo[i*2] = polyFrom[i].x;   polyTo[i*2+1] = polyFrom[i].y;
   }
}

// Copies from one world polygon to another
void CopyFromWPoly(double polyFrom[], int numPoints, POINT polyTo[])
```

```
{
  for (int i=0; i<numPoints; i++) {
    polyTo[i].x = polyFrom[i*2] + 0.5;
    polyTo[i].y = polyFrom[i*2+1] + 0.5;
  }
}

// Rotates a polygon by the number of degrees specified
// in Angle. The polygon must be in world coordinates.
void WRotatePoly(double poly[], int numPoints, double angle)
{
  double x, y, radians, cosTheta, sinTheta;
  radians = ToRadians(angle);
  cosTheta = cos(radians);   sinTheta = sin(radians);
  for (int i=0; i<numPoints; i++) {
    x = poly[i*2];     y = poly[i*2+1];
    poly[i*2] = x * cosTheta - y * sinTheta;
    poly[i*2+1] = x * sinTheta + y * cosTheta;
  }
}

// Translates a two-dimensional polygon by tx and ty.
// The polygon should be in world coordinates.
void WTranslatePoly(double poly[], int numPoints, double tx, double ty)
{
  for (int i=0; i<numPoints; i++) {
    poly[i*2] = poly[i*2] + tx;   poly[i*2+1] = poly[i*2+1] + ty;
  }
}

// Return TRUE if the coordinate pt is within "range" units from
// the coordinate "center"
BOOL PtInArea(POINT& pt, POINT& center, int range)
{
  return (center.x-range <= pt.x && pt.x <= center.x+range &&
    center.y-range <= pt.y && pt.y <= center.y+range) ? TRUE : FALSE;
}

// This function returns TRUE if the point pt is on a line segment
// that connects the points pt1 and pt2
BOOL PtOnLine(POINT& pt1, POINT& pt2, POINT& pt)
{
  double t, x, y, deltax = pt2.x - pt1.x;
  double deltay = pt2.y - pt1.y;
  if (fabs(deltax) > 0 && fabs(deltay) < fabs(deltax)) {
    t = (double)(pt.x - pt1.x) / (pt2.x - pt1.x);
    if (t >= 0 && t <= 1) {
      y = pt1.y + (pt2.y - pt1.y) * t;
      if (y-HANDLEWD <= pt.y && pt.y <= y+HANDLEWD)
        return TRUE;    // The point is near the line
    }
    return FALSE;
  }
```

```
  else if (fabs(deltay) > 0) {
    // The line is a vertical line
    t = (double)(pt.y - pt1.y) / (pt2.y - pt1.y);
    if (t >= 0 && t <= 1) {
      x = pt1.x + (pt2.x - pt1.x) * t;
      if (x-HANDLEWD <= pt.x && pt.x <= x+HANDLEWD)
        return TRUE;   // The point is near the line
    }
    return FALSE;
  }
  return FALSE;
}

// Offset the point pt by x and y
POINT OffsetPt(POINT& pt, int x, int y)
{
  pt.x += x;  pt.y += y;
  return pt;
}

// Scale the point pt by the scale factor
POINT ScalePt(POINT& scaledPt, POINT& pt, float scale)
{
  scaledPt.x = pt.x * scale + 0.5;  scaledPt.y = pt.y * scale + 0.5;
  return scaledPt;
}

// Scale the points in rect by the scale factor
RECT ScaleRect(RECT& scaledRect, RECT& rect, float scale)
{
  scaledRect.left = rect.left * scale + 0.5;
  scaledRect.top = rect.top * scale + 0.5;
  scaledRect.right = rect.right * scale + 0.5;
  scaledRect.bottom = rect.bottom * scale + 0.5;
  return scaledRect;
}
```

● GOBJLIST.H

```
// GOBJLIST.H: Defines a class that maintains a list of all the
// graphics figure objects that have been drawn.
#ifndef GOBJLISTH
#define GOBJLISTH

#include <stdio.h>
#include "gobject.h"
#include "draw.h"

// Maximum number of figures that can be placed in a scene
const int NUMGOBJECTS = 100;
// This class is used to maintain the list of figures currently
// displayed in the drawing window
class TGObjList {
```

```
public:
  TGObject* GObjects[NUMGOBJECTS]; // List of graphics figures
  TGObject* CopyBuffer;            // Cut and paste object buffer
  int NextObj;                     // Number of graphics objects
  int SelectedObj;                 // Currently selected object
  int PrevSelectedObj;             // Previously selected object
  TPaintContext* PC;
  BYTE Dirty;                      // TRUE if the drawing has changed
  TGObjList(TPaintContext* pc) {
    NextObj = 0;                   // The object list is empty
    SelectedObj = PrevSelectedObj = -1;  // No object is selected yet
    PC = pc;
    CopyBuffer = 0;                // The paste buffer is empty
    Dirty = FALSE;                 // The drawing window has not changed
  }
  ~TGObjList();
  void DisplayAll(HDC hDC);
  void Add(TGObject* Obj);
  void Delete();
  void DeleteAll();
  void FlipToBack();
  void FlipToFront();
  void Rotate(double angle);
  int Read(FILE* fp);
  void Save(FILE* fp);
  void Copy();
  BOOL Empty() { return (NextObj == 0) ? TRUE : FALSE; }
  BOOL ObjectSelected() { return (SelectedObj == -1) ? FALSE : TRUE; }
  int SetSelectedObj(int selectedObj);
  void Repaint(int obj, RECT* bounds);
};
#endif
```

• GOBJLIST.CPP

```
// GOBJLIST.CPP: The TGObjList class manages the TGObject graphics
// objects drawn in OODRAW.CPP.
#include <owl\applicat.h>
#include <owl\framewin.h>
#include <owl\dc.h>
#include "draw.h"
#include "gobjlist.h"
#include "gobject.h"

// Free each object in the figure list
TGObjList::~TGObjList()
{
  for (int i=0; i<NextObj; i++) delete(GObjects[i]);
}

// Display all of the graphics objects in the drawing window
void TGObjList::DisplayAll(HDC hDC)
{
```

```
    if (NextObj <= 0) return;
    for (int obj=0; obj<NextObj; obj++)
      GObjects[obj]->Display(hDC, PC->Zoom);    // Display each object
    if (SelectedObj >= 0)    // Draw handles around the selected object
      GObjects[SelectedObj]->DrawHandles(hDC, PC->Zoom, 0, 0);
}

// Set the selected object and return the previously selected object.
// This routine does not repaint the window, it just sets the index.
int TGObjList::SetSelectedObj(int selectedObj)
{
  int saveObj = SelectedObj;
  SelectedObj = selectedObj;
  return saveObj;
}

// Adds an object to the list of graphic objects in the drawing window
void TGObjList::Add(TGObject* obj)
{
  if (NextObj >= NUMGOBJECTS) {
    MessageBox(GetActiveWindow(), "Object list is full",
      GetApplicationObject()->GetName(), MB_OK);
    return;  // List is full. Do nothing.
  }
  GObjects[NextObj++] = obj;
  Dirty = TRUE;
}

// Delete the currently selected object from the object list. Update
// the screen after deleting the object from the list by erasing
// the drawing window and redrawing all remaining objects.
void TGObjList::Delete()
{
  if (SelectedObj == -1 && PrevSelectedObj == -1) return;
  // Restore the selected object, which gets reset after each
  // press of the rotate tool
  if (SelectedObj == -1) SelectedObj = PrevSelectedObj;
  RECT bounds;    // Save the bounds of the object about to be deleted
  CopyRect(&bounds, GObjects[SelectedObj]->GetBounds(FALSE));
  delete(GObjects[SelectedObj]);
  for (int i=SelectedObj; i<NextObj-1; i++)
    GObjects[i] = GObjects[i+1];
  NextObj--;
  SelectedObj = -1; // There is not a selected object
  Dirty = TRUE;
  Repaint(-1, &bounds); // Repaint the window where the object was
}

// Force the drawing window to repaint the object specified. If obj
// is -1 use the bounds parameter to specify the region to repaint.
void TGObjList::Repaint(int obj, RECT* bounds)
{
  RECT rect;
  if (obj >= 0)  // Use the specified object's bounds
```

```
      CopyRect(&rect, GObjects[obj]->GetBounds(FALSE));
    else
      CopyRect(&rect, bounds);
    OffsetRect(&rect, -PC->Offsx, -PC->Offsy);
    RECT scaledRect = ScaleRect(scaledRect, rect, PC->Zoom);
    InflateRect(&scaledRect, HANDLEWD, HANDLEWD);
    InvalidateRect(PC->DrawingWnd, &scaledRect, TRUE);
}

// Delete all objects in the object list. Clears the drawing window.
void TGObjList::DeleteAll()
{
    if (NextObj == 0) return;       // Empty list. No objects.
    for (int i=0; i<NextObj; i++) delete(GObjects[i]);
    NextObj = 0;
    SelectedObj = -1;
    Dirty = TRUE;
    InvalidateRect(PC->DrawingWnd, 0, TRUE); // Repaint the whole window
}

// Move the selected object to the back by copying it to the head
// of the object list
void TGObjList::FlipToBack()
{
    if (SelectedObj == -1 && PrevSelectedObj == -1) return;
    // Restore the selected object, which gets reset after each
    // press of the rotate tool
    if (SelectedObj == -1) SelectedObj = PrevSelectedObj;
    TGObject* temp = GObjects[SelectedObj];
    for (int i=SelectedObj; i>0; i--)
      GObjects[i] = GObjects[i-1];
    GObjects[0] = temp;
    SelectedObj = 0;
    Dirty = TRUE;
    Repaint(SelectedObj, 0); // Repaint area where object is
}

// Move the object to the front by putting it at the end of the
// object list and redrawing the area where the object is
void TGObjList::FlipToFront()
{
    if (SelectedObj == -1 && PrevSelectedObj == -1) return;
    // Restore the selected object, which gets reset after each
    // press of the rotate tool
    if (SelectedObj == -1) SelectedObj = PrevSelectedObj;
    TGObject* temp = GObjects[SelectedObj];
    for (int i=SelectedObj; i<NextObj-1; i++)
      GObjects[i] = GObjects[i+1];
    GObjects[i] = temp;
    SelectedObj = i;
    Dirty = TRUE;
    Repaint(SelectedObj, 0); // Repaint area where object is
}
```

```cpp
// Rotate the currently selected object about its center point. Note:
// Only polygons and lines can be supported.
void TGObjList::Rotate(double angle)
{
  if (SelectedObj == -1 && PrevSelectedObj == -1) return;
  // Restore the selected object, which gets reset after each
  // press of the rotate tool
  if (SelectedObj == -1) SelectedObj = PrevSelectedObj;
  // Get the bounds of the object before it is rotated
  RECT beforeBounds, afterBounds, clipRect;
  CopyRect(&beforeBounds, GObjects[SelectedObj]->GetBounds(TRUE));
  GObjects[SelectedObj]->Rotate(-angle);
  // Get the bounds of the newly rotated figure
  CopyRect(&afterBounds, GObjects[SelectedObj]->GetBounds(TRUE));
  Dirty = TRUE;
  // The clipping region is the union of the previous and
  // current bounds of the object. It's important to call GetBounds
  // above so that room is included for the handles,
  // otherwise, UnionRect will ignore vertical and horizontal lines
  // since their bounding boxes won't have any width or height.
  UnionRect(&clipRect, &beforeBounds, &afterBounds);
  Repaint(-1, &clipRect);
}


// Read the object data from the indicated file. Currently, this
// overwrites any existing object data. The return value is 1 if the
// function succeeds. Values less than 0 represent the following errors:
//       -1  : Incorrect file format
//       -2  : Unexpected end of file
int TGObjList::Read(FILE* fp)
{
  char buffer[MAXSTRING];
  POINT p[MAXPOLYSIZE*4];
  // The string "OODRAW2" must appear at the top of the file
  fscanf(fp, "%8s", buffer);
  if (lstrcmp(buffer, "OODRAW2") != 0) return -1;
  // Delete all the existing objects in the drawing. Remember if
  // there weren't any objects at all.
  BOOL objectsExist = (NextObj > 0) ? TRUE : FALSE;
  for (int i=0; i<NextObj; i++)
    delete(GObjects[i]);
  NextObj = 0;
  int objType, numObj, t1, t2, t3, t4, t5, t6, t7, j;
  COLORREF pc, bc;
  TGObject *obj;
  fscanf(fp, "%d", &numObj);
  for (i=0; i<numObj; i++) {      // Read the data
    if (EOF == fscanf(fp, "%d", &objType)) {
      // Force the window to repaint with what it did get
      // from the file if objects existed before
      if (objectsExist)
        InvalidateRect(PC->DrawingWnd, 0, TRUE);
      return -2;
    }
```

```
// Add the appropriate object to the figure list. Notice that the
// constructors used here are different than those used elsewhere.
switch(objType) {
  case LINEOBJ:
    fscanf(fp, "%d %ld %d %d %d %d", &t1, &pc, &t2,
      &t3, &t4, &t5);
    obj = new TLineObj(PC->DrawingWnd, t2, t3, t4, t5,
      t1, pc, PC, TRUE);
    Add(obj);
    break;
  case RECTANGLEOBJ:
    fscanf(fp, "%d %ld %ld %d %d %d %d", &t1, &pc, &bc, &t2,
      &t3, &t4, &t5);
    obj = new TRectangleObj(PC->DrawingWnd, t2, t3, t4, t5,
      t1, pc, bc, PC, TRUE);
    Add(obj);
    break;
  case EMPTYRECTANGLEOBJ:
    fscanf(fp, "%d %ld %d %d %d %d", &t1, &pc, &t2,
      &t3, &t4, &t5);
    obj = new TEmptyRectangleObj(PC->DrawingWnd, t2, t3, t4, t5,
      t1, pc, PC, TRUE);
    Add(obj);
    break;
  case EMPTYELLIPSEOBJ:
    fscanf(fp, "%d %ld %d %d %d %d", &t1, &pc, &t2,
      &t3, &t4, &t5);
    obj = new TEmptyEllipseObj(PC->DrawingWnd, t2, t3, t4, t5, t1, pc,
      PC, TRUE);
    Add(obj);
    break;
  case ELLIPSEOBJ:
    fscanf(fp, "%d %ld %ld %d %d %d %d", &t1, &pc, &bc, &t2,
      &t3, &t4, &t5);
    obj = new TEllipseObj(PC->DrawingWnd, t2, t3, t4, t5, t1, pc, bc,
      PC, TRUE);
    Add(obj);
    break;
  case POLYLINEOBJ:
    fscanf(fp, "%d %ld %d", &t1, &pc, &t2);
    for (j=0; j<t2; j++)
      fscanf(fp, "%d %d", &p[j].x, &p[j].y);
    obj = new TPolylineObj(PC->DrawingWnd, p, t2, t1, pc, PC, TRUE);
    Add(obj);
    break;
  case POLYGONOBJ:
    fscanf(fp, "%d %ld %ld %d", &t1, &pc, &bc, &t2);
    for (j=0; j<t2; j++)
      fscanf(fp, "%d %d", &p[j].x, &p[j].y);
    obj = new TPolygonObj(PC->DrawingWnd, p, t2, t1, pc, bc, PC, TRUE);
    Add(obj);
    break;
  case TEXTOBJ:
    // Color Left Top Right Bottom FontWd FontHt Strlen String
```

```
        fscanf(fp, "%ld %d %d %d %d %d %d %d ", &pc, &t1, &t2,
          &t3, &t4, &t5, &t6, &t7);
        for (j=0; j<t7; j++) // Read in the string
          fscanf(fp, "%c", &buffer[j]);
        buffer[j] = '\0';
        obj = new TTextObj(PC->DrawingWnd, t1, t2, t3, t4, t5, t6,
          buffer, pc, PC, TRUE);
        Add(obj);
        break;
      default:  // Invalid object
        // Force the window to repaint with what it did get
        // from the file if objects existed before
        if (objectsExist)
          InvalidateRect(PC->DrawingWnd, 0, TRUE);
        return -2;
    }
  }
  Dirty = FALSE;   // Start with a new, unchanged drawing
  // Force the window to completely repaint itself with
  // the new objects read from the file. Save a little
  // time by not erasing the window if objects didn't already
  // exist in the window.
  InvalidateRect(PC->DrawingWnd, 0, objectsExist);
  return 1;
}

// Save each object in the object list to a file
void TGObjList::Save(FILE* fp)
{
  fprintf(fp, "OODRAW2\n%d\n", NextObj);  // Write a header
  for (int i=0; i<NextObj; i++)           // Save each object's data
    GObjects[i]->Save(fp);
  Dirty = FALSE;   // The drawing was saved; reset the dirty flag
}

// Copy the currently selected object to the object buffer, CopyBuffer.
// If there is already an object in the copy buffer, delete it first.
void TGObjList::Copy()
{
  if (SelectedObj == -1) return;          // No object selected
  if (!CopyBuffer) delete CopyBuffer;     // Free any existing object
  // Copy the currently selected object to the object buffer
  CopyBuffer = GObjects[SelectedObj]->Dup();
}
```

• **GOBJTOOL.H**

```
// GOBJTOOL.H: Header file for GOBJTOOL.CPP.
#ifndef GOBJTOOLH
#define GOBJTOOLH

#include "draw.h"
#include "gobject.h"
```

```
#include "gobjlist.h"

// The tool that enables you to select and move objects
class TSelectObjTool : public TDrawingTool {
  BOOL Moving;          // The selected object is being moved
  BOOL Resizing;        // The selected object is being resized
  BOOL Reshaping;       // TRUE if the object is being reshaped
  int TestObj;          // Which object in list to test
  RECT OrigBounds;      // Original bounds of object
  RECT OrigBoundsWithFrame; // Bounds of object including its frame
  RECT Loc;             // Current location of object
  int HandleId;         // The handle of the object being resized
  HCURSOR UseCursor;    // Handle to the cursor to use while resizing
public:
  void Select(TPaintContext* pc);
  BOOL LButtonDown(POINT& pt);
  void MouseMove(POINT& pt);
  BOOL LButtonUp(POINT& pt);
  BOOL RButtonUp(POINT& pt) { return LButtonUp(pt); }
  BOOL PtOnRect(RECT* rect, POINT p);
  void Start();
  void Finish();
  void Update();
  HICON GetIcon();
  BOOL HasSize() { return FALSE; }  // No object's are created
  void UpdateCursor(POINT& pt);
};

class TSelectObj : public TGObject {
public:
  TSelectObj(BOOL allocObj): TGObject(0,0,0,0,0,0)
    { if (allocObj) Obj = new TSelectObjTool(); }
  BOOL HasSize() { return FALSE; } // No object's are created
};


// The tool that enables you to paste objects from the
// copy buffer
class TPasteObjTool : public TDrawingTool {
public:
  BOOL LButtonUp(POINT& pt);
  BOOL LButtonDown(POINT& pt) { return TRUE; }
  void MouseMove(POINT& pt) { }
  BOOL RButtonDown(POINT& pt) { return LButtonUp(pt); }
};

class TPasteObj : public TGObject {
public:
  TPasteObj(): TGObject(0,0,0,0,0,0) { Obj = new TPasteObjTool(); }
  ~TPasteObj() { delete Obj; }
};


// The following are several user messages that are used to
// communicate between some of the drawing tools and the figure list.
// These messages are used since the drawing tools (derived from
```

```
    // TDrawingTool) don't really know about the figure list. In the tools
    // above the figures list is accessed by typecasting the OWLWindow
    // field of the TPaintContext to a DrawingWindow (which contains a
    // pointer to the figure list). Either technique is valid.
    #define WM_UDELETE      (WM_USER + 1) // Delete an object
    #define WM_UDELETEALL   (WM_USER + 2) // Delete all objects
    #define WM_UFLIPTOBACK  (WM_USER + 3) // Move object to back
    #define WM_UFLIPTOFRONT (WM_USER + 4) // Move object to front
    #define WM_UROTATECW    (WM_USER + 5) // Rotate object -45 degrees
    #define WM_UROTATECCW   (WM_USER + 6) // Rotate object 45 degrees
    #define WM_UREADOBJLIST (WM_USER + 7) // Read object list file
    #define WM_USAVEOBJLIST (WM_USER + 8) // Save object list to a file

    // A tool for deleting the current object from the object list
    class TDeleteTool : public TDrawingTool {
    public:
      void Select(TPaintContext* pc) {
        TDrawingTool::Select(pc);
        // Send the drawing window a message to delete its
        // currently selected object
        SendMessage(PC->DrawingWnd, WM_UDELETE, 0, 0);
      }
      HICON GetIcon() {
        return LoadIcon(GetApplicationObject()->GetInstance(), "deletetool");
      }
    };

    class TDeleteObj : public TGObject {
    public:
      TDeleteObj(): TGObject(0,0,0,0,0,0) { Obj = new TDeleteTool(); }
      ~TDeleteObj() { delete Obj; }
    };

    // A tool for moving the current object to the back of the object list
    class TFlipToBackTool : public TDrawingTool {
    public:
      void Select(TPaintContext* pc) {
        TDrawingTool::Select(pc);
        SendMessage(PC->DrawingWnd, WM_UFLIPTOBACK, 0, 0);
      }
      HICON GetIcon() {
        return LoadIcon(GetApplicationObject()->GetInstance(),
          "fliptobacktool");
      }
    };

    class TFlipToBackObj : public TGObject {
    public:
      TFlipToBackObj(): TGObject(0,0,0,0,0,0) { Obj = new TFlipToBackTool(); }
      ~TFlipToBackObj() { delete Obj; }
    };

    // A tool for moving the current object to the front of the object list
```

```
class TFlipToFrontTool : public TDrawingTool {
public:
  void Select(TPaintContext* pc) {
    TDrawingTool::Select(pc);
    SendMessage(PC->DrawingWnd, WM_UFLIPTOFRONT, 0, 0);
  }
  HICON GetIcon() {
    return LoadIcon(GetApplicationObject()->GetInstance(),
      "fliptofronttool");
  }
};

class TFlipToFrontObj : public TGObject {
public:
  TFlipToFrontObj(): TGObject(0,0,0,0,0,0) { Obj = new TFlipToFrontTool();
}
  ~TFlipToFrontObj() { delete Obj; }
};

// A tool for rotating the current object counterclockwise 45 degrees
class TRotateCCWTool : public TDrawingTool {
public:
  void Select(TPaintContext* pc) {
    TDrawingTool::Select(pc);
    SendMessage(PC->DrawingWnd, WM_UROTATECCW, 0, 0);
  }
  HICON GetIcon() {
    return LoadIcon(GetApplicationObject()->GetInstance(),
      "rotateccwtool");
  }
};

class TRotateCCWObj : public TGObject {
public:
  TRotateCCWObj(): TGObject(0,0,0,0,0,0) { Obj = new TRotateCCWTool(); }
  ~TRotateCCWObj() { delete Obj; }
};

// A tool for rotating the current object clockwise 45 degrees
class TRotateCWTool : public TDrawingTool {
public:
  void Select(TPaintContext* pc) {
    TDrawingTool::Select(pc);
    SendMessage(PC->DrawingWnd, WM_UROTATECW, 0, 0);
  }
  HICON GetIcon() {
    return LoadIcon(GetApplicationObject()->GetInstance(),
      "rotatecwtool");
  }
};

class TRotateCWObj : public TGObject {
public:
```

```
    TRotateCWObj(): TGObject(0,0,0,0,0,0) { Obj = new TRotateCWTool(); }
    ~TRotateCWObj() { delete Obj; }
};

// A tool for saving the object list to a file
class TSaveObjListTool : public TDrawingTool {
public:
  void Select(TPaintContext* pc) {
    TDrawingTool::Select(pc);
    SendMessage(PC->DrawingWnd, WM_USAVEOBJLIST, 0, 0);
  }
  HICON GetIcon() {
    return LoadIcon(GetApplicationObject()->GetInstance(), "savetool");
  }
};

class TSaveObjListObj : public TGObject {
public:
  TSaveObjListObj(): TGObject(0,0,0,0,0,0) { Obj = new TSaveObjListTool();
}
  ~TSaveObjListObj() { delete Obj; }
};

// A tool for reading the object list from a file
class TReadObjListTool : public TDrawingTool {
public:
  void Select(TPaintContext* pc) {
    TDrawingTool::Select(pc);
    SendMessage(PC->DrawingWnd, WM_UREADOBJLIST, 0, 0);
  }
  HICON GetIcon() {
    return LoadIcon(GetApplicationObject()->GetInstance(), "readtool");
  }
};

class TReadObjListObj : public TGObject {
public:
  TReadObjListObj(): TGObject(0,0,0,0,0,0) { Obj = new TReadObjListTool();
}
  ~TReadObjListObj() { delete Obj; }
};
#endif
```

• GOBJTOOL.CPP

```
// GOBJTOOL.CPP: Interactive drawing tool derived from DRAW.CPP
// that save the figure drawn in the figure list (GObjList) that
// is maintained by GOBJLIST.CPP.
#include "draw.h"
#include "gobjlist.h"
#include "gobjtool.h"
#include "drawtool.h"
```

```
// The pointer tool has just been selected
void TSelectObjTool::Select(TPaintContext* pc)
{
  TDrawingTool::Select(pc);
  Moving = Resizing = Reshaping = FALSE;
  TGObjList* Figures =
    TYPESAFE_DOWNCAST(PC->OWLWindow,TDrawingWindow)->Figures;
  if (Figures->SelectedObj == -1) TestObj = 0; // No object is currently
    else TestObj = Figures->SelectedObj; // Use the first one in the list.
  ::SetCursor(hCursor);
}

// Override to avoid calling the selector functions if the object list
// is empty. Call the inherited function if the list is not empty.
BOOL TSelectObjTool::LButtonDown(POINT& pt)
{
  TGObjList* Figures =
    TYPESAFE_DOWNCAST(PC->OWLWindow,TDrawingWindow)->Figures;
  if (!Figures->Empty()) return TDrawingTool::LButtonDown(pt);
    else return FALSE;      // Signal the end of the operation
}

// Find the first object in the figure list, starting from the
// CurrentObj, that contains the point where the mouse button was
// pressed. The PtInRect() function does not consider the point to be
// inside the bounds of the rectangle if it lies on the bottom or
// right side. You can modify the code to check for these sides too.
void TSelectObjTool::Start()
{
  TGObjList* Figs =
    TYPESAFE_DOWNCAST(PC->OWLWindow,TDrawingWindow)->Figures;
  int selObj = Figs->SelectedObj;
  POINT pt, scaledPt;  // Scaled version of mouse location
  // Add in the current scroll position
  pt.x = Pt1.x + PC->Offsx;
  pt.y = Pt1.y + PC->Offsy;
  if (selObj >= 0) {    // Is there an object already selected
    CopyRect(&Loc, Figs->GObjects[selObj]->GetBounds(FALSE));
    CopyRect(&OrigBounds, Figs->GObjects[selObj]->GetBounds(FALSE));
    ::SetCursor(hCursor);
    POINT pt2;
    pt2.x = Pt1.x + PC->Offsx / PC->Zoom;
    pt2.y = Pt1.y + PC->Offsy / PC->Zoom;
    scaledPt = pt2;
    // See if the user has pressed the mouse while on the
    // resize handles of the currently selected object. If so,
    // the user wants to resize the object, so set a flag.
    if (GetKeyState(VK_CONTROL)&0x8000) {  // High bit set if key is down
      if ((HandleId=
        Figs->GObjects[selObj]->PtOnReshapeHandle(scaledPt, 1)) >= 0) {
        // The user can reshape some shapes by moving one of its points.
        // To move a point the user must hold down the "control" key
        // while pressing the mouse on the point to move.
```

```
        Reshaping = TRUE;
      }
      return;
    }
    else if ((HandleId=
      Figs->GObjects[selObj]->PtOnResizeHandle(scaledPt, 1, pt2)) >= 0) {
      // The point pt2 is the point that the object says is being moved
      Pt2 = pt2;
      Pt2 = OffsetPt(Pt2, -PC->Offsx/PC->Zoom, -PC->Offsy/PC->Zoom);
      Resizing = TRUE;
      return;
    }
    // If the user has pressed the mouse while on the border of the
    // currently selected object, the user wants to move the object
    if (Figs->GObjects[selObj]->PtOnFrame(&Loc, scaledPt)) {
      Pt2 = Pt1;
      Moving = TRUE;
      return;
    }
    // An object was already selected, and the user pressed the mouse
    // outside of the current object's frame. The user may want to
    // select another object. Deselect the currently selected object.
    int selectedObj = Figs->SelectedObj;
    Figs->SelectedObj = -1;  // Deselect all objects
    // Repaint the selected object without the highlighted frame
    CopyRect(&OrigBounds, Figs->GObjects[selectedObj]->GetBounds(FALSE));
    HDC hDC = GetDC(PC->OWLWindow->HWindow);
    Figs->GObjects[selectedObj]->DrawHandles(hDC, PC->Zoom, PC->Offsx,
      PC->Offsy);
    ReleaseDC(PC->OWLWindow->HWindow, hDC);
    Figs->SelectedObj = -1;
  }
  int startObj = TestObj;     // See which object was selected, if any
  Moving = FALSE;
  // Get the bounds of TestObj
  CopyRect(&OrigBoundsWithFrame, Figs->GObjects[TestObj]
    ->GetBounds(FALSE));
  CopyRect(&OrigBounds, Figs->GObjects[TestObj]->GetBounds(FALSE));
  do {
    // Add in the current scroll position
    pt.x = Pt1.x + PC->Offsx / PC->Zoom;
    pt.y = Pt1.y + PC->Offsy / PC->Zoom;
    scaledPt = pt;
    if (Figs->GObjects[TestObj]->PtInObject(scaledPt)) {
      // This is the object being pointed at. Draw a dashed
      // rectangle around it. Make this the selected object.
      CopyRect(&Loc, &OrigBounds);  // Copy the location of the object
      HDC hDC = GetDC(PC->OWLWindow->HWindow);
      Figs->GObjects[TestObj]->DrawHandles(hDC, PC->Zoom, PC->Offsx,
        PC->Offsy);
      ReleaseDC(PC->OWLWindow->HWindow, hDC);
      Figs->SelectedObj = TestObj;
      // Next time, try the next object in the list. Don't
      // forget to wrap around to the beginning of the list.
```

```
        TestObj++;
        if (TestObj >= Figs->NextObj) TestObj = 0;
        break;
      }
      else {
        // Try the next object in the list. Don't forget to
        // wrap around to the beginning of the list.
        TestObj++;
        if (TestObj >= Figs->NextObj) TestObj = 0;
        CopyRect(&OrigBoundsWithFrame, Figs->GObjects[TestObj]
          ->GetBounds(FALSE));
        CopyRect(&OrigBounds, Figs->GObjects[TestObj]->GetBounds(FALSE));
      }
  } while (TestObj != startObj);
}

// The mouse has moved. Update the position of the rectangle.
void TSelectObjTool::MouseMove(POINT& pt)
{
  TGObjList* Figs =
    TYPESAFE_DOWNCAST(PC->OWLWindow,TDrawingWindow)->Figures;
  int selObj = Figs->SelectedObj;
  if (selObj >= 0) {              // Is an object selected?
    if (Moving) {                // Is an object being moved?
      ::SetCursor(hCursor);      // Use the proper cursor
      Update();                  // If so, remove the bounding box
      // Move the bounding box by the amount that the
      // mouse has moved from its initial location at Pt1
      ScalePt(pt, pt, PC->Zoom);
      ScalePt(Pt1, Pt1, PC->Zoom);
      pt = PC->SnapToGrid(pt);
      Pt1 = PC->SnapToGrid(Pt1);
      ScalePt(pt, pt, 1/PC->Zoom);
      ScalePt(Pt1, Pt1, 1/PC->Zoom);
      POINT scaledPt, scaledOPt;
      ScalePt(scaledOPt, pt, 1/PC->Zoom);
      ScalePt(scaledPt, Pt1, 1/PC->Zoom);
      Loc.left = OrigBounds.left + (scaledOPt.x - scaledPt.x) * PC->Zoom;
      Loc.top = OrigBounds.top + (scaledOPt.y - scaledPt.y) * PC->Zoom;
      Loc.right = OrigBounds.right + (scaledOPt.x - scaledPt.x) *
        PC->Zoom;
      Loc.bottom = OrigBounds.bottom + (scaledOPt.y - scaledPt.y) *
        PC->Zoom;
      Pt2 = pt;
      Update();        // Display bounding box at new location
    }
    else if (Resizing) {
      ::SetCursor(hCursor);  // Use the proper cursor
      Update();                  // Remove the existing bounding box
      // This function adjusts the size of the Loc frame based
      // on the point pt and the handle being moved
      Figs->GObjects[selObj]->ResizeFrame(Loc, HandleId, pt, PC);
      Pt2 = pt;
```

```
        Update();
      }
    else if (Reshaping) {  // The select tool is resizing an object
      // Erase the current figure
      int oldROP = SetROP2(hDC, R2_XORPEN);
      HBRUSH hOldBrush = HBRUSH(SelectObject(hDC,
        GetStockObject(NULL_BRUSH)));
      Figs->GObjects[selObj]->Obj->Show(hDC, PC->Zoom, PC->Offsx,
        PC->Offsy);
      pt.x += PC->Offsx/PC->Zoom;    pt.y += PC->Offsy/PC->Zoom;
      // Update the location of the handle that is being moved
      Figs->GObjects[selObj]->Reshape(HandleId, pt);
      // Show the figure with its new shape
      Figs->GObjects[selObj]->Obj->Show(hDC, PC->Zoom, PC->Offsx,
        PC->Offsy);
      SetROP2(hDC, oldROP);
      SelectObject(hDC, hOldBrush);
    }
  }
}

// Display the bounding box at its latest location
void TSelectObjTool::Update()
{
  TGObjList* Figs =
    TYPESAFE_DOWNCAST(PC->OWLWindow,TDrawingWindow)->Figures;
  POINT pt2 = Pt2;
  ScalePt(pt2, Pt2, PC->Zoom);
  // Note: Only TLineObj does anything in Resize
  Figs->GObjects[Figs->SelectedObj]->Resize(hDC, pt2,
    HandleId, PC->Zoom, PC->Offsx, PC->Offsy);
  Figs->GObjects[Figs->SelectedObj]->DrawResizingObject(hDC, Loc,
    PC->Zoom, PC->Offsx/PC->Zoom, PC->Offsy/PC->Zoom, Moving);
}

// Display the object at its new location. When this routine
// is called hDC has already been released.
void TSelectObjTool::Finish()
{
  // Invalidate the portion of the window where the figure
  // originally was located. This effectively removes the
  // object from its initial position.
  RECT scaledRect;
  ScaleRect(scaledRect, OrigBounds, PC->Zoom);
  // Subtract off the window's scroll position
  OffsetRect(&scaledRect, -PC->Offsx, -PC->Offsy);
  // Add in the width of the resize handles. They aren't scaled.
  InflateRect(&scaledRect, HANDLEWD, HANDLEWD);
  // Invalidate the original bounds of the object at the end of this
  // function. Don't do it now; otherwise text objects won't be erased.
  RECT scaledRect2 = scaledRect;
  TGObjList* Figures =
    TYPESAFE_DOWNCAST(PC->OWLWindow,TDrawingWindow)->Figures;
  int selectedObj = Figures->SelectedObj;
```

```
        hDC = GetDC(PC->DrawingWnd);
        POINT scaledPt1, scaledPt2;
        ScalePt(scaledPt1, Pt1, 1/PC->Zoom);
        ScalePt(scaledPt2, Pt2, 1/PC->Zoom);
        if (Resizing) {
          // Scale the current object to fit in the box just sized.
          // The handle point does not change.
          POINT pt2;
          ScalePt(pt2, Pt2, PC->Zoom);
          // The lines use this routine to resize
          Figures->GObjects[selectedObj]->Resize(hDC, pt2,
            HandleId, PC->Zoom, PC->Offsx, PC->Offsy);
          // Rectangular objects and polygons use this call
          Figures->GObjects[selectedObj]->ScaleToRect(HandleId, Loc);
          Resizing = FALSE;
          // Get the object's new bounds. Don't use Loc as it is because
          // some objects, such as lines, don't use it for resizing.
          CopyRect(&Loc, Figures->GObjects[selectedObj]->GetBounds(FALSE));
          ScaleRect(scaledRect, Loc, PC->Zoom);
          OffsetRect(&scaledRect, -PC->Offsx, -PC->Offsy);
        }
        else if (Reshaping) {
          // Only text objects use the following function call. It forces a
          // text edit window to be displayed so the user can edit the text.
          Figures->GObjects[selectedObj]->Reshape(0, POINT(), 1);
          Figures->GObjects[selectedObj]->UpdateBounds();
          CopyRect(&Loc, Figures->GObjects[selectedObj]->GetBounds(FALSE));
          ScaleRect(scaledRect, Loc, PC->Zoom);
          OffsetRect(&scaledRect, -PC->Offsx, -PC->Offsy);
          Reshaping = FALSE;
        }
        else {
          // Translate the figure by the difference between these
          // two device points
          POINT diffPt;
          diffPt.x = (scaledPt2.x-scaledPt1.x)*PC->Zoom;
          diffPt.y = (scaledPt2.y-scaledPt1.y)*PC->Zoom;
          Figures->GObjects[selectedObj]->Translate(diffPt.x, diffPt.y);
          Figures->GObjects[selectedObj]->UpdateBounds();
          CopyRect(&Loc, Figures->GObjects[selectedObj]->GetBounds(FALSE));
          // Subtract off the window's scroll position
          ScaleRect(scaledRect, Loc, PC->Zoom);
          OffsetRect(&scaledRect, -PC->Offsx, -PC->Offsy);
          Moving = FALSE;
        }
        ReleaseDC(PC->DrawingWnd, hDC);
        // Invalidate the area where the object is now located so that
        // the object is repainted correctly at its new location
        InflateRect(&scaledRect, HANDLEWD, HANDLEWD);
        InflateRect(&scaledRect2, HANDLEWD, HANDLEWD);
        InvalidateRect(PC->DrawingWnd, &scaledRect2, TRUE);
        InvalidateRect(PC->DrawingWnd, &scaledRect, TRUE);
      }
```

```
// Repaint the object at its new location if it has been moved.
// Otherwise, simply release the device context.
BOOL TSelectObjTool::LButtonUp(POINT& pt)
{
  Pt2 = pt;
  TGObjList* Figures =
    TYPESAFE_DOWNCAST(PC->OWLWindow,TDrawingWindow)->Figures;
  if (Figures->SelectedObj >= 0 && Moving) {
    Update();       // Remove bounding box
    ReleaseDC(PC->DrawingWnd, hDC);
    ReleaseCapture();
    Finish();       // Display the object at its new location
  }
  else if (Resizing) {
    Update();       // Remove bounding box
    ReleaseDC(PC->DrawingWnd, hDC);
    ReleaseCapture();
    Finish();       // Display the object at its new location
  }
  else if (Reshaping) {
    Update();       // Remove bounding box
    ReleaseDC(PC->DrawingWnd, hDC);
    ReleaseCapture();
    Finish();       // Display the object at its new location
  }
  else {
    ReleaseDC(PC->DrawingWnd, hDC);
    ReleaseCapture();
  }
  DeleteObject(hPen); // Delete TDrawingTool::LButtonDown's pen
  return FALSE;
}

// Switch to a mouse cursor that indicates what action will take place
// if the mouse is used. The point pt is in window coordinates.
void TSelectObjTool::UpdateCursor(POINT& pt)
{
  TGObjList* Figs =
    TYPESAFE_DOWNCAST(PC->OWLWindow,TDrawingWindow)->Figures;
  int selObj = Figs->SelectedObj;
  if (selObj >= 0) {
    // An object is selected, but no action has been taken yet. Make
    // sure the proper cursor is shown based on the mouse's location.
    POINT savePt, pt2;
    savePt = pt;
    POINT scaledPt;  // Scaled version of mouse location
    int handleId;
    // Add in the current scroll position
    pt.x += PC->Offsx;    pt.y += PC->Offsy;
    ScalePt(scaledPt, pt, 1/PC->Zoom);
    pt2.x = savePt.x + PC->Offsx;    pt2.y = savePt.y + PC->Offsy;
    // See if the user has pressed the mouse while on the
    // resize handles of the currently selected object. If so,
    // the user wants to resize the object, so set a flag.
```

```
        if (GetKeyState(VK_CONTROL)&0x8000) {  // High bit set if key is down
          if (
            Figs->GObjects[selObj]->PtOnReshapeHandle(scaledPt, 1) >= 0) {
            // The user can reshape some shapes by moving one of its points.
            // To move a point the user must hold down the "control" key
            // while pressing the mouse on the point to move.
            SelectCursor(SIZEFRAME);
            ::SetCursor(hCursor);
          }
          else { // The mouse is outside of the object use a regular cursor
            SelectCursor(-1);
            ::SetCursor(hCursor);
          }
          return;
        }
        else if ((handleId=Figs->GObjects[selObj]->PtOnResizeHandle(
          scaledPt, PC->Zoom, pt2)) >= 0) {
          SelectCursor(handleId);
          ::SetCursor(hCursor);
          return;
        }
        // If the user has pressed the mouse while on the border of the
        // currently selected object, the user wants to move the object
        RECT bounds;
        pt.x = (savePt.x+PC->Offsx) / PC->Zoom;
        pt.y = (savePt.y+PC->Offsy) / PC->Zoom;
        CopyRect(&bounds, Figs->GObjects[selObj]->GetBounds(FALSE));
        if (Figs->GObjects[selObj]->PtOnFrame(&bounds, pt)) {
          SelectCursor(SIZEFRAME);
          ::SetCursor(hCursor);
          return;
        }
        else { // The mouse is outside of the object use a regular cursor
          SelectCursor(-1);
          ::SetCursor(hCursor);
        }
      }
      else { // The mouse is outside of the object use a regular cursor
        SelectCursor(-1);
        ::SetCursor(hCursor);
      }
}

HICON TSelectObjTool::GetIcon()
{
  return LoadIcon(GetApplicationObject()->GetInstance(), "pointertool");
}

// Paste the figure in the object buffer at the current mouse
// location. Force the drawing window to repaint itself at
// the new figure's location.
BOOL TPasteObjTool::LButtonUp(POINT& pt)
{
```

```
TGObjList* Figures =
  TYPESAFE_DOWNCAST(PC->OWLWindow,TDrawingWindow)->Figures;
// If there isn't an object in the buffer, then quit
if (!Figures->CopyBuffer) return FALSE;
// If the list is full display a warning and exit
if (Figures->NextObj >= NUMGOBJECTS) {
  MessageBox(GetActiveWindow(), "Object list is full",
    GetApplicationObject()->GetName(), MB_OK);
  return FALSE;  // List is full. Do nothing.
}
// Make a copy of the object buffer to paste
TGObject* obj = Figures->CopyBuffer->Dup();
// Translate the figure by the difference between the current
// location of the mouse and the object's original midpoint
RECT bounds;
CopyRect(&bounds, obj->GetBounds(FALSE));
obj->Translate(pt.x-(bounds.left+bounds.right)/2,
  pt.y-(bounds.top+bounds.bottom)/2);
// Add the object to the object to the figure list
Figures->Add(obj);
// Call its Display() function to display the function.
// This is okay to do here because the pasted object
// is always drawn on top of all the other objects.
HDC hDC = GetDC(PC->DrawingWnd);
obj->Display(hDC, PC->Zoom);
ReleaseDC(PC->DrawingWnd, hDC);
// Always terminate the drawing process by returning FALSE.
// This prevents the other mouse-related drawing functions
// from being called.
return FALSE;
}
```

• OODRAW.H

```
// OODRAW.H: Header file for OODRAW.CPP.

#define CM_PRINT 105
#define CM_SELECT 110
#define CM_LINE 113
#define CM_TEXT 114
#define CM_RECT 115
#define CM_EMPTYRECT 116
#define CM_ELLIPSE 117
#define CM_EMPTYELLIPSE 118
#define CM_POLYLINE 119
#define CM_POLYGON 120
#define CM_COPY 200
#define CM_PASTE 201
#define CM_DELETE 202
#define CM_DELETEALL 203
#define CM_TOOLPAL 121
#define CM_COLORPAL 122
#define CM_TOBACK 123
```

```
#define CM_TOFRONT 124
#define CM_ROTATE 125
#define CM_DUPLICATE 126
#define CM_GRID 127
#define CM_SNAPTOGRID 128

#define CM_VIEW25 130
#define CM_VIEW50 131
#define CM_VIEW100 132
#define CM_VIEW200 133
#define CM_VIEWFITINWINDOW 134
```

• OODRAW.CPP

```cpp
// OODRAW.CPP: An object-oriented Windows drawing program.
#include <owl\applicat.h>
#include <owl\framewin.h>
#include <owl\dc.h>
#include <owl\docview.h>
#include <owl\docview.rc>
#include <owl\printer.h>    // For OWL's printer object
#include <string.h>
#include "draw.h"           // The basic drawing tools
#include "gobject.h"        // Each figure is an object
#include "gobjlist.h"       // The object list
#include "gobjtool.h"       // Tools customized to manipulate objects
#include "matrix.h"         // Matrix operations
#include "drawtool.h"       // Defines the drawing window class
#include "oodraw.h"

const int NUMCOLORSWIDE = 9;
const int NUMCOLORSHIGH = 2;

// The colors in the color palette
const COLORREF DefColors[18 /*NUMCOLORSHIGH*NUMCOLORSWIDE*/] = {
  // Note: The first color position holds the currently
  // selected color. The color below it shows the current
  // fill pattern. The color below is index location 1.
  RGB(0,0,0), RGB(255,255,255),      // Draw color and fill color
  RGB(255,255,255), RGB(0,0,0),      // White and black
  RGB(128,128,128), RGB(64,64,64),   // Gray and dark gray
  RGB(255,0,0), RGB(128,0,0),        // Reds
  RGB(0,255,0), RGB(0,128,0),        // Greens
  RGB(0,0,255), RGB(0,0,128),        // Blues
  RGB(255,255,0), RGB(128,128,0),    // Yellows
  RGB(0,255,255), RGB(0,128,128),    // Cyans
  RGB(255,0,255), RGB(128,0,128)};   // Magentas

// A palette of colors. The current pen color is shown in the top-left
// cell. The current brush color is shown in the bottom-left cell. To
// change the pen color press the left mouse button over the color
// desired. To select another brush color press the right mouse button
// while over the desired color.
```

```
class TColorPalette : public TFrameWindow {
  int ColorWd, ColorHt;
  TPaintContext* PC;      // The painting parameters
  COLORREF Colors[NUMCOLORSWIDE*NUMCOLORSHIGH];
public:
  int WndWd, WndHt;       // Width and height of palette
  TColorPalette(TWindow* parent, const char* title,
    TPaintContext* pc);
  void Paint(TDC& dc, BOOL, TRect&);
  void EvLButtonDown(UINT, TPoint& pt);
  void EvRButtonDown(UINT, TPoint& pt);
  void EvClose();

  DECLARE_RESPONSE_TABLE(TColorPalette);
};

DEFINE_RESPONSE_TABLE1(TColorPalette, TFrameWindow)
  EV_WM_RBUTTONDOWN,
  EV_WM_LBUTTONDOWN,
  EV_WM_CLOSE,
END_RESPONSE_TABLE;

#define NUMICONSWIDE 2    // Number of icons left to right in palette
#define NUMICONSHIGH 8    // Number of icons stacked in palette
#define EXTRA 1           // Additional tools not displayed in palette

// Provides a palette of tools. Each tool is represented by
// an icon. This is the same type of palette created in Chapter 12.
class TToolsPalette : public TFrameWindow {
  HICON HIcons[NUMICONSWIDE*NUMICONSHIGH+EXTRA];
  int IconWd, IconHt;
public:
  int WndWd, WndHt;    // Width and height of palette
  TPaintContext* PC;
  int ToolNdx;         // Index of the currently select tool
  TGObject* Tools[NUMICONSWIDE*NUMICONSHIGH+EXTRA];
  TToolsPalette(TWindow* parent, const char* title,
    TPaintContext* pc);
  void HighlightIcon(HDC hDC, int i);
  void Paint(TDC& dc, BOOL, TRect&);
  void EvLButtonDown(UINT, TPoint&);
  void EvClose();

  DECLARE_RESPONSE_TABLE(TToolsPalette);
};

DEFINE_RESPONSE_TABLE1(TToolsPalette, TFrameWindow)
  EV_WM_LBUTTONDOWN,
  EV_WM_CLOSE,
END_RESPONSE_TABLE;

class TOODrawWindow : public TFrameWindow {
public:
```

```
        TToolsPalette* ToolPalette;
        TColorPalette* ColorPalette;
        TDrawingWindow* DrawingWindow;
        TDrawingTool* Tool;
        TPaintContext* PC;
        TGObjList* Figures;
        TPrinter* Printer;           // Use an OWL printer object
        char TitleBarStr[126];       // Object file being edited
        // The Paste operation tool is included in the main window's
        // object for convenience. Note: The Copy operation does not have
        // a comparable tool in the tool palette, although you could make one.
        TPasteObjTool PasteTool;
        TOODrawWindow(TWindow *parent, const char* title);
        ~TOODrawWindow();
        void SetTitleTo(const char *str);
        void EvSize(UINT, TSize&);
        void SetupWindow();
        void CmFileNew();
        void CmFileOpen();
        void CmFileSave();
        void CmFileSaveAs();
        void CmPrint();
        void CmCopy();
        void CmPaste();
        void CmDelete();
        void CmDeleteAll();
        void CmToolPal();
        void CmColorPal();
        void CmGrid();
        void CmSnapToGrid();
        void CmView25();
        void CmView50();
        void CmView100();
        void CmView200();
        void CmFitInWindow();
        BOOL CanClose();
        // These functions manage the menu checkmarks
        void CeEnableCopy(TCommandEnabler& ce);
        void CeEnablePaste(TCommandEnabler& ce);
        void CeEnableDelete(TCommandEnabler& ce);
        void CeEnableDeleteAll(TCommandEnabler& ce);
        void CeCheckFitInWindow(TCommandEnabler& ce);
        void CeCheckView25(TCommandEnabler& ce);
        void CeCheckView50(TCommandEnabler& ce);
        void CeCheckView100(TCommandEnabler& ce);
        void CeCheckView200(TCommandEnabler& ce);
        void CeCheckToolPal(TCommandEnabler& ce);
        void CeCheckColorPal(TCommandEnabler& ce);
        void CeCheckGrid(TCommandEnabler& ce);
        void CeCheckSnapToGrid(TCommandEnabler& ce);

        DECLARE_RESPONSE_TABLE(TOODrawWindow);
    };
```

```
DEFINE_RESPONSE_TABLE1(TODrawWindow, TFrameWindow)
  EV_WM_SIZE,
  EV_COMMAND(CM_FILENEW, CmFileNew),
  EV_COMMAND(CM_FILEOPEN, CmFileOpen),
  EV_COMMAND(CM_FILESAVE, CmFileSave),
  EV_COMMAND(CM_FILESAVEAS, CmFileSaveAs),
  EV_COMMAND(CM_PRINT, CmPrint),
  EV_COMMAND(CM_COPY, CmCopy),
  EV_COMMAND(CM_PASTE, CmPaste),
  EV_COMMAND(CM_DELETE, CmDelete),
  EV_COMMAND(CM_DELETEALL, CmDeleteAll),
  EV_COMMAND(CM_TOOLPAL, CmToolPal),
  EV_COMMAND(CM_COLORPAL, CmColorPal),
  EV_COMMAND(CM_GRID, CmGrid),
  EV_COMMAND(CM_SNAPTOGRID, CmSnapToGrid),
  EV_COMMAND(CM_VIEWFITINWINDOW, CmFitInWindow),
  EV_COMMAND(CM_VIEW25, CmView25),
  EV_COMMAND(CM_VIEW50, CmView50),
  EV_COMMAND(CM_VIEW100, CmView100),
  EV_COMMAND(CM_VIEW200, CmView200),
  EV_COMMAND_ENABLE(CM_COPY, CeEnableCopy),
  EV_COMMAND_ENABLE(CM_PASTE, CeEnablePaste),
  EV_COMMAND_ENABLE(CM_DELETE, CeEnableDelete),
  EV_COMMAND_ENABLE(CM_DELETEALL, CeEnableDeleteAll),
  EV_COMMAND_ENABLE(CM_VIEWFITINWINDOW, CeCheckFitInWindow),
  EV_COMMAND_ENABLE(CM_VIEW25, CeCheckView25),
  EV_COMMAND_ENABLE(CM_VIEW50, CeCheckView50),
  EV_COMMAND_ENABLE(CM_VIEW100, CeCheckView100),
  EV_COMMAND_ENABLE(CM_VIEW200, CeCheckView200),
  EV_COMMAND_ENABLE(CM_TOOLPAL, CeCheckToolPal),
  EV_COMMAND_ENABLE(CM_COLORPAL, CeCheckColorPal),
  EV_COMMAND_ENABLE(CM_GRID, CeCheckGrid),
  EV_COMMAND_ENABLE(CM_SNAPTOGRID, CeCheckSnapToGrid),
  EV_WM_HSCROLL,
  EV_WM_VSCROLL,
END_RESPONSE_TABLE;

// Constructor for the tools palette
TToolsPalette::TToolsPalette(TWindow* parent, const char* title,
  TPaintContext* pc) : TFrameWindow(parent, title)
{
  // A tool palette is a visible, pop-up window, with a caption
  Attr.Style = WS_POPUPWINDOW | WS_CAPTION | WS_VISIBLE;
  // Create the tools that the icons represent. The tools
  // are displayed left to right, top to bottom.
  Tools[0] = new TSelectObj(TRUE);
  Tools[1] = new TDeleteObj;
  Tools[2] = new TLineObj(TRUE);
  Tools[3] = new TTextObj(TRUE);
  Tools[4] = new TEmptyRectangleObj(TRUE);
  Tools[5] = new TRectangleObj(TRUE);
  Tools[6] = new TEmptyEllipseObj(TRUE);
  Tools[7] = new TEllipseObj(TRUE);
```

```
      Tools[8] = new TPolylineObj(TRUE);
      Tools[9] = new TPolygonObj(TRUE);
      Tools[10] = new TFlipToFrontObj;
      Tools[11] = new TFlipToBackObj;
      Tools[12] = new TRotateCCWObj;
      Tools[13] = new TRotateCWObj;
      Tools[14] = new TReadObjListObj;
      Tools[15] = new TSaveObjListObj;
      // Note the trick here. The Paste tool is appended to the list of draw-
      // ing tools, but an icon for it is not displayed. This gives the Paste
      // tool a consistent interface with the other drawing tools, but avoids
      // having an extra icon. The menu is used to select the Paste tool.
      Tools[NUMICONSWIDE*NUMICONSHIGH] = new TPasteObj;
      // Get a handle to each tool's icon
      for (int i=0; i<NUMICONSHIGH*NUMICONSWIDE+EXTRA; i++)
        HIcons[i] = Tools[i]->Obj->GetIcon();
      IconWd = GetSystemMetrics(SM_CXICON);
      IconHt = GetSystemMetrics(SM_CYICON);
      // Size the window so that it can hold NUMICONSWIDE columns of
      // NUMICONSHIGH rows of icons
      WndWd = IconWd * NUMICONSWIDE + GetSystemMetrics(SM_CXBORDER) * 2;
      WndHt = IconHt * NUMICONSHIGH + GetSystemMetrics(SM_CYBORDER) +
        GetSystemMetrics(SM_CYCAPTION);
      ToolNdx = 0;      // Index of currently selected tool
      PC = pc;
      PC->Tool = Tools[ToolNdx]->Obj;    // Default tool
      // Don't call Select() yet. The drawing window
      // has not been initialized.
    }


    // Paint the icons in the window
    void TToolsPalette::Paint(TDC& dc, BOOL, TRect&)
    {
      for (int j=0; j<NUMICONSHIGH; j++)
        for (int i=0; i<NUMICONSWIDE; i++)
          DrawIcon(dc, i*IconWd, j*IconHt, HIcons[j*NUMICONSWIDE+i]);
      HighlightIcon(dc, ToolNdx);
    }


    // Invert the icon specified in the tool palette. This
    // technique indicates which icon is selected.
    void TToolsPalette::HighlightIcon(HDC hDC, int i)
    {
      RECT rect;
      rect.top = i / NUMICONSWIDE * IconHt;
      rect.left = i % NUMICONSWIDE * IconWd;
      rect.bottom = rect.top + IconHt;
      rect.right = rect.left + IconWd;
      InvertRect(hDC, &rect);
    }


    // The mouse was pressed while over the toolbox palette.
    // Determine which icon is selected and save the index to this icon.
```

```
void TToolsPalette::EvLButtonDown(UINT, TPoint& pt)
{
  // Whenever a new tool is selected, the selected object is disabled
  TGObjList* Figs = TYPESAFE_DOWNCAST(PC->OWLWindow,TDrawingWindow)
    ->Figures;
  int selectedObj = Figs->SelectedObj;
  Figs->SelectedObj = -1;
  HDC hDC;
  if (selectedObj != -1) {
    hDC = GetDC(PC->DrawingWnd);
    SetROP2(hDC, R2_XORPEN);
    Figs->GObjects[selectedObj]->DrawHandles(hDC, PC->Zoom,
      PC->Offsx, PC->Offsy);
    ReleaseDC(PC->DrawingWnd, hDC);
  }
  Figs->PrevSelectedObj = selectedObj;
  int ix = pt.x / IconWd;
  int iy = pt.y / IconHt;
  int i = iy * NUMICONSWIDE + ix;
  hDC = GetDC(HWindow);
  PC->Tool->Deselect();
  HighlightIcon(hDC, ToolNdx);    // Restore highlighted icon
  ToolNdx = i;
  PC->Tool = Tools[ToolNdx]->Obj;
  HighlightIcon(hDC, ToolNdx);    // Highlight this new tool's icon
  ReleaseDC(HWindow, hDC);
  // Select this tool using the current paint context
  PC->Tool->Select(PC);
  // Tell the drawing window which tool object was just selected
  TYPESAFE_DOWNCAST(PC->OWLWindow,TDrawingWindow)->CurrObjTool =
    Tools[ToolNdx];
}

// When the user selects the close button on the tool palette don't
// really close the window. Instead, make the parent window execute
// the CmToolPal function, which hides the window.
void TToolsPalette::EvClose()
{
  TYPESAFE_DOWNCAST(Parent,TOODrawWindow)->CmToolPal();
}

// Constructor for the color palette
TColorPalette::TColorPalette(TWindow* parent, const char* title,
  TPaintContext* pc) : TFrameWindow(parent, title)
{
  Attr.Style = WS_POPUPWINDOW | WS_CAPTION | WS_VISIBLE;
  ColorWd = GetSystemMetrics(SM_CXICON) / 2;
  ColorHt = GetSystemMetrics(SM_CYICON) / 2;
  // Size the window so that it can hold NUMCOLORSWIDE columns
  // of NUMCOLORSHIGH rows of color patches
  WndWd = ColorWd * NUMCOLORSWIDE + GetSystemMetrics(SM_CXBORDER) * 2;
  WndHt = ColorHt * NUMCOLORSHIGH + GetSystemMetrics(SM_CYBORDER) +
    GetSystemMetrics(SM_CYCAPTION);
```

```
    for (int i=0; i<NUMCOLORSWIDE*NUMCOLORSHIGH; i++)
      Colors[i] = DefColors[i];
  PC = pc;
  PC->PenColor = Colors[0];
  PC->BrushColor = Colors[1];
}

// Paint the color palette in the window. The colors are painted
// column by column, left to right. Remember, the first column
// contains the currently selected drawing and fill color.
void TColorPalette::Paint(TDC& dc, BOOL, TRect&)
{
  RECT rect;
  HBRUSH hBrush;
  for (int i=0; i<NUMCOLORSWIDE; i++)
    for (int j=0; j<NUMCOLORSHIGH; j++) {
      rect.left = i*ColorWd;      rect.top = j*ColorHt;
      rect.right = rect.left + ColorWd;
      rect.bottom = rect.top + ColorHt;
      hBrush = CreateSolidBrush(Colors[i*NUMCOLORSHIGH+j]);
      FillRect(dc, &rect, hBrush);
      DeleteObject(hBrush);
    }
}

// The left mouse button was pressed while over the color palette.
// Determine which color was selected. This becomes the current
// pen color.
void TColorPalette::EvLButtonDown(UINT, TPoint& pt)
{
  RECT rect;
  HDC hDC = GetDC(HWindow);
  // Determine which color cell the user has clicked on
  int ix = pt.x / ColorWd;
  int iy = pt.y / ColorHt;
  int i = ix * NUMCOLORSHIGH + iy;
  // Display the color selected in the top-left box.
  // Use a pure color for the pen color.
  Colors[0] = GetNearestColor(hDC, Colors[i]);
  ReleaseDC(HWindow, hDC);
  // If there is an object currently selected in the drawing
  // window, change that object's color. Otherwise, change
  // the global color setting in the PC structure.
  TDrawingWindow* dWin = TYPESAFE_DOWNCAST(PC->OWLWindow,TDrawingWindow);
  if (dWin->Figures->ObjectSelected()) {
    TGObject *obj =
      dWin->Figures->GObjects[dWin->Figures->SelectedObj];
    ((TDrawingTool *)obj->Obj)->PC->PenColor = Colors[0];
    // Repaint the figure with the new color. First, get the
    // bounds of the figure.
    CopyRect(&rect, dWin->Figures->GObjects
      [dWin->Figures->SelectedObj]->GetBounds(TRUE));
    RECT scaledRect = ScaleRect(scaledRect, rect, PC->Zoom);
```

```
      OffsetRect(&scaledRect, -PC->Offsx, -PC->Offsy);
      ::InvalidateRect(dWin->HWindow, &scaledRect, FALSE);
    }
    else {
      // Update the color in the painting context structure
      PC->PenColor = Colors[0];
      // Force the palette to display the new drawing color
      rect.left = 0;          rect.top = 0;
      rect.right = ColorWd;  rect.bottom = ColorHt;
      ::InvalidateRect(HWindow, &rect, FALSE);
    }
}

// The right mouse button was pressed while over the color palette.
// Determine which color was selected. It becomes the current
// brush color. It is displayed in the bottom-left box in the palette.
void TColorPalette::EvRButtonDown(UINT, TPoint& pt)
{
  RECT rect;
  // Determine which color cell the user has clicked on
  int ix = pt.x / ColorWd;
  int iy = pt.y / ColorHt;
  int i = ix * NUMCOLORSHIGH + iy;
  // Display the color selected in the bottom-left box
  Colors[1] = Colors[i];
  // If there is an object currently selected in the drawing
  // window, change that object's brush color. Otherwise, change
  // the global brush color setting in the PC structure.
  TDrawingWindow* dWin =
    TYPESAFE_DOWNCAST(PC->OWLWindow,TDrawingWindow);
  if (dWin->Figures->ObjectSelected()) {
    // Set the selected object to the current fill color
    TGObject *obj =
      dWin->Figures->GObjects[dWin->Figures->SelectedObj];
    ((TDrawingTool *)obj->Obj)->PC->BrushColor = Colors[1];
    // Repaint the figure with the new color
    CopyRect(&rect, dWin->Figures->GObjects[dWin->Figures->SelectedObj]->
      GetBounds(TRUE));  // Get the bounds of the object
    RECT scaledRect = ScaleRect(scaledRect, rect, PC->Zoom);
    OffsetRect(&scaledRect, -PC->Offsx, -PC->Offsy);
    ::InvalidateRect(dWin->HWindow, &scaledRect, FALSE);
  }
  else {
    // Update the brush color in the painting context structure
    PC->BrushColor = Colors[1];
    // Force the palette to display the new brush color
    rect.left = 0;          rect.top = ColorHt;
    rect.right = ColorWd;  rect.bottom = ColorHt * 2;
    ::InvalidateRect(HWindow, &rect, FALSE);
  }
}

// Tell the parent window to hide the color palette
void TColorPalette::EvClose()
```

```
{
  TYPESAFE_DOWNCAST(Parent,TOODrawWindow)->CmColorPal();
}


// Use OWL's TPrintOut object to support printing the drawing window
class TWindowPrintout : public TPrintout {
public:
  TDrawingWindow* Window;
  BOOL Scale;
  TWindowPrintout(const char* title, TDrawingWindow* window);
  void GetDialogInfo(int& minPage, int& maxPage,
    int& selFromPage, int& selToPage) {
    minPage = maxPage = selFromPage = selToPage = 0;
  }
  void PrintPage(int page, TRect& rect, unsigned flags);
  void SetBanding(BOOL banding) { Banding = banding; }
  BOOL HasPage(int pageNum) { return pageNum == 1; }
};

TWindowPrintout::TWindowPrintout(const char* title,
  TDrawingWindow* window): TPrintout(title)
{
  Window = window;
  Scale = TRUE;
}


// Override the PrintPage function to print each page. In this case
// there is only one page.
void TWindowPrintout::PrintPage(int /*page*/, TRect& rect,
  unsigned /*flags*/)
{
  SIZE oldVExt, oldWExt;
  int prevMode = ::SetMapMode(*DC, MM_ISOTROPIC);
  ::SetViewportExtEx(*DC, PageSize.cx, PageSize.cy, &oldVExt);
  // Scale the drawing window's paper to the size of the actual paper
  ::SetWindowExtEx(*DC, PAPERWD*50+1, PAPERHT*50+1, &oldWExt);
  ::IntersectClipRect(*DC, 0, 0, PAPERWD*50+1, PAPERHT*50+1);
  ::DPtoLP(*DC, (POINT *)(&rect), 2);
  // Temporarily turn off the grid and any selected objects
  // when printing the drawing
  BOOL oldGridOn = Window->SetGridOn(FALSE);
  int saveSelectedObj = Window->Figures->SetSelectedObj(-1);
  Window->Paint(*DC, FALSE, rect);  // Print the drawing
  // Restore the selected object(s) and grid setting
  Window->SetGridOn(oldGridOn);
  Window->Figures->SetSelectedObj(saveSelectedObj);
  ::SetWindowExtEx(*DC, oldWExt.cx, oldWExt.cy, 0);
  ::SetViewportExtEx(*DC, oldVExt.cx, oldVExt.cy, 0);
  ::SetMapMode(*DC, prevMode);
}


// Constructor for the program's main window object
TOODrawWindow::TOODrawWindow(TWindow* parent, const char* title)
  : TFrameWindow(parent, title)
```

```
{
  // The drawing program consists of three windows: a tool
  // palette, a color palette, and a drawing window.
  PC = new TPaintContext;
  ToolPalette = new TToolsPalette(this, "Tools", PC);
  ColorPalette = new TColorPalette(this, "Colors", PC);
  Figures = new TGObjList(PC);    // Create the list of figures
  // Set up the drawing window. Pass it a pointer to the painting
  // context and the list of figures so that it can access the
  // currently selected tools and the list of figures
  DrawingWindow = new TDrawingWindow(this, "", PC, Figures);
  Printer = new TPrinter;         // Allocate a printer object
  AssignMenu("MENU_1");           // Set up the menu
  PC->SetSnapToGrid(DrawingWindow->GridWd/GRIDINCWD,
    DrawingWindow->GridHt/GRIDINCHT);
}


TOODrawWindow::~TOODrawWindow()
{
  delete Printer;  // Delete the printer object
}

// Add the currently open filename to the main window's caption
void TOODrawWindow::SetTitleTo(const char *str)
{
  wsprintf(TitleBarStr, "OODRAW: %s", str);  // Append the string
  ::SetWindowText(HWindow, TitleBarStr);     // Display the new title
}

void TOODrawWindow::SetupWindow()
{
  TFrameWindow::SetupWindow();      // Call the parent's setup routine
  PC->OWLWindow = DrawingWindow;                // Remember which window
  PC->DrawingWnd = DrawingWindow->HWindow;   // is the drawing window
  PC->Tool->Select(PC);            // Select the default drawing tool
  SetTitleTo(DrawingWindow->GetFilename());  // Set the window's title
}

// When creating the program's environment, position the three
// component windows so that the tool palette is at the top right,
// the color palette is at the bottom left, and the drawing
// window is as big as possible.
void TOODrawWindow::EvSize(UINT, TSize&)
{
  RECT rect;
  ::GetClientRect(HWindow, &rect);
  int border = GetSystemMetrics(SM_CYCAPTION) + 2;
  // Fit drawing window inside main window. Force it to
  // repaint itself by setting last parameter to TRUE.
  ::MoveWindow(DrawingWindow->HWindow, 0, 0,
    rect.right, rect.bottom, TRUE);
  // Because the palettes are pop-up windows, the X and Y locations in
  // MoveWindow are screen coordinates, not client coordinates. We want
  // to place the palettes relative to the main program's client
```

```
      // coordinates so we must call ClientToScreen to convert them. Child
      // windows, on the other hand (such as DrawingWindow), are specified
      // in client coordinates. Compare the three constructors to see how
      // the windows are defined.
      POINT p;
      // Place the tool palette at the top right
      p.x = rect.right - ToolPalette->WndWd - border;
      p.y = border;
      ::ClientToScreen(HWindow, &p);
      ::MoveWindow(ToolPalette->HWindow, p.x, p.y,
        ToolPalette->WndWd, ToolPalette->WndHt, TRUE);
      // Place the color palette at the bottom of the window
      p.x = border;
      p.y = rect.bottom - ColorPalette->WndHt - border;
      ::ClientToScreen(HWindow, &p);
      ::MoveWindow(ColorPalette->HWindow, p.x, p.y,
        ColorPalette->WndWd, ColorPalette->WndHt, TRUE);
    }

    // Clear the object list. You can call the figure list function
    // directly or use a message as is done here.
    void TOODrawWindow::CmFileNew()
    {
      if (CanClose()) {
        // Use the CanClose function to test whether the user wants
        // to save the current drawing
        ::SendMessage(DrawingWindow->HWindow, WM_UDELETEALL, 0, 0);
        Figures->Dirty = FALSE;
        DrawingWindow->SetFilename("UNTITLED.OOD");
        SetTitleTo(DrawingWindow->GetFilename());
      }
    }

    // Send a message to the drawing window to read an object file
    void TOODrawWindow::CmFileOpen()
    {
      if (CanClose() &&  // Call CanClose to save the current drawing
        ::SendMessage(DrawingWindow->HWindow, WM_UREADOBJLIST, 0, 0) == 1) {
        SetTitleTo(DrawingWindow->GetFilename());
      }
    }

    // Send a message to the drawing window to save itself to a file. If
    // the filename is UNTITLED.OOD, then bring up the Save As dialog box.
    void TOODrawWindow::CmFileSave()
    {
      // Save the drawing using the current filename
      ::SendMessage(DrawingWindow->HWindow, WM_USAVEOBJLIST, 0, 0);
    }

    // Force the Save As dialog box to appear and save the current drawing.
    // Set the application window's caption to the name of the file.
    void TOODrawWindow::CmFileSaveAs()
    {
```

```
    if (::SendMessage(DrawingWindow->HWindow, WM_USAVEOBJLIST, 1, 0) == 1)
      SetTitleTo(DrawingWindow->GetFilename());  // Update window caption
}

// Print the current drawing window
void TOODrawWindow::CmPrint()
{
  if (Printer) {    // If the printer object exists
    TWindowPrintout printout(DrawingWindow->GetFilename(), DrawingWindow);
    printout.SetBanding(TRUE);
    Printer->Print(DrawingWindow, printout, TRUE);
  }
}

// Copy the currently selected object into the paste buffer
void TOODrawWindow::CmCopy()
{
  Figures->Copy();
}

// Check the View 25% menu option if it is selected
void TOODrawWindow::CeCheckView25(TCommandEnabler& ce)
{
  ce.SetCheck((DrawingWindow->ZoomMode == VIEW25) ?
    TCommandEnabler::Checked : TCommandEnabler::Unchecked);
}

// Display the figures at half scale
void TOODrawWindow::CmView25()
{
  if (DrawingWindow->SetZoom(VIEW25) != VIEW25) {
    RECT rect;
    ::GetClientRect(DrawingWindow->HWindow, &rect);
    ::InvalidateRect(DrawingWindow->HWindow, 0, TRUE);
    DrawingWindow->Scroller->ScrollTo(0, 0);
    POINT pt;
    pt.x = 8.0 * .25;   pt.y = 8.0 * .25;
    pt = PC->SnapToGrid(pt);
    DrawingWindow->Scroller->XUnit = pt.x;
    DrawingWindow->Scroller->YUnit = pt.y;
    DrawingWindow->Scroller->SetRange(DrawingWindow->GridWd*PAPERWD/8.0,
      DrawingWindow->GridHt*PAPERHT/8.0);
    // Update the offsets for the scroll bars
    PC->Offsx = (int)(DrawingWindow->Scroller->XPos *
      DrawingWindow->Scroller->XUnit);
    PC->Offsy = (int)(DrawingWindow->Scroller->YPos *
      DrawingWindow->Scroller->YUnit);
  }
}

// Check the View 50% menu option if it is selected
void TOODrawWindow::CeCheckView50(TCommandEnabler& ce)
{
```

```cpp
    ce.SetCheck((DrawingWindow->ZoomMode == VIEW50) ?
      TCommandEnabler::Checked : TCommandEnabler::Unchecked);
}

// Display the figures at half scale
void TOODrawWindow::CmView50()
{
  if (DrawingWindow->SetZoom(VIEW50) != VIEW50) {
    RECT rect;
    ::GetClientRect(DrawingWindow->HWindow, &rect);
    ::InvalidateRect(DrawingWindow->HWindow, 0, TRUE);
    DrawingWindow->Scroller->ScrollTo(0, 0);
    POINT pt;
    pt.x = 8.0 * 0.5;   pt.y = 8.0 * 0.5;
    pt = PC->SnapToGrid(pt);
    DrawingWindow->Scroller->XUnit = pt.x;
    DrawingWindow->Scroller->YUnit = pt.y;
    DrawingWindow->Scroller->SetRange(DrawingWindow->GridWd*PAPERWD/8.0,
      DrawingWindow->GridHt*PAPERHT/8.0);
    // Update the offsets for the scroll bars
    PC->Offsx = (int)(DrawingWindow->Scroller->XPos *
      DrawingWindow->Scroller->XUnit);
    PC->Offsy = (int)(DrawingWindow->Scroller->YPos *
      DrawingWindow->Scroller->YUnit);
  }
}

// Check the View 100% menu option if it is selected
void TOODrawWindow::CeCheckView100(TCommandEnabler& ce)
{
  ce.SetCheck((DrawingWindow->ZoomMode == VIEW100) ?
    TCommandEnabler::Checked : TCommandEnabler::Unchecked);
}

// Display the figures without any zoom factor
void TOODrawWindow::CmView100()
{
  DrawingWindow->SetZoom(VIEW100);
  PC->Offsx = 0;   PC->Offsy = 0;
  ::InvalidateRect(DrawingWindow->HWindow, 0, TRUE);
  POINT pt;
  pt.x = 8.0;   pt.y = 8.0;
  pt = PC->SnapToGrid(pt);
  DrawingWindow->Scroller->XUnit = pt.x;
  DrawingWindow->Scroller->YUnit = pt.y;
  DrawingWindow->Scroller->SetRange(DrawingWindow->GridWd*PAPERWD/8.0,
    DrawingWindow->GridHt*PAPERHT/8.0);
  // Update the offsets for the scroll bars
  PC->Offsx = (int)(DrawingWindow->Scroller->XPos *
    DrawingWindow->Scroller->XUnit);
  PC->Offsy = (int)(DrawingWindow->Scroller->YPos *
    DrawingWindow->Scroller->YUnit);
}
```

```cpp
// Check the View 200% menu option if it is selected
void TOODrawWindow::CeCheckView200(TCommandEnabler& ce)
{
  ce.SetCheck((DrawingWindow->ZoomMode == VIEW200) ?
    TCommandEnabler::Checked : TCommandEnabler::Unchecked);
}

// Set the zoom factor to a factor of 2
void TOODrawWindow::CmView200()
{
  if (DrawingWindow->SetZoom(VIEW200) != VIEW200) {
    RECT rect;
    ::GetClientRect(DrawingWindow->HWindow, &rect);
    PC->Offsx += (rect.right-rect.left) / 4;
    PC->Offsy += (rect.bottom-rect.top) / 4;
    ::InvalidateRect(DrawingWindow->HWindow, 0, TRUE);
    POINT pt;
    pt.x = 8.0 * 2;   pt.y = 8.0 * 2;
    pt = PC->SnapToGrid(pt);
    DrawingWindow->Scroller->XUnit = pt.x;
    DrawingWindow->Scroller->YUnit = pt.y;
    DrawingWindow->Scroller->SetRange(DrawingWindow->GridWd*PAPERWD/8.0,
      DrawingWindow->GridHt*PAPERHT/8.0);
    // Update the offsets for the scroll bars
    PC->Offsx = (int)(DrawingWindow->Scroller->XPos *
      DrawingWindow->Scroller->XUnit);
    PC->Offsy = (int)(DrawingWindow->Scroller->YPos *
      DrawingWindow->Scroller->YUnit);
  }
}

// Check the Fit in window menu option if it is selected
void TOODrawWindow::CeCheckFitInWindow(TCommandEnabler& ce)
{
  ce.SetCheck((DrawingWindow->ZoomMode == FITINWINDOW) ?
    TCommandEnabler::Checked : TCommandEnabler::Unchecked);
}

// Scale the drawing window's page to fit in the window
void TOODrawWindow::CmFitInWindow()
{
  RECT rect;
  ::GetClientRect(DrawingWindow->HWindow, &rect);
  double scalex, scaley;
  scalex = (double)(rect.right-rect.left)/PAPERWD/DrawingWindow->GridWd;
  scaley = (double)(rect.bottom-rect.top)/PAPERHT/DrawingWindow->GridHt;
  scalex *= 0.9;   // Reduce the scale factor a little so that some of
  scaley *= 0.9;   // the background appears around the drawing window
  // Choose the smaller scale factor
  double scale = (scalex > scaley) ? scaley : scalex;
  DrawingWindow->SetZoom(FITINWINDOW, scale);
  ::GetClientRect(DrawingWindow->HWindow, &rect);
  ::InvalidateRect(DrawingWindow->HWindow, 0, TRUE);
```

```
    DrawingWindow->Scroller->ScrollTo(0, 0);
    POINT pt;
    pt.x = 8.0 * scale;    pt.y = 8.0 * scale;
    pt = PC->SnapToGrid(pt);
    DrawingWindow->Scroller->XUnit = pt.x;
    DrawingWindow->Scroller->YUnit = pt.y;
    DrawingWindow->Scroller->SetRange(DrawingWindow->GridWd*PAPERWD/8,
      DrawingWindow->GridHt*PAPERHT/8);
    // Update the offsets for the scroll bars
    PC->Offsx = (int)(DrawingWindow->Scroller->XPos *
      DrawingWindow->Scroller->XUnit);
    PC->Offsy = (int)(DrawingWindow->Scroller->YPos *
      DrawingWindow->Scroller->YUnit);
}

// Use the Paste tool to copy what's in the object buffer
// (ObjBuffer) to the window
void TOODrawWindow::CmPaste()
{
  HDC hDC = GetDC(ToolPalette->HWindow);
  PC->Tool->Deselect();
  // Restore highlighted icon
  ToolPalette->HighlightIcon(hDC, ToolPalette->ToolNdx);
  ReleaseDC(ToolPalette->HWindow, hDC);
  // Switch to the Paste tool
  ToolPalette->ToolNdx = NUMICONSWIDE*NUMICONSHIGH;
  PC->Tool = ToolPalette->Tools[ToolPalette->ToolNdx]->Obj;
  // No reason to highlight the Paste tool's icon because
  // it doesn't have one
  PC->Tool->Select(PC);
}

// Delete the current object. Compare this function with CmDeleteAll
// shown next. This function accesses the figure list directly.
void TOODrawWindow::CmDelete()
{
  PC->Tool->Deselect();
  Figures->Delete();
}

// Delete all objects in the drawing window. Send a message
// to the drawing window for it to delete the list itself.
void TOODrawWindow::CmDeleteAll()
{
  PC->Tool->Deselect();
  ::SendMessage(DrawingWindow->HWindow, WM_UDELETEALL, 0, 0);
}

// Enable the Copy menu item when an object is selected
void TOODrawWindow::CeEnableCopy(TCommandEnabler& ce)
{
  ce.Enable((Figures->ObjectSelected()) ? 1 : 0);
}
```

```
// Enable the Paste menu item when an object is in the copy buffer
void TOODrawWindow::CeEnablePaste(TCommandEnabler& ce)
{
  ce.Enable((Figures->CopyBuffer) ? 1 : 0);
}

// Enable the Delete menu item when an object is selected
void TOODrawWindow::CeEnableDelete(TCommandEnabler& ce)
{
  ce.Enable((Figures->ObjectSelected()) ? 1 : 0);
}

// Enable the Delete all menu item when there objects exist
void TOODrawWindow::CeEnableDeleteAll(TCommandEnabler& ce)
{
  ce.Enable((Figures->NextObj) ? 1 : 0);
}

// Place a checkmark next to the Tool palette menu option if the
// tool palette window is visible
void TOODrawWindow::CeCheckToolPal(TCommandEnabler& ce)
{
  ce.SetCheck((::IsWindowVisible(ToolPalette->HWindow)) ?
    TCommandEnabler::Checked : TCommandEnabler::Unchecked);
}

// Toggle whether the tool palette is displayed
void TOODrawWindow::CmToolPal()
{
  if (::IsWindowVisible(ToolPalette->HWindow))
    ::ShowWindow(ToolPalette->HWindow, SW_HIDE);
  else {  // Display the tool palette, but don't make it active
    ::ShowWindow(ToolPalette->HWindow, SW_SHOWNOACTIVATE);
    ::InvalidateRect(ToolPalette->HWindow, 0, TRUE);
  }
}

// Place a checkmark next to the Color palette menu option if the
// color palette window is visible
void TOODrawWindow::CeCheckColorPal(TCommandEnabler& ce)
{
  ce.SetCheck((::IsWindowVisible(ColorPalette->HWindow)) ?
    TCommandEnabler::Checked : TCommandEnabler::Unchecked);
}

// Toggle whether the color palette is displayed
void TOODrawWindow::CmColorPal()
{
  if (::IsWindowVisible(ColorPalette->HWindow))
    ::ShowWindow(ColorPalette->HWindow, SW_HIDE);
  else {  // Display the color palette, but don't make it active
    ::ShowWindow(ColorPalette->HWindow, SW_SHOWNOACTIVATE);
    ::InvalidateRect(ColorPalette->HWindow, 0, TRUE);
```

```
      }
    }

    // Place a checkmark next to the Grid menu option if GridOn is TRUE
    void TOODrawWindow::CeCheckGrid(TCommandEnabler& ce)
    {
      ce.SetCheck((DrawingWindow->GridOn) ?
        TCommandEnabler::Checked : TCommandEnabler::Unchecked);
    }

    // Toggle whether the drawing window displays a grid
    void TOODrawWindow::CmGrid()
    {
      DrawingWindow->GridOn = (DrawingWindow->GridOn) ? FALSE : TRUE;
      // Force the drawing window to repaint itself with the new setting
      ::InvalidateRect(DrawingWindow->HWindow, 0, TRUE);
    }

    // Place a checkmark next to the Snap to grid menu option if
    // SnapOn is TRUE
    void TOODrawWindow::CeCheckSnapToGrid(TCommandEnabler& ce)
    {
      ce.SetCheck((DrawingWindow->PC->SnapOn) ?
        TCommandEnabler::Checked : TCommandEnabler::Unchecked);
    }

    // Toggle whether the drawing window snaps the figures to the grid
    void TOODrawWindow::CmSnapToGrid()
    {
      DrawingWindow->PC->SetSnapToGridOn(
        (DrawingWindow->PC->SnapOn) ? FALSE : TRUE);
    }

    // OWL calls this virtual function just before it closes the window.
    // If it returns TRUE the window is closed, otherwise the close operation
    // is stopped. Before closing, the code tests whether a drawing exists.
    // If one does, the user is asked if they want to save the drawing. If
    // so, the drawing is saved to a user specified file, before closing.
    BOOL TOODrawWindow::CanClose()
    {
      if (Figures->Dirty) {    // Were there changes made to the drawing?
        char buffer[256];
        wsprintf(buffer, "Save changes to %s?", DrawingWindow->GetFilename());
        switch (::MessageBox(HWindow, buffer, "OODRAW",
          MB_YESNOCANCEL | MB_ICONQUESTION)) {
          case IDYES:                      // Save the object list
            if (::SendMessage(DrawingWindow->HWindow, WM_USAVEOBJLIST, 0, 0)
              <= 0)
              return FALSE; // The save operation failed; don't close
                            // the window
            break;
          case IDNO: return TRUE;      // Don't save the figure list
          case IDCANCEL: return FALSE; // Abort the close window operation
```

```
    }
  }
  return TRUE;
}

class TOODrawApp : public TApplication {
public:
  TOODrawApp() : TApplication() { }
  void InitMainWindow();
};

void TOODrawApp::InitMainWindow()
{
  EnableCtl3d();
  MainWindow = new TOODrawWindow(0, "OODraw");
}

int OwlMain(int /*argc*/, char* /*argv*/[])
{
  return TOODrawApp().Run();
}
```

• OODRAW.RC

```
/* OODRAW.RC: Resource file for the OODRAW program */
#include "windows.h"
#include <owl\docview.rc>
#include <owl\printer.rh>
#include <owl\printer.rc>
#include <owl\except.rc>
#include <owl\inputdia.rc>   /* Required for the TInputDialog object */
#include "oodraw.h"

/* The program's menu: */
MENU_1 MENU PRELOAD MOVEABLE DISCARDABLE
{
 POPUP "&File"
 {
  MENUITEM "&New", CM_FILENEW
  MENUITEM "&Open...", CM_FILEOPEN
  MENUITEM "&Save", CM_FILESAVE
  MENUITEM "Save &as...", CM_FILESAVEAS
  MENUITEM SEPARATOR
  MENUITEM "&Print", CM_PRINT
  MENUITEM SEPARATOR
  MENUITEM "E&xit", CM_EXIT
 }
 POPUP "&Edit"
 {
  MENUITEM "&Copy", CM_COPY
  MENUITEM "&Paste", CM_PASTE
  MENUITEM SEPARATOR
```

```
 MENUITEM "&Delete", CM_DELETE
 MENUITEM "Delete &all", CM_DELETEALL
}
POPUP "&View"
{
 MENUITEM "&Fit in window", CM_VIEWFITINWINDOW
 MENUITEM "&25%", CM_VIEW25
 MENUITEM "&50%", CM_VIEW50
 MENUITEM "&100%", CM_VIEW100
 MENUITEM "&200%", CM_VIEW200
 }
 POPUP "&Tools"
 {
 MENUITEM "&Tool palette", CM_TOOLPAL
 MENUITEM "&Color palette", CM_COLORPAL
 MENUITEM "&Grid", CM_GRID
 MENUITEM "&Snap to grid", CM_SNAPTOGRID
 }
}


/* Icons used in the program: */
linetool ICON line.ico
emptyrectangletool ICON rect.ico
rectangletool ICON fillrect.ico
emptyellipsetool ICON ellipse.ico
ellipsetool ICON fillelli.ico
polylinetool ICON polyline.ico
polygontool ICON polygon.ico
pointertool ICON pointer.ico
deletetool ICON cut.ico
fliptofronttool ICON flipfrnt.ico
fliptobacktool ICON flipback.ico
savetool ICON savetool.ico
readtool ICON read.ico
texttool ICON text.ico
rotateccwtool ICON rotccw.ico
rotatecwtool ICON rotcw.ico
```

FIFTEEN

Introduction to Three-Dimensional Graphics

F or the most part, we've focused on two-dimensional graphics applications. Although we've been able to create impressive graphics displays, you may be eager to expand your windows into three dimensions. After all, the world is three dimensional. In the next several chapters we'll explore the requirements for displaying three-dimensional objects in Windows.

In this chapter, we'll develop a powerful C++ class that contains everything we need for displaying three-dimensional, wire-frame objects from any vantage point. We'll also explain some of the terminology used in three-dimensional graphics. In Chapter 16, we'll build a Windows application around this three-dimensional object. Then in Chapter 17, we'll expand the program further by adding the option of displaying the three-dimensional objects as solids.

ADDING THE THIRD DIMENSION

In the drawing program presented in Chapter 14, the objects that we created were all defined using only the X and Y dimensions. This gave us objects with specific heights and widths. Now we'll add depth to our objects by including a third dimension, Z.

In this chapter, we'll develop a C++ class called **TThreeD** that will allow us to view *wire-frame* objects, as shown in Figure 15.1. The soure code for **TThreeD** is included in the source files THREED.H and THREED.CPP. To develop the three-dimensional program, however, we need to build a handful of new tools and explore various issues related to three-dimensional graphics.

457

Figure 15.1 The TThreeD class displays three-dimensional views.

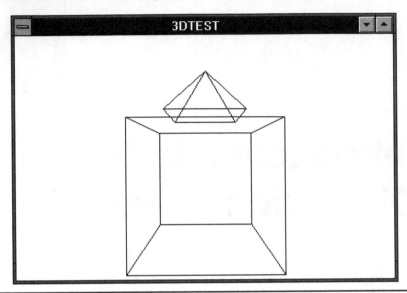

USING A CAMERA MODEL

Rendering a view of a three-dimensional object is similar to taking a picture of an object with a camera. For instance, both approaches create a two-dimensional view of a three-dimensional scene. In our case, the computer determines what to display by applying a *camera model* to a three-dimensional representation of a scene.

The camera model mimics the behavior of a pinhole camera, where everything in view is in focus. We'll assume that the camera is located somewhere in world coordinates at a location called the *from* point, and that the camera is looking directly toward a location called the *at* point. The camera model also specifies a viewing angle that defines how much of the scene is captured on the *viewing plane*. Finally, our camera model includes a parameter called an *up* vector that defines the orientation of the viewing plane—with relation to the coordinate system. Figure 15.2 illustrates each of these viewing parameters as they appear in world coordinates.

Actually, since we are interested in the way objects appear with respect to the screen, we will use another coordinate system, called *eye coordinates*. This set of coordinates has its origin at the *from* point, and the *at* point is on the positive Z axis, as shown in Figure 15.3. The term "eye coordinates" is used because the coordinate system is oriented with respect to the viewer—in our case, the camera.

Figure 15.2 The from, at, up, and viewing angle parameters in world coordinates.

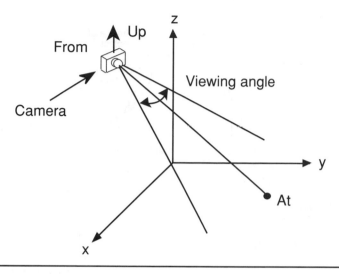

Finally, our camera model uses a perspective projection of all objects, creating our two-dimensional representation of the scene. The two-dimensional scene is created by projecting all objects onto the viewing plane along rays that extend out from the *from* point, as shown in Figure 15.4. Because we will be using perspective projection, objects will appear distorted, as illustrated in Figure 15.1, helping to give the natural sense of depth.

Figure 15.3 The viewing parameters as they appear in eye coordinates.

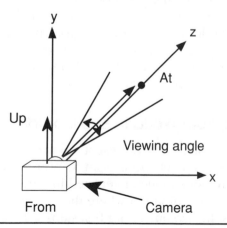

Figure 15.4 Projecting a three-dimensional object into two dimensions.

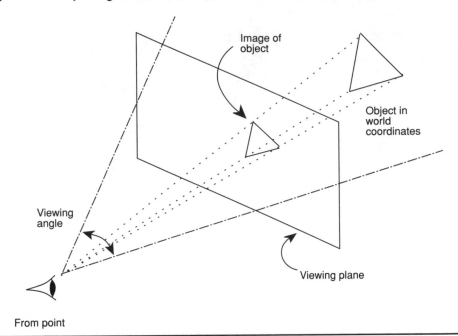

Image of
object

Object in
world
coordinates

Viewing
angle

Viewing plane

From point

Objects in Three Dimensions

To keep things simple, we'll work exclusively with three-dimensional, wire-frame objects, like those shown in Figure 15.1. Each object is represented by a series of three-dimensional coordinate triplets that are connected by line segments to create the outlines of an object.

Each point, or *vertex* as it is usually called, is specified as an (X,Y,Z) coordinate in world coordinates. The goal of a three-dimensional graphics package, therefore, is to transform these coordinates into two-dimensional screen coordinates and then connect them with line segments. This process requires numerous steps, which we'll cover in the next several sections.

Transforming from World to Eye Coordinates

As mentioned before, we'll represent each object as a series of connected vertices, where each point specifies an X, Y, and Z value in world coordinates. However, we are not so much interested in where these points are located in world coordinates as we are in where they are with respect to the viewer—in eye coordinates. In fact, one of our first steps will be to transform object points from the world coordinate system to an eye coordinate system. By doing this, we can easily determine which objects are in view and how they will appear.

Unfortunately, transforming a three-dimensional point from world coordinates to eye coordinates is not a trivial matter. Basically, we need to apply a series of transforms that can align the world coordinate system with the eye coordinate system. This task can be broken into the following steps:

1. Translate the world coordinate system so that the location of the viewer (the *from* point) is at the origin of the eye coordinate system.

2. Rotate the X axis so that the *at* point will lie on the positive Z axis.

3. Rotate the Y axis similarly.

4. Rotate the Z axis.

At this point, objects can be projected onto the viewing plane situated along the Z axis. The projection process is described in greater detail later.

Although the steps just described can be used to transform between world and eye coordinates, they require numerous mathematical operations. On some PCs, these calculations can make a system too slow to be practical.

Instead, we'll use a vector algebra technique that reduces the number of mathematical operations that must be made. The process begins, as before, by translating the viewer in the world coordinate system to the origin of the eye coordinates; however, to align the coordinate axes, we will not use a series of rotations. Instead, we'll replace these three steps with one step, as shown in Figure 15.5. We won't derive the matrix expression V that replaces the rotations described above, but let's look at what it is doing.

Essentially, the matrix V specifies how the unit vectors A_1, A_2, and A_3 can be aligned to the eye coordinate system, as Figure 15.6 illustrates. Therefore, by applying the matrix V shown in Figure 15.5, after translating the world coordinates, we can transform all world coordinates to eye coordinates.

In addition, we will apply the matrix

$$\begin{bmatrix} D & 0 & 0 & 0 \\ 0 & D & 0 & 0 \\ 0 & 0 & 1 & 0 \\ 0 & 0 & 0 & 1 \end{bmatrix}$$

where D is

$$\frac{1}{\tan(\text{viewing\_angle}/2)}$$

after converting points to eye coordinates. This matrix operation adjusts the scene according to the viewing angle so that the objects extend between the

Figure 15.5 These operations convert world coordinates to eye coordinates.

Step 1: Translate points by $(-f_x, -f_y, -f_z)$

Step 2: Multiply result from Step 1 by V_{4x4} where

$$V = \begin{bmatrix} a_{1x} & a_{1x} & a_{1x} & 0 \\ a_{1x} & a_{1x} & a_{1x} & 0 \\ a_{1x} & a_{1x} & a_{1x} & 0 \\ 0 & 0 & 0 & 1 \end{bmatrix}$$

$$(A_1) \quad (A_2) \quad (A_3)$$

To compute A_1, A_2, and A_3, let A' be a vector where $A' = A - F$ and

$$A_1 = \frac{A' \times U}{\| A' \times U \|}$$

$$A_2 = \frac{(A' \times U) \times A'}{\| (A' \times U) \times A' \|}$$

$$A_3 = \frac{A'}{\| A' \|}$$

lines Y=Z, Y=-Z, X=Z, and X=-Z; this makes clipping a lot easier. We'll look at this approach next.

Fortunately, we can combine the operations shown in Figure 15.5 and the matrix shown previously into a handful of equations. These resulting equations are used in **TThreeD**'s member function **TransformSeg** that transforms line segments from world to eye coordinates. To reduce the execution time, many of the values in **TransformSeg** are precalculated in the **SetEye** function. Therefore, you must call **SetEye** prior to transforming any line segments. A series of functions that implement the low-level vector operations required in THREED are included in the files VECTOR.H and VECTOR.CPP. A list of the routines in VECTOR.CPP is shown in Table 15.1.

Clipping in Three Dimensions

So far, Windows has provided us with clipping algorithms to handle clipping of graphics figures as they are displayed. However, now we must develop our

Figure 15.6 This figure illustrates vectors before and after the vector V is applied.

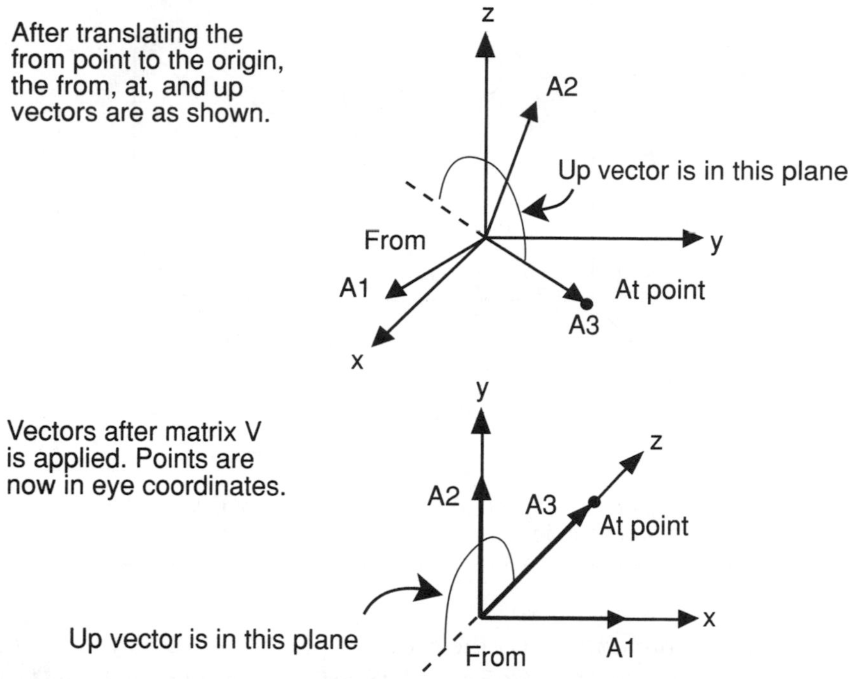

After translating the from point to the origin, the from, at, and up vectors are as shown.

Up vector is in this plane

From

A1

A2

A3

At point

z

y

x

Vectors after matrix V is applied. Points are now in eye coordinates.

A2

A3

At point

Up vector is in this plane

From

A1

y

z

x

own code to clip objects in three dimensions. Essentially, we want to ignore all objects that do not project onto the projection plane or clip edges of objects that extend beyond the border of our "picture."

To accomplish this, THREED.CPP includes the routines **Clip3D** and **Code** that clip three-dimensional line segments in eye coordinates to a *viewing pyramid*, as shown in Figure 15.7. Note that all objects within the viewing

Table 15.1 Functions in VECTOR.CPP

Function	Description
Cross	Calculates the cross product of two vectors
Divide	Divides a vector by a scalar
Dot	Calculates the dot product of two vectors
Mag	Returns the magnitude of a vector
Normalize	Normalizes a vector
Subtract	Subtracts two vectors

Figure 15.7 The viewing pyramid is used to clip objects in three dimensions.

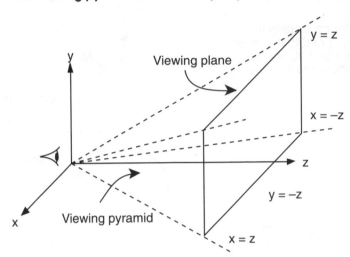

Objects are clipped to the viewing pyramid, which is a
region bounded by the planes y=z, y=–z, x=z, and x=–z.

pyramid are projected onto the viewing plane and displayed on the screen. You'll find calls to **MoveToEx** and **LineTo** at the end of **Clip3D** to display each line segment. Let's take a closer look at how the code works.

After we transform a line segment from world coordinates to eye coordinates, we'll pass it through the clipping process, which begins by calling **Clip3D**. Then **Clip3D** calls **Code** to determine the side of the viewing pyramid on which the endpoints of the line segment fall. If one of the coordinates falls outside the viewing pyramid, the appropriate flag in the variable **c** is set to indicate that the line might cross the edge of the viewing pyramid and must be clipped.

The clipping is performed in **Clip3D** by calculating where the line segment intersects the viewing pyramid. This intersection is then used as the new endpoint of the line; the resulting line is passed through the process again until the line is trimmed so that it is completely within the viewing pyramid. Then the line is displayed. As mentioned before, this is done at the end of **Clip3D**. Note that three-dimensional clipping is required so that we can ignore all objects that are behind the viewer—as well as those that extend out of view.

APPLYING PERSPECTIVE PROJECTION

All objects in the three-dimensional viewing program are displayed using perspective projection. The basic idea is to project all objects onto the viewing

Figure 15.8 Use this operation to project objects onto the viewing plane.

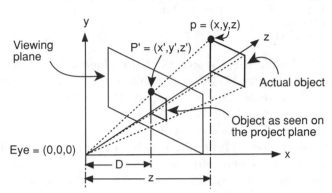

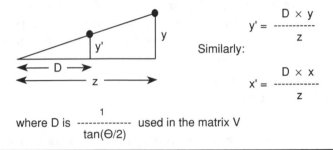

The cross section of the yz plane from the figure above is shown below
From similar triangles:

$$y' = \frac{D \times y}{z}$$

Similarly:

$$x' = \frac{D \times x}{z}$$

where D is $\dfrac{1}{\tan(\Theta/2)}$ used in the matrix V

plane, as shown earlier in Figure 15.4. Note that objects will be displayed only if a line connecting them and the viewer passes through the viewing plane. Objects that do not intersect this region are clipped, as described in the last section.

Assuming that we have a line segment that is within the viewport on the viewing plane, how do we know what size to draw it? Fortunately, we can use a simple geometric property of similar triangles, as shown in Figure 15.8. Based on these values, a point (X,Y,Z) maps to (X/Z,Y/Z) on the viewing plane. This point is then converted to window coordinates using the routine **WORLDtoPC**, as is done in **Clip3D**. Note that we need to make sure Z is not zero, so that we don't divide by zero! Once the points are converted to window coordinates, the line segment is displayed using **MoveToEx** and **LineTo**.

CREATING OBJECT FILES

The **TThreeD** class will be able to display three-dimensional objects that are stored in special text files. The object files have the following format:

```
NumberOfColors
<List of RGB triples>
NumberOfVertices    NumberOfConnections
<List of vertices>
<List of connections>
```

The top of the file lists the colors of the objects. We won't use the color information until Chapter 17, but we'll make our low-level routine compatible with files that do provide color information. The first value in the file indicates how many RGB triplets follow. For now, we'll expect that the file begins with a zero, indicating that no color information is specified.

The next two values indicate the number of vertices in the objects and the number of connections between the vertices, respectively. After this header information is a list of the vertices that make up the objects. Each vertex is represented by three **double** values that correspond to the X, Y, and Z values of the point in world coordinates. The number of vertices in this list is specified by the value in the header mentioned earlier. Next is a series of indices into this list of vertices. The indices specify which vertices should be connected to one another. Essentially, they describe how the points that were read should be connected to draw the object. For example, if a triangle has these vertices

(0.0, 1.0, 0.1)	Vertex 1
(1.0, 0.0, 0.1)	Vertex 2
(1.0, 0.1, 1.0)	Vertex 3

and we want to connect them in this order, then the list of connections would appear as:

```
1 2 3 1 -1
```

This indicates that vertex 1 is connected to vertex 2, which is connected to vertex 3, which in turn is connected to vertex 1. The last value, -1, is used to signal the end of the surface. This value will be used in Chapter 17, but for now, we'll simply ignore it. The number of connections in this case is five.

A valid object file for the triangle, therefore, would be:

```
0
9  5
0.0    1.0    0.1
1.0    0.0    0.1
1.0    0.1    1.0
1    2    3    1    -1
```

The member function **Read3DObject** is provided to read these values into the variables listed in Table 15.2. The coordinates are stored in **Points** and the connectivity list is placed in the array **Connect**. The figure, therefore, is displayed by drawing lines between the coordinates in the order specified by **Connect**.

Table 15.2 Variables Used to Store Objects

Variable	Description
Vertices	Number of vertices in object
Length	Number of connections in vertices
Points	Array of vertices that is stored in world coordinates
Connect	Array of indices into the Points array that specifies how the vertices are to be connected

DISPLAYING A THREE-DIMENSIONAL OBJECT

Now that you know how **TThreeD** reads a three-dimensional object from a file, we'll explain how **Points** and **Connect** are used to display an object. This is accomplished by the nested **while** loops in the member function **View**, as shown here.

```
while (i<Length) {
  startOfSide = i;    i++;
  while (Connect[i] > 0) {
    TransformSeg(hDC, &Points[Connect[i-1]],
      &Points[Connect[i]], pc1, pc2);
    i++;
  }
  // Close off the polygon
  TransformSeg(hDC, &Points[Connect[i-1]],
    &Points[Connect[startOfSide]], pc1, pc2);
  // Skip the negative value in the Connect array; it'll be
  // used in Chapter 16 to specify the polygon's color.
  i++;
}
```

The outer **while** loop sequences through the list of vertex connections contained in **Connect**. Remember that the negative values in **Connect** are used to denote the end of a series of connected points. The inner **while** loop sequences through the list of connected vertices until a negative marker is found. For each pair of connected points, **TransformSeg** is called to transform the two points and to display a line connecting them if it is visible:

```
TransformSeg(hDC, &Points[Connect[i-1]],
  &Points[Connect[i]], pc1, pc2);
```

When a negative value is reached in the **Connect** array, the last point is connected back to the first by the lines:

```
TransformSeg(hDC, &Points[Connect[i-1]],
  &Points[Connect[startofside]], pc1, pc2);
```

This process continues until all values in **Connect** are used.

The **Display** function is a high-level routine that you can call to paint a three-dimensional object that has been read into memory. The **Display** function reveals an important part of the **TThreeD** class. It sets the device context to the **MM_ISOTROPIC** mapping mode so that figures are displayed within the window regardless of the window's size and regardless of the screen's aspect ratio.

Setting the Viewing Parameters

Several parameters must be set for the three-dimensional viewing package to work properly. For instance, before an object can be viewed, values for **From**, **At**, **Up**, and **Angle** must be supplied. To simplify things, each of these is given a default value in **TThreeD**'s constructor, or values are automatically calculated for **From**, **At**, **Up**, and **Angle**. For example, the at location is set by **SetAt** each time a new object is read into memory. It calls the routine **MinMax** to determine the bounds of the object and then sets the at point to the middle of the object. Similarly, **SetFrom** sets the *from* point far enough away from the object so that the entire object will appear in the window.

Overview of TThreeD

The **TThreeD** class contains all the functionality you need for displaying three-dimensional wire-frame objects. The class definition contains numerous data members and a dozen member functions. Here is its complete definition:

```
// A three-dimensional viewing class
class TThreeD {
public:
  double A, B, C, D, DVal;
  VECTOR From, At, Up;          // Viewing parameters
  double Angle;                 // The viewing angle
  VECTOR A1, A2, A3;            // Used in three-dimensional transform
  int Connect[NUMCONNECTIONS];  // Vertex connections
  VECTOR Points[NUMVERTICES];   // Vertices
  int Vl, Vt, Vr, Vb;          // Screen boundaries of viewing area
  int Length;                   // Number of vertex connections
  int Vertices;                 // Number of vertices
  double ObjMinx, ObjMaxx;     // Extent of three-dimensional object
  double ObjMiny, ObjMaxy;
  double ObjMinz, ObjMaxz;
  double Offsx, Offsy, Offsz;   // Transform variables
  VECTOR Dist;                  // Distance between the from and at points
  TThreeD();
  void Display(HDC hDC, RECT& rect); // High level display routine
  virtual int Read3DObject(char *filename);
  void MinMax();
```

```
    void WORLDtoPC(double xw, double yw, POINT& pc);
    int Code(double x, double y, double z);
    void SetAt();
    virtual void SetFrom();
    void SetEye();
    virtual void View(HDC hDC);
    void TransformSeg(HDC hDC, VECTOR *v1, VECTOR *v2,
      POINT& pc1, POINT& pc2);
    virtual void Clip3D(HDC hDC, double x1, double y1, double z1,
      double x2, double y2, double z2, POINT& pc1, POINT& pc2);
};
```

The data members store such information as the object's coordinates, its extents, the viewing parameters, and various intermediate calculations. Most of the member functions are used internally. The two noted exceptions are **Read3DObject** and **Display**. You can call **Read3DObject** to read an object's data file into the class's data members.

Notice that several functions in **TThreeD** are virtual functions. We'll override these routines in Chapter 17 in order to display solid surfaces.

Testing the TThreeD Class

Before ending this chapter, we need to test the **TThreeD** class to ensure that it's working properly. The program 3DTEST.CPP uses the **TThreeD** class to display the object stored in TEST1.DAT, which is listed at the end of this section. Figure 15.1 displays the output of 3DTEST.CPP.

The 3DTEST program is extremely simple. The **TThreeDWindow**, derived from OWL's **TWindow** class, pops up a window and uses **TThreeD** to display the TEST1.DAT object. The **TThreeD** object is dynamically allocated in **TThreeDWindow**'s constructor. After this object is allocated, the **Read3DObject** routine is called to read the TEST1.DAT file. In addition, the functions **SetAt** and **SetFrom** are called to automatically select reasonable *from* and *at* points:

```
ThreeD = new TThreeD;    // Create a TThreeD object
if (ThreeD->Read3DObject(FILENAME)) {
  ThreeD->SetAt();
  ThreeD->SetFrom();
}
else {
  ::MessageBox(HWindow, "Failed to open file", "Error",
    MB_OK | MB_ICONEXCLAMATION);
  PostQuitMessage(0);
}
```

If an error occurs while reading a file, the **Read3DObject** constructor displays an error message and forces the application to terminate by calling Windows' **PostQuitMessage** function.

To compile 3DTEST.CPP, you'll need to place the files THREED.CPP, VECTOR.CPP, and 3DTEST.CPP in a project file. In the next chapter, we'll develop a more extensive three-dimensional viewing application, which will allow you to select the persepective.

• TEST1.DAT

```
0
13 51
1.0    1.0    1.0    1.0    1.0    0.0
1.0    0.0    0.0    1.0    0.0    1.0
0.0    1.0    1.0    0.0    1.0    0.0
0.0    0.0    0.0    0.0    0.0    1.0
0.8    0.2    1.1    0.8    0.8    1.1
0.2    0.8    1.1    0.2    0.2    1.1
0.5    0.5    1.5
1    5    8    4   -1    5    6    7    8   -1    6    2    3    7   -1
1    4    3    2   -1    8    7    3    4   -1    6    5    1    2   -1
9   10   13   -1   10   11   13   -1   11   12   13   -1   12    9   13   -1
12  11   10    9   -1
```

• THREED.H

```cpp
// THREED.H: Header file for THREED.CPP.
#ifndef THREEDH
#define THREEDH
#include "vector.h"

#define EM_FILEOPENERROR -100
#define EM_FILETOOBIG -101
#define NUMCONNECTIONS 400      // An object can have this many
#define NUMVERTICES 450         // vertices and connections.
#define VL 0                    // Borders of viewing region on
#define VR 1000                 // the screen. These four variables
#define VT 0                    // correspond to the left, right,
#define VB 1000                 // top, and bottom pixel boundaries
                                // of the viewing region.
// A three-dimensional viewing class
class TThreeD {
public:
  double A, B, C, D, DVal;
  VECTOR From, At, Up;              // Viewing parameters
  double Angle;                     // The viewing angle
  VECTOR A1, A2, A3;                // Used in three-dimensional transform
  int Connect[NUMCONNECTIONS];      // Vertex connections
  VECTOR Points[NUMVERTICES];       // Vertices
  int Vl, Vt, Vr, Vb;               // Screen boundaries of viewing area
  int Length;                       // Number of vertex connections
  int Vertices;                     // Number of vertices
  double ObjMinx, ObjMaxx;          // Extent of three-dimensional object
  double ObjMiny, ObjMaxy;
```

```
    double ObjMinz, ObjMaxz;
    double Offsx, Offsy, Offsz;      // Transform variables
    VECTOR Dist;                     // Distance between the from and at points
    TThreeD();
    void Display(HDC hDC, RECT& rect); // High-level display routine
    virtual int Read3DObject(char* filename);
    void MinMax();
    void WORLDtoPC(double xw, double yw, POINT& pc);
    int Code(double x, double y, double z);
    void SetAt();
    virtual void SetFrom();
    void SetEye();
    virtual void View(HDC hDC);
    void TransformSeg(HDC hDC, VECTOR* v1, VECTOR* v2,
      POINT& pc1, POINT& pc2);
    virtual void Clip3D(HDC hDC, double x1, double y1, double z1,
      double x2, double y2, double z2, POINT& pc1, POINT& pc2);
};
#endif THREEDH
```

• THREED.CPP

```
// THREED.CPP: A three-dimensional viewing package. Displays
// wire-frame, three-dimensional views of objects using perspective
// projection. Objects are read from files and displayed according
// to the settings of the from, at, up, and viewing angle.

#include <windows.h>
#include <stdio.h>
#include <math.h>
#include "threed.h"

// Return the larger of two values
inline double MaxOf(double val1, double val2) {
  return (val1 > val2) ? val1 : val2;
}

// The constructor sets up various default values for the camera model
TThreeD::TThreeD()
{
  Vb = VB;  Vt = VT;                // Set up the dimensions of
  Vr = VR;  Vl = VL;                // the viewing region
  A = (Vr - Vl) / (1 + 1);          // Set viewport and window
  B = Vl - A * (-1);                // mapping variables
  C = (Vt - Vb) / (1 + 1);
  D = Vb - C * (-1);
  // Set default values for from, at, and up vectors
  From.x = 1.0;  From.y = 0.0;  From.z = 0.0;
  At.x = 0.0;    At.y = 0.0;    At.z = 0.0;
  Up.x = 0.0;    Up.y = 0.0;    Up.z = 1.0;
  Angle = 60.0 * 0.017453293;       // Convert to radians
}
```

```
// High-level routine to display a three-dimensional object
// already read into memory. Sets up the mapping mode and
// then calls View to display the object.
void TThreeD::Display(HDC hDC, RECT& rect)
{
  // Use the isotropic mapping mode so that the X and Y dimensions
  // of equal sizes will appear the same within the window
  SetMapMode(hDC, MM_ISOTROPIC);
  // Set the logical coordinates of the window. Normally
  // our logical coordinates will be between 0 and 1, but
  // since we need integer coordinates we'll use 0 to 1000.
  SetWindowExtEx(hDC, VR-VL, VB-VT, 0);
  // Now set the viewport to use the largest square that fits in the
  // window. The origin defaults to the top left of the viewport.
  if (rect.right <= rect.bottom) {
    SetViewportOrgEx(hDC, 0, (rect.bottom-rect.right)/2, 0);
    SetViewportExtEx(hDC, rect.right, rect.right, 0);
  }
  else {
    SetViewportOrgEx(hDC, (rect.right-rect.bottom)/2, 0, 0);
    SetViewportExtEx(hDC, rect.bottom, rect.bottom, 0);
  }
  SetEye();
  View(hDC);      // Display the figure
}


// Convert clipped world coordinates to the window's coordinates
void TThreeD::WORLDtoPC(double xw, double yw, POINT& pc)
{
  pc.x = (int)(A * xw + B);
  pc.y = (int)(C * yw + D);
}


// Return the minimum and maximum values in the Points array
// for the X, Y, and Z axes
void TThreeD::MinMax()
{
  ObjMinx = 32000;  ObjMiny = 32000; ObjMinz = 32000;
  ObjMaxx = -32000; ObjMaxy = -32000; ObjMaxz = -32000;
  for (int i=1; i<=Vertices; i++) {
    if (Points[i].x > ObjMaxx) ObjMaxx = Points[i].x;
      else if (Points[i].x < ObjMinx) ObjMinx = Points[i].x;
    if (Points[i].y > ObjMaxy) ObjMaxy = Points[i].y;
      else if (Points[i].y < ObjMiny) ObjMiny = Points[i].y;
    if (Points[i].z > ObjMaxz) ObjMaxz = Points[i].z;
      else if (Points[i].z < ObjMinz) ObjMinz = Points[i].z;
  }
}


// Routine to provide a default value for the at point. It
// is set to the midpoint of the extents of the object.
void TThreeD::SetAt()
{
  MinMax();
```

```
    At.x = (ObjMinx+ObjMaxx) / 2.0;
    At.y = (ObjMiny+ObjMaxy) / 2.0;
    At.z = (ObjMinz+ObjMaxz) / 2.0;
}

// Routine that provides a default value for the from point. It
// is dependent on the at point and the view angle.
void TThreeD::SetFrom()
{
    const double WIDTH = 1.8;  // Ratio used to determine from point
                // It is based on size of object
    From.x = At.x + (ObjMaxx-ObjMinx) / 2.0 + WIDTH *
        MaxOf((ObjMaxz-ObjMinz)/2.0, (ObjMaxy-ObjMiny)/2.0);
    From.y = At.y;
    From.z = At.z;
}

// There must be a valid object in the Points array before calling this
// function. It sets up the various variables used in transforming an
// object from world to eye coordinates.
void TThreeD::SetEye()
{
    VECTOR temp;
    DVal = cos(Angle/2.0) / sin(Angle/2.0);
    Dist = Subtract(&At, &From);
    double amarkmag = Mag(&Dist);
    A3 = Divide(&Dist, amarkmag);
    temp = Cross(&Dist, &Up);
    double tempmag = Mag(&temp);
    A1 = Divide(&temp, tempmag);
    temp = Cross(&A1, &A3);
    tempmag = Mag(&temp);
    A2 = Divide(&temp, tempmag);
    Offsx = -A1.x * From.x - A1.y * From.y - A1.z * From.z;
    Offsy = -A2.x * From.x - A2.y * From.y - A2.z * From.z;
    Offsz = -A3.x * From.x - A3.y * From.y - A3.z * From.z;
}

const int NOEDGE = 0x00;
const int LEFTEDGE = 0x01;
const int RIGHTEDGE = 0x02;
const int BOTTOMEDGE = 0x04;
const int TOPEDGE = 0x08;

// Return a code specifying which edge in the viewing pyramid was
// crossed. There may be more than one.
int TThreeD::Code(double x, double y, double z)
{
    int c = NOEDGE;
    if (x < -z) c |= LEFTEDGE;
    if (x > z)  c |= RIGHTEDGE;
    if (y < -z) c |= BOTTOMEDGE;
    if (y > z)  c |= TOPEDGE;
    return(c);
}
```

```
// Clip the line segment in 3D coordinates to the viewing pyramid.
// The clipped coordinates are returned as screen coordinates
// in the variables (pc1.x,pc1.y) and (pc2.x,pc2.y).
void TThreeD::Clip3D(HDC hDC, double x1, double y1, double z1,
  double x2, double y2, double z2, POINT& pc1, POINT& pc2)
{
  int c, c1, c2;
  double x, y, z, t;
  c1 = Code(x1, y1, z1);
  c2 = Code(x2, y2, z2);
  while (c1 != NOEDGE || c2 != NOEDGE) {
    if ((c1 & c2) != NOEDGE)  // The line is not in the viewing
      return;                 // pyramid. Don't draw anything.
    c = c1;
    if (c == NOEDGE) c = c2;
    if ((c & LEFTEDGE) == LEFTEDGE) {  // Crosses left edge
      t = (z1 + x1) / ((x1 - x2) - (z2 - z1));
      z = t * (z2 - z1) + z1;
      x = -z;
      y = t * (y2 - y1) + y1;
    }
    else if ((c & RIGHTEDGE) == RIGHTEDGE) {
      // Crosses right edge of the viewing pyramid
      t = (z1 - x1) / ((x2 - x1) - (z2 - z1));
      z = t * (z2 - z1) + z1;
      x = z;
      y = t * (y2 - y1) + y1;
    }
    else if ((c & BOTTOMEDGE) == BOTTOMEDGE) {
      // Crosses bottom edge of the viewing pyramid
      t = (z1 + y1) / ((y1 - y2) - (z2 - z1));
      z = t * (z2 - z1) + z1;
      x = t * (x2 - x1) + x1;
      y = -z;
    }
    else if ((c & TOPEDGE) == TOPEDGE) {
      // Crosses top edge of the viewing pyramid
      t = (z1 - y1) / ((y2 - y1) - (z2 - z1));
      z = t * (z2 - z1) + z1;
      x = t * (x2 - x1) + x1;
      y = z;
    }
    if (c == c1) {
      x1 = x;  y1 = y;  z1 = z;
      c1 = Code(x, y, z);
    }
    else {
      x2 = x;  y2 = y;  z2 = z;
      c2 = Code(x, y, z);
    }
  }
  if (z1 != 0) {
    WORLDtoPC(x1/z1, y1/z1, pc1);
    WORLDtoPC(x2/z2, y2/z2, pc2);
```

```
    }
    else {
      WORLDtoPC(x1, y1, pc1);
      WORLDtoPC(x2, y2, pc2);
    }
    MoveToEx(hDC, pc1.x, pc1.y, 0);
    LineTo(hDC, pc2.x, pc2.y);
  }

  // Transform the segment connecting the two vectors into
  // the viewing plane. Clip3D clips and draws the line if visible.
  void TThreeD::TransformSeg(HDC hDC, VECTOR* v1, VECTOR* v2,
    POINT& pc1, POINT& pc2)
  {
    double x1, y1, z1, x2, y2, z2;
    x1 = (v1->x * A1.x + A1.y * v1->y + A1.z * v1->z + Offsx) * DVal;
    y1 = (v1->x * A2.x + A2.y * v1->y + A2.z * v1->z + Offsy) * DVal;
    z1 =  v1->x * A3.x + A3.y * v1->y + A3.z * v1->z + Offsz;
    x2 = (v2->x * A1.x + A1.y * v2->y + A1.z * v2->z + Offsx) * DVal;
    y2 = (v2->x * A2.x + A2.y * v2->y + A2.z * v2->z + Offsy) * DVal;
    z2 =  v2->x * A3.x + A3.y * v2->y + A3.z * v2->z + Offsz;
    Clip3D(hDC, x1, y1, z1, x2, y2, z2, pc1, pc2);
  }

  // Increment through the Points array, which contains the vertices of the
  // object and display them as you go. This will draw out the object.
  void TThreeD::View(HDC hDC)
  {
    int i=1, startOfSide;
    POINT pc1, pc2;
    while (i<Length) {
      startOfSide = i;   i++;
      while (Connect[i] > 0) {
        TransformSeg(hDC, &Points[Connect[i-1]],
          &Points[Connect[i]], pc1, pc2);
        i++;
      }
      // Close off the polygon
      TransformSeg(hDC, &Points[Connect[i-1]],
        &Points[Connect[startOfSide]], pc1, pc2);
      // Skip the negative value in the Connect array; it'll be
      // used in Chapter 16 to specify the polygon's color.
      i++;
    }
  }

  // Read in a file describing a polygon which adheres to the
  // format described in Chapter 15. Return 1 if file is read
  // successfully; otherwise, return a negative error flag.
  int TThreeD::Read3DObject(char* filename)
  {
    int i, skipNumColors, r, g, b;
    FILE *infile;
    if ((infile=fopen(filename, "r")) == NULL)
```

```
      return EM_FILEOPENERROR;
  fscanf(infile, "%d", &skipNumColors);  // Skip this field
  // Skip colors if they exist
  for (i=0; i<skipNumColors; i++)
    fscanf(infile, "%d %d %d", &r, &g, &b);
  fscanf(infile, "%d %d", &Vertices, &Length);
  if (Vertices >= NUMVERTICES || Length >= NUMCONNECTIONS)
    return EM_FILETOOBIG;
  for (i=1; i<=Vertices; i++)
    fscanf(infile, "%lf %lf %lf", &Points[i].x,
      &Points[i].y, &Points[i].z);
  for (i=1; i<=Length; i++)
    fscanf(infile, "%d", &Connect[i]);
  fclose(infile);
  return TRUE;
}
```

• VECTOR.H

```
// VECTOR.H: Header file for VECTOR.CPP.
#ifndef VECTORH
#define VECTORH

struct VECTOR {
  double x, y, z;
};
double Mag(VECTOR *v);
VECTOR Subtract(VECTOR *v1, VECTOR *v2);
VECTOR Cross(VECTOR *v1, VECTOR *v2);
VECTOR Divide(VECTOR *v, double num);
void Normalize(VECTOR *v);
double Dot(VECTOR *v1, VECTOR *v2);
#endif
```

• VECTOR.CPP

```
// VECTROR.CPP: Vector operations.
#include <stdio.h>
#include <math.h>
#include <stdlib.h>
#include "vector.h"

// Calculate the magnitude of the vector
double Mag(VECTOR *v)
{
  return sqrt(v->x * v->x + v->y * v->y + v->z * v->z);
}

// Subtract the two vectors
VECTOR Subtract(VECTOR *v1, VECTOR *v2)
{
  VECTOR d;
  d.x = v1->x - v2->x;
```

```
    d.y = v1->y - v2->y;
    d.z = v1->z - v2->z;
    return d;
}

// Cross multiply the two vectors v1 and v2
VECTOR Cross(VECTOR *v1, VECTOR *v2)
{
    VECTOR c;
    c.x = v1->y * v2->z - v2->y * v1->z;
    c.y = v1->z * v2->x - v2->z * v1->x;
    c.z = v1->x * v2->y - v2->x * v1->y;
    return c;
}

// Divide the scalar number into the vector v
VECTOR Divide(VECTOR *v, double num)
{
    VECTOR result;

    if (num != 0) {
        result.x = v->x / num;
        result.y = v->y / num;
        result.z = v->z / num;
    }
    return result;
}

// Normalize the vector v
void Normalize(VECTOR *v)
{
    double d = sqrt(v->x * v->x + v->y * v->y + v->z * v->z);
    if (d != 0) {
        v->x = v->x / d;
        v->y = v->y / d;
        v->z = v->z / d;
    }
}

// Calculate the dot product of the two vectors v1 and v2
double Dot(VECTOR *v1, VECTOR *v2)
{
    return v1->x * v2->x + v1->y * v2->y + v1->z * v2->z;
}
```

• 3DTEST.CPP

```
// 3DTEST.CPP: Tests the TThreeD class by displaying a wire-frame view
// of an object in a window. The file displayed has the name TEST1.DAT.
#include <owl\applicat.h>
#include <owl\framewin.h>
#include <owl\dc.h>
#include <stdio.h>
#include "threed.h"
```

```
#define FILENAME "TEST1.DAT"

class TThreeDWindow : public TWindow {
  TThreeD* ThreeD;
public:
  TThreeDWindow(TWindow* parent, const char* title);
  ~TThreeDWindow() { delete ThreeD; }
  void Paint(TDC& dc, BOOL, TRect&);
  void EvSize(UINT, TSize&) { ::InvalidateRect(HWindow, 0, FALSE); }

  DECLARE_RESPONSE_TABLE(TThreeDWindow);
};

DEFINE_RESPONSE_TABLE1(TThreeDWindow, TWindow)
  EV_WM_SIZE,
END_RESPONSE_TABLE;

TThreeDWindow::TThreeDWindow(TWindow* parent, const char* title)
  : TWindow(parent, title)
{
  ThreeD = new TThreeD;    // Create a TThreeD object
  if (ThreeD->Read3DObject(FILENAME)) {
    ThreeD->SetAt();
    ThreeD->SetFrom();
  }
  else {
    ::MessageBox(HWindow, "Failed to open file", "Error",
      MB_OK | MB_ICONEXCLAMATION);
    PostQuitMessage(0);
  }
}

void TThreeDWindow::Paint(TDC& dc, BOOL, TRect&)
{
  RECT rect;
  ::GetClientRect(HWindow, &rect);
  ::FillRect(dc, &rect, HBRUSH(GetStockObject(WHITE_BRUSH)));
  ThreeD->Display(dc, rect);
}

class TThreeDApp : public TApplication {
public:
  TThreeDApp() : TApplication() { };
  void InitMainWindow();
};

void TThreeDApp::InitMainWindow()
{
  MainWindow = new TFrameWindow(0, "3DTEST", new TThreeDWindow(0, ""));
}

int OwlMain(int /*argc*/, char* /*argv*/[])
{
  return TThreeDApp().Run();
}
```

SIXTEEN

A Wire-Frame Viewer

In Chapter 15, we introduced the **TThreeD** class, giving you all the low-level details necessary for displaying wire-frame, three-dimensional objects. In addition, we presented a simple test program that uses **TThreeD** to display a fixed, three-dimensional view of an object. In this chapter, we'll create a more sophisticated wire-frame viewing application. The new program, 3DVIEW.CPP, is still built around the **TThreeD** class; however, it contains several new features. In the next chapter, we'll expand our three-dimensional application further to support solid surfaces.

OVERVIEW OF **3DVIEW.CPP**

As Figure 16.1 suggests, the 3DVIEW program is quite different from its counterpart in Chapter 15. Its major new features are:

- A menu system
- A dialog box that enables the user to specify the object file to be displayed
- Multiple views of objects using Windows' Multiple-Document Interface (MDI) standard
- A dialog box that enables the user to customize the viewing parameters
- A print option
- Custom icons for the viewing windows

Table 16.1 lists the commands available in 3DVIEW. You can access these options through the program's menu. The code for the menus—and the program's dialog boxes—are included in the resource file 3DVIEW.RC. There's nothing unusual about the resource file, so we'll move on to discuss the 3DVIEW program.

Figure 16.1 3DVIEW.CPP builds upon THREED.CPP, created in Chapter 15.

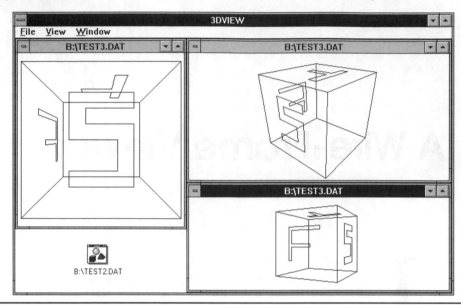

Displaying Multiple Views

The drawing program in Chapter 14 does not allow you to have more than one painting window open at a time. This helps keep our code simple. However, some applications demand multiple windows. In our three-dimensional program,

Table 16.1 Menu Options Included in 3DVIEW.CPP

Menu Option	Description
Open	Opens a new view and displays it in a window
Close All	Closes all view windows
Print	Prints the currently active view
Exit	Exits the program
Perspective	Pops up a dialog box that you can use to change the viewing parameters
Move In	Moves the from point toward the object
Move Out	Moves the from point away from the object
Tile	Tiles the currently displayed view windows
Cascade	Overlaps the currently displayed view windows

we'll want to display different views of a scene at the same time—much in the same way a word processor can display several files at once. Of course, we want all windows to share the same viewing features provided by the **TThreeD** class. Fortunately, Windows provides a perfect solution for this—its Multiple Document Interface (MDI) standard. The MDI standard enables an application to pop up any number of child windows that automatically share the same capabilities.

An MDI application has a structure that's a bit different from what you've seen before. An MDI program consists of three types of windows: a single background *frame,* an interior *client window,* and multiple *child windows,* as shown in Figure 16.2. The frame serves as the foundation of the application. Inside it is the client window that provides menu- and application-specific details. Within the client window, you can display multiple child windows. In our case, each child window contains the **TThreeD** class so that each one can display a three-dimensional view.

Writing an MDI application with OWL is relatively simple because OWL includes the **TMDIFrame** and **TMDIClient** classes, which handle many of the details of an MDI application for you. We'll assign a **TMDIFrame** object to the application's **MainWindow** variable and derive our own version of **TMDIClient** to support our application's menu options. The **TMDIClient** class serves as an intermediary between **TThreeDWindow**, which is derived from OWL's **TMDIChild** class, and the **TMDIFrame** object. An encapsulated view of 3DVIEW's object hierarchy is presented in Figure 16.3. At first glance, the object hierarchy may appear to be hopelessly complicated. However, it's really not that much different than what you've been using. For instance, the

---

Figure 16.2 An MDI application consists of a frame window, a client window, and any number of child windows.

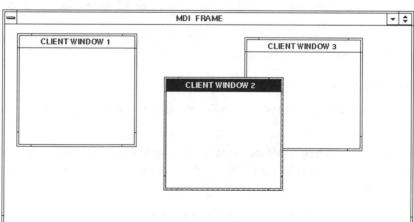

Figure 16.3 This figure illustrates the object hierarchy used in 3DVIEW.

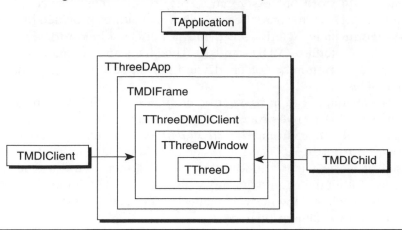

TThreeDWindow class used here is similar to the **TThreeDWindow** class we used in Chapter 15. The new classes are the intermediate classes that support Windows' MDI. Let's step through the class hierarchy from the top down.

The **TThreeDApp** class is derived from **TApplication** in order to provide some of the application-level details of the program and contains a **TMDIFrame** object. This object, in turn, includes a **TThreeDMDIClient** object that serves two purposes: to provide the MDI's client window and to respond to 3DVIEW's menu options. In addition, the **ThreeDMDIClient** object can have any number of **TThreeDWindow** window objects—which represent the child windows. Each **TThreeDWindow** object contains the logic for displaying three-dimensional objects through the **TThreeD** class. Whew! You may want to read through this discussion again and match the components with Figure 16.3 so that you have a good understanding of how the various classes in 3DVIEW interact.

Now let's look at the code. A **TThreeDApp** object sets its **MainWindow** to a **TThreeDMDIClient** object:

```
void TThreeDApp::InitMainWindow()
{
  MainWindow = new TMDIFrame(Name, "MENU_1", *new TThreeDMDIClient);
}
```

Remember, **TThreeDMDIClient** is derived from **TMDIFrame** in order to process the menu selections for the child windows. Here's the MDI client class definition:

```
class TThreeDMDIClient : public TMDIClient {
public:
```

```
    TTransferStruct TransferStruct;
    TThreeDMDIClient();
    char Filename[128];
protected:
    void CmFileOpen();
    void CmPerspective();
    void CmMoveIn();
    void CmMoveOut();
    void CmPrint();
    void CeEnableViewOptions(TCommandEnabler& ce);

    DECLARE_RESPONSE_TABLE(TThreeDMDIClient);
};
```

The **TThreeDMDIClient** class contains several message-response member functions that respond to the program's menu commands. There are also a few predefined menu functions that the **TMDIClient** class provides—we're using these functions "as is." The **CM_TILECHILDREN** command is one example. It tiles the client windows within the frame window. The resource file has an entry for this command, but we don't have to supply any code for it since we're inheriting it from **TMDIClient**. The **CM_CHANGECHILD** message, on the other hand, is explicitly overridden by **TThreeDMDIClient** to enable you to change the scene in a client window. The **CM_MOVEIN** and **CM_MOVEOUT** commands are unique to 3DVIEW and move the *from* point toward and away from the object. Finally, **CM_PRINT** prints the currently active view. Some of the **CM_XXXXX** constants the resource file uses are defined in OWL's header files MDI.RH and WINDOW.RH. Other constants are defined in 3DVIEW.H.

The child windows, **TThreeDWindow**, are derived from OWL's MDI child window class **TMDIChild**:

```
class TThreeDWindow : public TMDIChild {
public:
    TThreeD* ThreeD;        // A three-dimensional viewing object
    char FileName[MAXPATH];
    TThreeDWindow(TThreeDMDIClient* parent, const char* title);
    virtual ~TThreeDWindow() { delete ThreeD; };
    void Paint(TDC& dc, BOOL, TRect&);
    void EvSize(UINT, TSize&);

    DECLARE_RESPONSE_TABLE(TThreeDWindow);
};
```

As this class definition shows, each child window manages its own three-dimensional object through the **TThreeD** class. You might want to modify the code so that the windows can share **TThreeD** objects if you're planning on displaying multiple views of the same object.

Opening a View

You can create a new view of an object by selecting the Open menu option. As the 3DVIEW.RC resource file dictates, this menu item sends a **CM_FILEOPEN** message to **TThreeDMDIClient**. The **CmFileOpen** function in **TThreeDMDIClient** responds to this message:

```
void TThreeDMDIClient::CmFileOpen()
{
  FILE *fp;
  Filename[0] = '\0';
  TFileOpenDialog::TData FilenameData(
    OFN_FILEMUSTEXIST | OFN_HIDEREADONLY | OFN_PATHMUSTEXIST,
    "Figures (*.FIG)|*.DAT|", 0, "", "DAT");
  TFileOpenDialog *fileDlg = new TFileOpenDialog(this, FilenameData);
  if (fileDlg->Execute() == IDOK) {
    // Open the file
    if ((fp = fopen(FilenameData.FileName, "r")) == NULL) {
      ::MessageBox(HWindow, "Could not open file", 0, MB_OK);
      return;
    }
    else {
      lstrcpy(Filename, FilenameData.FileName);
      (new TThreeDWindow(this, Filename))->Create();
      fclose(fp);
    }
  }
}
```

This routine pops up a file open dialog box, enabling the user to enter the name of a file to read. If the filename is valid and the specified file can be opened, the code allocates a **TThreeDWindow** object, passing it the filename the user has entered. (Remember, a **TThreeDWindow** is a child window.) The call to **Create** constructs the child window. The **TThreeDWindow** constructor takes the filename specified and reads its object data into memory and initializes the *from* and *at* points. If there is an error reading the file, the function displays an error message. In case you're wondering, the three-dimensional view is displayed in **TThreeDWindow**'s **Paint** function. We'll look at this function later.

CHANGING THE PERSPECTIVE

The Perspective menu option pops up the dialog box shown in Figure 16.4. You can use this dialog box to change the viewing parameters used in a client window. The format for the dialog box is specified in the 3DVIEW.RC resource file and its code is encapsulated in the **TSettingsDlg** class. A transfer buffer is used, as we have done in the past, to copy data to and from the dialog box. The constructor in **TSettingsDlg** initializes the transfer buffer's values to the

Figure 16.4 The Viewing Parameters dialog box allows the user to change the viewing parameters for a client window.

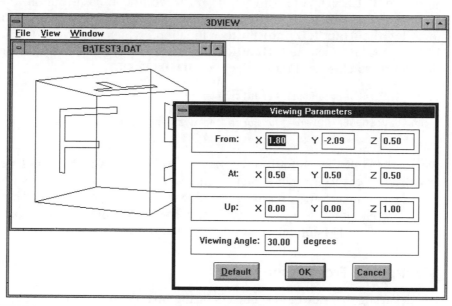

corresponding variables in **TThreeD**. It also dynamically allocates **TButton** and **TEdit** objects for the various button and editing fields specified for the dialog box in the resource file.

The **CmPerspective** function, included in **TThreeDMDIClient**, pops up a **TSettingsDlg** dialog box and copies its data to the appropriate client window. How does the function know which child window to communicate with? Fortunately, OWL can retrieve a pointer to the currently active window by calling the function **GetActiveMDIChild**. For convenience, **CmPerspective** copies the return value of **GetActiveMDIChild** into the variable **obj**. Notice that **CmPerspective** pops up the dialog box, passing it the **obj** pointer so that the dialog box uses the data from the **GetActiveMDIChild**:

```
void TThreeDMDIClient::CmPerspective()
{
  TThreeDWindow* obj = (TThreeDWindow *)GetActiveMDIChild();

  int resp = GetModule()->ExecDialog(new TSettingsDlg(this, ID_DIALOG,
    obj));
```

The Viewing Parameters dialog box contains the three buttons: OK, Cancel, and Default. Selecting the Cancel button aborts the operation. However, if the OK button is selected, the data from the transfer buffer is copied into the appropriate variables in the **TThreeD** object contained in the **obj** object. The **atof** function converts the character data in the transfer buffer to the floating-point values stored in **TThreeD**. Alternatively, if you select the Default button, the *from* and *at* points are reset to their original values. Notice that **TSettingsDlg** includes the **HandleDefaultButton** function, which is invoked when the Default button is selected. **HandleDefaultButton** calls **Destroy** to force the dialog box to close and return the code **ID_DEFAULT**:

```
void TSettingsDlg::HandleDefaultButton()
{
  Destroy(ID_DEFAULT);    // Force the dialog box to terminate
}
```

If the OK or Default buttons are selected, **CmPerspective** calls **InvalidateRect** to force the client window to repaint with the possibly new viewing parameters the user has entered in the Viewing Parameters dialog box.

We've skipped over a few statements in **CmPerspective** that control the window when it is minimized. We'll return to these later.

Moving the From Point

Besides using the Viewing Parameters dialog box, you can incrementally change the *from* point by selecting the Move In and Move Out menu options. These two commands move the *from* point along a line that passes through the *at* point. Again, these routines use the **GetActiveMDIChild** variable maintained by OWL so that the functions update the currently active client window. After modifying the *from* point, the two routines call **InvalidateRect** to update the scene.

PRINTING A WIRE-FRAME VIEW

The last of **TThreeDMDIFrame**'s functions, **CmPrint**, sends the currently active view to the printer. We're taking a fairly simple approach here. The function retrieves a handle to a printer device context using **GetPrinterDC**, which searches the WIN.INI file for the printer device statement and then creates a printer device context for the printer:

```
HDC CreatePrinterDC()
{
  char prnStr[80], *device, *driver, *port;
  GetProfileString("windows", "device", NULL, prnStr, 80);
  if ((device=strtok(prnStr, ",")) != 0 &&
    (driver=strtok(NULL, ",")) != 0 &&
    (port=strtok(NULL, ",")) != 0)
    return CreateDC(driver, device, port, NULL);
  return 0;     // No printer found
}
```

The printer device context is then simply passed along to **TThreeD**'s **View** function to display the view.

Of course, since the device context represents the printer and not the display, the output gets sent to the printer. Surrounding the call to **View** are calls to the printer function **Escape**, which start the printing process, eject the page, and terminate the printing operation:

```
if (Escape(hPrnDC, STARTDOC, 6, "3DVIEW", NULL) > 0) {
  // Display the wire-frame view on the printer
  TThreeDWindow* obj = (TThreeDWindow *)GetActiveMDIChild();
  obj->ThreeD->View(hPrnDC);
  if (Escape(hPrnDC, NEWFRAME, 0, NULL, NULL) > 0)
    Escape(hPrnDC, ENDDOC, 0, NULL, NULL);
}
```

Although the code doesn't trap for printer errors, it is amazing what you can do with so few statements. If you want more thorough printer support, you might want to integrate OWL's **TPrintout** object into the application; we used this approach in Chapter 14's drawing program.

BUILDING THE WIRE-FRAME PROGRAM

 To compile 3DVIEW.CPP, you'll need the files listed in Table 16.2. In addition, you must create a project file that contains the files 3DVIEW.CPP, THREED.CPP, and 3DVIEW.RC, VECTOR.CPP.

Sample Objects

This section lists two object data files that you can test with 3DVIEW. The first, TEST2.DAT, displays the object shown in Figure 16.5:

Table 16.2 Files Used to Compile 3DVIEW.CPP

Filename	Chapter	Place in Project File
THREED.H	15	No
THREED.CPP	15	Yes
3DVIEW.H	16	No
3DVIEW.CPP	16	Yes
3DVIEW.RC	16	Yes
VECTOR.H	15	No
VECTOR.CPP	15	Yes

```
0
13 51
1.0    1.0    1.0    1.0    1.0    0.0
1.0    0.0    0.0    1.0    0.0    1.0
0.0    1.0    1.0    0.0    1.0    0.0
0.0    0.0    0.0    0.0    0.0    1.0
0.8    0.2    1.1    0.8    0.8    1.1
0.2    0.8    1.1    0.2    0.2    1.1
0.5    0.5    1.5
1     5     8     4    -1     5     6     7     8    -1
6     2     3     7    -1     1     4     3     2    -1
8     7     3     4    -1     6     5     1     2    -1
9    10    13    -1    10    11    13    -1    11    12
13    -1    12     9    13    -1    12    11    10     9    -1
```

The following object data file, TEST3.DAT, generates the object shown in Figure 16.6:

```
0
38 63
1.0    1.0    1.0    1.0    1.0    0.0
1.0    0.0    0.0    1.0    0.0    1.0
0.0    1.0    1.0    0.0    1.0    0.0
0.0    0.0    0.0    0.0    0.0    1.0
0.25   0.0    0.25   0.25   0.0    0.75
0.75   0.0    0.75   0.75   0.0    0.7
0.3    0.0    0.7    0.3    0.0    0.5
```

Figure 16.5 This object was created by the file TEST2.DAT.

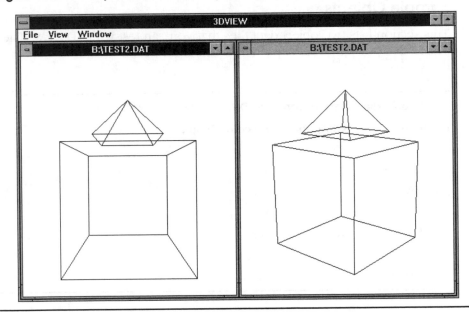

Figure 16.6 This object was created by TEST3.DAT.

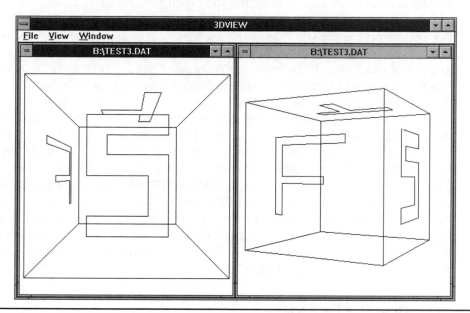

```
0.6    0.0    0.5    0.6    0.0    0.45
0.3    0.0    0.45   0.3    0.0    0.25
1.0    0.3    0.2    1.0    0.3    0.3
1.0    0.6    0.3    1.0    0.6    0.5
1.0    0.3    0.5    1.0    0.3    0.8
1.0    0.7    0.8    1.0    0.7    0.7
1.0    0.4    0.7    1.0    0.4    0.6
1.0    0.7    0.6    1.0    0.7    0.2
0.4    0.3    1.0    0.4    0.6    1.0
0.2    0.6    1.0    0.2    0.7    1.0
0.8    0.7    1.0    0.8    0.6    1.0
0.5    0.6    1.0    0.5    0.3    1.0
1    5    8    4    -1    5    6    7    8    -1
6    2    3    7    -1    1    4    3    2    -1
8    7    3    4    -1    6    5    1    2    -1
9   10   11   12    13   14   15   16   17   18   -1
19  20   21   22    23   24   25   26   27   28   29   30   -1
31  32   33   34    35   36   37   38   -1
```

Using 3DVIEW

After you've successfully compiled 3DVIEW.CPP, you're ready to try displaying
an object. To view one of the object data files listed in the previous section,
select the Open option in the File pull-down menu. Enter the desired filename
in the dialog box and select the OK button. The object associated with the data

file will appear in a new client window. You can open up other copies of the same file or another file by selecting the Open menu option again.

Try experimenting with each of the viewing parameters by selecting the Perspective option from the View pull-down menu. Using the Viewing Parameters dialog box, you can specify your own *from* point, *at* point, *up* vector, and viewing angle. For example, try changing the *from* point to (2,2,2) or even (0,0,0). The latter value should take you inside the object! You might also want to change the viewing angle, which effectively allows you to zoom in and out on an object. If you've experimented with the settings a little too much, simply select the Default button to restore the viewing parameters to their default settings.

Notice that, when you move very close to the object, its image is clipped to an imaginary square within the client window. The size of the square is set by Windows since 3DVIEW uses the **MM_ISOTROPIC** mapping mode. However, the **Clip3D** function in 3DVIEW clips the line segments to this square. Refer to Chapter 14 for a discussion of **Clip3D**. In the next chapter, we'll bypass the clipping portion of **Clip3D** so that the scene can fill the entire display window. Of course, the notion of a resizable viewing plane doesn't quite match a realistic camera model.

Extending the Program

You might try adding ehancements to the three-dimensional viewing package. For instance, you could add routines to interactively draw three-dimensional objects. The difficulty here lies in determining a clean way to draw the objects. You will probably want to use several windows that show the object at different perspectives in order to give yourself a good idea of what the object looks like.

You could also improve the user interaction by providing icons or hot keys to incrementally change the viewing parameters. For instance, you might add a hot key that performs the same action as the Move In menu option and another hot key that performs the Move Out menu option.

Another possible extension of the program is to add color or fill patterns to the objects that are drawn. This, in fact, is the focus of the next chapter as we present a technique for drawing *solid* objects.

• 3DVIEW.RC

```
// 3DVIEW.RC: Resource file for 3DVIEW.CPP.
#include "3dview.h"
#include "owl\mdi.rh"
#include "owl\window.rh"

ID_DIALOG DIALOG 46, 20, 202, 132
CAPTION "Viewing Parameters"
```

```
STYLE WS_POPUP | WS_CLIPSIBLINGS | WS_CAPTION | WS_SYSMENU | DS_MODALFRAME
BEGIN
  EDITTEXT ID_FROMX, 70, 12, 26, 13
  EDITTEXT ID_FROMY, 114, 12, 26, 13
  EDITTEXT ID_FROMZ, 160, 12, 26, 13
  EDITTEXT ID_ATX, 70, 39, 26, 13
  EDITTEXT ID_ATY, 114, 39, 26, 13
  EDITTEXT ID_ATZ, 160, 39, 26, 13
  EDITTEXT ID_UPX, 70, 65, 26, 13
  EDITTEXT ID_UPY, 114, 65, 26, 13
  EDITTEXT ID_UPZ, 160, 65, 26, 13
  EDITTEXT ID_VIEW, 70, 91, 26, 13
  DEFPUSHBUTTON "OK", IDOK, 86, 113, 32, 14
  PUSHBUTTON "Cancel", IDCANCEL, 139, 113, 30, 14
  PUSHBUTTON "&Default", ID_DEFAULT, 30, 113, 36, 14
  RTEXT "From:", -1, 26, 13, 23, 12
  RTEXT "At:", -1, 26, 40, 23, 12
  RTEXT "Up:", -1, 26, 66, 23, 12
  RTEXT "Viewing Angle:", -1, 18, 92, 48, 12
  LTEXT "degrees", -1, 100, 92, 28, 12
  RTEXT "Y", -1, 106, 14, 5, 11
  RTEXT "X", -1, 62, 14, 5, 11
  RTEXT "Z", -1, 152, 14, 5, 11
  CONTROL "", -1, "static", SS_BLACKFRAME, 12, 9, 178, 19
  RTEXT "Y", -1, 106, 41, 5, 11
  RTEXT "X", -1, 62, 41, 5, 11
  RTEXT "Z", -1, 152, 41, 5, 11
  CONTROL "", -1, "static", SS_BLACKFRAME, 12, 36, 178, 19
  RTEXT "Y", -1, 106, 67, 5, 11
  RTEXT "X", -1, 62, 67, 5, 11
  RTEXT "Z", -1, 152, 67, 5, 11
  CONTROL "", -1, "static", SS_BLACKFRAME, 12, 62, 178, 19
  CONTROL "", -1, "static", SS_BLACKFRAME, 12, 88, 178, 19
END

MENU_1 MENU
{
 POPUP "&File"
 {
  MENUITEM "&Open", CM_FILEOPEN
  MENUITEM SEPARATOR
  MENUITEM "&Print", CM_PRINT
  MENUITEM SEPARATOR
  MENUITEM "E&xit", CM_EXIT
 }

 POPUP "&View"
 {
  MENUITEM "&Perspective", CM_PERSPECTIVE
  MENUITEM "Move &in", CM_MOVEIN
  MENUITEM "Move &out", CM_MOVEOUT
 }
 POPUP "&Window"
 {
```

```
    MENUITEM "&Cascade", CM_CASCADECHILDREN
    MENUITEM "&Tile", CM_TILECHILDREN
    MENUITEM "Arrange &icons", CM_ARRANGEICONS
    MENUITEM SEPARATOR
    MENUITEM "Close &all", CM_CLOSECHILDREN
  }
}
```

• 3DVIEW.H

```
// 3DVIEW.H: Header file for 3DVIEW.CPP and 3DVIEW.RC.

#define CM_FILEOPEN 200
#define CM_PERSPECTIVE 201
#define CM_MOVEIN 202
#define CM_MOVEOUT 203
#define CM_PRINT 204


#define ID_DIALOG 210
#define ID_SETTINGS 211
#define ID_FROMX 212
#define ID_FROMY 213
#define ID_FROMZ 214
#define ID_ATX 215
#define ID_ATY 216
#define ID_ATZ 217
#define ID_UPX 218
#define ID_UPY 219
#define ID_UPZ 220
#define ID_VIEW 221
#define ID_DEFAULT 222
```

• 3DVIEW.CPP

```
// 3DVIEW.CPP: Wire-frame viewing program. Displays wire-frame, three-
// dimensional views of objects using perspective projection. Objects
// are read from files and displayed according to the settings of the
// from and at points, the up vector, and the viewing angle. You can have
// more than one view open at a time. The user can select the
// perspective and camera parameters used to display the object.
#include <owl\dialog.h>
#include <owl\applicat.h>
#include <owl\framewin.h>
#include <owl\dc.h>
#include <owl\opensave.h>
#include <owl\edit.h>
#include <owl\button.h>
#include <owl\mdi.h>
#include <stdio.h>
#include <string.h>
#include <math.h>
#include <dir.h>
```

```
#include "vector.h"
#include "threed.h"
#include "3dview.h"
                                // A real number in a dialog box can have
const MAXREALLEN = 11;          // one less than this many characters
// Structure used to copy data to and from the persepective dialog
struct TTransferStruct {
  char Fromx[MAXREALLEN];
  char Fromy[MAXREALLEN];
  char Fromz[MAXREALLEN];
  char Atx[MAXREALLEN];
  char Aty[MAXREALLEN];
  char Atz[MAXREALLEN];
  char Upx[MAXREALLEN];
  char Upy[MAXREALLEN];
  char Upz[MAXREALLEN];
  char View[MAXREALLEN];
};

class TThreeDMDIClient : public TMDIClient {
public:
  TTransferStruct TransferStruct;
  TThreeDMDIClient();
  char Filename[128];
protected:
  void CmFileOpen();
  void CmPerspective();
  void CmMoveIn();
  void CmMoveOut();
  void CmPrint();
  void CeEnableViewOptions(TCommandEnabler& ce);

  DECLARE_RESPONSE_TABLE(TThreeDMDIClient);
};

DEFINE_RESPONSE_TABLE1(TThreeDMDIClient, TMDIClient)
  EV_COMMAND(CM_FILEOPEN, CmFileOpen),
  EV_COMMAND(CM_PERSPECTIVE, CmPerspective),
  EV_COMMAND(CM_MOVEIN, CmMoveIn),
  EV_COMMAND(CM_MOVEOUT, CmMoveOut),
  EV_COMMAND(CM_PRINT, CmPrint),
  EV_COMMAND_ENABLE(CM_PERSPECTIVE, CeEnableViewOptions),
  EV_COMMAND_ENABLE(CM_MOVEIN, CeEnableViewOptions),
  EV_COMMAND_ENABLE(CM_MOVEOUT, CeEnableViewOptions),
  EV_COMMAND_ENABLE(CM_PRINT, CeEnableViewOptions),
END_RESPONSE_TABLE;

class TThreeDWindow : public TMDIChild {
public:
  TThreeD* ThreeD;        // A three-dimensional viewing object
  char FileName[MAXPATH];
  TThreeDWindow(TThreeDMDIClient* parent, const char* title);
  virtual ~TThreeDWindow() { delete ThreeD; };
```

```
  void Paint(TDC& dc, BOOL, TRect&);
  void EvSize(UINT, TSize&);

  DECLARE_RESPONSE_TABLE(TThreeDWindow);
};

DEFINE_RESPONSE_TABLE1(TThreeDWindow, TMDIChild)
  EV_WM_SIZE,
END_RESPONSE_TABLE;

// A dialog box that enables the user to set the various viewing parameters
class TSettingsDlg : public TDialog {
public:
  TSettingsDlg(TWindow* parent, int resourceId, TThreeDWindow* obj);
  void HandleDefaultButton();

  DECLARE_RESPONSE_TABLE(TSettingsDlg);
};

DEFINE_RESPONSE_TABLE1(TSettingsDlg, TDialog)
  EV_COMMAND(ID_DEFAULT, HandleDefaultButton),
END_RESPONSE_TABLE;

// The obj variable is a pointer to the child window object that was
// in focus at the time the dialog box was created.
TSettingsDlg::TSettingsDlg(TWindow* parent, int resourceId,
  TThreeDWindow* obj) : TDialog(parent, resourceId), TWindow(parent)
{
  // Move the child's data into the transfer buffer
  TThreeDMDIClient *p = TYPESAFE_DOWNCAST(Parent,TThreeDMDIClient);
  sprintf(p->TransferStruct.Fromx, "%4.2lf", obj->ThreeD->From.x);
  sprintf(p->TransferStruct.Fromy, "%4.2lf", obj->ThreeD->From.y);
  sprintf(p->TransferStruct.Fromz, "%4.2lf", obj->ThreeD->From.z);
  sprintf(p->TransferStruct.Atx, "%4.2lf", obj->ThreeD->At.x);
  sprintf(p->TransferStruct.Aty, "%4.2lf", obj->ThreeD->At.y);
  sprintf(p->TransferStruct.Atz, "%4.2lf", obj->ThreeD->At.z);
  sprintf(p->TransferStruct.Upx, "%4.2lf", obj->ThreeD->Up.x);
  sprintf(p->TransferStruct.Upy, "%4.2lf", obj->ThreeD->Up.y);
  sprintf(p->TransferStruct.Upz, "%4.2lf", obj->ThreeD->Up.z);
  // Convert radians to degrees
  double degAngle = obj->ThreeD->Angle * 57.2958;
  sprintf(p->TransferStruct.View, "%4.2lf", degAngle);
  new TButton(this, ID_DEFAULT); // Tell OWL about the default button
  new TEdit(this, ID_FROMX, sizeof(p->TransferStruct.Fromx));
  new TEdit(this, ID_FROMY, sizeof(p->TransferStruct.Fromy));
  new TEdit(this, ID_FROMZ, sizeof(p->TransferStruct.Fromz));
  new TEdit(this, ID_ATX, sizeof(p->TransferStruct.Atx));
  new TEdit(this, ID_ATY, sizeof(p->TransferStruct.Aty));
  new TEdit(this, ID_ATZ, sizeof(p->TransferStruct.Atz));
  new TEdit(this, ID_UPX, sizeof(p->TransferStruct.Upx));
  new TEdit(this, ID_UPY, sizeof(p->TransferStruct.Upy));
  new TEdit(this, ID_UPZ, sizeof(p->TransferStruct.Upz));
  new TEdit(this, ID_VIEW, sizeof(p->TransferStruct.View));
```

```
    SetTransferBuffer(&(p->TransferStruct));
}

// The default button was pressed; use the default settings
void TSettingsDlg::HandleDefaultButton()
{
  Destroy(ID_DEFAULT);   // Force the dialog box to terminate
}

// Initialize the transfer buffer in the MDI constructor
TThreeDMDIClient::TThreeDMDIClient(): TMDIClient()
{
  memset(&TransferStruct, 0x00, sizeof(TransferStruct));
}

// Clear the object list. You can call the figure list function
// directly or use a message as is done here.
void TThreeDMDIClient::CmFileOpen()
{
  FILE *fp;
  Filename[0] = '\0';
  TFileOpenDialog::TData FilenameData(
    OFN_FILEMUSTEXIST | OFN_HIDEREADONLY | OFN_PATHMUSTEXIST,
    "Figures (*.FIG)|*.DAT|", 0, "", "DAT");
  TFileOpenDialog *fileDlg = new TFileOpenDialog(this, FilenameData);
  if (fileDlg->Execute() == IDOK) {
    // Open the file
    if ((fp = fopen(FilenameData.FileName, "r")) == NULL) {
      ::MessageBox(HWindow, "Could not open file", 0, MB_OK);
      return;
    }
    else {
      lstrcpy(Filename, FilenameData.FileName);
      (new TThreeDWindow(this, Filename))->Create();
      fclose(fp);
    }
  }
}

// Allow the user to change the viewing parameters. Pop up a dialog
// box that enables the user to alter the various settings. Force the
// current child window that is in focus, if there is one, to redraw
// itself with these new settings.
void TThreeDMDIClient::CmPerspective()
{
  TThreeDWindow* obj = (TThreeDWindow *)GetActiveMDIChild();

  int resp = GetModule()->ExecDialog(new TSettingsDlg(this, ID_DIALOG,
    obj));
  if (resp != IDCANCEL) {
    if (resp == IDOK) {
      char buffer[256];
      wsprintf(buffer, "%s", TransferStruct.View);
      // The user pressed the OK button. Copy the new view
```

```
            // parameters to the active child window.
            obj->ThreeD->From.x = atof(TransferStruct.Fromx);
            obj->ThreeD->From.y = atof(TransferStruct.Fromy);
            obj->ThreeD->From.z = atof(TransferStruct.Fromz);
            obj->ThreeD->At.x = atof(TransferStruct.Atx);
            obj->ThreeD->At.y = atof(TransferStruct.Aty);
            obj->ThreeD->At.z = atof(TransferStruct.Atz);
            obj->ThreeD->Up.x = atof(TransferStruct.Upx);
            obj->ThreeD->Up.y = atof(TransferStruct.Upy);
            obj->ThreeD->Up.z = atof(TransferStruct.Upz);
            // Convert angle to radians when updating view angle
            obj->ThreeD->Angle = atof(TransferStruct.View) * 0.0174533;
              wsprintf(buffer, "%f", obj->ThreeD->Angle);
        }
      else {     // User must have selected Default settings
          obj->ThreeD->SetAt();
          obj->ThreeD->SetFrom();
          obj->ThreeD->Angle = 60.0 * 0.017453293;  // Use radians
        }
        ::InvalidateRect(GetActiveMDIChild()->HWindow, 0, TRUE);
    }
}

// Enable the view menu options when there is an open MDI window
void TThreeDMDIClient::CeEnableViewOptions(TCommandEnabler& ce)
{
  ce.Enable((GetActiveMDIChild()==0) ? 0 : 1);
}

// Interactively move the from point towards or away from
// the at point, depending upon the user input.
void TThreeDMDIClient::CmMoveIn()
{
  const double INC = 0.9;
  TThreeDWindow* obj = (TThreeDWindow *)GetActiveMDIChild();
  double nux = obj->ThreeD->At.x + INC *
    (obj->ThreeD->From.x - obj->ThreeD->At.x);
  double nuy = obj->ThreeD->At.y + INC *
    (obj->ThreeD->From.y - obj->ThreeD->At.y);
  double nuz = obj->ThreeD->At.z + INC *
    (obj->ThreeD->From.z - obj->ThreeD->At.z);
  if (nux == obj->ThreeD->At.x && nuy == obj->ThreeD->At.y
    && nuz == obj->ThreeD->At.z)
    ::MessageBox(HWindow, "Cannot move to here", "Error", MB_OK);
  else {
    obj->ThreeD->From.x = nux;
    obj->ThreeD->From.y = nuy;
    obj->ThreeD->From.z = nuz;
    ::InvalidateRect(obj->HWindow, 0, TRUE);
  }
}

// Interactively move the from point towards or away from
// the at point, depending upon the user input.
```

```
void TThreeDMDIClient::CmMoveOut()
{
  const double INC = 1.1;
  TThreeDWindow* obj = (TThreeDWindow *)GetActiveMDIChild();
  double nux = obj->ThreeD->At.x + INC *
    (obj->ThreeD->From.x - obj->ThreeD->At.x);
  double nuy = obj->ThreeD->At.y + INC *
    (obj->ThreeD->From.y - obj->ThreeD->At.y);
  double nuz = obj->ThreeD->At.z + INC *
    (obj->ThreeD->From.z - obj->ThreeD->At.z);
  if (nux == obj->ThreeD->At.x && nuy == obj->ThreeD->At.y &&
    nuz == obj->ThreeD->At.z)
    ::MessageBox(HWindow, "Cannot move to here", "Error", MB_OK);
  else {
    obj->ThreeD->From.x = nux;
    obj->ThreeD->From.y = nuy;
    obj->ThreeD->From.z = nuz;
    ::InvalidateRect(obj->HWindow, 0, TRUE);
  }
}

// Create a printer device context
HDC CreatePrinterDC()
{
  char prnStr[80], *device, *driver, *port;
  GetProfileString("windows", "device", NULL, prnStr, 80);
  if ((device=strtok(prnStr, ",")) != 0 &&
    (driver=strtok(NULL, ",")) != 0 &&
    (port=strtok(NULL, ",")) != 0)
    return CreateDC(driver, device, port, NULL);
  return 0;     // No printer found
}

// Print the window
void TThreeDMDIClient::CmPrint()
{
  HDC hPrnDC = CreatePrinterDC();
  if (!hPrnDC) {   // Failed to set up printer
    ::MessageBox(0, "Could not find printer", "Error", MB_OK);
    return;
  }
  if (Escape(hPrnDC, STARTDOC, 6, "3DVIEW", NULL) > 0) {
    // Display the wire-frame view on the printer
    TThreeDWindow* obj = (TThreeDWindow *)GetActiveMDIChild();
    obj->ThreeD->View(hPrnDC);
    if (Escape(hPrnDC, NEWFRAME, 0, NULL, NULL) > 0)
      Escape(hPrnDC, ENDDOC, 0, NULL, NULL);
  }
  DeleteDC(hPrnDC);
}

// Constructor for each pop up (child) window
TThreeDWindow::TThreeDWindow(TThreeDMDIClient* parent, const char* title)
  : TMDIChild(*parent, title)
```

```
{
  ThreeD = new TThreeD;
  _fstrcpy(FileName, title);
  if (ThreeD->Read3DObject(FileName)) {
    ThreeD->SetAt();
    ThreeD->SetFrom();
  }
  else {
    ::MessageBox(HWindow, "Failed to read file", "Error",
      MB_OK | MB_ICONEXCLAMATION);
  }
}

// The window was resized, redraw the scene
void TThreeDWindow::EvSize(UINT sizeType, TSize& size)
{
  TMDIChild::EvSize(sizeType, size);
  ::InvalidateRect(HWindow, 0, TRUE);
}

// Paint the child's window
void TThreeDWindow::Paint(TDC& dc, BOOL, TRect&)
{
  RECT tect;
  ::GetClientRect(HWindow, &rect);
  ThreeD->Display(dc, rect);    // Display the figure
}

class TThreeDApp : public TApplication {
public:
  TThreeDApp(const char* name) : TApplication(name) { };
  void InitMainWindow();
};

void TThreeDApp::InitMainWindow()
{
  MainWindow = new TMDIFrame(Name, "MENU_1", *new TThreeDMDIClient);
}

int OwlMain(int /*argc*/, char* /*argv*/ [])
{
  return TThreeDApp("3DVIEW").Run();
}
```

SEVENTEEN

Rendering Solid Objects

Displaying objects as wire frames is a quick way to render three-dimensional scenes. However, to make the scenes more realistic, we need to display the surfaces of the objects as well. In this chapter, we'll extend the 3DVIEW program we developed in the last chapter and the **TThreeD** class from Chapter 15 so that we can display solid objects.

We'll begin by describing what's necessary to make the transition from wire-frame to solid objects. Then, we'll get into the application-level details of a new solid modeling program, 3DSOLID. We'll also present two object data files that are specially designed to illustrate the features of the new program.

Adding Solid Modeling

We already have the basic code for displaying three-dimensional objects contained in the **TThreeD** class. However, to display solid, three-dimensional objects, we'll need to make the following changes:

- Add a color value for each polygon in the object file.
- Display objects using filled polygons rather than line segments.
- Shade the polygons that make up the object according to the color of the object and the angle of its surface with respect to the light source.
- Paint the polygons in the correct order so that closer surfaces overlap more distant surfaces.

Removing Hidden Surfaces

Rendering solid objects is more difficult than displaying wire frames. A key reason is that you simply can't display the object surfaces in any order that you choose. You must display the objects so that surfaces behind closer ones are not displayed, or are at least covered. This process is called *hidden surface removal*.

You can take several approaches to remove hidden surfaces. One sensible approach is to sort an object's polygons based on their distance from the viewer, the *from* point. Then the polygons can be painted one at a time, starting from the polygon farthest away. This technique is known as the *painters algorithm*. Although simple, the painters algorithm is not guaranteed. Figure 17.1 illustrates two potential pitfalls. One problem occurs when several polygons overlap so that no single polygon is clearly behind all the others. Similarly, the painters algorithm may not work correctly if one polygon pierces another. In addition, from a computational standpoint, the painters algorithm is not the best approach since the polygons must be re-sorted every time the viewer's location is changed.

Another technique is *Z buffering*. Often implemented in hardware, this approach uses an extensive two-dimensional array that stores the distance to each point in the generated image. A pixel on the screen is painted and the Z buffer is updated only if its distance is closer than the current distance stored in the Z buffer. To use this technique, we would need to write our own polygon display routine so that it would use a Z buffer.

To avoid these problems, we'll implement an algorithm known as *Binary Space Partitioning* (*BSP*). This technique avoids each of the problems that the painters and Z buffer algorithms suffer from.

THE BSP APPROACH

The BSP algorithm consists of two parts. In the first stage, the object's polygons are organized into a specially ordered binary tree. Then, the tree is traversed according to the location of the viewer in order to display the correct scene.

Figure 17.1 The painters algorithm cannot display these two scenes correctly.

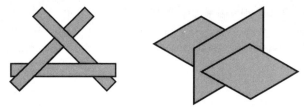

The technique revolves around the notion of *separation planes*. Polygons behind a separation plane are drawn first and those in front are painted last. Each node of the binary tree represents one polygon of the object and doubles as a separation plane. Two branches extend from each node of the BSP tree: one points to the polygons on the back side of the separation plane and the other branch points to the polygons on the front side. Displaying the scene requires traversing the binary tree in the correct order. For each node, it is determined whether the viewer is in front of or behind the separtion plane and traverses its branches accordingly—displaying the polygons behind the separation plane (with respect to the viewer) first.

This probably sounds much like a painters algorithm. It is. However, the BSP algorithm goes one step further. If a polygon is not completely on one side of the separation plane, then the polygon is divided into two. The part behind the separation plane is placed on one branch of the tree and the other piece is placed on the branch that corresponds with the polygons on its front side.

Let's look at an example. Assume you want to build a BSP tree for the four polygons shown in Figure 17.2. You can select any of the polygons as the first separation plane. We'll choose polygon A and create a node for it. Next, we'll select polygon B. It (polygon B) is behind A, so it is placed on A's back list. Now let's consider polygon C; it's on the front side of B, so it is placed on B's back pointer. The polygon D, however, is split by C into two pieces, D1 and

Figure 17.2 This figure illustrates how to buildi a BSP tree.

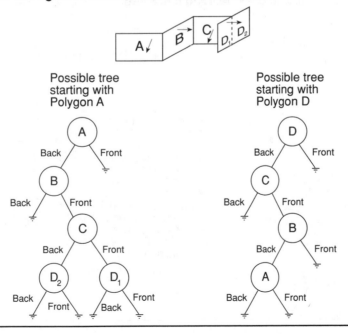

D2, since it is neither completely in front of or behind polygon C. Polygons D1 and D2, therefore, are added to the front and back pointers of C, respectively.

This process would be repeated if there were any other polygons. Notice that the tree created depends on the order in which we consider the polygons. For instance, the other tree in Figure 17.2 is a valid BSP tree for the same scene; however, the polygons were processed in the order D, C, B, and then A.

Painting the scene is simply a matter of traversing the tree correctly. At each node of the tree, you must determine whether the viewer (the *from* point) is in front of or behind the polygon represented by the node. The result of this calculation selects which branch of the tree to take. Whichever branch is on the side opposite the viewer is traversed first and its polygons are displayed. Then, the polygon for the node itself is painted, followed by the polygons in front. In this way, the scene is drawn in the correct order. Figure 17.3 walks through the display process for two different views.

One advantage of the BSP algorithm: the tree only needs to be built once for each collection of objects; you do not have to rebuild the tree each time the view changes. The order in which the tree is traversed depends on the location of the viewer. Each time the *from* point is changed, the program generates a different scene.

As you might guess, the BSP algorithm is not trivial and requires an extensive amount of code. If you are at all cautious about working with

---

Figure 17.3 Displaying a scene using a BSP tree.

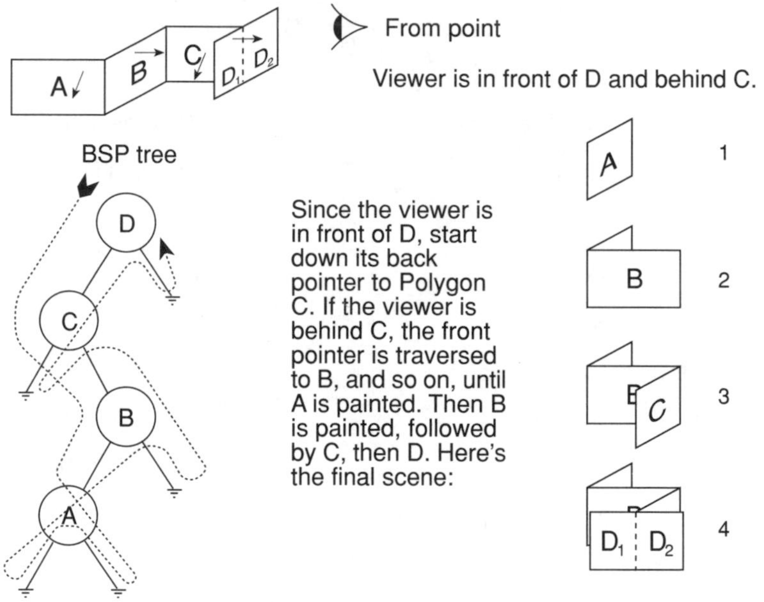

From point

Viewer is in front of D and behind C.

BSP tree

Since the viewer is in front of D, start down its back pointer to Polygon C. If the viewer is behind C, the front pointer is traversed to B, and so on, until A is painted. Then B is painted, followed by C, then D. Here's the final scene:

pointers, you may find the code a challenge. In addition, the BSP trees can get quite large for complex scenes. The size of the tree depends on two factors: the number of polygons in the scene and the number of polygons that are split. The latter number tends to vary greatly with the order in which the polygons are added to the tree. Another problem with the technique: the polygon splitting can give the scene a "shattered glass" appearance. I'll provide a suggestion on how to fix this problem at the end of this chapter.

There are also a few restrictions on the scenes that you can display. First, the polygons that make up the object must be planar. Therefore, we'll break up the figures into triangles so that we're always guaranteed planar polygons. In addition, the objects must be convex—in other words, they can't have depressions.

THE TThreeDSolid Class

The details of the BSP algorithm are encapsulated in the **TThreeDSolid** class. This class is derived from **TThreeD** and inherits much of its ability for handling three-dimensional objects. The new functions in **TThreeDSolid** are provided to support the rendering of solids.

The **TThreeDSolid** class also contains a handful of new data members. The **TriL** pointer holds a linked list of the triangles in the scene and the **Tree** pointer points to the root of the BSP tree. Both of these structures are built in the overridden **Read3DObject** function. In addition, **TThreeDSolid** contains several new variables to control the lighting. We'll discuss these variables in a later section.

The bulk of the **TThreeDSolid** class is dedicated to its numerous functions that support the BSP tree. These are listed in Table 17.1. Rather than review their code in detail, we'll take the high road and discuss, in general terms, what the important functions do.

Working with Triangles

To keep our code simple, objects will always be represented as a series of triangular polygons. By using triangles, we'll be assured that the polygons are always planar, as the BSP algorithm requires.

A key part of the BSP algorithm determines whether polygons are in front of or behind the current polygon being considered as the separation plane. But what do "in front of" and "behind" really mean? We'll assume that a polygon is in front of another if it is in the direction of the triangle's *normal*. (A normal is a vector that is perpendicular to the triangle's surface.) To be consistent in the way normals are used, we'll always specify the triangles in our data file by listing the vertices of the triangle in a counterclockwise direction and calculate the normal, as shown in Figure 17.4.

Table 17.1 Member Functions in the TThreeDSolid Class

Function	Description
Read3DObject	Reads an object file and builds the BSP tree
View	Overridden in order to call TraverseTree
CalcPlaneEqs	Precomputes the D term of the plane equation for each triangle
DisposeBSP	Frees the nodes of a BSP tree
MakeBSPNode	Creates and initializes a BSP node
AddList	Adds a triangle node to a temporary list
CalcSign	Determines which side of a plane a point is on
Intersect	Calculates where a line intersects a plane
InsertTriangle	Adds a triangle and its data to a temporary list of triangles
Split	Splits a triangle polygon into two or more pieces
MakeBSPTree	High-level function to create a BSP tree
CalcTriNormals	Precomputes the normal for each triangle
PrecomputeCentroids	Precomputes the centroid of each triangle
WorldToDisplay	Calculates where a world point is located in the display window
ComputeColor	Computes the shade of a color to use for a polygon
DisplayTriangle	Displays a triangle patch
TraverseTree	Traverses the BSP tree and displays the scene based on the current from point

Figure 17.4 We'll be using this technique to calculate the normal of a triangle.

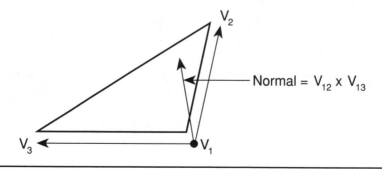

Adding Color to the Object Files

The **Read3DObject** function is partly overridden in order to read the colors of the polygons. Up to this point, we haven't used this feature of the file format. Specifying object colors requires two steps. First, the number of colors used by the polygons is listed at the beginning of the file. Following this is a list of the RGB colors used. Second, the negative number that has been used to signal the end of the polygon object is now employed as an index into the list of colors. For instance, the following header defines a palette of three colors:

```
3
255  0  0
0  255  0
0  0  255
```

Each color is specified as an RGB triplet. In this example, the first color is red, the second green, and the last blue. Then, to display a blue triangle, you might use the polygon sequence

```
1  2  3 -3
```

where the numbers 1, 2, and 3 point to the vertext list and −3 instructs 3DSOLID that it should use the third color in the list of colors—blue. The colors are stored in the **ColorPal** array starting at index location 1.

The rest of the file format is the same as before. Notice, however, that **Read3DObject** cannot read object files from previous chapters because the polygons are not specified as triangles.

Building a BSP Tree

The **Read3DObject** routine takes the steps necessary to build and initialize the BSP tree. First, it builds a linked-list copy of the triangles in the scene. Then, **Read3DObject** passes this list to **MakeBSPTree**, which actually constructs the BSP tree. In addition, **Read3DObject** precomputes the normals, centroids, and part of the plane equation for each triangle so that, when displaying a view, they don't have to be recomputed.

The **MakeBSPTree** function labels the first triangle in the list of triangles passed to it as the current separation plane. It then sorts the remaining polygons into the **frontList** and **backList** linked lists, depending on whether the polygons are in front of or behind the separation plane. Next, the separation plane is added to the BSP tree and **MakeBSPTree** is called again to process the **frontList** and **backList** lists and return their BSP subtrees.

```
node = MakeBSPNode(root->T);  // Add node for the root triangle
if (!node) {
  MessageBox(GetActiveWindow(), "MakeBSPTree: Out of Memory",
```

```
    GetApplicationObject()->GetName(), MB_OK | MB_ICONEXCLAMATION);
  return node;
}
node->Outside = MakeBSPTree(frontList);
node->Inside = MakeBSPTree(backList);
```

The **CalcSign** function helps to determine which side of the separation plane the polygons are on. It is called once for each vertex in a triangle to solve the plane equation for the separation plane using the vertex coordinate. The sign of the result reveals which side of the separation plane the vertex is on.

If **CalcSign** returns values with different signs for vertices in the same triangle, then that triangle crosses over the separation plane. In this case, the triangle is split into two or three pieces, as illustrated in Figure 17.5, by the function **Split**. These new triangular pieces are added to the front and back lists and processed like the other polygons. Notice that the splitting is performed so that it always creates triangles. This explains why a single triangle is split into three pieces, rather than two.

Displaying the Triangles

Displaying a scene is still initiated by the **View** member function in **TThreeD**. However, **View** is overridden in **TThreeDSolid** in order to call **TraverseTree**, which recursively winds its way through the BSP tree, displaying the triangles in the BSP tree as it proceeds. The key to the function is the calculation of the dot product between the triangle's normal and vector **S**—the line of sight to the triangle. Figure 17.6 shows the relationship between these two vectors. The sign of the dot product indicates which side of the polygon the viewer is located. If the *from* point is on the front side, the back polygons are displayed first. Otherwise, the front polygons are displayed first.

Figure 17.5 Splitting a triangle to the separation plane.

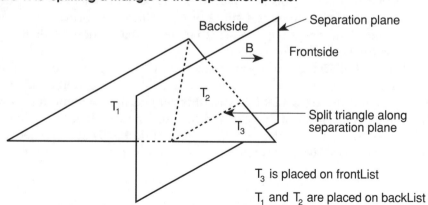

```
if (tree) {
  s.x = From.x - tree->Tri->V1.x;
  s.y = From.y - tree->Tri->V1.y;
  s.z = From.z - tree->Tri->V1.z;
  Normalize(&s);
  if (Dot(&s, &tree->Tri->Normal) > 0) { // The eye is in front
    TraverseTree(hDC, tree->Inside);        // of the polygon
    DisplayTriangle(hDC, tree->Tri);
    TraverseTree(hDC, tree->Outside);
  }
  else {                                  // The eye is in back
    TraverseTree(hDC, tree->Outside);       // of the polygon
    DisplayTriangle(hDC, tree->Tri);
    TraverseTree(hDC, tree->Inside);
  }
}
```

The **DisplayTriangle** function handles the details required to paint each triangle. This function first calls **ComputeColor**—we'll get to this function in a bit—to retrieve the polygon's color. Then, it calls **WorldToDisplay** to convert each of the triangle's vertices, which are in world coordinates, to the window's coordinates. Next, it creates and selects a solid brush that matches the color returned by **ComputeColor**. Finally, it displays a filled triangle by calling **Polygon**.

One notable feature missing from 3DSOLID is clipping to the viewing pyramid, which we did in the earlier programs. We've left this out because clipping polygons is slightly more complex than clipping line segments, which we did in **TThreeD**. An advantage of letting Windows perform the clipping is that the scene can cover the entire window. The drawback is that you can't zoom inside the object without getting incorrect results. You could fix this by clipping triangles that extend behind the viewer using a function similar to **Split**.

Figure 17.6 The line of sight and triangle's normal determine which side of the polygon the viewer is located.

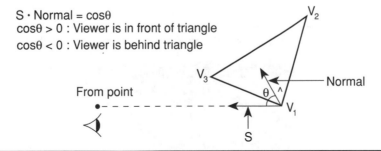

$S \cdot Normal = \cos\theta$
$\cos\theta > 0$: Viewer is in front of triangle
$\cos\theta < 0$: Viewer is behind triangle

ADDING A LIGHTING MODEL

The BSP algorithm enables you to paint the polygons that represent a three-dimensional object in the correct order. However, to render realistic scenes, you must account for the shading of surfaces as well. If an object is green, for instance, and you paint all sides of the object the same green, the sides will merge and you won't have any sense of depth. You must adjust the color of angled polygons as we did for the three-dimensional bar charts in Chapter 9.

We'll introduce a lighting model to determine the shade of each polygon. The brightness of the color depends on how bright an imaginary light is, the orientation of the surfaces, and how reflective the object is supposed to be. All of these factors are encapsulated in the lighting model we'll use.

We'll assume that a single, distant light source illuminates the scene evenly. The position of the light is stored in the vector **Light** in the **TThreeDSolid** class. The overall amount that the light source illuminates the scene is known as the *ambient light* portion of the illumuation. In general, the brighter the light is, the brighter the surface must be drawn.

The surface shade also depends on the properties of the surface and how much it scatters light at various angles—with respect to the light source. This is the *diffuse* component of the light. The closer the surface's normal points to the light source, the brighter the object should be drawn. A smoother, mirror-like object, for instance, would reflect more light when directly facing a light than a rough surface would refelect. The lighting model also darkens objects that face away from the light.

The 3DSOLID program contains two parameters that enable you to specify the amount of contribution that the ambient and diffuse light provide. These two variables, which must be between 0 and 1, are called **Ambient** and **Diffuse** and are located in the **TThreeDSolid** class. Their values are initialized in **TThreeDSolid**'s constructor. Typically, the ambient light contribution is greater than the diffuse contribution.

The 3DSOLID program includes two dialog boxes for setting the position of the light and the **Ambient** and **Diffuse** variables. These are implemented by the **TLightLocDlg** and **TLightingDlg** objects and are shown in Figures 17.7 and 17.8.

Figure 17.7 You use the Light Location dialog box to set the location of the light source.

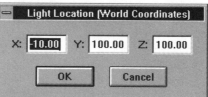

Figure 17.8 You use the Lighting dialog box to set the levels of ambient and diffuse lighting.

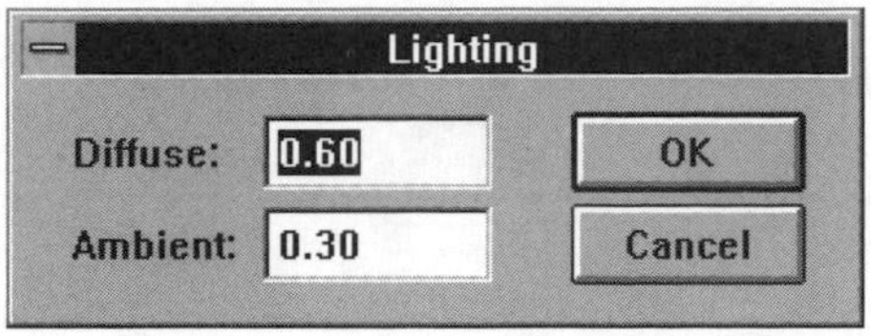

ADDING A TOOLBAR

One of the new features included in 3DSOLID is a toolbar at the top of the application window. The toolbar consists of the toolbar itself and a series of buttons. Each button is linked to some event in the program—usually a menu option. Therefore, when you click on a toolbar button it generates an event that looks like you actually selected its corresponding menu option.

We'll use OWL's **TControlBar** to add a toolbar to our application. This class takes care of most of the work of managing the toolbar. We do, however, have to tell the toolbar which buttons to create, supply bitmaps for them, and tell the toolbar which events belong to the buttons.

Adding a toolbar to an OWL-based MDI application takes four steps. The first step is to derive the frame window from OWL's **TDecoratedMDIFrame** class rather than some other class, such as **TMDIFrame**. The application object's **MainWindow** in 3DSOLID, in fact, is set to a **TDecoraterMDIFrame** window:

```
void TThreeDApp::InitMainWindow()
{
  TDecoratedFrame* Frame =
    new TDecoratedMDIFrame(Name, "COMMANDS", *new TThreeDMDIClient);
  MainWindow = Frame;
```

Second, the application's **InitMainWindow** function allocates a **TControlBar** object and assigns it to the frame window:

```
TControlBar* ControlBar = BuildControlBar(Frame, TControlBar::Horizontal);
Frame->Insert(*ControlBar, TDecoratedFrame::Top);
```

Third, we must create a bitmap for each button. We'll define separate .BMP (bitmap) files for each bitmap and tie them together in the resource file. In addition, you should give the bitmap the same resource identifier that you plan to use for the command it corresponds to. For instance, the resource identifier for the file open command in 3DSOLID has a value of **CM_FILEOPEN**, which is the same identifier for the File menu's Open command.

Figure 17.9 These three bitmaps are used in the toolbar's buttons.

The fourth step is to allocate a **TButtonGadget** object for each button in the toolbar and add the object to the toolbar by calling **TControlBar**'s **Insert** function. For example, the following statement creates a button for the file open command and adds it to the toolbar:

```
cb->Insert(*new TButtonGadget(CM_FILEOPEN, CM_FILEOPEN));
```

An equivalent statement exists for each button.

Figure 17.9 shows each of the bitmaps used in 3DSOLID's toolbar.

COMPILING AND USING 3DSOLID

The complete code for the BSP algorithm and the 3DSOLID program are located in the source files 3DSOLID.RC, 3DSOLID.H, and 3DSOLID.CPP. Notice that 3DSOLID includes its own resource file, 3DSOLID.RC, since it introduces two new dialog boxes and their corresponding menu entries.

Table 17.2 lists all the files you'll need to compile 3DSOLID. You'll need to create a project file with the files 3DSOLID.CPP, THREED.CPP, VECTOR.CPP, and 3DSOLID.RC. Because the program is so large, you can't compile the program with the small memory model. Instead, compile it with the large memory model and use the DLL libraries as you did for the OODRAW program in Chapter 14.

Figure 17.10 shows the environment of the 3DSOLID program. In many ways, it is similar to its wire-frame counterpart in Chapter 15. This program

Table 17.2 Files Used to Compile the Program 3DSOLID.CPP

Filename	Chapter	Include in Project File
3DSOLID.H	17	No
3DSOLID.CPP	17	Yes
3DSOLID.RC	17	Yes
THREED.H	15	No
THREED.CPP	15	Yes
VECTOR.CPP	15	Yes
VECTOR.H	15	No

Figure 17.10 The 3DSOLID program creates this environment.

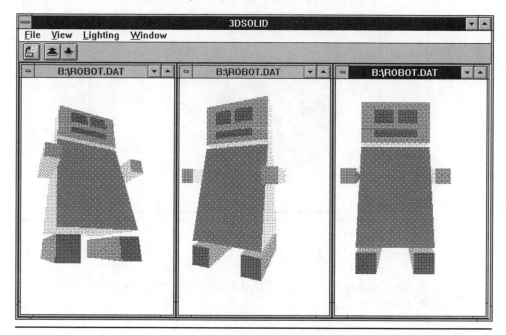

does, however, contain two new dialog boxes that control the lighting parameters. You probably won't need to change their settings unless you want to achieve some special effect.

Sample Solid Objects

This section provides two sample object files that adhere to the special file format described in this chapter. Remember, the scene is divided into triangles. The first object file, STEST1.DAT, generates the scene shown in Figure 17.11. Here is its data:

```
1
100 200 0
6   16
1.0   0.0   1.0
1.0   1.0   1.0
1.0   0.0   0.0
1.0   1.0   0.0
0.0   1.0   0.0
0.0   1.0   1.0
1   4   3   -1
1   2   4   -1
2   6   4   -1
6   5   4   -1
```

Figure 17.11 This object was created by the file STEST1.DAT.

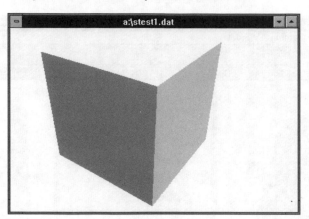

To duplicate Figure 17.11, set the *from* point to (2.2,1.7,1.7) and use a viewing angle of 30 degrees.

The next object file, STEST2.DAT, renders the scene shown in Figure 17.12. Its data is:

```
2
0 0 200
200 0 0
12 56
1.0   1.0   1.0   1.0   1.0   0.0
1.0   0.0   0.0   1.0   0.0   1.0
0.0   1.0   1.0   0.0   1.0   0.0
0.0   0.0   0.0   0.0   0.0   1.0
-1.5 -1.5   1.2   2  -1.5   1.2
2    2   1.2  -1.5   2   1.2
1   3   2  -1   1   4   3   -1   7   6   3   -1   2   3   6   -1
5   1   6  -1   1   2   6   -1   8   5   6   -1   8   6   7   -1
4   7   3  -1   4   8   7   -1   4   5   8   -1   4   1   5   -1
11  10  12  -2  12  10   9   -2
```

The light source in Figure 17.12 is set to (-10,100,50) and the *from* point is set to (4.25,1.87,1.7), with a viewing angle of 30 degrees.

Enhancing 3DSOLID

There are many ways you can expand upon the 3DSOLID program. The most useful would probably involve providing better shading. Due to the splitting of the polygons and the fact that figures are specified as a list of triangles, the objects may appear fractured if the light is close. The problem is that the shades of the triangle patches do not blend well. Each polygon uses a single,

Figure 17.12 This scene was created by the file STEST2.DAT.

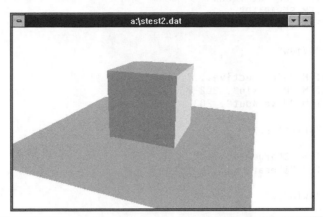

constant fill color. A more realistic approach is to vary the shading within each polygon.

One solution is to calculate the surface color at each vertex of the polygon and then perform a linear interpolation for the values in between. Named after its developer, this technique is known as Gouraud shading. To implement Gouraud shading, you'll have to provide your own fill routine for displaying triangles.

You also won't be able to rely on Windows' dithering to provide shades of colors, because you'll be plotting pixels in your fill routine. Since you'll want as many shades of colors available at one time as you can get, you'll probably want to use a logical palette filled with the colors you need. Unfortunately, this will mean that a standard VGA won't be sufficient to display objects shaded this way. To make your program useful on a wide variety of display devices, you'll probably want to supply a menu option that selects between constant shading and Gouraud shading.

Finally, to save space, a few of the functions from 3DVIEW are not included in 3DSOLID. For instance, the program cannot display a wire-frame view. It would be simple, however, to add a menu option that selects between solid and wire-frame views and inherits the wire-frame code from the **TThreeD** class.

• 3DSOLID.RC

```
/* 3DSOLID.RC: Resource file for 3DSOLID.RC */

COMMANDS MENU
{
 POPUP "&File"
 {
  MENUITEM "&Open...", 201
```

```
     MENUITEM SEPARATOR
     MENUITEM "&Print", 204
     MENUITEM SEPARATOR
     MENUITEM "E&xit", 24310
    }
    POPUP "&View"
    {
     MENUITEM "&Perspective...", 209
     MENUITEM "Move &in", 202
     MENUITEM "Move &out", 203
    }
    POPUP "&Lighting"
    {
     MENUITEM "&Parameters...", 208
     MENUITEM "&Location...", 207
    }
    POPUP "&Window"
    {
     MENUITEM "&Cascade", 24361
     MENUITEM "&Tile", 24362
     MENUITEM "Arrange &icons", 24364
     MENUITEM SEPARATOR
     MENUITEM "Close &all", 24365
    }
  }

210 DIALOG 46, 20, 248, 115
STYLE DS_MODALFRAME | WS_POPUP | WS_CLIPSIBLINGS | WS_CAPTION | WS_SYSMENU
CAPTION "Viewing Parameters"
{
 EDITTEXT 212, 70, 12, 26, 13
 EDITTEXT 213, 114, 12, 26, 13
 EDITTEXT 214, 160, 12, 26, 13
 EDITTEXT 215, 70, 39, 26, 13
 EDITTEXT 216, 114, 39, 26, 13
 EDITTEXT 217, 160, 39, 26, 13
 EDITTEXT 218, 70, 65, 26, 13
 EDITTEXT 219, 114, 65, 26, 13
 EDITTEXT 220, 160, 65, 26, 13
 EDITTEXT 221, 70, 91, 26, 13
 DEFPUSHBUTTON "OK", 1, 200, 8, 40, 14
 PUSHBUTTON "Cancel", 2, 200, 25, 40, 14
 PUSHBUTTON "&Default", 222, 200, 62, 40, 14
 RTEXT "From:", -1, 26, 13, 23, 12
 RTEXT "At:", -1, 26, 40, 23, 12
 RTEXT "Up:", -1, 26, 66, 23, 12
 RTEXT "Viewing angle:", -1, 18, 93, 48, 12
 LTEXT "degrees", -1, 100, 93, 28, 12
 RTEXT "Y", -1, 106, 14, 5, 11
 RTEXT "X", -1, 62, 14, 5, 11
 RTEXT "Z", -1, 152, 14, 5, 11
 CONTROL "", -1, "STATIC", SS_BLACKFRAME | WS_CHILD | WS_VISIBLE, 12, 9,
    178, 19
 RTEXT "Y", -1, 106, 41, 5, 11
```

```
   RTEXT "X", -1, 62, 41, 5, 11
   RTEXT "Z", -1, 152, 41, 5, 11
   CONTROL "", -1, "STATIC", SS_BLACKFRAME | WS_CHILD | WS_VISIBLE, 12, 36,
     178, 19
   RTEXT "Y", -1, 106, 67, 5, 11
   RTEXT "X", -1, 62, 67, 5, 11
   RTEXT "Z", -1, 152, 67, 5, 11
   CONTROL "", -1, "STATIC", SS_BLACKFRAME | WS_CHILD | WS_VISIBLE, 12, 62,
     178, 19
   CONTROL "", -1, "STATIC", SS_BLACKFRAME | WS_CHILD | WS_VISIBLE, 12, 88,
178, 19
}

230 DIALOG 89, 56, 142, 41
STYLE DS_MODALFRAME | WS_POPUP | WS_CAPTION | WS_SYSMENU
CAPTION "Lighting"
{
  EDITTEXT 101, 42, 7, 38, 12
  EDITTEXT 102, 42, 23, 38, 12
  DEFPUSHBUTTON "OK", 1, 94, 6, 40, 14
  PUSHBUTTON "Cancel", 2, 94, 22, 40, 14
  LTEXT "Diffuse:", -1, 9, 9, 30, 8
  LTEXT "Ambient:", -1, 9, 25, 30, 8
}

231 DIALOG 80, 60, 141, 51
STYLE DS_MODALFRAME | WS_POPUP | WS_CAPTION | WS_SYSMENU
CAPTION "Light Location (World Coordinates)"
{
  EDITTEXT 103, 19, 10, 27, 12
  EDITTEXT 104, 61, 10, 27, 12
  EDITTEXT 105, 105, 10, 27, 12
  DEFPUSHBUTTON "OK", 1, 25, 31, 40, 14
  PUSHBUTTON "Cancel", 2, 75, 31, 40, 14
  LTEXT "X:", -1, 9, 12, 8, 8
  LTEXT "Y:", -1, 51, 12, 8, 8
  LTEXT "Z:", -1, 95, 12, 8, 8
}

201 BITMAP "fileopen.bmp"
202 BITMAP "movein.bmp"
203 BITMAP "moveout.bmp"
```

● 3DSOLID.H

```
// 3DSOLID.H: Header file for 3DSOLID.CPP.

#define CM_FILEOPEN 201
#define CM_MOVEIN 202
#define CM_MOVEOUT 203
#define CM_PRINT 204
#define CM_SOLID 206
#define CM_LIGHTLOC 207
```

```
#define CM_LIGHTING 208
#define CM_PERSPECTIVE 209

#define ID_DIALOG 210
#define ID_SETTINGS 211
#define ID_FROMX 212
#define ID_FROMY 213
#define ID_FROMZ 214
#define ID_ATX 215
#define ID_ATY 216
#define ID_ATZ 217
#define ID_UPX 218
#define ID_UPY 219
#define ID_UPZ 220
#define ID_VIEW 221
#define ID_DEFAULT 222

#define LIGHTING_DLG 230
#define ID_DIFFUSE 101
#define ID_AMBIENT 102
#define LIGHTLOC_DLG 231
#define ID_LIGHTX 103
#define ID_LIGHTY 104
#define ID_LIGHTZ 105
```

• 3DSOLID.CPP

```
// 3DSOLID.CPP: Displays a solid representation of a three-dimensional
// object. Implements the BSP algorithm described in Chapter 17 in order
// to display the surfaces of objects correctly. Compile with VECTOR.CPP,
// 3DSOLID.RC, and THREED.CPP.
#include <owl\applicat.h>
#include <owl\framewin.h>
#include <owl\dc.h>
#include <owl\opensave.h>
#include <owl\edit.h>
#include <owl\button.h>
#include <owl\mdi.h>
#include <stdio.h>
#include <stdlib.h>
#include <string.h>
#include <math.h>
#include <io.h>
#include <dir.h>
#include <owl\buttonga.h>     // For OWL's button gadgets
#include <owl\controlb.h>     // For the control bar
#include <owl\decmdifr.h>     // Decorated MDI frames
#include "vector.h"
#include "threed.h"
#include "3dsolid.h"

#define EM_FILEOPENERROR -100
#define EM_FILETOOBIG -101
```

```
#define EM_TOOMANYCOLORS -102      // Too many colors in object file
#define TOL 0.001
#define NUM_SHADES 255

// Return the larger of two values
inline double MaxOf(double val1, double val2) {
  return (val1 > val2) ? val1 : val2;
}
const MAXREALLEN = 11;      // A real number in a dialog box field can
struct TTransferStruct {   // have one less than this many characters
  char Fromx[MAXREALLEN];
  char Fromy[MAXREALLEN];
  char Fromz[MAXREALLEN];
  char Atx[MAXREALLEN];
  char Aty[MAXREALLEN];
  char Atz[MAXREALLEN];
  char Upx[MAXREALLEN];
  char Upy[MAXREALLEN];
  char Upz[MAXREALLEN];
  char View[MAXREALLEN];
};

typedef VECTOR Point;
struct TRIANGLE {
  Point V1, V2, V3;    // The three vertices of the triangle
  VECTOR Normal;       // The normal of the triangle
  double d; // The d term of the plane which contains the triangle
  Point Centroid;      // Centroid of the triangle
  int ColorNdx;        // Index of triangle's color
  TRIANGLE *Next;
};

struct TLIST {          // Points to the triangle list data in TriL
  TRIANGLE *T;          // Points to a specific triangle in the TriL
  TLIST *Next;          // Next TLIST structure
};

struct BSPNode {
  TRIANGLE *Tri;
  BSPNode *Inside, *Outside;
};

struct RGBCOLOR {
  BYTE r, g, b;
};

struct TLightingTransfer {
  char Diffuse[MAXREALLEN], Ambient[MAXREALLEN];
};

struct TLightLocTransfer {
  char x[MAXREALLEN], y[MAXREALLEN], z[MAXREALLEN];
};
```

```
// This class supports solid three-dimensional objects
class TThreeDSolid : public TThreeD {
public:
  TRIANGLE* TriL;    // List of triangles in drawing
  BSPNode* Tree;     // Pointer to the root of the BSP tree
  RGBCOLOR ColorPal[NUMCOLORS]; // Color palette for polygons
  int NumColors;                // Number of colors in ColorPal
  double Ambient, Diffuse;      // Contributions of light. 0 <= >= 1.0
  VECTOR Light;                 // Location of light
  TThreeDSolid();
  int Read3DObject(char *filename);
  void View(HDC hDC);
  void CalcPlaneEqs();
  void DisposeBSP(BSPNode* tree);
  BSPNode *MakeBSPNode(TRIANGLE* tri);
  void AddList(TLIST* *tlist, TRIANGLE* tri);
  double CalcSign(Point& p, TRIANGLE* tri);
  void Intersect(TRIANGLE* tri, Point& v1, Point& v2, Point& loc);
  void InsertTriangle(TLIST* *tlist, Point& v1, Point& v2,
    Point& v3, TRIANGLE* copyFrom);
  void Split(TLIST* *frontList, TLIST* *backList, double signV1,
    double signV2, double signV3, TRIANGLE* sepPlane, TRIANGLE* tri);
  BSPNode* MakeBSPTree(TLIST* l);
  void CalcTriNormals();
  void PrecomputeCentroids();
  void WorldToDisplay(double x, double y, double z, int& xr, int& yr);
  COLORREF ComputeColor(Point& p, VECTOR& normal, int colorNdx);
  void DisplayTriangle(HDC hDC, TRIANGLE* tri);
  void TraverseTree(HDC hDC, BSPNode* tree);
};

// The application's client window class
class TThreeDMDIClient : public TMDIClient {
public:
  TTransferStruct TransferStruct;
  TLightingTransfer LightingTransfer;
  TLightLocTransfer LightLocTransfer;
  TThreeDMDIClient();
  void CmFileOpen();
  void CmPerspective();
  void CmMoveIn();
  void CmMoveOut();
  void CmPrint();
  void CmLighting();
  void CmLightLoc();
  void CeEnableViewOptions(TCommandEnabler& ce);

  DECLARE_RESPONSE_TABLE(TThreeDMDIClient);
};

DEFINE_RESPONSE_TABLE1(TThreeDMDIClient, TMDIClient)
  EV_COMMAND(CM_FILEOPEN, CmFileOpen),
  EV_COMMAND(CM_PRINT, CmPrint),
  EV_COMMAND(CM_PERSPECTIVE, CmPerspective),
```

```
    EV_COMMAND(CM_MOVEIN, CmMoveIn),
    EV_COMMAND(CM_MOVEOUT, CmMoveOut),
    EV_COMMAND(CM_LIGHTING, CmLighting),
    EV_COMMAND(CM_LIGHTLOC, CmLightLoc),
    EV_COMMAND_ENABLE(CM_PRINT, CeEnableViewOptions),
    EV_COMMAND_ENABLE(CM_PERSPECTIVE, CeEnableViewOptions),
    EV_COMMAND_ENABLE(CM_MOVEIN, CeEnableViewOptions),
    EV_COMMAND_ENABLE(CM_MOVEOUT, CeEnableViewOptions),
    EV_COMMAND_ENABLE(CM_LIGHTING, CeEnableViewOptions),
    EV_COMMAND_ENABLE(CM_LIGHTLOC, CeEnableViewOptions),
END_RESPONSE_TABLE;

// The class for each MDI child window
class TSolidWindow : public TMDIChild {
public:
  char Filename[MAXPATH];
  TThreeDSolid* ThreeD;
  TSolidWindow(TMDIClient* parent, const char* title);
  virtual ~TSolidWindow() { delete ThreeD; }
  void Paint(TDC& dc, BOOL, TRect&);
  void EvSize(UINT sizeType, TSize& size);

  DECLARE_RESPONSE_TABLE(TSolidWindow);
};

DEFINE_RESPONSE_TABLE1(TSolidWindow, TMDIChild)
  EV_WM_SIZE,
END_RESPONSE_TABLE;

// Enables the user to set the location of the light source
class TLightLocDlg : public TDialog {
public:
  TLightLocDlg(TWindow* parent, int menuResId, TSolidWindow* win);
};

// Enables the user to set the various viewing parameters
class TPerspectiveDlg : public TDialog {
public:
  TPerspectiveDlg(TWindow* parent, int menuResId, TSolidWindow* win);
  void HandleDefaultButton();

  DECLARE_RESPONSE_TABLE(TPerspectiveDlg);
};

DEFINE_RESPONSE_TABLE1(TPerspectiveDlg, TDialog)
  EV_COMMAND(ID_DEFAULT, HandleDefaultButton),
END_RESPONSE_TABLE;

// Enables the user to set the various lighting parameters
class TLightingDlg : public TDialog {
public:
  TLightingDlg(TWindow* parent, int menuResId, TSolidWindow* win);
};
```

```
// Initialize the three transfer buffers used to send and
// receive data from the dialog boxes in the program
TThreeDMDIClient::TThreeDMDIClient()
{
  memset(&TransferStruct, 0x00, sizeof(TransferStruct));
  memset(&LightingTransfer, 0x00, sizeof(LightingTransfer));
  memset(&LightLocTransfer, 0x00, sizeof(LightLocTransfer));
}

// This OWL function enables all view-related menu options
// when there is at least one MDI child window
void TThreeDMDIClient::CeEnableViewOptions(TCommandEnabler& ce)
{
  ce.Enable((GetActiveMDIChild()==0) ? 0 : 1);
}

// The win variable is a pointer to the child window object that was
// in focus at the time the dialog box was created
TPerspectiveDlg::TPerspectiveDlg(TWindow* parent, int menuResId,
  TSolidWindow* win) : TDialog(parent, menuResId)
{
  TThreeDMDIClient* p = TYPESAFE_DOWNCAST(parent,TThreeDMDIClient);
  // Move the child's data into the transfer buffer
  sprintf(p->TransferStruct.Fromx, "%4.2lf", win->ThreeD->From.x);
  sprintf(p->TransferStruct.Fromy, "%4.2lf", win->ThreeD->From.y);
  sprintf(p->TransferStruct.Fromz, "%4.2lf", win->ThreeD->From.z);
  sprintf(p->TransferStruct.Atx, "%4.2lf", win->ThreeD->At.x);
  sprintf(p->TransferStruct.Aty, "%4.2lf", win->ThreeD->At.y);
  sprintf(p->TransferStruct.Atz, "%4.2lf", win->ThreeD->At.z);
  sprintf(p->TransferStruct.Upx, "%4.2lf", win->ThreeD->Up.x);
  sprintf(p->TransferStruct.Upy, "%4.2lf", win->ThreeD->Up.y);
  sprintf(p->TransferStruct.Upz, "%4.2lf", win->ThreeD->Up.z);
  // Convert radians to degrees
  double DegAngle = win->ThreeD->Angle * 57.2958;
  sprintf(p->TransferStruct.View, "%4.2lf", DegAngle);
  new TButton(this, ID_DEFAULT); // Tell OWL about default button
  new TEdit(this, ID_FROMX, sizeof(p->TransferStruct.Fromx));
  new TEdit(this, ID_FROMY, sizeof(p->TransferStruct.Fromy));
  new TEdit(this, ID_FROMZ, sizeof(p->TransferStruct.Fromz));
  new TEdit(this, ID_ATX, sizeof(p->TransferStruct.Atx));
  new TEdit(this, ID_ATY, sizeof(p->TransferStruct.Aty));
  new TEdit(this, ID_ATZ, sizeof(p->TransferStruct.Atz));
  new TEdit(this, ID_UPX, sizeof(p->TransferStruct.Upx));
  new TEdit(this, ID_UPY, sizeof(p->TransferStruct.Upy));
  new TEdit(this, ID_UPZ, sizeof(p->TransferStruct.Upz));
  new TEdit(this, ID_VIEW, sizeof(p->TransferStruct.View));
  SetTransferBuffer(&(p->TransferStruct));
}

// Called when the user selects the Default button
void TPerspectiveDlg::HandleDefaultButton()
{
  Destroy(ID_DEFAULT);    // Force the dialog box to terminate
}
```

```
// Allow the user to change the viewing parameters. Pop up
// a dialog box that enables the user to alter the various
// settings. Force the current child window that is in focus,
// if there is one, to redraw itself with these new settings.
void TThreeDMDIClient::CmPerspective()
{
  TSolidWindow* win = (TSolidWindow *)GetActiveMDIChild();
  if (!win) return;    // No view to change
  switch (TPerspectiveDlg(this, ID_DIALOG, win).Execute()) {
    case IDOK:
      // The user pressed the OK button. Copy the new view
      // parameters to the active child window.
      win->ThreeD->From.x = atof(TransferStruct.Fromx);
      win->ThreeD->From.y = atof(TransferStruct.Fromy);
      win->ThreeD->From.z = atof(TransferStruct.Fromz);
      win->ThreeD->At.x = atof(TransferStruct.Atx);
      win->ThreeD->At.y = atof(TransferStruct.Aty);
      win->ThreeD->At.z = atof(TransferStruct.Atz);
      win->ThreeD->Up.x = atof(TransferStruct.Upx);
      win->ThreeD->Up.y = atof(TransferStruct.Upy);
      win->ThreeD->Up.z = atof(TransferStruct.Upz);
      // Convert angle to radians when updating view angle
      win->ThreeD->Angle = atof(TransferStruct.View) * 0.0174533;
      ::InvalidateRect(win->HWindow, 0, TRUE);
      break;
    case ID_DEFAULT:   // The user selected the Default button
      win->ThreeD->SetAt();
      win->ThreeD->SetFrom();
      win->ThreeD->Angle = 60.0 * 0.0174533;  // Angle is 60 degrees
      ::InvalidateRect(GetActiveMDIChild()->HWindow, 0, TRUE);
      break;
  }
}

// CmFileOpen responds to the File|Open menu option. It asks the
// user to enter the name of a file to read, opens the file,
// and creates a TSolidWindow that automatically reads the file
// and displays the figure in a new window.
void TThreeDMDIClient::CmFileOpen()
{
  FILE* fp;
  TFileOpenDialog::TData FilenameData(
    OFN_FILEMUSTEXIST | OFN_HIDEREADONLY | OFN_PATHMUSTEXIST,
    "Figures (*.DAT)|*.DAT|", 0, "", "DAT");
  TFileOpenDialog *fileDlg = new TFileOpenDialog(this, FilenameData);
  if (fileDlg->Execute() == IDOK) {  // Open the file
    if ((fp = fopen(FilenameData.FileName, "r")) == 0) {
      ::MessageBox(HWindow, "Could not open file",
        GetApplicationObject()->GetName(), MB_OK | MB_ICONEXCLAMATION);
      return;
    }
    else {   // Create a new window
      TSolidWindow* child = new TSolidWindow(this, FilenameData.FileName);
      child->Create();
```

```
      fclose(fp);
    }
  }
}

// Constructor for the MDI child window class
TSolidWindow::TSolidWindow(TMDIClient* parent, const char* title) :
  TMDIChild(*parent, title)
{
  strcpy(Filename, title);
  ThreeD = new TThreeDSolid;
  if (!ThreeD) {
    ::MessageBox(parent->HWindow, "Out of Memory",
      GetApplicationObject()->GetName(), MB_OK | MB_ICONEXCLAMATION);
    return;
  }
  switch (ThreeD->Read3DObject(Filename)) {
    case 0:
      ::MessageBox(parent->HWindow, "Out of Memory",
        GetApplicationObject()->GetName(), MB_OK | MB_ICONEXCLAMATION);
      break;
    case 1:  // The figure was successfully read from the file
      ThreeD->SetAt();   // Initialize the At and From points
      ThreeD->SetFrom();
      break;
    case EM_FILEOPENERROR:
      ::MessageBox(parent->HWindow, "Error opening file",
        GetApplicationObject()->GetName(), MB_OK | MB_ICONEXCLAMATION);
      break;
    case EM_FILETOOBIG:
      ::MessageBox(parent->HWindow, "Object in file is too large",
        GetApplicationObject()->GetName(), MB_OK | MB_ICONEXCLAMATION);
      break;
    case EM_TOOMANYCOLORS:
      ::MessageBox(parent->HWindow, "Too many colors in file",
        GetApplicationObject()->GetName(), MB_OK | MB_ICONEXCLAMATION);
      break;
  }
}

// Paint the MDI window
void TSolidWindow::Paint(TDC& dc, BOOL, TRect&)
{
  RECT rect;
  if (::IsIconic(HWindow)) return;  // Don't repaint if it's an icon
  ::GetClientRect(HWindow, &rect);
  // Use the isotropic mapping mode so that the X and Y dimensions of
  // equal sizes will appear the same within the window
  SetMapMode(dc, MM_ISOTROPIC);
  // Set the logical coordinates extend from 0 to 1000.
  SetWindowExtEx(dc, 1000, 1000, 0);
  if (rect.right <= rect.bottom) {
    SetViewportExtEx(dc, rect.right, rect.right, 0);
    SetViewportOrgEx(dc, 0, (rect.bottom-rect.right)/2, 0);
```

```
  }
  else {
    SetViewportExtEx(dc, rect.bottom, rect.bottom, 0);
    SetViewportOrgEx(dc, (rect.right-rect.bottom)/2, 0, 0);
  }
  ThreeD->SetEye();
  ThreeD->View(dc);      // Display the figure
}

// Sets up the dimensions of the window and various default values
TThreeDSolid::TThreeDSolid() : TThreeD()
{
  Ambient = 0.30; Diffuse = 0.60;
  Light.x = -10.0;  Light.y = 100;  Light.z = 100;
}

// Repaint the window when it is resized
void TSolidWindow::EvSize(UINT sizeType, TSize& size)
{
  TMDIChild::EvSize(sizeType, size);
  ::InvalidateRect(HWindow, 0, TRUE);
}

// Interactively move the from point towards or away from
// the at point, depending upon the user input.
void TThreeDMDIClient::CmMoveIn()
{
  const double INC = 0.9;
  TSolidWindow* win = (TSolidWindow *)GetActiveMDIChild();
  if (!win) return;
  double nux = win->ThreeD->At.x + INC *
    (win->ThreeD->From.x - win->ThreeD->At.x);
  double nuy = win->ThreeD->At.y + INC *
    (win->ThreeD->From.y - win->ThreeD->At.y);
  double nuz = win->ThreeD->At.z + INC *
    (win->ThreeD->From.z - win->ThreeD->At.z);
  if (nux == win->ThreeD->At.x && nuy == win->ThreeD->At.y &&
    nuz == win->ThreeD->At.z)
    ::MessageBox(HWindow, "Cannot move to here",
      GetApplicationObject()->GetName(), MB_OK | MB_ICONEXCLAMATION);
  else {
    win->ThreeD->From.x = nux;
    win->ThreeD->From.y = nuy;
    win->ThreeD->From.z = nuz;
    ::InvalidateRect(win->HWindow, 0, TRUE);
  }
}

// Interactively move the from point towards or away from
// the at point, depending upon the user input
void TThreeDMDIClient::CmMoveOut()
{
  const double INC = 1.1;
  TSolidWindow* win = (TSolidWindow *)GetActiveMDIChild();
```

```
  if (!win) return;
  double nux = win->ThreeD->At.x + INC *
    (win->ThreeD->From.x - win->ThreeD->At.x);
  double nuy = win->ThreeD->At.y + INC *
    (win->ThreeD->From.y - win->ThreeD->At.y);
  double nuz = win->ThreeD->At.z + INC *
    (win->ThreeD->From.z - win->ThreeD->At.z);
  if (nux == win->ThreeD->At.x && nuy == win->ThreeD->At.y &&
    nuz == win->ThreeD->At.z)
    ::MessageBox(HWindow, "Cannot move to here",
      GetApplicationObject()->GetName(), MB_OK | MB_ICONEXCLAMATION);
  else {
    win->ThreeD->From.x = nux;
    win->ThreeD->From.y = nuy;
    win->ThreeD->From.z = nuz;
    ::InvalidateRect(win->HWindow, 0, TRUE);
  }
}

// Create a printer device context
HDC CreatePrinterDC()
{
  char prnStr[80], *device, *driver, *port;
  GetProfileString("windows", "device", 0, prnStr, 80);
  if ((device=strtok(prnStr, ",")) != 0 &&
    (driver=strtok(0, ",")) != 0 && (port=strtok(0, ",")) != 0)
   return CreateDC(driver, device, port, 0);
  return 0;
}

// Print the window
void TThreeDMDIClient::CmPrint()
{
  HDC hPrnDC = CreatePrinterDC();
  if (!hPrnDC) {    // Failed to set up printer
    ::MessageBox(GetActiveWindow(), "Could not find printer",
      GetApplicationObject()->GetName(), MB_OK | MB_ICONEXCLAMATION);
    return;
  }
  if (Escape(hPrnDC, STARTDOC, 7, "3DSOLID", 0) > 0) {
    TSolidWindow* win = (TSolidWindow *)GetActiveMDIChild();
    if (!win) {
      win->ThreeD->View(hPrnDC);
      if (Escape(hPrnDC, NEWFRAME, 0, 0, 0) > 0)
        Escape(hPrnDC, ENDDOC, 0, 0, 0);
    }
  }
  DeleteDC(hPrnDC);
}

// Read in a file describing a polygon that adheres to the
// standard described in Chapter 17. Return 1 if the file is read
// successfully; otherwise return an error flag.
int TThreeDSolid::Read3DObject(char *filename)
```

```
{
  int i;
  FILE* infile;
  if ((infile=fopen(filename, "r")) == 0)
    return EM_FILEOPENERROR;
  fscanf(infile, "%d", &NumColors);
  if (NumColors >= NUMCOLORS) return EM_TOOMANYCOLORS;
  if (NumColors > 0)     // No color palette if 0 or negative
    for (i=1; i<=NumColors; i++)
      fscanf(infile, "%d %d %d", &ColorPal[i].r,
        &ColorPal[i].g, &ColorPal[i].b);
  fscanf(infile, "%d %d", &Vertices, &Length);
  if (Vertices >= NUMVERTICES || Length >= NUMCONNECTIONS)
    return EM_FILETOOBIG;
  for (i=1; i<=Vertices; i++)
    fscanf(infile, "%lf %lf %lf", &Points[i].x,
      &Points[i].y, &Points[i].z);
  for (i=1; i<=Length; i++)
    fscanf(infile, "%d", &Connect[i]);
  fclose(infile);
  TRIANGLE *tri, *t;
  TLIST *nu, *triList = 0;
  TriL = 0;        // Create the list of triangle data for the BSP tree
  i=1;
  while (i<Length) {
    t = new TRIANGLE;
    if (!t) return 0;  // Out of memory
    t->V1 = Points[Connect[i]];
    t->V2 = Points[Connect[i+1]];
    t->V3 = Points[Connect[i+2]];
    t->ColorNdx = -Connect[i+3];
    i += 4;
    t->Next = TriL;
    TriL = t;
  }
  tri = TriL; // Create a TLIST list of all the triangles in TriL
  while (tri) {
    nu = new TLIST;
    if (!nu) return FALSE;
    nu->T = tri;
    nu->Next = triList;
    triList = nu;        // Insert at head of list
    tri = tri->Next;
  }
  CalcTriNormals();
  CalcPlaneEqs();
  Tree = MakeBSPTree(triList);
  nu = triList;          // Free the TLIST structures
  while (nu) {
    triList = nu->Next;
    free(nu);
    nu = triList;
  }
```

```
    // Precompute values so that it's faster to display the objects
    PrecomputeCentroids();
    return TRUE;
}

// Precompute the d term in the plane equation for each polygon.
// The normal of the plane and a point on the plane--one of
// its vertices--are used to solve for d.
void TThreeDSolid::CalcPlaneEqs()
{
    TRIANGLE* tri = TriL;
    while (tri) {
        tri->d = -(tri->Normal.x * tri->V1.x +
            tri->Normal.y * tri->V1.y + tri->Normal.z * tri->V1.z);
        tri = tri->Next;
    }
}

// Dispose of the BSP tree
void TThreeDSolid::DisposeBSP(BSPNode* tree)
{
    if (tree) {
        DisposeBSP(tree->Outside);
        DisposeBSP(tree->Inside);
        free(tree);
    }
}

// Create a new node for the BSP tree
BSPNode* TThreeDSolid::MakeBSPNode(TRIANGLE* tri)
{
    BSPNode *node = new BSPNode;
    if (!node) return node;
    node->Tri = tri;    // Point to the triangle's data
    node->Outside = 0;  node->Inside = 0;
    return node;
}

// Add the triangle to the triangle list
void TThreeDSolid::AddList(TLIST** tlist, TRIANGLE* tri)
{
    TLIST *l = *tlist, *nuL, *back = *tlist;
    nuL = new TLIST;
    if (!nuL) {
        MessageBox(GetActiveWindow(), "AddList: Out of Memory",
            GetApplicationObject()->GetName(), MB_OK | MB_ICONEXCLAMATION);
        return;
    }
    nuL->T = tri;
    nuL->Next = 0;
    if (l) {
        while (l) {
            back = l;
            l = l->Next;
```

```
    }
    back->Next = nuL;
  }
  else                // List is empty. This is the first node.
    *tlist = nuL;
}

// Calculate the sign that indicates which side of the separation
// plane vertex p is on. Note that a tolerance value is used to account
// for arithmetic round off errors by the computer. This function uses
// the fact that a plane equation is: ax + by + cz + d = 0. If p is
// on the plane and plugged into the equation, the result will be 0.
// If p is not on the plane, the sign of the result indicates which
// side of the plane the point is on.
double TThreeDSolid::CalcSign(Point& p, TRIANGLE* tri)
{
  double value = p.x * tri->Normal.x + p.y * tri->Normal.y +
    p.z * tri->Normal.z + tri->d;
  if (labs(value) < TOL) return 0.0; // The point is on the plane
    else return value;  // The sign of the value indicates which
}                       // side p is on

// Uses a parameteric equation to determine where a line intersects the
// plane. The two vertices v1 and v2 are the endpoints of the line.
void TThreeDSolid::Intersect(TRIANGLE* tri, Point& v1,
  Point& v2, Point& loc)
{
  double t = -(tri->Normal.x * v1.x + tri->Normal.y * v1.y +
    tri->Normal.z * v1.z + tri->d) / (tri->Normal.x * (v2.x - v1.x) +
    tri->Normal.y * (v2.y - v1.y) + tri->Normal.z * (v2.z - v1.z));
  if (t >= -TOL && t <= 1 + TOL) {
    loc.x = v1.x + t * (v2.x - v1.x);
    loc.y = v1.y + t * (v2.y - v1.y);
    loc.z = v1.z + t * (v2.z - v1.z);
  }
}

// Insert the triangle formed by the vertices v1, v2, and v3 to
// the beginning of the triangle list, TriList. Add an appropriate
// pointer to this TRIANGLE structure to the end of TLIST.
void TThreeDSolid::InsertTriangle(TLIST** tlist,
  Point& v1, Point& v2, Point& v3, TRIANGLE* copyFrom)
{
  // Add a new triangle structure to the beginning of the
  // list of triangles in the figure
  TRIANGLE* nuT = new TRIANGLE;
  if (!nuT) {
    MessageBox(GetActiveWindow(), "InsertTriangle: Out of Memory",
      GetApplicationObject()->GetName(), MB_OK | MB_ICONEXCLAMATION);
    return;
  }
  nuT->Next = TriL;
  TriL = nuT;
```

```
      nuT->V1 = v1;    nuT->V2 = v2;    nuT->V3 = v3;
      nuT->Normal = copyFrom->Normal;
      nuT->d = copyFrom->d;  nuT->ColorNdx = copyFrom->ColorNdx;
      // Append a pointer to this triangle data in the list of
      // triangles. This triangle must be appended because
      // the head of the list is being used.
      AddList(tlist, nuT);
}

// Split the triangle by the plane specified
void TThreeDSolid::Split(TLIST** frontList, TLIST** backList,
   double signOfV1, double signOfV2, double signOfV3,
   TRIANGLE* sepPlane, TRIANGLE* tri)
{
   Point p, p2;
   if (signOfV1 == 0) {         // The plane goes through vertex V1
      Intersect(sepPlane, tri->V2, tri->V3, p);
      if (signOfV2 > 0) {       // Make right half on front side
         InsertTriangle(frontList, tri->V1, tri->V2, p, tri);
         InsertTriangle(backList, tri->V1, p, tri->V3, tri);
      }
      else {
         InsertTriangle(backList, tri->V1, tri->V2, p, tri);
         InsertTriangle(frontList, tri->V1, p, tri->V3, tri);
      }
   }
   else if (signOfV2 == 0) {   // The plane goes through vertex V2
      Intersect(sepPlane, tri->V1, tri->V3, p);
      if (signOfV1 > 0) {       // Make right half on front side
         InsertTriangle(frontList, tri->V1, tri->V2, p, tri);
         InsertTriangle(backList, p, tri->V2, tri->V3, tri);
      }
      else {
         InsertTriangle(backList, tri->V1, tri->V2, p, tri);
         InsertTriangle(frontList, p, tri->V2, tri->V3, tri);
      }
   }
   else if (signOfV3 == 0) {    // The plane goes through vertex V3
      Intersect(sepPlane, tri->V1, tri->V2, p);
      if (signOfV1 > 0) {       // Make right half on front side
         InsertTriangle(frontList, tri->V1, p, tri->V3, tri);
         InsertTriangle(backList, p, tri->V2, tri->V3, tri);
      }
      else {
         InsertTriangle(backList, tri->V1, p, tri->V3, tri);
         InsertTriangle(frontList, p, tri->V2, tri->V3, tri);
      }
   }
   else if (signOfV1 > 0 && signOfV3 > 0) {  // Vertex V2 on other side
      Intersect(sepPlane, tri->V1, tri->V2, p);
      Intersect(sepPlane, tri->V2, tri->V3, p2);
      InsertTriangle(frontList, tri->V1, p, tri->V3, tri);
      InsertTriangle(frontList, p, p2, tri->V3, tri);
      InsertTriangle(backList, p, tri->V2, p2, tri);
```

```
    }
    else if (signOfV1 < 0 && signOfV3 < 0) {  // Vertex V2 on other side
      Intersect(sepPlane, tri->V1, tri->V2, p);
      Intersect(sepPlane, tri->V2, tri->V3, p2);
      InsertTriangle(backList, tri->V1, p, tri->V3, tri);
      InsertTriangle(backList, p, p2, tri->V3, tri);
      InsertTriangle(frontList, p, tri->V2, p2, tri);
    }
    else if (signOfV2 > 0 && signOfV3 > 0) {  // Vertex V1 on other side
      Intersect(sepPlane, tri->V1, tri->V2, p);
      Intersect(sepPlane, tri->V1, tri->V3, p2);
      InsertTriangle(frontList, p, tri->V3, p2, tri);
      InsertTriangle(frontList, p, tri->V2, tri->V3, tri);
      InsertTriangle(backList, tri->V1, p, p2, tri);
    }
    else if (signOfV2 < 0 && signOfV3 < 0) {  // Vertex v1 on other side
      Intersect(sepPlane, tri->V1, tri->V2, p);
      Intersect(sepPlane, tri->V1, tri->V3, p2);
      InsertTriangle(backList, p, tri->V3, p2, tri);
      InsertTriangle(backList, p, tri->V2, tri->V3, tri);
      InsertTriangle(frontList, tri->V1, p, p2, tri);
    }
    else if (signOfV1 > 0 && signOfV2 > 0) {   // Vertex V3 on other side
      Intersect(sepPlane, tri->V2, tri->V3, p);
      Intersect(sepPlane, tri->V1, tri->V3, p2);
      InsertTriangle(frontList, tri->V1, tri->V2, p, tri);
      InsertTriangle(frontList, tri->V1, p, p2, tri);
      InsertTriangle(backList, p2, p, tri->V3, tri);
    }
    else if (signOfV1 < 0 && signOfV2 < 0) {  // Vertex v3 on other side
      Intersect(sepPlane, tri->V2, tri->V3, p);
      Intersect(sepPlane, tri->V1, tri->V3, p2);
      InsertTriangle(backList, tri->V1, tri->V2, p, tri);
      InsertTriangle(backList, tri->V1, p, p2, tri);
      InsertTriangle(frontList, p, p2, tri->V3, tri);
    }
  }
}

// Make the BSP tree structure
BSPNode* TThreeDSolid::MakeBSPTree(TLIST* l)
{
  TLIST *backList=0, *frontList=0, *root, *tri;
  double signOfV1, signOfV2, signOfV3;
  BSPNode* node;
  if (!l) return 0;
  else {
    root = l;  // Set the root as the first triangle in the list
    tri = root->Next;
    while (tri) {
      signOfV1 = CalcSign(tri->T->V1, root->T);
      signOfV2 = CalcSign(tri->T->V2, root->T);
      signOfV3 = CalcSign(tri->T->V3, root->T);
      if (signOfV1 >= 0 && signOfV2 >= 0 && signOfV3 >= 0)
        AddList(&frontList, tri->T);    // Triangle is in front of root
```

```
          else if (signOfV1 <= 0 && signOfV2 <= 0 && signOfV3 <= 0)
            AddList(&backList, tri->T);     // Triangle is in back of root
          else
            Split(&frontList, &backList, signOfV1, signOfV2, signOfV3,
              root->T, tri->T);
          tri = tri->Next;
        }
        node = MakeBSPNode(root->T);  // Add node for the root triangle
        if (!node) {
          MessageBox(GetActiveWindow(), "MakeBSPTree: Out of Memory",
            GetApplicationObject()->GetName(), MB_OK | MB_ICONEXCLAMATION);
          return node;
        }
        node->Outside = MakeBSPTree(frontList);
        node->Inside = MakeBSPTree(backList);
        TLIST* p = frontList;
        while (p) {
          frontList = p->Next;  free(p);  p = frontList;
        }
        p = backList;
        while (p) {
          backList = p->Next;   free(p);  p = backList;
        }
      }
      return node;
}


// Convert world coordinates to display coordinates
void TThreeDSolid::WorldToDisplay(double x, double y, double z,
  int& xr, int& yr)
{
  double xc = (x * A1.x + A1.y * y + A1.z * z + Offsx) * DVal;
  double yc = (x * A2.x + A2.y * y + A2.z * z + Offsy) * DVal;
  double zc = x * A3.x + A3.y * y + A3.z * z + Offsz;
  double xm = xc / zc;
  double ym = yc / -zc;
  xr = 400 * xm + 400;
  yr = 400 * ym + 400;
}


// Calculate the normals of the triangles
void TThreeDSolid::CalcTriNormals()
{
  TRIANGLE* tri = TriL;
  VECTOR d1, d2;
  while (tri) {
    d1 = Subtract(&tri->V1, &tri->V2);
    d2 = Subtract(&tri->V1, &tri->V3);
    tri->Normal = Cross(&d1, &d2);
    Normalize(&tri->Normal);
    tri = tri->Next;
  }
}
```

```
// Precompute the centroids of all the triangles
void TThreeDSolid::PrecomputeCentroids()
{
  TRIANGLE* t = TriL;
  while (t) {
    t->Centroid.x = (t->V1.x + t->V2.x + t->V3.x) / 3.0;
    t->Centroid.y = (t->V1.y + t->V2.y + t->V3.y) / 3.0;
    t->Centroid.z = (t->V1.z + t->V2.z + t->V3.z) / 3.0;
    t = t->Next;
  }
}

// Return the color to paint a polygon. Only ambient and diffuse
// lighting is used. You are looking at point p and the variable
// "normal" is the normal of the polygon. colorNdx specifies the
// desired color of the polygon.
COLORREF TThreeDSolid::ComputeColor(Point& p, VECTOR& normal,
  int colorNdx)
{
  VECTOR l;
  double lDotN;
  l = Subtract(&Light, &p); // Find vector from light to point p
  Normalize(&l);
  lDotN = Dot(&l, &normal);
  // Calculate diffuse lighting contribution to object's color
  if (lDotN <= 0) lDotN *= -Diffuse * NUM_SHADES;
    else lDotN *= Diffuse * NUM_SHADES;
  // Add ambient coefficient
  int Red = (int)(ColorPal[colorNdx].r + Ambient * NUM_SHADES + lDotN);
  int Green = (int)(ColorPal[colorNdx].g + Ambient * NUM_SHADES + lDotN);
  int Blue = (int)(ColorPal[colorNdx].b + Ambient * NUM_SHADES + lDotN);
  if (Red > 255) Red = 255;
  if (Green > 255) Green = 255;
  if (Blue > 255) Blue = 255;
  return RGB(Red, Green, Blue);
}

// Display the triangle
void TThreeDSolid::DisplayTriangle(HDC hDC, TRIANGLE* tri)
{
  POINT t[4];  // Screen coordinates of triangle to display
  COLORREF Color = ComputeColor(tri->Centroid,tri->Normal,tri->ColorNdx);
  WorldToDisplay(tri->V1.x, tri->V1.y, tri->V1.z, t[0].x, t[0].y);
  WorldToDisplay(tri->V2.x, tri->V2.y, tri->V2.z, t[1].x, t[1].y);
  WorldToDisplay(tri->V3.x, tri->V3.y, tri->V3.z, t[2].x, t[2].y);
  t[3].x = t[0].x;    t[3].y = t[0].y;    // Close of the triangle
  // Create the correct brush and display the triangle
  HBRUSH hBrush = CreateSolidBrush(Color);
  HBRUSH hOldBrush = HBRUSH(SelectObject(hDC, hBrush));
  HPEN hOldPen = HPEN(SelectObject(hDC, GetStockObject(NULL_PEN)));
  Polygon(hDC, t, 4);    // Display the triangle
  SelectObject(hDC, hOldPen);
  SelectObject(hDC, hOldBrush);
```

```
        DeleteObject(hBrush);
}

// Display the figure stored in the BSP tree
void TThreeDSolid::View(HDC hDC)
{
    TraverseTree(hDC, Tree);
}

// Traverse a BSP tree, rendering a three-dimensional scene
void TThreeDSolid::TraverseTree(HDC hDC, BSPNode* tree)
{
    VECTOR s;
    if (tree) {
        s.x = From.x - tree->Tri->V1.x;
        s.y = From.y - tree->Tri->V1.y;
        s.z = From.z - tree->Tri->V1.z;
        Normalize(&s);
        if (Dot(&s, &tree->Tri->Normal) > 0) { // The eye is in front
            TraverseTree(hDC, tree->Inside);       // of the polygon
            DisplayTriangle(hDC, tree->Tri);
            TraverseTree(hDC, tree->Outside);
        }
        else {                                  // The eye is in back
            TraverseTree(hDC, tree->Outside);   // of the polygon
            DisplayTriangle(hDC, tree->Tri);
            TraverseTree(hDC, tree->Inside);
        }
    }
}

// Display a dialog box that allows the user to change the diffuse
// and ambient lighting parameters
void TThreeDMDIClient::CmLighting()
{
    TSolidWindow* win = (TSolidWindow *)GetActiveMDIChild();
    if (!win) return;    // No view to change
    switch (TLightingDlg(this, LIGHTING_DLG, win).Execute()) {
        case IDOK:
            // The user pressed the OK button. Copy the new view
            // parameters to the active child window.
            TThreeDSolid* solid = (TThreeDSolid *)win->ThreeD;
            solid->Diffuse = atof(LightingTransfer.Diffuse);
            solid->Ambient = atof(LightingTransfer.Ambient);
            // Force these lighting parameters between 0 and 1, inclusive
            if (solid->Diffuse < 0) solid->Diffuse = 0;
            if (solid->Diffuse > 1) solid->Diffuse = 1;
            if (solid->Ambient < 0) solid->Ambient = 0;
            if (solid->Ambient > 1) solid->Ambient = 1;
            ::InvalidateRect(win->HWindow, 0, TRUE);
            break;
    }
}
```

```
// This dialog box controls the lighting parameters. The win variable
// is a pointer to the child window object that was in focus at the
// time the dialog box was created.
TLightingDlg::TLightingDlg(TWindow* parent, int menuResId,
  TSolidWindow* win) : TDialog(parent, menuResId)
{
  // Move the child's data into the transfer buffer
  TThreeDMDIClient* p = TYPESAFE_DOWNCAST(parent,TThreeDMDIClient);
  TThreeDSolid* solid = (TThreeDSolid *)win->ThreeD;
  sprintf(p->LightingTransfer.Diffuse, "%4.2lf", solid->Diffuse);
  sprintf(p->LightingTransfer.Ambient, "%4.2lf", solid->Ambient);
  new TEdit(this, ID_DIFFUSE, sizeof(p->LightingTransfer.Diffuse));
  new TEdit(this, ID_AMBIENT, sizeof(p->LightingTransfer.Ambient));
  SetTransferBuffer(&(p->LightingTransfer));
}

// Pop up a dialog box to change the lighting location
void TThreeDMDIClient::CmLightLoc()
{
  TSolidWindow* win = (TSolidWindow *)GetActiveMDIChild();
  if (!win) return;  // No view to change
  switch (TLightLocDlg(this, LIGHTLOC_DLG, win).Execute()) {
    case IDOK:
      // The user pressed the OK button. Copy the new view
      // parameters to the active child window.
      TThreeDSolid* solid = (TThreeDSolid *)win->ThreeD;
      solid->Light.x = atof(LightLocTransfer.x);
      solid->Light.y = atof(LightLocTransfer.y);
      solid->Light.z = atof(LightLocTransfer.z);
      ::InvalidateRect(win->HWindow, 0, TRUE);
      break;
  }
}

// This dialog box is used to set the location of the light source.
// The win variable is a pointer to the child window object that
// was in focus at the time the dialog box was created.
TLightLocDlg::TLightLocDlg(TWindow* parent, int menuResId,
  TSolidWindow* win) : TDialog(parent, menuResId)
{
  TThreeDMDIClient* p = TYPESAFE_DOWNCAST(parent,TThreeDMDIClient);
  TThreeDSolid* solid = (TThreeDSolid *)win->ThreeD;
  // Move the child's data into the transfer buffer
  sprintf(p->LightLocTransfer.x, "%4.2lf", solid->Light.x);
  sprintf(p->LightLocTransfer.y, "%4.2lf", solid->Light.y);
  sprintf(p->LightLocTransfer.z, "%4.2lf", solid->Light.z);
  new TEdit(this, ID_LIGHTX, sizeof(p->LightLocTransfer.x));
  new TEdit(this, ID_LIGHTY, sizeof(p->LightLocTransfer.y));
  new TEdit(this, ID_LIGHTZ, sizeof(p->LightLocTransfer.z));
  SetTransferBuffer(&(p->LightLocTransfer));
}

class TThreeDApp : public TApplication {
public:
```

```
  TThreeDApp(const char* name): TApplication(name) { }
  void InitMainWindow();
};

// Build a toolbar for the application
TControlBar* BuildControlBar(TWindow *parent,
  TControlBar::TTileDirection direction)
{
  // Create the toolbar from OWL's TControlBar class
  TControlBar* cb = new TControlBar(parent, direction);
  // Add buttons to open a file and move the from point in and out
  cb->Insert(*new TButtonGadget(CM_FILEOPEN, CM_FILEOPEN));
  cb->Insert(*new TSeparatorGadget);   // Add a separator between buttons
  cb->Insert(*new TButtonGadget(CM_MOVEIN, CM_MOVEIN));
  cb->Insert(*new TButtonGadget(CM_MOVEOUT, CM_MOVEOUT));
  return cb;
}

void TThreeDApp::InitMainWindow()
{
  TDecoratedFrame* Frame =
    new TDecoratedMDIFrame(Name, "COMMANDS", *new TThreeDMDIClient);
  MainWindow = Frame;
  EnableCtl3d(TRUE);   // Use Microsoft's 3D control styles
  // Place a toolbar at the top of the application's window
  TControlBar* ControlBar = BuildControlBar(Frame,
    TControlBar::Horizontal);
  Frame->Insert(*ControlBar, TDecoratedFrame::Top);
}

int OwlMain(int /*argc*/, char* /*argv*/[])
{
  return TThreeDApp("3DSOLID").Run();
}
```

Index

Disk Order Form

If you want to avoid typing in the programs in this book, you can order the *Windows Graphics Companion Disk*. This disk includes all the source code presented in the book, ready for you to experiment with.

To receive your disk, fill out the form below (or write the information on a separate sheet of paper) and mail it along with $15 in check or money order to Robots Etc, P.O. Box 122, Tempe, AZ 85280. Make checks payable to Robots Etc.

For phone orders or further information, call (602) 966-0695 or fax (602) 966-0769. Call for details on rush delivery.

Please send me _____ copies of the *Windows Graphics Companion Disk* at $15 each. Make checks payable to Robots Etc. (Checks must be in U.S. funds drawn on a U.S. bank.)

Diskette Size: ___ 5-1/4" (1.2MB) ___ 5-1/4" (360K) ___ 3-1/2" (1.44MB)

_____
Name

_____
Address

_____
City   State   Zip

_____
Country   Telephone

Send to: Robots Etc, P.O. Box 122, Tempe, AZ 85280
Please allow 2-4 weeks for delivery

John Wiley & Sons, Inc., is not responsible for orders placed with Robots Etc.